De Gruyter Handbook of European Union Environmental Policy

De Gruyter Contemporary Social Sciences Handbooks

Volume 21

De Gruyter Handbook of European Union Environmental Policy

Edited by
Anthony R. Zito and Ekaterina Domorenok

DE GRUYTER

ISSN 2747-9269
ISBN 978-3-11-132124-0
e-ISBN 978-3-11-132152-3 (PDF)
e-ISBN 978-3-11-132160-8 (EPUB)

Library of Congress Control Number: 2026931247

Bibliographic information published by the Deutsche Nationalbibliothek
The Deutsche Nationalbibliothek lists this publication in the Deutsche Nationalbibliografie;
detailed bibliographic data are available on the Internet at http://dnb.dnb.de.

De Gruyter and Walter de Gruyter GmbH are part of De Gruyter Brill.
www.degruyterbrill.com

Questions about General Product Safety Regulation:
productsafety@degruyterbrill.com

Cover image: Wlad74 / iStock / Getty Images Plus
Printing: CPI books GmbH, Leck

MIX
Papier | Fördert gute Waldnutzung
FSC® C083411
www.fsc.org

Contents

Section B **Policy actors**

Section C **Policies**

Section D **Policy pathways and dynamics**

List of abbreviations

AGRI	(Committee on) Agriculture and Rural Development
ALDE	Alliance of Liberals and Democrats for Europe
AAQC	Ambient Air Quality and Cleaner Air Directive
BATNEEC	Best available techniques not entailing excessive cost
BAT	Best available technology
CBAM	Carbon Border Adjustment Mechanism
CCS	Carbon Capture and Storage
CEE	Central and Eastern Europe
CAS	Chemical Abstracts Service
CSO	Civil society organization
CLP	Classification, labeling, and packaging
COICOP	Classification of Individual Consumption by Purpose
CCIS	Climate Change and International Security
CPI	Climate Policy Integration
COREPER	Committee of Permanent Representatives
CAMM	Common agenda for migration and mobility
CAP	Common Agricultural Policy
COP	Conference of the Parties
CJEU	Court of Justice of the European Union
CoM	Covenant of Mayors
CO_2e	CO_2 equivalents
CRMs	Critical raw materials
CRMA	Critical Raw Materials Act
DMPs	Deliberative mini publics
DG	Directorate-General
DG DEVCO	Directorate-General Development and Cooperation-EuropeAid
DMC	Domestic material consumption
EMAS	Eco-management and audit scheme
ESR	Effort-Sharing Regulation
EPBD	Energy Performance of Buildings Directive
ETS	Emissions Trading System
ETS2	Emissions trading scheme for buildings, road transport and additional sectors
ECCP	Energy and Climate Change Package
EAP	Environment Action Programme
ENVI	(Committee on the) Environment, Public Health and Food Safety
ENGO	Environmental non-governmental organization
EPI	Environmental policy integration
CEFIC	European Chemical Industry Council
ECHA	European Chemicals Agency
ECI	European Citizens' Initiative
ECF	European Climate Foundation
EC	European Commission
ECR	European Conservatives and Reformists Group
EEC	European Economic Community
EEA	European Environment Agency
EEB	European Environmental Bureau
EFSA	European Food Safety Authority

https://doi.org/10.1515/9783111321523-001

EGD	European Green Deal
ENP	European Neighbourhood Policy
IMPEL	European Network for the Implementation and Enforcement of Environmental Law
EP	European Parliament
EPP	European People's Party
EPSU	European Public Services Union
EU	European Union
EUWI	European Union Water Initiative
ENF	Europe of Nations and Freedom
EFD(D)	Europe of Freedom and (Direct) Democracy
ETS	Emissions Trading System
F2F	Farm to Fork
FEC	Financial and Economic Crisis
FF55	Fit for 55
FoE	Friends of the Earth
GM	Gender mainstreaming
GAM	Global approach to migration
GAMM	Global approach to migration and mobility
GCCA	Global Climate Change Alliance
GCM	Global Compact for Safe, Orderly and Regular Migration
GFC	Global financial crisis
G10	Green 10
GHG	Greenhouse gas
GUE-NGL	Greens and The Left
GDP	Gross domestic product
IRA	Inflation Reduction Act
IEEP	Institute for European Environmental Policy
IMO	International Maritime Organization
IOM	International Organization for Migration
IPCC	Intergovernmental Panel on Climate Change
IWRM	Integrated water resources management
JRC	Joint Research Centre
JHA	Justice and Home Affairs
LULUCF	Land Use, Land Use Change, and Forestry
MEP	Member of the European Parliament
MFF	Multiannual Financial Framework
MEA	Multilateral environmental agreement
MLG	Multilevel governance
NRL	Nature Restoration Law
NZIA	Net-Zero Industry Act
NEPI	New environmental policy instrument
NEB	New European Bauhaus
NextGenEU	Next Generation EU
NGO	Non-governmental organization
NI	Non-Inscrits
OLP	Ordinary legislative procedure
OECD	Organization for Economic Co-operation and Development
PES	Party of European Socialists
PFAS	Perfluoroalkyl and polyfluoroalkyl substances
PV	Photovoltaic

PDD	Platform on Disaster Displacement
PEB	Pro-environmental behaviour
S&D	Progressive Alliance of Socialists and Democrats
PPPA	Public policy and public administration
PPS	Purchasing power standards
QMV	Qualified majority voting
QCA	Qualitative Comparative Analysis
REEs	Rare earth elements
RRF	Recovery and Resilience Facility
REACH	Registration, Evaluation, Authorisation and Restriction of Chemicals
R&D	Research and development
RBMP	River basin management plan
STS	Science and technology studies
SG	Secretariat-General
SEA	Single European Act
SEM	Single European Market
SME	Small and medium-sized company
SDGs	Sustainable Development Goals
SUR	Sustainable Use of Plant Protection Products Regulation
TSCA	Toxic Substances Control Act
TSD	Trade and sustainable development
UEN	Union for Europe of the Nations
UN	United Nations
UNEP	United Nations Environmental Programme
UNFCCC	United Nations Framework Convention on Climate Change
UAEU	Urban Agenda for the EU
VA	Voluntary Agreement
WsFD	Waste Framework Directive
WPP	Waste Prevention Programme
WFD	Water Framework Directive
WHO	World Health Organization
WWF	World Wildlife Fund

Anthony R. Zito and Ekaterina Domorenok

Handbook introduction: European Union environmental policy in times of turbulence

1 European Union environmental policy: significance of the sector and its study

Environmental policy, in all its dimensions, represents the response to the clearest and most urgent existential threat to the survival of Earth and all species inhabiting it. Studying policy is essential to analyse the means used by particular actors to achieve goals that tackle general or specific problems.

This handbook examines one of the key policymaking players on the international stage. The European Union (EU), as both a leading historical and current contributor to this global environmental threat, as well as arguably the most consistent global political leader in the last three decades for environmental response, demands scrutiny and understanding of its policy processes and outlook. The EU's contribution to the world's environmental problems is inarguable. For example, EU annual consumption (i. e. final demand of goods and services) caused 3.5 billion tons of global CO_2 emissions, roughly 9 percent of worldwide emissions (European Commission, 2024). Each European citizen produces 4.8 ton of waste each year, (European Environment Agency, 2024a), with EU waste exports increasing by 77 percent between 2004 and 2021 (European Environment Agency, 2024b).

Beyond the impact of the EU on the planet, EU environmental policy has a separate significance as an academic field of study. There are several dimensions to this. First, the majority of the global elite and population increasingly view environmental issues as fundamental global priorities (64 percent of the global population viewed climate change as a global emergency in 2021; see United Nations Development Programme, 2021). This challenges the notion in neofunctional and intergovernmental expectations (approaches defined in Chapter 2) that transnational cooperation tends towards the more technical "low" politics and low-visibility politics of harmonization, rather than to questions of national security (Weale, 1999; Zito, 1999). The environment and climate are increasingly framed as questions of security. Second, not only has environmental policy been one of the most successful areas of expansion for European political integration (both in terms of the scope of coverage of these policies as well as the depth of their impact), it has also acted as a significant source of legitimacy and potential EU identification for the European integration project as a whole (Lenschow and Sprungk, 2010). The third dimension is that EU environmental policy studies has presented a challenge to international relations approaches that have emphasized more zero-sum, transactional and competitive politics, highlighting the potential for transnational cooperation and learning (Jachtenfuchs, 1996). At no point has any scho-

https://doi.org/10.1515/9783111321523-002

lar dismissed the importance of interests and bargaining, but EU environmental policy scholarship has given more focus to the importance of such dynamics as knowledge and problem-solving. It is not coincidental that new notions of policy-learning and governance have been a particular feature in the study of EU environmental policy.

While there is a strong case to be made about the importance of EU environmental policy to the planet, the process of European integration and EU academic research, this handbook is published at a time when the policy area faces a period of uncertainty in terms of its long-term direction. This is reflected in a range of studies questioning if the governance area is facing policy dismantling, stagnation, turbulence and crisis (terms defined in Chapters 4 and 37, as well as, for example, Gravey and Jordan, 2020; Burns, Eckersley and Tobin, 2020; Lenschow, Burns and Zito, 2020). There are a range of questions confronting the policy area generated by external factors, such as the invasion of Ukraine, and internal ones, such as austerity politics. For example, there is a question of how well environmental policy actors are handling environmental goals due to issues of capacity and resources (e. g., environmental actors lacking the resources to deliver policies to the appropriate standard), as well as questions of whether the chosen environmental goals are the most appropriate ones (e. g., focusing on pollution sources may ignore more fundamental problems of consumption). These factors range from the rise of political movements that emphasize right-wing, anti-Green, populist, Eurosceptic and other values to an international and national range of economic, political, social, security and other crises, which often pose aims that are seen as competing with environmental ones (e. g. energy security through fossil fuels).

In grappling with these vital analytical threads, the *Handbook on European Union Environmental Policy* engages with the broader analytical question of how those studying and practising environmental policymaking understand the turbulent period facing the EU and the planet. Do the dramatic challenges that all humanity faces currently in this Anthropocene epoch force a commensurate change in the analytical approaches of academics and policy approaches by EU actors? Even if one accepts that many aspects of EU environmental policy have been successful in remedial protection of the environment, do the often "end of pipe" solutions (e. g. fitting climate capture mechanisms on fossil fuel facilities) have the required capacity to deal with the massive challenge of climate change and biodiversity loss? Should policy actors and scholars who follow them be shifting their focus and priorities to more integrated approaches that focus on reshaping human production and consumption processes? On the other hand, do the current challenges and political and environmental turbulence risk both policy actors and scholars overlooking difficult and important lessons learnt about environmental problems and their resolution? Does the current EU environmental policy tradition (and its academic study) overlook vital elements of human and nonhuman communities?

In responding to these questions, the *Handbook* takes a pluralistic view towards theoretical and analytical frameworks but required all authors to isolate the key dynamics that drive environmental policymaking, with a focus on the political behaviour and interaction of a diverse set of policy actors, specific EU dynamics that place both opportunities and constraints on policy making and innovation and the core understandings of the policy problem underlying specific EU policy priorities. The *Handbook* chapters both reflect on and frame the potential directions for analytical, conceptual and empirical innovation on these topics. An underlying question of the book is whether students of the EU should rethink assumptions, categorizations and other policy studies' conceptualizations and how to develop this new and/or interdisciplinary thinking. The chapters assess whether there are important gaps in the study of their respective topic(s) but also whether scholars are keeping clearly in view the policy implications and challenges of the fast-moving EU environmental policy developments and research.

2 The arc of EU environmental policy

The authors of the *Handbook on European Union Environmental Policy* have been asked to take a long-term perspective on how the field has evolved. This is important because the *Handbook* takes the perspective that ideational (i. e., new philosophies and policy principles) and institutional decisions (i. e. the creation of new organizational structures and rules) taken in context can have substantial consequences over time. Demarcation of eras varies, but most scholars generally divide the trajectory into the roughly the same time periods adopted here (Hildebrand, 1993; Knill and Liefferink, 2007; Zito, 1999; Zito, Burns and Lenschow, 2019).

1957 – 1972: Pre-framing of the environmental policy problem

The founding treaties creating the European Communities in 1957 (to avoid confusion, this chapter will continue to use the acronym EU to refer to the overall integration project) make only limited mention of environmental policy in a way that suggests that Member States had scope to consider protections to "health and life" of living things (Rehbinder and Stewart, 1985). The notion of an environmental issue as a policy problem that required the establishment of a policy sector had yet to be framed. Accordingly, the extant Treaties of the European Communities make certain references, e. g. the Euratom Treaty referring to worker and public health. The Treaty establishing the European Economic Community contains a Preamble and Articles 2, 100 and 235 that became interpreted as justifying environmental action, sometimes involving a considerable stretch in interpretation (Hildebrand, 1993; McCormick, 2001). As the *Handbook* chapters explore, the environmental policy sector was inserted in pre-existing European Communities Treaties, institutions, laws and principles, such that questions of integrating varying and sometimes clashing priorities were inherent in the policy development. A small number of measures ensued that to varying degrees can be described as environmental, such as Directive 70/157/EEC on vehicle sound and exhaust emissions. Directives have remained the vital environmental policy tool to the present. A directive specifies goals and objectives that Member States are required to transpose to their national legislation while giving the Member States scope to individually translate the provisions into their domestic context. Directives differ from regulations in EU terminology, as regulations are directly applicable and binding in their entirety for Member States.

1972 – 1987: Environmental framing in and out of the common market context

The first EU Environmental Action Program crystallized the actual framing of the environment as a distinct policy problem requiring its own policy organization and response (Council of the European Communities, 1973). With this policy focus becoming a greater concern for the European public and rising up the European political agenda, the initial six Member States and the three prospective enlargement states were beginning to create national environmental policies that raised questions about distortions to the common market (Andersen and Liefferink, 1997). In the context of the Member State developments and the public concern for environmental incidents, such as the 1986 Sandoz toxic spill into the Rhine river, the European Communities steadily adopted environmental legislation at a gradually increasing rate towards 1991. These steps occurred without an explicit treaty mention until the Single European Act (SEA) in 1987 (Haigh, 2011). From 1972 to 2002, the dominant EU instruments continued to be various forms of regulations, especially directives that were prescriptive in nature. In the 1970s and early 1980s, this effort tended to focus on producing standards to limit emissions, but there are exceptions such as the directives on wild birds and their habitats. After the mid-1980s, the EU undertook a considerable expansion of policy instruments that had a greater focus on preventing pollution (McCormick, 2001).

1987 – 1999: Governance expansion

As indicated above, the SEA (European Communities, 1987) changed the institutional dynamics by enshrining environmental competence into the EU treaty system. However, this was not the only major institutional shift. Another institutional step was the increasing prominence of the EU as an international actor, both in terms of how it shaped EU-level political interactions as well as its global impact. Although the EU had been a signatory to important treaties such as the 1979 Convention on Long-Range Transboundary Air Pollution, other international actors only recognized the EU as a full international partner by the time of the 1992 United Nations Conference on Environment and Development, at which a Convention on Climate Change (as well as one on Biodiversity) was signed (Sbragia with Damro, 1999).

Although this period saw many years of expanded environmental initiatives and amendments of extant legislation, various reactions to environmental policy expansion and European integration (e.g. the failure of the first Danish referendum on the Maastricht Treaty) occurred more generally. A strong element was the inherent tension in the balance of governing between the EU and the constituent Member States. The French and United Kingdom governments drew up a list of EU laws to roll back in the 1990s (Wurzel, 2002). Although the SEA referred to general principles with respect to environmental policy action (European Communities 1987, Article 4), the Maastricht Treaty that established the European Union explicitly enshrined the principles of subsidiarity that guide whether the EU should take policy steps or leave such measures to the Member States. Subsidiarity operates according to the following principles: (1) the area in question does not fall within the Union's exclusive competence; (2) Member States cannot achieve satisfactorily the intended objectives of the proposed action; and (3) the EU consequently can undertake the action more successfully (European Union, 2007, Article 5(3)).

Another important dimension was the economic sector and the Member State government reaction to issues of implementation of EU legislation and questions of effectiveness of environmental design. This period saw a greater weighting—for example, by the Commission after the Jacques Delors era—on implementation, which strongly shaped subsequent EU environmental policy efforts. A further challenging dynamic, one more focused on the global environmental policy sector, was the criticism of the design and burdens of environmental regulation in the EU and its Member States and beyond. Economic interests and actors as well as other policy actors emphasized questions of competitiveness and effectiveness, suggesting the need to take more flexible approaches to regulations while also considering instruments targeting informational and market incentives in a less intrusive, prescriptive and economically burdensome fashion (Jordan, Wurzel and Zito, 2013). A core argument of our *Handbook* chapters is that, with the exception of a few instruments such as the Emissions Trading Scheme, EU environmental policy has expanded through instruments that emphasize rules and some degree of prescription; furthermore, Directive 2003/87/EC created the Trading Scheme, and rules are fundamental in underpinning this market.

1999 – 2019: Facing the challenges

We view 1999 as the start of a new environmental policy era, with the adoption of the Euro forcing a prioritization of Euro Member countries' economies and the resignation of the Santer Commission leadership (Zito, Burns and Lenschow, 2019). While previous enlargements had a mixed impact on EU environmental policy expansion, the sheer size of the 2004 and 2007 enlargements created additional decision-making challenges around reaching agreement on directives as well as a much wider divergence in environmental ambitions, contexts and traditions. The shift in priorities away from environmental policy expansion as a result of these institutional, political and policy developments was followed by a swarm of external crises and political changes. These included the global economic crisis after 2007, the direct security impact of Russia's interventions in Georgia, Ukraine and elsewhere, the more indirect impact of migration and other consequences of the Arab Spring and various conflicts in Africa and the Middle East, Brexit and the first Trump Administration.

There are many dynamics that shape EU environmental policy governance in this period, but we have selected the following to highlight for discussion in the *Handbook*. First is the issue of the trajectory of EU environmental policy during this turbulence and beyond. There is a strong academic debate, which is taken up in this handbook, about the degree to which this period has witnessed a decrease of EU initiatives or even a dismantling of the institution. Some of the core literature suggests that the European Commission and other actors have framed policy proposals, for example, in terms of narratives of "better regulation" that are compatible with notions of economic recovery and competitiveness (Knill, Steinebach and Fernández-i-Marín, 2020).

A second dynamic has been the growing dominance of the climate crisis on the environmental agenda. Although from an environmental perspective, climate policy interacts with a whole range of other environmental concerns, from biodiversity to waste policy, the political and policy prioritization of the climate issue has made it a standalone issue. Evidence includes, for example, the institutional transformation of the Directorate-General for Climate Action as distinct from the Directorate-General for Environment. The implications of the positioning of climate vis à vis the environmental and other EU policy priorities and policy sectors (e.g. migration policy and economic growth) are a core interest for a growing body of academic study and strongly feature in this handbook. To what extent has the climate crisis squeezed out both the policy and scholarly focus on other environmental crises that both Europe and the globe face, and what are the longer-term implications of this priority shift?

The need for balancing environmental and economic priorities has culminated in a major EU initiative containing a range of visions, targets and proposals that demarcates the start of the current EU environmental era: the European Green Deal (EGD). At its core the EGD echoes Franklin Delano Roosevelt's "New Deal" vision of harnessing political power and progressive politics to boost economic prosperity—in this case to enhance the environment (Schlesinger Jr., 1958). The European Commission and the Council of the European Union (2025) explicitly framed the EGD as a growth strategy. The EGD involves a large package of policy initiatives that also move the EU towards a green transition and climate neutrality by 2050, highlighting the need to also address the social costs and risks associated with environmental degradation and climate change. The package stresses an industrial plan and investment to achieve such targets while also acknowledging the importance of restructuring the economic process through such means as the circular economy concept (defined in Chapter 36) and healthy and affordable food. The policy agenda of the current era has at its heart the question of how far and to what degree the EU will implement the EGD in the face of internal and external turbulence (Domorenok and Graziano, 2023).

2019 and into the future

Although the EGD seemed to signal a renewed, concerted and multidimensional environmental policy approach, this agenda-setting has been made more problematic because of ongoing global turbulence. This includes, but is not restricted to, the Covid-19 crisis, Russia's 2022 invasion of Ukraine and the greater political weight given to populist notions in the Member States (von Homeyer, Oberthür and Jordan, 2021). In June 2025, the Council of the EU (2025) approved a negotiating position for the Commission's proposed Omnibus I simplification package to, among other things, amend EGD measures in order to lighten the regulatory burdens and boost competitiveness (European Commission, 2025).

With the apparent success of vested corporate and agricultural interests in pushing for ratcheting down the EGD programme, the question of democratic participation and attitudes toward environmental policy is now more pressing than ever. To what extent does the increased political presence of populist politicians reflect public attitudes towards the environment and climate change (Kulin and Johansson Sevä, 2024; Huber et al., 2021)? Does the rise of populism reflect a larger lack of trust in European political leaders, civil servants and experts that can fuel both the populist movement as well as resistance to environmental policy change? This question of a disconnect between policymakers and the range of European communities does not require belief in a populist discourse. Most critical environmental policy issues (climate, water, waste, air pollution etc.) require some form of discussion and policymaking at a transnational level using bilaterial and multilateral venues. It is apparent that the resulting decisions from this transnational decision-making do not have a material and emotional resonance with the various communities that are impacted by these policy choices when compared to community engagement in more local practices (Kiss *et al.*, 2022).

Whatever the outlook of the public and elites towards environmental policy priorities, the evidence mounts of the deepening of global, multilevel and intersecting crises for the biosphere: climate, biodiversity and land use, water quality, air and waste emissions, plastic and toxics are all created, nested problems. For example, the EU's monitoring report for 2024 suggests that waste and microplastic generation is increasing and that the planned reduction of nitrates is unlikely (European Environmental Agency, 2025).

Beyond the question of the political will to tackle these policy problems are a range of intrinsic policy challenges. The tradition of tackling pollution sources and emissions has brought the EU considerable policy success, but the harder questions of the consumption and production approaches of the EU and the Global North more generally remain. The story of farmers' protests against EU policy and the shifting stance of the European People's Party towards a more critical view of the Nature Restoration Law suggest the difficulty of pursuing these measures (Finger et al., 2024). The aftermath of the decision to adhere to economic stability that resulted in austerity measures in a range of EU Member States as well as in the European Commission, leaves a fundamental question about the capacity of the multiple levels of environmental governance to pursue the extant policy objectives.

The multiplicity of nested environmental problems and political resistance raises an even more fundamental analytical challenge: are both EU environmental policy makers and scholars too fixed on traditional, end of pipe and human-centred solutions? Scholars such as Biermann (2021) question the fundamental understanding behind European and international public policy that differentiates humans from nature. Such interrogation poses challenges about the role and importance of the nonhuman and the survival of the most substantial portion of the planet. The EU's ongoing focus on the compatibility of economic growth with environmental protection through the means of technocentric and anthropocentric policy approaches, such as ecological modernization, suggests that these inherent tensions will remain in future EU environmental policy.

The ongoing marginalization of women, indigenous populations, the poor, future generations and refugees, particularly in the Global South, deepens this policy conundrum for the EU. Although this critique from many perspectives (intersectional, neocolonial and others) holds true for all of the Global North's environmental policy (e. g. Govaert, 2024; Lombardo and Verloo, 2009), this challenge is particularly telling for an EU integration project that takes pride in the effort to be a global leader shaping international norms, particularly on such issues as environmental policy problems (Delreux and Happaerts, 2016; Manners, 2002). Although greater emphasis on environmental and social justice has found its way into EU rhetoric, as can be seen in the EGD project (European Council and the Council of the European Union, 2025), the policy reality is that EU efforts to achieve its policy objectives continue to rely heavily on policy activity in the Global South (such as the use of foreign carbon credits; see Weise and Sahlberg, 2025) and on environmental displacement (such as biofuels, the extraction of rare earth minerals and the export of waste), rather than fundamentally changing EU consumption and production patterns.

3. *Handbook* themes and organization

Overarching Handbook themes

The *Handbook* is organized into four sections. Each section contains an introduction that navigates the different chapters in each section. An overview of each chapter is given in these section introductions.

Section A contains chapters that review and discuss theoretical and conceptual issues that inform past and ongoing research on EU environmental policy. The organization of the section begins with some of the more traditional ways of thinking about EU environmental policy before bringing in approaches that challenge these outlooks. Accordingly, the section starts by looking at some of the longstanding integration theories and policy paradigms, particularly ecological modernization. The section chapters assess how the EU has sought to manage competing demands and turbulence through both knowledge and learning. The section ends with chapters that point out fundamental tensions in the EU environmental approach that raise questions about the long-term viability of the EU's current policy approach.

Section B focuses on actors and organizations involved in shaping the EU's environmental sector. The contributions in this section ask about the conditions and factors that lead policy actors to become drivers for policy change, as well as those conditions that induce these actors to become opponents and veto points. We start by looking at the core EU-level policymaking institutions and core institutional participants before introducing actor dynamics that cross multiple levels in the EU policy process. Section B ends with chapters that start to push the conventional wisdom (often technocratically oriented) of who constitutes the EU environmental policy actor sphere, raising the question of the role, for example, of foundations, the general public as environmental citizens and the nonhuman policy actor.

Section C drills down into substantive policymaking, studying more specific EU efforts to deal with environmental policy questions and problems. Out of the huge range of specific environmental policies that the EU has undertaken, we decided to focus on core policy priorities and environmental crises. Thus, particular attention is given to the climate and biodiversity crises as well as the ongoing challenges of protecting water and food while tackling the impact of chemicals and waste. Given the high complexity found in each of these policy problems, there is a danger of understanding these particular problems as being siloed. In order to stress the intersection of every environmental policy problem with other policy sectors and the transnational impact of EU action and inaction, we have included chapters on how the EU has responded to climate-triggered migration, on the EU energy sector, as well as on the EU's external environmental policy that helps tie the section together.

The final section, Section D, tackles the broader dynamics that explain how various EU policy processes generate policy outputs and outcomes. We asked the chapter authors to look at the underlying dynamics that only manifest over time and that are not sufficiently examined in EU studies. Thus, we ask the question of whether the climate crisis has displaced other environmental policy issues. We also look at the role and evolution of policy integration, the Single Market, regulatory instruments and policy implementation in shaping EU environmental policy. Finally, the section examines how new understandings of the circular economy and democratic governance may shift the EU trajectory going forward.

Approach to the individual Handbook chapters

The editors selected the *Handbook* authors for their current, cutting-edge expertise in their subject areas. The editors suggested a general topic for each author but gave the chapter authors a free hand (analytical approach, methods, level of analysis) as to how

they assessed the trajectory of EU policymaking for their chosen topic. Authors were asked to cover these elements at some point in their chapter:
- Offer a brief orientation to the chapter topic and core themes over time;
- Outline the EU's historical and intellectual development the area;
- Discuss and critique past research contributions with a focus on the EU effort;
- Assess the key changes and dynamics (the state of the actual environment, international dynamics, new scientific understandings) that require integration into the EU effort;
- Isolate the current and future challenges and opportunities for EU focused research in the area;
- Outline important future alternative conceptual and analytical approaches; and
- Reflect on policy challenges, with the option of offering policy recommendations.

Although all of the authors make judgements about the policy and academic study of their given topic, the premise of the book is to raise questions and challenges about the trajectory of EU environmental policy rather than offer definitive verdicts. As a number of chapters suggest, the EU and all of its policy sectors are experiencing policy turbulence that requires both policy actors and students of policy to take a flexible, adaptative approach to understanding the EU environmental policy processes and outcomes. Readers should read the *Handbook* with the view of formulating and taking forward their own policy understandings and research agendas.

References

Andersen, M.S. and Liefferink, D. (1997) 'Introduction: The impact of the pioneers on EU environmental policy', in: Andersen, M.S. and Liefferink, D. (eds.) *European environmental policy: the pioneers.* Manchester: Manchester University Press, pp. 1–35.

Biermann, F. (2021) 'The future of "environmental" policy in the Anthropocene: Time for a paradigm shift', *Environmental Politics*, 30(1), pp. 58–77.

Burns, C., Eckersley, P. and Tobin, P. (2020) 'EU environmental policy in times of crisis', *Journal of European Public Policy*, 27(1), pp. 1–19.

Council of the European Communities (1973) 'Declaration of the Council of the European Communities and of the representatives of the governments of the Member States meeting in the council of 22 November 1973 on the Programme of Action of the European Communities on the environment', *Official Journal of the European Communities*, No. C 113, pp. 1–53.

Council of the European Union (2025) 'Simplification: Council agrees position on sustainability reporting and due diligence requirements to boost EU competitiveness', Press Release 23 June 2025 22:12. Available at: https://www.consilium.europa.eu/en/press/press-releases/2025/06/23/simplification-council-agrees-position-on-sustainability-reporting-and-due-diligence-requirements-to-boost-eu-competitiveness (Accessed: 12 July 2025).

Delreux, T. and Happaerts, S. (2016) *Environmental policy and politics in the European Union.* London: Palgrave.

Domorenok, E. and Graziano, P. (2023) 'Understanding the European Green Deal: A narrative policy framework approach', *European Policy Analysis*, 9(1), pp. 9–29.

European Commission (2024) 'Greenhouse gas emission statistics—carbon footprints', Eurostat Explained. Available at: https://ec.europa.eu/eurostat/statistics-explained/index.php?title=Greenhouse_gas_emission_statistics_-_carbon_footprints (Accessed: 10 November 2024).

European Commission (2025) 'Omnibus package', Brussels: European Commission. Available at: https://finance.ec.europa.eu/news/omnibus-package-2025-04-01_en#:~:text=On%2026%20February%202025%2C%20the%20European%20Commission%20adopted,simplifying%20EU%20rules%2C%20enhancing%20competitiveness%20and%20attracting%20investment (Accessed: 25 June 2025).

European Communities (1987) 'Single European Act', *Official Journal of the European Communities* No. L 169, pp. 1–28.

European Council and the Council of the European Union (2025) *European Green Deal.* Brussels: General Secretariat of the Council. Available at: https://www.consilium.europa.eu/en/policies/european-green-deal/ (Accessed: 25 June 2025).

European Environment Agency (2024a) 'Waste and recycling'. Available at: https://www.eea.europa.eu/en/topics/in-depth/waste-and-recycling?activeTab=fa515f0c-9ab0-493c-b4cd-58a32dfaae0a (Accessed: 10 November 2024).

European Environment Agency (2024b) 'Waste management'. Available at: https://www.eea.europa.eu/publications/zero-pollution/production-consumption/waste-management (Accessed: 10 November 2024).

European Environment Agency (2025) *Zero pollution monitoring and outlook 2025.* EEA-JRC report 13/2024. Luxembourg: Publications Office of the European Union. Available at: https://www.eea.europa.eu/en/analysis/publications/zero-pollution-monitoring-and-outlook-report (Accessed: 25 June 2025).

European Union (2007) 'Treaty of Lisbon amending the Treaty on European Union and the Treaty establishing the European Community, signed at Lisbon, 13 December 2007', *Official Journal of the European Union* C 306, pp. 1–271.

Finger, R.,Fabry, A., Kammer, M., Candel, J., Dalhaus, T. and Meemken, E.M. (2024) 'Farmer protests in Europe 2023–2024', *EuroChoices*, 23(3), pp. 59–63.

Govaert, L. (2024) 'Neocolonialism in disguise? The European Commission's trade and sustainable development discourse', *European Foreign Affairs Review*, 29(3), pp. 331–360.

Gravey, V. and Jordan, A. (2020) 'Policy dismantling at EU level: reaching the limits of "an ever-closer ecological union"?', *Public Administration*, 98(2), pp. 349–362.

Haigh, N (ed.) (2011) *Manual of environmental policy: the EC and Britain.* London: Cartermill Publishing.

Hildebrand, P. (1993) 'The European community's environmental policy, 1957 to "1992": From incidental measures to an international regime?' *Environmental Politics*, 1(4), pp. 13–44.

Huber, R.A., Maltby, T., Szulecki, K. and Ćetković, S. (2021) 'Is populism a challenge to European energy and climate policy? Empirical evidence across varieties of populism', *Journal of European Public Policy*, 28(7), pp. 998–1017.

Jachtenfuchs, M. (1996) *International policy-making as a learning process? The European Union and the greenhouse effect.* Farnham: Ashgate Publishing.

Jordan, A., Wurzel, R. and Zito, A. (2013) 'Still the century of "new" environmental policy instruments? Exploring patterns of innovation and continuity', *Environmental Politics*, 22(1), pp. 155–173.

Kiss, B., Sekulova, F., Hörschelmann, K., Salk, C.F., Takahashi, W. and Wamsler, C. (2022) 'Citizen participation in the governance of nature-based solutions', *Environmental Policy and Governance*, 32(3), pp. 247–272.

Knill C and Liefferink D (2007) *Environmental politics in the European Union.* Manchester: Manchester University Press.

Knill, C., Steinebach, Y. and Fernández-i-Marín, X. (2020) 'Hypocrisy as a crisis response? Assessing changes in talk, decisions and actions of the European Commission in EU environmental policy', *Public Administration*, 98(2), pp. 363–377.

Kulin, J. and Johansson Sevä, I. (2024) 'Rightwing populist attitudes and public support for climate policies in Western Europe: Widening the scope using the European Social Survey', *PLOS Climate*, 3(10), e0000443.

Lenschow, A., Burns, C. and Zito, A. (2020) 'Dismantling, disintegration or continuing stealthy integration in European Union environmental policy?', *Public Administration*, 98(2), pp. 340 – 348.

Lenschow, A. and Sprungk, C. (2010) 'The myth of a green Europe', *Journal of Common Market Studies*, 48(1), pp. 133 – 154.

Lombardo, E. and Verloo, M. (2009) 'Institutionalizing intersectionality in the European Union? Policy developments and contestations', *International Feminist Journal of Politics*, 11(4), pp. 478 – 495.

Manners, I. (2002) 'Normative power Europe: A contradiction in terms?', *Journal of Common Market Studies*, 40(2), pp. 235 – 258.

McCormick, J. (2001) *Environmental policy in the European Union.* Houndmills: Palgrave.

Rehbinder, E. and Stewart, R. (1985) *Environmental protection policy, volume two: Integration through law: Europe and the American federal experience.* Berlin: De Gruyter.

Sbragia, A. with Damro, C. (1999) 'The changing role of the European Union in international environmental politics: Institution building and the politics of climate change. *Environment and Planning C: Government and Policy*, 17(1), pp. 53 – 68.

Schlesinger Jr., A. (1958). *The age of Roosevelt: The coming of the New Deal.* Boston: Houghton Mifflin.

United Nations Development Programme (UNDP) (2021) 'World's largest survey of public opinion on climate change: A majority of people call for wide-ranging action'. Available at: https://www.undp.org/press-releases/worlds-largest-survey-public-opinion-climate-change-majority-people-call-wide-ranging-action (Accessed: 16 March 2025).

von Homeyer, I., Oberthür, S. and Jordan, A. (2021) 'EU climate and energy governance in times of crisis: Towards a new agenda', *Journal of European Public Policy*, 28(7), pp. 959 – 979.

Weale, A. (1999) 'European environmental policy by stealth: The dysfunctionality of functionalism?', *Environment and Planning C: Government and Policy*, 17(1), pp. 37 – 51.

Weise, Z. and Sahlberg, J. (2025) 'EU climate chief lobbied Germany to back weakened 2040 goal', *Politico*, 2 June. Available at: https://www.politico.eu/article/eu-climate-chief-wopke-hoekstra-germany-2040-climate-target-carbon-credits/?utm_source=email&utm_medium=alert&utm_campaign=EU%20climate%20chief%20lobbied%20Germany%20to%20back%20weakened%202040%20goal (Accessed: 6 July 2025).

Wurzel, R. (2002) *Environmental policy-making in Britain, Germany and the European Union.* Manchester: Manchester University Press.

Zito, A.R. (1999) 'Task expansion: A theoretical overview', *Environment and Planning C: Government and Policy*, 17(1), pp. 19 – 35.

Zito, A.R., Burns, C. and Lenschow, A. (2019) 'Is the trajectory of European Union environmental policy less certain?' *Environmental Politics*, 28(2), pp. 1 – 21.

Section A **Changing perspectives and issues in environmental policy**

Introduction: Changing perspectives and issues in environmental policy

This section outlines the key theoretical debates and major developments in the evolution of European Union (EU) environmental policy over the past decades. It opens with a chapter by **Anthony Zito**, who sets the stage by tracing the evolution of theoretical approaches to EU environmental policy, highlighting both enduring conceptual frameworks and emerging analytical challenges. **Zito** offers a concise review of the main schools of thought that have shaped the field, identifying three major theoretical streams: i) EU integration studies, influenced by international relations, political economy and comparative politics; ii) public policy and public administration; and iii) environmental studies. He underscores the role of intellectual context in shaping theoretical perspectives, with particular attention to the influence of networks, institutions and ideas. His chapter also identifies key analytical and thematic gaps and outlines possible future trajectories for research in EU environmental policy.

Diving deeper into theoretical perspectives that can capture the nature and trajectories of environmental policy, the chapter by **Helge Jörgens** and **Inês Rocha Trindade** develops a typology of environmental policy paradigms, reflecting on how EU environmental policies respond to pressing challenges such as climate change, biodiversity loss and resource depletion. The typology is structured around two key dimensions: a) the conception of the human–nature relationship (anthropocentric vs. ecocentric) and b) the nature of proposed solutions (technological vs. behavioral). The resulting four paradigms (Technological Anthropocentrism, Behavioral Anthropocentrism, Technological Ecocentrism and Behavioral Ecocentrism*)* are illustrated with concrete policy examples. Their framework provides a valuable lens through which to analyze the normative underpinnings of EU environmental policymaking.

Vivian Gravey's contribution brings in the concept of *turbulence* to interpret recent shifts in EU environmental governance, particularly with regard to the European Green Deal (EGD). Drawing from public administration literature, **Gravey** argues that turbulence—as opposed to 'crisis'—offers a more effective conceptual tool for understanding the complex and often unstable policy environment. She demonstrates that, rather than 'governing with turbulence' or adapting governance to turbulence, the von der Leyen Commission (I) pursued a rigid, top-down strategy in the final months of its mandate. This approach, she contends, weakened both environmental ambition and institutional coherence. Her chapter argues that by connecting broader contextual shifts, organizational tensions and conflicting timescales, turbulence enables environmental scholars to capture how the general EU picture constrains the achievable responses to the twin climate and biodiversity emergencies.

In her chapter, **Zora Kovacic** explores the contested role of scientific evidence in EU environmental policy. Drawing on policy document analysis, fieldwork and interviews conducted in collaboration with the European Environment Agency and the

https://doi.org/10.1515/9783111321523-003

Joint Research Centre, **Kovacic** reveals that what counts as policy-relevant evidence is often the result of negotiation among competing policy priorities. Her chapter shows that economic and environmental rationales are frequently misaligned and that, in practice, institutional knowledge brokers tend to select evidence aligned with economic imperatives to advance environmental goals. Against this backdrop, she raises a fundamental question: is the EGD a genuinely transformative project or merely a green veneer over traditional economic policy?

A complementary perspective on knowledge use is offered by **Katharine Rietig**, who investigates the role of learning in EU environmental policy. Her chapter reviews how the literature on policy-learning has evolved, emphasizing the importance of the learning dynamic in facilitating environmental policy change. Through the case of the greening of the Common Agricultural Policy, **Rietig** illustrates how learning can occur at any stage of the policy cycle. She shows how actors adapt their strategies, incorporate new knowledge and even revise core beliefs, highlighting the dynamic interplay between experience and policy transformation.

The normative evolution of EU environmental policy is addressed in the chapters by **Ian Bailey** and by **Annica Kronsell** and **Gunnhildur Magnusdottir**. **Bailey** analyzes the values underpinning the EU's approach to reconciling environmental protection and economic growth. He traces the shifting balance of these values since the inception of EU environmental policy in 1972, focusing on treaty provisions, environmental action programs and the rhetorical and practical emphasis on economic competitiveness. His chapter argues that ecological modernization and econocentric framings have become dominant, often marginalizing alternative approaches that do not serve the EU's economic growth agenda. **Kronsell and Magnusdottir** bring in an ecofeminist and feminist-institutionalist lens to examine how the EGD frames gender and environmental concerns. Their analysis reveals that, while the EGD incorporates nature more explicitly than gender, both are constrained by the EGD's prevailing techno-economic logic and path-dependent ecological modernization framework. They argue that the limited integration of nature and gender reflects deeper structural biases; consequently, they call for a fundamental rethinking of both environmental integration and gender equality principles in EU environmental policymaking.

One of the wider challenges EU environmental policy faces is the degree of democratic input that is included, which the chapter by **Diarmuid Torney, Aron Buzogány and Louisa Parks** tackles. They trace the EU's initial neglect of democratic principles in environmental policymaking and highlight a gradual institutional shift toward participatory and deliberative mechanisms aimed at addressing legitimacy deficits. While the EGD places significant emphasis on democratic engagement, the authors argue that substantial gaps remain, particularly in the inclusiveness and effectiveness of participatory and deliberative processes.

Anthony R. Zito

Navigating the streams? Theoretical approaches and European Union environmental policy studies

Abstract: This chapter analyzes the evolution of theoretical conceptualizations of European Union (EU) environmental policy over time and outlines the current and future conceptual challenges facing EU environmental policy studies. While various approaches have shaped the field's theoretical thinking, the chapter argues that three core theoretical streams have defined the terms of the field: EU integration studies (often channeling developments in international relations, political economy and comparative politics), public policy and public administration, and environmental studies. Stressing the importance of intellectual circumstances in framing how academics theorize, the chapter charts, decade by decade, many of the prominent theoretical works examining EU environmental policy, focusing on such approaches as the role of networks, institutions and ideas. The chapter emphasizes the key questions that this literature has pursued before discussing some thematic and analytical gaps that need highlighting and future theoretical trajectories for environmental policy research.

Keywords: European integration theories; public policy theories; environmental studies theories; institutions; ideas

1 Introduction

This chapter explores the evolution of theoretical conceptualizations of European Union (EU) environmental policy over time and assesses the past, current and future conceptual questions facing EU environmental policy studies. While strong theorizing of elements of EU environmental policy has occurred, these efforts have often followed particular analytical tracks and puzzles that overlook others. This chapter offers a heuristic framework to help students of EU environmental policy and integration studies understand some of the larger dynamics. The chapter aligns with Rosamond (2007) in paying attention to the intellectual circumstances, or 'scholarly contingency', that academics face when they write. This includes observing events and attempting to understand and contextualize these events.

This chapter offers one way of understanding the theoretical evolution of the field and how different approaches have interacted with each other. A wide range of disciplinary approaches (from sociology, geography, planning, economics and so forth) have shaped this theoretical thinking. Nevertheless, the interaction of three core theoretical dynamics or streams (here I am inspired by the image of Kingdon's 1984 multiple streams approach) has shaped the study of EU environmental policy: EU integration studies (often channeling developments in international relations, international

https://doi.org/10.1515/9783111321523-004

political economy and/or comparative politics), public policy and public administration, and environmental studies. In each of these three streams, we find academics developing their theoretical ideas, partly in response to contemporary events but also to influential academic publications that preceded their own efforts.

Other disciplines have had significant input in the field, but they have tended to be either transmitted or incorporated through at least one of the three core theoretical streams that drive the field. The image, and it is only a heuristic image, depicts the trajectory of academic thinking over time as it is found in academic exchange and publication in that subfield; academics from the other two streams will borrow and transfer theoretical ideas at various points. Each stream will ebb and flow as new ideas, questions and EU phenomena (e.g. Eastern enlargement) occur. The streams will merge and diverge at various points. The influences and ripples that happen in one stream may cascade into the other streams although often with a temporal delay. Many scholars who have had significant theoretical influence in this field do not neatly fit into the three streams: for example, Philip Lowe (rural studies, e.g., Brouwer and Lowe, 2000), Albert Weale (political theory, e.g., 1996) and Arthur Mol (sociology, e.g., Mol and Liefferink, 1993). At most we can say that the publication in the academic space of EU environment policy has meant that a wide range of thinkers and disciplines have engaged with academics, venues and ideas operating in the three streams. This chapter also cannot cover all the important theories in operation in this field, so the selection has concentrated on the earlier, highly significant examples of theoretical concepts that address certain core research questions.

The next section proceeds to map important theoretical works in terms of discussions in the streams. It does so chronologically, therefore stressing the importance of the intellectual circumstances and disciplinary dynamics as academics react to the evolution of EU policy. Three contextual periods for EU studies are roughly demarcated around certain core theoretical questions and themes: explaining EU environmental policy expansion and its drivers (1974–1998), coping with the sector expansion in practice (1998–2007), navigating increasing turbulence (2007 to now). This temporal differentiation shares the outlook of Lenschow's 2021 overview but carries a much more micro focus on the evolution of theories reflecting scholarly circumstances. The third section discusses core theoretical themes over time and theoretical absences. The fourth and concluding section makes suggestions for future research.

2 Chronology and intellectual context of EU environmental theorization

EU environmental policy expansion and growth, 1972–1998

The period from 1972 to 1984 witnessed the European Community expand legally binding legislation without an explicit treaty basis (Knill and Liefferink, 2007); interesting-

Table 1: Overview of 1972–1998 dynamics.

Circumstances	Questions	Theoretical approaches
1972–1984: Binding legislation without explicit treaty basis	What dynamics and actors drive this integration?	– Environmental stream: federal institutionalist response
1987 onwards: Single European Act spurs integration (and integration theory), gives legal status to environmental policy	What dynamics are giving impetus to this policy area?	– Combine Integration and Policy streams with environmental streams: contextual analysis – Combine integration and environmental streams: integration theories, more general international relations theories, ideational and interest group approaches
	How do national administrative systems respond to this integration and shape it?	– Combine Integration and Environmental streams: institutional, national styles – States seek advantages through market
1989: Fall of Berlin Wall 1992: First Danish Referendum on Maastricht Treaty, Anglo-French pushback against Community regulation 1995: Molitor Report	Some academics posing questions, but no strong trend in any of the three streams until next era	– Academics in streams react in next era

ly, the academic theoretical interest in the policy and integration streams did not track this development. In the environmental studies stream, by contrast, academics (particularly legal scholars and practitioners) were noting the striking growth in quite demanding supranational regulation as well as other strategic communications (n.b. Haigh, 1984; Johnson and Corcelle, 1989). Nevertheless, these works did not take a theoretical stance. Although not explicitly making a theoretical statement, legal scholars Rehbinder and Stewart (1985) offered a comparative federal institutionalist analysis, acknowledging the importance of comparing dynamics such as interstate commerce (comparing the United States' history to Europe's) for triggering efforts to prevent potential barriers to trade created by state environmental legislation. Although not the focus of the authors, their argument provided one answer to the analytical question of what dynamics and actors were driving EU environmental policy expansion. Accordingly, Rehbinder and Stewart helped start the theoretical study of how certain dynamics (in this case market-building and trade) can affect environmental policy creation, influencing environmental and federalism scholars such as Liberatore (1991) and Kelemen (2004).

Influenced by these authors and the blending of integration and policy studies by Majone (e.g., 1991), Liberatore (1991) laid out several contextual reasons for the growth of EU environmental policy, before enmeshing her integration and environmental policy analysis in classic policy stream concerns. Liberatore raised a number of policy issues that the EU policy sector will have to confront *over time*; these include the need for more approaches that seek to cure environmental pollution problems versus those that seek to prevent them, how to integrate environmental priorities not only across environmental media (i. e., water versus air) but also across policy sectors, who wins and who loses as a result of regulation and how one achieves effective implementation. Only with greater recognition in European environment and integration contexts and streams would these policy challenges (i. e., what does policy expansion mean in practice?) start being the focus of the next scholarly period.

A related but separate theoretical strand arose with regulatory studies that bridged policy and environmental streams by focusing on the importance of national administrations and how they shape Member State environmental behavior. These studies, only two of which are mentioned here, focused on national regulatory systems but had important commentary on the European Community impact on these national institutions and processes. Accordingly, Brickman, Jasanoff and Ilgen (1985) discussed the Community role in shaping national chemical regulation, emphasizing the characteristics of national institutions, the political strategies of interest groups and the wielding of scientific information. They also stressed the Community role as a supranational federation that can push harmonization. Vogel (1986) also focused on regulation, making the argument that states have favored and routinized approaches to policy problems over time, which Richardson termed "policy styles" (Richardson, Gustafsson and Jordan, 1982). Accordingly, the United Kingdom (UK) national administration has a traditional approach to protecting the environment, but the British style was being challenged and shaped by the UK's EU membership.

In terms of spurring theoretical studies forward, the 1985 development and subsequent ratification of the Single European Act (SEA) gave Community environmental policy aims explicit treaty recognition, but, even more importantly for this field, triggered a renewed if delayed Anglo-American interest in the integration streams. It is important to stress that hugely significant steps in EU integration occurred throughout the 1970s and 1980s, but the SEA ratification triggered a renewal of integration theory after Haas (1975) and other influential integration stream scholars turned away from studying EU integration in the 1970s. In the integration stream, the two dominant theories of the 1960–1974 period, neofunctionalism and intergovernmentalism, also received renewed importance. Neofunctionalism continued to stress the importance of supranational institutions and learning dynamics that induce populations to welcome the benefits of integration (see especially Mutimer, 1989), while various versions of intergovernmental theories continued to stress the driving role of interdependent Member States in pushing integration to fulfill national interests (see especially Moravcsik, 1993).

Two other contextual and disciplinary developments are worth mentioning. Within the environmental stream, the publication of the Brundtland Report and the advance of the idea of sustainable development triggered various conceptual developments within Community environmental policy and the environmental studies stream (World Commission on Environment and Development, 1987). The Brundtland Report frames it as development that meets present needs without jeopardizing the needs of future generations (World Commission on Environment and Development, 1987, Chair's Forward, point 27). Baker et al. (1997, p. 26) tease out the theoretical strands of the Brundtland Report and other conceptualizations of sustainable development, noting how the very ambiguity of this political idea makes it a powerful tool for building political consensus because individual policymakers have a large degree of flexibility in interpreting what the commitment means.

Simultaneously, international relations and other politics scholars were questioning the focus on material interests and highlighting the importance of beliefs, norms, rules and values—operating under various labels including new institutionalism, ideational approaches, constructivism and so forth (for example, March and Olsen, 1983; Wendt, 1992; Goldstein and Keohane, 1993). These viewpoints influenced the convergence of the integration and the public policy streams over time. One of the important theoretical arguments embedded in institutionalist approaches is the notion of path dependency. If we apply path dependency to the European Community integration and policy process, we would expect the following dynamic: policy and organizational choices made at the start of the environmental policy history generate institutionalized commitments and constituent interests; these choices and commitments become harder to unravel over time and determine subsequent policy decisions (Weale, 1996; Peters, 2005). European Community structures and legislation consist of rules and norms that embody identities, values and interests, and accordingly define the appropriate action for policymakers to take.

In this period of streams convergence, the 1992a Judge special issue deliberately sought to assess the 'interconnectedness' of the emerging environmental policies with the Community integration process and politics in the aftermath of the SEA project (Judge, 2020, pp. xi–xii). Interestingly, the importance of Judge 1992a confirms Rosamond's (2016) argument to beware of viewing retrospectively the integration stream in this time period solely as a theoretical battle between intergovernmentalism and neofunctionalism. It is true that numerous works in this field have genuflected toward these two traditional integration arguments, but much of the work we discuss here does not take the two approaches as their analytical core. The Judge special issue is also prescient in highlighting the limits of integration as it shapes policy, looking at the struggles to integrate environmental priorities with economic ones (Weale and Williams, 1992) and the challenges of effective implementation (Collins and Earnshaw, 1992).

Judge and his colleagues deployed policy analysis, comparative politics, electoral and participatory politics and political economy into the integration analysis of environmental policy and environmental politics (Judge, 2020). Using ideational and institutional analysis, Weale and Williams (1992) offer a prescient case about the limits of EU environmental policy expansion. They juxtapose the ideational expectations of ecological modernization (defined briefly here as an approach viewing environmental protection as preconditions for economic growth—see Chapter 3 for a detailed examination) with the actual failure to fully integrate environmental policy aims in the Single Market. In mixing these approaches the authors note the importance of economic actors in defining problems and the role of organizational (which follows the line about how institutions are set up—i. e. a form of institutional analysis) and bureaucratic politics (e. g., the implications of the Commission Directorate-General for Environment was a junior, less influential player). Van der Straaten (1992) focuses also on the ideational dimension by assessing how the Single Market program could overcome the limitations of the traditional neoclassical economics paradigm and its lack of understanding of environmental value. With a focus on lobbying and alliance-building in the European Community context, Boons (1992), Mazey and Richardson (1992) and Judge (1992b) respectively bring in elements of networks (defined here as clusters of individuals, groups, organizations and institutions that maintain a relationship based on shared interests, ideas and other connections and that influence policy actions) and power relations between differing industrial and other interests, non-governmental organizations (NGOs), strategies and alliances, and institutional political strategies and coalition-building.

Following closely after with a greater focus on the international dynamics and implications of how the European Communities have pushed environmental policy, Liefferink, Lowe and Mol (1993) edited a volume that sought to analytically frame the three converging streams at the time. In their two theoretical survey chapters, Mol and Liefferink give greater weight to developments in the integration stream given the volume's stronger international focus (Mol and Liefferink, 1993; Liefferink and Mol, 1993). They assess the comparative merits of realism (focusing on how states dominate international politics in their quest for security and focus on 'high' politics) and the neo-Marxist assumptions of *dependencia* and world-systems approaches (contending that the polarization between capitalist Global North countries and the poorer Global South leads the Global South toward dependency and underdevelopment). They lean toward the international relations movement from the integration stream to focus on global interdependence and its policy characteristics of networks and regimes working in particular policy issues (as indicated by Haas, 1975 and Keohane and Nye, 1977) and the importance of comparing the Community's federal characteristics to other systems (in particular Scharpf, 1988).

These theoretical suggestions have continuing resonance with the study of EU environmental policy, but other chapters in Liefferink, Lowe and Mol (1993) put forward explanations of EU policy dynamics that have often had greater resonance. Borrowing from sociology and systems theory and reflecting the move toward more construed and ideational views of the world, Jachtenfuchs and Huber (1993, pp. 36–37) introduced the concept of learning to the study of European Community policy, focusing on how 'issue frames' (cognitive structures that give meaning to events the actors observe) shape how policy actors perceive and act upon reality. They argued that a major frame shift occurred between 1988–1991 with respect to the Community climate policy. Weale (1993) takes a similar tack in viewing ecological modernization as an important example of a belief system, meaning a set of interrelated ideas that inform policy action and that actors use to explain and justify this policy action. Grant (1993) combined the ideational elements of the push for globalization and regulatory harmonization with the importance of understanding the power of transnational corporations, while Rucht (1993) focused on the policy and political impact NGOs can have through transnational cooperation. In this same edited volume, Mazey and Richardson (1993) extended Richardson's policy-style argument to ask if the EU was developing a pragmatic policy style for grappling with environmental questions, focusing on the openness of the European Commission (EC) to all interest groups, the overall Community stress on consultation processes and a tendency to break environmental issues down into more manageable, technical elements. Finally, Buller, Lowe and Flynn (1993) offered one of the earliest usages of the concept of Europeanization in our three streams, making the point that a critical dynamic in European integration in general but also particularly in environmental studies is how European integration impacts different administrative cultures and the relevant constituent interests in the environment sector. Thus, they argue that European environmental efforts have helped to centralize UK environmental administration while aiding the process of decentralization of the French management.

The recognition of the importance of the state and how national administrations guide or obstruct implementation was taken up by a range of scholars. Particularly important for both of these strands was the teaching and writings of Héritier. Héritier (1995) argued for the essential importance of understanding the linkage between Community and Member State policymaking; political actors and contexts in both levels seek to influence and are being influenced by policy decisions at the other level. Influenced by the German, more actor-orientated policy network tradition, she and her collaborators focused on networks of rational actors exchanging material and non-material (e. g., knowledge) resources within the context of institutional/legal barriers, social norms and specific policy contexts, revealing how national actors might gain a competitive advantage by driving Community policies that reflect national practice (Héritier, Knill and Mingers, 1996). Héritier (1995) differentiated Member States in terms of whether they were 'leaders' or 'laggards' – an assessment that very much depended on the specific policy and national contexts as well as external factors. A great deal of analytical examination has followed this differentiation of state approaches (see for example Chapter 12).

It is worth noting that some scholars continued to engage with some of the bigger European integration questions. One example is Jonathan Golub (1996) who sought to assess the relative merits of the theoretical explanations focused on supranational institutions (in this case the EC and European Parliament versus those focused on state-centered explanations and intergovernmentalism). He found that entrepreneurial and agenda shaping efforts of the supranational bodies can wield influence, but the intergovernmental bodies retain the power, unless the supranational institutions use the institutional mechanisms of the EU process to disrupt the decision-making. One of the interesting concepts to persist from the integration stream is the neofunctionalist concept of spillover. While the creator of neofunctionalism discredited his own theory (Haas, 1975), his concept of spillover has remained in use (e. g., Weale, 1999). Spillover's expectation is that, when national interest groups and populations witness how European integration benefits them in one policy sector, they will see how other related policy areas touched by integration development would be improved by further integration. At a more fundamental political level the elites and population groups will also learn to appreciate these benefits and be willing to grant a greater extension of integration into other policy problems.

A prominent example of a work that seeks to explain European environmental integration through a greater focus on the policy stream is Pollack (1994), who combines Lowi's public policy dynamics typology with Scharpf's institutional analysis of voting rules to understand EU policy expansion, with environment being one of the preeminent areas. Pollack argued that extensive EU rulemaking (regulatory policies) reflects the spillover dynamic created by Member State policies that disrupted the Common Market.

Wrestling with expansion in practice, 1998 – 2007

As the previous section clearly indicates, there has been a strong theoretical tradition in the confluence of the academic streams for looking beyond grand integration theories and for recognizing the long-term challenges that EU environmental policymaking faces. It is arguable that much of the theoretical developments used in EU environmental policy studies currently derive from these core arguments; consequently, the next sections are relatively smaller in scope. Nevertheless, a series of developments

Table 2: Overview of 1998 – 2007 dynamics.

Circumstances	Questions	Theoretical approaches
1997: EU pushes ambitious aims at the Kyoto Conference	What kind of global leader can the EU be?	– Theorizing the EU as a global leader
1999: 11 Member States adopt Euro Santer Commission resigns	What dynamics and actors drive this integration? How do national administrative systems respond to this integration and shape it? How to improve EU environmental policy implementation? How to integrate EU environmental policy into other EU priorities?	– Institutions, ideas, interests, networks and other actors/dynamics drive integration – Institutional path-dependent explanations – Implementation analysis – Europeanization dynamics – Policy instrument analysis – Policy integration analysis
2004, 2007: 12 new Member States join	What is the future for EU environmental policy governance?	– EU environmental governance

created an intellectual context where the academic focus shifted. Part of this impetus comes from events that occurred before 1998, the ramifications of which set a political and policy context that was different from the enthusiasm for various aspects of integration after ratification of the Single European Act. After the difficulties of negotiating and ratifying the Maastricht Treaty, actors complained about burdens of Community/EU environmental regulation. This was exemplified by the 1992 Anglo-French efforts to push back against EU regulation and the 1995 Molitor Report reflecting the political pressure to simplify EU regulation (European Commission, 1995; Wurzel, 2002, p. 59). The 1999 collapse of the Santer Commission raised a host of questions about EU management and both EU and Member State administrative capacity, such as whether the EU had become overextended and unable to deliver its policy agenda. These contextual dynamics, together with the enormous adjustment required both from the EU and new Member States between 2004 and 2007, suggested a move toward policy implementation and consolidation over policy expansion. Nevertheless, EU environmental policy also saw a simultaneous enlargement of scope as the EU moved to becoming a prominent global leader on climate and other environmental topics as seen in the 1997 Kyoto negotiations (Sbragia with Damro, 1999).

In the midst of this context change, scholars continued to study the EU environmental expansion that was still ongoing in this period. Many scholars turned to the approaches developed in the three theoretical streams, seeking to refine those explanations. For example, Zito (2000) and Wurzel (2002) explored the importance of expert networks and policy entrepreneurship to overcome EU and Member State institutional blockages. These network approaches came from the public policy and integration streams but tended to focus on expertise and knowledge as a key driver in pushing environmental policy outputs. Expert networks can take a range of forms. Some network approaches focus on actors linked to each other by their roles and frequent contact. In this network interaction, network members will exchange and combine their respective resources (including knowledge and power) in order to influence the various stages of the policy process. Wurzel (2002) used the term policy networks that was prevalent, particularly in comparative politics and public policy, during this period. A different approach to networks is to put greater weight on the knowledge and ability to create a scientific consensus that underpins a policy idea. The epistemic community argument and the advocacy coalition framework expect that a network of professionals use their recognized expertise and authoritative claims to such expertise to persuade other actors (Zito, 2018; Sabatier, 1998).

While many scholars pursued these explanations for continued EU environmental policy expansion, the changes in the EU context and the academic discussions in the policy stream led to other questions. There was a greater focus on assessing the effectiveness of the EU environmental policy architecture and investigating what conditions and measures were associated with more effective implementation and delivery (e. g., Jordan, 1999; Knill and Lenschow, 1998). Knill and Lenschow (1998) tackled the issues of implementation by typologizing the regulatory style (interventionist versus mediating) and regulatory structures (whether administrative competencies are concentrated or fragmented vertically and/or horizontally) of EU policy tools and assessing the (mis-)match between these tools and the styles and structures of national administrations. Börzel (2003) followed this conceptual agenda with a stronger focus on failures of compliance, testing a range of explanations, including political and social institutions and culture, administrative capacity and the fragmented, politicized nature of the policy process in the Member States. Finding that rather than a problem confined to newer, poorer Member States, older, traditional Member States have faced significant issues of compliance as well, Börzel argued that there was a misfit between EU rules and Member State policy traditions and legislation and the degree of societal mobilization around the policy.

One of the major challenges of creating consistent and positive policy outcomes for the environment has centered around the difficulties of integrating environmental policies and aims with other policy sectors and aims, such as agriculture and transportation. These other policy sectors usually have a significant impact on environmental policies and problems (e.g., Lenschow, 1997). Lenschow (1997) used the policy networks concept to assess how groupings of policy actors sought to integrate environmental concerns into Cohesion and Structural Funds but faced different levels of institutional constraint, which defined success. Lenschow and Zito (1998) recalibrated the investigation into processes that integrated environmental policy into other EU aims by giving a greater weight to the role of ideas. They utilized the concept of policy framing (as promulgated by Schön and Rein, 1994). This approach expects policymakers, when facing situations where the policy basis in knowledge is contestable and uncertain, to co-construct a narrative enabling the policymakers to assess the problem, formulate solutions and cajole other policy actors to embrace this solution.

In examining questions such as the degree of transformation we see in Member State administrations, policy processes and interest group configurations, scholars have turned to the concept of Europeanization found in the integration stream (Jordan and Liefferink, 2004). Though defined variously one standard definition of Europeanization is "the domestic adaptation to European regional integration" (Vink and Graziano, 2008, p. 7). Another standard formulation of Europeanization is to assess domestic structures in terms of policy (broader policy goals and policy instruments), politics (how civil society and the public engage with integration processes) and polity (focusing on government and institutional interactions and administration) (Börzel and Risse, 2003; Börzel, 2008). One of the core analytical investigations focused on how and in what direction Europeanization occurs: for example, do we see convergence or divergence of Member States and which conditions shape these outcomes?

Many academics wanted to place these questions in a wider integration and public policy context to assess the degree that European integration was transforming Member State domestic policy and governance (e.g., Börzel and Risse, 2003; Jordan, 2002) and how to govern more efficiently and democratically (e.g., Jachtenfuchs, 2001). Jachtenfuchs (2001, p. 246) defines governance "as the intentional regulation of social relationships and the underlying conflicts by reliable and durable means and institutions, instead of the direct use of power and violence". Much of this governance approach has focused on governing without a central, hierarchical authority. Scholars have found the EU's multilevel, multi-institutional policy process to be an appropriate context of such studies. Equally, EU policymakers caught between the desire to enhance EU policy while dealing with popular mistrust of political institutions, also pushed the idea of governance (European Commission, 2001). Jordan and Schout (2006) combine network analysis with the study of policy integration to articulate the coordination mechanisms that the EU multilevel governance process needs to pursue. Their findings caution that governance and coordination mechanisms will fare poorly where EU and Member State administrative capacity is lacking.

The focus on environmental policy instruments constitutes another effort to investigate how to make environmental policy effective. This analytical focus came from a combination of the policy and environmental streams: namely, the Organization for Economic Cooperation and Development (e. g., 1999) and a range of institutes and researchers looking for environmental tools, particularly market-based and informational instruments that could replace and/or supplement traditional forms of regulation. The focus in this literature has often been on the design and contextualization of new instruments (e. g., Ellerman and Buchner, 2007). Other scholarship has focused on how instruments have spread in the EU and wider global context, often looking at how such tools are diffused or transferred from one jurisdiction to another (Tews, Busch and Jörgens, 2003; Jordan *et al.*, 2003).

While the examination of policy instruments brought in a range of international dynamics, a number of scholars decided to theorize the EU as a global actor. Vogler (1999, pp. 27–28), argues that there are four crucial characteristics of 'actorness' that can help evaluate the degree to which the EU qualifies. His typology includes volition (the capacity to make choices and exhibit purposive behavior), autonomy (the degree of ability to act independently of Member States), ability to employ policy instruments (that can influence other international actors) and formal and informal recognition by other third-party actors. Taking a more institutionalist approach to compare EU international activity to that of the United States, Sbragia with Damro (1999) find that the EU's process of institution building (which combines both supranational and Member State perspectives and interests) has led to a development of inclusive pre-negotiation positions that facilitate treaty ratification and implementation. Skjærseth and Wettestad (2002) use the international relations framework regime analysis to gauge how effective the EU is in implementing its policies at the Member State level.

Increasing Turbulence, 2007 to now

Much of the theoretical work on EU environmental policy has focused on the implications of external and internal pressures that have impacted EU governance (a handful are listed in Table 3). Many critics of EU integration in the previous era were focused on internal questions of EU policy competence and effectiveness. In our ongoing era, the global economic crisis, which particularly hit hard certain vulnerable EU Member States such as Greece, and other crises such as the rise of migration flows after the Arab Spring and other circumstances all raise questions about the EU's political and policy priorities. These dynamics have coincided with renewed concerns about EU economic competitiveness and whether EU regulations are justified in their aims, standards and design.

At the same time, the EU has continued to propose ambitious programs and targets, particularly concerning the climate as embodied by the European Green Deal. The questions raised about the impact of crises and the degree of green ambition that the EU has going forward have led to a range of integration stream scholarship (e. g., Burns, Eckersley and Tobin, 2020). Chapter 4 by Gravey looks extensively at these arguments about the EU's ability to weather such crises and pressures. A large body of literature has studied whether EU institutions are actually dismantling or decreasing environmental policy measures. Chapter 37 by Tobin and Minas covers the debate's concepts and findings.

An interesting part of this conversation looks at the performative element of EU actors, which raises the question of how much of EU policy activity rests in the realm of symbolic and rhetorical policy positioning. Knill, Steinebach and Fernández-I-Marín (2018) find that the European Commission continues to take a very public stance about promoting environmental goals while avoiding the adoption of new and/or more ambitious policies and the enforcement Member State compliance. Lenschow and Sprungk (2010) take a similar track to pose broader questions about mythmaking

Table 3: Overview of 2007 onwards dynamics.

Circumstances	Questions	Theoretical approaches
2007: start of the Global Financial Crisis 2008, 2014: Russian actions in Georgia, then Ukraine	How does the EU continue to promote environmental policy in the face of turbulence and increased environmental urgency?	– Learning literature – Turbulence analysis
2010: Victor Orban, Fidesz come into power in Hungary 2011: Migration crisis after Arab Spring 2016: Brexit. Election of the first Trump Administration	Does EU environmental policy face moving backwards?	– Policy Dismantling – Postfunctionalism – Ecocentric ideas – Critical Ecology – Intersectional perspectives – Decolonization studies
2019: EC announces European Green Deal 2022: Second Russian attack on Ukraine	Can the EU maintain its strategy of combining economic growth and environmental protection in the face of rising environmental problems and politicization? How does a green strategy fit into the global security challenge?	

in the European integration stream. Mythmaking involves constructing longer-term narratives that embody political meanings and explain EU integration and policy thinking over time. They argue that the EU has pursued the myth of a 'Green Europe' to boost EU legitimacy, which enhances environmental wellbeing in the Member States while also buttressing the European 'brand'. This helps make Europe distinct internally and globally, reinforcing a common European identity.

The European integration stream has given considerable attention to the rise of populist political figures and parties and, more importantly, the political dynamics that drive what is usually an anti-EU stance. Hooghe and Marks (2009) argue that the extent of European integration and its effects have increased in such a demonstrable way that the public and political parties are much more focused on European integration as a site of political contestation. Consequently this has created a much greater concern about the loss of national control and identity. The authors coin the concept of postfunctionalism to capture the politicization and party competition that now exists and can impact EU-level environmental policymaking. As handbook Chapter 11 on parties indicates, future conceptual and empirical work in EU environmental policy studies is required to explore how nationalist and populist attitudes shape EU efforts. Tosun and Debus (2021) caution us against accepting a one-dimensional view of right-wing populist parties, noting the Austrian Freedom Party, which combines anti-EU and anti-expert narratives with a desire to protect nature in particular circumstances.

In recognizing the politicization of EU integration, one must acknowledge also the longstanding popularity of environmental policies among the public and the continued importance of the EU environmental effort. Many EU environmental scholars who make important conceptual contributions pursue this approach by examining Member State contestation and leadership (e.g., Wurzel, Liefferink and di Lullo, 2019), Member State compliance, enforcement, monitoring and implementation (Börzel and Buzogány, 2019; Hofmann, 2019, Schoenefeld and Jordan, 2019) and policy instruments (Domorenok, 2019). There is also a strong theoretical interest in how learning shapes policy change even in the face of the political and policy challenges (e.g., Rietig, 2021). Chapter 6 by Rietig offers an intensive examination of the learning approach.

All the above lines of inquiry contribute significant understanding of EU environmental policy. Nevertheless, academic research being done particularly in the integration and environmental theoretical streams suggests some clear gaps in EU environmental policy studies. We expect that events and political circumstances will trigger theoretical innovation in the directions suggested by the literature discussed below.

Scholars such as Bierman (2021) are making arguments in the environmental stream, questioning the anthropocentric focus found in environmental policymaking. He argues for the need to break down the artificial separation of humanity from the rest of nature that currently is embedded in environmental governance and ideology. Several handbook chapters in Section A articulate conceptual alternatives. Duit, Feindt and Meadowcroft (2016) take a different tack by conceptualizing the idea of an environmental state, where the policy system has features such as an active and strong system of regulatory intervention, a systematic but specialized administrative apparatus, a strategy of promoting ideas and funding knowledge and open arena for contestation and discussion of environmental values. Yet another environmental literature that raises critical questions about the EU environmental governance approach is political ecology. Political ecology has a normative ambition to overturn the tendency of political economy to overlook or marginalize environmental values and priorities and seeks to give critical weight to actors marginalized in current policy debates (Sultana, 2021).

Political ecology authors such as Sultana (2021) are raising normative questions drawn heavily from intersectional studies. Intersectional studies are increasingly deployed in the integration theoretical stream. Lombardo and Rolandsen Agustín (2012) define the intersectional approach as one without a predetermined approach to framing inequality; it follows the key principle of looking at how inequalities intersect and are mutually constitutive rather than evaluating them separately. Finally, EU environmental policy studies need to develop critical tools for understanding two dimensions. First, much of the environmental cost of human activity falls upon the poorest communities and most vulnerable biospheres in the Global South; second, much of the rare earth deposits needed to counteract complex environmental problems are in areas where poor communities labor in extractive industries, often in the Global South. Making a wider point about the European and EU political project of integration and individual nation-building, Bhambra (2022) argues that the decolonization of Europe can occur only when the colonial histories of Europe are explicitly tackled by European elites and society, necessitating that the people of Europe understand that Europe, and therefore the integration project, have been constituted by the colonial histories. Just as ecologists would argue there is a false separation between humanity and nature, European history and development cannot be separated from its colonial past. As environmental failures and competition for scarce resources reverberate from the Global South to the world of the Global North, including the EU, these critical approaches from the environmental and integration streams will become more vital for studying environmental policy.

3 Conclusion

This chapter has surveyed much of the core theorization that has occurred in EU environmental policy studies. In order to understand why scholars adopt particular approaches, we have examined two different contextual dynamics. First is the global political context in which events have significant political, environmental, economic and social impacts on EU integration and environmental policy trajectories. Second, academics have drawn heavily, but not exclusively, from environmental studies, public policy research and comparative politics and international relations analysis that has been harnessed to study European integration. At various points these intellectual trajectories merge and separate, hence the image of a theoretical stream. Understanding the sequence of events and approaches helps one to recognize why perspectives dominate and may help us predict which approaches are more likely to appear on the horizon.

In the 1970s, integration studies had largely dissipated, with major scholars such as Haas abandoning regional integration studies. Viewing the European Community as a public policy actor had not yet gained a large following. Nevertheless, environmental scholars recognized the importance of European Community efforts. With the renewed academic attention toward European integration in the mid-1980s, we see a return to the deployment of international relations approaches but also a greater use of comparative and public policy perspectives to study EU integration. Not only did scholars acknowledge the global political significance of the Single European Act, they also began to catch up with the burgeoning policy architecture that the EU was creating in several policy sectors, including the environment. With the EU confronting various political difficulties and questions about the effectiveness of this project, we see many scholars from 1999–2007 move away from the more macro-international relations explanations of EU integration and toward public policy analysis that focuses on governance, implementation, policy instruments etc. It is probable that the ongoing political upheaval, particularly with its ramifications for the Global South, and the rise of important environment-triggered events, will give EU environmental policy scholars the stimulus to adopt newer theoretical tools.

References

Baker, S., Kousis, M., Richardson, D. and Young, S. (1997) 'Introduction: The theory and practice of sustainable development in EU perspective', in: Baker, S., Kousis, M., Richardson, D. and Young, S. (eds.) *The politics of sustainable development.* London: Routledge, pp. 1–40.

Bhambra, G. (2022) 'A decolonial project for Europe', *Journal of Common Market Studies*, 60(2), pp. 229–244.

Biermann, F. (2021) 'The future of "environmental" policy in the Anthropocene: Time for a paradigm shift', *Environmental Politics*, 30(1), pp. 58–77.

Börzel, T. (2003) *Environmental leaders and laggards in Europe: Why there is (not) a 'Southern problem'.* Aldershot: Ashgate.

Börzel, T. (2008) 'Environmental policy', in: Graziano, P. and Vink, M. (eds.) *Europeanization: New research agendas.* London: Palgrave Macmillan, pp. 226–238.

Börzel, T. and Buzogány, A. (2019) 'Compliance with EU environmental law: The iceberg is melting', *Environmental Politics*, 28(2), pp. 315–341.

Börzel, T. and Risse, T. (2003) 'Conceptualizing the domestic impact of Europe', in: Featherstone, K. and Radaelli, C. (eds.) *The politics of Europeanization.* Oxford: Oxford University Press, pp. 57–80.

Boons, F. (1992) 'Product-oriented environmental policy and networks: Ecological aspects of economic internationalisation', *Environmental Politics*, 1(4), pp. 84–105.

Bhambra, G.K. (2022) 'A decolonial project for Europe', *Journal of Common Market Studies*, 60(2), pp. 229–244.

Brickman, R., Jasanoff, S. and Ilgen, T. (1985) *Controlling chemicals: The politics of regulation in Europe and the United States.* Ithaca: Cornell University Press.

Brouwer, F. and Lowe, P. (eds.) (2000) *CAP regimes and the European countryside: Prospects for integration between agricultural, regional, and environmental policies.* Wallingford: CABI Publishing.

Buller, H., Lowe, P. and Flynn, A. (1993) 'National responses to the Europeanisation of environmental policy: a selective review of comparative research', in: Liefferink, D., Lowe, P. and Mol, A. (eds.) *European integration and environmental policy.* London: Belhaven Press, pp. 175–195.

Burns, C., Eckersley, P. and Tobin, P. (2020) 'EU environmental policy in times of crisis', *Journal of European Public Policy*, 27(1), pp. 1–19.

Collins, K. and Earnshaw, D. (1992) 'The implementation and enforcement of European community environment legislation', *Environmental Politics*, 1(4), pp. 213–249.

Domorenok, E. (2019) 'Voluntary instruments for ambitious objectives? The experience of the EU Covenant of Mayors', *Environmental Politics*, 28(2), pp. 293–314.

Duit, A., Feindt, P. and Meadowcroft, J. (2016) 'Greening Leviathan: The rise of the environmental state?' *Environmental Politics*, 25(1), 1–23.

Ellerman, A. and Buchner, B. (2007) 'The European Union emissions trading scheme: Origins, allocation and early results' *Review of Environmental Economics and Policy*, 1(1), pp. 66–87.

European Commission (1995) 'Report of the group of independent experts on legislative and administrative simplification', *COM*(95) 288. Brussels: Commission of the European Communities.

European Commission (2001) 'European governance: A white paper', *COM*(200(1) 428 final. *Official Journal* C 287, pp. 1–29.

Goldstein, J. and Keohane, R. (eds.) (1993) *Ideas and foreign policy: Beliefs, institutions, and political change.* Ithaca: Cornell University Press.

Golub, J. (1996) 'State power and institutional influence in European integration: Lessons from the packaging waste directive', *Journal of Common Market Studies*, 34(3), pp. 313–339.

Grant, W. (1993) 'Transnational companies and environmental policy making: The trend of globalisation, in: Liefferink, D., Lowe, P. and Mol, A. (eds.) *European integration and environmental policy.* London: Belhaven Press, pp. 59–74.

Haas, E. (1975) *The obsolescence of regional integration theory.* Research Series no. 25. Berkeley: Institute of International Studies, University of California.

Haigh, N. (1984) *EEC environmental policy and Britain: An essay and a handbook.* London: Environmental Data Services.

Héritier, A. (1995) '"Leaders" and "laggards" in European clean air policy', in: Unger, B. and van Waarden, F. (eds.) *Convergence or diversity? Internationalization and economic policy response.* Aldershot: Avebury, pp. 278–304.

Héritier, A., Knill, C. and Mingers, S. (1996) *Ringing the changes in Europe: Regulatory competition and the transformation of the state. Britain, France, Germany.* Berlin: Walter de Gruyter.

Hofmann, A. (2019) 'Left to interest groups? On the prospects for enforcing environmental law in the European Union', *Environmental Politics*, 28(2), pp. 342–364.

Hooghe, L. and Marks, G. (2009) 'A postfunctionalist theory of European integration: From permissive consensus to constraining dissensus', *British Journal of Political Science*, 39(1), pp. 1–23.

Jachtenfuchs, M. (2001) 'The governance approach to European integration', *Journal of Common Market Studies*, 39(2), pp. 245–264.

Jachtenfuchs, M. and Huber, M. (1993) 'Institutional learning in the European Community: The response to the greenhouse effect', in: Liefferink, D., Lowe, P. and Mol, A. (eds.) *European integration and environmental policy.* London: Belhaven Press, pp. 36–58.

Johnson, S. and Corcelle, G. (1989) *The environmental policy of the European Communities.* London: Graham and Trotman.

Jordan, A. (1999) 'The implementation of EU environmental policy: A policy problem without a political solution?', *Environment and Planning C: Government and Policy*, 17(1), pp. 69–90.

Jordan, A. (2002) *The Europeanization of British environmental policy: a departmental perspective.* Houndmills: Palgrave Macmillan.

Jordan, A. and Liefferink, D. (2004) 'Europeanization and convergence', in: Jordan, A. and Liefferink, D. (eds.) *Environmental policy in Europe: The Europeanization of national environmental policy.* London: Routledge, pp. 224 – 245.

Jordan, A. and Schout, A. (2006) *The coordination of the European Union: Exploring the capacities of networked governance.* Oxford: Oxford University Press.

Jordan, A., Wurzel, R., Zito, A. and Brückner, L. (2003) 'European governance and the transfer of "new" environmental policy instruments (NEPIs) in the European Union', *Public Administration*, 81(3), pp. 555 – 574.

Judge, D. (ed.) (1992a) 'A green dimension for the European Community: Political issues and processes', *Environmental Politics*, 1(4), pp. 1 – 249.

Judge, D. (1992b) '"Predestined to save the Earth": The Environment Committee of the European Parliament', *Environmental Politics*, 1(4), pp. 186 – 212.

Judge, D. (2020) 'Foreword', in: Zito, A., Burns, C. and Lenschow, A. (eds.) *The future of European Union environmental politics and policy.* London: Routledge, pp. xi–xii.

Kelemen, R. (2004) *The rules of federalism: Institutions and regulatory politics in the EU and beyond.* Cambridge, MA: Harvard University Press.

Keohane, R. and Nye, J. (1977) *Power and interdependence: World politics in transition.* Boston: Little, Brown.

Kingdon, J. (1984) *Agendas, alternatives, and public policies.* Boston, MA: Little, Brown.

Knill, C. and Lenschow, A. (1998) 'Coping with Europe: The impact of British and German administrations on the implementation of EU environmental policy', *Journal of European Public Policy*, 5(4), pp. 595 – 614.

Knill, C. and Liefferink, D. (2007) *Environmental politics in the European Union: Policy-making, implementation and patterns of multi-level governance.* Manchester: Manchester University Press.

Knill, C., Steinebach, Y. and Fernández-I-Marín, X. (2020) 'Hypocrisy as a crisis response? Assessing changes in talk, decisions, and actions of the European Commission in EU environmental policy', *Public Administration*, 98(2), pp. 363 – 377.

Lenschow, A. (1997) 'Variation in EC environmental policy integration: Agency push within complex institutional structures', *Journal of European Public Policy*, 4(1), pp. 109 – 127.

Lenschow, A. (2021) 'Studying EU environmental policy', in: Jordan, A. and Gravey, V. (eds.) *Environmental Policy in the EU: Actors, institutions and processes.* Fourth Edition. London: Earthscan, pp. 51 – 71.

Lenschow, A. and Sprungk, C. (2010) 'The myth of a green Europe'. *Journal of Common Market Studies*, 48(1), pp. 133 – 154.

Lenschow, A. and Zito, A. (1998) 'Blurring or shifting of policy frames? Institutionalization of the economic-environmental policy linkage in the European Community', *Governance*, 11(4), pp. 415 – 441.

Liberatore, A. (1991) 'Problems of transnational policymaking: Environmental policy in the European Community', *European Journal of Political Research*, 19(2 – 3), pp. 281 – 305.

Liefferink, D., Lowe, P. and Mol, A. (eds.) (1993) *European integration and environmental policy.* London: Belhaven Press.

Liefferink, D. and Mol, A. (1993) 'Environmental policy making in the European Community: An evaluation of theoretical perspectives', in: Liefferink, D., Lowe, P. and Mol, A. (eds.) *European Integration and Environmental Policy.* London: Belhaven Press, pp. 99 – 113.

Lombardo, E. and Rolandsen Agustín, L. (2012) 'Framing gender intersections in the European Union: What implications for the quality of intersectionality in policies?', *Social Politics*, 19(4), pp. 482 – 512.

Majone, G. (1991) 'Cross-national sources of regulatory policymaking in Europe and the United States', *Journal of Public Policy*, 11(1), pp. 79 – 106.

March, J. and Olsen, J. (1983) 'The new institutionalism: Organizational factors in political life', *American Political Science Review*, 78(3), pp. 734 – 749.

Mazey, S. and Richardson, J. (1992) 'Environmental groups and the EC: Challenges and opportunities', *Environmental Politics*, 1(4), pp. 109–128.
Mazey, S. and Richardson, J. (1993) 'EC policy making: an emerging European policy style?', in: Liefferink, D., Lowe, P. and Mol, A. (eds.) *European integration and environmental policy.* London: Belhaven Press, pp. 114–125.
Mol, A. and Liefferink, D. (1993) 'European environmental policy and global interdependence: A review of theoretical approaches', in: Liefferink, D., Lowe, P. and Mol, A. (eds.) *European Integration and Environmental Policy.* London: Belhaven Press, pp. 17–35.
Moravcsik, A. (1993) 'Preferences and power in the European Community: A liberal intergovernmentalist approach', *Journal of Common Market Studies*, 31(4), pp. 473–524.
Mutimer, D. (1989) '1992 and the political integration of Europe: Neofunctionalism reconsidered', *Journal of European Integration*, 13(1), pp. 75–101.
Organization for Economic Cooperation and Development (1999) *Economic instruments for pollution control and natural resources management in OECD countries: A survey.* Paris: OECD.
Peters, B.G. (2005) *Institutional theory in political science: The 'new institutionalism'.* London: Continuum.
Pollack, M. (1994) 'Creeping competence: The expanding agenda of the European Community', *Journal of Public Policy*, 14(2), pp. 95–145.
Rehbinder, E. and Stewart, R. (1985) *Environmental protection policy, volume 2: Integration through law: Europe and the American federal experience.* Berlin: De Gruyter.
Richardson, J., Gustafsson, G. and Jordan, G. (1982) 'The concept of policy style', in: Richardson, J. (ed.) *Policy styles in Western Europe.* London: Allen and Unwin, pp. 1–16.
Rietig, K. (2021) *Learning in governance: Climate policy integration in the European Union.* Cambridge, MA: MIT Press.
Rosamond, B. (2007) 'European integration and the social science of EU studies: The disciplinary politics of a subfield', *International Affairs*, 83(2), pp. 231–252.
Rosamond, B. (2016) 'Field of dreams: The discursive construction of EU studies, intellectual dissidence and the practice of "normal science"', *Journal of Common Market Studies*, 54(1), pp. 19–36.
Rucht, D. (1993) '"Thinking globally, act locally"? Needs, forms and problems of cross-national cooperation among environmental groups', in: Liefferink, D., Lowe, P. and Mol, A. (eds.) *European Integration and Environmental Policy.* London: Belhaven Press, pp. 75–95.
Sabatier, P. (1998) 'The advocacy coalition framework: Revisions and relevance for Europe', *Journal of European Public Policy*, 5(1), 98–130.
Sbragia, A. with Damro, C. (1999) 'The changing role of the European Union in international environmental politics: Institution building and the politics of climate change', *Environment and Planning C: Government and Policy*, 17(1), pp. 53–68.
Scharpf, F. (1988) 'The joint-decision trap: Lessons from German federalism and European integration', *Public Administration*, 66(3), pp. 239–278.
Schön, D. and Rein, M. (1994) *Frame reflection: Toward the resolution of intractable policy controversies.* New York: Basic Books.
Schoenefeld, J. and Jordan, A. (2019) 'Environmental policy evaluation in the EU: Between learning, accountability, and political opportunities?' *Environmental Politics*, 28(2), pp. 365–384.
Skjærseth, J. and Wettestad, J. (2002) 'Understanding the effectiveness of EU environmental policy: how can regime analysis contribute?', *Environmental Politics*, 11(3), pp. 99–120.
Sultana, F. (2021) 'Political ecology 1: From margins to center', *Progress in Human Geography*, 45(1), pp. 156–165.
Tews, K., Busch, P.-O. and Jörgens, H. (2003) 'The diffusion of new environmental policy instruments', *European Journal of Political Research*, 42(4), pp. 569–600.
Tosun, J. and Debus, M. (2022) 'Right-wing populist parties and environmental politics: Insights from the Austrian Freedom Party's support for the glyphosate ban', *Environmental Politics*, 30(1–2), pp. 224–244.

van der Straaten, J. (1992) 'A sound European environmental policy: Challenges, possibilities and barriers', *Environmental Politics*, 1(4), pp. 65–83.
Vink, M. and Graziano, P. (2008) 'Challenges of a new research agenda', in: Graziano, P. and Vink, M. (eds.) *Europeanization: New research agendas.* London: Palgrave Macmillan, pp. 3–20.
Vogel, D. (1986) *National styles of business regulation: A case study of environmental protection.* Ithaca: Cornell University Press.
Vogler, J. (1999) 'The European Union as an actor in international environmental politics', *Environmental Politics*, 8(3), pp. 24–48.
Weale, A. (1993) 'Ecological modernisation and the integration of European environmental policy', in: Liefferink, D., Lowe, P. and Mol, A. (eds.) *European integration and environmental policy.* London: Belhaven Press, pp. 196–216.
Weale, A. (1996) 'Environmental rules and rule-making in the European Union', *Journal of European Public Policy*, 3(4), pp. 594–611.
Weale, A. (1999) 'European environmental policy by stealth: The dysfunctionality of functionalism?' *Environment and Planning C: Government and Policy*, 17(1), pp. 37–51.
Weale, A. and Williams, A. (1992) 'Between economy and ecology? The Single Market and the integration of environmental policy', *Environmental Politics*, 1(4), pp. 45–64.
Wendt, A. (1992) 'Anarchy is what states make of it: The social construction of power politics', *International Organization*, 46(2), pp. 391–425.
World Commission on Environment and Development (1987) *Our common future: Report of the 1987 World Commission on Environment and Development.* Oslo: United Nations.
Wurzel, R. (2002) *Environmental policy-making in Britain, Germany and the European Union: The Europeanisation of air and water pollution control.* Manchester: Manchester University Press.
Wurzel, R., Liefferink, D. and di Lullo, M. (2019) 'The European Council, the Council and the Member States: Changing environmental leadership dynamics in the European Union', *Environmental Politics*, 28(2), pp. 248–270.
Zito, A. (2000) *Creating environmental policy in the European Union.* Houndmills: Macmillan.
Zito, A. R. (2018) 'Instrument constituencies and epistemic community theory', *Policy and Society*, 37(1), pp. 36–58.

Helge Jörgens and Inês Rocha Trindade

Policy ideas, policy paradigms and principles in search of a policy

Abstract: The recognition that today's best practice in environmental policymaking is insufficient to adequately address the persistent and potentially disruptive challenges of climate change, biodiversity loss and resource depletion has triggered a debate about future European Union (EU) environmental governance. Will new policy paradigms complement ecological modernization as the dominant approach, or will incremental change of the existing policy repertoire prevail? Against this backdrop, we develop a typology of potential future environmental policy paradigms. The typology distinguishes approaches to environmental policymaking along two dimensions: 1) their perspective on the relationship between humans and nature, which can be *anthropocentric* or *ecocentric*; and 2) the character of the proposed solutions, which can be *technological* or *behavioral.* We outline the four paradigms and illustrate them with examples of existing or proposed environmental policies and instruments.

Keywords: Environmental policy; policy paradigms; ecological modernization; EU environmental policy; sufficiency

1 Introduction

Fifty years after the beginning of modern environmental policy, the fight against environmental degradation and climate change stands at a crossroads. The substantial successes in European Union (EU) environmental policy, which marked the period from the early 1980s to the mid-2000s in areas such as pollution control, energy efficiency and resource management, are losing momentum. Their main recipe for success had been a set of eco-efficiency-based policies that belong to the "ecological modernization" paradigm. Ecological modernization refers to the policy-driven innovation and diffusion of technologies that have a positive impact on the environment by increasing the efficiency of energy and resource use (Jänicke and Jörgens, 2023, pp. 69–70). The greatest strength of ecological modernization policies was their compatibility with economic growth. Policies under the ecological modernization paradigm were at least partially successful in reconciling economic growth and environmental preservation by systematically making products, processes and services more eco-efficient. Instead of slowing down economic growth, the ecological modernization paradigm triggered an impressive "*growth of the limits*" (Jänicke and Jörgens, 2023, p. 68).

However, in recent years (and particularly in light of the threat of global warming and the international consensus to keep global temperature rise below 2°C or even 1.5° C) the gap between environmental goals and actual improvements is widening (UN En-

https://doi.org/10.1515/9783111321523-005

vironment, 2019a). In the face of the "increasing scale, global reach and speed of change in [many] drivers of environmental change" (UN Environment, 2019b, p. 7), the former strengths of the ecological modernization approach to environmental policymaking have turned into weaknesses. First, due to its reliance on relative rather than absolute reductions in emissions and resource consumption, positive environmental effects are increasingly being outweighed by absolute growth. Second, its strong dependence on the availability of feasible technological solutions (Fisher and Freudenburg, 2001; Mol and Jänicke, 2009) reduces its effectiveness in areas such as climate change, biodiversity loss and land use where technological innovation is either not available, still in an experimental stage of development, too expensive or strongly conflicting with entrenched polluter interests.

The realization that the current approach to environmental policy is insufficient to adequately address the persistent and potentially disruptive challenges of climate change, biodiversity loss and resource depletion has triggered a debate about the future of environmental policy (Biermann, 2021). Will new policy paradigms replace or complement ecological modernization as the dominant approach, or will incremental change of the existing policy repertoire prevail?

To contribute to this debate, we develop a typology of potential future environmental policy paradigms. The typology distinguishes approaches to environmental policymaking along two dimensions: 1) their perspective on the relationship between humans and the natural environment, which can be *anthropocentric* or *ecocentric*; and 2) the character of the proposed solutions, which can be *technological* or *behavioral*. The chapter will outline the four paradigms and illustrate them with examples of actual environmental policies and measures in the EU.

2 Analysis of paradigmatic environmental policy change

New environmental policy paradigms can potentially overcome the shortcomings of today's environmental policies under the ecological modernization paradigm. Following Hall (1993, p. 279), we define a policy paradigm as an interpretive "framework of ideas and standards that specifies not only the goals of policy and the kind of instruments that can be used to attain them but also the very nature of the problems they are meant to be addressing". Paradigmatic policy change thus occurs when not only policy instruments and their settings are altered, but so is the overarching *leitmotiv* of policymaking in a particular policy area, that is, "a particular set of ideas that recognize some social interests as more legitimate than others and privilege some lines of policy over others" (Hall, 1993, p. 292).

How do we recognize paradigmatic environmental policy change in the EU when we see it? To operationalize paradigmatic environmental policy change, we propose to develop a typology of interpretive frameworks of environmental policymaking and assign empirically observable policies to each of these potential policy paradigms. If we can identify a coherent set or cluster of proposed or adopted policies that fit one of the potential paradigms rather than focusing on the adoption or modification of individual environmental and climate policies, we can interpret this as a new environmental policy paradigm. We thus conceive of policy paradigms as clusters of environmental policies in the EU that can be assigned to a distinguishable interpretive framework or *leitmotiv.*

So far, comparative research on environmental and climate policy change has only sporadically examined paradigmatic policy change (Busch and Jörgens, 2005; Holzinger, Knill and Arts, 2008; Jörgens, Lenschow and Liefferink, 2014). A main reason for this *lacuna* has been the conceptualization of the dependent variable as individual policies rather than clusters of policies that follow a similar logic of intervention. By focusing on clusters of EU policies which share an interpretive framework (i. e., a common understanding of the type of intervention regarded as necessary to address climate change and of the main objectives of government action in this policy domain), we are better equipped to observe paradigmatic policy change beyond single or small-n comparative case studies.

The following section deductively develops a typology of potential paradigms in environmental policymaking and identifies examples of concrete policies that fit the interpretive framework of each of the potential paradigms.

3 A typology of potential environmental policy paradigms

We propose to distinguish approaches to environmental policymaking along two dimensions. First, policies may differ in terms of their worldview with regard to the relationship between humans and nature, which can be *anthropocentric* or *ecocentric* (Eckersley, 1992). Second, they may differ with regard to their logic of intervention, i. e., the character of the proposed solutions, which can be *technological* or *behavioral.* Each of the resulting four environmental policy types represents a set of beliefs, values and principles that guide the way that policy problems and solutions are conceived.

Regarding the first dimension, the relationship between humans and nature can be understood from a more human-centered perspective or from a more ecosystems-centered perspective. The *anthropocentric* perspective assumes that human beings are at the center of existence and that all other living beings and nonliving things have instrumental value. This perspective is characterized by a utilitarian approach toward the environment where nature exists primarily as a resource for human needs and where environmental conservation is mainly a means to ensure human welfare and ultimately the survival of the human species. By contrast, the *ecocentric* perspective believes that human beings are only one element of wider ecosystems and that all of nature has intrinsic value. Ecocentrism thus implies a more holistic perspective, with a nonutilitarian approach toward nature. It is not limited to a biocentric view, which focuses mainly on living organisms, but focuses also on environmental systems as a whole, including their abiotic aspects (Washington et al., 2017). By favoring an integrative and systemic approach, ecocentrism does not emphasize the superiority of one element over another but rather the importance of each element in the functioning of an entire ecosystem. It is important to note that anthropocentrism and ecocentrism "merely represent the opposing poles of a wide spectrum of differing orientations towards nature" (Eckersley, 1992, p. 33). Between these two extremes, we find mixed positions, some of which tend more toward ecocentrism, while others are more closely linked to anthropocentrism.

The second dimension focuses on a given policy or policy instrument's dominant logic of intervention. We distinguish between *technological* and *behavioral* solutions. While the former sees technological innovation as the main driver of environmental improvements, the latter emphasizes the need for behavioral changes at the individual or collective level. *Technological solutions* have long been a priority in environmental and climate policy because they are compatible with existing market structures and institutional frameworks and require only indirect behavioral changes. Technological solutions, as we understand them, not only encompass technological innovation, which is driven by human knowledge, but also natural innovation, where humans take a more systemic or broader view of knowledge and mimic nature's solutions (van der Jagt et al., 2020). While technological innovation has been an important driver of environmental progress in recent decades, many reports and a growing body of literature indicate that technological solutions alone may be insufficient to achieve climate goals.

A second logic of intervention, therefore, emphasizes *behavioral solutions.* Drawing on contributions from behavioral economics, behavioral science and psychology, behavioral policy refers to solutions that target psychological and cognitive mechanisms. Behavioral insights have been applied to a wide range of policy areas, including consumer protection, food safety, climate change, public health and others (Straßheim and Beck, 2019). Behavioral solutions in environmental policy vary in scope. Transition-based approaches to behavioral change aim to make individual consumption and lifestyle choices more eco-efficient, for example through nudges, education or information campaigns but also through changes in transport, energy or housing infrastructures as tools to influence individual choices. These options promote behavioral change without fundamentally changing the socioeconomic, political or ideational structures of society. In contrast, transformation-based approaches seek to collectively reshape consumption patterns and address unsustainable political, social or economic structures that perpetuate unsustainable individual habits and social norms. Transformation-based approaches, which are still more hypothetical than real, include collective redefinitions of lifestyles (e. g. sufficiency, vegetarianism, voluntary simplicity) and economic priorities (post-growth, degrowth) as ways to move beyond the "modern, industrial, consumerist, capitalist state" (Princen, 2022, p.6).

Based on these distinctions, *Table 1* identifies four potential environmental policy paradigms.

Table 1: A typology of potential environmental policy paradigms.

Worldview \ Logic of intervention	Technological Solutions	Behavioral Solutions
Anthropocentric	***"Technological Anthropocentrism"*** - Ecological Modernization - Green Growth - Geoengineering ("Ecological Modernization 2.0") - Eco-efficiency	***"Behavioral Anthropocentrism"*** - Eco-efficient Behavior - Green and Inclusive Economy - Circular Economy - Changed Infrastructures
Ecocentric	***"Technological Ecocentrism"*** - Nature-Based Solutions - Nature Restoration - Bioeconomy	***"Behavioral Ecocentrism"*** - Eco-Sufficiency Lifestyles - Wellbeing Dissociated from Growth - Post- and Degrowth - Post-Capitalism

The first paradigm, *technological anthropocentrism*, focuses on leveraging technological advancements to address environmental challenges with a primary emphasis on human-centric benefits and eco-efficiency gains. Policies involve the development and use of advanced technologies to reduce environmental impacts by increasing the eco-efficiency of production processes, products and services rather than attempting to change the behavior of producers and consumers. This paradigm has become manifest in the concept of ecological modernization, which has been dominant in environmental policymaking since the late 1980s (Jänicke and Jörgens, 2023). Since the anchoring of the sustainable development principle in the Maastricht and Amsterdam Treaties, the ecological modernization paradigm has been the strategic framework for a multitude of EU environmental policy strategies and measures whose overarching goal is the reconciliation of environmental protection and economic growth (Baker, 2007; Gouldson and Murphy, 1996; see Chapter 7). While the ecological modernization paradigm was already prominent in the EU's Fourth Environmental Action Program (EAP), it was the Fifth EAP that turned it into the EU's principal environmental strategy (Machin, 2019). With their guiding principle of green growth, the Europe 2020 strategy (Delreux and Happaerts, 2016) and the European Green Deal (EGD) (Fitch-Roy and Bailey, 2023) broadly continued the tendencies of seeking environmental protection by increasing eco-efficiency and prioritizing human needs when formulating goals. For technological anthropocentric strategies like ecological modernization to work there must be institutionalized mechanisms of environmental policy integration. This means the systematic "integration of environmental policy goals and concerns into other concurrent policy fields [...] such as transport, industry or agriculture" (see also Lafferty and Hovden, 2003, p. 9; Steinbacher, 2023, p. 124). One of the most ambitious and earliest attempts at institutionalizing cross-sectoral attention to environmental concerns was the EU's Cardiff Process of Environmental Policy Integration, which was adopted in 1998 at the European Council meeting (Jacob and Volkery, 2004; Chapter 33).

More recently, technological anthropocentrism has opened to technologies of carbon dioxide removal (Meadowcroft and Langhelle, 2010) and solar geoengineering (Jinnah and Nicholson 2019). These technologies have not yet been deployed on a large scale and are still largely theoretical and speculative (Möller, 2023) but promise to compensate for weaknesses in the ecological modernization strategy, such as efficiency's only relative gains (Jänicke and Jörgens, 2023) and rebound effects (Herring and Sorrell, 2009). These large-scale technological interventions that would deliberately modify the Earth's climate system are discussed under the terms *geoengineering* or *climate engineering* (Burns and Nicholson, 2017; The Royal Society, 2009). In contrast to all other approaches, climate engineering does not attempt to reduce emissions but aims to break the causal chain between emissions and potentially harmful environmental change (Dessler and Parson, 2005). Policies include attempts to reduce the amount of sunlight absorbed by the earth's atmosphere (solar radiation management) (Jinnah et al., 2019) and programs to remove CO_2 from the atmosphere and store it safely, ranging from ocean iron fertilization (Abate, 2013) and large-scale afforestation to bioenergy with carbon capture and storage (Michaelson, 2013). Despite an early discussion of carbon capture and storage, the EU has been reluctant to engage in a debate, let alone adopt policies, aimed at carbon removal (Geden, Peters and Scott, 2019).

Among the EU policies that can be subsumed under the technological anthropocentrism paradigm, the EU Emissions Trading System (ETS) of 2005 stands out. It seeks technological rather than behavioral change, and its ambition, while leading the world, is best described as "too little, too late" from an ecocentric point of view (Oberthür and Homeyer, 2023, p. 463; Wettestad and Jevnaker, 2018). Similarly, the EU's green energy policy (Chapter 26) predominantly focuses on technological change on the demand side and raising the energy efficiency of buildings rather than targeting energy-intensive behavior. In his review of EU policies promoting more sustainable behaviors in energy end-users, Bertoldi (2020, p. 457) concludes that the "majority of these policies are designed to improve the technical efficiency of the equipment or systems and not to encourage more efficient behavioral practices".

The second paradigm, *behavioral anthropocentrism*, emphasizes the need to change human behavior to achieve environmental goals while maintaining an anthropocentric perspective. Policies under this paradigm focus on infrastructural changes that encourage individuals and communities to adopt conservation-oriented lifestyles, those which promote sustainable consumption and waste reduction for the benefit of human societies. Concepts of a green and/or circular economy are prominent under this paradigm (Fairbrass and Vasilakos, 2021). Rather than relying on marginal increases in the eco-efficiency of products, processes and services, these policies aim for a "comprehensive restructuring of public and private infrastructures" (Jänicke and Jörgens, 2023, p. 78) and an "upgrading of the entire production system to environmental and resource-saving processes and products" (Jänicke, 2012, p. 14). While non-incremental and based on an absolute rather than a relative decoupling of economic growth from environmental pollution and resource consumption, these programs are (at least theoretically) compatible with continued, albeit dematerialized, economic growth (Ferguson, 2015; Jackson and Victor, 2019). Policies under this paradigm include large-scale investments in national energy, transport or building infrastructures (for a detailed review of building sector policy instruments, see Lucon et al., 2014; Ürge-Vorsatz, Koeppel and Mirasgedis, 2007) or attempts to systematically integrate environmental indicators into systems of national accounts (United Nations Statistical Commission, 2018).

The EU has been instrumental in adding a behavioral component to the technology-oriented approach of ecological modernization. For example, its Circular Economy Action Plan, originally adopted in 2015 and updated in 2020 (see Chapter 36), focuses on guidelines for green public procurement and consumer information requirements to make consumption patterns more environmentally friendly (European Commission, 2020a). The EU Taxonomy Regulation (Regulation 2020/852) aims to change investor behavior to redirect capital flows toward sustainable projects. The Energy Efficiency Directive (2012/27/EU, amended in 2018 and 2023) includes measures to change energy consumption behaviors, such as mandatory energy audits for large companies and consumer information programs about energy efficiency (see Chapter 26). Other recent EU policies aimed at changing behavioral patterns while maintaining a predominantly anthropocentric focus include the Single-Use Plastics Directive (Directive 2019/904) and the Farm to Fork Strategy under the EGD (COM/2020/381 final and European Commission, 2020b).

The third paradigm, *behavioral ecocentrism*, emphasizes changing human behavior to align with ecological principles, adopting an ecocentric perspective. It represents a more radical approach than behavioral anthropocentrism in that it emphasizes the intrinsic value of nature and promotes human behavior change, prioritizing ecological integrity over economic growth. Behavioral policies within this paradigm aim to address unsustainable economic and social conditions that perpetuate a mainstream culture of unsustainability that is difficult to change through voluntary behavior change alone. This includes the collective redefinition of lifestyles as well as rethinking the fundamental political and economic principles that underly societal organization. The onus is on policymakers to change framework conditions and generate collective change (Princen, 2022). This paradigm emphasizes that, while built infrastructures are crucial for behavioral change, changes to the collective imagination, governance models and social structures are ultimately needed to guarantee widespread and long-lasting environmental behavior change.

Here, individuals' lifestyle choices are seen as a potential lever to reduce emissions and resource consumption. At its core stands the idea of sufficiency (Büchs and Koch, 2017; Fuchs et al., 2023; Princen, 2003; Spangenberg and Lorek, 2019), i.e., "the reduction of consumption on an individual level in order to contribute to ecological sustainability" (Heindl and Kanschik, 2016, p. 43). Changes in environmental behavior aim at absolute reduction rather than the substitution of behaviors. Policy ideas in this category are based on notions of degrowth, slow living and ecological sufficiency; policies either attempt to change individual lifestyles by "limiting the consumption of environmentally unsound goods and services" (Spengler, 2016, p. 922) or define and impose limits on ecologically harmful economic activities (Alexander, 2012; Koch, 2020). While scholars agree that sufficiency "needs to be supported by [...] policy frameworks" (Lorek and Spangenberg, 2019, p. 26), we still lack empirical assessments of the extent to which policies based on the sufficiency principle have found their way into policy mixes at the European or the national levels. Following Heyen et al. (2013, pp. 14–17), we can distinguish four types of instruments for sufficiency policy: regulatory instruments (e.g., product bans, car bans in city centers, speed limits, regulation of planned obsolescence), economic instruments (e.g., kerosene taxes, property taxes, personal carbon allowances), planning and infrastructure provisions (e.g., priority lanes for car-sharing, vegetarian offerings in public canteens) and information-based instruments (e.g., public campaigns to eat less meat or to lower room temperature by 1 °C in winter) (see also Maitre-Ekern and Dalhammar, 2016, for the regulation of planned obsolescence; Parag, Capstick and Poortinga, 2011, for personal carbon allowances). Focusing mainly on the consumption side, Sandberg (2021, p. 6) distinguishes between policies aimed at absolute reductions of consumption, modal shifts from one consumption mode to another that is less resource intensive, product longevity and sharing practices.

While less prevalent in EU environmental policy than anthropocentric approaches to behavioral change, several policies and initiatives contain elements that align with behavioral ecocentrism principles of sufficiency, degrowth and ecological limits. In the field of product-specific regulations, the EU has developed policies that aim to incentivize consumers to repair goods instead of replacing them with new ones. Measures of this sort were included in the 2009 Ecodesign Directive (Directive 2009/125/EC) and the EU Circular Economy Action Plan (European Commission, 2020a) and strengthened in 2024 with the so-called "Right to Repair" Directive (Directive (EU) 2024/1799) (see Chapter 36). The EU's Farm to Fork Strategy (European Commission, 2020b) encourages shifts toward less resource-intensive diets without, however, going beyond information-based policy instruments (see Chapter 28). Personal carbon trading (also referred to as personal carbon allowances) has the potential to provide a strong regulatory framework for making individual lifestyles more sufficient, but has not yet found its way onto the EU climate policy agenda (Fuso Nerini et al., 2021). So far, only the United Kingdom has undertaken a systematic review of personal carbon allowances as a climate policy instrument (Fawcett, 2010). Finally, the Energy Sufficiency Policy Database (Best et al., 2022) contains several energy policies based on the eco-sufficiency principle that can be subsumed under the behavioral ecocentrism paradigm.

The fourth paradigm, *technological ecocentrism*, combines a focus on technological innovation with an ecocentric, nature-based worldview. It seeks technological solutions that not only benefit human societies but are inspired by nature and simultaneously prioritize the intrinsic value of nature. This worldview is most explicitly expressed by the European Union's concept of nature-based solutions, which it describes as "nature-based 'frugal technologies'" and "bioinspired technologies, replicating and simulating the ecosystem's natural restorative capacity" (European Commission, 2015, pp. 12, 61). Policies under this paradigm focus on how nature and ecosystem processes can serve as an inspiration for technologies that leverage natural processes and ecosystems to address environmental challenges (European Commission, 2015; van der Jagt et al., 2020). The ecocentric rationale behind nature-inspired innovation is that solutions for human development can emerge from nature itself. The European Commission defines nature-based solutions as meaning "innovating with nature" and developing solutions "inspired and supported by" natural systems (European Commission, n.d.)

Several technological advances exemplify this paradigm. Nature-based solutions and also biomimicry apply nature's designs and processes to areas such as green infrastructure, biomimetic materials and regenerative agriculture, promoting ecological balance rather than exploitation. Ecological restoration technologies, such as rewilding, carbon sequestration and reforestation, actively restore ecosystems and enhance biodiversity. Finally, decentralized and locally adaptive technologies, such as permaculture systems and community-led conservation, build ecological resilience while living within the limits of local ecosystems. These principles have shaped EU policy since the early 2000s with the "ecosystem-based approach" and have been present in research and innovation funding through programs such as "Horizon 2020" and "Horizon Europe". More recently, nature-based solutions have also been a key part of the EGD, particularly in relation to biodiversity and climate change.

Table 2 summarizes the main features of each of the four potential environmental policy paradigms and identifies their key ideas, the interpretive framework they apply to identify the nature of the problem to be addressed, their key policy objectives, the type of instruments used and the institutional requirements each paradigm presupposes. This characterization does not only rely on existing environmental policies but also considers policy proposals being discussed in the political arena.

4 Conclusion and future research

This chapter has developed a typology of potential future environmental policy paradigms to address the growing inadequacy of current approaches to tackle persistent

Table 2: Policy paradigms in environmental and climate governance.

Policy paradigm	Ideas	Interpretive framework	Policy objectives	Policy instruments	Institutional requirements
Technological Anthropocentrism	- Instrumental value of nature - Utilitarian perspective - Eco-efficiency/Optimization - Green Tech Innovation/Eco-efficiency technologies (products processes and services) - Geoengineering	Increase compatibility of environmental protection and economic growth	Increase eco-efficiency or eco-resilience through technological innovation	Top-runner program, energy efficiency labeling etc. Afforestation programs, carbon dioxide removal, solar radiation management etc.	Institutional mechanisms for environmental policy integration
Behavioral Anthropocentrism	- Instrumental value of nature - Utilitarian perspective - Green consumption - Indirect behavior change - Changing infrastructures to enable modal shifts - Substitution/shift old habits/objects for new ones	Absolute decoupling of growth from emissions/ resource consumption. Beyond growth/post-growth New economic narratives around growth Green and Inclusive Growth	Transformation of infrastructures to enable behavioral change	Energy transition to renewables, improve public transport infrastructure, build infrastructures for reuse and recycling (circular economy)	Green Deal type long-term investment program

Table 2 *(Continued)*

Policy paradigm	Ideas	Interpretive framework	Policy objectives	Policy instruments	Institutional requirements
Behavioral Ecocentrism	- Intrinsic value of nature - Nonutilitarian perspective - Sufficient consumption/lifestyles - Green citizenship/ agents of change - Direct behavior change - Create new habits (avoid, reduce, absolute reduction)	Apply the idea of sufficiency to individual lifestyles and the economy as a whole Degrowth, solidarity economy, sharing economy, cooperatives, commons	Change lifestyles and consumption patterns; impose limits on economic activities; political and economic restructuring of the state	Individual carbon allowances, bans on disposable plastic bags etc.	Modification of national accounts to include non-material aspects like well-being Redefining property rights Constitutional embedding of ecological rights
Technological Ecocentrism	- Intrinsic value of nature - Nonutilitarian perspective - Low tech - Environmental and social co-benefits/ ecosystem and community resilience	Restoration of nature and ecosystems services, ecological economics	Using technological innovation to develop nature-based solutions to environmental problems	Technology-based policies to enhance, restore, or protect natural ecosystems; e. g. promotion of green roofs, permeable pavements or urban wetlands	Modification of national accounts to include ecosystems services

environmental challenges. We argue that the ecological modernization paradigm, which has dominated EU environmental policy since the 1980s, faces fundamental limitations in addressing the scale and urgency of climate change, biodiversity loss and resource depletion. While this paradigm successfully reconciled environmental protection with economic growth through eco-efficiency improvements, its reliance on technological solutions and relative rather than absolute reductions has proven insufficient for achieving the transformational changes required to meet ambitious climate targets.

The four-paradigm typology presented here—distinguished along dimensions of worldview (anthropocentric vs. ecocentric) and intervention logic (technological vs. behavioral)—provides a framework for understanding potential pathways that complement or move beyond ecological modernization. Each paradigm offers distinct approaches. Technological anthropocentrism continues the efficiency-focused tradition while incorporating emerging technologies such as geoengineering. Behavioral anthropocentrism emphasizes transforming infrastructure to enable sustainable consumption patterns. Behavioral ecocentrism promotes sufficiency-based approaches that challenge growth-oriented assumptions and lifestyles. Technological ecocentrism harnesses nature-based solutions that prioritize ecological integrity.

Our overview of existing EU policies shows that while anthropocentric approaches remain dominant, elements of all four paradigms are already present in the European policy landscape. The EGD, Circular Economy Action Plan and various sustainability directives demonstrate how policy paradigms can coexist and complement each other. However, policies aligned with ecocentric worldviews, particularly those emphasizing sufficiency and absolute consumption reduction, remain relatively marginal in mainstream EU environmental governance. The analysis suggests that the future of EU environmental policy likely lies not in the replacement of ecological modernization by a single alternative paradigm but rather in the strategic combination of approaches from multiple paradigms. This paradigmatic pluralism may be necessary to address the diverse and interconnected nature of contemporary environmental challenges, each requiring different types of interventions across various scales and sectors.

Several paths for future research emerge from this analysis:

- Empirical assessment of policy implementation: while we have identified policy examples that align with each paradigm, systematic empirical research is needed to assess the extent to which coherent clusters of policies reflecting specific paradigms have been adopted and implemented across EU Member States. This research should examine not only policy adoption but also implementation effectiveness and outcomes.
- Political feasibility analysis: future research should investigate the political and institutional conditions that facilitate or constrain the adoption of policies from different paradigms. This includes examining the role of policy entrepreneurs, interest groups, institutional arrangements and public opinion in shaping paradigmatic policy change. Particular attention should be paid to understanding

why ecocentric approaches face greater political resistance and how their political feasibility can be increased.

- Policy mixes across paradigms: research is needed on how policies from different paradigms can be effectively combined within coherent policy mixes. This includes studying potential synergies and conflicts between paradigmatic approaches, optimal sequencing of interventions and institutional requirements for managing paradigmatic diversity.
- Evaluating effectiveness: comparative studies should assess the relative effectiveness of policies aligned with different paradigms in achieving environmental outcomes. This research should move beyond individual policy evaluation to examine the cumulative effects of paradigm-coherent policy clusters.
- Dynamic analysis of paradigm shifts: longitudinal research should examine the conditions under which paradigmatic change occurs in environmental policy. This includes studying learning processes, crisis-induced change and the role of external shocks in creating windows of opportunity for paradigmatic innovation.

References

Abate, R.S. (2013) 'Ocean iron fertilization; science, law, and uncertainty', in: Burns, W.C.G. and Strauss, A.L. (eds.) *Climate change geoengineering: Philosophical perspectives, legal issues, and governance frameworks*. Cambridge: Cambridge University Press, pp. 221–251.

Alexander, S. (2012) 'Planned economic contraction: The emerging case for degrowth', *Environmental Politics*, 21(3) pp. 349–368.

Baker, S. (2007) 'Sustainable development as symbolic commitment: Declaratory politics and the seductive appeal of ecological modernisation in the European Union', *Environmental Politics*, 16(2), pp. 297–317.

Bertoldi, P. (2020) 'Overview of the European Union policies to promote more sustainable behaviours in energy end-users', in: Lopes, M., Antunes, C.H. and Janda, K.B. (eds.) *Energy and behaviour: Towards a low carbon future*. London: Academic Press, pp. 451–477.

Best, B. et al. (2022) 'Building a database for energy sufficiency policies', *F1000Research*, 11(229).

Biermann, F. (2021) 'The future of 'environmental' policy in the Anthropocene: Time for a paradigm shift', *Environmental Politics*, 30(1–2), pp. 61–80.

Büchs, M. and Koch, M. (2017) *Postgrowth and wellbeing: Challenges to sustainable welfare*. Cham: Palgrave Macmillan.

Burns, W. and Nicholson, S. (2017) 'Bioenergy and carbon capture with storage (BECCS): The prospects and challenges of an emerging climate policy response', *Journal of Environmental Studies and Sciences*, 7(4), pp. 527–534.

Busch, P.-O. and Jörgens, H. (2005) 'The international sources of policy convergence: Explaining the spread of environmental policy innovations', *Journal of European Public Policy* 12(5), pp. 860–884.

Delreux, T. and Happaerts, S. (2016) *Environmental policy and politics in the European Union*. London: Palgrave Macmillan.

Dessler, A.E. and Parson, E.A. (2005) *The science and politics of global climate change: A guide to the debate*. Cambridge: Cambridge University Press.

Eckersley, R. (1992) *Environmentalism and political theory: Toward an ecocentric approach*. London: UCL Press.

European Commission (2015) *Towards an EU research and innovation policy agenda for nature-based solutions & re-naturing cities: Final report of the Horizon 2020 Expert Group on 'nature-based solutions and re-naturing cities' (full version).* Brussels: European Commission.

European Commission (2020a) 'A new circular economy action plan: For a cleaner and more competitive Europe', *COM*(2020) 98 final. Available at: https://eur-lex.europa.eu/legal-content/EN/TXT/?uri=celex:52020DC0098 (Accessed: 18 June 2025).

European Commission (2020b) *Farm to Fork Strategy: For a fair, healthy and environmentally-friendly food system* Available at: https://food.ec.europa.eu/document/download/472acca8-7f7b-4171-98b0-ed76720d68d3_en?filename=f2f_action-plan_2020_strategy-info_en.pdf (Accessed: 18 June 2025).

European Commission (n.d.) *Nature-based solutions.* Available at: https://research-and-innovation.ec.europa.eu/research-area/environment/nature-based-solutions_en (Accessed: 18 June 2025).

Fairbrass, J. and Vasilakos, N. (eds.) (2021) *Emerging governance of a green economy: Cases of European implementation.* Cambridge: Cambridge University Press.

Fawcett, T. (2010) 'Personal carbon trading: A policy ahead of its time?', *Energy Policy* 38(11), pp. 6868–6876.

Ferguson, P. (2015) 'The green economy agenda: Business as usual or transformational discourse?', *Environmental Politics*, 24(1), pp. 17–37.

Fisher, D.R. and Freudenburg, W.R. (2001) 'Ecological modernization and its critics: Assessing the past and looking toward the future', *Society and Natural Resources*, 14, pp. 701–709.

Fitch-Roy, O. and Bailey, I. (2023) 'Green growth and competitiveness in EU climate policy: Paradigm shift or "*plus de la même chose*"?', in: Rayner, T., Szulecki, K., Jordan, A.J. and Oberthür, S. (eds.) *Handbook on European Union climate change policy and politics.* Cheltenham: Edward Elgar, pp. 173–186.

Fuchs, D., Lorek, S., Mamut, P. and Rossmoeller, A. (2023) 'Fifty shades of sufficiency: Semantic confusion and no policy', in: Jörgens, H., Knill, C. and Steinebach, Y. (eds.) *Routledge handbook of environmental policy.* London: Routledge, pp. 347–357.

Fuso Nerini, F., Fawcett, T., Parag, Y. and Ekins, P. (2021) 'Personal carbon allowances revisited', *Nature Sustainability*, 4(12), pp. 1025–1031.

Geden, O., Peters, G.P. and Scott, V. (2019) 'Targeting carbon dioxide removal in the European Union', *Climate Policy*, 19(4), pp. 487–494.

Gouldson, A. and Murphy, J. (1996) 'Ecological modernization and the European Union', *Geoforum*, 27(1), pp. 11–21.

Hall, P.A. (1993) 'Policy paradigms, social learning, and the state: The case of economic policymaking in Britain', *Comparative Politics*, 25(3), pp. 275–296.

Heindl, P. and Kanschik, P. (2016) 'Ecological sufficiency, individual liberties, and distributive justice: implications for policy making', *Ecological Economics*, 126, pp. 42–50.

Herring, H. and Sorrell, S. (eds.) (2009) *Energy efficiency and sustainable consumption: The rebound effect.* Basingstoke: Palgrave Macmillan.

Heyen, D.A. et al. (2013) 'When less is more. Sufficiency—need and options for policy action', *Oeko-Institute's Working Paper 3/2013.*

Holzinger, K., Knill, C. and Arts, B. (eds.) (2008) *Environmental policy convergence in Europe. The impact of international institutions and trade.* Cambridge: Cambridge University Press.

Jackson, T. and Victor, P.A. (2019) 'Unraveling the claims for (and against) green growth', *Science* 366(6468), pp. 950–951.

Jacob, K. and Volkery, A. (2004) 'Institutions and instruments for government self-regulation: Environmental policy integration in a cross-country perspective', *Journal of Comparative Policy Analysis: Research and Practice*, 6(3), pp. 291–309.

Jänicke, M. (2012) '"Green growth": From a growing eco-industry to economic sustainability', *Energy Policy*, 48, pp. 13–21.

Jänicke, M. and Jörgens, H. (2023) 'Ecological modernization and beyond', in: Jörgens, H., Knill, C. and Steinebach, Y. (eds.) *Routledge handbook of environmental policy*. London: Routledge, pp. 68 – 87.

Jinnah, S. and Nicholson, S. (2019) 'Introduction to the symposium on "geoengineering: governing solar radiation management"', *Environmental Politics*, 28(3), pp. 385 – 396.

Jinnah, S. et al. (2019) 'Governing climate engineering: A proposal for immediate governance of solar radiation management', *Sustainability*, 11(14), 3954.

Jörgens, H., Lenschow, A. and Liefferink, D. (eds.) (2014) *Understanding environmental policy convergence: The power of words, rules and money*. Cambridge: Cambridge University Press.

Koch, M. (2020) 'The state in the transformation to a sustainable postgrowth economy', *Environmental Politics*. 29(1), pp. 115 – 133.

Lafferty, W.M. and Hovden, E. (2003) 'Environmental policy integration: Towards an analytical framework', *Environmental Politics*, 12(3), pp. 1 – 22.

Lorek, S. and Spangenberg, J.H. (2019) 'Identification of promising instruments and instrument mixes to promote energy sufficiency. EUFORIE—European Futures for Energy Efficiency', *Deliverable 5.5. EUFORIE—European Futures for Energy Efficiency*.

Lucon, O. et al. (2014) 'Buildings', in: Edenhofer, O. et al. (eds.) *Climate change 2014: mitigation of climate change. Working Group III contribution to the fifth assessment report of the Intergovernmental Panel on Climate Change*. New York: Cambridge University Press, pp. 671 – 738.

Machin, A. (2019) 'Changing the story? The discourse of ecological modernisation in the European Union', *Environmental Politics*, 28(2), pp. 208 – 227.

Maitre-Ekern, E. and Dalhammar, C. (2016) 'Regulating planned obsolescence: A review of legal approaches to increase product durability and reparability in Europe', *Review of European, Comparative & International Environmental Law*, 25(3), pp. 378 – 394.

Meadowcroft, J. and Langhelle, O. (eds.) (2010) *Caching the carbon: The politics and policy of carbon capture and storage*, Cheltenham: Edward Elgar.

Michaelson, J. (2013) 'Geoengineering and climate management: From marginality to inevitability', in: Burns, W.C.G. and Strauss, A.L. (eds.) *Climate change geoengineering: philosophical perspectives, legal issues, and governance frameworks*. Cambridge: Cambridge University Press, pp. 81 – 114.

Mol, A.P.J. and Jänicke, M. (2009) 'The origins and theoretical foundations of ecological modernisation theory', in: Mol, A.P.J., Sonnenfeld, D.A. and Spaargaren, G. (eds.) *The ecological modernisation reader: Environmental reform in theory and practice*. London: Routledge, pp. 17 – 27.

Möller, I. (2023) 'Geoengineering and public policy: Framing, research, and deployment', in: Jörgens, H. Knill, C. and Steinebach, Y. (eds.) *Routledge handbook of environmental policy*. London: Routledge, pp. 381 – 399.

Oberthür, S. and von Homeyer, I. (2023) 'From emissions trading to the European green deal: The evolution of the climate policy mix and climate policy integration in the EU', *Journal of European Public Policy*, 30(3), pp. 445 – 468.

Parag, Y., Capstick, S. and Poortinga, W. (2011) 'Policy attribute framing: A comparison between three policy instruments for personal emissions reduction', *Journal of Policy Analysis and Management*, 30(4), pp. 889 – 905.

Princen, T. (2003) 'Principles for sustainability: From cooperation and efficiency to sufficiency', *Global Environmental Politics*, 3(1), pp. 33 – 50.

Princen, T. (2022) 'Sufficiency and the state: A prospective project', *Frontiers in Sustainability* 3, 956139.

Sandberg, M. (2021) 'Sufficiency transitions: A review of consumption changes for environmental Sustainability', *Journal of Cleaner Production*, 293, 126097.

Spangenberg, J.H. and Lorek, S. (2019) 'Sufficiency and consumer behaviour: From theory to policy', *Energy Policy*, 129, pp. 1070 – 1079.

Spengler, L. (2016) 'Two types of 'enough': Sufficiency as minimum and maximum', *Environmental Politics*, 25(5), pp. 921 – 940.

Steinbacher, C. (2023) 'Analytical perspectives on environmental policy integration', in: Jörgens, H. Knill, C. and Steinebach, Y. (eds.) *Routledge handbook of environmental policy*. London: Routledge, pp. 122–135.

Straßheim, H. and S. Beck (eds.) (2019) *Handbook of behavioural change and public policy*. Cheltenham: Edward Elgar.

The Royal Society (2009) *Geoengineering the climate: Science, governance and uncertainty*. London: The Royal Society.

UN Environment (2019a) *Global environment outlook—GEO-6: Healthy planet, healthy people*. Cambridge: Cambridge University Press.

UN Environment (2019b) *Global environment outlook GEO-6: Summary for policymakers*. Cambridge: Cambridge University Press.

United Nations Statistical Commission (2018) *Global assessment of environmental-economic accounting and supporting statistics 2017. Background document. Statistical Commission, forty-ninth session, 6–9 March 2018*. New York: StatCom.

Ürge-Vorsatz, Koeppel, S. and Mirasgedis, S. (2007) 'Appraisal of policy instruments for reducing buildings' CO 2 Emissions', *Building Research & Information*, 35(4), pp. 458–477.

van der Jagt, A.P., Raven, R., Dorst, H. and Runhaar, H. (2020) 'Nature-based innovation systems', *Environmental innovation and societal transitions*, 35, pp. 202–216.

Washington, H. et al. (2017) 'Why ecocentrism is the key pathway to sustainability', *The Ecological Citizen*, 1(1), pp. 35–41.

Wettestad, J. and Jevnaker, T. (2018) 'EU emissions trading: Frontrunner—and 'black sheep'?', in: Wettestad, J. and Gulbrandsen, L.H. (eds.) *The evolution of carbon markets: Design and diffusion*. London: Routledge, pp. 30–52.

Viviane Gravey

Turbulence: A new normal for European Union policymaking?

Abstract: This chapter assesses the emerging public administration literature on turbulence and how governments (should) respond to it. Taking as an example the fraught delivery of the nature parts of the European Green Deal, it argues that turbulence, more than crisis, is a useful lens to consider the current challenging context for making European Union (EU) environmental policy. By connecting broader contextual shifts, organizational tensions and conflicting timescales, turbulence enables environmental scholars to capture how the general EU picture constrains the achievable responses to the twin climate and biodiversity emergencies. However, the solutions to turbulence—robust governance strategies—put forward by turbulence scholars are a bad fit for a political system like the EU. The chapter shows how the von der Leyen Commission wielded such a robust governance strategy in the last few months of its first term, with deleterious consequences for both environmental ambition and the integrity of the European project. This chapter urges EU environmental scholars to both build on and contribute to broader EU studies, as environmental policies are both critical to the EU's identity and a particular target of the current anti-EU backlash.

Keywords: Turbulence; environmental policy; robust governance; crisis

1 Introduction

The European Union (EU) and its predecessors have a long history of crises and of the changes these crises brought. From the French refusal to ratify the European Defence Community in 1954 and the Danish 'no' vote to the Maastricht Treaty in 1991 to the 2008 global financial crisis, the EU is used to crises. But the last fifteen years have seen an unrelenting assault of crises coming from different directions, with complex moving parts, layering on top of each other and interacting with one another.

European integration scholars have tried to make sense of this 'poly-crisis' or "conglomerate of crisis" (Falkner, 2016), studying the emerging 'crisification' of European governance (the emergence of networks of civil servants supplemented by experts tasked with keeping watch over emerging crises and driving crisis response (Rhinard, 2019)). If the EU is in a situation of 'perma-disaster', then crisis is not the correct lens to employ to comprehend the situation (Dobbs, Gravey and Petetin, 2021). A crisis implies an acute event, born from either external shock or internal discord, which has a relatively clear beginning and once resolved, can be resorbed (Saurugger, 2014). There is a pre-crisis and post-crisis normal—a return to a more 'ordinary' situation. What if no 'ordinary' exists in Brussels anymore, and instead a constant stream of crises exists with no semblance of normalcy?

https://doi.org/10.1515/9783111321523-006

To make sense of the challenges facing the EU today, this chapter suggests stepping out of the European studies cannon and engaging with recent developments in the broader public policy and public administration (PPPA) literature. Despite the EU's special features, it faces many similar challenges to other political systems, and our analysis of the EU is enriched by fostering exchanges between our environmental niche in European studies, the broader European studies community and wider PPPA debates. In this chapter, I demonstrate this by applying a PPPA concept, turbulence, to EU environmental policies and the European Green Deal (EGD). Other such bridges between political science subfields could, for example, help to critically assess the delivery of a just transition and the democratic credentials of EU environmental action and therefore offer promising avenues for research.

This chapter portrays an EU facing a highly turbulent situation. It argues for the added explanatory value that considering this context as one of turbulence, not crisis or crises, provides. Considering turbulence and its response can help environmental scholars reconnect our specific, sectoral analysis with the wider EU picture, analyzing both how that broader context constrains the achievability of a green transition and how environmental policy developments tell a wider story of where the EU is headed.

Having set out the diagnostic—a highly turbulent situation—the chapter then considers potential responses or cures. It summarizes the growing literature on robust governance and governing with turbulence and discusses its application to the EU. Analyzing the development of the EGD and its fraught delivery in the last months of the first von der Leyen Commission, the chapter addresses two research questions: Is the EGD, both in its design and delivery, an example of a robust response to turbulence? To what extent do EU responses to turbulence risk weakening environmental ambition and European integration more widely?

2 Environmental action in a turbulent EU

Scholars investigating turbulence contend that turbulence is likely in democratic governance; changes in governing parties, economic success or societal mobilization will always lead to some level of uncertainty, inconsistency, surprise and unpredictability. However, in recent years democratic governments have been experiencing greater and more frequent spikes in turbulence. This chapter builds on the work of Ansell and co-authors and defines turbulence as resting on three characteristics: shifting parameters, intercurrence (or unexpected interdependence) and temporal complexity.

The first characteristic, shifting parameters, helps distinguish turbulence from crisis. Hence, while crises are 'extraordinary' events that exist in contrast to 'ordinary' time, the balance between the routine and the turbulent is now so skewed that turbulence is in itself a 'new normal'. No quiet, ordinary time remains; instead, the ground keeps shifting under decision-makers' feet (Ansell and Trondal, 2018). This means that prepared plans and typical solutions suddenly are not applicable or relevant for decision-makers. When nevertheless adopted, these solutions end up having unexpected outcomes (Lund and Andersen, 2023). This leads to a constant game of catch-up and having to revise policy on the fly, recently illustrated by the multitudinous, ad hoc Covid-19 containment policy revisions and innovations (Ansell, Sørensen and Torfing, 2021). While EU scholarship and politicians have often expressed the 'positive' impact that crises have on pushing forward the European integration project, constantly shifting grounds can undermine the EU in terms of both how and what decisions are taken (and how credible or legitimate they are).

Second, this "increasingly volatile context for complex problem-solving" (Ansell, Sørensen and Torfing, 2021, p. 951) is fueled by 'intercurrence', that is unforeseen, surprising and not necessarily conducive "institutional entanglements" at different scales and "unexpected interdependences" between issues or institutions (Ansell and Trondal, 2018, p. 45). New stakeholders may suddenly erupt in a policy network or be pushed out. Decisions that look 'good' at one level of governance may raise alarm bells at a lower or higher level, or indeed a solution that looks 'good' in one part of government may be highly problematic for another. In an EU context, this raises concerns of subsidiarity. European integration that increasingly supports the competences of subnational entities makes the EU particularly susceptible to intercurrence. So too does the churn of planned or snap domestic elections across its twenty-seven Member States, making for a very fluid composition of the Council of the European Union and the European Council, which can change dramatically over the lifetime of a policy proposal.

Third, decision-makers are increasingly faced with temporal complexity, concerned with both clashing time horizons—exemplified with Covid recovery planning having to balance the provision of urgent support to affected professions and 'build back better' in the medium term with an eye towards net-zero by 2050 (Dobbs, Gravey and Petetin, 2021)—and shifting tempos within organizations between periods of high and low demand and capacity that constrains policy choice and delivery.

These three characteristics can lead to different forms of turbulence that are readily apparent in the EU. Ansell and co-authors posited three forms: environmental (or contextual), organizational and scalar (Ansell and Trondal, 2018). Dobbs, Gravey and Petetin (2021) suggested the EU is facing all three as well as a fourth form of policy turbulence. The EU is facing environmental turbulence as both the Covid-19 pandemic and the Russian invasion of Ukraine have profoundly shaken its domestic agenda. This is leading to a dramatic shift in discourse towards security of supply (of food, of energy) and interdependence. The EU is also facing organizational turbulence. Within the EU institutions themselves, restructuration and centralization of power within the Commission is profoundly changing how policies are made but also enforced. Additionally, the growing number of populist governments in the Council (and their growing weight in the European Parliament (EP)) is leading to a rise in 'unpolitics', with political actors refusing to abide by both formal and informal rules and undermining the EU decision-making process (Zaun and Ripoll Servent, 2023). The EU is further facing scalar turbulence, i.e., turbulence whereby decisions at one level of governance impact another. This is exemplified by decisions in one EU Member State impacting its neighbors (such as diverging decisions regarding opening or closing internal EU borders during different crises, from the refugee crisis to Covid-19). Finally, policies themselves, especially wide-ranging, innovative policies, can foster turbulence in adjacent policy fields (for example, UK farming communities leaving not only the EU but the Common Agricultural Policy fueled turbulence) (Gravey, Petetin and Dobbs, 2021). This makes addressing turbulence particularly difficult as responding to some forms of turbulence can fuel other turbulence. As the following EGD analysis shows, the adoption of the EGD, partly a response to turbulence, disrupted EU agricultural policy and lead to a sharp backlash from farming unions and farmers in early 2024, which shaped the policy debate ahead of the June 2024 EP elections.

By drawing on these contextual, scalar, organizational and policy dimensions, turbulence is a much richer concept than crisis, and is particularly well suited to study what is happening to the EU. First, it does not presuppose a sudden end of either the crisis or of the EU itself. Second, the interconnections between those dimensions are particularly visible in the EU, which is recent and fragile enough that turbulence can easily spread and reinforce itself. Hence, environmental policy scholars need to pay attention to both how the broader EU context may reshape our research field, and vice versa (see Chapter 2). Third, turbulence also offers a way to study changes to EU environmental policy in terms of how the EU responds to turbulence and what it is ready to abandon to tackle turbulence, even if only in the short term.

3 Responding to turbulence in a robust fashion

Decision-makers facing turbulent situations grapple with difficult choices. Put simply (although it is never as simple in practice and from the viewpoint of decision-makers themselves), they have to decide to govern *against* or *with* turbulence (Dobbs, Gravey and Petetin, 2021). They either have to try to maintain or regain as much stability as possible or choose a more robust path of transformation and reinvention to keep on delivering some (but not all) objectives and values. This is what Ansell et al. are conceptualizing as 'robust governance', i. e.: "The ability of one or more decisionmakers to uphold or realize a public agenda, function, or value in the face of the challenge and stress from turbulent events and processes through the flexible adaptation, agile modification, and pragmatic redirection of governance solutions" (Ansell, Sørensen and Torfing, 2021, p. 952).

This section introduces the robust governance concept (and how it differs from resilience) and how it can be analyzed (strategies for robust governance), before highlighting the two critical challenges robust governance poses for EU environmental action: to the integrity of the EU and to its environmental ambitions.

In choosing 'robust' governance and robustness as an answer to turbulence, Ansell and co-authors echo other public policy scholars investigating how to mix durability and flexibility (Jordan and Moore, 2020). Building on the work of, e. g., Howlett and Ramesh (2022), they distinguish between resilience or static robustness and a more dynamic form of robustness (Ansell, Sørensen and Torfing, 2023). That first static/resilient approach is focused on the ability to *bounce back* to a stable status quo, akin to what Dobbs, Gravey and Petetin (2021) argue is the aim of governing *against* turbulence, trying to limit its most egregious effects and hoping to continue as much as possible with business as usual. Conversely, dynamic robustness is not so backward facing. It is instead about transformation and bouncing *forward*. Thus, Howlett and Ramesh (2022, p. 25) describe dynamic robustness as "changes in goals as well as means in order to allow policies to adapt more broadly by altering their form in response to changing circumstances."

Authors writing about turbulence and robustness wield numerous adjectives to capture this imperative for change, from nimble to innovative and transformative. For Ansell et al. governing in situations of turbulence is "not for control freaks" (Ansell, Sørensen and Torfing, 2021, p. 955) as governments suddenly lose a lot of the control they may be used to (or think is in reach in more routine times). Far from following routine processes, in turbulent times, decision-making loops are much shorter; governments cannot afford to wait for the 'best' practice and full data but need to make decisions quickly, with reduced stakeholder engagement, and be prepared to revise decisions as quickly (Ansell, Sørensen and Torfing, 2021, p. 956). While robust governance shares with 'muddling through' its iterative nature, it is not limited to minor departures from the status quo (Bendor, 2015). Robustness calls for potentially radical changes, which may require stepping outside normal procedures to ensure the continued delivery of (revised/recommitted to) objectives. The type of procedural shortcuts and lack of transparency that these answers suggest needs to be offset by frequent and clear communication (Ansell, Sørensen and Torfing, 2023).

Both of these strategies are easier said than done in the EU context. First, procedures matter, even more so in a community of law like the EU. Not only are procedures critical to the legitimacy of the EU institutions themselves ("throughput legitimacy", Schmidt, 2013), but they are the results of hard-fought compromises to manage competing interests (small and large Member States, various parties etc.) and agreed-upon policies that go beyond the lowest common denominator. Second, EU institutions, both by design and in practice, are rather bad at communicating with European citizens.

Regarding the first, Rhinard's work on crisification and its impact on the quality of EU decision-making offers a cautionary tale. Studying the crisis-mapping and crisis-responding units and procedures blooming in European institutions, Rhinard identified that "a logic of urgency rather than bargaining or deliberation creeps into decision-making arenas", with choices having to be made quickly, with real life consequence, a paucity of facts and genuine dilemmas and by a much narrower group of decision-makers with limited engagement with stakeholders (Rhinard, 2019, p. 11). Ansell et al. argue that robust governance is a balancing act of legitimacies, juggling between "the importance of political/democratic steering (majority rule), knowledge concerns (expert rule), the interests of particularly affected parties (stakeholder rule), and the impartiality in law application (the rule of law)" (Ansell, Sørensen and Torfing,

2023, p. 202). That balance in the EU is in flux with a growing politicization of what was traditionally an elite-driven technocratic project and had become a hyper-consensual project famous for taking a long time to agree on policies—and for those policies to then 'stick' and be hard to dismantle (Gravey and Jordan, 2016).

Far from leaving politics to its Member States, the EU is now the site of "politics against policy" and even "politics against polity" (Schimdt, 2018, p. 1548). Populist actors engage in 'unpolitics' whereby they reject the very foundations of how agreements are made in the Council of the European Union (rejecting consensual norms, refusing to compromise and undermining solutions) (Zaun and Ripoll Servent, 2023), while simultaneously more mainstream political actors struggle (or indeed refuse) to contain them (Kelemen, 2020). The ground may be shifting under foot for *all* governance levels, but the ground is particularly brittle below the EU's feet. The EU is thus facing both demands to do 'more' and 'more quickly' in times of crisis (Rhinard, 2019) and greater scrutiny and pushback regarding what it has done, why and at what cost.

How should the EU respond to turbulence? In order to analyze whether a governance response is 'robust' or not, the emerging literature has identified various strategies. Most of these strategies are based on studies of decision-making during the Covid-19 pandemic and decisions often made by frontline administrators (see e. g., Capano and Toth, 2023; Previtali and Salvati, 2023). They may not readily translate to strategies pursuable at other governance levels, but they offer a useful starting point.

These can be grouped into four overarching categories: experimentation, coordination, prioritization and procedural innovation. The experimentation category concentrates on thinking outside the box and developing new solutions/instruments (e. g., prototyping or modularization) or repurposing existing ones (*bricolage*) (Ansell, Sørensen and Torfing, 2021; Previtali and Salvati, 2023). The second set concerns the scaling up of these new solutions (e. g., strategic polyvalence, scalability) but also fine-tuning the balance between local innovation and coordination at higher government levels (e. g., 'bounded'; Ansell, Sørensen and Torfing, 2021, or 'coordinated'; Capano and Toth, 2023, autonomy). Here, autonomy and coordination are balanced such that the center only steps in when part of the system malfunctions, or to support learning from/diffusion of innovation in one part of system to others). While experimentation and coordination/facilitation strategies are mostly single-issue focused, the prioritization strategies go to the heart of the political choice incumbent on government in turbulent times: not all objectives and values can be delivered. Policies and instruments can be reframed to fit with political priorities or conversely to be downgraded through a reordering of policy priorities between what is 'necessary' versus what is 'nice to have'. This re-ordering also pertains to procedures and to how decisions are made. In turbulent times decision-makers may not have the same amount, type or quality of data, may not have the time to engage with a wide-range of stakeholders etc. Thus, robustness strategies concern not only the *type* of policies agreed upon but *how* they are agreed upon.

This third category, prioritization, is where critical policy consequences for EU environmental action arise (Dobbs, Gravey and Petetin, 2021). Not every instrument, objective or even value will be retained. A robust governance response is one that prioritizes some objectives, values or instruments, keeps some static, reinvents others and fully abandon yet others. It is in the frequent recalibration and revision of the objectives and means of public action that decision-makers can ride the turbulence wave. This can be presented very positively, such as when Ansell et al. write of the "the flexible adaptation, agile modification, and pragmatic redirection of governance solutions" (Ansell, Sørensen and Torfing, 2021, p. 252). However, this formulation often hides the political, and indeed potentially "tragic", choices (Rhinard, 2019, p. 627) inherent in such pragmatic redirection.

The fourth category, procedural innovation, concerns the institutional and organizational dimensions of those changes. The Covid-19 pandemic demonstrated that not only policy outcomes but how policies are agreed upon had changed—with often profound procedural innovation happening in short order. This raises the question of who decides which path to aim for? Who decides what instruments, values or objectives get discarded, and which are worth preserving, even at great cost? Second, who decides who is to be tasked with these major decisions and how can decision-makers responding to turbulence be held accountable for their choices?

Capano's analysis of Italy's early Covid-19 response illustrates the importance of these two different faces of Ansell et al.'s pragmatic redirection. Capano emphasizes that, facing a crisis with little preparation or directly relevant experience, Italian decision-makers went with what they knew best and that "the existing characteristics of the policy and political system, with all their pros and cons, prevail(ed)" (Capano, 2020, p. 326). More generally, we posit that a high turbulence setting will be revelatory of decision-makers deep-seated preferences.

4 Nimble or brittle? The EGD as response to turbulence

This chapter considers the implications for EU environmental action of the current high turbulence affecting the EU. To do so, it focuses first on the EGD as the flagship environmental strategy of the von der Leyen Commission (interestingly, also its flagship economic strategy) and then in particular on the nature dimension of the European Green Deal. While this chapter argues that *all* environmental policymaking in the EU will be caught in turbulence, the effect of turbulence—and the response to it—will be more readily visible in such a high-profile policy. Due to the sequencing of legislative work on the EGD and its headline objective of climate neutrality by 2050, most of the existing literature on the EGD has focused on its climate dimensions: the Carbon Border Adjustment Mechanism, the Climate Pact and the Climate Law (see e.g. Dupont, Oberthür and von Homeyer, 2020; Dupont et al., 2024). As such, to better understand what the EGD does for environmental and not just climate action, we should consider its nature dimension (see Chapter 8).

Dobbs, Gravey and Petetin (2021) suggested the EGD as announced in 2019 could be a way for the European Commission to govern *with* turbulence, harnessing the chaotic environment, intercurrence and to jump *forward* to a 'better' Europe, achieving nature recovery, climate neutrality and a just societal transition. As such, this chapter asks whether the EGD is, in both its design and delivery, a robust answer to turbulence and the extent to which EU responses to turbulence risk weakening environmental ambition and European integration more widely.

To answer these questions, this chapter focuses on the last semester of the 2019–2024 European Parliament, i. e., the sequence from the last few months of the Spanish Presidency of the Council in late 2023 up to the June 2024 European Elections, which saw, as is typical at the end of each legislature, a spur in legislative activity to try to finalize some files in time while abandoning or profoundly rewriting others. This analysis first surveys the overall EGD legislative agenda before focusing on its nature dimension exemplified by three legislative case studies: the withdrawn Sustainable Use of Plant Protection Products Regulation (SUR), the Nature Restoration Law (NRL) and the snap reform of the Common Agricultural Policy (CAP).

The European Green Deal (see also Chapter 20) was one of the six main priorities of the first von der Leyen Commission, Europe's 'man on the moon' moment aiming for climate neutrality and living well within planetary boundaries by 2050. It has spawned the most Commission initiatives (167 out of 661) but at about 50 percent has a low completion rate (European Parliament, 2023). These numbers reveal the breadth of the work undertaken by European institutions as part of the EGD—167 initiatives including 138 legislative proposals across a wide range of economic and environmental issues (European Parliament, 2024). In that respect, the EGD has had the potential to be transformative, offering not just a resilient but a robust path forward for Europe. Hence the EGD, itself a response to turbulence, has apparently been able to withstand the growing turbulence that enfolded the EU during its delivery. Announced in late 2019, the EGD could have easily been sidelined during the Covid-19 pandemic or the Russian invasion of Ukraine in February 2022. This did not happen. Instead, EGD delivery proceeded, reinforced by the agreement of the Next Generation EU (NextGenEU) financial package. NextGenEU, presented as a "once in a lifetime chance to emerge stronger from the pandemic, transform our economies and societies, and design a Europe that works for everyone" (European Union, n.d.), is a transformative program that exemplifies two robustness strategies: experimentation (both in terms of EU-wide borrowing and in the scaling up of green and digital transition through targeted investments) and facilitation (fostering coordinated autonomy with a central role for Member States in delivering those investments via the adoption of National Recovery and Resilience Plans submitted to the European Commission).

At first glance EGD legislative progress appears very positive, as only five files have officially been withdrawn or blocked. Nevertheless, many files did not proceed smoothly—or at all. We note the high number of files proposed too late for work to be done—twenty-one announced, twenty-four tabled—which could indicate either workload issues within the Commission (Guillot, 2021) or prioritization of certain files and areas of work following the Commission's political judgement. For example, the fact that the Commission did not produce a proposal for a revision of its flagship chemical regulation REACH despite consultations closing in 2022 shows a clear decision to delay a reform unpopular with industry (European Commission, 2021). The EGD remains a work in progress: the second von der Leyen Commission will decide whether it maintains tabled/announced files in its work program and the changing balance of power within the Council and the EP will decide the fate of the twenty-four files 'close to adoption'.

EGD legislative progress is further in question when we turn to its nature dimension. Our three policy case studies reached very different outcomes along very different timelines. The SUR proposal, tabled in June 2022, was rejected in the European Parliament plenary in November 2023; it then continued progressing in the Council until the European Commission withdrew it in February 2024. The Nature Restoration Law, proposed in June 2022, was finally agreed upon in the Council two years later in June 2024 after months of uncertainty despite a political agreement in trilogue between the two legislators in November 2023. The snap CAP reform proposal was published in mid-March 2024 and finished its legislative passage barely two months later in mid-May 2024. Each of these case studies demonstrates the use of robust governance strategies by EU actors and the risk attached to those.

All case studies show evidence of procedural innovation—indeed, procedural shortcuts—highlighting the fragility of EU decision-making conventions. With SUR, the Parliament Plenary endorsed the views of the Committee on Agriculture and Rural Development (AGRI) over the compromise report produced by the lead Committee on the Environment, Public Health and Food Safety (ENVI). The file was rewritten to such an extent that the ENVI rapporteur recommended voting against it. While it is rare for the Plenary to significantly diverge from the lead committee, what followed next is almost unheard of: the Plenary voted against sending the file back to committee. By refusing to do so, the Plenary effectively ended its first reading, leaving the file's fate to the Council. The Council discussed next steps but did not go much further before Commission President Ursula von der Leyen announced in February 2024 it would withdraw the file to assuage farmers' protests.

With the snap CAP reform, the Commission first ignored its usual practice of broad consultation, only consulting the four farming organizations represented at the EU level, with both the organic and small farmers organizations (IFOAM and ECVC) complaining that they were 'consulted but not heard'. The Commission then ignored its normal requirements for impact assessment as well. The Parliament legal service endorsed the latter move, which however is the basis of an ongoing ClientEarth action against the Commission. To ensure the proposal made it through the Parliament in time for the final plenary session, the AGRI Committee agreed to forego the normal translation of the proposal and endorsed the Council's position with no amendments, sending it directly to the Plenary. The Plenary voted to reject a debate on the text and agreed to it in full.

Finally, with NRL the Council stepped outside expected norms. Despite a provisional political agreement between the Council and Parliament reached in trilogue in November 2023, the Council only adopted the law in June 2024. The Council coalition favoring NRL had floundered in early 2024, with the Belgian Presidency and especially Prime Minister de Croo working to undermine the law, calling it a 'bad law' and suggesting it should be reopened in the next legislature. De Croo's position—with rumors he had reached out to Orban to oppose the NRL—shed light on divisions within Belgium, with the Flemish Environment minister calling on de Croo to ask von der Leyen to withdraw NRL (Guillot, 2024a), while the Brussels Region Environment minister pushed for its adoption (Guillot, 2024b). Similar divisions in another EU federal state, Austria, were instrumental to NRL's final adoption, with Austria's environment minister voting in favor of the law against her Chancellor's wishes, opening herself up to lawsuits in both Austria and at the EU level (Guillot, 2024c).

These examples illustrate both the ongoing turbulence in the EU and that EU actors are willing to compromise key values and functions to respond to turbulence. Each case reflects an effort to downgrade the priority of nature protection in the broader European Green Deal, especially where it directly impacts (conventional) farming interests. Although the NRL case and Austria's fraught position show these shortcuts can also be taken in favor of ambition. Each case is revelatory of the EU's ranked priorities (nature protection falling behind both agri-food production and climate action).

While some may argue this prioritization makes sense—ensuring climate action is on track before tackling other environmental challenges—this ignores both the interconnected nature of the climate and biodiversity crises and the fact that one of the main challenges for the EU's delivery of its climate neutrality objective is the very same agri-food sector it decided against reforming. Accordingly, these three cases reveal an EU buckling under pressure. Instead of seizing the opportunity to reform European agriculture in response to both the climate and biodiversity emergency and the Russian invasion of Ukraine, the EU is instead governing *against* turbulence and trying to maintain the EU farming status quo as long as possible. Due to the interconnected nature of environmental challenges, these decisions undermine the entire EGD—and its ability to help the EU withstand turbulence. The procedural shortcuts adopted in all three cases further reveal that Schmidt's "politics against policy" and "politics against polity" go hand in hand (2018, p. 1045), with efforts to undermine the transformative power of EGD's not stopping even when at risk of undermining EU decision-making rules. Building on Zaun and Ripoll Servent (2023) we note that the practice of 'unpolitics', conceptualized to make sense of fringe populists at EU level, appears to be increasingly popular with the mainstream.

5 Conclusion

This chapter surveyed the emerging turbulence literature in public administration, arguing that turbulence offered a useful lens for EU environmental scholars to account for the impact of broader EU developments. It argued that turbulence permeates all EU action. Addressing turbulence requires hard choices—questionable, political choices—for which EU actors should be held accountable. The chapter summarized the type of robust governance strategies emerging in the literature, arguing they are not a very good fit for a system like the EU and could be used to weaken environmental ambition.

It tested this hypothesis by looking at the final months of the von der Leyen Commission and the delivery of the nature parts of the EGD. It found that 'robust' governance strategies were used against environmental ambition and against EU decision-making conventions. Instead of governing *with* turbulence the EU is governing *against* it, trying to maintain and protect the status quo from turbulence instead of using turbulence to fuel the green transition (Dobbs, Gravey and Petetin, 2021). This example illustrates the need for continuous exchanges between EU environmental scholars and the broader field of EU studies and the disciplines, from International Relations to public administration etc. that feed into it. While EU environmental scholars should keep in mind developments in the broader field, environmental policies and politics are both a lightning rod for anti-EU backlash and an area where democratic innovations are most frequently used. This makes environmental scholarship a source of both early-warning signals and potential solutions for addressing the growing turbulence engulfing the European Union.

References

Ansell, C., Sørensen, E. and Torfing, J. (2021) 'The COVID-19 pandemic as a game changer for public administration and leadership? The need for robust governance responses to turbulent problems', *Public Management Review*, 23(7), pp. 949 – 960.

Ansell, C., Sørensen, E. and Torfing, J. (2023) 'Public administration and politics meet turbulence: The search for robust governance responses', *Public Administration*, 101(1), pp. 3 – 22.

Ansell, C.K. and Trondal, J. (2018) 'Governing turbulence: An organizational-institutional agenda', *Perspectives on Public Management and Governance*, 1(1), pp. 43 – 57.

Bendor, J. (2015) 'Incrementalism: Dead yet flourishing', *Public Administration Review*, 75(2), pp. 194 – 205.

Capano, G. (2020) 'Policy design and state capacity in the COVID-19 emergency in Italy: If you are not prepared for the (un)expected, you can be only what you already are', *Policy and Society*, 39(3), pp. 326 – 344.

Capano, G. and Toth, F. (2023) 'Thinking outside the box, improvisation, and fast learning: Designing policy robustness to deal with what cannot be foreseen', *Public Administration*, 101(1), pp. 90 – 105.

Dobbs, M., Gravey, V. and Petetin, L. (2021) 'Driving the European Green Deal in turbulent times', *Politics and Governance*, 9(3), pp. 316 – 326.

Dupont, C. *et al.* (2024) 'Three decades of EU climate policy: Racing toward climate neutrality?', *WIREs Climate Change*, 15(1), e863.

Dupont, C., Oberthür, S. and von Homeyer, I. (2020) 'The Covid-19 crisis: A critical juncture for EU climate policy development?', *Journal of European Integration*, 42(8), pp. 1095 – 1110.
European Commission (2021) *Chemicals legislation—revision of REACH Regulation to help achieve a toxic-free environment., European Commission—Have your say.* Available at: https://ec.europa.eu/info/law/better-regulation/have-your-say/initiatives/12959-Chemicals-legislation-revision-of-REACH-Regulation-to-help-achieve-a-toxic-free-environment_en (Accessed: 6 July 2024).
European Parliament (2023) *The six policy priorities of the von der Leyen Commission: an end of term assessment.* LU: Publications Office. Available at: https://data.europa.eu/doi/10.2861/763094 (Accessed: 6 July 2024).
European Parliament (2024) *A European Green Deal, legislative train schedule.* Available at: https://www.europarl.europa.eu/legislative-train/theme-a-european-green-deal (Accessed: 6 July 2024).
European Union (n.d.) *NextGenerationEU—European Union.* Available at: https://next-generation-eu.europa.eu/index_en (Accessed: 6 July 2024).
Falkner, G. (2016) 'The EU's current crisis and its policy effects: Research design and comparative findings', *Journal of European Integration*, 38(3), pp. 219 – 235.
Gravey, V. and Jordan, A. (2016) 'Does the European Union have a reverse gear? Policy dismantling in a hyperconsensual polity', *Journal of European Public Policy*, 23(8), 1180 – 1198.
Gravey, V., Petetin, L. and Dobbs, M. (2021) 'Quitter la PAC, comment et pour quoi faire ?: La (re) construction des politiques agricoles britanniques au cœur des turbulences du Brexit', *Politique européenne*, 73(3), pp. 150 – 178.
Guillot, L. (2021) *Eurocrats burn out under 'insane' Green Deal workload, POLITICO.* Available at: https://www.politico.eu/article/european-commission-green-deal-staff-burnout-workload/ (Accessed: 6 July 2024).
Guillot, L. (2024a) *Flemish minister asks Belgian PM to stall Green Deal files during EU presidency, POLITICO.* Available at: https://www.politico.eu/article/flanders-zuhal-demir-belgium-alexander-de-croo-green-deal-eu-presidency/ (Accessed: 6 July 2024).
Guillot, L. (2024b) *'Insane' and 'dangerous' to give up on EU nature law, says Belgian minister, POLITICO.* Available at: https://www.politico.eu/article/insane-dangerous-eu-nature-law-belgium-minister-alain-maron/ (Accessed: 6 July 2024).
Guillot, L. (2024c) *Rogue Austrian minister burns bridges to save EU nature law, POLITICO.* Available at: https://www.politico.eu/article/rogue-austria-environment-minister-leonore-gewessler-burns-bridges-save-eu-nature-restoration-law/ (Accessed: 6 July 2024).
Howlett, M. and Ramesh, M. (2022) 'Designing for adaptation: Static and dynamic robustness in policy-making', *Public Administration*, 101, pp. 23 – 35.
Jordan, A. and Moore, B. (2020) 'Designing durable policies: An instruments perspective', in: *Durable by design? Policy feedback in a changing climate.* Cambridge: Cambridge University Press, pp. 29 – 54.
Kelemen, R.D. (2020) 'The European Union's authoritarian equilibrium', *Journal of European Public Policy*, 27(3), pp. 481 – 499.
Lund, C.S. and Andersen, L.B. (2023) 'Professional development leadership in turbulent times: Public administration symposium: Robust politics and governance in turbulent times', *Public Administration*, 101(1), pp. 124 – 141.
Previtali, P. and Salvati, E. (2023) 'Governance robustness put to the test by Covid-19: The case of Local Area Plans in the Lombardy Region', *European Planning Studies*, 31(12), pp. 2637 – 2658.
Rhinard, M. (2019) 'The crisisification of policy-making in the European Union', *Journal of Common Market Studies*, 57(3), pp. 616 – 633.
Saurugger, S. (2014) 'Europeanisation in times of crisis', *Political Studies Review*, 12(2), pp. 181 – 192.
Schmidt, V.A. (2013) 'Democracy and legitimacy in the European Union revisited: Input, output and "throughput"', *Political Studies*, 61(1), pp. 2 – 22.

Schmidt, V.A. (2018) 'Rethinking EU governance: From "old" to "new" approaches to who steers integration', *Journal of Common Market Studies*, 56(7), pp. 1544 – 1561.

Zaun, N. and Ripoll Servent, A. (2023) 'Perpetuating crisis as a supply strategy: The role of (nativist) populist governments in EU policymaking on refugee distribution', *Journal of Common Market Studies*, 61(3), pp. 653 – 672.

Zora Kovacic

Negotiating expertise and policy goals in European Union environmental policies

Abstract: This chapter investigates the interface between science and policy in European Union environmental governance. Questioning the idea of a linear process from science to policymaking, it shows that what counts as policy-relevant evidence is part of a larger negotiation over policy priorities and environmental concerns.

Keywords: Evidence; science-policy interface; boundary organizations; precautionary principle; uncertainty

1 Introduction

This chapter investigates the interface between science and policy in European Union (EU) environmental governance. The relationship between science and policy is often described in idealized terms as 'get-the-facts-then-act' (Pielke, 2007). The idea that policy should be based on evidence rehearses a very specific understanding known as the modern model of policymakers regulating based on 'objective' scientific advice, as opposed to political, economic or social interests (Funtowicz and Strand, 2007). Science and Technology Studies (STS) scholars have long questioned the idea of the objectivity of science (Daston and Galison, 2010), arguing instead that science is better understood as a situated practice (Latour, 1993; Shapin and Schaffer, 2011). What comes to be seen as evidence is the result of a co-production between science and policy (Jasanoff, 2004). The term 'science-policy interface' is used here to indicate the shift away from the view that science provides facts to policy to a more nuanced understanding that scientific evidence and policy are mutually constitutive.

Focusing on the governance of complex environmental issues, Silvio Funtowicz and Jerome Ravetz (1993) further question the idea that science provides so-called facts to policy. In post-normal conditions, facts are uncertain and closely imbricated with value disputes and high stakes. For example, deforestation may have consequences for biodiversity loss and ecosystem health that are not perfectly predictable; it may involve a dispute between the economic benefits of timber extraction and the sacred value that the forest may hold for local populations (Martinez-Alier, 2002). What counts as evidence in this instance: economic benefit, ecological models of ecosystem resilience or anthropological accounts of local languages of valuation? Disputes speak of the challenge of harmonizing different policy goals, which may not always pull in the same direction, and of dealing with multiple types of evidence, which may not all provide the same level of certainty.

The modern model moreover presupposes that science speaks with one voice. When that is not the case, the plurality of voices within science destabilizes the mod-

https://doi.org/10.1515/9783111321523-007

ern model (Sarewitz, 2004). The environmental sciences do not share the same models, assumptions and data as economics, hence multiple facts emerge. The choice between 'environmental facts' and 'economic facts' to inform policy is a value-laden choice. A corollary of the modern model is the belief that facts speak for themselves and have the power to compel policymakers into action. If facts are endowed with such power, the insistence on the need for evidence-based policy has the effect of making the production and selection of evidence the site of power struggles (Stirling, 2008) and political negotiation over which facts inform policy.

This chapter explores the interconnections between negotiations of different policy goals and the use of scientific evidence in policy. The analysis is based on policy documents, interviews and field notes from collaborations with the European Environment Agency (EEA) and the European Commission's Joint Research Centre (JRC) (for more details please see Appendix I). My starting point is the critique of the modern model of science speaking truth to power, extending this critique to analyze the different roles that knowledge brokers may assume at the interface with policy. The literature overlooks this issue: when science speaks with many voices, the question is which voices get to speak to power. I then turn to a historical overview of EU environmental policy, showing that environmental voices are in tension with economic voices. Environmental facts get to speak to power by negotiating with economic interests and attempting to redirect mainstream policy tools. The presence of multiple facts leads to a situation in which the role of knowledge-brokering institutions may be understood as selecting (rather than passing on) policy-relevant evidence. I show that institutional knowledge brokers tend to select evidence that aligns with economic interests as a strategy to advance environmental interests. The following section demonstrates that environmental and economic facts are not always in harmony, and the discursive alignment between economic and environmental rationales produces policies based on contested evidence. I conclude by pointing to a critical debate: is the European Green Deal a great achievement or is 'green' a 'nice-to-have' ambition added on top of economic policy? I argue that it is both: a great achievement in political and temporary terms and a 'nice-to-have' in long-term EU growth strategies.

2 Understanding evidence-based policy

Critiques of the modern model and of knowledge-brokering between science and policy have not sufficiently dealt with the issue of pluralism in the scientific knowledge base. Issues of multiple, contrasting and uncertain kinds of evidence put those who inform policy in a difficult position and challenge the modern model of the science-policy interface. I start by exploring the theoretical implications of this issue. If science does not speak with one voice, how should one interpret the idea of evidence-based policy? Which type of evidence is policy based on and which evidence is discarded? How is evidence selected and by whom? In what follows, I combine the discussion of the different roles that experts advising policy can play (Pielke, 2007), the different models of the science-policy interface (Funtowicz and Strand, 2007) and the politics of uncertainty (Oreskes and Conway, 2011; Stirling, 2017).

Roger Pielke (2007) defines four ideal roles that experts can assume: the pure scientist, the science arbiter, the issue advocate and the honest broker. The pure scientist and the science arbiter act as if science and policymaking were (or ought to be) two separable realms. The pure scientist provides information to decision-makers and has no interest in which decisions are taken. In a situation with many scientific voices, the pure scientist provides an account of the many voices, even if this means contradictory information, and the decision-maker is left to sort out what to do. The pure scientist rehearses the demarcation model (Funtowicz and Strand, 2007), which rests on the effort to define separate roles for science (responsible for the facts) and policymaking (responsible for values).

The science arbiter provides information upon request, without intervening in which questions are asked. This role rests on the technocratic model, or what Funtowicz and Roger Strand (2007) call the framing model: science provides the information it is asked for; the information may be value-laden, but the value decisions are supposedly taken by the decision-maker when asking for information. Pielke (2007) argues that, in practice, both the pure scientist and the science arbiter slip into 'stealth issue advocacy' because scientific information is necessarily value-laden and cannot be separated from politics.

Hence, two other roles are identified: the issue advocate, who argues for a specific decision, and the honest broker, who presents information that clarifies the trade-offs of each decision. The issue advocate explicitly violates the value-neutrality of science and is not a role that EU knowledge-brokering institutions take. Examples of issue advocates include individuals such as Al Gore, who invoked the power of science to legitimize his political campaign, and nongovernmental organizations such as Greenpeace. The honest broker, which is what Pielke argues for, is a role only assumed in very special circumstances: for example, under the precautionary model (Funtowicz and Strand, 2007). The United Nations (UN) Conference on Environment and Development defined the precautionary principle as follows: "Where there are threats of serious or irreversible damage, lack of full scientific certainty shall not be used as a reason for postponing cost-effective measures to prevent environmental degradation" (United Nations, 1992). In this case, scientific advice goes beyond the presentation of facts and includes assessment of the consequences of policy (in)action.

The precautionary principle is also an example of "desperate modernity" (Strand, 2002), a situation in which institutions "pretend to believe" (Strand, 2002) in the modern model, because the separation of science and politics provides legitimacy to decision-making processes. The phrasing 'lack of full scientific certainty' in the definition of the precautionary principle avoids naming uncertainty and retains a primary role for science in informing policy (Fjelland, 2002; Funtowicz and Strand, 2007). The European Commission (EC) mentions uncertainty but demarcates very clearly the separate roles of science and policy in the following manner: "the precautionary principle is part of risk management, when scientific uncertainty precludes a full assessment of the risk and when decision-makers consider that the chosen level of environmental protection or of human, animal and plant health may be in jeopardy" (European Commission, 2000, p. 12). In other words, the precautionary principle belongs to *management*, to policymaking, as opposed to risk *assessment*, i. e., the scientific part. Policymaking is portrayed as based on science and, in cases of uncertainty, on high ethical standards, such as 'the chosen level of protection'.

The politics of uncertainty have been documented among others by Naomi Oreskes and Erik Conway (2011). They analyzed cases in which scientific uncertainty is overemphasized to undermine restrictive policies, as in the case of the tobacco industry overemphasizing the uncertainty of the link between smoking and cancer. The political mobilization of uncertainty may help explain the UN's careful avoidance of the mention of uncertainty and the EC's demarcation of uncertainty as something belonging to management not science.

The honest broker is an argument for the recognition of uncertainty and the limits of scientific knowledge (Jasanoff, 2007), of pluralism within the scientific knowledge base (Sarewitz, 2004) and of the non-neutrality of science advice (Pielke, 2007). Complex issues create uncertainty and a plurality of legitimate, yet non-equivalent, descriptions. The existence of multiple voices within science raises the question "who has the power to simplify complexity?" (Martinez-Alier, 2009, p. 87). When I talk about selecting policy-relevant evidence in contexts in which science does not speak with one voice, I do not suggest that facts are selected in the sense of fabricated or politically informed (although that happens); I am referring to the fact that knowledge-brokering is not a straightforward process of providing information. What comes to be seen as policy-relevant evidence is the result of continuous negotiations and power asymmetries (Stirling, 2008). In the next section, I narrate these negotiations as a history of tensions between environmental policy and economic policy.

3 EU environmental policy: a history of tensions

EU environmental policy emerged in the 1970s. At the time, environmental concerns were increasingly brought up in public and policy debate. In 1972, the Club of Rome drew attention to the tensions between economic growth and the material limits of a finite planet. The First Environment Action Program (EAP) dates back to the European Economic Community (EEC) and was adopted in 1973. The EEC introduced this common environmental policy to support the Common Market, driven by the concern that diverse environmental standards could result in trade barriers and competitive distortions (Johnson and Corcelle, 1989). The main focus of the First EAP was harmonizing standards. Notably, environmental policy was first conceived in service of economic interests and, more specifically, of the internal market (see Chapter 7 and Chapter 31). Christoph Knill and Duncan Liefferink argue that "policy makers, acting without any legislative authority, initially made a clever move to increase the EU's capacity to act by defining environmental policy as a trade problem" (2021, p. 23). This 'clever move', however, situated environmental policy from the start as a negotiation between environmental concerns and economic interests. The focus on the Common Market continued through the Second (1977–1981) and Third (1982–1986) EAP.

In 1981, the Directorate-General for the Environment was established, creating a space for environmental policy (Haigh, 2016). As an environmental policy space was being carved out, new principles other than purely economic ones were introduced. The First and Second EAP introduced two of the principles that drive European environmental regulation (Curmei and Kurrer, 2023), namely the prevention principle and the 'polluter pays' principle. Prevention requires the operators of activities that may have a harmful effect on the environment to take preventive measures. The 'polluter pays' principle corrects a market failure by making producers internalize the costs of environmental harm when this has already occurred. The 'polluter pays' principle is interesting because it uses market instruments to correct a market failure.

In 1992, the precautionary principle was introduced. The need to justify environmental policy based on 'objective evidence' is indicative of the tensions that environmental concerns create with other policies and of the conflictual and highly political nature of these tensions. So-called objective evidence is invoked to solve tensions, as if political problems were technical challenges with a unique answer. However, the requirement that (environmental) policy be based on hard evidence becomes difficult to sustain in the presence of uncertainty—a recurrent feature of environmental problems (Funtowicz and Ravetz, 1993). The precautionary principle responds to this challenge.

The mobilization of objective evidence (mentioned nineteen times in the Communication on the precautionary principle) and ethics are an expression of the tension between environmental regulation and other policies. To somewhat limit economic activity, one must have hard facts and irrefutable reasons to do so. Not all evidence is created equal; environmental evidence is presumed guilty (of halting economic progress) until proven innocent. This is a tension that is not exclusive to the EU. For example, the 113th United States Congress (2013–2015) proposed legislation "to prohibit the Environmental Protection Agency from proposing, finalizing, or disseminating regulations or assessments based upon science that is not transparent or reproducible" (Pereira and Saltelli, 2016, p. 129). The legislation questioned the assumption that science is reproducible and required it to be proven before evidence could be considered policy-relevant.

Interestingly, the EEC Communication on the precautionary principle explicitly speaks of balancing different policy goals in terms of dealing with a 'dilemma': "Decision-makers are constantly faced with the dilemma of balancing the freedoms and rights of individuals, industry and organizations with the need to reduce or eliminate the risk of adverse effects to the environment or to health" (European Commission, 2000, p. 2). Balancing in this context clearly signifies dealing with the tensions created by contrasting objectives.

The Fourth EAP (1987–1992) introduced the need to integrate environmental requirements into other policies, which carried through to the Fifth and Sixth EAP.

Nigel Haigh argues that 1987 is a turning point which brings environmental policy 'from obscurity to centrality' by making environmental protection a requirement of other policies. The "EU, having been created for reasons quite unconnected with the environment, now found it had a compelling new justification" due to the emergence of problems, such as acid rain, that could not "be handled by individual countries acting alone" (Haigh, 2016, p. 6). Nevertheless, bringing environmental policy to the center stage also enhances both the tensions with economic priorities and the 'dilemma' of balancing multiple and not always compatible objectives.

EU policy evolved in dialogue with international debates and emerging concepts, such as the idea of sustainable development, formally defined in the so-called Brundtland Report (World Commission on Environment and Development, 1987). The idea of development, as opposed to economic growth, emerged to draw attention to the need to correct the harmful social effects (such as inequality, poverty and social exclusion) of economic growth. The adjective 'sustainable' signals the need to correct the environmental harm of socioeconomic development (see Chapter 7). This is yet another example of the tension between economic, social and environmental priorities. In EU policy, the Fifth EAP (1993–2000), "Towards sustainability", endorsed the sustainable development concept. Crucially, sustainable development refers to "a continuous and balanced expansion without any suggestion that environmental constraints might limit such expansion" (Haigh, 2016, p. 4). The negotiation of different interests leads among other practices to the attempt of placing existing policy instruments *also* at the service of environmental policy and to a focus on creating synergies, at least at the discursive level.

One could speak of a shift in the 1990s from the conception of environmental policy at the service of economic interests to an alignment—or balancing act—between environmental and economic concerns and priorities. With the 1997 signing of the Kyoto Protocol, attention has been drawn more and more to environmental problems such as climate change, through which environmental challenges are framed as global problems. In the EU context, there has also been a similar shift in emphasis. The Sixth EAP (2002–2012), 'Our choice, our future', raises the status of environmental problems to primary policy concerns, focusing on climate change, biodiversity loss and excessive resource consumption.

The Seventh (2013–2021) and Eighth (2022–) EAPs promote the idea of "living well and within planetary boundaries". They aim to pursue the wellbeing of all Europeans while ensuring that economic activity stays within planetary boundaries. The concept of 'planetary boundaries' (Steffen et al., 2015) refers to the impact of human activities on the global ecosystem. Boundaries are the point beyond which the Earth system may not be able to self-regulate anymore. "Living well and within planetary boundaries" arguably expresses the understanding of sustainability as a relational balance between the socioeconomic system and the ecosystem. This relational understanding makes it necessary to balance different policy goals and brings the focus on the search for synergies between environmental and economic interests. Because policy and evidence are co-produced, the policy need for synergies becomes an important factor also in the selection of policy-relevant evidence.

4 The making of policy-relevant evidence in boundary organizations

The negotiation between different policy goals is also a negotiation about which evidence should come to 'inform' policy. Knowledge brokers play a central role in the definition of what counts as evidence and in the selection of policy-relevant evidence (Sarewitz, 2004; Pielke, 2007). Accordingly, for a closer look at the role of boundary organizations, whose mandate is to act as knowledge-brokers for the EC, I focus on the European Environment Agency and the Joint Research Centre. The JRC is referred to as the EC's "in-house science service" (Pereira and Saltelli, 2016). The EEA has the mandate of providing knowledge and evidence to the EC concerning environmental issues.

Both institutions have been defined as "boundary organizations" (Guston, 2001; Waterton and Wynne, 2004; Pereira and Saltelli, 2016). A boundary organization sits in between the worlds of science and policy, which the modern model portrays as separate. The idea of a boundary organization contributes to the imaginary of science and policymaking as separate realms, while being a place where knowledge and social orders are co-produced (Jasanoff, 2004). The interplay between the idea of a boundary and the work of co-production can be seen in the way that the work of knowledge-brokering is described. Both institutions use the rhetoric of the modern model of providing 'independent' and 'objective' evidence. At the same time, they are part and parcel of the co-production of science and policy, as attested by the aim to provide evidence that is 'timely' (that is, that coincides with political agendas), 'targeted' (meets the needs of 'key clients', which have evolved overtime from Member States to other EC Directorates-General) and 'reliable' (provides a basis for action upon which policymakers can rely) (Waterton and Wynne, 2004).

According to David Guston (2001), boundary organizations induce stability by successfully internalizing boundary negotiations. In other words, these organizations internalize the inherently political negotiation of what counts as policy-relevant evidence. The policy context in which evidence is to be used defines what counts as evidence. Co-production involves the important function, among others, of selecting evidence. I identify three strategies that are used to select policy-relevant evidence in EU boundary organizations:

(1) The selection of evidence can take the form of defining the attributes that policy-relevant evidence should have. Timely, targeted and reliable evidence are attributes of evidence based on policy needs (Waterton and Wynne, 2004). A prime example of this work is the EEA report "Knowledge for Action. Empowering the transition to a sustainable Europe" (European Environment Agency, 2021b), which reflects on the type of evidence needed to transition to sustainability. By upholding the

value of action, the EEA does not dismiss the scientific validity of critical and reflexive perspectives but deems them less policy-relevant because they are not actionable.

(2) A second strategy is to align evidence about environmental problems with the dominant political priorities. A respondent has described this alignment as the “desire to be close to power” (EEA interviews, 2020, see Appendix I). The EEA and the JRC are not the only knowledge brokers for EU policy. They compete (and may collaborate) with industries, Member States and their national environmental agencies, lobbies and scientific community experts. Providing policy-relevant evidence is also a means of demonstrating the policy relevance of these institutions, whose existence is often perceived as under threat (Waterton and Wynne, 2004). In this context, relevance is defined as being aligned with political priorities, as captured by the idea of “policy-based evidence” (Pereira and Saltelli, 2016).

The alignment of evidence and political priorities should not necessarily be read as a case of corruption and may be driven by good intentions. In the case of the circular economy (see Chapter 36), EEA officers argued that it was important to provide a ‘positive framing’ to environmental concerns. Although the economy cannot be 100 percent circular, the argument went, the circular economy idea was moving things in ‘the right direction’ (EEA interviews, 2018, see Appendix I). The ‘right direction’ in this context does not refer to the policy’s viability but to the visibility given to environmental concerns.

(3) A third strategy is to mobilize uncertainty and risk. This is the case of the risks of the ‘twin’ green and digital transitions, which the 2022 Strategic Foresight Report examines in depth (European Commission, 2022). The twin transition, which is part of the European Green Deal, refers to the idea of creating a synergy between the green and the digital transitions. In this case, evidence of risks helps legitimize and redefine the role of governing institutions as capable of steering the risky digital transition in the right (green) direction (Kovacic et al., 2024).

The precautionary principle discussed above is a special case in which uncertainty is elevated to high-level policy advice. Examples of using the precautionary principle in the selection of policy-relevant evidence are the reports “Late lessons from early warnings” by the EEA (2001, 2013). Another notable example is the JRC evaluation of the bioeconomy policies, which states that “the outcomes of human actions on societies and ecosystems, *including policy-driven actions*, are intrinsically difficult to anticipate” (Joint Research Centre, 2023, emphasis added). This assessment introduces a reflexive approach and explicitly acknowledges that policy action may itself be uncertain. These examples exist but are rare. The dominant practice is to align environmental facts with mainstream policy.

5 From tensions to improbable coalitions

What is the result of aligning evidence selection with policy needs? The balancing and negotiation of different interests create ‘improbable coalitions’. Zeitlin, Nicoli and Laffan (2019) introduce the idea of improbable coalitions to describe temporary coalitions formed between unlikely allies, for example, across the left and right divide in response to crises. I use it here to refer to coalitions between policy goals such as economic growth and environmental protection. Below, I show that improbable coalitions create the conditions for the emergence of environmental policies based on contradictory and sometimes contested evidence.

Improbable coalitions between policies emerge as a response to crises. In contexts of crisis and when political attention shifts toward recovering economic growth, as in the aftermath of the 2008 global financial crisis and of the Covid-19 pandemic, the tension between economic and environmental priorities puts environmental policy in an unfavorable position. Environmental concerns have historically been expressed as a 'stop!' message that refers to limits, planetary boundaries and resource scarcity. In contrast, economic policy is associated with a 'go!' message, which focuses on growth, innovation and progress (Kovacic, Strand and Völker, 2019). Consequently, when political priority turns toward economic recovery, environmental concerns and their 'stop!' message may become politically difficult to sustain.

Under these conditions, discursively turning trade-offs between environmental and economic goals into synergies may resolve policy negotiations. Examples of improbable coalitions include: (i) the circular economy (Kovacic, Strand and Völker, 2019), which discursively turns resource scarcity from a potential limit to growth into an opportunity for new 'circular' business models that relocate resource extraction within the economy (see Chapter 36); (ii) the twin transition (Kovacic et al., 2024), which, without forgetting the 'necessary' green transition, turns the tension of managing the 'unavoidable' digital transition into a synergy by hoping to put digital technology at the service of environmental challenges; and (iii) the REPowerEU plan (Vezzoni, 2023), which discursively turns the war-derived energy crisis into an opportunity to accelerate the transition toward renewable energy (see Chapter 26).

In all three examples, the policies were formulated after economic and geopolitical crises. The circular economy appears in EU policy after the 2007–2009 global financial crisis, and the economic and sovereign debt crises that followed in the eurozone. The REPowerEU plan is a response to the invasion of Ukraine by Russia and the energy crisis that ensued. The twin transition is championed by von der Leyen's geopolitical Commission and imbricated with the idea of strategic open autonomy.

Policy coalition, however, does not solve the differences in the evidence base which informs environmental, social and economic policies. All three examples rely on contested evidence. Many scholars (Kovacic, Strand and Völker, 2019; Giampietro and Funtowicz, 2020; Martinez-Alier, 2022) have criticized the circular economy idea, arguing that the economic process is entropic, not circular. That is, circularity violates the second law of thermodynamics; the idea of a circular economy is dismissed as a theoretical impossibility. The REPowerEU plan, which aims at reducing dependence on (Russian) gas imports by accelerating the transition toward renewable energies, ignores the fact that the increased penetration of intermittent energy sources is precisely what has increased the EU's dependence on gas. To adapt the electric grid to intermittent energy sources and avoid blackouts, a variety of strategies can be used, including electricity storage and the use of power plants that can produce electricity on demand, known as peak-loaders. Gas power plants are an example of peak-loaders. Because in the EU electricity storage was not available on a large enough scale at the time of the war in Ukraine, gas was used to fill in electricity production when intermittent energy sources were not available (He et al., 2018). Interestingly, in the case of the twin transition, the critique is offered by the EU evidence pool itself. The 2022 Strategic Foresight Report (European Commission, 2022) is entirely devoted to the analysis of the trade-offs between digitalization and sustainability.

Through alignment with policy priorities, evidence about the viability of the circular economy and the economic benefit of the twin transition is selected as policy-relevant. According to some policy officers, presenting environmental problems as an economic opportunity was seen as the "only way to get environmental concerns on the agenda during times of austerity" (Kovacic, Strand and Völker, 2019, p. 87). Evidence about tensions and uncertainties is often absent from high-level policy documents. Although in some cases good intentions may explain evidence selection, the circularity of EU economies has not increased (European Environment Agency, 2021a), gas imports have not decreased (although trade partners have been diversified) (European Environment Agency, 2024) and the twin transition may have the effect of putting environmental concerns on the back burner (Kovacic et al., 2024).

6 Conclusion

This chapter has advanced the idea that evidence and policy are better understood as co-produced rather than as a linear process that goes from facts to policymaking. Advancing environmental policy is not a matter of producing irrefutable evidence or of improving and diversifying the EU expertise that is offered to policy. Facts do not speak for themselves. Policy-relevant facts are allowed to speak to policy as part of a larger negotiation over policy priorities. Hence, producing policy-relevant evidence requires a deep understanding of the processes of co-production of evidence and policy, of what makes evidence policy-relevant and of the difficult choices involved in negotiating evidence and policy priorities.

As a research agenda, it is important to understand the science-policy interface as a site of co-production and the production of science for policy as an exercise of selecting policy-relevant evidence. Jasanoff's (2004) theory of co-production has been fruitfully applied to the study of the EEA (Waterton and Wynne, 2004). While the theory of co-production is a well-established academic field within STS, what pluralism within science means in a context of co-production has been less thoroughly studied. Some investigations in this area have become seminal works, such as Sarewitz's (2004) account of the multiple voices within science and of how policy-relevant evidence is selected, and Rayner's (2012) analysis of how 'uncomfortable knowledge' is eliminated from the science-policy interface. More recently, Giampietro and Funtowicz (2020) have argued that EU policy is drifting toward 'policy legends' (policy narratives based on folktales that express collective fears and desires), citing the circular bioeconomy. My own work on the circular economy (Kovacic, Strand and Völker, 2019) and the twin transitions (Kovacic et al., 2024) addresses this question. One potential step is to follow the processes of evidence and policy negotiation over time and enrich the notion of expertise as a situated practice (a practice that happens in a specific spatial and temporal context, tied to the experiences and embedded knowledge of those involved), which is much broader than a matter of 'knowing what' and much less distinct from politics than the modern model would portray.

The brief EU environmental policy overview shows that the dominant strategy has been to select evidence that aligns with policy priorities and try to create a synergy between environmental and economic policy goals, because environmental concerns tend to be at the losing end of the tension. This strategy enabled the EU to adopt the European Green Deal: the EU policy framework for the years 2019–2024, which aims to make the EU climate neutral by 2050 and boost green growth and innovation. To some extent, the European Green Deal can be seen as a great achievement: environmental concerns are at the forefront of the EU political agenda. Yet green policies are subordinated to geopolitical and economic interests. The EU supports the twinning of the digital and green transitions as a means of making EU digital technology competitive. This strategy can backfire. As long as being green helps achieve other economic and geopolitical objectives, environmental concerns stay on the policy ticket. When the alignment is no longer tenable, policies may lose the green element. The alignment with power makes environmental policy a 'nice-to-have' rather than a sign that environmental concerns are shaping EU policy.

References

Curmei, M.-M. and Kurrer, C. (2023) *Environment policy: General principles and basic framework.* Fact sheet 2.5.1. European Parliament. Available at: https://www.europarl.europa.eu/erpl-app-public/factsheets/pdf/en/FTU_2.5.1.pdf (Accessed: 25 July 2024).

Daston, L. and Galison, P. (2010) *Objectivity.* First paperback edition. New York, NY: Zone Books.

European Commission (2000) 'Communication from the Commission on the precautionary principle', *COM*(2000/0001) final. Brussels: Commission of the European Communities. Available at: https://eur-lex.europa.eu/legal-content/EN/TXT/?uri=celex%3A52000DC0001 (Accessed: 25 July 2024).

European Commission (2022) *2022* 'Strategic foresight teport. Twinning the green and digital transitions in the new geopolitical context', *COM*(2022/289) final. Brussels: Commission of the European Communities. Available at: https://eur-lex.europa.eu/legal-content/EN/TXT/?uri=CELEX:52022DC0289 (Accessed: 12 January 2024).

European Environment Agency (2001) *Late lessons from early warnings: The precautionary principle 1896–2000.* Issue Report No 22. Copenhagen: European Environment Agency.

European Environment Agency (2013) *Late lessons from early warnings: Science, precaution, innovation.* EEA Report 1/2013. Copenhagen: European Environment Agency.

European Environment Agency (2021a) *Growth without economic growth.* Briefing no. 28/2020. Copenhagen: European Environment Agency.

European Environment Agency (2021b) *Knowledge for action: Empowering the transition to a sustainable Europe.* EEA Report 10/2021. Copenhagen: European Environment Agency.

European Environment Agency (2024) *Governance in complexity. Sustainability governance under highly uncertain and complex conditions.* EEA Report 05/2024. Copenhagen: European Environment Agency.

Fjelland, R. (2002) 'Facing the problem of uncertainty', *Journal of Agricultural and Environmental Ethics*, 15(2), pp. 155 – 169.

Funtowicz, S. and Ravetz, J.R. (1993) 'Science for the post-normal age', *FUTURES*, 25(7), pp. 739 – 755.

Funtowicz, S.O. and Strand, R. (2007) 'Models of science and policy', in: Traavik, T. and Lim, L.C. (eds.) *Biosafety first: Holistic approaches to risk and uncertainty in genetic engineering and genetically modified organisms.* Trondheim: Tapir Academic Press.

Giampietro, M. and Funtowicz, S.O. (2020) 'From elite folk science to the policy legend of the circular economy', *Environmental Science & Policy*, 109, pp. 64 – 72.

Guston, D.H. (2001) 'Boundary organizations in environmental policy and science: An introduction', *Science, Technology, & Human Values*, 26(4), pp. 399 – 408.

Haigh, N. (2016) *EU environmental policy: Its journey to centre stage.* Milton Park, Abingdon, Oxon; New York, NY: Routledge.

He, C. et al. (2018) 'Coordination of interdependent electricity grid and natural gas network: A review', *Current Sustainable/Renewable Energy Reports*, 5(1), pp. 23 – 36.

Jasanoff, S. (ed.) (2004) *States of knowledge: The co-production of science and social order.* International library of sociology. London: Routledge.

Jasanoff, S. (2007) 'Technologies of humility', *Nature*, 450(7166), p. 33.

Johnson, S. and Corcelle, G. (1989) *The environmental policy of the European communities.* International environmental law and policy series. London; Boston: Graham & Trotman.

Joint Research Centre (2023) *Integrated bioeconomy land use assessment: Land system responses to bioeconomy-related policies, supporting policy with scientific evidence.* Available at: https://knowledge4policy.ec.europa.eu/projects-activities/integrated-bioeconomy-land-use-assessment_en (Accessed: 14 May 2024).

Knill, C. and Liefferink, D. (2021) 'The establishment of EU environmental policy', in: Jordan, A. and Gravey, V. (eds.) *Environmental policy in the EU: Actors, institutions and processes.* Fourth edition. Abingdon, Oxon; New York, NY: Routledge.

Kovacic, Z. et al. (2024) 'The twin green and digital transition: High-level policy or science fiction?', *Environment and Planning E: Nature and Space*, 7(6), pp. 2251 – 2278.

Kovacic, Z., Strand, R. and Völker, T. (2019) 'The circular economy in Europe: Critical perspectives on policies and imaginaries'. London and New York: Routledge.

Latour, B. (1993) *We have never been modern.* Boston, Massachusetts: Harvard University Press.

Martinez-Alier, J. (2002) *The environmentalism of the poor: A study of ecological conflicts and valuation.* Cheltenham, UK Northhampton, MA: Edward Elgar.

Martinez-Alier, J. (2009) 'Social metabolism, ecological distribution conflicts, and languages of valuation', *Capitalism Nature Socialism*, 20(1), pp. 58 – 87.

Martinez-Alier, J. (2022) 'Circularity, entropy, ecological conflicts and LFFU', *Local Environment*, 27(10 – 11), pp. 1182 – 1207.

Oreskes, N. and Conway, E.M. (2011) *Merchants of doubt: How a handful of scientists obscured the truth on issues from tobacco smoke to climate change.* Reprint edition. New York, London, Oxford, New Delhi, Sydney: Bloomsbury Publishing.

Pereira, Â.G. and Saltelli, A. (2016) 'Institutions on the verge: Working at the science policy interface', in: Benessia, A. et al. (eds.) *The rightful place of science: Science on the verge.* First edition. Tempe, AZ Washington, DC: Consortium for Science, Policy & Outcomes.

Pielke, R.A.J. (2007) *The honest broker: Making sense of science in policy and politics.* Cambridge University Press.

Rayner, S. (2012) 'Uncomfortable knowledge: The social construction of ignorance in science and environmental policy discourses', *Economy and Society*, 41(1), pp. 107–125.
Sarewitz, D. (2004) 'How science makes environmental controversies worse', *Environmental Science & Policy*, 7(5), pp. 385–403.
Shapin, S. and Schaffer, S. (2011) *Leviathan and the air-Pump: Hobbes, Boyle, and the experimental life.* Princeton: Princeton University Press.
Steffen, W. et al. (2015) 'Planetary boundaries: Guiding human development on a changing planet', *Science*, 347(6223), 1259855.
Stirling, A. (2008) '"Opening up" and "closing down": Power, participation, and pluralism in the social appraisal of technology', *Science, Technology & Human Values*, 33(2), pp. 262–294.
Stirling, A. (2017) 'Precautionary appraisal as a response to risk, uncertainty, ambiguity and ignorance', in: Spash, C.L. (ed.) *Routledge handbook of ecological economics.* London: Routledge.
Strand, R. (2002) 'Complexity, ideology, and governance', *Emergence*, 4(1–2), pp. 164–183.
United Nations (1992) *Report of the United Nations Conference on Environment and Development.* A/CONF.151/26. Rio de Janeiro: United Nations.
Vezzoni, R. (2023) 'Green growth for whom, how and why? The REPowerEU Plan and the inconsistencies of European Union energy policy', *Energy Research & Social Science*, 101, 103134.
Waterton, C. and Wynne, B. (2004) 'Knowledge and political order in the European Environment Agency', in: Jasanoff, S. (ed.) *States of knowledge: The co-production of science and social order.* International library of sociology. London: Routledge, pp. 87–108.
World Commission on Environment and Development (1987) *Our common future.* A/42/251 82e Environment. New York: United Nations, p. 374.
Zeitlin, J., Nicoli, F. and Laffan, B. (2019) 'Introduction: The European Union beyond the polycrisis? Integration and politicization in an age of shifting cleavages', *Journal of European Public Policy*, 26(7), pp. 963–976.

Appendix I

The empirical analysis presented in this chapter builds on a core set of policy documents contextualized with interviews and field notes from research projects the author was part of from 2016 to 2024. More specifically, within the Horizon2020 project MAGIC (2016–2020) twenty-eight interviews were carried out with policy officers from the European Commission, European Parliament and the European Environment Agency and 2 workshops were organized at the Joint Research Centre at Ispra, Italy (February 2018) and the European Environment Agency in Copenhagen, Denmark (May 2018). For this chapter, the author draws on interviews related to the circular economy and energy policies. From June 2020 to November 2024, the author collaborated in a series of service contracts between the European Centre for Governance in Complexity and the European Environment Agency, which included the organization of three workshops (February 2021 online; June 2024 online; November 2024 Brussels). Within the IBLUA project coordinated by the European Commission's Joint Research Centre (2024–2027), twenty-seven interviews were carried out with policy officers from the European Commission, academic researchers, interest groups and practitioners, and one workshop was organized in Brussels (July 2024). For this chapter, the author draws on interviews related to the European Green Deal. Notes from the workshops were consulted.

Katharina Rietig

Learning in European environmental policy

Abstract: Learning can be an important factor in the facilitation of effective environmental policy outcomes when actors reflect on new knowledge and previous experiences and may even change their perspectives and underlying beliefs as a result of this reflection. Learning can occur at any stage of the policy process, and drawing lessons from past experiences means that it tends to occur over a longer time frame, usually throughout a policymaking process and subsequent emerging policy reform processes. Learning can facilitate policymaking processes, avoid 'reinventing the wheel' and repeating past errors. To effectively influence the policy process, actors often use entrepreneurial policy strategies with or without acting as teachers. This chapter examines how scholarship on learning in public policy, especially on European Union environmental policy, has evolved and advanced our understanding of the role of learning in environmental policy change.

Keywords: Climate governance; EU environmental policy; learning; policy entrepreneur; policy process

1 Introduction

Learning is an important aspect of policy change and has gained increasing attention in the European Union (EU) environmental policy field for its role in facilitating or hindering policy outcomes (Challies et al., 2017; Domorenok and Zito, 2021; Koch and Lindenthal, 2011; Westerink, Pérez-Soba and van Doorn, 2020; Zaki and Dupont, 2023). Learning can occur when policymakers gain experience and knowledge while evaluating existing policies or identifying a need for new policies to address a specific problem. It usually requires some kind of conscious reflection on an input, such as new information or an experience (Rietig, 2021). The field of environmental policy is understood here as deliberately broad to also include environmental policy integration (Koch and Lindenthal, 2011), i. e., the integration of environmental objectives (see Chapter 33) into other relevant policy fields such as agriculture, energy and transport policy, as well as climate policy. Learning is particularly relevant as environmental policy often requires engagement with these adjacent policy fields. This consequently can increase the likelihood of competition of interests, usually environmental interests versus economic and/or social interests.

The central question this chapter addresses is how does learning matter in the policy process? Learning can occur at any stage of the policy process, and drawing lessons from past experiences means that it tends to occur over a longer time frame, usually throughout a policymaking process and later emerging policy reform processes. Actors who reflected on earlier experiences and knowledge, or even subsequently changed their beliefs, are in the ideal position to act as 'teachers' by sharing their les-

https://doi.org/10.1515/9783111321523-008

sons learned (Bomberg, 2007) at the European level, but also the international, national and sub-national governance levels (Rietig, 2025). This can facilitate policymaking processes and help actors avoid 'reinventing the wheel' and repeating past errors (Rietig, 2019). To effectively influence the policy process, actors tend to use policy-entrepreneurial strategies. The key actors are policymakers, but they frequently learn from experts, scientists and broader epistemic communities, especially in the area of the environment where drawing on scientific evidence plays an important role (Dunlop, 2009; Zaki and Dupont, 2023).

This chapter examines how public policy scholarship on learning, particularly on EU environmental policy, has evolved and advanced our understanding of the role of learning in environmental policy change. The literature on learning in public policy is closely linked to and has often been further advanced through empirical case studies of learning in EU environmental policymaking, implementation and evaluation. Therefore, it is important not to focus too narrowly on learning conceptualizations solely in environmental policy given their broader applicability. This chapter introduces key theoretical approaches to learning in policy change and discusses their applications in, and advancement through, the empirical EU environmental policy literature. It then uses the 'Learning in Governance Framework' (Rietig, 2021) as a meta-theoretical framework on learning and the policy reform process of greening the Common Agricultural Policy (CAP) as central environmental and climate policy integration to illustrate key points of learning in a policymaking process over a longer timeframe.

2 What is learning? Key conceptualizations used in EU environmental policy research

This section presents key learning conceptualizations identified as relevant in EU environmental policy. These conceptualizations, or 'types', of learning can be mapped along a continuum ranging from the individual level to the collective level (within organizations and broader society) and from accumulating knowledge through experiential learning based on reflection on experiences to changes in beliefs regarding policies and broader values.

Key conceptualizations of learning that frequently informed empirical research on EU environmental policy case studies emerged in the 1980s and 1990s. These themselves drew on learning conceptualizations and definitions from the 1970s around muddling through (policy changes made in small incremental steps), single/double loop learning (learning that involves a change in policy but only double loop learning changes underlying values; see Argyris and Schoen, 1978), experiential learning cycles and links between learning among individuals and transfer of learning onto an organizational level (March and Olsen, 1975). Conceptual advances in the 1980s and 1990s moved the focus on learning from the organizational learning literature toward the public policy literature both in the United States and Europe. Especially in the

2000s and 2010s, an increasing number of studies on EU environmental policy utilized and advanced conceptualizations of learning.

Each learning 'type' has its own definition. Accordingly, what exactly learning is varies based on its definition. This raises methodological challenges for identifying the presence of learning in a policy process and in evaluating its influence for affecting policy change. One major difference in learning definitions is how high the bar is set for learning to occur. If learning is assumed to be present everywhere and anytime, it becomes all-encompassing and loses some of its usefulness as an analytic concept. If the bar for learning is set very high with rare occurrences of learning, it is possible to miss out on some of the more 'everyday' or incremental aspects of learning which have impacts that are only seen in years, even decades after the learning happened (Rietig and Perkins, 2018). This also applies to the time frame of observation; learning requires time, and for learning to make a difference to policy change, it requires even more time. Thus, a time frame of a few months likely will result in little observable learning effects, while a time frame of several years or even decades will most likely present a wealth of learning at various points and stages. A timeframe of several decades means that learning becomes possibly indistinguishable from societal change. Consequently, a time frame of a few years has become the standard for identifying and assessing the role of learning in policy change (Radaelli, 2009; Rietig, 2021).

3 Political learning

A frequent aspect found in policy learning is 'political learning', i. e., when individuals and/or organizations learn to use the policy process to their advantage. Peter May popularized the concept of political learning, or "lessons about maneuvering within and manipulation of policy processes in order to advance an idea or problem" (May, 1992, p. 351). Essentially, through political learning individuals reflect on their previous experience or advice about the 'machinery' of policymaking and use this knowledge and experience to more effectively participate in the process, influencing the policy outcome using sophisticated political tactics. Political learning relates to tactical behavior. It includes judgments concerning whether proposals are politically feasible, i. e., have a realistic chance at succeeding and a good understanding of the policymaking process (May, 1992, p. 339). The political learning concept dates back several decades, drawing from earlier concepts of defensive avoidance (Janis and Mann, 1977), buck-passing and muddling through (Lindblom, 1979). Often, learning is predominantly symbolic or political in the sense that it leads to more effective participation in the policy process, but less often does learning mean arriving at normatively 'better' policy outcomes. A central finding from the EU literature is that, "Learning should not be correlated with policy improvement. It is obvious that policymakers have learned symbolically and politically" (Radaelli, 2009, p. 1161). Political learning is a common finding among empirical studies in EU environmental policy, a finding that also extends to how stakeholders who seek to influence the policy process by engaging in learning do so more effectively, including scientific experts (Zaki and Dupont, 2023).

4 Social learning

Social learning was identified in various areas of environmental policy such as ecosystem services (Westerink, Pérez-Soba and van Doorn, 2020). It relates to changing beliefs among individuals involved in the policymaking process or the overall shifting objectives of the individual's wider organization. The key agent for social learning is the social interaction of experts who are either bureaucrats, politicians or expert network members (Hall, 1993, p. 277). Hall defines social learning "as a deliberate attempt to adjust the goals or techniques of policy in response to past experience and new information. Learning is indicated when policy changes as the result of such a process" (Hall, 1993, p. 278). Key contributions (e.g., Bennett and Howlett, 1992; May, 1992; Zito and Schout, 2009) emphasized that "social learning requires showing that the dominant policy elite's beliefs have either been altered or reaffirmed in light of policy experience" (May, 1992, pp. 337–338).

5 Governance learning

New preferences for governance instruments motivated the concept of 'governance learning'. Learning about governance instruments can be relevant to, e.g., the involvement of stakeholders in the implementation of environmental policies (Challies et al., 2017) and is central to better understanding transnational networks of sub-national actors such as the Covenant of Mayors (Domorenok and Zito, 2021). It is defined as "learning about the major governance modes and how they can be employed effectively" (Schout 2009, p. 1125). Governance learning involves choosing which dominant form (mode) of governing works (market versus network versus state governing) in the policy area. It has two aspects, instrument learning and organizational learning. Following May (1992, p. 332), Schout defines instrument learning "as the development in instruments and entailing lessons about the viability of the individual policy instruments" (Schout, 2009, p. 1125). These include obtaining information about laws, soft coordination, such as the Open Method of Coordination, and steering through the use of tax incentives, innovation, fiscal policy and agencies (Schout, 2009, p. 1127). Governance learning refers to accumulating information and experience about bureaucratic capacities, standardization of objectives, training and horizontal coordination mechanisms such as task forces or teams.

6 Instrumental learning

'Instrumental learning' can be triggered when a government organization seeks to improve its administrative and governance performance. Dissatisfaction with the performance of policy programs can initiate a search for alternative modes of governance, i. e., "ways of doing business" (May 1992, p. 341). These types of policy failure can not only improve the modes of governance and the content of policy instruments but also provide opportunities for reflection on the overall objectives of the policy. Instrumental learning occurs in organizations that find themselves under the pressure to deliver. Policymakers used policy instruments and assessment tools such as Regulatory Impact Assessment when they want to improve the effectiveness and efficiency of regulation (Radaelli, 2009, p. 1149), thus using knowledge as an instrument to achieve a given policy objective.

7 Environmental policy integration as learning process

Frequently drawing on and further advancing some or several of the learning types introduced above, the empirical literature on environmental policy change in the EU offers diverse insights. Some of these include conceptualizing learning as an integral part of the policymaking process, which in turn becomes a learning process.

Within the broader EU learning scholarship, one set of literature conceptualizes Environmental Policy Integration (see Chapter 33) as learning (Fiorino, 2001; Nilsson and Persson, 2003; Nilsson, 2005). They define environmental policy integration "as a policy-learning process in which perspectives evolve and sectoral actors reframe their objectives, strategies, and decision-making processes toward sustainable development" (Nilsson and Persson 2003, p. 207). This conceptualization links back to Jachtenfuchs (1996): while Jachtenfuchs also includes the organizational level, Nilsson focuses implicitly on wider changes in the sociopolitical sphere. He uses a narrower definition of frames as "ways of selecting, organizing, interpreting, and making sense of a complex reality to provide guideposts for knowing, analysing, persuading and acting" (Nilsson 2005, p. 209) and limits this to wider changes in the policymaking environment. Yet, a key aspect of the "Environmental Policy Integration as learning" literature is its distinctive focus on the implementation of policies on the national and local level, taking a broader approach to learning across the full policy cycle. 'Learning by doing' and 'trial-and-error-learning' are typical occurrences in policy implementation. In a follow-up study Nilsson and Eckerberg (2007) provide an empirically thick analysis of environmental policy integration into energy, agriculture and biofuels policy in Sweden using the same learning frame. Environmental policy integration is concluded to be learning, but it happens in wider societal frame-changes. They acknowledge that, once the policymaking process is entered, political interests can take over and hinder learning.

8 No learning or non-learning

A common element to most studies on learning is their 'positive' focus on learning and less on hindering factors that make learning difficult although many conclude that learning was not as important or relevant for the environmental policy outcome than the title or hypothesis might lead the reader to expect. While the literature on explanations for policy change in the environmental realm other than learning is extensive and diverse, a relatively small body of literature originating mainly in management studies and social psychology is concerned with the opposite of learning (also referred to as 'non-learning') on the individual and organizational level. This includes avoiding reflection on an input, forgetting about previously acquired knowledge, reactive governing and simply 'muddling through' the process toward an outcome (e.g. Hedberg, 1981; Janis and Mann, 1977; Lindblom, 1979). This literature provides indirect links to the well-developed literature on power and more state-centered explanations for policy change. Unlearning occurs when individuals unconsciously or intentionally discard knowledge (Hedberg, 1981, p. 18). Potential reasons include that the expert in the field left the organization or decision-makers forgot that they dealt with a similar issue in another context. Frequently, empirical literature assessing the role of learning in EU environmental policymaking and/or implementation finds that the role of learning, e.g., around policies (McGowan, 2020), was limited or policy change was due to alternative explanations (e.g. interest group resistance, see Koch and Lindenthal, 2011, Rietig and Perkins, 2018).

9 Cross-cutting learning scholarship

More recently, we see a revived interest in learning in the EU environmental policy literature and beyond. It started from the conclusion that existing theoretical conceptualizations on learning were insufficient to help answer research questions. This 'new wave' of learning scholarship is more cross-cutting, draws on a wide spectrum of literature starting from the 1960s and includes interdisciplinary crossovers.

Dunlop and Radaelli (2013; Radaelli and Dunlop, 2013) offered a comprehensive overview of major streams of learning literature before developing their two-by-two conceptualization of different learning types. They differentiate between low/high problem tractability and certification of actors, arriving at four learning types (reflexive learning, learning through bargaining, epistemic learning, learning in the shadow of hierarchy). Learning does not always necessarily support policy change; it can also be dysfunctional (Dunlop and Radaelli, 2018). Each learning type can be further differentiated into four sub-elements: high/low learner's control over learning objectives and learner's high/low control over learning content, resulting in self-directed learning, informal learning, non-formal learning and formal learning (Dunlop and Radaelli, 2013).

Heikkila and Gerlak (2013) offer a theoretically grounded approach to defining and understanding collective-level learning. They see learning as a collective process, which may include acquiring information through diverse actions (e. g., trial and error), assessing or translating information and disseminating knowledge or opportunities across individuals in a collective. Learning can also be a collective product that emerges from the process, such as new shared ideas, strategies, rules, or policies (Gerlak and Heikkila, 2011, p. 5). Through the collective learning process, the transfer from individual learning products to collective learning outputs occurs. They propose a set of factors internal to the collective setting that may promote or inhibit learning, including institutional structure, social dynamics and the technological and functional domain. They also draw attention to exogenous factors like political, social and economic changes that may shape learning processes and products.

In addition, the 'Learning in Governance Framework' (Rietig and Perkins, 2018; Rietig, 2021) draws on the public policy literature on the Organizational Studies (Argyris and Schoen, 1978; March and Olsen, 1975) and non-learning literature (Janis and Mann, 1977), with the objective to go 'back to the basics' and offer a comprehensive yet intuitive meta-theoretical framework that includes all major elements and types of learning without adding more sub-types, such as social learning, government learning, governance learning or political learning. They differentiate between the individual and collective level, which can be further split into the level of the organization (e. g., a government department) and the sociopolitical level of wider society. Learning can take the form of gaining new knowledge (factual learning), new experience (experiential learning) and/or actors changing the way they see things, i. e., belief changes (constructivist learning). Beliefs include the very stable 'deep beliefs' in the form of world views, 'deeper beliefs' in the form of, e. g., prioritizing environmental protection, 'policy design beliefs' on, e. g., preferences of regulation-based emission standards over voluntary industry commitments and 'policy detail beliefs' regarding, e. g., preferences for a certain level of emission standards (Rietig, 2021).

The key element of this framework is the comparably 'high bar' for learning to occur as individuals and/or organizations need to actively reflect on the knowledge or experience-based input, which requires a conscious cognitive process as pre-condition for learning. If actors do not reflect on the input, learning cannot occur. There can still be policy change, but this may be the result of explanations other than learning, such as defensive avoidance, political bargaining/power politics, institutional machinery, simple time/resource constraints or following orders. Even if the individual did learn, this learning is not necessarily transferred to the organizational level or the policy outcome, as it may have been blocked by any of the above hindering factors (Rietig and Perkins, 2018).

This phase of consolidation in learning theories has been followed by an increasing number of empirical studies in EU environmental policy that sought to apply and test these meta-frameworks to various case studies. These studies found that learning matters in facilitating policy change but not all learning is 'positive' from a normative perspective, in the sense that it results or contributes to more effective environmental policies. Individuals and their organizations usually gain new knowledge and add new experiences. Depending on whether learning is defined as requiring the learning individual/organization to reflect on these stimuli or not, it is more or less likely to occur automatically. One common finding is that individuals and/or organizations learned to 'play politics better', i. e., improved their acumen in influencing the political decision-making process, or they gained new knowledge and experience about the content and/or design of policies (Koch and Lindenthal, 2011). It is also possible that they are 'forced' to learn through a hierarchical process, such as through the implementation of policies that were devised at other governance levels, which is particularly likely when Member States and subnational actors implement EU environmental policy (Dunlop and Radaelli, 2018).

Empirical studies on environmental policy also offered deeper insights into the agents of learning. Frequently, it is up to policy entrepreneurs to make policy change happen. These policy entrepreneurs likely learned in the past and subsequently use their previous learning to their advantage, effectively influencing the policy process to their organization's advantage (Rietig, 2021). Several empirical studies end their analysis with hypotheses for further research on how learning can be used to arrive at more effective policies or the implementation of existing policies. This is where 'teachers' and 'learning entrepreneurs' are invoked as agents of change that, following their own learning in the past, actively teach or provide a forum that facilitates learning among other policymakers (e. g., Bomberg, 2007; Rietig, 2025).

10 Learning in greening the EU Common Agricultural Policy

This case study zooms in on two reform cycles that illustrate broader learning patterns and mechanisms in EU environmental policy and where environmental policies are integrated into other policy areas. The EU Common Agricultural Policy (CAP) is a policy with most profound impacts on the environment and close interconnections, given that virtually all non-built-up spaces, with the exception of a very small percentage of national parks or otherwise protected areas across Europe, are lands used for agriculture and forestry (see Chapters 4, 23, 28). The CAP is also one of Europe's core policies ensuring food security, one of its oldest policy areas and one of the EU's largest expenditures in its seven-year budget. The CAP was reframed from its initial purpose to ensure food security to additionally conform with emerging and increasingly stringent environmental standards (Swinnen, 2008).

One of these core initiatives is 'greening' the CAP by increasing the share of EU funds dedicated to environmental protection, gradually moving from a voluntary greening approach toward connecting compliance with environmental standards to the provision of public funds to farmers. Two central reforms were the 2003 Fischler reforms, named after the Commissioner for Agriculture and Rural Development Franz Fischler (Swinnen, 2008) and the 2014 Greening the CAP reform led by Dacian Ciolos and his team at the Directorate-General for Agriculture within the European Commission (EC; for more details on the reform processes, see Rietig, 2021).

One recurring theme in the literature is the role of learning from facts and experiences on the individual level. This can include learning how to better use (or 'play') the policymaking process to achieve one's objectives or more basic learning that takes place through the acquisition of new facts such as the latest scientific evidence or beginning to work in a new policy area. Experiential learning is particularly common: reflection on one's own or other's previous experiences and subsequently changing an approach (i.e., reflection on past errors and their correction) or repeating strategies that were successful in the past.

In the 2003 Mid-Term Review of the CAP, the EC acted as policy broker by changing the framework conditions and creating hurting stalemates with the 'surprise reform proposal' approach of Commissioner Fischler (Feindt, 2010; Swinnen, 2008). This was an instance where Fischler had reflected upon earlier experiences with the Council of Agriculture Ministers and decided to use his wealth of knowledge in the negotiations to foster agreement on key greening elements. He drew on previous factual learning and reflected on his experiences with the 2000 CAP reform (Rietig, 2021). This was a common recurrence for individuals in key positions who learned from their past experiences and used their knowledge (e.g., a background in agricultural economics) to command an authority that went beyond their formal role in the process. This means that they acted as policy entrepreneurs to achieve their desired policy outcome. Factual learning also occurred on the organizational level going back to the 1990s MacSharry Reforms when the European Commission overall reflected on the emerging scientific consensus about the negative environmental impacts of the CAP and concluded that it requires reform through increasing environmental protection (Feindt, 2010).

Policy change in the CAP is a constant over regular reform cycles. As long as the EC promotes policy change, the institutional setting supports incremental changes and the evolution of paradigms (Feindt, 2010). Constructivist learning through changes in beliefs occurred both on the individual and organizational level when those whose primary objectives were focused on maintaining the CAP (e.g., in the Directorate-General for Agriculture, agriculture ministers) reflected upon and came to adjust their beliefs about policy design and policy details that, given the strong environmental lobby through environmental nongovernmental organizations (NGOs) and demands from Member States, the CAP needed to adapt if it were to maintain public acceptance and avoid being discontinued. This was a result of changing overall sociopolitical framework conditions, especially the rise of environmental actors, such as green parties and increasingly professional lobbying by environmental NGOs, and overall public concern and criticism of the CAP as being outdated and not in line with environmental values (Rietig, 2021). This subsequently increased support within the EC in favor of greening measures. The realization that the CAP needed to change to maintain public acceptance was a central driving factor of the 2014 Greening of the CAP for the 2014–2020 EU budget. The overall constructivist learning on the organizational level was driven by a 'public money for public goods' narrative that focused particularly on the environment and on addressing climate change through an increase in natural carbon sinks in the form of green vegetation and forest cover. The narrative shifted toward serving the public good, or 'the 97 percent' of the public and thus moving beyond catering to the interests of 'the 3 percent', i. e., the farm lobby and especially industrial agriculture conglomerates. This time, policy change was not driven by an individual policy entrepreneur such as Franz Fischler but by a small group of policy entrepreneurs working within Commissioner Ciolos' Agriculture Cabinet (Rietig, 2021). As in the previous case of Franz Fischler, their existing knowledge about agriculture and the CAP changed little during the policymaking process as they were already Europe's leading experts on the topic.

The level of pre-existing knowledge and experience is a crucial determinant for 'how much' learning occurs in any given EU environmental policymaking process. While the EC's factual and experiential expert learning remained limited, these types of learning were particularly dominant among Members of the European Parliament (MEPs). A novelty of the 2014 CAP reform was European Parliament (EP) involvement, which means that all MEPs engaged in steep experiential learning regardless of how long they have been serving in the EP. Furthermore, most MEPs involved in the greening discussions did not have a background in agriculture and thus engaged in a similarly steep level of factual learning about the CAP and different greening measures, such as increasing the conditionality of farm payments on good environmental management and practices.

11 Pathways forward for learning scholarship in EU environmental policy

In conclusion, we see several 'waves' of scholarly interest around learning. The 1990s and 2000s saw a phase of empirically testing the theoretical conceptions of learning, frequently referring back to key 1990s literature reviews and contributions (Bennett and Howlett, 1992; Hall, 1993; May, 1992) with different learning 'labels' such as political learning, governance learning and social learning. One recent development resulting from the revived interest in policy learning, especially in the public policy community, are an increasing number of workshops, conference panels, special journal issues (e. g., *Journal of Environmental Policy and Planning* 2019, *Environmental Politics* 2019, *Public Administration* 2020; *Journal of European Public Policy* 2023) and edited book volumes (Radaelli, Dunlop and Trein, 2018, Radaelli and Zaki, 2026) involving a new generation of scholars.

A theme that emerged in the late 2010s/early 2020s focuses on the drivers of learning, especially learning during a period of crisis (e.g., Dunlop and Radaelli, 2016; Kamkhaji and Radaelli, 2017). This resulted in several empirical applications to Covid-19 and the environmental crisis (Von Hagke et al., 2022; Zaki, Pattyn and Wayenberg, 2024) and more specifically the climate crisis (e.g., Müller, 2023) drawing on the learning literature discussed above.

A starting point for new empirical research would be to form hypotheses based on recurring themes and patterns in the EU environmental policy learning literature. The first hypothesis concerns the time frame for learning. Often individuals formed beliefs and gained expertise and experience long in the past, frequently in their youth or during their university education. This results in more incremental factual and experiential learning when these individuals are already experts. Second, factual learning and experiential learning exists in almost any EU environmental policy process once individuals reflect on a situation and subsequently react to it. Third, changes in beliefs are rare, especially to deep beliefs such as underpinning values and world views. Rather, individuals and organizations engage in experiential learning to 'better play politics' (often labeled 'political learning') and be more successful in preventing policy change or only allowing enough policy change so that it is still aligned with their deep core and deeper beliefs. They may change their beliefs about policy design and details to protect their deep core and deeper beliefs while conforming to wider societal changes and demands, such as in the case of greening the CAP (Rietig, 2021). These changes are often a response to public pressure from wider society and environmental NGOs/green parties. Fourth, entrepreneurial policy strategies remain dominant as individuals and organizations use rather 'conventional' power tactics to influence the policy process, drawing on their own learning in the past, rather than taking the time and making the effort to 'teach' others about the importance of addressing the environmental challenge. In terms of policy implications, this is where 'learning entrepreneurs' could be helpful agents for perpetuating policy changes where others learn why it is important to improve a particular environmental aspect rather than being at the receiving end of power politics. This, however, also means acknowledging the risk that other actors may not want to 'learn' and support the environmental policy but rather use the opportunity of being consulted to play their own power politics.

One major challenge that remains is around the methodological issues of identifying, differentiating and evaluating the impact of learning on a policy outcome or decision-making process. This is especially true with regards to the inclusion of quantitative methods in addition to the proven approaches of elite interviews with key actors and subsequent process-tracing of learning and other potential factors in the policy outcome. A further challenge is how to link learning across the individual and collective levels and connect the causal mechanisms that determine when, why, how and under what conditions learning is transferred from one level to the other. Furthermore, most of the literature has so far focused on detecting learning and determining its influence on the policy process. This raises the question of how the learning literature could be utilized in a more forward-thinking manner (Cashore et al., 2019) to facilitate and improve learning among individuals and organizations within the policymaking process as well as to support them in becoming and acting as learning entrepreneurs who facilitate others' reflections and learning. This forward-thinking approach to policy learning would allow for applying framework parameters that are similar across case studies in practice. These could include a timeframe for learning of several years, the identification of the central role of policy entrepreneurs in also facilitating other's learning as learning entrepreneurs and a focus on the type of belief changes that have the most profound impact on policy change beyond more incremental and omnipresent factual and experiential learning.

References

Argyris, C. and Schön, D. (1978) *Organizational learning: A theory of action perspective.* Reading: Addison-Wesley.

Bennett, C.J. and Howlett, M. (1992) 'The lessons of learning: Reconciling theories of policy learning and policy change', *Policy Sciences*, 25(3), pp. 275–294.

Bomberg, E. (2007) 'Policy learning in an enlarged European Union: Environmental NGOs and new policy instruments', *Journal of European Public Policy*, 14(2), pp. 248–268.

Cashore, B. et al. (2019) 'Designing stakeholder learning dialogues for effective global governance', *Policy & Society*, 38(1), pp. 118–147.

Challies, E., Newig, J., Kochskämper, E. and Jager, NW. (2017) 'Governance change and governance learning in Europe: Stakeholder participation in environmental policy implementation', *Policy & Society*, 36(2), pp. 288–303.

Domorenok, E. and Zito, A.R. (2021) 'Engines of learning? Policy instruments, cities and climate governance', *Policy Sciences*, 54(3), pp. 507–528.

Dunlop, C. (2009) 'Policy transfer as learning: Capturing variation in what decision-makers learn from epistemic communities', *Policy Studies*, 30(3), pp. 289–311.

Dunlop, C. and Radaelli, C. (2013) 'Systematising policy learning: From monolith to dimensions', *Political Studies*, 61(3), pp. 599–619.

Dunlop, C. and Radaelli, C. (2016) 'Policy learning in the Eurozone crisis: Modes, power and functionality', *Policy Sciences*, 49(2), pp. 107–124.

Dunlop, C. and Radaelli, C. (2018) 'The lessons of policy learning: Types, triggers, hindrances and pathologies', *Policy & Politics*, 46(2), pp. 255–272.

Dunlop, C., Radaelli, C. and Trein, P. (eds.) (2018) *Learning in public policy.* Cham: Springer International Publishing.

Feindt, P. (2010) 'Policy-learning and environmental policy integration in the common agricultural policy, 1973–2003', *Public Administration*, 88(2), pp. 296–314.

Fiorino, D. (2001) 'Environmental policy as learning: A new view of an old landscape', *Public Administration Review*, 61(3), pp. 322–334.

Gerlak, A. and Heikkila, T. (2011) 'Building a theory of learning in collaboratives: Evidence from the Everglades restoration programme', *Journal of Public Administration Research and Theory* 21, pp. 619–644.

Hall, P. (1993) 'Policy paradigms, social learning, and the state: The case of economic policymaking in Britain', *Comparative Politics* 25(3), pp. 275–296.

Hedberg, B. (1981) 'How organizations learn and unlearn', in: Nystrom, P. and Starbuck, W. (eds.) *Handbook of organizational design.* Oxford: Oxford University Press.

Heikkila, T. and Gerlak, A. (2013) 'Building a conceptual approach to collective learning: Lessons for public policy scholars', *Policy Studies Journal*, 41(3), pp. 484 – 512.

Jachtenfuchs, M. (1996) *International policy-making as a learning process? The European Union and the greenhouse effect.* Aldershot: Ashgate Publishing.

Janis, I. and Mann, L. (1977) *Decision making: A psychological analysis of conflict, choice, and commitment.* London: Macmillan Publishers.

Kamkhaji, J. and Radaelli, C. (2017) 'Crisis, learning and policy change in the European Union', *Journal of European Public Policy*, 24(5), pp. 714 – 734.

Koch, M. and Lindenthal, A. (2011) 'Learning within the European Commission: The case of environmental integration', *Journal of European Public Policy*, 18(7), pp. 980 – 998.

Lindblom, C. (1979) 'Still muddling, not yet through', *Public Administration Review*, 39(6), pp. 517 – 526.

March, J. and Olsen, J. (1975) 'The uncertainty of the past: Organizational learning under ambiguity', *European Journal of Political Research*, 3, pp. 147 – 171.

May, P. (1992) 'Policy learning and failure', *Journal of Public Policy*, 12(4), pp. 331 – 354.

McGowan, F. (2020) 'Policy learning or politics as usual? Explaining the rise and retrenchment of renewable electricity support policies in Europe', *Environmental Politics*, 29(4), pp. 589 – 608.

Müller, M. (2023) 'Crisis learning or reform backlog? The European Parliament's treaty-change proposals during the polycrisis', *Politics and Governance*, 11(4), pp. 311 – 323.

Nilsson, M. (2005) 'Learning, frames, and environmental policy integration: The case of Swedish energy policy', *Environment and Planning C: Government and Policy*, 23(2), pp. 207 – 226.

Nilsson, M. and Eckerberg, K. (eds.) (2007) *Environmental policy integration in practice: Shaping institutions for learning.* London: Earthscan.

Nilsson, M. and Persson, A. (2003) 'Framework for analysing environmental policy integration', *Journal of Environmental Policy & Planning*, 5(4), pp. 333 – 359.

Radaelli, C. (2009) 'Measuring policy learning: Regulatory impact assessment in Europe', *Journal of European Public Policy*, 16(8), pp. 1145 – 1164.

Radaelli, C. and C. Dunlop (2013) 'Learning in the European Union: Theoretical lenses and meta-theory', *Journal of European Public Policy*, 20(6), pp. 923 – 940.

Radaelli, C. and Zaki, B. (eds.) (2026) Handbook of Policy Learning. Cheltenham: Edward Elgar Publishing.

Rietig, K. (2019) 'Leveraging the power of learning to overcome negotiation deadlocks in global climate governance and low carbon transitions', *Journal of Environmental Policy & Planning*, 21(3), pp. 228 – 241.

Rietig, K. (2021) *Learning in governance: Climate policy integration in the European Union.* Cambridge: MIT Press.

Rietig, K. (2025) 'What next for international climate politics? Learning and multilevel reinforcing dynamics in the UNFCCC', *International Affairs*, 101(4), pp. 1301 – 1321.

Rietig, K. and Perkins, R. (2018) 'Does learning matter for policy outcomes? The case of integrating climate finance into the EU budget', *Journal of European Public Policy*, 25(4), pp. 487 – 505.

Schout, A. (2009) 'Organizational learning in the EU's multi-level governance system', *Journal of European Public Policy*, 16(8), pp. 1124 – 1144.

Swinnen, J. (ed.) (2008) *The perfect storm: The political economy of the Fischler reforms of the Common Agricultural Policy*. Brussels: Centre for European Policy Studies.

Von Hagke, C. et al. (2022) 'Learning from the COVID-19 pandemic crisis to overcome the global environmental crisis', *Sustainability*, 14(17), p. 10545.

Westerink, J., Pérez-Soba, M. and van Doorn, A. (2020) 'Social learning and land lease to stimulate the delivery of ecosystem services in intensive arable farming', *Ecosystem Services*, 44, 101149.

Zaki, B. and Dupont, C. (2023) 'Understanding political learning by scientific experts: A case of EU climate policy', *Journal of European Public Policy*, 31(7), pp. 1993 – 2025.

Zaki, B., Pattyn, V. and Wayenberg, E. (2024) 'Policy learning from evidence during polycrises: A case of EU environmental policy', *Policy Design and Practice*, 7(4), pp. 390 – 408.

Zito, A. and Schout, A. (2009) 'Learning theory reconsidered: EU integration theories and earning', *Journal of European Public Policy*, 16(8), pp. 1103 – 1123.

Ian Bailey

Synergies and tensions between the European Union's economic and environmental values

Abstract: This chapter offers critical reflections on the values underpinning the European Union's (EU) framing of the relationship between environmental protection and economic growth and the expression of these values in EU environmental policymaking. Three vantage points are used to analyze this relationship: (i) a chronological view of the values informing EU environmental policy since its inception in 1972; (ii) a declarative-substantive view comparing the goals and principles adopted in the EU treaties and environmental action program with key policies introduced to address the environmental effects of the EU's economic activities; and (iii) the use of economic and noneconomic framings in policy areas that have a less immediate bearing on the functioning and competitiveness of the EU economy. The chapter concludes by considering the main factors that have contributed to the privileging and embedding of ecological modernization and econocentric discourses within EU environmental policy and their effects in marginalizing ways of addressing environmental pressures that do not contribute to economic growth.

Keywords: Values; economic growth; environmental protection; ecological modernization and decoupling; European Green Deal

1 Introduction

The extent to which environmental concerns have permeated the European Union's (EU) governance system is a striking achievement when one considers that the early decades of European integration were concerned primarily with restoring political relations and promoting economic cooperation and that the EU lacked a legal basis for enacting common environmental policies until the Single European Act (SEA) came into force in 1987. Despite the progress made in developing its environmental *acquis*, the EU still has substantial ground to cover before it can claim to have reconciled its economic and environmental agendas. The European Environment Agency's 2020 *State of Nature* report charts a continued decline in biodiversity and many other environmental indicators (European Environment Agency, 2020), and the EU remains first and foremost an economic integration organization comprised of Member States that often hold divergent outlooks on environmental issues. Many of its environmental policies, meanwhile, still convey the impression that environmental problems are market failures that can be regulated away without deeper questioning of the EU's commitment to economic growth (Burns, Eckersley and Tobin, 2020; Machin, 2019).

An optimistic reading of this situation is that the EU's governing institutions are working proficiently within the requirements of the treaties and wider social and eco-

https://doi.org/10.1515/9783111321523-009

nomic constraints and that, with persistence, its policies will succeed in decoupling economic growth from environmental degradation (Fitch-Roy and Bailey, 2023). A bleaker assessment is that the EU's current value orientations—and the environmental policies they privilege—are inveterately wedded to economic growth and that environmental policy ambition and outcomes inevitably suffer when the two priorities collide (Burns, Eckersley and Tobin, 2020).

This chapter explores the value systems underpinning EU environmental policy in order to discern the extent to which either position reflects the EU's approach to the economy-environment relationship. Unpacking the belief system of a political entity like the EU is challenging because the values undergirding the discussion and management of issues are often virtue-signaled or undeclared. Difficulties also arise from the differential embeddedness of different types of values. Deep-core beliefs—such as concerns for human rights and democracy—provide basic ontological and normative building blocks for reasoning and are highly resistant to change. Policy-core beliefs —which arguably include growth-centered market economics and environmental protection—form a second layer of values that hold coalitions together, while secondary beliefs relate to specific aspects of problems, such as methods for addressing environmental problems, and are more negotiable (Ripberger et al., 2014; Zafonte and Sabatier, 1998). The challenge is to differentiate whether economic growth constitutes a deep-core or policy-core EU value and, from this, determine the EU's scope for critical reflection on its growth ambitions in the context of deepening ecological crises.

Three vantage points are used to decipher the values shaping the EU's environmental policies. First, a chronological viewpoint is used to explore which values have held sway at different times and how they have evolved. Second, a declarative-substantive viewpoint is used to compare the goals and principles expressed in high-level political statements against the more detailed policies introduced to achieve these aspirations. Finally, the chapter examines whether and in what ways the EU has moderated or modified its economic objectives in areas of environmental policy that theoretically have fewer economic ramifications. The main argument developed from this analysis is that environmental protection has moved closer to the heart of EU policy discourse and praxis (Lenschow, Burns and Zito, 2020), but that, for various reasons, econocentric leanings that foreground the necessity of growth-centered justifications for environmental policy and the feasibility of decoupling growth from environmental degradation have become increasingly embedded in the EU's environmental policy psyche. The chapter concludes by reflecting on some of the factors driving this orientation, their implications for EU environmental policymaking and directions for future research in the field.

2 The chronological view of the EU's environmental values

The inception and early years of EU environmental policy were strongly shaped by two factors that, when combined, provide early indicators of the values systems informing its approach to environmental policy: the European Economic Community's involvement in the United Nations (UN) Conference on the Human Environment in Stockholm in 1972; and the lack of a treaty basis for developing common environmental policies prior to the SEA (Hey, 2006). The Stockholm Conference added momentum to concerns that were already emerging in several Member States about the adverse effects of economic growth and consumerism (Meyer, 2017). However, Articles 100 and 235 of the Treaty of Rome largely restricted the Community's environmental policymaking capacity to measures affecting the establishment or functioning of the Common Market (see Chapter 31). Hildebrand (2002) contends that this uncertain jurisdictional basis corralled the early phases of Community environmental policy through legal necessity along an overridingly economic trajectory and toward a gradualist approach to environmental policy that frustrated the spirit of optimism the Stockholm Conference had generated about the feasibility of far-reaching policy change (Hey, 2006).

The inclusion of an environmental chapter in the SEA theoretically created opportunities for greater reflection on how the Community should balance its economic and environmental priorities, so too, in a sense, did the SEA's articles pertaining to the completion of the internal market—which prompted debate within the Commission on the need to address the anticipated environmental effects of the acceleration of the internal market's economic growth—and to the introduction of qualified majority voting in the Council on environmental policy (Hildebrand, 2002). Space constraints prevent a forensic dissection of the impact of these developments on the EU's outlook on the growth-environment question, but the general view is that the post-SEA era was characterized as much by continuity as by change. Although the SEA codified several important environmental principles—including the need to prioritize preventative action and ensure polluters paid for the environmental damage they caused—and reduced the need for environmental measures to secure unanimous support from the Member States, economic thinking remained central to EU environmental policy throughout the 1980s (Hey, 2006).

The emergence of the sustainable development agenda in the build-up to the UN Conference on Environment and Development in Rio de Janeiro in 1992 formed another important juncture in the EU's deliberations on the economy-environment relationship. The definition of sustainable development elaborated by the Brundtland Commission sought to put the economy, environment and social progress on an equal footing, and its adoption at the Rio Summit provided an opportunity for the EU to make a firm commitment to the concept in the Treaty on European Union (Maastricht) (Pallemaerts, 2013). Although this only partly materialized after the term 'sustainable and non-inflationary growth' was adopted instead, sustainable development continued to make headway in EU political discourse, including in the Fifth Environment Action Program, 'Towards Sustainability', which Hey (2006, p. 23) describes as having "all the necessary elements of a policy oriented towards 'ecological structural change'".

While the 1990s could be regarded as a period of greater reflection on sustainability issues and led, among other things, to the adoption of the environmental integration principle in the 1997 Treaty of Amsterdam, ambivalence toward tempering the EU's economic goals to accommodate environmental concerns persisted. Pallemaerts (2013) argues that the EU's sustainable development strategy co-existed uneasily for many years with the Lisbon Strategy adopted in 2000 to boost employment and productivity in the EU economy. Conversely, ecological modernization narratives (see Chapter 3) extolling the reciprocity of environmental protection and economic growth began to gain greater traction and were important in convincing poorer Member States to accept environmental measures they feared would hinder their development and economic convergence (Baker, 2007; Gouldson and Murphy, 1996). Ecological modernization's optimistic framings thus helped create more favorable political conditions for debate of environmental issues, policy experimentation, and institutional learning (see Chapter 6) about how to address environmental problems (Bailey, Gouldson and Newell, 2011; Leipold, 2021).

The final set of indications of the EU's stance on the decoupling thesis examined here concerns the EU's support for the green economy ethos, first, at the UN Rio+20 conference in 2012 and, more latterly, through the adoption of the European Green Deal (EGD) in 2019. A UN expert panel for the Rio+20 summit defined the green economy as a 'new economic growth paradigm' for moving from an economic system "that allowed, and at times generated crises towards a system that proactively addresses and prevents them" (Ocampo, 2011, p. 3). Notwithstanding Rio+20's emphasis on social inclusion and poverty reduction alongside environmental protection, green economy thinking has been criticized for ignoring basic contradictions between ever-expanding human activity and a finite world, for placing unwarranted faith in market mechanisms and technical expertise to solve environmental problems and for limiting society's ability to conceive responses to sustainability challenges that lie outside the economic sphere (e.g., Spash, 2012; Wilson, 2019). Despite these criticisms, the Commission's communication, "Rio+20: towards the green economy and better governance", was unambiguous in portraying the green economy as both radical and desirable:

> Responses to these challenges [of providing better lives for the global population and addressing environmental pressures] will not come from slowing growth, but rather from promoting the *right* kind of growth. There are compelling reasons to fundamentally rethink the conventional model of economic progress [...] A green economy offers an effective way of promoting sustainable development, eradicating poverty and addressing emerging challenges and outstanding implementation gaps. (European Commission, 2011, p. 5, original emphasis)

The following section discusses the EGD in more detail, but the main point to note here is its framing as a new growth strategy for transforming the EU into a fair and prosperous society where growth is decoupled from resource use and environmental impacts (European Commission, 2019). Summing up, the chronological view indicates that shifts have occurred from early positioning of the environment as a flanking policy to trade liberalization toward a situation where environmental concerns occupy a prominent place in the EU's strategic objectives. Despite this, environmental issues have consistently—and perhaps increasingly—been framed in ways that depict economic growth and competitiveness as prerequisites for, rather than threats to, environmental protection.

3 The declarative-substantive view: treaties, programs and policies

High-level political declarations often contain limited policy detail and employ expansive but pliable language in order to mediate the views of the different political groups involved in their negotiation (Baker, 2007). Consequently, their usefulness as lenses for understanding policymakers' underlying intentions can be quite limited. Their significance nevertheless lies in their capacity to generate norms that shape problem-perception and political decisions on issues addressed by declarations. The EU treaties provide a useful starting point for probing how the EU has framed the economy-environment relationship. As noted earlier, using the term *sustainable and non-inflationary growth* in the Treaty on European Union was highly contentious but indicated a belief that environmental protection complemented, rather than clashed with, the continued growth of the EU economy. Subsequent treaties have moved closer to the UN's formulation, though even the Lisbon Treaty's reference to *the sustainable development of Europe* continues to emphasize balanced economic growth as a key feature of the EU's approach to environmental sustainability (Benson and Adelle, 2013; Kenig-Witkowska, 2017).

Moving down the ladder of policy abstraction, the EU Environment Action Programs (EAP) equally indicate an incremental evolution in the EU's position on environmental protection and economic growth. The Fifth EAP, which ran between 1993 and 2000, emphasized *sustainable growth that respected the environment*, while the Sixth and Seventh EAPs (2002–2012 and 2014–2020) referred explicitly to *decoupling environmental pressures from economic growth* as the lynchpin of its environmental strategy. By the Eighth EAP (2022–2030), the EU had shifted toward the objective of ensuring that, by 2050 at the latest, the EU would operate a *well-being economy* where people live well within planetary boundaries, *growth is regenerative, climate neutrality has been achieved within the EU and inequalities have been significantly reduced.* Growth thus remains a core objective but with a more nuanced operationalization of its desired features (European Union, 2022).

Whatever weight one attaches to strategic political statements, the proving ground for the EU's ideals is the detailed policies introduced to achieve its environmental objectives. The EU's most recent and most expansive strategy, and arguably the clearest expression of its conviction that a mutually supportive relationship can be forged between growth and environmental protection, is the European Green Deal (EGD) launched in 2019. The Deal contains a compendium of new and existing initiatives for achieving climate neutrality in the EU by 2050 and was described in the European Commission's communication launching the Deal as "a new growth strategy that aims to transform the EU into a fair and prosperous society, with a modern, resource-efficient and competitive economy where there are no net emissions of greenhouse gases in 2050 and where economic growth is decoupled from resource use" (European Commission, 2019, p. 2).

The EGD's orientation toward the decoupling hypothesis can be illustrated by examining its circular economy package. The goal of the circular economy is to promote restorative and regenerative industrial systems that eliminate waste through product and materials design, reuse and recycling (see Chapter 36). However, the concept remains deeply contested: some question the practicality of creating nature-mimicking production systems, while others argue that circular economy narratives de-problematize and depoliticize questions concerning the sustainability of continued economic growth (Corvellec, Stowell and Johansson, 2022; Valenzuela and Böhm, 2017). Slightly more sympathetically, Kovacic, Strand and Völkder (2020) argue that lack of critical scrutiny of contested ideas forms a critical part of alliance-building between different branches of the Commission and consensus-building among the Member States (see Chapter 5). Either way, the EU has thrown its weight behind the circular economy for both economic and environmental reasons. The Commission's first circular economy plan, published in 2014, outlined fifty-four measures to promote the circular economy and trailed proposals to amend a number of existing directives, including the Waste Framework Directive and the Landfill, End-of-Life Vehicles and Waste Electrical and Electronic Equipment Directives, to strengthen their alignment with circular economy ideas (European Commission, 2014; Fitch-Roy and Bailey, 2023). While the 2014 plan hinted that circular economy practices could make growth more environmentally sustainable, the Commission's Circular Economy Action Plan published in 2020 was more unequivocal, arguing that it could increase EU Gross Domestic Product by 0.5 percent by 2030 while creating 700,000 new jobs (European Commission, 2020a).

The growth-inducing benefits of environmental measures have equally underpinned other elements of the EGD. For instance, key selling points for the green hydrogen and offshore wind strategies identified by the Commission were their potential to create millions of jobs and billions of Euros in cumulative investment (European Commission, 2020b, 2020c), while the Farm to Fork Strategy (see Chapter 4) was portrayed as 'a huge economic opportunity', in addition to yielding biodiversity, regional development and health benefits (European Commission, 2020d). Vezzoni (2023) argues that such rarefied narratives mask a host of possible adverse effects, not least the potential for the EU's renewable energy strategy to lock the EU into raw material import dependencies and intensive extractive activities that run contrary to green growth dematerializing narratives.

In contrast to its focus on production efficiency and technological innovation, the EGD initially made only passing mention of consumption in remarks on "redirect[ing] public investment, consumption and taxation to green priorities" (European Commission 2019, p. 17). Addressing the sustainability impacts of consumption nevertheless began to gain greater prominence with the adoption of the New Consumer Agenda in November 2020 (European Commission, 2020e). The essence of the Agenda's methodology is that providing consumers with greater information on the environmental impacts of products will enable them to make more informed purchasing choices, with the ongoing expectation that consumer sovereignty will influence production choices. The Agenda also trails initiatives to improve product durability by strengthening consumer rights, including an effective 'right to repair' under the Sustainable Product Policy and the extension of minimum liability periods for new and second-hand goods. Measures to improve the verifiability of green product claims made by companies have also emerged via the greenwashing and green claims directives (European Union, 2024). However, the Agenda appears to reject any notion of quantitative constraints on consumption:

> Consumers across Europe are showing a growing interest in contributing personally to climate neutrality, preserving natural resources and biodiversity, and reducing water, air and soil pollution. The challenge is to unlock this potential through measures that empower, support and enable every consumer, regardless of their financial situation, to play an active role in the green transition *without imposing a specific lifestyle* and without social discrimination. (European Commission, 2020e, p. 5, emphasis added)

Whether the EGD can achieve a genuine decoupling of growth from environmental degradation or further postpones debate on how the EU balances its economic and environmental values can only be judged once its measures have had more time to take effect. Hereu-Morales, Segarra and Valderrama (2023) nevertheless argue that the EGD contains major flaws in its interpretation of environmental sustainability and fails to acknowledge the challenges of transitioning to a circular economy, while its "focus on economic growth no matter what" increases the difficulties of conserving natural capital and "jeopardises efforts on sustainable development issues that do not imply a direct link with the economy" (Hereu-Morales, Segarra and Valderrama, 2023, p. 657). Samper, Schockling and Islar (2021), meanwhile, contend that the EGD extends the application of neoliberal ideas (prioritizing market over state solutions) to environmental issues to an unprecedented level and creates a dangerous over-reliance on corporate interests to achieve environmental goals.

4 Nature conservation: economic framings for a noneconomic problem?

Except for measures that intersect with agricultural and land-use policy, nature conservation theoretically has fewer direct implications for the EU economy and gives the EU greater scope to foreground non-material relationships between humans and nature in how it develops its conservation policies (Alblas and van Zeben, 2023). But to what extent has this happened and what factors have shaped the EU's approach to nature conservation (see Chapters 19 and 23)?

The EU's first nature protection legislation, the Birds Directive (adopted in 1979 and amended in 2009), arguably incorporates such sentiments in its requirement for the Member States to maintain the population of naturally occurring wild bird species and to preserve, maintain or re-establish a sufficient diversity and area of habitats for these species. Similarly, the Habitats Directive, which led to the creation of the Natura 2000 network, obliges Member States to maintain or restore natural habitats and wild fauna and flora species of Community interest to a favorable conservation status by designating, protecting and managing specified habitat types (Jackson, 2018). Both directives nevertheless stipulate that Member State measures should take account of economic, social and cultural requirements and regional and local characteristics.

By 2021, Natura 2000 sites accounted for around 18 percent of the EU's land area and 9 percent of its seas. However, the European Environment Agency's 2020 *State of ature* report (European Environment Agency, 2020) charts a continued decline in EU biodiversity, with only 50 percent of bird species and 15 percent of habitats enjoying favorable conservation status. Although Natura 2000 sites showed less deterioration than the EU average, Kati et al. (2015) identify a number of impediments to their effectiveness, including: variability in the designation of sites; lack of political will among local and national governments to implement measures; local stakeholder resistance to measures that impinge on economic and social concerns; underfunding and understaffing of management authorities and poor decision-making stemming from poor knowledge of conservation practices.

The EU's latest nature conservation strategy, the 'Biodiversity Strategy for 2030', was adopted with the ambition of ensuring that, "by 2050 all of the world's ecosystems are restored, resilient, and adequately protected" (European Commission, 2020 f, p. 3). Although it has sought to act as a norm-shaper for international conservation efforts by calling for a global commitment to biodiversity net-gain and the halt to further human-induced species losses, the Commission's communication accompanying the strategy launch again sent mixed messages about the EU's motivations. It describes protecting nature as a moral imperative but defines nature's value chiefly in terms of provisioning human needs and helping society to cope with global change, health threats and disasters (see Chapter 23). In contrast, the communication does not mention moral or legal obligations toward nature, despite a study the previous year by the

European Economic and Social Committee (2019) advocating an EU Charter of Rights for Nature.[1] Tellingly, the strategy argues that "[t]he business case for biodiversity is compelling", claiming that at a global level biodiversity conservation could increase the seafood industry's profits by over EUR 49 billion annually and save the insurance sector EUR 50 billion through wetland protection and reduced flood-damage (European Commission, 2020 f, p. 1).

This largely anthropocentric and econocentric framing notwithstanding, the nature restoration plan outlined in the Biodiversity Strategy sets out far-reaching proposals to restore at least 20 percent of the EU's land and sea areas by 2030 and all ecosystems in need of restoration by 2050. The strategy additionally formed the basis of a Commission proposal for a Nature Restoration Regulation in 2022 (European Commission, 2022) aimed at expanding norms of nature restoration beyond the species and habitats identified in the Habitats Directive to include, among other things, urban environments and agricultural ecosystems (Hoek, 2022). Supplementing the Biodiversity Strategy's headline targets, the Regulation requires Member States to restore at least 30 percent of habitats listed in the Regulation that are in poor condition by 2030, increasing to 60 percent in 2040 and 90 percent by 2050. Although the Regulation arguably represents a further advance toward the advocacy of noneconomic justifications for biodiversity conservation, it was only passed by the Council by a qualified majority following a change in position by Austria, which, along with several other Member States, previously withheld support for the Regulation citing concerns over its cost and effects on the agricultural sector (Kurmayer, 2024).

The challenges of shifting toward a more ecocentric approach to conservation are equally underscored by the EU's efforts to direct a greater proportion of Common Agricultural Policy (CAP) funding toward environmentally beneficial farming practices (Gravey, Adam and Hoerver, 2021). The process of 'greening the CAP' through the introduction of measures to enhance environmental protection on agricultural land began with the McSharry reforms in 1992 but, despite numerous revisions, the EU is widely regarded as having failed to constrain the adverse environmental impacts of farming. Rac, Erjavec and Erjavec (2024) argue that the latest reforms introduced under the EGD still fail to provide adequate support for environmentally friendly farming and that the uptake of CAP environmental payments remains uneven because of different discursive representations of the relationship between nature and farming across the EU. Whereas agriculture is portrayed at the EU level through a productivist lens that emphasizes food security, with the environment being used as a justification for CAP payments, countries such as Finland have adopted more ecological modernization narratives that emphasize synergetic relationships between farming incomes,

1 Epstein and Schoukens (2021) argue that although rights for nature are not explicitly recognized in EU law, nature does enjoy rights in the EU legal order by virtue of obligations contained within existing environmental laws. Epstein and Schoukens (2021) add that Court of Justice of the European Union rulings on the protection of wolves further indicate that nature enjoys some legal rights that cannot be entirely sidelined by human utilitarian interests.

competitiveness and environmental protection, while others, like Croatia, have depicted environmental measures as externally-imposed constraints on agricultural productivity.

Piecing the evidence together, even on issues where the economic stakes are lower and the ecological imperatives more pressing, the EU still seems reluctant to move away from conventional policy frames and toward environmental policymaking based on more ecological thinking (Warleigh-Lack, 2010). Warleigh-Lack argues that several factors have contributed to this: the constraining effects of the EU treaties on the scope for radical thinking; the historical and accumulative embedding of path-dependent values and norms among EU actors who express concern about the environmental effects of economic activities but are unwilling to reject materialism or to articulate a clear sense of human interdependencies with the nonhuman world and the practical difficulties of building solidarity among the Member States for framings that challenge the optimistic narratives of ecological modernization.

5 Conclusion

EU environmental policy has undergone profound changes, but one of its abiding features has been EU decision-makers' belief in the compatibility of environmental protection and economic growth. The chronological view particularly reveals how EU environmental policymaking was initially constrained by a lack of treaty authorization for measures that did not contribute to the functioning of the internal market. Sustainable development's emergence as a new paradigm in the early 1990s arguably presented an opportunity for the EU to redefine how it balanced its economic, social and environmental objectives but coincided with pressures to complete the single market. In the subsequent period, the values of ecological modernization appear increasingly to have developed a self-reinforcing logic.

Various factors help to explain this trend: the EU's jurisdictional limits; the need to demonstrate its willingness and capacity to address citizen and Member-State concerns and the economic strains of the global financial crisis, Covid-19 and the 2022 energy-price crisis. The troubles that beleaguered the EU Nature Restoration Regulation and CAP reforms equally provide clear illustrations of the challenges involved in tackling frictions between the EU's growth and environmental agendas.

Navigating these circumstances has required the EU to exhibit multiple forms of environmental policy leadership. Entrepreneurial leadership has been particularly important in reconciling different national positions, as, to an extent, has leadership-by-example in the aspirations of the EGD (Liefferink and Wurzel, 2017). However, the EU's intellectual leadership on environmental policy—its capacity to redefine interests through the promotion of new ideas—has been confined largely to problem-solving within the parameters of its prevailing values. Many of its higher-level policy declarations on environmental issues have been presented as radical, but the substantive policies underlying them have tended to reinforce, rather than question or meaningfully reform, the 'win-win' values of ecological modernization (Fitch-Roy and Bailey, 2023). Also striking is how these narratives have come to be seen as the only message that can galvanize the EU's environmental program. Leipold (2021) warns that fetishizing the notion of benign growth renders EU environmental policy prone to a creeping depoliticization in which subjective decisions are discursively constructed as matters of market rationality and technocracy rather than as topics of democratic debate. Ecological modernization is then presented as the only feasible solution, such that, as Machin (2019, p. 208) puts it, "Not only are political differences erased from the discourse, but the discourse is itself removed from political debate".

Debates on whether the EU is excessively wedded to a 'growth-first' outlook on environmental policy and how it might maneuver toward assigning environmental goals a more equivalent status to economic and social objectives will doubtless continue, but advancing them requires greater clarity on a number of issues. First, thoroughgoing analysis is needed of how and why decoupling growth from resource consumption and environmental degradation is (not) occurring across different spheres of EU policymaking. Second, critical examination is needed of alternative measures of societal progress and narratives that might help steer EU decision-making from its current econocentric direction. In many ways, these represent time-honored questions in the growth debate, but more geographically-grounded and politically-focused research is needed to deepen understanding of how the divergent interests that make up the EU might be encouraged to coalesce around a more transformative approach to environmental policymaking.

References

Alblas, E. and van Zeben, J. (2023) '"Farming out' biodiversity: Implementing EU Nature Law through agri-environmental schemes', *Earth System Governance*, 17, 100180, pp. 1–10.

Bailey, I., Gouldson, A. and Newell, P. (2011) 'Ecological modernisation, policy networks and the governance of the new carbon economy', *Antipode*, 43(3), pp. 682–703.

Baker, S. (2007) 'Sustainable development as symbolic commitment: Declaratory politics and the seductive appeal of ecological modernisation in the European Union', *Environmental Politics*, 16(2), pp. 297–317.

Benson, D. and Adelle, C. (2013) 'EU environmental policy after the Lisbon Treaty', in: Jordan, A. and Adelle, C. (eds.) *Environmental policy in the EU: Actors, institutions and processes.* Abingdon: Routledge, pp. 32–48.

Burns, C., Eckersley, P. and Tobin, P. (2020) 'EU environmental policy in times of crisis', *Journal of European Public Policy*, 27(1), pp. 1–19.

Corvellec, H. Stowell, A. and Johansson, N. (2022) 'Critiques of the circular economy', *Journal of Industrial Ecology*, 26(2), pp. 421–432.

Epstein, Y. and Schoukens, H. (2021) 'A positivist approach to rights of nature in the European Union', *Journal of Human Rights and the Environment*, 12(2), pp. 205–227.

European Commission (2011) 'Rio+20: Towards the green economy and better governance', *COM*(2011) 363 final. Available at: https://eur-lex.europa.eu/legal-content/EN/TXT/?uri=celex:52011DC0363 (Accessed: 29 May 2024).

European Commission (2014) 'Towards a circular economy: A zero waste programme for Europe, 2014', *COM*(2014/0398) final. Available at: https://eur-lex.europa.eu/legal-content/EN/TXT/?uri=celex:52014DC0398 (Accessed: 29 May 2025 2024).

European Commission (2019) 'The European green deal', *COM*(2019) 640 final. Available at: https://eur-lex.europa.eu/legal-content/EN/TXT/?uri=celex:52019DC0640 (Accessed: 22 August 2024).

European Commission (2020a) 'A new circular economy action plan for a cleaner and more competitive Europe', *COM*(2020) 98 final. Available at: https://eur-lex.europa.eu/legal-content/EN/TXT/?uri=celex:52020DC0098 (Accessed: 23 August 2024).

European Commission (2020b) 'A hydrogen strategy for a climate-neutral Europe', *COM*(2020) 301 final. Available at: https://eur-lex.europa.eu/legal-content/EN/TXT/?uri=celex:52020DC0301 (Accessed: 26 March 2024).

European Commission (2020c) 'An EU strategy to harness the potential of offshore renewable energy for a climate neutral future', *COM*(2020) 741 final. Available at: https://eur-lex.europa.eu/legal-content/EN/TXT/HTML/?uri=CELEX%3 A52020DC0741 (Accessed: 26 March 2024).

European Commission (2020d) *Farm to fork strategy: For a Fair, healthy and environmentally-friendly food system.* Available at: https://food.ec.europa.eu/system/files/2020-05/f2f_action-plan_2020_strategy-info_en.pdf (Accessed: 19 August 2024).

European Commission (2020e) 'New consumer agenda: Strengthening consumer resilience for sustainable recovery', *COM*(2020) 696 final. Available at: https://eur-lex.europa.eu/legal-content/EN/TXT/?uri=celex:52020DC0696 (Accessed: 29 August 2024).

European Commission (2020 f) 'EU biodiversity strategy for 2030: Bringing nature back into our lives', *COM*(2020) 380 final. Available at: https://eur-lex.europa.eu/legal-content/EN/TXT/?uri=celex:52020DC0380 (Accessed: 29 August 2024).

European Commission (2022) 'Proposal for a regulation of the European Parliament and of the Council on Nature Restoration,' *COM*(2022) 304 final. Available at: https://eur-lex.europa.eu/legal-content/EN/TXT/?uri=celex:52022PC0304 (Accessed: 29 August 2024).

European Economic and Social Committee (2019) *Towards an EU charter of the fundamental rights of nature.* Available at: https://doi.org/10.2864/499675 (Accessed: 29 August 2024)

European Environment Agency (2020) *State of nature in the EU.* Luxembourg: Publications Office of the European Union.

European Union (2022) 'Decision (EU) 2022/591 of the European Parliament and of the Council of 6 April 2022 on a General Union Environment Action Programme to 2030', *Official Journal of the European Union.* Available at: https://eur-lex.europa.eu/legal-content/EN/TXT/PDF/?uri=CELEX:32022D0591 (21 August 2024).

European Union (2024) 'Directive (EU) 2024/825 amending Directives 2005/29/EC and 2011/83/EU as regard empowering consumer for the green transition through better protection against unfair practices and through better information', *Official Journal of the European Union.* Available at: https://eur-lex.europa.eu/eli/dir/2024/825/oj (Accessed: 22 August 2024).

Fitch-Roy, O. and Bailey, I. (2023) 'Green growth and competitiveness in EU climate policy: Paradigm shift or "*plus de la même chose*"?'. In: Rayner, T., Szulecki, K., Jordan, A. and Oberthür, S. (eds.) *Handbook on European Union climate change policy and politics.* Cheltenham: Edward Elgar, pp. 173 – 186.

Gouldson, A. and Murphy, J. (1996) 'Ecological modernization and the European Union', *Geoforum*, 27(1), pp. 11 – 21.

Gravey, V., Adam, U. and Hoerber, T. (2021) 'The Long and winding road to greening the Common Agricultural Policy', in: Hoerber, T., Weber, G. and Cabras, I. (eds.) *Routledge handbook of European integration.* London: Routledge, pp. 376 – 393.

Hereu-Morales, J., Segarra, A. and Valderrama, C. (2023) 'The European (green?) deal: A systematic analysis of environmental sustainability', *Sustainable Development*, 32(1), pp. 647 – 661.

Hey, C. (2006) 'EU environmental policies: A short history of the policy strategies', in: Scheuer, S. (ed.) *EU environmental policy handbook: A critical analysis of EU environmental legislation.* Brussels: European Environmental Bureau, pp. 17 – 30.

Hildebrand, P. (2002) 'The European Community's environmental policy, 1957 to '1992': From Incidental Measures to an International Regime?', in: Jordan, A. (ed.) *Environmental policy in the European Union: Actors, institutions and processes.* London: Earthscan, pp. 13 – 36.

Hoek, N. (2022) 'A critical analysis of the proposed EU regulation on nature restoration: Have the problems been resolved?', *European Energy and Environmental Law Review*, 31(5), pp. 320 – 333.

Jackson, A. (2018) *Conserving Europe's wildlife: Law and policy of the Natura 2000 network of protected areas.* Abingdon: Routledge.

Kati, V. et al. (2015) 'The challenge of implementing the European network of protected areas Natura 2000', *Conservation Biology*, 29(1), pp. 260 – 270.

Kenig-Witkowska, M. (2017) 'The concept of sustainable development in the European Union policy and law', *Journal of Comparative Urban Law and Policy*, 1(1), pp. 64 – 80.

Kovacic, Z., Strand, R. and Völker, T. (2020) *The circular economy in Europe: Critical perspectives on policies and imaginaries.* Abingdon: Routledge.

Kurmayer, N.J. (2024) 'Nature restoration: Austrian conservatives charge Gewessler for abuse of office', *EurActiv.* Available at: https://www.euractiv.com/section/energy-environment/news/nature-restoration-austrian-conservatives-charge-gewessler-for-abuse-of-office/ (Accessed: 31 August 2024).

Leipold, S. (2021) 'Transforming ecological modernization "from within" or perpetuating it? The circular Economy as EU environmental policy narrative', *Environmental Politics*, 30(6), pp. 1045 – 1067.

Lenschow, A., Burns, C. and Zito, A.R. (2020) 'Dismantling, disintegration or continuing stealthy integration in European Union environmental policy?' *Public Administration*, 98(2), 340 – 348.

Liefferink, D. and Wurzel, R.K.W. (2017) 'Environmental leaders and pioneers: Agents of change?', *Journal of European Public Policy*, 24(7), 951 – 968.

Machin, A. (2019) 'Changing the story? The discourse of ecological modernisation in the European Union', *Environmental Politics*, 28(2), pp. 208 – 227.

Meyer, J.H. (2017) 'From nature to environment: International organizations and environmental protection before Stockholm', in: Kaiser, W. and Meyer, J.H. (eds.) *International organizations and environmental protection: Conservation and globalization in the twentieth century.* New York: Berghahn, pp. 31 – 73.

Ocampo, J. (2011) 'The transition to a green economy: Benefits, challenges and risks from a sustainable development perspective', p. 3. Available at: https://wedocs.unep.org/bitstream/handle/20.500.11822/9310/-Transition%20to%20a%20green%20economy:%20benefits,%20challenges%20and%20risks%20from%20a%20sustainable%20development%20perspective-2012UN-DESA,%20UNCTAD%20Transition%20GE.pdf?sequence=3&amp%3Bis (Accessed: 18 June 2024).

Pallemaerts, M. (2013) 'Developing more sustainably?', in: Jordan, A. and Adelle, C. (eds.) *Environmental policy in the EU: Actors, institutions and processes.* Abingdon: Routledge, pp. 346 – 366.

Rac, I., Erjavec, K. and Erjavec, E. (2024) 'Agriculture and environment: Friends or foes? Conceptualising agri-environmental discourses under the European Union's Common Agricultural Policy', *Agriculture and Human Values*, 41, pp. 147 – 166.

Ripberger, J., Gupta, K., Silva, C. and Jenkins-Smith, H. (2014) 'Cultural theory and the measurement of deep core beliefs within the advocacy coalition framework', *Policy Studies Journal*, 42(4), pp. 509 – 527.

Samper, J.A., Schockling, A., and Islar, M. (2021) 'Climate politics in green deals: Exposing the political frontiers of the European green deal', *Politics and Governance*, 9(2), pp. 8 – 16.

Spash, C.I. (2012) 'Green economy, red herring', *Environmental Values*, 21(2), pp. 95 – 99.

Valenzuela, F. and Böhm, S. (2017) 'Against wasted politics: A critique of the circular economy', *Ephemera: Theory And Politics In Organization*, 17(1), pp. 23 – 60.

Vezzoni, R. (2023) 'Green growth for whom, how and why? The REPowerEU Plan and the inconsistencies of European Union energy policy', *Energy Research & Social Science*, 101, 103134, pp. 1–15.
Warleigh-Lack, A. (2010). 'Greening the European Union for legitimacy? A cautionary reading of Europe 2020'. *Innovation: The European Journal of Social Science Research*, 23(4), pp. 297–311.
Wilson, M. (2019) 'The green economy: The dangerous path of nature commoditization', *Consilience: The Journal of Sustainable Development*, 21(1), pp. 86–99.
Zafonte, M. and Sabatier, P. (1998) 'Shared beliefs and imposed interdependencies as determinants of ally networks in overlapping subsystems', *Journal of Theoretical Politics*, 10(4), pp. 473–505.

Annica Kronsell and Gunnhildur Lily Magnusdottir

Integrating gender and nature in the European Green Deal: Unpacking the challenges of path-dependent eco-modernized framings

Abstract: The chapter explores how gender and nature/environment are understood and framed in the European Green Deal (EGD), with a specific focus on the use of gender mainstreaming and environmental policy integration as a tool for policy integration. The analysis reveals a greater integration of nature into the EGD than gender and that EGD's aim to leave no one behind appears to be gender-blind. Using ecofeminist and feminist institutionalist scholarship, the chapter demonstrates that, although environmental concerns are integrated, the EGD techno-economic norms and path-dependent ecological modernization are obstacles for integration of nature and gender. The analysis thus demonstrates the need for a fundamental rethinking of how gender equality and nature are understood in the context of the EGD.

Keywords: European Green Deal; just transition; environmental policy integration; gender mainstreaming

1 Introduction

Ecofeminists argue that the domination of nature is closely linked to the domination of humans by humans (MacGregor 2017, 2021; Merchant, 1980; Plumwood, 1993). This chapter asks if and how the European Green Deal (EGD), the European Union's (EU) response to the Paris Agreement, recognizes this link. Through the different EGD strategies and the Fit for 55 package for a green transition, the EU sets ambitious climate goals to become the first climate-neutral continent and leader of the global climate regime. The EGD also purports to be the EU's main roadmap to a green and just climate transition and important foundation in EU efforts to fulfil the United Nations' (UN) Sustainable Development Goals (SDGs), including gender equality goals.

EGD's focus on a just transition seeks to address inequities and inequalities. It signals an aspiration to be inclusive of the whole population in the transformative process toward climate objectives. This is crucial because the recognition of social differences, including gender, is a prerequisite for just climate strategies and should be recognized in striving for a 'just' transition. The climate crisis reveals vulnerabilities in European societies tied to gender, economic status, location, age and ethnicity (Heffernan et al., 2021). We use research on the EGD and its policies to explore the integration of environment and gender into EGD and its policies. The policy areas of environment and gender have previously developed independently, but they share a cross-

https://doi.org/10.1515/9783111321523-010

sectoral nature. Being cross-sectoral means that the problems they tackle are often generated in other policy areas.

The EU has long-standing treaty-based tools intended to facilitate cross-sectoral policy coordination. Environmental policy integration (EPI) is a tool that has been in place since early 1980s and stipulates that environmental concerns should be taken into consideration in all EU policies and sectors (Kronsell, 1997, pp. 127–128). Similarly, gender mainstreaming (GM) is a tool committing the EU to integrate gender concerns into all EU policies and throughout the policy cycle (Allwood, 2020; Arora-Jonsson and Sijapati, 2018; Jordan and Lenschow, 2010). The cross-sectoral character of both EPI and GM as policy instruments can generate particular challenges for the policy institutions where they are to be enacted.

At first glance of the whole picture, the engagement with sectors and the many environmental policies embraced in the EGD suggests that EPI has achieved its ambitions. In comparison, regarding GM, the EGD has remained at the declaratory level, speaking of a just future that aspires to 'putting people at the front' (European Commission, 2024a) while accompanied by policies where gender is invisible (Allwood and Kronsell, 2025; Heffernan et al., 2021). Yet, inequalities permeate all aspects of climate change, for example, in the various attempts at creating jobs in the green economy, which are primarily jobs in male-dominated sectors (EEB, 2021; EIGE, 2023; Magnusdottir and Kronsell, 2024). This chapter explores why this is the case by relying on a feminist institutional framework.

We rely on previous research and take examples from strategy documents, assessing both the social dimension of climate change and the environment. The aim is to discuss institutional factors that are relevant to how EPI and GM have been embraced in the EGD. The following section introduces GM and EPI as policy instruments and then summarizes research on how the EU has approached sector integration in particular with GM. Then we briefly survey the theoretical ideas and the analytical approach used in the subsequent analysis. The remaining analysis will focus on exploring how the two policy areas have or have not been integrated into the EGD and why this may be the case. It then discusses what is needed to overcome these challenges and the opportunities for future research it poses.

2 Parallel streams: Gender mainstreaming and environmental policy integration

Both environmental and gender issues are cross-sectoral issues, necessitating a recognition that problems in either domain cannot be effectively addressed in isolation. The trajectories of these policy fields are also similar. Initially, both emerged as flanking policies alongside the European Common Market, aiming to prevent distortions in the market's competitiveness (see Chapter 31). Competitiveness was thought to be hampered by different environmental or labor market standards in the Member States.

Common environmental policies were developed since the early 1970s, and the 1957 Treaty of Rome endorsed equal pay for equal work for similar reasons (Minto and Mergaert, 2018, p. 213). Given their cross-sectoral nature, policymakers in both environmental and gender issue areas have endeavored to integrate them into broader consideration within the EU, moving beyond the confines of the common market and the compartmentalized structure of the Commission's Directorate-Generals (DGs). Despite similarities in terms of the cross-sectoral character of these two areas, research on and policy for GM and EPI have been treated as isolated, parallel streams. Here, we seek to learn from both areas.

Environmental policy integration has long been a guiding principle of the EU, with a focus on policies beyond the traditional environmental policy domain, including agriculture, urban planning, transport and other policy domains (see Chapter 33). EPI is deemed necessary because research indicates that sector-specific policies often overlook environmental effects (Runhaar, Driessen and Uittenbroek, 2014, p. 233). Since the 1980s, EPI has enjoyed a relatively prominent legal status in the EU, enshrined in the Treaty of Maastricht 1993 (Rietig, 2013, p. 297), but it is also "one of the guiding axioms of green thinking and practice" (Jordan and Lenschow, 2010, p. 156). A related concept, climate policy integration (CPI), advocates for the integration of climate concerns into sectoral policy, effectively 'mainstreaming' them into existing policy fields (Runhaar, Driessen and Uittenbroek, 2014, p. 233).

The EGD is an interesting example of environmental policy integration. Environmental policy in the EU has become devoted mainly to climate policy, and climate policy has become EGD (see Chapter 30). The EGD is the EU's primary environmental strategy as underscored by its incorporation into the Environmental Action Program 2021–2030 which "endorses the EGD key policy goals" (Paleari, 2022, p. 218). EU climate policy was institutionalized in 2010 with DG Climate Action, a new separate Directorate-General of climate change within the EU Commission (see Chapter 10), which signaled the importance of climate issues in EU's environmental politics (Burns, Eckersley and Tobin, 2020; Magnusdottir and Kronsell, 2016). This role was strengthened, e.g., with the integration of climate concerns into EU's foreign policymaking (Jänicke and Wurzel, 2019) and as a key element of EU identity (Kreienkamp, Pegram and Coen, 2022, p. 736). This culminated with the 2019 EGD, aimed at positioning Europe as the first climate-neutral continent (European Commission, 2019). The EGD is geared to cross-sectoral integration of climate policy with sectors, for example, by requiring extensive coordination between the EU institutions and by relating to specific sectors such as industry, transport, energy and agriculture, but it also includes several nature and environmental policies in its package.

Gender mainstreaming is a mechanism similar to EPI, calling for the integration of gender into all policy areas. Policies that aim to integrate 'outside' concerns into existing policies and institutions challenge existing institutional practices and norms. GM emerged as an approach during a period when EU gender equality progress had reached a standstill. It first appeared in the Action Program for equal opportunities between women and men, 1991–1995, with the transformative goal to both strengthen and expand the reach of EU gender equality policies. Gender mainstreaming aimed to challenge the social construction of gender roles across all policies. This was a shift in focus. Instead of merely adding women to sectors where they were underrepresented, it sought to address gender inequality as rooted in EU institutional structures and pointed to their role in perpetuating inequality (Hubert and Stratigaki, 2016). Lomazzi and Crespi (2019) suggest that the GM's radical potential to make visible and challenge gender norms in institutional practices has not been fully utilized. GM is far from a success story. Instead of integrated, gender issues have been 'layered': where, for example, gender concerns are added on top of existing policies due to challenges, for instance, relating to institutional resilience around dominant gender norms and path-dependent policymaking. GM is most likely to fail if it does not allow for reflection with regard to practices and norms in policymaking, established power relations and knowledge production within the EU institutions (Magnusdottir and Kronsell, 2021, 2024).

Recent research on the EGD has demonstrated that despite the 'success' of EPI with the EGD climate policy, it has not been gender mainstreamed. Gender concerns in Fit for 55 and the 2021 Climate Law are limited (Allwood 2020, 2022, 2023). Moreover, policymakers, sector actors and the public seem largely unaware of potential gender effects, and efforts to learn about such effects have been rendered moot. Impact assessments were either not carried out at all, as happened with the 2021 Climate Law, or completely overlooked gender considerations as in the impact assessment accompanying the communication 'Stepping up the EU's Climate Action' (Allwood and Kronsell, 2025). The communication seems reluctant to take on gender equality while reiterating the need for a just transition. For example, the vulnerabilities of different groups in relation to the energy and transport dimensions of the EGD are pointed to through concepts like transport and energy poverty. The conclusion one must draw is that a just transition is about economic relations only and the call for compensation for 'poor' citizens. This chapter expands on this previous research by a closer scrutiny of the Social Climate Fund.

While environmental policy in the EU also faces challenges, in comparison to GM, EPI appears to have achieved more and been well integrated. In the EGD package there are eleven different policies dealing with broader environmental concerns. To our knowledge, there has been no research on the role of GM in these policies, and thus this chapter contributes the first analysis focusing on the Biodiversity Strategy and Nature Restoration Law. We also explore the social dimension of the EGD and the environment/nature dimension, with an interest in investigating the challenges of applying GM and EPI. As suggested earlier, GM and EPI defy practices and norms of institutions and are thus likely to benefit from an institutional approach.

3 Theoretical approach

Feminist institutionalism suggests that policies and strategies, such as the EGD, are gendered in the way policy and related institutions organize people, establish norms and sanction practices (Acker, 2012; Magnusdottir and Kronsell, 2021). In policy institutions, such as the EU, normative elements—problem frames, knowledge preferences and institutional practices—overlap with material forms of power—i.e., who gets to speak, decide and partake of resources. Here, we study the normative content of EGD policies. Norms are formal and informal rules, collective expectations, shared values and standards (Horne and Mollborn, 2020). They can be explicit or constitute silences—that of which nothing is said. Norms have an impact beyond policy, as they provide the frames within which policymakers take action. Their agency is embedded in the institutional context. Thus, any assumption that an increase in the number of female bodies in historically male dominated institutions will automatically change them is refuted. Representation or inclusiveness will be difficult to achieve unless some established institutional norms and narrow framings are changed.

When norms are deeply embedded in institutions this leads to path dependencies, for example, historically male-dominant institutions make masculinity a normality and very resilient (Ljungholm, 2017; Magnusdottir and Kronsell, 2024). Another example is norms of knowledge. Some knowledge is deemed rational and apolitical (e.g., knowledge based on natural science in the climate change context), while approaches such as feminist lenses are often deemed as political and less legitimate (Singleton and Magnusdottir, 2021). Ecofeminist scholarship is useful for highlighting the specific underlying norms and patterns that reproduce inequalities in order to tackle the causes of structural economic inequalities between men and women, humans and nature. Ecofeminism's central claim is that the exploitations of women and nature are similar and linked oppressions (Merchant, 1980; Plumwood, 1993). The domination of nature is closely tied to the domination of humans by humans. It is "a key factor in Western civilization's advance at the expense of nature", through a human self that perceives itself as a rational master, rendering nature as vegetative matter, inert and controllable, open to human manipulation and management (Merchant, 1980, p. 214, 245f).

The rich countries of the EU follow a path-dependent view that environmental goods and a just transition can be achieved through modified economic growth and efficient resource exploitation. This underlying rationality for governance—ecological modernization—is at the core of environmental governance (Jänicke and Jacob, 2004; Mol, 2002; Næss and Saglie, 2019). Many ecofeminist scholars have identified this as a key problem, as they stress the need for the transformation of economies, shifting from this strong focus on continued growth dependent on natural resources to 'a well-being economy' that cares for and prioritizes people and nature (Heffernan et al., 2021; Melin, Magnusdottir and Baard, 2022). From the feminist institutional perspective, ecological modernization is a gendered path dependence with resilient norms about how the economy constantly develops to become ever more efficient with the help of new (technological) innovations that benefit the market: the economy can continue to grow while climate and environmental effects are contained and reduced (Kronsell, 2024).

The following section explores the EGD package using the theoretical framework. We take examples from documents related to the Social Climate Fund, the Biodiversity Strategy and Nature Restoration Law. We scrutinize wordings in policy, looking for silences and how social difference and/or gender is articulated. If it is mentioned, we consider this to be evidence of a first step in GM, a recognition of a problem; if not, it is evidence of path dependency. We find evidence of the related path dependency of ecological modernization as we study framings in policy text, including how nature, humans, the economy and the social are perceived.

4 The promises of the European Green Deal and gendered path dependence

There were important indicators that the EGD would incorporate gender concerns as it acknowledged the distributional consequences of decarbonization. The imperative for a just transition prompted this (Kreienkamp, Pegram and Coen, 2022, p. 742). The overarching EGD objectives are achieving net-zero greenhouse gas (GHG) emissions by 2050 by decoupling economic growth from resource use and ensuring social justice by leaving 'no person or place behind'. It signaled a commitment to address both equality and equity issues through the simultaneous announcement of the EGD, with the new Gender Equality Strategy and the appointment of the first ever Commissioner for Equalities (von der Leyen, 2019). This raised hopes that the dual priorities of climate action and equalities would be addressed in an integrated manner (Müller and Tömmel, 2022, pp. 316, 319).

The EGD frames climate change in a way that suggests *gendered path dependence on ecological modernization.* The EGD considers economic development related to the strategies as a win-win for everyone while also emphasizing "economic growth decoupled from resource use" as one of three goals of the strategy (European Commission, 2024b). The EGD is an unprecedented attempt to drive the environmental transition within the EU. According to Kreienkamp, Pegram and Coen (2022, p. 742), EGD strategies are deeply transformative, extending beyond short-term emission reductions to focus on long-term socioeconomic change—in direct alignment with the Paris Agreement. It aims to "transform the EU into a fair and prosperous society, with a modern, resource-efficient and competitive economy [...]" (European Commission, 2019, p. 2). The EGD stresses the need for a just and inclusive transition in tandem with growth. However, when looking at the actual strategies, we learn that 'growth' is only to occur through decarbonization in sectors like energy, transport and agriculture. They are the sectors with the highest carbon emissions, so transformation is urgently needed, but they are also sectors almost completely dominated by men (EIGE 2023). Thus, it is likely that masculine norms have been normalized. Nowhere is this recognized; there is only silence. Nor is the omission of the low-carbon-emitting social sector discussed. An ecofeminist analysis emphasizes that strategies on sustainability and a just transition cannot be limited to sectors such as energy, transport and agriculture and securing jobs in these sectors. Attention should also be given to female dominated low-carbon sectors such as health care and education, which "[...] contribute to the wellbeing of different generations and the resilience and health of society in general" (Heffernan et al., 2021, p. 10). We argue that the path dependence of ecological modernization can explain this development.

How is nature framed in the EGD?

The importance of the environment in the EGD is shown in its initial statement: "Climate change and environmental degradation are an existential threat to Europe and the world" (European Commission, 2024b). Compared to the EGD's social and gender dimensions, the environmental agenda appears highly ambitious with as many as eleven 'actions' that involve "Protecting the environment and oceans with the Green Deal" (European Commission, 2024c). We have selected one of these policies, the EU's Biodiversity Strategy for 2030, because the European Commission (2024d) articulated it to be "a comprehensive, ambitious and long-term plan to protect nature and reverse the degradation of ecosystems".

Indeed, the strategy seems to reject the path dependence of ecological modernization as it does recognize the dependency between humans and nature and is set on: "Bringing nature into our lives" (European Commission, 2020, para. 1). The connection between humans and nature is addressed not in particularly critical terms: it does not fully recognize any of the previous destructive relations or exploitation of nature across Europe and underlying European wealth (see Chapter 19). However, the recognition of the interdependence between humans and nature is pronounced. The dependence is articulated as relevant for health reasons but also as a sink for carbon emissions. The message is mixed. The sink analogy is a rather instrumental view of nature as something society exploits for human purposes. It is, however, also possible to see some ideas relating to valuing nature for nature's own sake, particularly when referring to how to protect nature (European Commission, 2020, paras. 2–2.1). For example, it frames the importance of nature and biodiversity as a service to humans that rely on water, air, energy and other natural resources. It stresses that "Nature and biodiversity make life possible, provide health and social benefits and drive our economy. Nature is also our best ally in tackling the climate crisis". What this means is not clear (European Commission, 2020, paras. 2.2.8–2.2.9), and the strategy is ambiguous. It is both about protecting more nature areas for biodiversity and about economic benefits and job opportunities related to biodiversity protection. Thus, it does not question ecological modernization up front: "The plan will create jobs, reconcile economic activities with nature growth and help ensure the long-term productivity and value of our natural capital" (European Commission, 2020, para. 2.2). Farmers are perceived as playing a vital role yet recognized as associated with destructive practices that harm nature. They are assumed to benefit economically, with jobs, from the strategy. Foresters, too, are named as vital for providing the products and services critical for the circular bioeconomy (European Commission, 2020, paras. 2.2.1–2.2.4). Beyond farmers and foresters, little is said about which job opportunities these are and who they might benefit, even though the biodiversity strategy underscores that measures should operate "in a fair way and just for all" (European Commission, 2020, para. 2.2.6).

The strategy endorses what it calls a "principle of equality" (European Commission, 2020, para. 4.1). However, it turns more into wishful thinking to "ensure social justice, fairness and inclusiveness in line with the European Pillar of Social Rights" (European Commission, 2020, para. 5), as the principles are never substantiated. While the policy documents explicitly recognize equality, equity and justice principles, there is a lack of recognition of gender. The Biodiversity Strategy has not been gender mainstreamed, as it completely lacks gender awareness. This problematically reproduces a silence on the male dominance in the farming sector (FAO, 2024), and the masculine norms embedded in the agricultural sector can prevail unquestioned. Ownership, decision-making, income and entrepreneurship in agriculture are areas where men dominate across Europe (Prügl, 2011). This is not recognized or mentioned. An example is the Factsheet on the EGD benefits for farmers. As many as four images depict women, only one depicts a man and one a man and woman farming together, i. e., representing the family farm. This is an incorrect image of the state of EU farming where women run less than a third of farms (EIGE, 2017). While it is recognized that farming is important in maintaining the quality of the environment and in climate change, it is problematic not to take a gender and intersectional perspective. Studies have concluded that women farmers and younger farmers are more inclined to adopt sustainable agricultural practices, such as organic farming and other environmental practices (Unay-Gailhard and Bojnec, 2021).

How is the social framed in EGD?

The social dimension included in the EGD recognizes the need to address the climate impacts of the North, as in Agenda 2030. The call to leave no one behind appears to primarily build on the UN's SDGs rather than EU's existing gender mainstreaming goals. It is not in any other way attentive to the EU's internal, existing policy development on gender equality and equity, which Allwood and Kronsell (2025) call a "missed opportunity". The agenda of leaving no one behind in the EGD seems to have been wrongly perceived as something which has nothing to do with the gender equality work of the EU or Member States, leading to this disjuncture witnessed with the EGD (Allwood and Kronsell, 2025).

Within the EGD the policy that explicitly deals with the attempt to leave no one behind is the **Social Climate Fund. The Regulation (EU 2023/955), which established the Social Climate Fund, recognized gender and stated that (24):**

> Women are disproportionately affected by energy poverty and transport poverty, in particular single mothers, who represent 85 percent of single parent families, as well as single women, women with disabilities, and elderly women living alone. In addition, women have different and more complex mobility patterns. Single parent families with dependent children have a particularly high risk of child poverty. Gender equality and equal opportunities for all, and the mainstreaming of those objectives, as well as accessibility rights of persons with disabilities should be upheld and promoted throughout the preparation and implementation of Plans to ensure that no one is left behind. (European Union, 2023, Art. 24)

Nevertheless, when it comes to actual practices to be undertaken through the Social Climate Fund, the focus is primarily on economic measures connected to green growth. "The Social Climate Fund will dedicate EUR 65 billion from the EU budget, and over EUR 86 billion in total to support the most vulnerable citizens and small businesses with the green transition. This will ensure there are opportunities for everyone, by tackling inequality and energy poverty, and strengthening the competitiveness of European companies, leaving no one behind" (European Commission, 2024e). However, the impact will vary across countries and sectors. Feminist scholarship has stressed that this strong focus on green growth within the current market economy (Heffernan et al., 2021; Melin, Magnusdottir and Baard, 2022) is problematic. Strategies that are based on current market economy approach cannot be transformative as they reproduce existing path dependencies in policymaking institutions, such as tendencies to reproduce existing power relations based on the gender binary and the superiority of humans over nature (Magnusdottir and Kronsell, 2024; Melin and Magnusdottir, 2022). As an example, the regulation establishing the Social Climate Fund recognizes that women are disproportionately affected by energy poverty and transport poverty. However, it is left at the level of recognition, which is he first step of a GM strategy, but further action is needed.

Transport and energy poverty have much to do with a gendered economic system, and women are in general and on average poorer than men. Additionally, the labor market and the educational system are gendered. Women lack agency in the male-dominated sectors included in the green transition as is outlined in the EGD, which states that "[...] the economic and employment impacts of the green transition are expected to be positive. With the right accompanying polices in place, the transition could create around 1 million jobs in the EU by 2030 and 2 million jobs by 2050—particularly middle-skilled, middle-paying jobs, in construction and manufacturing" (European Commission, 2021). Since these economic sectors are dominated by men, women are less likely to benefit from strategic investments in the transport and energy sector, even though they may benefit from single measures to abate poverty. Hence, the Social Climate Fund does not outline a structural transition nor make full use of GM.

It is rather telling that the national authorities in each Member State that have been assigned responsibility for drawing up the social climate plans are mostly environmental, climate or energy authorities. Only one Member State, the Netherlands, has assigned this responsibility to the Ministry for Social Affairs and Employment. The social climate plans are in their initial stages as the Member States will submit these plans to the European Commission by June 2025 to receive funding from the Social Climate Fund. There is a risk that national environmental and energy authorities will continue with established institutional practices, which rest on ecological modernization, masculinity norms and reproduction of established knowledge, where agency is only given to a limited number of stakeholders within the green growth sphere. This conforms to how the energy and transport policies have been developed within the EU, where techno-economic norms have been reproduced in new policy documents and in new institutional settings, limiting the leeway for new knowledge or a deeper understanding of the intersectional nature of climate change. Feminist institutionalists would highlight that the EGD and its strategies were and are being developed and negotiated in a path-dependent institutional environment that is resistant to change.

5 Conclusions

When comparing GM and EPI and their impact for EGD policymaking and strategizing, it is apparent that EPI has achieved more in introducing environmental issues and concerns for nature into the EGD, while the GM approach has been of little importance to the EGD developments despite its proclaimed desire for a 'just transition'. The EPI of the EGD has resulted in a range of policies, and we have only focused on one of them, the biodiversity strategy. We see some indications of the path dependency of ecological modernization in the attention to the economy and jobs and how it is framed to be a win-win. The biodiversity strategy also recognizes norms that differ from this, stressing the human dependency and need for nature and natural resources, and for the protection of biodiversity, to some extent on its own merits. Yet, there is a remaining path dependence relating to how the social dimension is viewed: the social has no gender, it is invisible and so are other social differences based on class, age etc. Gender power is invisible when it is hidden behind farmers and foresters, problematically obscuring the fact that women and younger farmers may be much more inclined to adopt farming practices that lead to sustainability and biodiversity gains.

EGD reproduces gender along the lines of the continued importance of the classic breadwinner model, a stereotypical view of men. It is based on the traditional gender arrangement where the male is the primary or sole income-earner, and the female is assumed to take on the role of homemaker and caretaker. Indeed, when we looked for omissions and invisibilities in the EGD, the worry of leaving no one behind seems related to a concern for the working-class male, i. e., males that are tied to fossil fuel industries who, with the successful implementation of EGD, are at risk of unemployment. In reading the EGD documents it is apparent that there is a worry that climate measures, such as electrification and other restrictions, will lead to unemployment. Another ground for expecting this to be the case is that the social sector, where European women have most of their employment, is excluded from the EGD altogether (EIGE, 2023). Hence, the Social Climate Fund is likely to be used to compensate mostly this group of men. One idea for future research is to critically study the Member States' applications for the social climate fund.

We therefore suggest that policymakers make use of feminist approaches, highlighting the importance of representation of different groups in society in order to address the multilayered social dimensions of climate change. Similarly, policymakers need to be aware that the established majority views and approaches of powerful stakeholders and experts may be considered impartial and apolitical due to path-dependent techno-economic norms but reproduce knowledge influenced by ecological modernization. Finally, we suggest an ecofeminist understanding of a just transition, which would mean including policy areas such as the social, healthcare and education sectors into cross-sectoral climate policymaking and an increased emphasis on the well-being of people and nature.

References

Acker, J. (2012) 'Gendered Organizations and Intersectionality: Problems and possibilities', *Equality, Diversity and Inclusion* 31(3), pp. 214 – 224.

Allwood, G. (2020) 'Mainstreaming gender and climate change to achieve a just transition to a climate-neutral Europe', *Journal of Common Market Studies* 58(1), pp. 173 – 186.

Allwood, G. (2022) *How just and how equal? The EU's transition to climate justice and gender equality.* Brussels: Foundation for European Progressive Studies.

Allwood, G. (2023) *Climate mainstreaming: Climate and gender policy.* Brussels: Foundation for European Progressive Studies.

Allwood, G. and Kronsell, A. (2025) 'The European Green Deal through an equalities lens: A lost opportunity?', in: Abels, G., Kantola, J., Lombardo, E. and Müller, H. (eds.): *Towards a "union of equality": The European Commission under President Ursula von der Leyen (2019 – 2024).* Oxford: Oxford University Press.

Arora-Jonsson, S. and Sijapati, B. (2018) 'Disciplining gender in environmental organizations: The texts and practices of gender mainstreaming', *Gender, Work and Organization* 25(3), pp. 309 – 325.

Burns, C., Eckersley, P. and Tobin, P. (2020) 'EU environmental policy in times of crisis', *Journal of European Public Policy* 27(1), pp. 1 – 19.

EEB (2021) *Why the European Green Deal needs ecofeminism.* European Environmental Bureau. Available at: https://eeb.org/library/why-the-european-green-deal-needs-ecofeminism/ (Accessed: 24 September 2024).

EIGE (2017) *Agriculture and rural development.* European Institute for Gender Equality. Available at: https://eige.europa.eu/gender-mainstreaming/policy-areas/agriculture-and-rural-development (Accessed: 24 September 2024).

EIGE (2023) *EIGE gender index 2023: Thematic focus of gender equality and the socially fair transition of the European Green Deal.* Vilnius: European Institute for Gender Equality.

European Commission (2019) *The European Green Deal.* COM(2019) 640 final. Available at: https://eur-lex.europa.eu/legal-content/EN/TXT/PDF/?uri=CELEX:52019DC0640&from=EN (Accessed: 30 September 2024).

European Commission (2020) *EU biodiversity strategy for 2030.* COM(2020) 380 final. Available at: https://eur-lex.europa.eu/legal-content/EN/TXT/?uri=celex:52020DC0380 (Accessed: 9 March 2025).

European Commission (2021) *A socially fair transition.* Factsheet. Available at: https://commission.europa.eu/publications/delivering-european-green-deal_en (Accessed: 26 August 2024).

European Commission (2024a) *The European Green Deal.* Available at: https://commission.europa.eu/strategy-and-policy/priorities-2019–2024/story-von-der-leyen-commission/european-green-deal_en#protecting (Accessed: 30 September 2024).

European Commission (2024b) *European Green Deal. Striving to be the first climate-neutral continent.* Available at: https://commission.europa.eu/strategy-and-policy/priorities-2019–2024/european-green-deal_en (Accessed: 30 September 2024).

European Commission (2024c) *Protecting the environment and oceans with the Green Deal.* Available at: https://commission.europa.eu/strategy-and-policy/priorities-2019–2024/european-green-deal/protecting-environment-and-oceans-green-deal_en (Accessed: 30 September 2024).

European Commission (2024d) *Biodiversity strategy for 2030.* Available at: https://environment.ec.europa.eu/strategy/biodiversity-strategy-2030_en (Accessed: 26 August 2024).

European Commission (2024e) *Delivering the European Green Deal.* Available at: https://commission.europa.eu/strategy-and-policy/priorities-2019–2024/european-green-deal/delivering-european-green-deal_en (Accessed: 19 August 2024).

European Union (2023) *Regulation 2023/955 of the European Parliament and of the Council of 10 May 2023 establishing a Social Climate Fund and amending Regulation (EU) 2021/1060.* L 130/1. Available at: https://eur-lex.europa.eu/legal-content/EN/TXT/PDF/?uri=CELEX:32023R0955 (Accessed: 15 May 2024).

FAO (2024) *Gender equality and women's empowerment.* Food and agriculture organization of the United Nations. Available at: https://www.fao.org/gender/learning-center/thematic-areas/gender-equality-and-women-empowerment/ (Accessed: 30 September 2024).

Heffernan, R. et al. (2021) *A feminist European Green Deal—towards an ecological and gender just transition.* Bonn: Friedrich Ebert Stiftung.

Horne, C. and Mollborn, S. (2020) 'Norms: An integrated framework', *Annual Review of Sociology* 46(1), pp. 467–487.

Hubert, A. and Stratigaki, M. (2016) 'Twenty years of EU gender mainstreaming: Rebirth out of the ashes?', *FEMINA POLITICA—Zeitschrift für feministische Politikwissenschaft,* 25(2), pp. 21–36.

Jänicke, M. and Jacob, K. (2004) 'Lead markets for environmental innovations : A new role for the nation state', 4(1), *Global Environmental Politics*, 4(1), pp. 29–46.

Jänicke, M. and Wurzel, R. (2019) 'Leadership and lesson-drawing in the European Union's multilevel climate governance system', *Environmental Politics* 28(1), pp. 22–42.

Jordan, A. and Lenschow, A. (2010a). 'Environmental policy integration: A state of the art review', *Environmental policy and governance* 20(3), pp. 147–158.

Kreienkamp, J., Pegram, T. and Coen, D (2022) 'Explaining transformative change in EU climate policy: Multilevel problems, policies, and politics', *Journal of European Integration* 44(5), pp. 731–748.

Kronsell, Annica (1997) *Greening the EU—power practices, resistances and agenda setting.* Lund: Lund University Press.

Kronsell A (2024) 'Imagining a new gender contract for climate', in: Petö, A. Thissen, L. and Clavaud, A. (eds.) *Imagining a new gender equality contract: Feminism as a progressive glue.* Foundation for European Progressive Studies. Cham: Palgrave Macmillan.

Von der Leyen, U. (2019) 'My agenda for Europe: Political guidelines for the next European Commission 2019–2024.' *European Commission.* Available at https://commission.europa.eu/system/files/2020-04/political-guidelines-next-commission_en_0.pdf (Accessed: 23 May 2025).

Ljungholm, D.P. (2017) 'Feminist institutionalism revisited: The gendered features of the norms, rules, and routines operating within institutions', *Journal of Research in Gender Studies* 7(1), pp. 248 – 254.
Lomazzi, V. and Crespi, I. (2019) *Gender mainstreaming and gender equality in Europe.* Bristol: Bristol University Press.
MacGregor, S. (2017) *Routledge handbook of gender and environment.* London: Taylor and Francis.
MacGregor, S. (2021) 'Making matter great again? Ecofeminism, new materialism and the everyday turn in environmental politics', *Environmental Politics* 30(1 – 2), pp. 41 – 60.
Magnusdottir, G.L. and Kronsell, A. (2016) 'The double democratic deficit in climate policy-making by the EU Commission', *FEMINA POLITICA—Zeitschrift für feministische Politikwissenschaft* 25(2), pp. 64 – 77.
Magnusdottir, G.L. and Kronsell, A. (eds.) (2021) *Gender, intersectionality and climate institutions in industrialized states.* London: Routledge.
Magnusdottir, G.L. and Kronsell, A. (2024) 'Climate institutions matter: The challenges of making gender-sensitive and inclusive climate policies', *Cooperation and Conflict,* 59(3), pp. 361 – 378.
Melin, A., Magnusdottir, G.L. and Baard, P. (2022) 'Energy politics and justice: An ecofeminist ethical analysis of the Swedish parliamentarian debate', *Ethics, Policy and Environment.* Available at: doi:10.1080/21550085.2022.2115752.
Merchant, C. (1980) *The death of nature: Women, ecology and the scientific Revolution.* San Francisco: Harper.
Minto, R. and Mergaert, L. (2018) 'Gender mainstreaming and evaluation in the EU: Comparative perspectives from feminist institutionalism', *International Feminist Journal of Politics,* 20(2), pp. 204 – 220.
Mol, A.P.J (2002) 'Ecological modernization and the global economy', *Global Environmental Politics,* 2(2), pp. 92 – 115.
Müller, H. and Tömmel, I. (2022) 'Strategic leadership: Ursula von Der Leyen as President of the European Commission', in: Müller, H. and Tömmel, I. (eds.) *Women and leadership in the European Union,* Oxford: Oxford University Press, pp. 311 – 330.
Næss, P. and Saglie, I.L. (2019) 'Ecological modernisation', in: *The Routledge companion to environmental planning.* London: Routledge, pp. 63 – 72.
Paleari, S. (2022) 'The impact of the European Green Deal on EU environmental policy', *Journal of Environment and Development,* 31(2).
Plumwood, V. (1993) *Feminism and the mastery of nature.* London: Routledge.
Prügl, E. (2011) *Transforming masculine rule: Agriculture and rural development in the European Union.* Ann Arbor: University of Michigan Press.
Rietig, K. (2013) 'Sustainable climate policy integration in the European Union', *Environmental Policy and Governance,* 23(5).
Runhaar, H., Driessen, P. and Uittenbroek, C. (2014) 'Towards a systematic framework for the analysis of environmental policy integration', *Environmental Policy and Governance,* 24(4), pp. 233 – 246.
Singleton, B.E. and Magnusdottir, G.L. (2021) 'Take a ride into the danger zone? Assessing path dependency and the possibilities for instituting change at two Swedish government agencies', in: Magnusdottir, G.L. and Kronsell, A. (eds.) *Gender, intersectionality and climate institutions in industrialized state.* London and New York: Earthscan, Routledge.
Unay-Gailhard, İ. and Bojnec, Š. (2021) 'Gender and the environmental concerns of young farmers: Do young women farmers make a difference on family farms?', *Journal of Rural Studies,* 88, pp. 71 – 82.

Diarmuid Torney, Aron Buzogány and Louisa Parks

European Union environmental policy and democratic governance

Abstract: This chapter examines the relationship between democratic governance and European Union (EU) environmental policy, highlighting how democratic principles have influenced this area. We argue that, historically, considerations around democratic legitimacy have not been central to EU environmental policy. However, over time and because of its distinctive status as a complex, multilevel representative democracy, the EU has started to respond to democratic deficits by emphasizing participatory and deliberative aspects of democracy. We map these developments by considering EU environmental policy through the lenses of representative democracy, participatory democracy and deliberative democracy. These three approaches serve to elucidate and also partly periodize the evolution of the democratic dimensions of EU environmental policy, culminating in the development of the European Green Deal.

Keywords: EU environmental policy; democratic governance; representative democracy; participatory democracy; deliberative democracy

1 Introduction

The first question worth asking is why discuss democratic governance in relation to European Union (EU) environmental policies? Is not environmental policy, like any other policy area, simply subject to the ordinary legislative procedure in the EU's decision-making process? This was true until recently. Historically, democracy was not a central consideration in EU environmental policy, which developed as a collateral effect of economic integration that focused on achieving regulatory goals rather than integrating democratic principles. Yet, as environmental democracy gained prominence and political salience, the EU began to emphasize democratic principles, such as public participation, transparency and accountability, both within and outside its borders.

Paying attention to democratic governance and environmental policy is normatively important, because democracy performs better than autocracies in adopting ambitious climate policies. Research shows that higher levels of democratic quality are associated with better climate policy outcomes (Hanusch, 2018), while corporatist democracies, with their strong stakeholder participation, tend to have stronger environmental records (Scruggs, 2003; Escher and Walter-Rogg, 2020). This suggests that democratic governance, particularly in the EU, plays a crucial role in shaping the effectiveness of environmental policies. However, the type of democracy matters. Some democracies outperform others in the implementation of more ambitious and effective environmental policies. Empirical research demonstrates that social-liberal and

https://doi.org/10.1515/9783111321523-011

deliberative democracies adopt more ambitious environmental commitments than liberal democracies, prompting discussions about how democratic structures influence environmental performance (Povitkina and Jagers, 2022).

Understanding EU democratic governance is also crucial given that established decision-making and governance systems have failed to deliver appropriate climate policy responses at sufficient scale and speed (Dupont et al., 2024). They have also struggled to adequately include citizens in decision-making, contributing to rising mistrust (Kohler-Koch and Quittkat, 2013) and to climate movement demands for stronger and more inclusive responses (Buzogány and Scherhaufer, 2022; Parks, 2025). We are also witnessing a long democratic recession and a widespread perception that democracy is in crisis (Norris and Inglehart 2019). The rise in populism, increased political polarization and challenges to science and expertise following a decade of cascading polycrises (Lawrence et al., 2024) pose risks to democratic governance. Populist backlash is increasingly evident in a range of western democracies, with climate action drawing criticism as an elitist or socially unjust project. Climate change sceptics' claims and actions are on the rise, and populist radical right-wing actors have begun to backtrack and to challenge environmental policy agendas. A recent example is the EU's Nature Restoration Law, where agricultural and employment concerns clashed with biodiversity conservation goals (Schauenberg, 2023).

More generally, there is also a growing recognition that democracies face structural challenges in addressing climate change: e.g., the inbuilt myopia resulting from short electoral cycles, slow implementation due to complex and fragmented decision-making processes, inherent incrementalism or the unequal citizen representation because of financially powerful lobbies' disproportionate influence (Smith, 2021). Where publics prioritize other issues, moreover, politicians lack electoral incentives to engage in climate policies (Moore et al., 2024). More problematic is that environmental degradation is an "inevitable by-product of the limited temporal, spatial, epistemological, and community horizons of liberal democracies" (Eckersley, 2020, p. 218). Even the best performing environmental democracies will eventually hit the 'glass ceiling' of the fossil-based growth model (Hausknost and Hammond, 2020).

This chapter delves into various forms of democratic governance—representative, participatory, and deliberative—and their roles in shaping EU environmental policy. We explore how the EU's environmental governance framework has evolved and the role these different democratic approaches play in the EU's environmental and climate policies. The three sections provide an overview of how these democratic approaches have influenced EU environmental policy over time.

2 Representative democracy and EU environmental policy

To understand the nature of EU environmental policy, it is important to recall that the EU's political system is characterized, first and foremost, by the principle of representative democracy. Like its Member States, the EU is a representative democracy, where citizens directly elect representatives to the European Parliament (EP) and are also represented indirectly through the Council of the EU and the European Council, which consists of government representatives accountable to their respective national parliaments and, thus, indirectly, to EU citizens. The dynamics between political parties, parliaments and governments, both at the Member State and the EU level, shape EU environmental policy.

Representative institutions do care about their voters; responsiveness to societal interest has been a key driver of EU-level environmental and climate policy. Survey data suggests that European societies become greener with each generation (Lichtin, van der Brug and Rekker, 2023). Political parties are critical in shaping public opinion and legitimizing environmental policies (Carter, 2013; Farstad, 2018). An increasing presence of green parties in the EP and growing importance of green issues in all parties' manifestos have characterized the last four decades (see Chapter 11).

While broader societal trends and party entrepreneurship underpin the rise of environmental issues at the national and EU levels (Dennison and Kriesi, 2023), a multilevel governance structure characterizes EU environmental decision-making: it is where national governments and EU-level representative institutions, the EP and the European Council, closely cooperate in the legislative process. The EU's 'multilevel reinforcement' system (Schreurs and Tiberghien, 2007) has triggered positive effects among the different levels. Member State governments have enshrined environmental and climate policy goals in domestic legislation, making them subject to domestic parliamentary scrutiny. Similar developments also occur at the EU level, with the Council and the EP playing central roles. The EU's Environment Council, which brings together Ministers of Environment from the Member States, has played an important role in EU uptake of environmental policy since the 1980s (Wurzel, Liefferink and Di Lullo, 2019). The Council's Working Groups and the Committee of Permanent Representatives provide the Council's administrative backbone; they negotiate the legislative policy details before the Environment Council ministers discuss them (Andersen and Rasmussen, 1998). Leader-laggard dynamics have characterized these decision-making processes since the EU accession of Scandinavian countries and Austria. Together with Germany and the Netherlands, they became seen as pioneers of a common environmental policy (Andersen and Liefferink, 1997). This contrasted with the more lenient positions of the United Kingdom, the Southern European members and, later, the Eastern Europeans. The dynamic between leaders and laggards also impacted the Council's rotating presidency, affecting policy output and the EU's role in multilateral negotiations (Delreux, 2012).

As representative democracy's central institutions, parliaments and individual members of parliament have an important role to play in climate change politics as agents of transformational change (Moore et al., 2024). The EP being the EU's only directly elected supranational body, it plays a central role in connecting with and representing EU citizens. The literature often described the EP as an environmental champion playing a proactive legislative role by acting as a strong advocate for ambitious environmental policies, making strategic use of its powers and procedures and engaging with other EU institutions and the public (Burns, 2012; Delreux and Burns, 2019). The EP's Environment Committee has been regarded as a particularly influential promoter of environmental policies across the EU (Judge, 1992). More recent studies indicate trade-offs between the Parliament's role as an actor in the EU's power triangle and its internal politicization of the climate issue (Wendler, 2019). The stronger emphasis on climate issues has led to EP polarization among interests representing the economy, trade, agriculture and industry (Gravey and Buzogány, 2021). Most research shows that party ideologies play an important role: left-wing parties tend to be more environmentally ambitious than center-right and right-wing parties (Hix and Høyland 2013; Forchtner and Lubarda, 2023). With increased EP fragmentation due to the rising presence of radical forces, agreeing on common policies has become more complex and dependent on unstable majorities (Buzogány and Ćetković, 2021).

Beyond its policymaking role, the EP also holds other roles attributed to parliaments as representative institutions. Offering a unique transnational public sphere for agenda setting, argumentation and justification, the EP also fulfils debating functions where representatives speak and argue on behalf of those they represent. Analyses of parliamentary debate and voting behavior explore justifications for climate and energy policies put forward by representatives (Petri and Biedenkopf, 2021; Kinski and Servent Ripoll, 2022; Wendler, 2022). In addition, the EP has also actively engaged with nongovernmental organizations (NGOs) and the public to resist efforts to weaken environmental policies, with strong support from the Environment Committee and the Parliament as a whole (Burns, 2012, 2019). Research also highlights the EP's openness to the climate movement, emphasizing its role representing societal interests (Pollex and Berker, 2024).

While both the European Council and the Parliament hold their own sources of democratic legitimacy, the emergence of comitology, informal trilogues and crisis-led emergency legislation has thrown a shadow over some democratic aspects of democratic decision-making. The main effect has been from the strong leadership of the unelected European Commission and the European Court of Justice, which are often regarded as the main drivers of EU-level policy development. Despite the EP's increasing powers over time, this has not necessarily translated into the Parliament's ability and willingness to adopt greener policies consistently (Burns and Carter, 2010). To handle increasing institutional complexity, informal trilogues emerged as efficient ways to shorten the decision-making period and are now the standard operating procedure for reaching legislative decisions. Trilogues are, however, democratically questionable as they move debates out of the EP's public arena (Rosén and Stie, 2022). At the same time, trilogues also affect the Environment Council, which has no direct role, as rotating presidency officials represent the Council (Wurzel Liefferink and Di Lullo, 2019). Crisis-led decision-making processes and the use of emergency powers linked to the various crises of the past decade have also emerged as potential democratic problems because they might circumvent democratic decision-making. For instance, following the war in Ukraine, most emergency regulations adopted by the Council were to address short-term crisis effects, such as putting a cap on soaring prices and coordinating gas supplies. In fact, however, they touched upon rather long-standing obstacles to EU renewable energy goals (Buzogány, Ćetković and Maltby, 2023). These developments suggest the rise of emergency intergovernmentalism in environmental policy. The European Council expanded its role beyond the Treaty obligations during the 2020 and 2030 Climate and Energy Framework negotiations by setting emissions targets and determining policy instruments, which limited the roles of the European Commission and Parliament (see Chapter 30). However, under the European Green Deal (EGD), the Council reverted to its traditional role, altering the working dynamics among EU institutions, with the Commission regaining its leadership role once again (Pollex and Lenschow, 2024).

3 Participation, democracy, and EU environmental policy to the EGD

While the European Council and Parliament have clear roots in representative democracy, the European Commission does not. As democratic deficit debates developed over the years in the EU, the Commission in particular sought to boost its image of democratic legitimacy in other ways, most prominently through increased attention to participation. The following brief overview outlines the Commission's efforts to show its responsiveness to the claims and concerns of citizens at moments when the EU has been publicly challenged. In this logic, the increasing politicization of climate change governance and the widespread popular mobilizations on the theme emerge as important ingredients in the emphasis on participation contained in the 2019 EGD, where a new focus on democracy emerged in close connection with environmental policy. Below we consider how the Commission has addressed citizen participation in EU decision-making in line with marked moments of contestation since 2000. This historical account reveals two clear trends: an emphasis on the role of civil society organizations (CSOs) as both conduits for information about the EU and conveyors of citizens' voices up until the 2009 Lisbon Treaty, and a shift in emphasis toward the direct involvement of individual citizens after Lisbon. The next section takes up this latter theme concerning deliberative democracy.

The emphasis on the role of CSOs began with the July 2001 Commission White Paper on Governance outlining proposals to "bring citizens closer to the European institution" (European Commission, 2001). The White Paper followed mass protests at the European Council in Gothenburg, and the public health scandals regarding foot and mouth disease (and mad cow disease before it). The White Paper proposed improving the EU's democratic image through a range of measures but described CSO inclusion as key to improving the EU's legitimacy. This inclusion was conditional on CSOs complying with a series of good governance principles rooted in the values of representative democracy however, including representativity.[1] CSOs were also called upon to contribute to the better communication of the EU and its decisions, underlining a 'transmission belt' view where CSOs bring in citizens' views and relay information back to them (Albareda and Braun, 2019). Democratic legitimacy and participation were thus linked to the perception that the EU was happy to engage with open and transparent CSOs representing citizens' views but also that the EU would be seen as more legitimate if citizens understood it more fully. This approach continued in the following years. Citizen inclusion was funneled through CSOs in the Convention on the Future of Europe that proposed the 2004 draft Constitutional Treaty (for discussion see Bouza Garcia 2010). After referenda in France and the Netherlands rejected the Constitutional Treaty in 2005, signaling popular dissent once more, the Commission launched the European Transparency Initiative. The Commission's 'Plan D for democracy' (European Commission, 2005) made CSOs central but burdened them with demonstrating their democratic credentials, leading scholars to note that this appeared to shift the blame for the EU's opacity (Friedrich, 2011).

Environmental CSO actions echo this general picture, as seen in prominent examples (see Chapter 17). The sector had long been seen as a source of valuable expertise, with a revolving door relationship with the Directorate-General (DG) Environment in its early days, providing expert and dedicated staff to the EU (Ruzza, 2004). With the moves described above, scholarship on environmental CSO influence over decision-making noted that to secure influence, CSOs needed to display their democratic and expert credentials by forming alliances. These alliances appeared to be most influential in decision-making when they brought together groups with closer ties to individual members at national levels (who thus possessed the capacity to demonstrate their 'representativity' through actions such as petitions, small demonstrations and the like) and groups that specialized in providing expertise and engaging in advocacy work at the Commission and Parliament (Parks, 2015). These coalitions worked even better when set on a more permanent footing: e.g., the Green 10, whose members coordinated campaigns such as that around EU chemicals legislation, in which it mobilized citizens to flood a public consultation and provided expert information and complex advocacy (Parks, 2015). The strategies of environmental CSOs show how the Commission's moves on participation shape their work, since groups sought influence by demonstrating their closeness to citizens and their capacity to provide expertise to

1 On the imposition of the logics of liberal representative democracy on civil society actors and its consequences for their freedom and ability to take critical stances, see Mercer, 2002.

EU decision-makers, thereby signaling their suitability also as conveyors of information.

The focus on citizen participation via CSOs moved toward individual citizen participation after the so-called 'pause for reflection' that produced the 2009 Lisbon Treaty. Acting on proposals first brought by CSOs themselves in the earlier Convention on the Future of Europe, the Lisbon Treaty introduced a new instrument for direct participation—the European Citizens' Initiative (ECI). Petitions initiated through the ECI can prompt the EU to introduce new legislation provided they are signed by at least one million EU citizens and pass minimum thresholds in at least seven Member States. Although this clearly marks a shift to individual participation, with the vast majority of ECIs being ruled inadmissible or having failed (see ECI Campaign, 2024), CSOs have proven central to the successful organization of signature collection (Parks, 2015). One of the very first ECIs registered concerned environmental issues and was named Right2Water. This petition's central claim was that water should be recognized as a human right and a public good, and therefore not subject to market rules or logics. The European Public Services Union (EPSU), which had been working on water issues alongside other groups and activists since the early 1990s, drove the Right2Water ECI. The EPSU relied on its networks of national and local members for signature collection, and media attention in Germany led to over a million German signatures alone. This had an immediate impact on the Commission, which announced that it would remove water from its controversial Concessions Directive in July 2013 before the ECI had even closed for signature. This change in the Commission's approach to water suggests once more that, where a claim can be clearly attributed to citizens, a change in EU decisions is possible. However, other ECIs have had little impact by comparison, perhaps partly due to the complex rules that surround them (Parks, 2015).

Major EU contestation next arose with the financial crisis. The Commission did not move to open up participation at this point, since select EU Member States pushed to shift decision-making power to spaces beyond the influence of citizens. Scholars noted that citizen contestation of the austerity agenda shifted to national and local levels, partly as a consequence of CSOs' and citizens' perception of this democratic closure (della Porta and Parks, 2018). With the rapid spread of climate protests in 2019, however, the EU appeared to react very quickly, paying attention to participation and emphasizing the role of individual citizens. While its new participatory forums were framed as a reaction to youth protests (Machin, 2025), on closer examination, it seems that this reaction was longer in the making, comprising the wish to avoid the disunity of the financial crisis (della Porta, Parks and Portos, 2024) and a reaction to the continuing rise of right-wing populist forces (not to mention Brexit) (Ruzza, Berti and Cossarini, 2021). While the 2021–2022 Conference on the Future of Europe was a more general forum for participation, others were firmly within the EGD remit. The European Climate Pact envisages that individual citizens active in their communities will inform others about the EGD and therefore participate in its implementation (Çelik, 2025). Building on the European Citizens' Panels of the Conference and the popularity of climate assemblies across Europe, the Commission included rules about Member States holding public consultations in the 2018 Regulation on the Governance of the Energy Union and Climate Action (Oberthür et al., 2023), and local authorities are expected to guarantee citizen participation when developing Just Transition Plans. While the 2021 European Climate Law contains a nod to provisions for public participation at the EU level, the EGD suggests a potential new era in the EU approach to participation (Oberthür et al., 2025). Not only does the EGD emphasize individual citizens instead of CSOs, but it stresses individual engagement in shaping EU decisions at national and local levels. Moreover, there is a new emphasis on bringing individual citizens together to debate, which we discuss in depth below. In line with this shift, there have been few prominent campaigns by environmental CSOs in recent years, while climate protests and assemblies have arguably taken the spotlight (Parks, 2025).

4 Deliberative democracy and EU environmental policy

Deliberative forms of democracy shift our attention from the aggregation of preferences to the transformation of preferences. Bächtiger et al. (2018, p. 2) define deliberative democracy as being "grounded in an ideal in which people come together, on the basis of equal status and mutual respect, to discuss the political issues they face and, on the basis of those discussions, decide on the policies that will then affect their lives". Proponents of deliberative democracy have highlighted its particular suitability to helping shape climate change responses (Willis, Curato and Smith, 2022). According to Niemeyer (2013), engaging citizens in deliberation has been found to produce improved environmental outcomes. In the setting of deliberative forums, citizens' participation is facilitated in considering the interests of nonhuman agents, and deliberation has the potential to attune participants to complexity and taking a long-term view.

Research has focused particularly on so-called deliberative mini publics (DMPs), such as citizens' assemblies, citizens' juries and deliberative polling (Setälä and Smith, 2018). DMPs have at least two core design features: they are *deliberative*, in the sense of participants reaching their conclusions or recommendations via careful consideration and discussion of relevant evidence and information, and they are *representative* in the sense of constituting a representative subset of the wider population or maxi-public (Farrell et al., 2019). Empirical evidence shows that deliberative minipublics on climate change can be sites of deliberation, transforming the preferences of participants, and that participants increase understanding of opposing views (Willis, Curato and Smith, 2022). However, critical scholarship on DMPs and environmental issues has pointed to the risk that DMPs can serve to limit public deliberation through a reliance on expert knowledge and framings of policy problems and solutions and an over-emphasis on achieving consensus in deliberations (Blue, 2015; Machin, 2023).

Until recently, deliberative democratic approaches did not feature prominently in EU environmental policy. The EGD marked the first time that deliberative democracy has been given prominence in EU environmental policy (Buzogány, Parks and Torney, 2025). The Commission's communication on the EGD sets out in its opening paragraphs that the transition "must be just and inclusive. It must put people first, and pay attention to the regions, industries and workers who will face the greatest challenges. Since it will bring substantial change, active public participation and confidence in the transition is paramount if policies are to work and be accepted" (European Commission, 2019, p. 1). It later states that "(t)he Climate Pact will build on the Commission's ongoing series of citizens' dialogues and citizens' assemblies across the EU, and the role of social dialogue committees. It will continue to work to empower regional and local communities, including energy communities". Meanwhile, the European Democracy Action Plan identifies "[p]romoting democratic engagement and active participation beyond elections" among priority areas (European Commission, 2020, Section 2.4).

Nonetheless, in the environmental arena innovation and experimentation with deliberative democracy have principally occurred at Member State rather than EU level. Indeed, a range of climate-focused deliberative mini-publics has been held over the past decade in EU Member States at multiple levels of governance. National-level citizens' assemblies and citizens' juries have been held in Denmark, Ireland, France, Finland, Luxembourg, Sweden, Poland, Spain, Germany and Austria. Subnational assemblies have occurred in a much wider set of jurisdictions. According to one estimate, as of June 2024 a total of 143 local or regional climate assemblies have been convened in EU Member States (Smith, 2024, p. 4). Among the earliest of the current wave of climate assemblies in Europe occurred in Ireland in 2017. The Assembly produced a set of recommendations considerably more ambitious than policies operating at the time and has been credited with helping strengthen Ireland's climate change policies and governance (Devaney et al., 2020). The French Convention Citoyenne pour le Climat, which occurred in 2019–2020, was among the longest-running climate assemblies, meeting for a total of eight official sessions. While it gave significant agency to citizens themselves (Giraudet et al., 2022; Torney, 2021), the government response to the French climate assembly was criticized for not going far enough.

Building on this 'first wave' of climate assemblies—mostly in Europe—the literature offers a number of emerging themes. First, the differential impact of climate assemblies across countries has generated questions around the institutionalization of climate assemblies into broader policymaking systems (Boswell, Dean and Smith, 2023; Courant, 2022), including the potential to create permanent climate assemblies (Smith, 2024). Second, the inclusion of previously marginalized voices and perspectives, including future generations and children, has come into focus (Mallon et al. 2025; Reid, 2024). Third, scholarship has begun to investigate the ways in which citizens and citizenship are conceived of within climate assemblies and the EGD, with critics pointing to a peculiarly depoliticized version of citizenship embedded within the EGD (Machin, 2025).

5 Conclusion

This chapter examined the nexus between democratic governance and EU environmental policy, highlighting how different democratic principles have shaped the policy field. Historically, environmental policy within the EU was primarily driven by the logic of economic integration rather than by democratic principles. Environmental policies developed as a collateral effect of regulatory goals related to economic growth without much consideration of democratic processes such as public participation or transparency. However, over time the EU began to emphasize democratic values like transparency, public involvement and accountability more generally as it sought to tackle various crises of legitimacy. With the announcement of the EGD, environmental policy has, we argue, come to the forefront of the EU's attempts to build a democratic legitimacy framework by moving from an emphasis on transparency and participation to deliberation. Rather than foregrounding the potential advantages of democratic governance for environmental policy discussed in the literature, this chapter focused on the structural challenges that democracies face when dealing with climate change. We delved into three forms of democratic governance discussed in the EU context: representative, participatory and deliberative democracy.

The EU is a complex, multilevel representative democracy. The European Parliament, often regarded as an environmental champion in the literature, serves as the only directly elected EU institution and is tasked with representing the voices of EU citizens in policy discussions. Over the past decades, the Parliament has increasingly pushed for more ambitious environmental policies, frequently acting as a counterbalance to the more conservative positions of national governments, though there are signs that this is changing with the Parliament's shift to the right at the time of writing. At the same time, the Environment Council, representing the Member States, also plays a crucial role in negotiating environmental legislation. As a result of its multilevel nature, the EU decision-making process is highly complex, often involving informal trilogues—closed-door negotiations between the European Parliament, the European Council and the European Commission—which limit transparency and public participation. These informal decision-making channels, while efficient in speeding up legislative processes, are criticized for sidelining democratic debate, reducing accountability and concentrating decision-making power in unelected bodies, such as the European Commission and the European Court of Justice.

The European Commission, which has long been criticized for its lack of democratic legitimacy, has responded to such concerns about the EU's democratic deficit by promoting greater citizen participation. In the early 2000s, this was largely achieved through collaboration with civil society organizations, which were tasked with representing citizen concerns, providing expertise and communicating EU policies to the public. However, following the 2009 Lisbon Treaty, there was a shift toward more direct citizen involvement. One major innovation was the European Citizens' Initiative, a mechanism allowing EU citizens to directly petition for new legislation. While some ECIs, like the 'Right2Water' initiative, have successfully influenced EU policy, the majority have struggled to meet the required thresholds or have had limited impact.

The 2019 EGD marked a new phase in the EU's approach to participatory democracy, placing a stronger emphasis on direct citizen involvement in shaping and implementing climate policies. The EGD envisions a more inclusive governance model, with mechanisms like the European Climate Pact encouraging individual citizens to engage in environmental initiatives at local and national levels (Çelik, 2025; Tosun and Heinz-Fischer, 2025). Public consultations, citizens' panels and climate assemblies are increasingly used to ensure that diverse voices are heard in the policymaking process. This shift reflects the growing prominence of individual citizen activism. Deliberative democracy, a form of governance focused on transforming citizen preferences through discussion and collective decision-making, has also gained traction within the EU's environmental policy framework. Randomly selected deliberative citizens' assemblies have been seen as particularly successful in fostering deeper understanding and consensus on complex issues like climate change. Such deliberative democratic mechanisms have until now been experimented with mainly at the national level.

This chapter illustrates how the EU's environmental governance has evolved to integrate democratic principles more fully, complementing representative democracy with an increasing focus on participation and deliberation. Clear challenges persist, including questions of transparency and political polarization. While civil society is understood as comprising groups spanning from industry lobbies to environmental NGOs, the question of who has more influence on policies remains. There are clear rules for the groups that access decision-makers, but none that specify how their perspectives are taken up. Polarization, increasingly expressed in the European Parliament's make-up, has also driven actions against strong environmental policy in recent years, as debates about how the costs of the transition away from a fossil-fuel based economy come to the fore. Nevertheless, the EU's increasing emphasis on democratic engagement can be seen as a widening of democratic principles and the EGD's focus on participatory and deliberative democracy is a new development that adds new layers of input to addressing these issues. This raises a central question for the EU's evolving democratic legitimacy framework: whether deliberative inputs can move beyond consultation to exert tangible influence on policy outcomes.

Acknowledgements

This chapter was written within the framework of the RETOOL Horizon Europe project, which focuses on strengthening democratic governance for climate transitions (https://retoolproject.eu). The authors acknowledge funding for the RETOOL project from the European Union's HORIZON EUROPE Research and Innovation Programme under grant agreement No. 101132661.

References

Albareda, A. and Braun, C. (2019) 'Organizing transmission belts: The effect of organizational design on interest group access to EU policy-making', *Journal of Common Market Studies*, 57(3), pp. 468–485.

Andersen, M.S. and Liefferink, D. (1997) *European environmental policy: The pioneers.* Manchester: Manchester University Press.

Andersen, M.S. and Rasmussen, L.N. (1998) 'The making of environmental policy in the European Council', *Journal of Common Market Studies*, 36(4), pp. 585–605.

Bächtiger, A., Dryzek, J.S., Mansbridge, J. and Warren, M. (2018) 'Deliberative democracy: An introduction', in: Bächtiger, A., Dryzek, J.S., Mansbridge, J. and Warren, M. (eds.) *The Oxford handbook of deliberative democracy.* Oxford: Oxford University Press, pp. 1–31.

Blue, G. (2015) 'Public deliberation with climate change: Opening up or closing down policy options?', *Review of European Comparative & International Environmental Law*, 24(2), pp. 152–159.

Boswell, J., Dean, R. and Smith, G. (2023) 'Integrating citizen deliberation into climate governance: Lessons on robust design from six climate assemblies', *Public Administration*, 101(1), pp. 182–200.

Bouza Garcia, L. (2010) 'From civil dialogue to participatory democracy: The role of civil society organisations in shaping the agenda in the debates on the European Constitution', *Journal of Contemporary European Research*, 6(1), pp. 85–106.

Burns, C. and Carter, N., (2010) 'Is co-decision good for the environment? An analysis of the European Parliament's green credentials', *Political Studies*, 58(1), pp. 123–142.

Burns, C. (2012) 'The European Parliament: The European Union's environmental champion?', in: Jordan, A. and Adelle, C. (eds.) *Environmental policy in the European Union.* London: Earthscan, pp. 132–152.

Burns, C. (2019) 'In the eye of the storm? The European Parliament, the environment and the EU's crises', *Journal of European Integration*, 41(3), pp. 311–327.

Buzogány, A. and Ćetković, S. (2021) 'Fractionalized but ambitious? Voting on energy and climate policy in the European Parliament', *Journal of European Public Policy*, 28(7), pp. 1038–1056.

Buzogány, A., Ćetković, S. and Maltby, T. (2023) 'EU renewable energy governance and the Ukraine War: Moving ahead through strategic flexibility?', *Politics and Governance*, 11(4), pp. 263–274.

Buzogány, A., Parks, L. and Torney, D. (2025) 'Democracy and the European Green Deal', *Journal of European Integration*, 47(2), pp. 135–154.

Buzogány, A. and Scherhaufer, P. (2022) 'Framing different energy futures? Comparing Fridays for Future and Extinction Rebellion in Germany', *Futures*, 137, 102904.

Carter, N. (2013) 'Greening the mainstream: Party politics and the environment', *Environmental Politics*, 22(1), pp. 73–94.

Çelik, F.B. (2025) 'Unpacking democratic participation in the European Green Deal: The case of Climate Pact', *Journal of European Integration*, 47(2), pp. 173–192.

Courant, D. (2022) 'Institutionalizing deliberative mini-publics? Issues of legitimacy and power for randomly selected assemblies in political systems', *Critical Policy Studies*, 16(2), pp. 162–180.

della Porta, D. and Parks, L. (2018) 'Social movements, the European crisis, and EU political opportunities', *Comparative European Politics*, 16(1), pp. 85–102.

della Porta, D., Parks, L. and Portos, M. (2024) 'Social movements and Europeanisation: Framing "responsibility" and "responsiveness" in times of multiple crises', *Journal of European Public Policy*, 31(4), pp. 1100–1125.

Delreux, T. (2012) 'The rotating presidency and the EU's external representation in environmental affairs: The case of climate change and biodiversity negotiations', *Journal of Contemporary European Research*, 8(2), pp. 210–227.

Delreux, T. and Burns, C. (2019) 'Parliamentarizing a politicized policy: Understanding the involvement of the European Parliament in UN climate negotiations', *Politics and Governance*, 7(3), pp. 339–349.

Dennison, J. and Kriesi, H. (2023) 'Explaining Europe's transformed electoral landscape: Structure, salience, and agendas', *European Political Science Review*, 15(4), pp. 483 – 501.

Devaney, L., Torney, D., Brereton, P. and Coleman, M. (2020) 'Ireland's Citizens' Assembly on Climate Change: Lessons for deliberative public engagement and communication', *Environmental Communication*, 14(2), pp. 141 – 146.

Dupont, C. et al. (2024) 'Three decades of EU climate policy: Racing toward climate neutrality?', *WIREs Climate Change*, 15(1), e863.

ECI Campaign (2024) *Ongoing ECI*. The European Citizens' Initiative. Available at: https://citizens-initiative.eu/ongoing-eci/ (Accessed: 19 March 2025).

Eckersley, R. (2020) 'Ecological democracy and the rise and decline of liberal democracy: Looking back, looking forward', *Environmental Politics*, 29(2), pp. 214 – 234. Escher, R. and Walter-Rogg, M. (2020) *Environmental performance in democracies and autocracies: Democratic qualities and environmental protection*. Basingstoke: Palgrave MacMillan.

European Commission (2001) 'European governance—A white paper', *COM*(2001) 428 final. Available at: https://eur-lex.europa.eu/legal-content/EN/TXT/?uri=celex:52001DC0428 (Accessed: 04 July 2025).

European Commission (2005) 'The Commission's contribution to the period of reflection and beyond: Plan-D for democracy, dialogue and debate', *COM*(2005) 494 final. Commission of the European Communities. Available at: https://eur-lex.europa.eu/LexUriServ/LexUriServ.do?uri=COM:2005:0494:FIN:en:PDF (Accessed: 23 June 2025).

European Commission (2019) 'The European Green Deal', *COM*(2019) 640 final. Brussels: Commission of the European Union. Available at: https://eur-lex.europa.eu/legal-content/EN/TXT/?uri=CELEX%3A52019DC0640 (Accessed: 8 July 2025).

European Commission (2020) 'O*n the European democracy action plan', COM*(2020) 790 final. Brussels: Commission of the European Union. Available at: https://eur-lex.europa.eu/legal-content/EN/TXT/?uri=CELEX%3A52020DC0790 (Accessed: 8 July 2025).

Farstad, F.M. (2018) 'What explains variation in parties' climate change salience?' *Party Politics*, 24(6), pp. 698 – 707.

Farrell, D.M. et al. (2019) 'Deliberative mini-publics: Core design features', *Centre for Deliberative Democracy and Global Governance Working Paper.* Canberra: Centre for Deliberative Democracy and Global Governance.

Forchtner, B. and Lubarda, B. (2023) 'Scepticisms and beyond? A comprehensive portrait of climate change communication by the far right in the European Parliament', *Environmental Politics*, 32(1), pp. 43 – 68.

Friedrich, D. (2011) *Democratic participation and civil society in the European Union.* Manchester: Manchester University Press.

Giraudet, L.-G., et al. (2022) '"Co-construction" in deliberative democracy: Lessons from the French Citizens' Convention for Climate', *Humanities and Social Sciences Communications*, 9(207).

Gravey, V. and Buzogány, A. (2021) 'For farmers or the environment? The European Parliament in the 2013 CAP reform', *Politics and Governance*, 9(3), pp. 16 – 28.

Hanusch, F. (2018) *Democracy and climate change.* Abingdon: Routledge.

Hausknost, D. and Hammond, M. (2020) 'Beyond the environmental state? The political prospects of a sustainability transformation', *Environmental Politics*, 29(1), pp. 1 – 16.

Hix, S. and Høyland, B. (2013) 'Empowerment of the European Parliament', *Annual Review of Political Science*, 16, pp. 171 – 189.

Judge, D. (1992) '"Predestined to save the earth": The Environment Committee of the European Parliament', *Environmental Politics*, 1(4), pp. 186 – 212.

Kinski, L. and Servent Ripoll, A. (2022) 'Framing climate policy ambition in the European Parliament', *Politics and Governance*, 10(3), pp. 251 – 263.

Kohler-Koch, B. and Quittkat, C. (2013) *De-mystification of participatory democracy: EU-governance and civil society*. Oxford: OUP Oxford.

Lawrence, M., et al. (2024) 'Global polycrisis: The causal mechanisms of crisis entanglement', *Global Sustainability*, 7, e6.

Lichtin, F., van der Brug, W. and Rekker, R. (2023) 'Generational replacement and Green party support in Western Europe', *Electoral Studies*, 83. Available at: https://doi.org/10.1016/j.electstud.2023.102602.

Machin, A. (2023) 'Democracy, agony, and rupture: A critique of climate citizens' assemblies', *Politische Vierteljahresschrift*, 64, pp. 845–864.

Machin, A., (2025) 'The European Green Deal and the democratic imagination', *Journal of European Integration*, 47 (2), pp. 155–171.

Mallon, B., et al. (2025) 'Children and young people's assemblies against the backdrop of the European Green Deal: Opportunities for consolidating and extending a sustainable and democratic transition', *Journal of European Integration*, 47(2), pp. 319–337.

Mercer, C. (2002) 'NGOs, civil society and democratization: A critical review of the literature', *Progress in Development Studies*, 2(1), pp. 5–22.

Monaghan, E. (2012) 'Assessing participation and democracy in the EU: The case of the European Citizens' Initiative', *Perspectives on European Politics and Society*, 13(3), pp. 285–298.

Moore, B. et al. (2024) 'Politicians and climate change: a systematic review of the literature', *WIREs Climate Change*, e908.

Niemeyer, S. (2013) 'Democracy and climate change: What can deliberative democracy contribute?', *Australian Journal of Politics and History*, 59(3), pp. 429–448.

Norris, P. and Inglehart, R. (2019) *Cultural backlash: Trump, Brexit, and authoritarian populism*. Cambridge: Cambridge University Press.

Oberthür, S., Moore, B., von Homeyer, I. and Söebech, Ó. (2023) *Towards an EU climate governance framework to deliver on the European Green Deal*. Brussels: GreenDeal-NET. Available at: https://www.greendealnet.eu/node/205 (Accessed: 19 March 2025).

Oberthür, S., Von Homeyer, I., Schewe, L. and Moore, B. (2025) 'Public participation in EU climate governance: The underexploited potential of national energy and climate plans', *Journal of European Integration*, 47(2), pp. 257–276.

Parks, L. (2015) *Social movement campaigns on EU policy, in the corridors and in the streets*. Basingstoke: Palgrave Macmillan.

Parks, L. (2025) 'How the climate movement shaped the EU: Protest cycles and democratic spaces in the European Green Deal', *Journal of European Integration*, 47(2), pp. 299–318.

Petri, F. and Biedenkopf, K. (2021) 'Weathering growing polarization? The European Parliament and EU foreign climate policy ambitions', *Journal of European Public Policy*, 28(7), pp. 1057–1075.

Pollex, J. and Berker, L.E. (2024) 'The European Parliament and Fridays for Future: Analysing reactions to a new environmental movement by Europe's climate policy champion', *Journal of European Integration*, 46(8), pp. 1–18.

Pollex, J. and Lenschow, A. (2024) 'When talk meets actions—Return to Commission leadership in EU environmental policy-making with the European Green Deal', *Journal of European Public* Policy. Available at: https://doi.org/10.1080/13501763.2024.2402866.

Povitkina, M. and Jagers, S.C. (2022) 'Environmental commitments in different types of democracies: The role of liberal, social-liberal, and deliberative politics', *Global Environmental Change*, 74, 102523.

Reid, K. (2024) *Children and young people's participation in climate assemblies*. Knowledge Network on Climate Assemblies Guidance Document. Available at: https://knoca-staging.webflow.io/guidances-documents/children-and-young-peoples-participation-in-climate-assemblies (Accessed: 21 January 2025).

Rosén, G. and Stie, A.E. (2022) 'Balancing seclusion and inclusion: EU trilogues and democratic accountability', *Journal of European Public Policy*, 29(3), pp. 383–404.

Ruzza, C. (2004) *Europe and civil society: Movement coalitions and European governance*. Manchester: Manchester University Press.

Ruzza, C., Berti, C. and Cossarini, P. (eds.) (2021) *The impact of populism on European institutions and civil society*. Basingstoke: Palgrave Macmillan.

Schauenberg, T. (2023) *Farmers revolt against EU's historic nature restoration law*. Bonn: Deutsche Welle. Available at: https://www.dw.com/en/farmers-revolt-against-eus-historic-nature-restoration-law/a-65735393 (Accessed: 21 January 2025).

Schreurs, M.A. and Tiberghien, Y. (2007) 'Multi-level reinforcement: Explaining European Union leadership in climate change mitigation', *Global Environmental Politics*, 7(4), pp.19 – 46.

Scruggs, L. (2003) *Sustaining abundance: Environmental performance in industrial democracies*. Cambridge: Cambridge University Press.

Setälä, M., and Smith, G. (2018) 'Mini-Publics and deliberative democracy', in: Bächtiger, A., Dryzek, J.S., Mansbridge, J. and Warren, M. (eds.) *The Oxford handbook of deliberative democracy*. Oxford: Oxford University Press, pp. 300 – 314.

Smith, G. (2021) *Can democracy safeguard the future?* Hoboken: John Wiley & Sons.

Smith, G. (2024) *Climate assemblies: Emerging trends, challenges and opportunities: A report of the Knowledge Network on climate assemblies*. Available at: https://www.knoca.eu/current-trends/climate-assemblies-emerging-trends-challenges-and-opportunities (Accessed: 21 January 2025).

Torney, D. (2021) 'Deliberative mini-publics and the European Green Deal in turbulent times: The Irish and French climate assemblies', *Politics and Governance*, 9(3), pp. 380 – 390.

Tosun, J. & Heinz-Fischer, C., (2025). *European Climate Pact Ambassadors: Motivations, Strategies, and Experiences*: Policy Press.

Wendler, F. (2019) 'The European Parliament as an arena and agent in the politics of climate change: Comparing the external and internal dimension', *Politics and Governance*, 7(3), pp. 327 – 338.

Wendler, F. (2022) *Framing climate change in the EU and US after the Paris Agreement*. Springer.

Willis, R., Curato, N. and Smith, G. (2022) 'Deliberative democracy and the climate crisis', *Wiley Interdisciplinary Reviews: Climate Change*, 13(2), e759.

Wurzel, R.K.W., Liefferink, D. and Di Lullo, M. (2019) 'The European Council, the Council and the Member States: Changing environmental leadership dynamics in the European Union', *Environmental Politics*, 28(2), pp. 248 – 270.

Section B **Policy actors**

Introduction: Policy actors

This section examines the complex constellation of policy actors that shape European Union (EU) environmental policy. Beyond analyzing the policymaking dynamics among the key EU institutions—the European Commission, European Parliament and European Council—it also offers a broader overview of other relevant stakeholders that influence the formulation and implementation of environmental policy across various territorial levels and subfields. The later chapters start to challenge some of the predominant considerations of who or what should be a stakeholder.

The chapter by **Alexander Bürgin** investigates the evolving leadership role of the European Commission. It argues that, beyond the personal attributes of the Commission President, organizational reforms have enabled a more centralized and top-down style of leadership. These reforms have bolstered the Commission's ability to take unified positions and exert greater influence in interinstitutional negotiations. **Bürgin** further demonstrates how a strengthened focus on enforcement and capacity-building, supported by advancements in digital technology and data processing, has enhanced the Commission's ability to monitor Member State compliance.

The role of the European Parliament (EP) is explored in the chapter by **Neil Carter and Fay Farstad**, which unpacks the internal and external factors influencing the EP's involvement in environmental policy. Tracing its evolution from the 1980s through the European Green Deal, their chapter examines how ideological divides, national interests, EU enlargement and successive crises have shaped the EP's environmental stance. Using the 'Fit for 55' climate package as a case study, the authors underscore the EP's continued relevance in steering EU environmental ambitions and call for deeper understanding of the internal and interinstitutional politics that shape its actions.

Intergovernmental bargaining and the formation of alliances among Member States are critically assessed in the chapter by **Rüdiger K.W. Wurzel, Duncan Liefferink and Maurizio di Lullo**. The authors differentiate between environmental 'leaders', who seek to shape collective EU positions and 'pioneers' primarily driven by domestic concerns. Their chapter examines how leadership dynamics play out in key forums, such as the Environment Council and the European Council, particularly in high-stakes climate negotiations and explains how certain states can help overcome political gridlock.

Taking a broader conceptual lens, **Peter Eckersley** investigates how multilevel power relations influence environmental policy outcomes across state and non-state actor organizational boundaries. His chapter presents a heuristic framework that connects three conceptions of power—'power over', 'power to', and 'power with'—to monocentric, polycentric and multilevel governance perspectives, respectively. Drawing on examples from EU environmental policy over recent decades, **Eckersley** argues that the EU has moved away from a monocentric approach in certain areas with im-

https://doi.org/10.1515/9783111321523-012

plications for the governance configurations and policy instruments seeking to deliver policy.

Policy implementation challenges are explored by **Tanja Börzel and Andreas Hofmann**, who analyze Member State compliance with EU environmental law. Drawing on original empirical data from infringement procedures and third-party enforcement, their chapter highlights how administrative capacity and political will affect compliance. It illustrates how even traditionally green countries like Germany, the Netherlands and Sweden have been recently showing resistance to EU environmental mandates due to the costs of green transitions and a shift toward decentralized enforcement mechanisms.

The role of cities and local authorities in achieving EU environmental goals is examined by **Jeroen van der Heijden**. Drawing from urban environmental governance literature, **van der Heijden** critically assesses the tools and incentives the EU provides to mobilize local action, particularly after the Paris Agreement and in light of the European Green Deal. His chapter highlights the substantial increase in environmental and climate measures that address the city level of EU governance since 2015 while noting that the relevant academic literature has struggled to understand the complex and multilevel nature of EU environmental policy in which cities with many differing contexts reside.

Thibaut Joltreau and Andy Smith turn to the role of business actors and corporate engagement in EU environmental policymaking. Their chapter examines how institutional contexts and political opportunity structures shape corporate strategies. They argue that long-term relationships with EU institutions, along with industry-specific characteristics, significantly influence how firms define and act upon environmental priorities.

The influence of civil society organizations, including think tanks, non-governmental organizations and foundations, is addressed in the chapter by **Nathalie Berny**. Identifying three logics of engagement (mobilization, maintenance and access to decision-making), her chapter offers a comprehensive view of lobbying in the field of EU environmental policy, extending beyond institutional channels to include public advocacy and research activities. **Berny** highlights how EU environmental legislation has supported the emergence of a transnational civil society network, also raising broader questions about democratic legitimacy and representation.

The democratic dimensions of environmental policymaking, particularly in relation to citizenship, are analyzed in the chapter by **Amanda Machin**. Building on the concept of critical green citizenship, her chapter develops a typology of environmental imaginaries and explores how citizens engage with and influence EU environmental policy. **Machin** offers new insights into the participatory potential and democratic challenges of the European Green Deal and suggests avenues for further research in this underexplored area.

The section concludes with the chapter by **Núria Almiron** and **Eze Paez**, which examines the so far understudied topic of the normative and practical treatment of nonhuman animals within EU environmental policy. They critique the current anthropocentric approach, arguing that it often overlooks individual animal interests, leading to ethically questionable practices, such as culling, insect farming or certain forms of rewilding. The authors propose an alternative policy framework that better integrates animal welfare, offering concrete recommendations for ethical governance of human–nonhuman relations and animal agriculture.

Alexander Bürgin

The European Commission and its sources of entrepreneurial leadership in the European Union

Abstract: The European Commission's influence on European Union environmental policy developments is shaped by institutional, situational and ideational factors, as well as the personal leadership qualities of the Commission president. Two recent developments are conducive for the Commission's entrepreneurial leadership. First, organizational reforms have enabled a more top-down steering of the Commission. This more effective management of the Commission has contributed to a more united appearance, strengthening the Commission's influence in interinstitutional legislative brokering. Second, the Commission's stronger focus on enforcement and capacity-building and changes in environmental reporting and data processing, enabled by digital technology advances, have strengthened the Commission's capacity to monitor Member State compliance.

Keywords: European Commission; leadership; agenda setting; decision-making; implementation

1 Introduction

The European Commission's main functions in the European Union's (EU) internal governance are initiating legislation and monitoring Member State implementation. The extent to which it can use these functions to shape policy developments is an ongoing debate. Some scholars regard the Commission's influence as being 'in decline' since the 1990s, offering five main explanations: a more assertive role of the European Council (e. g., Bickerton, Hodson and Puetter, 2015), a more autonomous European Parliament (EP); (e. g., Bauer and Ege, 2012, p. 405), an unfavorable political context due to increasing public discomfort with the EU (e. g., Ershova, Yordanova and Khokhlova, 2023), the Commission's increased size after Eastern Enlargement and, partly as a consequence of these factors, the lack of ambition of the Commission presidents, who consider themselves primarily to be policy managers rather than policy entrepreneurs (e. g., Tömmel, 2013). Regarding environmental policy, scholars have questioned whether the environment remained among the Commission's priorities (e. g., Burns, Eckersley and Tobin, 2020; Gravey and Jordan, 2020; Steinbach and Knill, 2017; Zito, Burns and Lenschow, 2019). However, other scholars highlight the Commission's ongoing leadership ambitions and influence, referring to various factors, including the expansion of EU competences since Maastricht, the Commission agenda-setting strategies, a more hierarchical internal organization and the increase of Commission

https://doi.org/10.1515/9783111321523-013

executive powers (e.g., Blom-Hansen and Senninger, 2021; Bürgin, 2018; Nugent and Rhinard, 2019).

Quantitative studies on the Commission's influence reveal a mixed picture. According to Buket Oztas and Amie Kreppel (2022), around 60 percent of the 1,266 legislative priorities listed in the Commission's annual work program between 2000 and 2014 were translated into legislative outcomes and almost 40 percent of these lacked explicit congruence with the legislative priorities of the Council and the European Parliament. However, they also conclude that the Commission's legislative priorities in this period have increasingly frequently failed to be translated into EU polices, unless they directly addressed the publicly stated policy priorities of other the two co-legislators. Similarly, using an analysis of quantitative data on sixty legislative proposals, Stefanie Bailer (2014) argues that the Commission's ability to defend the content of its original proposals depends primarily on the constellation of Member State positions, while the Commission's resources such as expertise and experience influence only marginally the Commission's legislative success.

The reason for these mixed results is a complex interplay between the inter- and intra-institutional setting, the situational context, the Commission's strategies and its president's personal leadership skills. While research on the Commission has mainly focused on its ability to influence policy decisions, it has neglected another venue for impact: the Commission's capacity to enforce the implementation of existing laws. The Commission's monitoring activities do not represent simply technical but rather political actions that have important influence in the EU system (Nugent and Rhinard, 2019, p. 214). In the following, I refer to the main scientific debates and findings regarding the Commission's influence on policy decisions and its proper implementation. I highlight two recent development that have contributed to the Commission's influence in the EU system: the 'presidentialization' of the Commission and improvements in its compliance monitoring capacity that have been enabled by advances in digitalization.

2 Agenda setting and legislative brokering

Interinstitutional relations

As concerns the interinstitutional political power structure, a common view is that Member States strengthened intergovernmental cooperation in the Council at the Commission's expense. Compared to the past, European Council summits are more frequent, better coordinated by an elected president and more directly involved in daily policymaking (Puetter, 2015); new modes of governance such as the *Open Method of Coordination* have increased importance (Wille, 2013, p. 208).

The EP's increasing influence and the perception of its changed role are additional institutional factors, highlighted as being detrimental to Commission leadership. Formerly a natural ally of the Commission in the struggle between the supranationalist institutions and the intergovernmentalist Council, the EP has become progressively more interested in the political agenda-setting and executive powers vested in the Commission (Bauer and Ege, 2012, p. 405; Tömmel, 2013, p. 801). Having no initiative rights of its own, the EP often presses Commissioners to issue new directives addressing the EP's concerns. The Commission often accedes, fearing that the EP could otherwise use the powers granted by the Lisbon Treaty to block the Commission's policy initiatives.

However, the consequences of the changed roles of European Council and EP are not necessarily negative for the Commission's legislative influence. Even if the European Council's involvement in agenda setting has grown in the post-Maastricht era, its internal divisions due to increased heterogeneity after Eastern enlargement often reduce the scope for agreement to vaguely defined guidelines and principles (see Chapter 12). More substantive policy discussions therefore require Commission input more than ever (Peterson, 2015, p. 197; Nugent and Rhinard, 2019, 2016). Consequently, cooperation between the two institutions has increased recently, allowing the Commission to retain substantial capacity for policy initiative (e.g., Thaler, 2016). Moreover, as a Commission proposal is more easily accepted than modified, the Commission has conditional agenda-setting power if a qualified majority in the Council prefers the Commission proposal to the status quo.

The EP's ability to gradually overcome the interinstitutional rivalry that shaped its relationship with the Council since the early 1970s (Pollack and Slominski, 2015, pp. 261–262) does not preclude a strong alliance between EP and Commission. On the contrary, higher levels of professionalism and expertise have improved the EP's potential for a strategic alliance with the Commission in the policy negotiations with Member States (Dinan, 2016, p. 111; Bürgin, 2019). While the loss of a common majority for the European People's Party and European Socialists after the 2019 election complicates majority-building, it also represents a window of opportunity for the Commission to promote ambitious environmental policies, as this situation has strengthened the Greens (Buzogany and Cetkovic, 2021).

Intra-institutional leadership

The coherence of the Commission's position increases its influence in the negotiations with Council and Parliament (Knodt, Ringel and Müller, 2020, p. 791). However, in the past, the Commission often appeared as fragmented, with weak top-down leadership and power widely dispersed within the College and between the services (e.g., Kassim et al., 2017). There were two main institutional factors that constrained Commission top-down steering. First, regarding the relations with the College of Commissioners, the Commission president is not the head of a government and therefore lacks a prime minister's hierarchical authority over his ministerial colleagues within a particular Member State. This is illustrated by the conflict between Commission President Barroso and Climate Commissioner Hedegaard with Energy Commissioner Oettinger in 2013 on the level of the CO_2 reduction goal for 2030 and whether it should be legally binding or just advisory (Bürgin, 2014). Second, concerning Commission services, the president's cabinet and the secretariat-general's (SG) role in the coordination of services have been limited. The SG has traditionally been the main guardian of collegiality, serving and supporting the College, rather than the president's personal service. Therefore, it has had limited involvement in internal policy negotiation within the directorates-general (DGs), leaving the president operating at some distance from interdepartmental affairs. This absence of centralized political authority has encouraged DGs to pursue their own agendas. For instance, while the legally binding Environmental Policy Integration (EPI) principle (see Chapter 33) requires intense cross-departmental exchange, due to rival portfolio interests, DGs regularly tried to circumvent internal coordination.

In response, the Amsterdam, Nice and Lisbon Treaties have strengthened the Commission president's internal leadership, providing the office holder with a de facto veto over national candidate Commissioners and discretion over task allocation. In addition to these treaty provisions, organizational reforms have aimed at directly strengthening the president. During the Barroso I Commission, the SG was transformed into an administrative command center for the president, playing a more interventionist role in ensuring inter-service coordination (Kassim et al., 2013, p. 186). These reforms were further developed by Juncker's introduction of seven vice presidents, each mandated to steer and co-ordinate teams of Commissioners working on specific priority projects. Additionally, Juncker further increased the SG's staff and allocated it an important agenda-setting power as chair of all inter-service steering groups, dealing with priority initiatives included in the Commission's work program.

Some scholars were initially skeptical about the reform impact on the Commission president's leadership capacity, highlighting the path dependency of routine DG activities (Ellinas and Suleiman, 2012, p. 73; Trondal, 2012). However, a widespread view now is that these organizational reforms have contributed to a more top-down steering of the Commission (e.g., Baracani, 2023; Blom-Hansen and Senninger, 2021; Bürgin, 2020, 2018; Kassim et al., 2017), affecting the internal policymaking process in two main ways. First, with the increase in the Commission president's power to exercise political leadership within the Commission, policy prioritization has become much more dependent on the president's own personal political agenda. For instance, despite growing resistance among the member states and in the EP after the 2024 election against a climate policy, perceived as overambitious, von der Leyen allocated the post of the Executive Vice-President for a Clean, Just and Competitive Transition to Spain's deputy prime minister, the Socialist Teresa Ribera, an outspoken advocate of climate action, tasked to lead a project team dealing, inter alia, with the 90 % emission-reduction target for 2040. Anticipating a right-wing backlash, von der Leyen assigned Climate, Net Zero and Clean Growth to Wopke Hoekstra, a Dutch conservative, who will, however, work under Ribera's oversight. Second, the introduction of project teams led by vice presidents has promoted an earlier policy coordination among cabinets and Commissioners. This provides stronger policy guidance to the services and contributes to improved consistency and coherence of policy proposals, which is particularly relevant for cross-portfolio initiatives in the field of climate action (e.g., Bürgin, 2020, p. 387; Bürgin, 2018, pp. 844–846; Rietig and Dupont, 2021).

The presidentialization of policy control, in turn, strengthens the Commissions' influence in inter-institutional relations. Negotiations between institutions on legislative proposals generally take the form of tripartite meetings ('trilogues') between Parliament, the Council and the Commission. Their purpose is to reach a provisional agreement on a text acceptable to both the Council and the Parliament. Research on trilogue negotiations shows that strong institutional cohesion increases an institution's chance to secure its policy preferences in the legislative process (e.g., Delreux and Laloux, 2018). Therefore, the Commission's ability to safeguard its own preferences in the trilogues has benefitted from an earlier coordination at the political level, mainly organized by the Cabinet of the Vice-Presidents, which has improved the process management of building strong and coherent trilogue positions (Panning, 2021, p. 34).

The situational context

The current situational context is considered to constrain generally the Commission's policy entrepreneurship. As Euroskepticism has become a persistent phenomenon within the integration process, it has become more difficult for the Commission to suggest controversial policy initiatives, as Member States intend to avoid the costs of disregarding public preferences over EU integration levels (e.g., Ershova, Yordanova and Khokhlova, 2023). Following this line of argument, the strained budget situation of several Member States in the aftermath of the 2008/2009 economic crisis has been considered as a reason for the Commission's reduced environmental policy legislative agenda and waning ambitions in this field (e.g., Čavoški, 2015; Steinbach and Knill, 2017).

However, the increasingly Euroskeptic public also represents an opportunity for the Commission to provide agenda-setting leadership. Absent a strong German-France axis and with internal divisions within the Council, the Commission can present itself as a leader offering a vision for the general EU direction (e.g., Nugent and Rhinard, 2016, p. 1202). The extent to which the situational context can strategically be used as a window of opportunity for policy entrepreneurship depends on the Commission president's personal leadership qualities and political experience (e.g., Tömmel, 2020). Scholars largely agree that the Commission presidents who followed Jacques Delors and his exceptional leadership—Jacques Santer, Romano Prodi and José Barroso—were rather weak, despite achieving certain successes (e.g., Kassim et al., 2017; Müller 2016). In contrast, the Juncker presidency has been assessed as successful in the sense that he carved out a new, more political role for the Commission president; he also exploited the difficult situational context to close ranks within the Commission (e.g., Tömmel, 2020). Similarly, Ursula von der Leyen's performance, and particularly her push for an ambitious climate policy, has been judged positively (e.g., Baracani,

2023; Kassim, 2023; Silander, 2023). For instance, in April 2020, she coupled the negotiations on a recovery fund addressing the threat of a Corona-induced recession with negotiations on the 2021–2027 Multiannual Financial Framework (MFF). These negotiations were stalled, inter alia, due to a foreseen budget share of around 30 percent for climate policy that some Member States criticized as overly ambitious. The coupling increased the pressure for a MFF agreement, as any delay would affect the urgently needed disbursement of the Recovery Fund (Dupont, Oberthür and von Homeyer, 2020, p. 1096).

Ideational resources

While institutional and situational factors and the Commission president's personal qualities shape the room to maneuver, the Commission's influence also depends on ideational resources that enable the Commission to exert 'intellectual leadership' by relying on ideas "to shape the way in which participants in institutional bargaining understand the issue at stake and to orient their thinking about options available" (Baracani, 2023, p. 1454). Scholars have highlighted several ideational resources that contribute to the Commission's discursive power (see Chapters 3 and 6). First, the better the Commission can frame its proposal as an appropriate solution for a salient problem, the greater its legitimacy. The increasing public awareness of environmental problems and climate change provides a favorable contextual condition for policy entrepreneurship. For instance, the von der Leyen Commission could build its proposal for a European Green Deal committing to carbon neutrality on the global momentum around the climate emergency, such as the 2018 warning issued by the Intergovernmental Panel on Climate Change that the world needed to reach net-zero emissions by 2050 to avoid a climate catastrophe and the societal mobilization triggered by the Friday's for Future movement the same year (Eckert, 2021).

Moreover, the Commission's discursive power depends on its issue-specific expertise. The Commission has developed networks with various stakeholders, such as business associations, non-governmental organizations (NGOs) and think tanks. Involving interest group expertise in policy drafting provides the Commission with opportunities to find allies for dealing with the Council and Parliament (Binderkrantz, Blom-Hansen and Senninger. 2021). Furthermore, being able to draw on expert knowledge from EU agencies such as the European Environment Agency (EEA) has become central to the Commission in legitimizing their proposals because it lends authority to policy positions (Jevnaker and Saerbeck, 2019). Similarly, the Commission uses impact assessments of all major legislative proposals, covering the potential economic, social and environmental benefits and costs of the proposed policy, as well as ex post legislative evaluation. These tools enable accountability and foster learning but also serve as legitimation strategy for policy proposals, by providing substance for the claim that Commission proposals are evidence-based (Schönfeld and Jordan, 2019).

Finally, with an argumentation based on commonly shared norms and values, the Commission can exercise normative pressure on Member States to act in line with such normative standards. For instance, the commonly accepted norm of providing directional leadership in international climate diplomacy helped to legitimize the Commission's proposal for more ambitious emissions reduction targets ahead of international climate conferences, in line with arguments that EU commitments could be leverage in talks with other large emitters (e. g., Tobin, Torney and Biedenkopf, 2023).

3 Implementation and compliance monitoring

Implementing powers and comitology

The Commission's executive competencies mainly stem from two legal instruments: implementing acts and delegated acts. Prior to adopting an implementing act, the Commission submits a draft for approval by Member State representatives in a comitology committee, while the EP has no veto powers. By contrast, the Commission adopts delegated acts after consulting national experts in a comitology committee and then submits these acts for ex post control by the Council and the EP, which both have a veto right.

While some scholars consider the comitology committees as control mechanisms designed by EU member governments to supervise the Commission in its executive duties, others consider them as fora in which national officials can deliberate with Commission officials over solutions to common policy problems (see Pollack, 2003). Usually, both these legal instruments combine nonpolitical administrative and technical aspects. Yet, the EU Taxonomy Climate Delegated Act, which established the criteria for determining the conditions under which a specific economic activity qualifies as sustainable, enabling, or harmful, illustrates that administrative laws may also trigger political contestation (Eckert, 2023).

Legal enforcement and capacity building

Major implementation deficits exist in EU environmental policy; for a large majority of the Member States, the environment currently represents the leading policy area for pending infringement procedures (see Chapters 9 and 14). Noncompliance is the result of state capacity limitations and the government reluctance to bear the compliance costs (e. g., Börzel et al., 2010). Member States must report to the Commission, which, in cases of noncompliance, can launch an infringement procedure before the Court of Justice (CJEU), which may eventually lead to financial penalties; however, few cases reach this stage.

The implementation literature is generally skeptical regarding the Commission's ability to effectively enforce EU laws (e.g., Börzel and Buzogany, 2019, p. 326; Falkner, 2018; Jordan and Tosun, 2012, p. 249). When Member States report incorrectly, the Commission has limited capacities to verify the data and follow up non-compliance cases (Martens, 2008, p. 640). Furthermore, constant pressure on certain Member States to implement community laws might endanger their political support for further ambitious policy proposals (e.g., Kelemen and Pavone, 2023).

Due to the infringement process's limitations and confrontational character, since 2004 the Commission has wielded its enforcement powers more selectively based on political considerations (e.g., Zhelyazkova and Schrama, 2023) and has increasingly used capacity-building measures instead. Administrative networks have been established to enhance such capacities and improve coordination between public and private actors, and between EU, national and subnational levels of government. For instance, the European Network for the Implementation and Enforcement of Environmental Law (IMPEL), established in 1992 and comprising national and European environmental authorities, aims to promote the exchange of information and experience and has developed 'best-practice' rules as regards inspection, monitoring, reporting and enforcement of environmental legislation. In this administrative network, the Commission acts as a guide and coordinator, aiming to convince the national officials of what it perceives as the most desirable courses of action (Martinsen, Mastenbroek and Schrama, 2022). Furthermore, the Commission became an active driver of capacity-building measures for NGOs and subnational actors, providing financial aid and access to the policy formulation process (e.g., Kern and Bulkeley, 2009, p. 312). Additionally, the Commission encouraged 'outsourcing' enforcement to environmental NGOs by systematically promoting their access to national courts (Hofmann, 2019, p. 342).

The effect of such capacity building measures remains ambivalent. Some evidence indicates that these measures have contributed to a narrower implementation gap (Börzel and Buzogany, 2019). For instance, local and regional authorities' increasing expertise strengthened their role in the coordinating EU environmental policy at the national level (Jänicke and Quitzow, 2017, p. 128). 'Bottom-up' enforcement of environmental NGOs has been central for promoting effective compliance with environmental laws (Kingston et al., 2023). However, to what extent and under what conditions the Commission can play an effective role in these administrative networks remains understudied (Mastenbroek and Martinsen, 2018).

Data access and data processing

The Commission's knowledge of the Member States' implementation performance is a precondition for both an effective compliance enforcement via the infringement procedure and more targeted capacity-building measures. Nevertheless, two main data-related problems have hampered the Commission's awareness of the Member States' situations previously. First, the Commission has lacked access to timely data. Only around half of the 181 reporting obligations in the fifty-eight pieces of EU environmental law, reviewed in the Commission's 2017 Fitness Check, were required at intervals of two years or less (European Commission, 2018, p. 3). Moreover, Member States' insufficient administrative capacities have contributed to poor response rates to main reporting obligations and delays of several years were normal (Bürgin, 2021). Second, inconsistency in Member States' reporting has challenged the Commission when assessing their implementation performance. The Commission frequently criticized the unevenness of Member State monitoring efforts and the patchy, often out-of-date information provided (European Commission, 2017, p. 4).

To address these deficits, the Commission since 2008 has launched several initiatives to modernize and simplify the collection, exchange and use of data and information required for the design and implementation of environmental policy. While several studies have highlighted the potential of advances in digital technologies for promoting environmental protection and sustainability (e.g., Finck and Mueller, 2023; Conelly et al., 2016), the interaction between technical change and political change in the era of Big Data has remained largely neglected (Höchtl, Parycek and Schöllhammer, 2016, p. 147). One study that explicitly addresses the impact of digitalized data processing on the Commission's compliance monitoring capacity reveals three positive effects (Bürgin, 2021). First, quicker data access has been achieved by increased levels of publicly available data, the EEA's transformation into a data-processing hub and data harvesting at EU level, a technological solution to accessing data at national or local level that bypasses the need for active Member State reporting. Instead, software programs automatically extract large amount of data from national websites, providing the Commission with faster and more flexible access to data, while minimizing Member State reporting obligations. Second, indicator, rather than textual-based, reporting contributed to improved comparability and accuracy of data. Finally, data generated through Copernicus, the European satellite system for monitoring the Earth, offer new opportunities for real-time data access from sources other than the Member States. For instance, the steadily improved quality of satellite pictures allows a more precise monitoring of the EU's Natura 2000 habitats, a biodiversity safety network.

4 Conclusion

While the complexity of intervening factors rules out general assessments on the Commission's influence on policy developments, two recent developments have contributed to the Commission's standing in EU governance. First, internal organizational reforms, such as the new filter function attributed to the vice presidents, the earlier coordination among the cabinets and a more assertive SG role in the inter-service coordination, have increased the Commission president's power to exercise political direction over the Commission. Consequently, the ambition levels of the Commission's environmental policy agenda now depend much more on the Commission president's priorities. Furthermore, a more effective management of the Commission also contributes to a more united appearance, strengthening Commission influence in interinstitutional relations. Deep Council divisions, the fracturing of the European party landscape and the weakening of the Franco-German axis have enabled the Commission to be more in the driver's seat than in the last decades. Future research must show how stable the current Commission comeback as policy entrepreneur will be in the long-term.

Second, the Commission's influence on EU environmental policy is not only reflected in its ability to promote new legislation but also by its capacity to enforce implementation of existing environmental laws. The Commission's stronger focus on enforcement and capacity building has narrowed the implementation gap, even if implementation deficits in the environmental policy sector persist. Moreover, recent changes in environmental reporting and data processing, enabled by advances in digital technology, have strengthened the Commission's capacity to monitor Member State compliance. However, improvements in the Commission's compliance monitoring capacity are very recent and still patchy. Despite the recent advances in data collection and processing technology, the tangible effects on the Commission's monitoring capacity should not be overstated; the monitoring capacity itself is only one of several factors influencing Member States' implementation performance. Consequently, further research, in particular case studies, are required to explore the extent to which the Commission's improved monitoring capacities can deliver substantial improvements in the implementation of EU law. The effect of knowledge management on policy learning in policy networks represents a particularly interesting research avenue.

References

Bailer, S. (2014) 'An agent dependent on the EU Member States? The determinants of the European Commission's legislative success in the European Union', *Journal of European Integration*, 36(1), pp. 37–53.

Baracani, E. (2023) 'Ideational agenda-setting leadership: President von der Leyen and the EU response to the invasion of Ukraine', *West European Politics*, 46(7), pp. 1451–1474.

Blom-Hansen, J. and Senninger, J. (2021) 'The Commission in EU policy preparation', *Journal of Common Market Studies*, 59(3), pp. 625–642.

Bauer, M.W. and Ege, J. (2012) 'Politicization within the European Commission's bureaucracy', *International Review of Administrative Sciences*, 78(3), pp. 403–424.

Becker, S., Bauer, M.W., Connolly, S. and Kassim, H. (2016) 'The Commission: Boxed in and constrained, but still an engine of integration', *West European Politics*, 39(5), pp. 1011–1031.

Bickerton, C., Hodson, D. and Puetter, U. (2015) 'The new intergovernmentalism: European integration in the Post-Maastricht era', *Journal of Common Market Studies*, 53(4), pp. 703–722.

Binderkrantz, A.S., Blom-Hansen, J. and Senninger, R. (2021) 'Countering bias? The EU Commission's consultation with interest groups', *Journal of European Public Policy*, 28(4), pp. 469–488.

Börzel, T.A. and Buzogány, A. (2019) 'Compliance with EU environmental law: The iceberg is melting', *Environmental Politics*, 28(2), pp. 315 – 341.

Börzel, T.A., Hofmann, T., Panke, D. and Sprungk, C. (2010) 'Obstinate and inefficient: Why member states do not comply with European law', *Comparative Political Studies*, 43(11), pp. 1363 – 1390.

Bürgin, A. (2021) 'Modernization of environmental reporting as a tool to improve the European Commission's regulatory monitoring capacity', *Journal of Common Market Studies*, 59, pp. 354 – 370.

Bürgin, A. (2020) 'The impact of Juncker's reorganization of the European Commission on the internal policy-making process: Evidence from the Energy Union project', *Public Administration*, 98, pp. 378 – 391.

Bürgin, A. (2019) 'The implications of the better regulation agenda for the European Parliament's intra- and interinstitutional power relations', *Journal of European Integration*, 41(2), pp. 187 – 202.

Bürgin, A. (2018) 'Intra- and inter-institutional leadership of the European Commission president: An assessment of Juncker's organizational reforms', *Journal of Common Market Studies*, 56, pp. 837 – 853.

Bürgin, A. (2014) 'National binding renewable energy targets for 2020, but not for 2030 anymore: Why the European Commission developed from a supporter to a brakeman', *Journal of European Public Policy*, 22(5), pp. 690 – 707.

Burns, C., Eckersley, P. and Tobin, P. (2020) 'EU environmental policy in times of crisis', *Journal of European Public Policy*, 27(1), pp. 1 – 19.

Buzogány, A. and Ćetković, S. (2021) 'Fractionalized but ambitious? Voting on energy and climate policy in the European Parliament', *Journal of European Public Policy*, 28(7), pp. 1038 – 1056.

Čavoški, A. (2015) 'A post-austerity European Commission: No role for environmental policy?', *Environmental Politics*, 24(3), pp. 501 – 505.

Connelly, R., Playford, C.J., Gayle, V. and Dibben, C. (2016) 'The role of administrative data in the big data revolution in social science research', *Social Science Research*, 59, pp. 1 – 12.

Delreux, T. and Laloux, T. (2018) 'Concluding early agreements in the EU: A double principal-agent analysis of trilogue negotiations', *Journal of Common Market Studies*, 56(2), pp. 300 – 317.

Dupont, C., Oberthür, S. and von Homeyer, I. (2020) 'The Covid-19 crisis: A critical juncture for EU climate policy development?', *Journal of European Integration*, 42(8), pp. 1095 – 1110.

Dinan, D. (2016) 'Governance and institutions: A more political commission', *Journal of Common Market Studies*, 54(Annual Review), pp. 101 – 116.

Eckert, S. (2023) 'Business and private finance: Their role in the EU's climate transition', in: Rayner, T., Szulecki, K., Jordan, A.J. and Oberthür, S. (eds.) *Handbook on European Union Climate Change Policy and Politics*. Cheltenham: Edward Elgar.

Eckert, S. (2021) 'The European Green Deal and the EU's regulatory power in times of crisis', *Journal of Common Market Studies*, 59(S1), pp. 81 – 91.

Ellinas, A. and Suleiman, E. (2012) *The European Commission and bureaucratic autonomy: Europe's custodians*. New York: Cambridge University Press.

European Commission (2018) 'Proposal for a regulation of the European Parliament and of the Council on the alignment of reporting obligations in the field of environment policy', *COM*(2018) 381 final. Available at: https://ec.europa.eu/environment/legal/reporting/pdf/1_EN_ACT_part1.pdf (Accessed: 22 October 2024).

European Commission (2017) 'Actions to streamline environmental reporting', *SWD*(2017) 312 final. Available at: https://ec.europa.eu/environment/legal/reporting/pdf/action_plan_env_issues.pdf (Accessed: 22 October 2024).

Ershova, A., Yordanova, N. and Khokhlova, A. (2023) 'Constraining the European Commission to please the public: Responsiveness through delegation choices', *Journal of European Public Policy*. Available at: https://doi.org/10.1080/13501763.2023.2224399.

Falkner, G. (2018) 'A causal loop? The Commission's new enforcement approach in the context of non-compliance with EU law even after CJEU judgments', *Journal of European Integration*, 40 (6), pp. 769–784.
Finck, M. and Mueller, M.S. (2023) 'Access to data for environmental purposes: Setting the scene and evaluating recent changes in EU data law', *Journal of Environmental Law*, 35(1), pp. 111–128.
Gravey, V. and Jordan, A. (2020) 'Policy dismantling at EU level: Reaching the limits of "an ever-closer ecological union"?', *Public Administration*, 98(2), pp. 349–362.
Höchtl, J., Parycek, P. and Schöllhammer, R. (2016) 'Big data in the policy cycle: Policy decision making in the digital era', *Journal of Organizational Computing and Electronic Commerce*, 26(1–2), pp. 147–169.
Hofmann, A. (2019) 'Left to interest groups? On the prospects for enforcing environmental law in the European Union', *Environmental Politics*, 28(2), pp. 342–364.
Jänicke, M. and Quitzow, R. (2017) 'Multi-level reinforcement in European climate and energy governance: Mobilizing economic interests at the sub-national levels', *Environmental Policy and Governance*, 27(2), pp. 122–136.
Jevnaker, T. and Saerbeck, B. (2019) 'EU agencies and the Energy Union: Providing useful information to the Commission?', *Politics and Governance*, 7(1), pp. 60–69.
Jordan, A. and Tosun, J. (2012) 'Policy implementation', in: Jordan, A and Adelle, C. (eds.) *Environmental policy in the EU: Actors, institutions and processes.* London: Routledge, pp. 273–292.
Kassim, H. (2023) 'The von der Leyen Commission: An early assessment', in: Costa, O. and Van Hecke, S. (eds.) *The EU political system after the 2019 European elections.* Palgrave Studies in European Union Politics. Cham: Palgrave Macmillan, pp. 187–205.
Kassim, H. et al. (2017) 'Managing the house: The presidency, agenda control and policy activism in the European Commission', *Journal of European Public Policy*, 24(5), pp. 653–674.
Kassim, H., et al. (2013) *The European Commission of the twenty-first century.* Oxford: Oxford University Press.
Kelemen, R.D. and Pavone, T. (2023) 'Where have the guardians gone? Law enforcement and the politics of supranational forbearance in the European Union', *World Politics*, 75(4), pp. 779–825.
Kern, K. and Bulkeley, H. (2009) 'Cities, Europeanization and multi-level governance: Governing climate change through transnational municipal networks', *Journal of Common Market Studies*, 47(2), pp. 309–332.
Kingston, S., Alblas, E., Callaghan, M. and Foulon, J. (2023) 'Empowering through law: Environmental NGOs as regulatory intermediaries in EU nature governance', *Transnational Environmental Law*, 12, pp. 469–497.
Knodt, M., Ringel, M. and Müller, R. (2020) '"Harder" soft governance in the European Energy Union', *Journal of Environmental Policy & Planning*, 22(6), pp. 787–800.
Mastenbroek, E. and Martinsen, D.S. (2018) 'Filling the gap in the European administrative space: The role of administrative networks in EU implementation and enforcement', *Journal of European Public Policy*, 25(3), pp. 422–435.
Martens, M. (2008) 'Administrative integration through the back door? The role and influence of the European Commission in rransgovernmental networks within the environmental policy field', *Journal of European Integration*, 30(5), pp. 635–651.
Martinsen, D.S., Mastenbroek, E. and Schrama, R. (2022) 'The power of "weak" institutions: Assessing the EU's emerging institutional architecture for improving the implementation and enforcement of joint policies', *Journal of European Public Policy*, 29(10), pp. 1529–1545.
Müller, H. (2016) 'Between potential, performance and prospect: Revisiting the political leadership of the EU Commission president', *Politics and Governance*, 4(2), pp. 68–79.
Nugent, N. and Rhinard, M. (2019) 'The "political" roles of the European Commission', *Journal of European Integration*, 41(2), pp. 203–220.
Nugent, N. and Rhinard, M. (2016) 'Is the European Commission really in decline?', *Journal of Common Market Studies*, 54(5), pp. 1199–1215.

Oztas, B. and Kreppel, A. (2022) 'Power or luck? The limitations of the European Commission's agenda setting power and autonomous policy influence', *Journal of Common Market Studies*, 60(2), pp. 408 – 426.

Panning, L. (2021) 'Building and managing the European Commission's position for trilogue negotiations', *Journal of European Public Policy*, 28(1), pp. 32 – 52.

Peterson, J. (2015) 'The Commission and the new intergovernmentalism: Calm within the storm', in: Bickerton, C.J., Hodson, D. and Puetter, U. (eds.) *The new intergovernmentalism*. Oxford: Oxford University Press, pp. 185 – 207.

Pollak, J. and Slominski, P. (2015) 'The European Parliament: Adversary or accomplice of the new intergovernmentalism?', in: Bickerton, C.J., Hodson, D. and Puetter, U. (eds.) *The new intergovernmentalism*. Oxford: Oxford University Press, pp. 245 – 262.

Pollack, M.A. (2003) 'Control mechanism or deliberative democracy? Two images of comitology', *Comparative Political Studies*, 36(1 – 2), pp. 125 – 155.

Ponzano, P., Hermann, C. and Corona, D. (2012) 'The power of initiative of the European Commission: A progressive erosion?', *Notre Europe Studies and Research*, 2012(89), pp. 56 – 71.

Puetter, U. (2015) 'The European Council: The centre of new intergovernmentalism', in: Bickerton, C.J., Hodson, D. and Puetter, U. (eds.) *The new intergovernmentalism*. Oxford: Oxford University Press, pp. 165 – 184.

Rietig, K. and Dupont, C. (2021) 'Presidential leadership styles and institutional capacity for climate policy integration in the European 'mission', *Policy and Society*, 40(1), pp. 19 – 36.

Seele, P. and Lock, I. (2017) 'The game-changing potential of digitalization for sustainability', *Sustainable Science*, 12(2), pp. 183 – 185.

Schoenefeld, J.J. and Jordan, A.J. (2019) 'Environmental policy evaluation in the EU: Between learning, accountability, and political opportunities?', *Environmental Politics*, 28(2), pp. 365 – 384.

Silander, D. (2022) 'The European Commission on sustainable development. A new normative power in its making?', *Forum for Social Economics*. Available at: https://doi.org/10.1080/07360932.2022.2032255.

Steinebach, Y. and Knill, C. (2017) 'Still an entrepreneur? The changing role of the European Commission in EU environmental policy-making', *Journal of European Public Policy*, 24(3), pp. 429 – 446.

Thaler, P. (2016) 'The European Commission and the European Council: Coordinated agenda setting in European energy policy', *Journal of European Integration*, 38(5), pp. 571 – 585.

Tobin, P., Torney, D. and Biedenkopf, K. (2023) 'EU climate leadership: Domestic and global dimensions', in: Rayner, T., Szulecki, K., Jordan, A.J. and Oberthür, S. (eds.) *Handbook on European Union climate change policy and politics*. Cheltenham: Edward Elgar.

Tömmel, I. (2020) 'Political leadership in times of crisis: The Commission presidency of Jean-Claude Juncker', *West European Politics*, 43(5), pp. 1141 – 1162.

Tömmel, I. (2013) 'The presidents of the European Commission: Transactional or transforming leaders?', *Journal of Common Market Studies*, 51(4), pp. 789 – 805.

Trondal, J. (2012) 'On bureaucratic centre formation in government institutions. Lessons from the European Commission', *International Review of Administrative Sciences*, 78(3), pp. 425 – 445.

Wille, A. (2013) *The normalization of the European Commission*. Oxford: Oxford University Press.

Zito, A.R., Burns, C. and Lenschow, A. (2019) 'Is the trajectory of European Union environmental policy less certain?', *Environmental Politics*, 28(2), pp. 187 – 207.

Zhelyazkova, A. and Schrama, R. (2023) 'When does the EU Commission listen to experts? Analysing the effect of external compliance assessments on supranational enforcement in the EU', *Journal of European Public Policy*, pp. 1 – 29.

Neil Carter and Fay Farstad

Political parties and European Union environmental policy: The role of the European Parliament

Abstract: This chapter focuses on the role of the European Parliament (EP) and political parties within it in shaping European Union (EU) environmental policy. The chapter explores a range of variables that explain the environmental behavior of the EP and its parties: left-right differences, national interests, the impact of enlargement, and the series of crises that have disrupted the EU since 2008. We chart the emergence and development of the EP as a purported environmental champion from when the environment rose up the political agenda in the 1980s and 1990s, through the 2000s when the rise of both Green and populist far-right parties contributed to the wider fragmentation of party stability of the chamber, to finally discussing the contemporary relevance of European political parties and the EP for EU environmental policy, using the EU's Fit for 55 climate package as a case study. We conclude by reflecting on the outcome of the 2024 European elections and its implications for the future of the EU's environmental ambitions.

Keywords: European Parliament; political parties; environmental policy; climate policy; European Green Deal

1 Introduction

This chapter examines the important role of the European Parliament (EP)—the only directly elected European Union (EU) institution—and political parties in the development of EU environmental policy. The EU's growing importance as an environmental actor from the 1980s onwards set the context for the EP to develop a reputation as an 'environmental champion' through its efforts to shape the political agenda and to strengthen the environmental content of new legislation, while simultaneously pushing to strengthen its own institutional powers. Efforts to establish the validity of the EP's green credentials and to explore the tension between its ambition and its influence, have shaped much of the literature in this field. In recent years, several factors have raised doubts about the EP's continuing commitment to its positive green agenda: the evolution of interinstitutional behavior, enlargement, a plethora of crises and the growing fragmentation of political groupings in the EP. Yet the outcome of the 'green election' in 2019 countered these doubts. European elections are a key moment when parties can exercise policy influence, and the 2019 election occurred during high levels of public concern about climate change and paved the way for President von der Leyen's European Green Deal (EGD), which she had promised in order to secure cross-party support for her candidacy.

https://doi.org/10.1515/9783111321523-014

This chapter examines the development of the EP's role as an environmental champion alongside the evolution of its powers. Given the encompassing nature of the EGD, the latter part of the chapter will focus in more detail on one major element of it—climate policy—and, specifically, key parts of the Fit for 55 climate package (supplemented by an online appendix detailing the positions of the European Parliament on key pieces of FF55 legislation). The concluding discussion will draw on the EGD case study and the 2024 European Parliament elections to assess the contemporary challenges and opportunities facing the parties within the EP.

2 The emergence of an environmental champion

During the 1980s and 1990s the EP established a reputation as an environmental champion in the wider context of the growing importance of the EU as an environmental political actor. The entry into force of the Single European Act (SEA) in 1987 prompted a huge increase in environmental policies designed to ensure a level playing field across the common market by preventing countries from lowering their environmental standards to secure a competitive advantage over rivals. Environmental legislation became increasingly Europeanized: the domestic policies of Member States have been shaped by EU legislation and, as part of the regulatory competition that has characterized EU decision-making, Member States in turn have sought to upload their own national models of legislation to the European level (Jordan and Liefferink, 2004).

A parallel process saw a series of Treaty reforms that significantly expanded the formal legislative powers of the European Parliament, moving it from being little more than a 'talking shop' to a co-legislator with the power to negotiate with the Council of Ministers in most policy areas. Indeed, the Parliament's prominent role in environmental policy contributed to it achieving its long-term strategic goal of expanding its powers while also helping to establish its reputation as an environmental champion. The activities of its influential Committee on Environment, Public Health and Food Safety (ENVI) played a key role in achieving both these outcomes (Burns, 2021).

ENVI is responsible for producing reports on environmental policies proposed by the Commission. During the long tenure of UK Labour Member of the European Parliament (MEP) Ken Collins as chair (1979–1984, 1989–1999), ENVI built a close relationship with the Commission that enabled the EP to exploit the new powers it gained first under the cooperation procedure and later the co-decision procedures (now the ordinary legislative procedure). The ongoing dialogue established with the Committee, later a trilogue with the Council and often supplemented by committee members producing their own initiative reports or commissioning expert reports on key topics, enabled the Committee to carve out a powerful agenda-setting role that included pushing the Commission to introduce directives banning the use of lead in petrol and the import of skins from seal pups (Judge, 1992). It also exercised its growing legislative powers by demonstrating a willingness to strengthen proposals. The Committee—and the broader Parliament—was relatively receptive to lobbying by environmental nongovernmental organizations (ENGOs), which often struggled to gain a sympathetic hearing in the Commission and Council. Moreover, the presence in Parliament of a steadily growing group of Green MEPs who were particularly keen to influence the Environment Committee also contributed to the EP's reputation as an environmental champion (Burns, 2021).

However, these claims about the EP's environmental credentials were largely based on a handful of case studies. While the EP was clearly playing an agenda-setting role, there was only sketchy empirical evidence for its positive legislative impact. Could it be that some MEPs were engaging in performative politics (e.g., seal pups) while in practice exercising limited influence over very important, albeit often technical and mundane, legislative detail (Weale et al., 2000)? This knowledge gap was addressed by several quantitative studies that were primarily testing wider claims about the impact of new decision-making procedures on the power of the EP. For example, Tsebelis and Kalandrakis (1999) found that the EP exercised considerable influence on nine pieces of chemical legislation passed through the (now defunct) cooperation procedure, securing adoption, in whole or part, of around half of its amendments in the final legislation—although these were not all beneficial to the environment.

Burns and Carter (2010) developed a typology for assessing the environmental content of amendments, which they applied to nine pieces of environmental legislation adopted under different procedures and found that the EP consistently tried to strengthen environmental legislation. This general tendency to pursue a progressive environmental agenda was confirmed by a mass study of 7,065 EP amendments adopted to all environmental legislation under the ordinary legislative procedure (OLP) between 1999–2009 (Burns et al., 2013). After excluding the 51% of amendments that were environmentally 'neutral' (i.e., technical in nature), 46% were classified as seeking to strengthen environmental protection. While most (35%) would make legislation only marginally stronger, some 11% would have a substantive beneficial impact. By contrast, just 3% of EP proposed amendments would have weakened environmental legislation (Burns et al., 2013, pp. 944–945).

3 The European Parliament's shifting environmental ambition

However, as its powers had increased, the Parliament appeared to have become less ambitious in its environmental demands: for example, by proposing fewer amendments that would strengthen environmental protection and fewer important/highly important amendments in 2004–2009 compared to 1999–2004 (Burns et al., 2013, pp. 944–945). Yet the EP had also become more successful in getting its amendments adopted between these two parliamentary sessions.

Several factors contributed to this shift in the EP's approach. Institutional factors were clearly significant. The Commission was now required to provide an explicit justification for its proposals and to engage in wider stakeholder consultation, which indicated it might be crafting 'better' legislation (Burns et al., 2013). The period 1999–2009 also saw the consolidation of new OLP procedures and the normalization of a more informal approach to decision-making whereby the Commission, Council and Parliament communicated with each other much earlier in the process. As the aim of these trilogues is to negotiate an agreed upon text, the Council in particular was encouraged to engage more constructively with the Parliament. However, as a result the EP seemed to be proposing weaker amendments to the plenary, as it became more adept at recognizing which amendments the Council would be willing to accept and where the two institutions could negotiate compromises that were acceptable to all sides (Burns and Carter, 2010; Ripoll Servant, 2018, see Chapter 11). That said, despite the Parliament's increased powers, the Commission seemed to put more emphasis on anticipating and accommodating the Council's preferences, so EP amendments (particularly the greenest ones) that fell outside the preference set of the Commission and Council tended not to fare well (Burns et al., 2013).

Three broader factors were also in play. First, EU *enlargements* in 2004 and 2007 brought in twelve new Member States, mostly from Central and Eastern Europe (CEE). These new members were poorer and less economically developed than most existing Member States and they faced the huge burden of implementing the environmental *acquis communautaire.* Although there was little immediate impact on the EP's approach to environmental policy, it coincided with a growing reluctance by ENVI to engage in direct conflict with the Council (Burns, Carter and Worsfold, 2012). The passage of the major Energy and Climate Change Package (ECCP) (2007–2009) prompted more organized opposition from CEE governments and MEPs, notably from Poland, which was heavily dependent on fossil fuels for its energy supply. The result was the inclusion of several derogations for CEE states in the final legislation.

The second factor was *crisis.* The passage of the ECCP coincided with the financial and economic crisis through 2007–2008, which reduced the appetite for radical action on climate change across many Member States and MEPs, both east and west, particularly where measures had significant cost implications. One outcome was that fewer pieces of environmental legislation were launched, thereby reducing the potential for the EP to exercise influence (see Chapter 37; also Burns, 2019). Moreover, divisions over contentious issues emerged within some political groups, notably the center-right European People's Party (EPP) when German MEPs tried to water down parts of the ENVI report on the Emissions Trading System, even though the Irish rapporteur Avril Doyle was an EPP group member.

The third factor was *ideology.* Political parties in the EP generally behave along ideological rather than national lines (Hix, Noury and Roland, 2007). To secure majority support for amendments the political groups need to cooperate with each other. The longstanding dominance of the EPP and the center-left Progressive Alliance of Socialists and Democrats (S&D) meant that this 'grand coalition' provided considerable stability to EP policymaking. However, shifts did occur. The EPP's replacement of the S&D as the largest political group in 1999 alongside ENVI being chaired by a series of EPP members between 1999 and 2009 may have contributed to a decline in the EP's environmental radicalism. Voting records indicate that several party groups, particularly the EPP and the liberal Alliance of Liberals and Democrats for Europe (ALDE), became less sympathetic to environmental protection. During 2004–2009 the EPP consistently voted more closely on ENVI roll-call votes with the right-wing Union for Europe of the Nations (UEN) (81 % of votes) and ALDE (70 %) than with the Party of European Socialists (PES) (60 %), which is generally seen as more 'pro-environment', and less than 50 percent of the time with the Greens and The Left (GUE-NGL) (Burns, Carter and Worsfold, 2012). The expansion of the party groups to include MEPs from the new Member States probably encouraged this shift in position.

Since 2009, each of these factors has grown increasingly important in shaping events across the EU and, specifically, the EP's behavior. Post-enlargement, several new Member States, notably the Visegrad states of Hungary, Poland, Czechia and Slovakia, have regularly worked together to oppose progressive environmental measures. This ministerial resistance in the Council may have generated anticipatory compliance by the Commission, leading it to weaken its proposals in the face of likely Council opposition. During this period, the EU has also experienced multiple crises: the Eurozone crisis (following the financial and economic crisis), for example, required bailouts to several debt-ridden states; additionally, there was an ongoing migration crisis, repeated waves of populist protests and growth in radical right parties that question many of the core assumptions of the EU project. All of this was later compounded by the Covid-19 pandemic and the Russian invasion of Ukraine. Lastly, the growth of radical right and Eurosceptic conservative parties—but also the Greens/European Free Alliance (EFA)—have together contributed to a broader fragmentation of EP party groupings.

Some observers feared that this combination of developments would exert a negative impact on the EP's environmental ambition and even lead to some environmental policy dismantling (Lenschow, Burns and Zito, 2020). Burns (2019) analyzed all environmental legislation between 2004 and 2016, assessing whether the environmental ambition became stronger or weaker between the proposal and adoption of a policy. While she found little evidence of any explicit efforts by the EP to weaken environmental policy, there were also few examples of legislation being strengthened by the EP. Most academic attention has focused on assessing the EP's impact over EU energy and climate change policy, which has increasingly come to dominate the EU's environmental policy agenda since the 2000s. One institutional impact of this shift is that ENVI increasingly has to work with other committees, thereby providing the opportunity for other actors to express concerns over effects of climate measures on competitiveness in, for example, trade, agriculture or industry. Consequently, the growing scope for political division over climate policy, especially as the number of climate skeptic radical right MEPs has grown, has encouraged interest in the way EP political groups behave.

A study of roll call voting in the eighth EP (2014–2019) found that greater fragmentation and polarization had not prevented the EP from advocating ambitious goals in its negotiations with the Commission and Council across ten of the twelve key pieces of energy and climate policy legislation examined (Buzogány and Ćetković, 2021). This finding is explained by the high degree (over 90 percent) of internal cohesion among major political groups (EPP, S&D, ALDE, Greens/EFA), whereas groups on the radical left and right were far more internally divided and therefore less able to influence EP positions. Thus, fragmentation had actually enabled the more progressive groups—S&D, ALDE, Greens/EFA—to play a key role in building majorities for EP positions, although they often involved compromises to win EPP support (Buzogány and Ćetković, 2021).

Similarly, a study of plenary debates held prior to the annual United Nations (UN) climate conferences where EP resolutions are adopted found that despite the growth of radical right MEPs the level of ambition remained broadly unchanged during 2009–2019. Indeed, the majority of MEPs regarded the EU as a global climate policy leader (Petri and Biedenkopf, 2021). This finding may indicate that plenary speeches are an opportunity for individual MEPs to grandstand, making performative speeches calling for radical action, whereas the lower profile activity of building compromises on 'domestic' environmental legislation requires inter-institutional cooperation that inevitably veers towards compromise and moderation (see also Wendler, 2019). Nevertheless, their discursive analysis does identify a clear polarization across political groups between those advocating higher EU ambition (EPP, S&D, ALDE, Greens/EFA, GUE/NGL) and those seeking low ambition (the European Conservatives and Reformists Group (ECR), Europe of Freedom and (Direct) Democracy (EFD(D)), Europe of Nations and Freedom (ENF) and 'Non-Inscrits' (NI)), with the latter questioning the EU's responsibility to reduce emissions and expressing concern about the damage to competitiveness from climate mitigation policies (Petri and Biedenkopf, 2021). It is important to note that, while the EP has limited influence over the EU's foreign policy, these plenary debates are one means of doing so. The consent procedure, whereby the EP's approval is required before some international treaties involving the EU can enter into force, may encourage the Commission and Council to include EP positions in climate negotiations. Other mechanisms it uses include sending parliamentary delegations to UN climate negotiations and producing its own initiative reports (Delreux and Burns, 2019).

Overall, the evidence confirms that there is substance to the epithet that the EP was an environmental champion during the 2000s and 2010s, while also identifying an apparent decline in its radicalism.

4 The Parliament and the European Green Deal

The EU elections in 2019 saw the EP and political groups gain renewed significance. The elections took place during high levels of public concern about climate change and became a key topic in Ursula von der Leyen's bid for Commission President. To secure cross-party support from the EP, von der Leyen made a series of ambitious environmental commitments and promised to make combating climate change a key Commission policy goal. However, despite her environmental overtures, von der Leyen was elected by only 383 votes, just slightly above the absolute majority of 374 required to be elected, and far short of the 422 votes her predecessor Jean-Claude Juncker received in 2014. Von der Leyen was supported by the three mainstream, pro-EU groups—EPP, S&D and Renew Europe (formerly ALDE)—while MEPs from the Greens/EFA, as well as the right-wing and left-wing parties, largely voted against.

Once elected, von der Leyen nevertheless remained true to her promise, and on December 11, 2019 announced the European Green Deal. The EGD was framed as a green growth strategy to create new jobs, but it included the central goal of making the EU the world's first climate-neutral continent by 2050. To reach the 'net-zero' target by 2050, the EU adopted a Climate Act, which also set out an interim goal of reducing net emissions by 55 percent by 2030 compared to 1990-levels. The Commission subsequently published its landmark Fit for 55 (FF55) climate package, which collectively aims to make the EU 'fit' to achieve the interim target. The EGD is not just a climate strategy, however, but includes a wide range of cross-cutting environmental proposals relating to: clean, affordable and secure energy; a circular economy; energy efficiency in buildings; sustainable mobility; food and farming; biodiversity protection; pollution control as well as sustainable finance (European Commission, 2019). The EGD sets out proposals for new or revised directives, regulations, laws and strategies, and started what has been referred to as a 'legislative tsunami' (Hodgson, 2021).

Following the launch of the EGD, the Commission was also forced to respond to the Covid-19 pandemic, the Russian invasion of Ukraine and ensuing energy crisis and competition for business investment from the generous subsidies awarded by the United States Inflation Reduction Act. At each turn, however, the answer from the Commission was more, not less, ambition. In several speeches, Commissioner Frans Timmermans—responsible for climate action and EGD—argued that these crises only made the EGD more pertinent and important. For example, the Covid-19 recovery package Next Generation EU earmarked funds for climate change and biodiversity protection investments. Similarly, the REPowerEU plan set out measures for weaning the EU off its dependency on Russian gas and accelerate the deployment of renewable energy, while the EU's Green Deal Industrial Plan aimed to enhance the competitiveness of Europe's net-zero industry in relation to other powers, such as the United States. The EP also used its additional budgetary powers to pursue progressive climate policies. During negotiations for approving the 2021–2022 annual budget, the EP successfully pressed for the inclusion of "achieving climate neutrality by 2025" as a budget priority. Similarly, in negotiations for the multiannual financial framework for 2021–2027 (where EP approval is required via the assent procedure) it was able to increase funding for the EGD (Petri, Zapletalová and Biedenkopf, 2023).

Although certainly not without its critics (radical right-wing parties condemn it for going too far, while the left, greens and parts of the ENGO sector despair that it does not go far enough), the EGD was widely commended for its ambitious targets and its breadth of scope. Taking the FF55 climate package as an example, we provide a preliminary and high-level examination of EP positions on key pieces of FF55 legislation, with the view to assessing whether the EP still acts as an environmental champion. We focus on climate policy because it is both a central and contentious part of the EGD and the FF55 package includes a wide range of policy proposals allowing us to analyze various relationships of interest within the EP. (For an analysis of other parts of the EGD, for example the EU's nature restoration law and pesticides legislation, see Chapter 4.)

However, as the FF55 package itself encompasses a wide range of policy areas, we focus our analysis on the key proposals within the package that cover the main emission sources in the EU (see Chapter 20): the Effort-Sharing Regulation (ESR); the revisions to the EU Emissions Trading Scheme (ETS, in this chapter also ETS1 for distinction purposes); the new emissions trading scheme for buildings, road transport and additional sectors (ETS2); the Land Use, Land Use Change and Forestry (LULUCF) Regulation and important innovations such as the Carbon Border Adjustment Mechanism (CBAM).

Tables 1–6 (see Online Appendix) present a simplified overview of the positions of the main EU institutions on the key FF55 proposals and show the final outcomes of the trilogue negotiations. For the details of each proposal and position, see Farstad et al. (2024). Our overview indicates that the EP generally tried to increase the ambition of the various FF55 proposals. While the Council largely endorsed or attempted to water down the Commission's original proposal, the EP sought more ambitious targets,[1] a broader scope,[2] earlier introductions,[3] and generally attempted to secure early and continuous progress.[4]

There is one notable exception, however, namely the EP's position on the new ETS2, where it did seek to water down ambitions. Although the EP suggested an earlier introduction of the ETS2 than the Commission's original proposal, it wished to exempt private buildings and transport until 2029. It also wanted a price cap of EUR 50 on emissions allowances. Both suggested changes would significantly decrease the effectiveness of the scheme. The EP's foot-dragging in this case is perhaps understandable; multiple observers have sharply criticized the ETS2 for potentially increasing the costs

---

1 One example is for the ETS1.

2 For example, which voyages, ships and greenhouse gases should be included in the ETS1 and which products should be covered by the CBAM.

3 For example, when shipping should be included in the ETS1 and when the ETS2 should be established. The EP also wanted a faster phase-out of free emission allowances due to the CBAM.

4 This included proposing a tougher baseline for setting annual emission limits under the ESR and suggesting reduced flexibility. The EP also opposed combining agriculture and LULUCF into a new Agriculture, Forestry and Other Land Use sector, as they argued this risked hiding emissions from the agricultural sector behind forest sinks, reducing incentives for agriculture to reduce emissions, and that it was risky to lean too heavily on a sector vulnerable to natural disturbances such as forest fires.

of heating and fuel for citizens, which were already increasing as a result of the Russian invasion of Ukraine and rising inflation. Despite the establishment of a Social Climate Fund, designed to compensate vulnerable groups with funds earned from the scheme, many MEPs were wary of the potential backlash from voters. The EP's (and the Council's) objections were met with partial understanding from the Commission, and the final outcome was substantially watered down compared to the Commission's original proposal. Several observers were nonetheless surprised the new ETS2 was approved at all, given the widespread opposition.

The final FF55 decisions were fairly classic EU compromises, with both the Council and EP receiving concessions, yet the outcomes were not too far off the Commission's intention. The EP managed to negotiate a tougher ETS1 target; the inclusion of more voyages, vessels and greenhouse gases in the shipping component of the ETS1; the inclusion of more products (such as hydrogen) in the CBAM and a more progressive phase-out of free emission allowances; and it ensured that flexibilities under the ESR were significantly tightened. Overall, therefore, the final FF55 package demonstrated that the EP can still be considered an environmental champion, with the EGD placing it center stage in EU politics.

5 Looking forwards: beyond the 2024 European Elections

Getting the FF55 package successfully through the trilogue negotiations was only the first hurdle. The effective implementation of the EGD will very much continue to depend on the composition of the EP after the 2024 EU elections, as several parts of the FF55 package will be reviewed and potentially adjusted over time, and other parts will need to be developed further through more detailed secondary legislation (see the Online Appendix for details). A review of the manifestos of the different EP party families for the 2024 EU elections reveals that climate change had slipped down the political agenda somewhat, with defense, economic security and the EU's strategic autonomy as the most salient issues. Following a global pandemic, the outbreak of war and an energy crisis in Europe, record inflation and increasing geopolitical competition, the lower salience of climate change is perhaps not surprising. Overall, however, climate change and the environment still featured prominently in manifestos. The fact that the issue remained high on the agenda behind topical issues such as defense and economic security perhaps demonstrated that climate change is unlikely to drop back to its pre-2019 status as a secondary issue. Indeed, these high-profile issues were frequently discussed with reference to climate and environment, with security and defense policies being linked to energy security, for example, and economic security being linked to energy poverty and green growth.

Running up to the 2024 election, there was also a growing backlash against the ambitions and tempo of the EGD, most notably from farmers staging large-scale protests across Europe over the environmental requirements of the EU's new farming policies. The opposition to the new ETS2 discussed above also flags an important issue in regards to the kind of policy measures that came to dominate the agenda. Whereas previously the costs and impacts of a large part of EU climate legislation had fallen primarily on businesses and states, increasingly costs were now being felt directly by citizens: for example, the costs of new heat pumps, electrical vehicles, and higher fuel and electricity prices. Likewise, key environmental legislation such as the Farm to Fork strategy and nature restoration law set significant limits on land use and economic activities such as farming. This shift potentially made MEPs less enthusiastic about the EGD agenda. In response to the protests, von der Leyen made several U-turns, such as watering down elements of the EU's Farm to Fork strategy. Moreover, the 2019 election happened in the wake of the publication of the Intergovernmental Panel on Climate Change's 1.5 degree report and Greta Thunberg's Fridays for Future movement taking to the streets, giving the greens a surge in popularity. In contrast, the run-up to the 2024 election saw mushrooming support for nationalist, Euroskeptic, populist and radical right-wing parties, both in the EP and in key Member States (POLITICO, 2024).

In any event, while radical right parties made significant gains in key Member States such as Germany, France and Italy, they did not achieve the EU-wide landslide indicated by the polls. The center-right EPP tightened its grip on the chamber and the center-left S&D largely held firm, meaning that despite the decimation of the liberal Renew group, the pro-EU 'centrist coalition' (EPP, S&D and Renew) retained its majority, paving the way for von der Leyen's second term without the need for support from the radical right. Indeed, EU leaders gave their approval for von der Leyen soon after the election, and she then swiftly secured a comfortable majority in the 720-seat EP when 401 MEPs voted in favor and 284 against. Significantly, while not all centrist MEPs voted in line with their party group, von der Leyen's majority was boosted by support from the Greens/EFA group. Ironically, although the Greens/EFA lost more than a dozen MEPs, dropping to the sixth largest political group in the chamber, they may play an influential role due to the delicate balance of power in the 2024–2029 EP.

However, if the two radical right political groups, the European Conservatives and Reformists and the Patriots for Europe, voted together, they would form the second largest force in the EP. Despite the disagreements and rivalries among the various far-right parties that have previously impeded their ability to act as a coherent bloc, the broad opposition of most right-wing MEPs to stronger climate targets and their widespread criticism of the EGD means that the future environmental ambitions of both the EP and Commission may be tempered. Although the main elements of climate legislation contained in the FF55 package were passed before the 2024 election—making them difficult to revoke —the rightwards shift of the chamber could influence the implementation of these policies through the more detailed secondary legislation. There will also be key stages where new initiatives are proposed and existing policies reviewed that will provide opportunities for opponents to water down ambitions.

Moreover, environmental policies such as the Farm to Fork strategy and the EU's nature restoration law have already been diluted in response to protests from industry and heavily impacted Member States. Overall, the election results suggest the negative impact of a populist backlash against the EGD, or at the very least an EGD 'fatigue', which is likely to constrain environmental ambitions for the 2024–2029 term. This seems especially relevant considering that other important issues have ascended the political agenda, such as economic competitiveness, trade and defense. For example, the Commission's 2025 'Omnibus' packages (European Commission, 2025), which the Commission argues will simplify EU rules, particularly for small and medium-sized enterprises, have received criticism for watering down the ambitions of the EGD (Costa, 2025). On a more positive note, at the Member State–level the election results are likely to have made politicians more attuned to the distributional impacts of environmental and climate policy, which might increase efforts to shield vulnerable groups from high costs of fuel and heating. Moreover, the EU's new climate law should at least partially ensure progress on climate change.

6 Conclusion

This chapter has analyzed the role of the European Parliament and its political parties in shaping EU environmental policy. We have charted how the European Parliament established its 'environmental champion' credentials in the post-Single European Act–era as part of its wider efforts to expand its formal powers. Over the last two decades the EP has secured those formal powers and tempered its green credentials in the face of changing contexts: polycrises, enlargement and fragmentation of party groups. Yet there has been no significant dismantling of environmental policy, and the 2019–2024 parliament largely saw it renew its green reputation through its treatment of the European Green Deal. Although the 2024 EU elections and rightward shift of the parliament (and the Commission and Council) may limit future ambitions, the majority held by the pro-EU and centrist 'coalition' of the EPP, S&D and Renew (supplemented by the Greens/EFA), combined with the continued leadership of Commission President Ursula von der Leyen, may provide continuity in the EU's environmental agenda. However, the rightward shift has enabled EPP politicians to push for some reframing of the EGD. Thus, the Commission's February 2025 proposal for a Clean Industrial Deal was presented as a follow-up to the EGD, but with a new pro-business focus on increasing business competitiveness and enabling economic growth (Lynes 2025).

The 2024 elections certainly underscored the enduring importance of the European Parliament for the future of the EU's environmental ambitions. Future research should delve deeper into the role of political parties within the European Parliament. There remain significant gaps in our understanding of how parties and MEPs adopt their environmental positions: for example, are these primarily shaped by ideological or party-political factors, country or regional representation or other factors such as lobbying? It will also be important to analyze whether and how the radical right groups in the EP influence the ambition of key environmental legislation and how the Commission, the Council and other parties in the EP respond. Crucially, with the far right politically ascendant across many Member States, will the two radical right groups in the EP become a more coherent force on environmental issues? And will the center-right EPP be dragged rightwards to vote more frequently with the ECR and Patriots for Europe on environmental legislation? At a point where decisive action is needed on the environment and climate change, can the European Parliament stay the course?

References

Burns, C. (2019) 'In the eye of the storm? The European Parliament, the environment and the EU's crises', *Journal of European Integration*, 41 (3), pp. 311–327.

Burns, C. (2021) 'The European Parliament', in: Jordan, A. and Gravey, V. (eds.) *Environmental policy in the EU: Actors, institutions and processes.* Fourth Edition. London: Routledge, pp. 128–146.

Burns, C. and Carter, N. (2010) 'Is co-decision good for the environment? An analysis of the European Parliament's green credentials', *Political Studies*, 58(1), pp. 123–142.

Burns, C., Carter, N. and Worsfold, N. (2012) 'Enlargement and the environment: The changing behaviour of the European Parliament', *Journal of Common Market Studies.* 50(1), pp. 54–70.

Burns, C., Carter, N., Davies, G. and Worsfold, N. (2013) 'Still saving the earth? The European Parliament's environmental record', *Environmental Politics*, 22(6), pp. 935–954.

Buzogány, A., and Ćetković, S. (2021) 'Fractionalized but ambitious? Voting on energy and climate policy in the European Parliament', *Journal of European Public Policy*, 28(7), pp. 1038–1056.

Costa, M. (2025) 'EU omnibus sustainability proposal: Why experts are concerned', *Green Central Banking.* Available at: https://greencentralbanking.com/2025/02/26/eu-sustainability-omnibus-proposal/ (Accessed: 10 June 2025).

Delreux, T. and Burns, C. (2019) 'Parliamentarizing a politicized policy: Understanding the involvement of the European Parliament in UN climate negotiations' *Politics and Governance*, 7(3), pp. 339–349.

European Commission (2019) 'The European Green Deal', *COM*(2019) 640 final. Available at: https://eur-lex.europa.eu/legal-content/EN/TXT/?uri=COM%3A2019%3A640%3AFIN (Accessed: 16 May 2024).

European Commission (2025) *Commission simplifies rules on sustainability and EU investments, delivering over €6 billion in administrative relief.* Available at: https://finance.ec.europa.eu/publications/commission-simplifies-rules-sustainability-and-eu-investments-delivering-over-eu6-billion_en (Accessed: 10 June 2025)

Farstad, F. et al. (2024) 'EUs klimaregelverk vedtatt: Hva nå for Norge?', *CICERO Report* 01:24. Available at: https://nva.sikt.no/registration/0198cc51c921-54d8ca20-4458-4721-96a3-a84edf9819b3. (Accessed: 25 June 2025).

Hix, S., Noury, A. and Roland, G. (2007) *Democratic politics in the European Parliament.* Cambridge: Cambridge University Press.

Hodgson, R. (2021) 'What to expect in this autumn's green policy "tsunami"', *ENDs Europe*, 3 September.

Jordan, A. and Liefferink, D. (eds.) (2004) *Environmental policy in Europe: The Europeanization of national environmental policy.* London: Routledge.

Judge, D. (1992) '"Predestined to save the earth": The environment committee of the European Parliament', *Environmental Politics*, 1(4), pp. 186–212.

Lenschow, A., Burns, C. and Zito, A. (2020) 'Dismantling, disintegration or continuing stealthy integration in European Union environmental policy?', *Public Administration*, 98(2), pp. 340–348.

Lynes, M. (2025) 'Interview: Clean industrial deal puts EPP's Ehler in the driving seat', *The Parliament Magazine*, 14 May. Available at: https://www.theparliamentmagazine.eu/news/article/interview-clean-industrial-deal-puts-epps-ehler-in-the-driving-seat (Accessed: 9 June 2025).

Petri, F. and Biedenkopf, K. (2021) 'Weathering growing polarisation? The European Parliament and EU foreign climate policy ambitions', *Journal of European Public Policy*, 28(7), pp. 1057 – 1075.

Petri, F., Zapletalová, V. and Biedenkopf, K. (2023) 'The European Parliament: A strong internal actor with external ambitions', in: Rayner, T. Szulecki, K. Jordan, A. and Oberthür, S. (eds.) *Handbook on European Union Climate Change Policy and Politics*. Cheltenham: Edward Elgar, pp. 53 – 67.

POLITICO (2024) *Poll of Polls—EU Election 2024*. Available at: https://www.politico.eu/europe-poll-of-polls/european-parliament-election/ (Accessed: 21 February 2024).

Ripoll Servant, A. (2018) *The European Parliament*. London: Palgrave.

Tsebelis, G. and Kalandrakis, A. (1999) 'The European Parliament and environmental legislation: The case of chemicals', *European Journal of Political Research*, 36(1), pp. 119 – 154.

Weale, A. et al. (2000) *Environmental governance in Europe*. Oxford: Oxford University Press.

Wendler, F. (2019) 'The European Parliament as an arena and agent in the politics of climate change: Comparing the external and internal dimension', *Politics and Governance*, 7(3), pp. 327 – 338.

Rüdiger K.W. Wurzel, Duncan Liefferink and Maurizio di Lullo

Environmental leadership and intergovernmental bargaining in the European Union

Abstract: This chapter offers a critical assessment of intergovernmental bargaining between European Union (EU) Member States in the environmental policy field. It analyzes these dynamic intergovernmental relationships and focuses on different alliances between Member States in EU environmental policy. The chapter explains how environmental leaders can try to overcome political stalemates in the Council of the EU—and most of all the Environmental Council—as well as the European Council, which has become involved in the high politics of climate policy issues in recent years. It differentiates between environmental leaders who purposefully aim to attract followers and environmental pioneers who are primarily concerned about their own domestic environmental policies. The chapter assesses what types of environmental leadership and pioneership the EU and its Member States have provided.

Keywords: Environmental leaders, pioneers and followers; intergovernmental bargaining; Member States; Council of the European Union; European Council

1 Introduction

Environmental leadership literature emerged out of a body of general leadership literature, which initially focused primarily on powerful political leaders such as American presidents (Burns 1978, 2003; Blondel, 1987; Mascuilli, 2009; Rhodes and 't Hart, 2014). In contrast, much of the early environmental leadership literature, which was heavily influenced by international relations studies, mainly analyzed what role states and/or international institutions play during the negotiation and adoption of international environmental agreements and regimes (Young, 1991; Underdal, 1994; Malnes, 1995). The European Union (EU) featured only infrequently in early environmental leadership studies for two main reasons. First, the EU adopted a common environmental policy only relatively late compared to early environmental leader states such as Sweden, the United States (US) and Japan, which had instituted fairly ambitious domestic environmental policies already by the early 1970s (Weidner and Jänicke, 2002; Schreurs, 2003; Jänicke, 2005). Second, the EU was purposefully designed as a 'leaderless Europe' which "deliberately shun[ned] the institution of an overriding leadership" (Hayward, 2008, p. 1). This made it challenging, although not impossible,

Note: The views expressed by Maurizio di Lullo are his personal views and not those of the Council of the EU.

https://doi.org/10.1515/9783111321523-015

for the EU to develop its own environmental leadership capabilities. Much of the early EU environmental leadership literature therefore focused mainly on Member States that acted as environmental leaders and how they tried to influence EU environmental policy (Héritier, Knill and Mingers, 1996; Andersen and Liefferink, 1997; Liefferink and Andersen, 1998; Schreurs and Tiberghien, 2007; Knill, Heichel and Arndt, 2012; Liefferink and Wurzel, 2017; Liefferink et al., 2023).

As the EU increasingly developed more comprehensive environmental policy measures, the literature shifted its focus towards the Europeanization of Member States' environmental policies and politics (Knill and Lenschow, 1998; Börzel, 2000; Zito, 2000; Jordan and Liefferink, 2004). A more general, not specifically EU-related literature focused on the transfer and diffusion of domestic environmental innovations by European and non-European environmental leader states (Vogel, 1995; Weidner and Jänicke, 2002; Jänicke, 2005; Biedenkopf, 2012; Hanf and Jansen, 2014).

The EU's initial lack of a common environmental policy became painfully apparent at the 1972 United Nations (UN) Stockholm Conference where Member States spoke with different voices (Bungarten, 1987, p. 142). The Heads of State or Government (e.g., the French president, German chancellor and Italian prime minister) of the EU's Member States subsequently gave the starting signal for a common environmental policy at a Paris meeting in October 1972 (Bungarten, 1978, pp. 135–143; Rehbinder and Stewart, 1985, pp. 16–17; Hildebrand, 1992; Delreux and Happaerts, 2016; Knill and Liefferink, 2021). As explained below, the Heads of Government or State rarely get involved in EU environmental issues which are widely perceived as relatively technical, low politics issues. Instead, it is the Council of the EU (Council, hereon) that is involved on a day-to-day basis in the EU environmental lawmaking process.

Although domestic and foreign EU environmental policies are closely interlinked (Delreux and Happaerts, 2016), this chapter focuses mainly on domestic EU environmental policy (for EU external environmental policy see Chapter 29). It proceeds as follows. The next section highlights intergovernmental bargaining. An assessment of the role of environmental leaders, pioneers and followers follows. The remaining sections focus on the Council and the European Council before the Conclusion offers a summary and an outlook for possible future research directions.

2 Intergovernmental bargaining

Intergovernmental bargaining between Member States has always been a prominent feature of EU environmental policymaking. It occurs mainly within EU institutions —primarily, the Council and the European Council (see below)—and outside EU institutions in bilateral or multilateral relations. Importantly, it centers not only on the level of stringency for EU environmental standards but also on nationally preferred environmental regulatory styles, policy instruments and institutional structures (Héritier, Knill and Mingers, 1996; Knill and Lenschow, 1998; Jordan and Liefferink, 2005; Wurzel, Zito and Jordan, 2013). For example, in the 1980s major political disagreements occurred between Germany and the United Kingdom (UK) about the EU's environmental policy. Germany preferred uniform EU-wide environmental limits derived from the best available technology (BAT) principle which constitutes an important action-guiding principle in German domestic environmental policy; the UK pushed for more flexible environmental quality objectives cost-effective policy measures that fitted its domestic best practicable means and best available techniques not entailing excessive cost (BATNEEC) principles (Weale, 1992; Héritier, Knill and Mingers, 1996; Knill and Lenschow, 1998; Weale et al., 2000; Wurzel, 2002). Consequently, the resulting EU environmental laws referred to both the BAT principle and the BATNEEC principle.

The EU's consensus-seeking decision-making style (Hayes-Renshaw and Wallace, 2006; Lewis, 2022; Wurzel, Liefferink and Torney, 2019) frequently leads to the adoption of common environmental laws, which stipulate derogations, exemptions, differentiated implementation deadlines, review clauses and vague phrases that allow for a wide interpretation of legal obligations during implementation (Wurzel, 2021, p. 81). Package deals and side payments (e.g., additional funding from the EU's structural funds in exchange for support for certain environmental policy measures) usually help the EU to resolve intractable intergovernmental stalemates (Wurzel, Liefferink and Torney, 2019; Dieters, 2021). This helps explain why the EU has been frequently able to get agreement from reluctant Member States who may otherwise have tried to block adoption of EU environmental policy measures. It is one important reason for why EU environmental laws are usually significantly more ambitious than the lowest common denominator (Dieters, 2021).

Since the early 1970s, Denmark, Germany and the Netherlands have widely been seen as a 'green trio' that expanded into a 'green sextet' when Austria, Finland and Sweden joined the EU in 1995 (Andersen and Liefferink, 1997; Liefferink and Andersen, 1998; Liefferink and Wurzel, 2017). Within the EU, however, there are no semipermanent alliances of environmental leader states across a wide range of environmental issues. Instead, such alliances "have to be formed on an issue-by-issue basis and remain liable to defection" (Liefferink and Andersen, 1998, p. 262). The environmental leaders among Member States nevertheless often end up supporting similar EU environmental measures even without formal coordination (Liefferink and Wurzel, 2017, p. 955). The EU's environmental leader states have exerted significant influence on EU environmental policy despite remaining in a minority among Member States.

On the international level there has been a "'historical come-and-go' of environmental pioneers" (Liefferink et al., 2009, p. 679). Since the 1970s, the US has oscillated between acting as an environmental leader and laggard (Selin and VanDeever, 2021). No such extreme swings between environmental leader and laggard positions have (as yet), or at least not within such relatively short time spans, occurred with any EU Member States, although changes in government have frequently triggered alterations in the environmental ambitions and positions of those Member States, especially in Southern Europe and Central and Eastern Europe. For example, in Spain Socialist and Conservative governments have regularly adopted somewhat different national positions on EU environmental issues. The same applies to the Polish right-wing populist Justice and Law Party and the liberal-conservative Civic Platform (see also Chapter 11).

Some of the EU's erstwhile environmental leaders have considerably watered down their environmental ambitions since the 1990s. For example, Germany became more cost conscious since reunification occurred between the former East and West Germanys in 1990 (Wurzel, 2008a, 2021, p. 87). In the 1980s Germany acted as the main pusher for more ambitious EU car emission limits (Holzinger, 1994; Wurzel, 2002). Denmark and the Netherlands supported its efforts (Liefferink, 1996). However, in the 2020s, Germany lobbied hard against EU legislation that demanded the phasing out of combustion engines in cars in favor of electric vehicles by 2035 (Dieters, 2021). Important differences exist on this issue amongst political parties in Germany. Since the 2000s, the Netherlands has lowered its environmental leadership ambitions by offering mainly 'cost-free leadership' (Liefferink and Birkel, 2011) or 'fading leadership' (Wiering, Liefferink and Beijen, 2018).

Although the Franco-German alliance is frequently seen as the engine for deeper European integration, the regular bilateral meetings between French and German Environment Ministers have not tangibly impacted EU environmental policy (Wurzel, 2008a). This is largely because France and Germany have often adopted differing positions on environmental issues (Héritier, Knill and Mingers, 1996; Wurzel, 2021, p. 76). Similarly, the Weimar Triangle, which France, Germany and Poland established in 1991, has rarely focused on environmental issues despite demands from environmental groups for a 'Green Weimar Triangle' (Germanwatch, 2024).

Denmark, Finland and Sweden frequently discuss environmental issues within the Nordic Council (Iceland, Norway, Faroe Islands, Greenland and Åland Islands are also members). During their EU accession negotiations in the early 1990s, Austria, Finland, Norway and Sweden regularly met to coordinate their negotiation strategies, for which environmental issues constituted a priority area. However, since Austria, Finland and Sweden joined in 1995—Norway failed to join following the 'no' vote in a referendum—they no longer meet regularly before important EU meetings. This is partly because semipermanent alliances of environmental leader states are widely considered to be detrimental to finding compromises within the Council and European Council (Liefferink and Wurzel, 2017; Wurzel, Liefferink and Torney, 2019; Wurzel, 2021).

However, in the 2010s, the Visegrád countries (Czechia, Hungary, Poland and Slovakia) challenged this informal norm by developing highly institutionalized coordination mechanisms to agree on common policy stances on EU policies, including environmental policy (Braun, 2014; Wurzel, Liefferink and Di Lullo, 2019; Wurzel, Di Lullo and Liefferink, 2023, pp. 47–48). The Visegrád group also reached out to other countries (including Bulgaria, Croatia and Romania) while trying to water down EU climate policies. Tobin and colleagues (2023, p. 187 and passim) have termed this type of conduct 'negative climate leadership', although environmental leadership has traditionally been defined as (environmental policy) action, which tries to solve a collective action problem (Young, 1991; Underdal, 1994; Liefferink and Wurzel, 2017).

3 Different types of environmental leadership and pioneership

To understand better how environmental leaders and pioneers can act as 'agents of change' (Liefferink and Wurzel, 2017), we need to focus on the different types of environmental leadership and pioneership which they can exhibit. Different, often overlapping, typologies exist. While Young (1991) differentiates between structural, entrepreneurial and intellectual leadership, Underdal (1994) identifies coercive, instrumental and unilateral leadership. Grubb and Gupta (2000) focus on structural, instrumental and directional leadership, and Parker and colleagues (2015) distinguish between structural, directional, idea-based and instrumental leadership.

For this chapter we have adopted Liefferink and Wurzel's (2017) fourfold typology which differentiates between: (1) structural, (2) entrepreneurial, (3) cognitive and (4) exemplary leadership and distinguishes between environmental leaders, who actively seek to attract followers, and environmental pioneers who do not do so (see also Wurzel, Connelly and Liefferink, 2017; Wurzel, Liefferink and Di Lullo, 2019; Wurzel, Di Lullo and Liefferink, 2023; Tobin, Torney and Biedenkopf, 2023; Leenders, Liefferink and Smeets, 2024). There is wide agreement that environmental leaders and pioneers can offer different types of leadership sequentially or simultaneously. Although environmental leadership and pioneership have been attributed also to non-state actors (Liefferink and Wurzel, 2017; Wurzel, Connelly and Liefferink, 2017; Wurzel, Liefferink and Torney, 2019; Torney, 2019; Tobin, Torney and Biedenkopf, 2023), this chapter focuses merely on states.

First, structural leadership and pioneership are primarily associated with economic and military power; the latter plays no significant role for EU environmental policy. Secondly, entrepreneurial leadership and pioneership require the use of negotiation and diplomatic skills to broker compromises that are acceptable to others. Thirdly, cognitive leadership and pioneership demand the generation and provision of ideas and expertise which can redefine actors' interests and preferences. Fourthly, exemplary leadership and pioneership necessitate the setting of good examples. However, while exemplary *leadership* takes place with the intention of attracting followers, this is not the case for exemplary *pioneership*, which instead is aimed primarily at domestic environmental problem-solving. Policy transfer literature in particular has identified examples of unintentional exemplary pioneership (Tews, Busch and Jörgens, 2003; Jänicke, 2005; Biedenkopf, 2012).

Within the EU, Denmark has frequently acted as an environmental pioneer by adopting unilaterally ambitious domestic environmental policies. Germany by contrast has, mainly due to competitiveness concerns for its large manufacturing industry, repeatedly made its environmental leadership conditional on other Member States adopting the same or similar policy measures (Andersen and Liefferink, 1997; Liefferink and Andersen, 1997; Liefferink and Wurzel, 2017; Wurzel, 2021, p. 87). The EU's Single European Market (SEM) rules severely constrain Member States' ability to adopt unilaterally more stringent product standards because they can create barriers to trade which are prohibited under SEM rules that protect the free movement of goods, people, services and capital. Only public emergencies (e.g., an environmental catastrophe) allow Member States to adopt restrictions on the free movement of goods. In contrast, Member States are largely free to adopt their own domestic process standards, which set (environmental) standards for how products are produced, unless the EU has already adopted common process standards (Rehbinder and Stewart, 1985; Scharpf, 1996; Wurzel, 2008a; Dieters, 2021).

Denmark tested the limits of imposing restrictions on the free movement of products on environmental grounds when it introduced a more stringent national bottles deposit-and-recycling scheme: it restricted the number of different types of bottles that could be sold in Denmark by domestic producers and foreign importers, the latter considering the Danish law to be discriminatory and a barrier to trade for their products. The European Court of Justice (which was renamed Court of Justice of the EU by the 2009 Lisbon Treaty) largely sided with Denmark although it emphasized the need for proportionality when adopting such national environmental measures (Liefferink and Andersen, 1998, p. 257).

Leenders and colleagues (2024) have introduced the term 'sequential leadership' for the dynamic that environmental leaders can engender into the EU environmental policy making process when they each offer different leadership types sequentially. When the EU extended its emissions trading scheme (ETS) to buildings, road transport and additional sectors (ETS2), Denmark provided cognitive leadership, Germany offered exemplary and structural leadership, and the Commission and rotating Presidencies exhibited cognitive and entrepreneurial leadership (Leenders, Liefferink and Smeets, 2024).

Research has focused more strongly on environmental leaders than on followers although there are exceptions (Karlson et al., 2012; Parker, Karlsson and Hjerpe, 2015; Torney, 2015, 2019; Liefferink et al., 2023). Important reasons for it constitute the "methodological and evidential challenges associated with convincingly identifying followers and followership" (Wurzel, Liefferink and Torney, 2019, p. 12). It is methodologically challenging to show that particular actions by environmental leaders have indeed caused environmental followers to emulate environmental leaders. Importantly, environmental followers which adopt the environmental innovations originally developed by environmental leaders can themselves start promoting those environmental innovations (Leenders, Liefferink and Smeets, 2024). Moreover, environmental followers may actually further advance the innovation originally generated by environmental leaders. A good example is Germany's initial outright opposition to the EU ETS (Wurzel, 2008b) and subsequent environmental (co-)leadership during the revisions and extension of the EU ETS (Leenders, Liefferink and Smeets, 2024; Wettestad, 2025).

4 Council of the European Union

Although legally speaking there is only one Council, the ministers responsible for particular policy areas meet separately in different Council formations. The first meeting of the Member States' ministers responsible for environmental policy took place in 1973 (Bungarten, 1978). The ministerial meetings constitute only the tip of the iceberg of the Council system, which is "at the institutional heart of decision-making in the EU" (Lewis, 2022, p. 156). The Committee of the Permanent Representatives of the Governments of the Member States to the EU (COREPER), which is made up of national officials from the Member States' Permanent Representations in Brussels, prepares ministerial meetings. Their work is supported by approximately 250 Council working groups which are attended by Member State officials from the relevant national ministries. The Environment Working Group was established in 1973.

The Working Groups and COREPER try to achieve as much consensus as possible on dossiers before the Ministers in the Council discuss them. Estimates range from 65 percent to up to 90 percent for the number of dossiers that are agreed on in principle already by the working groups and/or COREPER (Hayes-Renshaw and Wallace, 2006, p. 53; Häge, 2008, p. 554). Such dossiers are then put on the Council's agenda as so-called A-points which are normally adopted by the ministers without further discussion, although Member States can call for a vote (which happens only infrequently). Despite qualified majority voting (QMV) now being formally applicable to most EU environmental dossiers, the Council usually adopts its decisions by consensus. The frequent meetings between Member State officials within the elaborate Council system and the regular ministerial meetings encourage the adoption of problem-solving approaches instead of pure intergovernmental bargaining (Scharpf, 2011). This is not to downplay the importance of intergovernmental bargaining in the Council which however is both a negotiating forum for member governments *and* an EU institution (Hayes-Renshaw and Wallace, 2006; Lewis, 2022; Wurzel, 2021, p. 76).

The six-monthly presidency, which rotates between Member States, chairs all meetings of the Council including working groups, COREPER and ministerial Council meetings. The exception is the Foreign Affairs Council which is chaired by the High Representative for Foreign Affairs and Security Policy. The presidency used to chair also European Council meetings until the 2009 Lisbon Treaty established an elected president for the European Council. The presidency involves the following, at times conflicting, main roles: (1) manager and administrator, (2) point of contact (for other Member States and EU institutions), (3) honest broker, (4) initiator and (5) external representative (Wurzel, 1996, 2021; Hayes-Renshaw and Wallace, 2006; Lewis, 2022).

The Council Secretariat supports the presidencies, offering administrative support and advice and providing continuity. Especially the large Member States (e.g., France and, until Brexit, the UK) tend to make use of the initiator role while small Member States and the Council Secretariat usually emphasize the centrality of the honest broker and mediator role. The initiator role allows presidencies to shape the Council's agenda (Tallberg, 2006). Presidency holders can try to slow down or speed up, which is more difficult because it also strongly depends on the actions of other EU actors (such as the Commission and EP), progress on particular dossiers without violating the honest broker role. Occasionally such violations nevertheless occur. For example, the 1999 German EU presidency took off the Council's agenda the end-of-life vehicles directive, which imposed recycling obligations on car producers, fearing that it might negatively impact Germany's largest automobile company, although this action merely temporarily slowed down the adoption process of the directive (Wurzel, 2000). However, such violations of the honest broker norm tend to constitute exceptions which prove the rule.

The Council has developed relatively strong entrepreneurial environmental leadership capacities as a result of regular ministerial meetings and frequent COREPER and Council Working Group meetings. It has also acquired considerable structural leadership capacities, as the Council has authoritative decision-making powers when it adopts (together with the EP) EU environmental laws. The Council's cognitive leadership capacity appears more limited. Member States (and the Commission) tend to provide more strong cognitive leadership (Wurzel, Liefferink and Torney, 2019). During its EU presidency in 1992 the UK launched the Cardiff strategy according to which all non-Environment Council formations had to report on how they could integrate environmental requirements into their dossiers. Consequently, joint councils (e.g., joint Energy and Environment Councils) briefly flourished in the 1990s. This was in line with the idea that environmental policy is a typical cross-sectoral policy whose requirements ought to be taken seriously in all EU policies. However, no formal joint councils have taken place since the early 2000s (Wurzel, 2021, p. 84). By the early 2010s, the Cardiff strategy (or environmental policy integration as it became known) was 'as dead as a dodo' (Interview, UK official, 2012; Wurzel, Liefferink and Torney 2019, p. 259; Wurzel, Di Lullo and Liefferink, 2023, p. 43). The need for climate policy integration has become an important issue since the adoption of the European Green Deal in 2019 (see Chapter 30). Whether it will suffer a similar fate as the unsuccessful Cardiff strategy remains to be seen. The fact that a 30% share of the EU's multiannual financial framework for 2021–2027 ought to be devoted to climate-related measures increases the chances for success for climate policy integration (see also Chapters 20 and 33). However, economic pressures and the EU's functionalist integration logic, which is reflected in the Council's different formations, militate against climate policy integration efforts.

5 European Council

The European Council is attended by the Heads of State or Government of the Member States as well as the president of the European Council and the European Commission president. The High Representative of the Union for Foreign Affairs and Security Policy also attends the European Council when foreign affairs issues are on its agenda.

Since the 2009 Lisbon Treaty, the European Council has normally held four formal meetings per year. It can organize additional meetings at short notice, for example, in crisis situations (such as the financial crisis, Covid-19 pandemic and Russia's full-scale invasion of Ukraine).

After the European Council gave the starting signal for a common environmental policy in 1972 (Bungarten, 1978), it only occasionally concerned itself with environmental issues (Wurzel, Liefferink and Torney, 2019; Wurzel, Di Lullo and Liefferink, 2023). One relatively rare example includes the 1992 European Council meeting in Edinburgh, which issued a detailed declaration on the correct interpretation of the principle of subsidiarity. It triggered the publication of an Anglo-Franco hit list of (environmental and other) laws to be repatriated, although none of these laws targeted was eventually scrapped (Wurzel, 2021, p. 86). One important reason for the infrequent interventions by the European Council in environmental policy is that the EU (environmental) laws are adopted by the Council (together with the EP), whereas the European Council provides the general political guidelines which determine the overall political direction of the EU. Moreover, environmental issues are often regarded as 'low politics' issues that require a relatively high degree of technical expertise. The Council (and especially its Environment Working Group) can generate more easily this type of expertise than the European Council, which normally focuses primarily on 'high politics' issues such as foreign policy issues. However, the European Council has occasionally acted as an arbiter and/or final decision-maker for dossiers on which the Council has failed to reach agreement due to unbridgeable differences between Member States within the Council. For example, on EU climate policy, the European Council has repeatedly had to identify compromise solutions which were acceptable to both the richer Western European Member States, most of which were keen to adopt ambitious EU climate policy measures, and the poorer Central and Eastern European Member States, which were concerned about the possible negative impact of such measures on their domestic economic development (Wurzel, Liefferink and Torney, 2019, p. 253).

Since the 2000s, the European Council has increasingly involved itself in climate policy issues. This was the case, for example, with regard to the climate and energy package for 2020, for which major disagreements between some Member States remained unresolved at the Council level in 2008. The European Council issued a fairly detailed compromise proposal that was subsequently adopted by the Council and EP, although the European Council does not have any formal rights to issue instructions to the Council and/or EP during the EU lawmaking process. Since then, additional fairly detailed interventions by the European Council on EU climate policy followed (Wurzel, Liefferink and Torney, 2019; Wurzel, Di Lullo and Liefferink, 2023).

6 Conclusion

Environmental leaders and pioneers have been able to exert considerable influence on EU environmental policies. There is relatively wide agreement that Denmark, Germany and the Netherlands used to make up a 'green trio' which was extended to a 'green sextet' when Austria, Finland and Sweden joined the EU. However, the environmental ambitions of some environmental leaders and pioneers have waned over time and/or never been very strong on particular issues. All environmental leaders and pioneers have some (environmental) blind spots, which can vary in size across time.

Importantly, environmental leaders and pioneers have not formed any semipermanent alliances for fear that this could make more challenging the search for consensus within the Council. The Visegrád countries, concerned that what they consider to be overly ambitious EU climate policies might negatively impact their economies, have challenged the informal norm that semipermanent alliances between Member States should not be formed within the Council. It remains to be seen whether the Visegrád countries' institutionalized coordination mechanisms for agreeing on common stances on EU (environmental) policies before Council and European Council meetings will endure, given that they are a Member State grouping whose interests diverge fairly sharply on other EU policy issues (such as Russia's full-scale war on Ukraine, for which Poland and Hungary have adopted diametrically opposed positions).

The environmental leaders and pioneers have provided structural, entrepreneurial, cognitive and exemplary environmental leader- and pioneership, either sequentially or simultaneously. While structural leadership capacities are strongly dependent on power resources (which tend to be concentrated in the larger Member States), this is not necessarily the case for entrepreneurial, cognitive and exemplary environmental leadership and pioneership. It helps explain why relatively small Member States (e.g., Denmark and Sweden) have been relatively successful influencing EU environmental policy.

Future research could focus more strongly on the dynamic effects that environmental leaders/pioneers can engender in the EU environmental policymaking process by offering different types of environmental leadership/pioneership sequentially and/or simultaneously. This may also include the role of nonstate actors, such as business or nongovernmental organizations, acting as leaders/pioneers (cf. Wurzel, Liefferink and Torney, 2019). Relatively little is also known about the interrelations between environmental leaders/pioneer and followers who, over time, may possibly overtake the initial environmental leaders/pioneers in terms of their environmental ambitions. Intergovernmental bargaining between environmental leaders/pioneers and environmental laggards can lead to decisional deadlock, which may not easily be resolvable by environmental followers joining the group of Member States with high environmental ambitions.

References

Andersen, M.S. and Liefferink, D. (eds.) (1997) *European environmental policy: The pioneers.* Manchester: Manchester University Press.

Biedenkopf, K. (2012) 'Environmental leadership through the diffusion of pioneering policy', in: Gallagher, D. (ed.) *Environmental leadership. A reference handbook.* London: Sage, pp. 105 – 112.

Blondel, J. (1987) *Political leadership: Towards a general analysis.* London: Sage.

Börzel, T.A. (2000) 'Why there is no Southern problem', *Journal of European Public Policy*, (7)1, pp. 141 – 162.

Braun, M. (2014) 'EU climate norms in East-Central Europe', *Journal of Common Market Studies*, 52(3), pp. 455 – 560.

Bungarten, H.H. (1978) *Umweltpolitik in Westeuropa.* Bonn: Europa Union Verlag.

Burns, C., Eckersley, P. and Tobin, P. (2020) 'EU environmental policy in times of crisis', *Journal of European Public Policy*, 27(1), pp. 1 – 19.

Burns, J.M. (1978) *Leadership.* New York: Harper & Row.

Burns, J.M. (2003) *Transforming leadership.* New York: Grove Press.

Delreux, T. and Happaerts, S. (2016) *Environmental policy and politics in the European Union.* London: Palgrave Macmillan.

Dieters, H. (2021), 'Policy making', in: Jordan, A. and Gravey, V. (eds.) *Environmental policy in the EU.* Abingdon: Routledge, pp. 186 – 202.

Germanwatch (2024) *Green Weimar Triangle should become a driving force for EU climate policy*, Germanwatch. Available at: https://www.germanwatch.org/en/90954 (Accessed: 25 March 2025).

Gupta, A. and Grubb, M. (eds.) (2000) *Climate change and European leadership.* Dordrecht: Kluwer Publishers.

Häge, F. (2008) 'Who decides in the Council of the European Union?', *Journal of Common Market Studies*, 46(3), pp. 533 – 558.

Hanf, K. and Jansen, A.-I. (2014), *Governance and environment in Western Europe.* Abingdon: Routledge.

Hayes-Renshaw, F. and Wallace, H. (2006) *The council of ministers.* Second edition. Basingstoke: Palgrave Macmillan.

Hayward, J. (ed.) (2008) *Leaderless Europe.* Oxford: Oxford University Press.

Héritier, A., Knill, C. and Mingers, S. (1996) *Ringing the changes in Europe.* Berlin: Walter de Gruyter.

Holzinger, K. (1994) *Politik des kleinsten gemeinsamen Nenners? Umweltpolitische Entscheidungprozesse in der EU am Beispiel der Einführung des Katalysators.* Berlin: Sigma.

Hildebrand, P. (1992) 'The European Community's dnvironmental policy, 1957 – 1992', *Environmental Politics*, 1(4), pp. 13 – 44.

Interview, UK official (2012) Interview (by the first named author) with a UK permanent representation official in 2012.

Jänicke, M. (2005) 'Trend-setters in environmental policy: The character and role of pioneer countries', *European Environment*, 15(2), pp. 129 – 142.

Jordan, A. and Liefferink, D. (eds.) (2004) *Environmental policy in Europe: The Europeanization of national environmental policy.* Abingdon: Routledge.

Karlsson, C., Hjerpe, M., Parker, C.F. and Linnér, B-O. (2011) 'The legitimacy of leadership in international climate change negotiations', *Ambio*, 41, pp. 46 – 55.

Knill, C. and Lenschow, A. (1998) 'Coping with Europe: The impact of British and German administrations on the implementation of EU environmental policy', *Journal of European Public Policy*, 5(4), pp. 595 – 614.

Knill, C., Heichel, S. and Arndt, D. (2012) 'Really a front-runner, really a straggler? Of environmental leaders and laggards in the European Union and beyond', *Energy Policy*, 48, pp. 36 – 45.

Knill, C. and Liefferink, D. (2021) *The establishment of EU environmental policy*, in: Jordan, A. and Gravey, V. (eds.) *Environmental policy in the EU.* Fourth edition. Abingdon: Routledge, pp. 13–32.

Leenders, E., Liefferink, D. and Smeets, S. (2024) 'Leadership in EU policy-making: A deep dive into the extension of the EU emissions trading system', *Journal of European Public Policy*, 31, pp. 1–23.

Lewis, J. (2022) 'The European Council and the Council of European Union', in: Cini, M. and Pérez-Solórzano Borragán, N. (eds.) *European Union politics.* Sixth edition. Oxford: Oxford University Press, pp. 156–174.

Liefferink, D. (1996) *Environment and the nation state. The Netherlands, the European Union and acid rain.* Manchester: Manchester University Press.

Liefferink, D. and Andersen, M.S. (1998) 'Strategies of the "green" member states in EU environmental policy-making', *Journal of European Public Policy*, (5)2, pp. 254–270.

Liefferink, D., Arts, B., Kamstra, J. and Ooijevaar, J. (2009) 'Leaders and laggards in environmental policy', *Journal of European Public Policy*, 16(5), pp. 677–700.

Liefferink, D. and Birkel, K. (2011) 'The Netherlands: A case of "cost-free leadership"', in: Wurzel, R. and Connelly, J. (eds.), *The European Union as a leader in international climate change politics.* Abingdon: Routledge, pp. 147–162.

Liefferink, D. and Wurzel, R. (2017) 'Environmental leaders and pioneers: Agents of change?', *Journal of European Public Policy*, 24(7), pp. 951–968.

Liefferink, D. et al. (2023) 'Leaders, pioneers and followers in environmental governance', in: Jörgens, H., Knill, C. and Steinebach, Y. (eds.) *Routledge handbook of environmental policy.* Abingdon: Routledge, 237-248.

Malnes, R. (1995) '"Leader" and "entrepreneur" in international negotiations: A conceptual analysis', *European Journal of International Relations*, 1(1), pp. 87–112.

Masciulli, J. (2009) *The Ashgate research companion to political leadership.* London: Ashgate.

Parker, C., Karlsson, C. and Hjerpe, M. (2015) 'Climate change leaders and followers: Leadership recognition and selection in the UNFCCC negotiations', *International Relations*, 29(4), pp. 434–454.

Rehbinder, E. and Stewart, R. (1985) *Integration through law: Europe and the American federal experience.* Berlin: Walter de Gruyter.

Rhodes, R.A.W. and 'T Hart, P. (eds.) (2014) *The Handbook of political leadership.* Oxford: Oxford University Press.

Scharpf, F.W. (1996) 'Negative and positive integration in the political economy of European Welfare States', in: Marks, G., Scharpf, F.W., Schmitter, P.C. and Streeck, W. (eds.) *Governance in the European Union.* London: Sage, pp. 15–39.

Scharpf, F.W. (2011) 'Introduction: The problem-solving capacity of multi-level governance', *Journal of European Public Policy*, 4(4), pp. 520–538.

Schreurs, M. (2003) *Environmental politics in Japan, Germany and the United States.* Cambridge: Cambridge University Press.

Schreurs, M. and Tiberghien, Y. (2007) 'Multi-Level reinforcement: Explaining European Union leadership in climate change mitigation', *Global Environmental Politics*, 7(4), pp. 19–46.

Selin, H. and VanDeever, S. (2021) 'Climate change politics and policies in the United States: Forward, reverse and through the looking glass', In: Wurzel, R., Andersen, M.S. and Tobin, P. (eds.) *Climate governance across the globe.* Abingdon: Routledge, pp. 123–140.

Tallberg, J. (2006) *Leadership and negotiations in the European Un*ion. Abingdon: Routledge.

Tews, K., Busch, P.-O. and Jörgens, H. (2003) 'The diffusion of new environmental policy instruments', *European Journal of Political Research*, 42(4), pp. 569–600.

Tobin, P., Torney, D. and Biedenkopf, K. (2023) Leadership: Global and domestic dimensions, in: Rayner, T. Szulecki, K., Jordan, A. and Oberthür, S. (eds.) *Handbook on European Union climate change policy and politics.* Cheltenham: Edward Elgar, pp. 187–200.

Torney, D. (2015) *European climate leadership in question: Policies toward China and India.* Massachusetts: MIT Press.

Torney, D. (2019) 'Follow the leader? Conceptualising the relationship between leaders and followers in polycentric climate governance', *Environmental Politics*, 28(1), pp. 167–186.

Underdal, A. (1994) 'Leadership theory: Rediscovering the arts of management', in: Zartman, W.I. (ed.) *International multilateral negotiation.* San Francisco: Jossey-Bass, pp. 178–197.

Vogel, D. (1995) *Trading up. Consumer and Environmental Regulation in a Global Economy.* Cambridge, Massachusetts: Harvard University Press.

Weale, A. (1992) *The new politics of pollution.* Manchester: Manchester University Press.

Weale, A., et al. (2000) *Environmental governance in Europe.* Oxford: Oxford University Press.

Weidner, H. and Jänicke, M. (eds.) (2002) *Capacity building in national environmental policy: A comparative study of 17 countries.* Berlin: Springer.

Wettestad, J. (2025) 'EU emissions trading for transport and buildings: Saved by synergistic institutional interaction?', *Journal of Common Market Studies*, 6(3), pp. 915–931.

Wiering, M., Liefferink, D. and Beijen, B. (2018) 'The internal and external face of Dutch environmental policy: a case of fading environmental leadership?', *Environmental Science and Policy*, 81, pp. 18–25.

Wurzel, R. (1996) 'The role of the EU Presidency in the environmental field', *Journal of European Public Policy*, (3)2, pp. 272–291.

Wurzel, R. (2000) 'Flying into unexpected turbulence: The German EU presidency in the environmental field', *German Politics*, 9(3), pp. 22–42.

Wurzel, R. (2002) *Environmental policy-making in Britain, Germany and the European Union.* Manchester: Manchester University Press.

Wurzel, R. (2008a) 'Environmental policy: EU actors, leader and laggard states', in: Hayward, J. (ed.) *Leaderless Europe.* Oxford: Oxford University Press, pp. 66–88.

Wurzel, R. (2008b) *The politics of emissions trading in Britain and Germany.* London: Anglo-German Foundation.

Wurzel, R. (2021) 'The Council, European Council and member states', in: Jordan, A. and Gravey, V. (eds.) *Environmental policy in the EU.* Fourth edition. London: Routledge, pp. 75–92.

Wurzel, R., Zito, A. and Jordan, A. (2013) *Environmental governance in Europe. A comparative analysis of new environmental policy instruments.* Cheltenham: Edward Elgar.

Wurzel, R., Connelly, J. and Liefferink, D. (eds.) (2017) *The European Union in international climate change politics.* Abingdon: Routledge.

Wurzel, R. Liefferink, D. and Torney, D. (2019) 'Pioneers, leaders and followers in multilevel and polycentric climate governance', *Environmental Politics.* 28(1), pp. 248–270.

Wurzel, R., Liefferink, D. and Di Lullo, M. (2019) 'The European Council, the Council and the Member States: Changing Environmental Leadership Dynamics in the European Union', *Environmental Politics.* 28(2), pp. 248–270.

Wurzel, R., Di Lullo, M. and Liefferink, D. (2023) 'The European Council, Council and Member States: Jostling for influence', in: Rayner, T., Szulecki, K., Jordan, A. and Oberthür, S. (eds.), *Handbook on European Union climate change policy and politics.* Cheltenham: Edward Elgar, pp. 38–52.

Young, O.R. (1991) 'Political leadership and regime formation: On the development of institutions in international society', *International Organization*, 45(3), pp. 281–308.

Zito, A. (2000) *Creating environmental policy in the European Union.* Basingstoke: Palgrave Macmillan.

Peter Eckersley

Multilevel governance, polycentricity, power, and European Union environmental policy

Abstract: Power relations between governing actors play a key role in decision-making. However, the literatures on polycentric, monocentric and multilevel governance have often neglected the importance of these relationships in shaping policy outcomes. This chapter places a broad understanding of power—one that incorporates power over, power to and power with—in the center of these debates. It shows how these three different conceptualizations of power correspond to more monocentric, polycentric and multilevel governance perspectives, respectively, as well as to preferences for different types of policy instruments (namely 'sticks', 'sermons' and 'carrots'). By bringing these literatures together and drawing on examples from European Union (EU) environmental policy over recent decades, the chapter presents a heuristic framework for understanding the linkages between typologies of power, governance and policy instruments. The framework can help to organize future research into (environmental) policy and governance, both within the EU and more broadly.

Keywords: Multilevel governance; polycentricity; monocentricity; power; policy instruments

1 Introduction

Scholars and policymakers have consistently emphasized that the European Union (EU) operates within a 'multilevel' context, particularly in the sphere of environmental policy (Jordan, 2000; Bulkeley and Betsill, 2003; Jänicke, 2017). More recent studies suggest that this context has become increasingly fragmented and 'polycentric', in that numerous governing authorities operate within the policy landscape, and they often seek to develop their own responses to environmental problems (Jordan et al., 2018; Tobin, Huitema and Kellner, 2024). This presents policymakers with challenges of coordination and steering when they seek to address environmental problems (Wurzel, Zito and Jordan, 2013), which are perhaps less obvious in more 'monocentric' contexts where central actors exert greater control. Relatedly, critiques of both multilevel and polycentric governance argue that neither perspective takes sufficient account of the importance of power relations between governing actors and therefore do not help to explain which actors exert the most influence over decision-making (Zito, 2015; Eckersley, 2018; Morrison et al., 2017).

This chapter will show how a broad conceptualization of power—one that incorporates power *over*, power *to*, and power *with* (Partzsch, 2017)—can help to explain the behavior of governing actors in classic monocentric, polycentric and multilevel governance arrangements. By extension, it can help to generate a better understand-

https://doi.org/10.1515/9783111321523-016

ing of the structures, actors, policy instruments and potential benefits and drawbacks involved in contrasting approaches to environmental policymaking. The chapter begins by setting out some of the key concepts and actors associated with multilevel, polycentric and monocentric governance, treating the three characterizations as ideal types. It then shows how the distribution of resources between governing actors influences the exercise of power (*over*, *to* and *with*) in policymaking and corresponds to more monocentric, polycentric and multilevel governance approaches respectively. Drawing on empirical examples from previous studies, it suggests that these power relationships and governance approaches may be reflected in policy design and the choice of policy instruments that actors adopt to tackle (environmental) problems. It then summarizes some of the normative drawbacks and benefits of the three different models.

2 Multilevel, polycentric and monocentric governance

With its origins in the study of EU regional policy (Marks, 1993), *multilevel* governance emphasizes the importance of collaboration across state and nonstate organizational boundaries to increase societal capacity to act. For several decades, scholars have stressed the importance of such arrangements for tackling 'wicked' (environmental) issues, such as climate change, given that individual governments are unable to address them alone (Lenschow, 1999; Jänicke, 2017). A multilevel perspective allows us to sketch out which actors are involved in policymaking and implementation and paint a more comprehensive picture of how societies are trying to address these challenges (Bulkeley and Betsill, 2003; Wurzel, Zito and Jordan, 2013). One common characterization proposes two contrasting types of multilevel governance, based on the institutional structures that predominate within a jurisdiction: Type I, in which static, multipurpose public authorities operate within a fairly rigid constitutional framework; and Type II, in which relationships between ad hoc and task-specific organizations are more fluid and dynamic (Hooghe and Marks, 2003). However, there has only been limited theorization about how and why the different types might emerge and evolve (Bache and Flinders, 2022), and they serve largely as illustrative heuristics rather than explanatory theoretical tools (Zito, 2015; Eckersley, 2017). Nonetheless, multilevel governance is based on an implicit assumption that the state plays the most important role in governing, and that studies should focus their attention on how governments seek to coordinate and steer public activities across different levels, in the pursuit of policy objectives (Homsy and Warner, 2018).

Polycentric governance also stresses that policymaking is dispersed across multiple centers of authority. Compared to the multilevel literature, however, it tends to place greater emphasis on the autonomy of different organizations and the importance of private and voluntary actors (Heinen, Arlati and Knieling, 2022). Based initially on the work of Elinor Ostrom (2010), polycentric governance suggests that these centers of authority can exercise substantial autonomy when governing their specific domains. By implication, state institutions do not necessarily coerce or steer these actors to work toward particular policy goals. Instead, governments expect (or hope) that autonomous actors will develop their own innovative practices and approaches to tackling societal problems at the local level (van der Heijden, 2018). Although critics have argued that this governance landscape is more likely to result in uncoordinated policymaking and 'free-riding' (Galaz et al., 2012), other scholars have countered that polycentricity represents a more realistic interpretation of how global environmental governance operates (Jordan et al., 2018).

Monocentric governance is often portrayed as the opposite of polycentricity, in that it involves strong central actors that can coerce others through hierarchical mechanisms in line with traditional state-centric approaches to governing (Tollefson, Zito and Gale, 2012). Based on this principle, scholars have sought to locate different governance arrangements along a spectrum of poly- and monocentricity, depending on the degree to which individual actors can exercise autonomy (Morrison et al., 2017; Kern et al., 2024). Monocentric contexts contrast with the fragmented institutional landscape of polycentric governance, even though power and authority will always be dispersed to some extent and therefore 'pure' monocentric systems are unlikely to exist in practice (Tobin, Huitema and Kellner, 2024).

For illustrative and comparative purposes, this chapter treats all three perspectives—multilevel, polycentric and monocentric governance—as ideal types. Given that multilevel governance implies a stronger coordinating role for central state actors than polycentricity but nonetheless recognizes that responsibilities and functions are dispersed within networks, I locate it between the two poles of mono- and polycentricity.[1] While both the EU more generally and individual Member States more particularly almost certainly exhibit elements of all three types of governance, the chapter shows how different conceptualizations of power within each model could help to explain contrasting approaches to policymaking. It then draws on examples from elsewhere in this volume and the wider literature to illustrate how they might operate in practice.

1 Given the dominance of fixed state institutions in 'Type I' multilevel governance arrangements and the more flexible and *ad hoc* nature of 'Type II' contexts, we could also locate the former toward the monocentric end of the spectrum and associate the latter more closely with polycentricity (Heinen, Arlati and Knieling, 2022). However, since these sub-types have the same theoretical roots and studies do not tend to apply them analytically, I group them together under the broad heading of multilevel governance for the purposes of this chapter.

3 Power and policy instruments in governance networks

Scholars have criticized multilevel and polycentric interpretations of governance due to their lack of a power dimension (Galaz et al., 2012; Eckersley, 2018; Morrison et al., 2017). Given that these characterizations tend to focus on identifying and sketching out policymaking actors within the governance landscape, rather than necessarily analyzing which of them are most influential and why, we can see how this is a valid criticism. Nonetheless, drawing on interdependence theory, we can examine the resources that each actor possesses and begin to appreciate how power relationships can shape decision-making contexts (Rhodes, 1981). Individual actors that possess most of the necessary resources to achieve their objectives can often exercise considerable power; conversely, if they need to rely heavily on other organizations for crucial or scarce resources, they occupy a weaker position within the governance network. The extent to which governing actors need to access resources from each other will influence whether relations between them are highly *inde*pendent, more *interde*pendent or largely *de*pendent (Eckersley, 2017, 2018).

This chapter suggests that power *over* and *de*pendence might be more important within highly monocentric arrangements, whereas applying power *to* and *inde*pendence perspectives can help us understand polycentric contexts better, and power *with* and *interde*pendence is more closely associated with multilevel governance. Furthermore, these different characterizations of power and governance contexts may also be reflected at the level of policy. Specifically, different types of policy instrument (such as those set out in Vedung's (1998) classic 'sticks, carrots and sermons' characterization) may be more closely associated with monocentric, multilevel and polycentric governance respectively. The remainder of this chapter sets out how these concepts relate to each other, illustrated by examples of EU environmental policy.

Power over, sticks and monocentric governance

Power *over* refers to a longstanding political science literature that understands power relations in coercive and hierarchical terms. Dahl (1957, pp. 202–203) argued that "*A* has power over *B* to the extent that he [*sic*] can get *B* to do something that *B* would otherwise not do". Shortly afterwards, Bacharach and Baratz (1963) expanded this definition to posit that actors can also exercise considerable power by controlling the political agenda and determining which issues come up for debate and consideration. Later, Lukes (1974) added a third dimension to interpretations of power *over*. He argued that existing power structures become so embedded in societal narratives, discourses and ideas that they have become 'hidden', and less influential individuals often submit to them subconsciously, contributing toward their own domination.

We can see how this interpretation of power applies in highly monocentric contexts, where strong central authorities can coerce public bodies and societal actors to act in a particular way and may also monitor and ensure compliance through hierarchical mechanisms. In the EU context this could manifest itself through regulations and directives; although Member States are responsible for implementing this legislation, it can still be enforced through the EU's legal apparatus. Within states, similar regulatory policies (i. e., 'sticks') are also illustrative of more monocentric governance arrangements. The United Kingdom's (UK) Clean Air Act 1956, which banned dark smoke emissions caused by the burning of coal in homes, factories, trains and boats (Longhurst et al., 2016), is a notable example.

Although governments at all levels usually rely on a mix or blend of different policy types to achieve their objectives, particularly in the environmental sector (Howlett and Rayner, 2007; Eckersley, Harrison and Poberezhskaya, 2023), a preference for regulations may well indicate that the governance context is located toward the monocentric end of the spectrum. Additionally, the central authority in this context possesses most of the resources required to govern (i. e., the ability to regulate and enforce compliance). Since other actors are much weaker, they are highly *de*pendent on this central authority to develop policies and initiatives that will address problems appropriately and effectively. By implication, monocentric actors can introduce policies fairly quickly and easily (because other actors are not able to muster sufficient opposition to resist them), and coercive regulations are often effective in changing behavior. However, they may be insufficiently tailored to local contexts, and stringent regulations are sometimes difficult to enforce (Heyes, 2000).

Power to, sermons and polycentric governance

We can also talk about power in terms of *em*powerment: providing individual actors with the resources to achieve their objectives (to "get things done", Parsons, 1963, p. 232) without necessarily coercing or dominating others (Morriss, 2002). This conceptualization of power suggests that where resources are distributed more symmetrically across the governance landscape, relationships between actors are placed on a more equal footing and those that might otherwise be fairly marginalized and power*less* can exert more influence (Partzsch, 2017). As a result, actors can operate *inde*pendently of each other in the pursuit of their own objectives, provided they possess the necessary resources to do so (Eckersley et al., 2025). By emphasizing autonomy and a lack of central hierarchy, this understanding of power is highly relevant for polycentric governance arrangements, in which individual actors develop their own approaches to tackling societal problems.

Instead of restrictive regulations, voluntary or informational initiatives (i. e., sermons) are more common in these contexts, since they give actors greater freedom from coercive control. Scholars have debated the prevalence and efficacy of such 'new' policy instruments for some time (Jordan, Wurzel and Zito, 2005; Wurzel, Zito and Jordan, 2013), and there is little doubt that they form an important part of the policy mix—not least because they are less likely to trigger societal opposition than hierarchical regulations (Eckersley, Harrison and Poberezhskaya, 2023). At the global level, for example, the Paris Agreement, which relies on individual states setting their own targets for reductions in greenhouse gas emissions and climate neutrality and cannot be enforced by a hierarchical central actor, is often cited as a key illustration of how polycentric governance operates in practice (Jordan et al., 2018). Perhaps reflecting the limited extent to which they can exert power in local governance contexts, municipal governments may also be keener to adopt sermons than sticks (Kirschke and Kosow, 2022; Chapter 15). However, although voluntary instruments may be politically popular, a lack of coercion means that some actors may 'free-ride' and not change their behavior, and therefore policies often fail to address the problem they intended to solve (Steinebach, 2022).

Power with, carrots and multilevel governance

Although Mary Parker Follett conceptualized the idea of power *with* long before Dahl (see Metcalf and Urwick, 1941), scholars have only begun to engage with it quite recently (Partzsch, 2017). As with power *to*, power *with* does not interpret the concept in terms of societal domination or hierarchy. Rather than prioritizing individual interests, however, it stresses the importance of concerted and collaborative action in the pursuit of common objectives. Although this perspective is sometimes portrayed in terms of societal resistance to oppression and violence (e.g., Arendt, 1970), we can see how it could also apply to state and societal actors working together for the common good. This requires cooperation, knowledge-sharing and collective learning and a belief that collective efforts will exceed those of individual actors (Abizadeh, 2023).

The emphasis on collaboration and mutual support to generate collective power suggests that it is most applicable in multilevel governance contexts, which stress (albeit often implicitly) the importance of policy coordination between tiers of government, between state and societal actors and between the domestic and the international (Piattoni, 2009). This perspective emphasizes the *interde*pendent nature of governance relationships, and the fact that all actors can contribute to the success (or otherwise) of policy initiatives (Eckersley et al., 2025). At the same time, we can see that it may be difficult to mobilize and steer the numerous different organizations that are involved in any single sector to ensure that policy is coherent and coordinated. Nonetheless, mutual assistance and support through (re)distributive instruments (i.e., carrots) such as funding schemes, financial incentives or capacity-building initiatives may help to achieve this outcome. Such policies can ensure that resources are spread out appropriately between different actors, thereby enabling them to undertake activities that contribute toward common societal goals. One example would be the German federal government's *Kommunalrichtlinie* initiative, which has provided funding to hundreds of municipalities across the country to develop climate protection and adaptation plans and also to employ officers to oversee these functions (Kern, Eckersley and Haupt, 2023). Given the important role that state and nonstate actors at all levels need to play in combating wicked issues such as climate change, perhaps it is not surprising that scholars have tended to adopt a multilevel governance perspective to examine policy in this sector (Bulkeley and Betsill, 2003; Kern, 2019).

4 Monocentric, polycentric and multilevel governance in EU environmental policy

Scholars have suggested that the EU, along with its Member States and much of the industrialized world, may be following a general trend away from monocentricity and sticks toward polycentricity and sermons (Jordan et al., 2018). Indeed, the bloc introduced a range of regulatory standards in its early decades, including on lead in petrol, water quality, air pollution and vehicle exhaust emissions, initially in the guise of harmonizing trade barriers (Wurzel, 2008) before pivoting toward voluntary policies more recently (Moore et al., 2021). This initial preference for sticks may be partly because the EU's governance arrangements were more monocentric in character: it had far fewer Member States and the Commission played an active role in policymaking (Deters, 2019). In the early years and decades, these core actors retained important policymaking resources and sought to exert power *over* polluting industries (and Member States) through stringent regulations. For their part, more ambitious Member States were highly *de*pendent on the EU to establish minimum environmental standards that would apply across the common market and therefore prevent other countries from establishing a competitive economic advantage by failing to act on environmental pollution.

However, as the bloc grew in size and incorporated more liberal market economies such as the UK, which were less inclined to agree to regulations, the EU began to embrace other types of environmental instrument. In particular, the Fifth Environmental Action Program that came into force in 1993 placed greater emphasis on economic and voluntary policies, partly due to Member State pressure for deregulation (Knill and Liefferink, 2007). Another trend has been toward greater flexibility in implementation through the principle of subsidiarity (Jordan, 2000) and a greater reliance on framework directives (for example, in air and water quality, Moore et al., 2021). Perhaps the most prominent example of a voluntary policy is the EU's ecolabeling scheme, which enables organizations to gain accreditation for the sustainability of the goods and services they provide, on the basis that they reach certain standards (Preziosi et al., 2019). These developments show how power and resources have been increasingly dispersed across a more polycentric governance landscape, in that Member States, industries and subnational entities have greater autonomy to act *inde*pendently of each other (power *to*), albeit within an overall framework that seeks to encourage environmental protection.

Such debates on policy instruments have sometimes run in parallel with studies into the 'dismantling' of environmental policy (Gravey and Jordan, 2016) and the extent to which this may have occurred following several decades of expansion (Zito, Burns and Lenschow, 2020). Although the EU environmental *acquis* may not have actually weakened in recent years, Burns, Eckersley and Tobin (2020) identified a 'slowing' of progress, which they attributed partly to the 2004 enlargement that made it more difficult to reach consensus on ambitious policies. Other factors, including the impact of the 2008 financial crisis and the increasing complexity of environmental problems that governments seek to address, have undoubtedly played a role in this process. Nonetheless, a more fragmented and polycentric governance context appears to have contributed toward a situation in which individual Member States (and the polluters that reside within them) are better placed to exercise the power *to* further their own objectives rather than necessarily prioritize the interests of EU citizens (power *with*) or be constrained by EU institutions (power *over*).

One exception to this trend has been in the area of climate mitigation (see Chapter 20), where the EU has continued to play a leading role on the global stage and introduced various mechanisms and instruments over recent decades. Foremost amongst these have been the Emissions Trading System (ETS) and the Green Deal, both of which are redistributive carrots. The ETS was established in 2005, following unsuccessful attempts at introducing a carbon tax, and it remains the world's largest cap-and-trade scheme for greenhouse gas emissions (Moore et al., 2021). The scheme sets an overall limit on these emissions and distributes allowances to industries, who are then able to trade these allowances with each other in a market (Hepburn et al., 2006). For its part, the Green Deal represents a break from the EU's recent trajectory toward sermons, in that it emphasizes the economic benefits to all citizens of transitioning to a more sustainable economy and achieving carbon neutrality. This policy package commits to substantial investment to help transform industries across the bloc and also seeks to involve and mobilize actors from across the governance landscape (Domorenok and Graziano, 2023) and thereby generate power *with*. Although this shift toward redistributive carrots may be initially limited to climate mitigation, an issue that has broad support from governments and citizens across the continent (Jordan and Gravey 2021), this most recent example may herald a return to more multilevel approaches in other areas of environmental policy.

5 Discussion and conclusions

Overall, we can see how monocentric, polycentric and multilevel governance arrangements correspond to power *over*, *to* and *with* and may ultimately manifest themselves at the policy level through regulations, voluntary instruments and (re)distributive initiatives respectively. This chapter treats all three governance arrangements (and, by extension, the different characterizations of power and the various types of policy) as 'ideal types' and therefore recognizes that jurisdictions are likely to exhibit elements of each of them. Nonetheless, Table 1 summarizes the above discussion and provides a heuristic to distinguish between the different concepts and organize future research.

Table 1: Power relationships and policy instruments in monocentric, polycentric and multilevel governance arrangements.

	Monocentric	**Polycentric**	**Multilevel**
Dominant power dynamic	Power *over*	Power *to*	Power *with*
Dominant principles	Hierarchy, compliance, control	Empowerment, autonomy	Cooperation, coordination
Resource distribution	Concentrated in central authority	Distributed across the governance landscape	Located in governance networks
Key actors and relationships	Peripheral actors *dependent* on central state authority	Individual state and societal actors operate *independently* of each other	State and societal actors operate *inter*dependently in governance networks
Dominant policy instrument types	Regulatory (sticks)	Voluntary (sermons)	(Re)distributive (carrots)
Policy examples	Limits on vehicle exhaust emissions	Eco-labeling	Green Deal
Potential benefits	Opportunity for decisive and effective action	Opportunity for innovation and tailored solutions	Opportunity for mobilization and policy coherence
Potential drawbacks	Societal opposition; inflexibility	Free riding; lack of action; incoherence	Steering can be difficult

As Table 1 suggests, the three different governance arrangements, as well as the various policy types, have their distinct benefits and drawbacks. Notably, each of these are related to the dominant power relationships that operate within them: opposition is more likely where monocentric actors seek to exercise excessive power *over* societal actors; polycentricity may lead to free-riding because potential polluters have the power *to* decide for themselves whether to change their behavior and steering can be difficult in multilevel arrangements, particularly if actors struggle to collaborate and agree on the policy goals that they should seek to achieve through power *with*. On reflection, therefore, perhaps we should not be surprised that all three governance contexts are present (albeit probably to varying degrees) in the EU and its Member States. Indeed, some kind of hybrid governance arrangement, as well as a mixture of policy types, may well represent the most effective approach for tackling societal problems. This is particularly the case in the environmental sector where, for example, transboundary air and water pollution render monocentric approaches insufficient, steering through multilevel governance structures may be difficult and a lack of hierarchical enforcement would increase the risk that offenders will free-ride. Different problems will require different solutions, and political and institutional contexts will also influence decisions around instrument choice. Indeed, we can see how policymakers face a significant challenge in selecting the most appropriate and effective blend of solutions to environmental problems, in terms of both the hybrid approach at the macro-level of governance and also the policy mix at the micro-level of instruments.

6 Conclusions

The EU appears to have shifted away from monocentricity and sticks toward an increasing reliance on polycentricity and sermons, probably due in part to the addition of new members over recent decades, which has made it more difficult to reach agreement on hierarchical regulations. However, the most recent example of the Green Deal suggests that it may be moving back away from polycentricity and toward a more multilevel approach, given the importance of redistributive carrots and the need to mobilize actors from across the governance landscape to tackle climate change.

It remains to be seen whether this trajectory will continue and extend to other areas of environmental policy. Since redistributive policies necessitate budgetary commitments, they require unanimous support from all twenty-seven Member States and the EU institutions to take effect, which is difficult to achieve. Despite this, however, the cumulative nature of EU environmental law means that older regulations are still in force and newer ones (such as CO_2 emissions performance standards for new vehicles) continue to join them, meaning that sticks still comprise a bigger share of the environmental *acquis* than 'newer' instruments (Moore et al., 2021). As such, the hybrid remains very much intact, even though the EU may have evolved in a polycentric direction over recent years.

Some may argue that the existence of such hybrids merely confirms that environmental policy operates within polycentric contexts. Nonetheless, it would be useful to examine the extent to which each of the three ideal types of monocentric, polycentric and multilevel governance may be present in different geographic, legal and policymaking circumstances. Such studies would be extremely welcome and could help to generate important knowledge about how different jurisdictions (in the EU and elsewhere) are trying to tackle public problems. Indeed, the framework presented in Table 1 should be applicable in other policy sectors and therefore help to address bigger questions about how different actors may be exercising power in policymaking contexts and—ultimately—how societies are governed. Additionally, although this chapter does not seek to formulate detailed policy prescriptions to tackle specific problems in particular locations, the framework could provide a useful heuristic for policymakers who aim to identify which approaches might be most appropriate for their own specific contexts—at the EU, Member State and subnational levels.

This chapter has drawn on a range of studies and perspectives on polycentric, monocentric and multilevel governance, power, policy instruments and EU environmental policy. It was unable to explore any of them in great depth due to limited space, but readers may wish to find out more about these topics from elsewhere in this volume and within wider scholarship. In particular, those with interests in polycentric environmental governance should consult the edited volume by Jordan et al. (2018) and a recent special issue of *Global Environmental Politics*, starting with Tobin, Huitema and Kellner's (2024) introductory article. Additionally, Heinen, Arlati and Knieling (2022), as well as Homsy and Warner (2018), provide useful contrasts between polycentricity and multilevel governance at a conceptual level. Piattoni (2009), Bache and Flinders (2022) and Papadopoulos, Tortola and Geyer (2024) outline how the multilevel governance perspective has evolved over time, and Kern (2019) sets out how an effective multilevel system might operate for climate policy, emphasizing the importance of mutual support across and between tiers and organizations. Additionally, Morrison et al. (2017) and Partzsch (2017) offer valuable insights into how actors can wield power in different ways in (polycentric) environmental policy contexts. For more on the evolution of EU environmental policy, the volume edited by Jordan and Gravey (2021), and especially the chapter by Moore et al. (2021) on the types of instruments it has adopted over time, is particularly helpful. Finally, Capano and Howlett's (2020) overview of perspectives on policy instruments should give readers useful insights into this literature.

In most cases, these recommendations only provide some of the most recent perspectives on these issues, and they therefore build on a large body of work by numerous other scholars. Nonetheless, they offer useful food for thought for academics and policymakers interested in these important topics.

References

Abizadeh, A. (2023) 'The grammar of social power: Power-to, power-with, power-despite and power-over', *Political Studies*, 71(1), pp. 3–19.

Arendt, H. (1970) *On violence.* New York: Harcourt Publishing.

Bacharach, P. and Baratz, M.S. (1963) 'Decisions and nondecisions: An analytical framework', *American Political Science Review*, 57(3), pp. 632–642.

Bache, I. and Flinders, M. (2022) 'Multilevel governance', in: Ansell, C. and Torfing J. (eds.) *Handbook on theories of governance.* Cheltenham: Edward Elgar, pp. 528–539.

Bulkeley, H. and Betsill, M. (2003) *Cities and climate change: Urban sustainability and global environmental governance.* London: Routledge.

Burns, C., Eckersley, P. and Tobin, P. (2020) 'EU environmental policy in times of crisis', *Journal of European Public Policy*, 27(1), pp. 1–19.

Capano, G. and Howlett, M. (2020) 'The knowns and unknowns of policy instrument analysis: Policy tools and the current research agenda on policy mixes', *SAGE Open*, 10(1), pp. 1–13.

Dahl, R.A. (1957) 'The concept of power', *Behavioral Science*, 2(3), pp. 201–215.

Deters, H. (2019) 'European environmental policy at 50: Five decades of escaping decision traps?', *Environmental Policy and Governance*, 29(5), pp. 315–325.

Domorenok, E. and Graziano, P. (2023) 'Understanding the European Green Deal: A narrative policy framework approach', *European Policy Analysis*, 9(1), pp. 9–29.

Eckersley, P. (2017) 'A new framework for understanding subnational policy-making and local choice', *Policy Studies*, 38(1), pp. 76–90.

Eckersley, P. (2018) 'Who shapes climate policy? Unpicking governance arrangements in English and German cities', *Environmental Politics*, 27(1), pp. 139–160.

Eckersley, P., Harrison, O. and Poberezhskaya, M. (2023) 'A new framework to understand the drivers of policy mixes in multilevel contexts: The case of urban air pollution', *Environmental Policy and Governance*, 33(2), pp. 178–190.

Eckersley, P. et al. (2025) 'Accountability as a function of power relations in governance networks', *Public Administration*, 103(3), pp. 906–922.

Galaz, V. et al. (2012) 'Polycentric systems and interacting planetary boundaries', *Ecological Economics*, 81, pp. 21–32.

Gravey, V. and Jordan, A. (2016) 'Does the European Union have a reverse gear? Policy dismantling in a hyperconsensual polity', *Journal of European Public Policy*, 23(8), 1180–1198.

Heinen, D., Arlati, A. and Knieling, J. (2022) 'Five dimensions of climate governance: A framework for empirical research based on polycentric and multi-level governance perspectives', *Environmental Policy and Governance*, 32(1), pp. 56–68.

Hepburn, C. et al. (2006) 'Auctioning of EU ETS phase II allowances: How and why?', *Climate Policy*, 6(1), pp. 137–160.

Heyes, A. (2000) 'Implementing environmental regulation: Enforcement and compliance', *Journal of Regulatory Economics*, 17(2), pp. 107–129.

Homsy, G.C. and Warner, M.E. (2018) 'Cities and sustainability: Polycentric action and multilevel governance', *Urban Affairs Review*, 51(1), pp. 46–73.

Hooghe, L. and Marks, G. (2003) 'Unravelling the central state, but how? Types of multi-level governance', *American Political Science Review*, 97(2), pp. 233–243.

Howlett, M. and Rayner, J. (2007) 'Design principles for policy mixes: Cohesion and coherence in "new governance arrangements"', *Policy and Society*, 26(4), pp. 1–18.

Jänicke, M. (2017) 'The multi-level system of global climate governance—the model and its current state', *Environmental Policy and Governance*, 27(1), pp. 108–121.

Jordan, A. (2000) 'The politics of multilevel environmental governance: Subsidiarity and environmental policy in the European Union', *Environment and Planning A*, 32(7), pp. 1307–1324.

Jordan, A. and Gravey, V. (eds.) (2021) *Environmental policy in the EU: Actors, institutions and processes.* Abingdon: Earthscan.

Jordan, A., Huitema, D., van Asselt, H. and Forster, J. (2018) *Governing climate change.* Cambridge: Cambridge University Press.

Jordan, A.J., Wurzel, R.K.W. and Zito, A. (2005) 'The rise of new policy instruments in comparative perspective: Has governance eclipsed government?', *Political Studies*, 53(3), pp. 477–496.

Kern, K. (2019) 'Cities as leaders in EU multilevel climate governance: Embedded upscaling of local experiments in Europe', *Environmental Politics*, 28(1), pp. 125–145.

Kern, K., Eckersley, P. and Haupt, W. (2023) 'Diffusion and upscaling of municipal climate mitigation and adaptation strategies in Germany', *Regional Environmental Change*, 23(28).

Kern, K., Eckersley, P., Kochskämper, E. and Haupt, W. (2024) 'Unpacking polycentric climate governance: tracing the evolution of transnational municipal networks over time', *Global Environmental Politics*, 24(3), pp. 121–143.

Kirschke, S. and Kosow, H. (2022) 'Designing policy mixes for emerging wicked problems: The case of pharmaceutical residues in freshwaters', *Journal of Environmental Policy & Planning*, 24(5), pp. 486–497.

Knill, C. and Liefferink, D. (2007) *Environmental politics in the European Union: Policy-making, implementation and patterns of multi-level governance.* Manchester: Manchester University Press.

Lenschow, A., (1999) 'Transformation in European environmental governance', in: Kohler-Koch, B. and Eising, R. (eds.) *The transformation of governance in the European Union.* London: Routledge, pp. 37 – 58.

Longhurst, J.W.S. et al. (2016) 'Progress with air quality management in the 60 years since the UK Clean Air Act, 1956: Lessons, failures, challenges and opportunities', *International Journal of Sustainable Development and Planning*, 11(8), pp. 491 – 499.

Lukes, S. (1974) *Power: A radical view.* London: MacMillan Press.

Marks, G. (1993) 'Structural policy and multi-level governance in the EC', in: Cafruny, A. and Rosenthal, G. (eds.) *The state of the European Community, volume 2: The Maastricht debates and beyond.* Boulder, CO: Lynne Rienner, pp. 391 – 410.

Metcalf, H.C. and Urwick, L. (1941) *Dynamic administration: The collected works of Mary Parker Follett.* New York: Harper and Brothers.

Moore, B.M. et al. (2021) 'Governing with multiple policy instruments?' In: Jordan, A., and Gravey, V. (eds.) *Environmental policy in the EU: Actors, institutions and processes.* Fourth edition. Abingdon: Earthscan, pp. 219 – 346.

Morrison, T. et al. (2017) 'Mitigation and adaptation in polycentric systems: Sources of power in the pursuit of collective goals', *WIREs Climate Change* 8(5), e479.

Morriss, P. (2002) *Power: A philosophical analysis.* Manchester: Manchester University Press.

Ostrom, E. (2010) 'Polycentric systems for coping with collective action and global environmental change', *Global Environmental Change*, 20(4), pp. 550 – 557.

Papadopoulos, Y., Tortola, P.D. and Geyer, N. (2024) 'Taking stock of the multilevel governance research programme: A systematic literature review', *Regional and Federal Studies,* pp. 1 – 33. Available at: https://doi.org/10.1080/13597566.2024.2334470.

Parsons, T. (1963) 'On the concept of political power', *Proceedings of the American Philosophical Society,* 107(3), pp. 232 – 262.

Partzsch, L. (2017) '"Power with" and "power to" in environmental politics and the transition to sustainability', *Environmental Politics*, 26(2), pp. 193 – 211.

Piattoni, S. (2009) 'Multi-level governance: A historical and conceptual analysis', *European Integration,* 31(2), pp. 163 – 180.

Preziosi, M. et al. (2019) 'The role of environmental practices and communication on guest loyalty: Examining EU-Ecolabel in Portuguese hotels', *Journal of Cleaner Production*, 237, 117659.

Rhodes, R.A.W., (1981) *Control and power in central-local relations.* Farnborough: Gower.

Steinebach, Y. (2022) 'Instrument choice, implementation structures, and the effectiveness of environmental policies: A cross-national analysis', *Regulation and Governance*, 16(1), pp. 225 – 242.

Tobin, P., Huitema, D. and Kellner, E. (2024) 'The empirical realities of polycentric climate governance: Introduction to the special issue', *Global Environmental Politics*, 24(3), pp. 1 – 23.

Tollefson, C., Zito, A.R. and Gale, F. (2012) 'Symposium overview: Conceptualizing new governance arrangements', *Public Administration*, 90(1), pp. 3 – 18.

van der Heijden, J. (2018) 'City and subnational governance', in: Jordan, A., Huitema, D., van Asselt, H. and Forster, J. (eds.) *Governing climate change.* Cambridge: Cambridge University Press, pp. 81 – 96.

Vedung, E. (1998) 'Policy instruments: Typologies and theories', in: Bemelmans-Videc, M.-L., Rist, R. C. and Vedung, E. (eds.) *Carrots, sticks, and sermons: Policy instruments and their evaluation.* Transaction Publishers, pp. 21 – 58.

Wurzel, R.K.W. (2008) 'Environmental policy: EU actors, leader and laggard states', in: Hayward, J. (ed.) *Leaderless Europe.* Oxford: Oxford University Press, pp. 66 – 88.

Wurzel, R.K.W., Zito, A.R. and Jordan, A. (2013) *Environmental governance in Europe: A comparative analysis of new environmental policy instruments.* Cheltenham: Edward Elgar.

Zito, A.R. (2015) 'Multi-level governance, EU public policy and the evasive dependent variable', in: Ongaro, E. (ed.) *Multi-level governance: the missing linkages.* Bingley: Emerald, pp. 15–39.

Zito, A.R., Burns, C. and Lenschow, A., (eds.) (2020) *The future of European Union environmental politics and policy.* London: Routledge.

Tanja Börzel und Andreas Hofmann

Beyond leaders and laggards: Member State compliance with European Union environmental law

Abstract: This chapter explores the challenges European Union (EU) Member States face in complying with EU environmental law, emphasizing both administrative capacity and political willingness. While administrative capacity is essential for compliance, political will becomes a key factor in states with strong governance structures. Traditionally, countries like Germany, the Netherlands and Sweden have been seen as environmental leaders, but growing resistance to the costs of green transitions challenges this perception. The chapter takes issue with the conventional "leader-laggard" framework and offers a more nuanced assessment of compliance patterns. Using empirical data from infringement procedures and third-party enforcement, it highlights discrepancies between Commission priorities and domestic legal actions. Additionally, case studies of Germany, the Netherlands and Sweden illustrate decentral enforcement efforts that largely bypass EU institutions. This analysis broadens the understanding of compliance with EU environmental law beyond simplistic categorizations.

Keywords: Compliance; litigation; European Commission; environmental law; interest groups

1 Introduction

This chapter investigates current challenges European Union (EU) Member States face in complying with EU environmental law. Such challenges can arise both from the lack of administrative capacity of implementing authorities and from the unwillingness of authorities to comply with obligations that either require substantial investments or place costs on important constituents. Our starting observation is that administrative capacity is a necessary condition for compliance. Political willingness should therefore become decisive primarily in places that have substantial administrative capacities. Such willingness to comply has increasingly come under strain in countries normally assumed to be leaders in EU environmental policy, as the costs for adjusting to the requirements of a green economy and the distribution of such costs among different societal groups have become more evident.

As governments with strong administrative capacities and environmental ambitions face backlash over the allocation of such adjustment costs, traditional understandings of leaders and laggards in EU environmental policy (Wurzel, Liefferink and Di Lullo, 2019, pp. 259–261) should be reconsidered. The current Dutch 'nitrogen crisis', for instance, has triggered significant political repercussions and was precipi-

https://doi.org/10.1515/9783111321523-017

tated by a legal conflict over Dutch authorities' compliance with EU obligations to protect areas within the Natura 2000 network. Nominally 'green' countries, such as Germany, the Netherlands and Sweden, face difficult political balancing acts in squaring environmental obligations with equitable burden-sharing across constituencies. Focusing on such distinctions, the chapter provides a more nuanced overview of the state of compliance than simple labels such as 'leaders' and 'laggards' suggest.

After reviewing theoretical assumptions about the drivers of noncompliance with environmental obligations, a first empirical section reviews available data on the state of Member State compliance with EU environmental law. We complement data on the Commission's use of the infringement procedure with data on third-party enforcement. Data on preliminary references in the environmental field provide an indication of what private actors see as compliance deficits in their respective countries. These are quite different from Commission enforcement priorities. However, data on preliminary references also tell only part of the story. Most court cases about EU law do not get referred to the Court of Justice of the European Union, and some nonetheless lead to significant legal innovation. We therefore present a qualitative analysis of decentral enforcement, with minimal involvement of EU institutions, in three cases: Germany, the Netherlands and Sweden.

2 Why Member States fail to comply

The literature on compliance has focused on three different sets of factors to explain state compliance with international norms and rules: the preferences of states, their power and their capacity to act upon these preferences (Chayes and Chayes, 1993; Raustiala and Slaughter, 2002; Simmons, 1998; Tallberg, 2002). On a theoretical level, preference and capacity-based arguments tend to be treated as competing or alternative explanations of noncompliance (Chayes and Chayes, 1993; Checkel, 2001; Downs, Rocke and Barsoom, 1996). Yet, empirically, a growing number of studies find that willingness and capacity are equally relevant (Börzel, 2021b; Börzel, et al., 2010; Linos, 2007; Mbaye, 2001). Noncompliance only becomes an issue when states are incapable or unwilling to cope with adjustment costs. Costs arise when compliance with EU law requires institutional and behavioural changes at the domestic level due to a 'misfit' between EU and domestic regulations (Duina, 1997; Knill, 1998; Thomson, 2007).

Environmental laggards face higher adjustment costs than environmental leaders as the former have neither the ambition nor the power to shape EU environmental law (Börzel, 2003). Their willingness and capacity to comply with costly EU environmental legislation is also weaker. The EU's traditional environmental laggards, such as Greece, Portugal, Italy, Belgium, France or Poland, differ with regard to the technical, administrative and financial resources required to ensure compliance. They all suffer, however, from bureaucratic inefficiency, as these resources are dispersed among various public agencies (e.g. ministries) and levels of government (Börzel, 2003; Egeberg, 1999; Mastenbroek, 2003; Haverland and Romeijn, 2007; Steunenberg and Toshkov, 2009; Zhelyazkova, Kaya and Schrama, 2016). Corruption further undermines their capacity to comply with EU law, since political favoritism is likely to determine the enforcement of (costly) EU legislation (Kaeding, 2006; Linos, 2007; Mbaye, 2001).

Low environmental ambitions and limited administrative capacity also negatively affect the political willingness of environmental leaders to cope with adjustment costs. Nevertheless, even the EU's traditional environmental leaders (the Netherlands, Denmark, Sweden, Finland, Austria and Germany), who lack neither ambition nor capacity, increasingly struggle with adjustment costs. Overall, EU legislation has become less ambitious (Börzel, 2021b, pp. 96–140). Simultaneously, adjustment costs are likely to be more politicized in all EU Member States due to the way in which they are allocated among domestic groups.

3 Data

To explore our argument, we combine an analysis of large-N data with qualitative case studies. Compliance is difficult to measure. It is most visible in conflicts over compliance. Such conflicts, however, require a complainant. The presence or absence of complainants is a central source of bias in compliance research. Many studies have relied on infringements reported by the Commission to assess Member State compliance with EU law (Börzel et al., 2010; Mbaye, 2001; Sverdrup, 2004; Tallberg, 2002; Thomson, 2007). Commentators have highlighted potential biases in Commission data resulting from the Commission's limited capacity to detect and pursue noncompliance (Hartlapp and Falkner, 2009; König and Mäder, 2014; Thomson, 2007) and from its changes in priorities in the allocation of resources to monitoring and enforcement (Hofmann, 2019; Kelemen and Pavone, 2023; Zhang, 2022). Commission data are only the tip of the iceberg of noncompliance in the EU, and we have no way of knowing how big the iceberg is (Hartlapp and Falkner, 2009). Nonetheless, infringement proceedings cover many different types of noncompliance, and there is no indication that the Commission displays favoritism toward individual governments.

We use the Berlin Infringement Database (Börzel, 2021a), which contains all infringement files opened between 1978 and 2017 that have advanced to at least the 'reasoned opinion' stage by March 7, 2019. It gives detailed information on the more than 13,300 infringement procedures initiated by the Commission. While it does not allow for a measurement of the size of the noncompliance iceberg, it arguably covers all those cases that lie at its core. As the most comprehensive database on infringement procedures, it allows for the analysis of variation across time, Member States, policy sectors, type of legal act and type of violation. We complement this with current data from the Commission's public infringement database.[1]

While Commission action is at the heart of central enforcement of EU law, the Court of Justice of the European Union (CJEU) laid the foundation for a decentral enforcement mechanism. In declaring EU law supreme to national law and directly effective, the CJEU gave citizens, groups and companies the opportunity to challenge public authorities before national courts for alleged infringements of EU law (Alter, 2001; Conant, 2002; Pavone, 2024; Weiler, 1981). National courts can resolve conflicts between national and EU law themselves, unless they doubt the validity of the EU legal act in question (only the CJEU can annul EU legal acts). National courts of last instance are obliged to refer a case to the CJEU only where the interpretation of EU law is unclear. Lower courts can refer questions whenever they find it necessary. National courts therefore hold a central role in the enforcement of EU legal obligations, and this process does not always require a reference to the CJEU. However, decentral enforcement does require two things: complainants that would bring cases, and national judges that are receptive to arguments based in EU law. Using national preliminary reference rates as an indicator, judicial receptivity appears to vary significantly across countries (Dyevre and Lampach, 2021; Kelemen and Pavone, 2016). An organized civil society with strong legal consciousness is also likely to be a robust predictor of decentral enforcement efforts (Börzel, 2006; Conant, et al., 2018). Systematic data on national environmental litigation is unavailable. Below, we use data on preliminary reference procedures, well aware that this, too, is biased along the lines outlined above. We use the IUROPA Project's (Brekke et al., 2023) CJEU database platform (Fjelstul et al., 2024), specifically information on all preliminary reference cases decided until the end of 2023.

4 What we know about the state of compliance

Commission infringement procedures

First, we revisit data on Commission enforcement of EU environmental law. Figure 1 displays the number of environmental infringement cases each Commission has referred to the CJEU during their term of office. As recent studies have highlighted, the Commission has pursued steadily fewer infringement cases since the end of the Prodi Commission (Falkner, 2018; Hofmann, 2019; Kelemen and Pavone, 2023). While the Prodi Commission referred 187 so-called 'discretionary' infringement cases (those not involving late transposition) to the CJEU, the von der Leyen I Commission did so in only fifty-nine cases. There is, however, disagreement on how to interpret

1 R-code for the combination of these data and for all analyses below can be accessed at https://github.com/ahofmann-eu/centralised_enforcement.

these findings. Fewer infringement procedures may indicate an improvement in Member State compliance (Börzel and Buzogány, 2019). The reduction has also been linked to diminishing EU legislative activity and ambition (Börzel, 2021b, pp. 105–109). Much of the Commission's enforcement activity focusses on the transposition of directives (European Commission, 2023). Even though overall transposition rates are high (above 90 percent), late transposition accounts for about two-thirds of the opening of infringement cases. Since the early 2000s, the Commission has de facto automated the initiation of infringement procedures in late transposition cases (European Commission, 2007, p. 9). Figure 1 shows that late transposition cases in the field of environmental law have largely disappeared—the von der Leyen I Commission only referred one such case to the CJEU. A combination of fewer transposition deadlines and better Member State performance explain the decline in this type of case; Member States now notify transposition measures largely on time (but not necessarily correctly). In fact, to buy time some Member States notify the Commission of transposition measures before they have been taken (Falkner et al., 2005; Zhelyazkova, Kaya and Schrama, 2017). Consequently, timely transposition may be associated with more rather than less noncompliance (Zhelyazkova, Kaya and Schrama, 2017; Zhelyazkova and Yordanova, 2015).

The findings are different for discretionary infringement cases—those initiated for incorrect transposition or bad application of EU law. As Figure 1 indicates, for the field of environmental law, discretionary infringement procedures have remained steady since the drop after the Barroso I Commission, with about fifty to sixty such cases referred to the CJEU per term. This indicates that Member State compliance, at best, has improved only to the extent of formal notification.

What has changed, however, is the geographic focus of Commission enforcement action. This is evident in Figure 2. While the Barroso I Commission still maintained a pattern prevalent in the central enforcement of environmental law since the southern enlargements of the 1980s (i.e., many more cases pursued against Italy, Spain and Greece), the von der Leyen I Commission had a much less clear geographic focus. Figure 2 indicates that the focus has shifted toward the countries of central and eastern Europe (CEE). In its first term, the von der Leyen Commission referred almost as many cases against eastern countries to the CJEU as cases against southern countries. The decrease in infringement action that took place after Barroso I happened uniquely with regard to the 'old' Member States, while the absolute number of cases against 'new' Member States—on an overall lower level—has in fact increased since the 2004 enlargement, which is mostly attributed to problems of practical application (Falkner, Treib and Holzleitner, 2008). The traditional green leaders of the EU, the BeNeLux countries, Germany and Austria (Wurzel, Liefferink and Di Lullo, 2019),[2] are now hardly ever targets of Commission enforcement action.

2 We include France in this group, as the pattern of infringement procedures against France does not match that of the Southern countries Greece, Italy, Spain and Portugal.

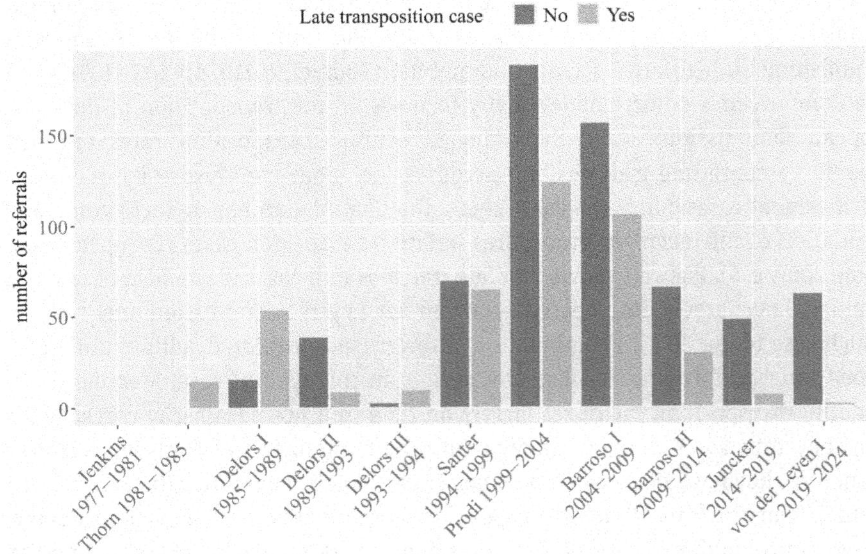

Figure 1: Referrals to CJEU in environmental infringement cases.

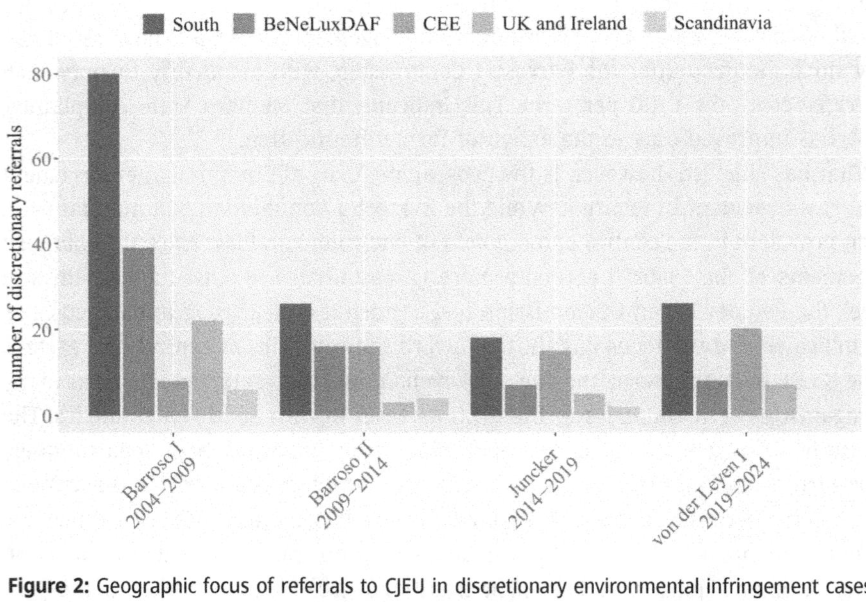

Figure 2: Geographic focus of referrals to CJEU in discretionary environmental infringement cases.

Preliminary reference procedures

In order to 'triangulate' Commission infringement data as a potential indicator for compliance problems, we move next to data on preliminary reference cases involving

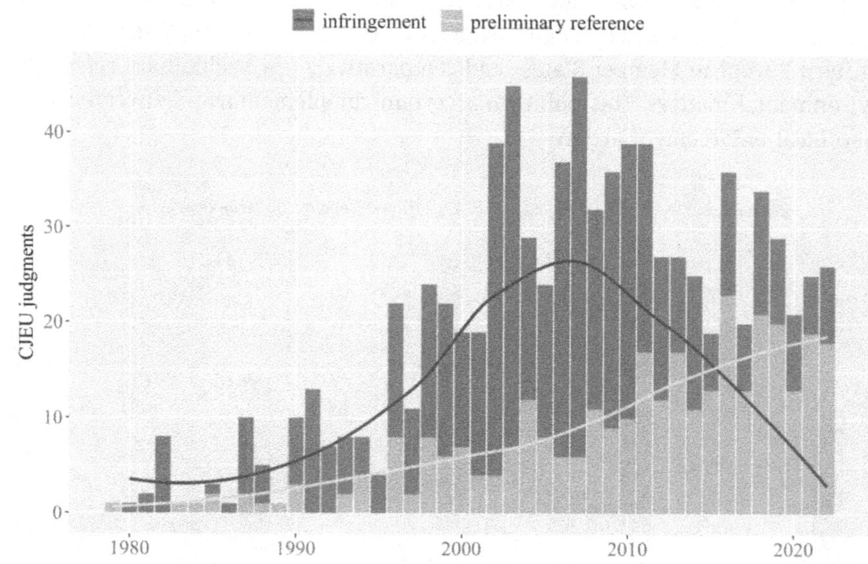

Figure 3: Central and decentral enforcement of EU environmental law.

issues of environmental law. Legislative implementation and judicial enforcement of the Aarhus Convention since 2003 have given private actors, in particular environmental nongovernmental organizations (ENGOs), an opportunity to rely on EU environmental law in national court proceedings, which may get referred to the CJEU (Hofmann, 2019). While such data are highly indicative of national conflicts over compliance, they also contain biases (see above). Figure 3 compares the number of CJEU judgments in infringement and preliminary reference procedures concerning EU environmental law. The light grey columns depict the number of judgments in preliminary reference cases, the black columns judgments in infringement cases. We added separate LOESS curves to visualize trends. Since the start of the Barroso II Commission, preliminary reference cases outnumber infringement cases. The average annual number of judgments in preliminary reference cases has increased from ten between 2008 and 2012 to eighteen between 2018 and 2022, while the average number of judgments in infringement cases in the same periods has dropped from twenty-three to nine. The overall number of CJEU judgments in environmental cases has remained broadly constant since the early 2000s, some annual peaks and troughs notwithstanding. These developments provide another piece of the puzzle concerning the 'true' life of EU environmental law in Member States.

Preliminary reference cases have a very different geographic profile than Commission action. Figure 4 shows the origins of preliminary reference cases by region. Most cases (between 50 and 60 percent) come from the BeNeLux countries, Germany, Austria or France. These are Member States with strong civil society engagement in environmental matters. The numbers skew toward countries with good conditions for decentral enforcement, but they also show that compliance problems exist in countries that are hardly targeted by Commission enforcement action. Conversely, southern and eastern European Member States send comparatively few preliminary references in environmental matters. This points to a certain complementarity between central and decentral enforcement action.

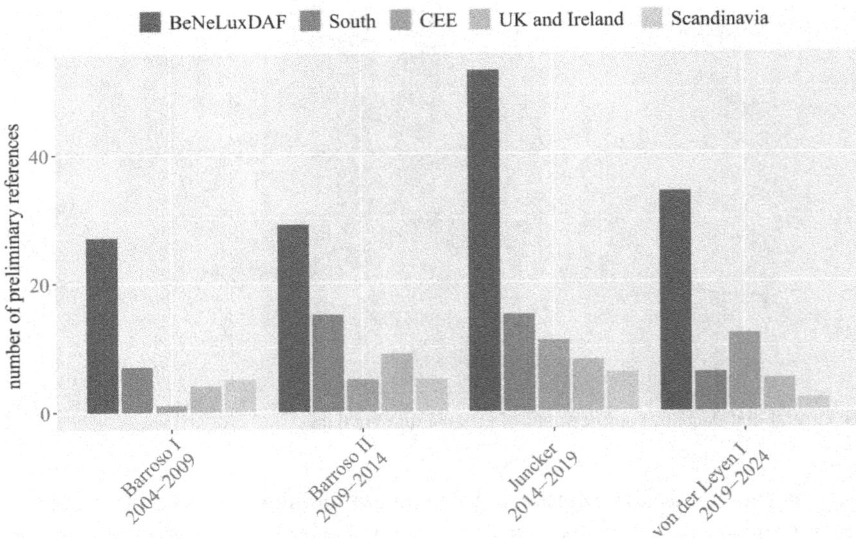

Figure 4: Preliminary references by origin.

5 Case studies

Given the absence of systematic data on national environmental litigation, we do not know how representative preliminary reference cases are of the total number of cases litigated domestically based on EU environmental law. Many conflicts over compliance never leave the national judicial system, even where such conflicts exist. To demonstrate the relevance of such conflicts over compliance, we present cases from three traditional environmental leaders—Germany, the Netherlands and Sweden. A central theme in all three case studies will be government reluctance to impose costs on important constituencies and civil society organizations' efforts to leverage EU law to force authorities to do so.

Ambient air quality in Germany

The EU has legislated air quality standards since the 1980s. Vehicle emissions are an important source of air pollution. Since the phase-out of lead in fuels, the most harmful pollutants in vehicle emissions are nitrogen oxides and soot (particulate matter). The EU first introduced limits on particulate matter in 1980 (European Union, 1980) and nitrogen oxides in 1985 (European Union, 1985). The 1996 Directive on ambient air quality assessment and management (European Union, 1996) introduced concrete requirements for national authorities to draw up action plans where limit values were exceeded, outlining measures to reduce pollution to limit values in as short a time as possible. Limit values and management procedures were recast in 2008 in a comprehensive directive on "ambient air quality and cleaner air for Europe" (European Union, 2008). Nonetheless, as late as 2018, more than fifty German cities exceeded nitrogen oxide emission limits (Töller, 2021, p. 488). In the early 2010s, taking action was low on the list of the responsible authorities' political priories. Awareness of the harmful effects of nitrogen oxides was low, and few citizens complained. Measures to reduce emissions would either require costly investments in public infrastructure and fleets or impose restrictions that would be unpopular with drivers and local businesses (Töller, 2021, pp. 497–498).

In this situation, a German ENGO, Environmental Action Germany (Deutsche Umwelthilfe, DUH), started specializing in litigation to enforce compliance with emission limit values. DUH first supported legal action by an individual to force the state of Bavaria to implement air quality measures for the city of Munich. The German Federal Administrative Court asked the CJEU for clarification concerning the right of individuals to challenge air quality and action plans. In 2008, the CJEU held that individuals indeed have a right to require authorities to create action plans (*Janecek*, case C-237/07, 2008). This single reference set off a cascade of national litigation campaigns. DUH subsequently started initiating litigation itself against insufficient air quality plans. In 2013, the Federal Administrative Court confirmed that DUH, following the CJEU's case-law on the Aarhus Convention, had standing to do so. DUH proceeded to initiate legal action against action plans in over forty German cities (Töller, 2021, p. 497). It was successful in every single case that reached a judgment (Töller, 2021, p. 499). One of its central demands was that authorities implement driving bans for diesel cars in areas where limit values had been exceeded. In 2018, the Federal Administrative Court confirmed that authorities needed to consider such measures, provided that the measures were proportionate. Such bans are highly controversial, not least since the German car industry had focused on diesel technologies and bans seriously disrupt the primary and secondary markets for diesel cars, impacting owners and producers alike. Despite local court rulings and the financial penalties accrued since, the Bavarian government has refused to consider diesel bans for the city of Munich (*Süddeutsche Zeitung*, 2019). DUH therefore asked courts whether coercive detention could be a possible penalty for noncompliant public officials. The Higher Administrative Court of Bavaria referred this case to the CJEU, who hedged on the possibility of coercive detention—this would be possible only where national law explicitly and predictably allowed for it; EU law would not empower national courts to order such measures (*Deutsche Umwelthilfe*, case C-752/18, 2019). DUH itself described the purpose of this litigation as seeking to clarify possible remedies against recalcitrant public authorities rather than detention of public officials per se.

The Commission, too, became active in enforcing air quality standards but only after DUH's litigation campaign was in full swing. In 2015, the Commission sent a letter of formal notice to the German government. It referred the case to the CJEU in 2018, which found against Germany in 2021. By this stage, DUH had already initiated forty-seven cases in German courts, and nitrogen oxide emissions were in decline (Bothner, Töller and Schnase, 2022).

Nitrate deposition in the Netherlands

The Habitats Directive (European Union, 1992), together with the Birds Directive (European Union, 2009), are the central pieces of EU legislation governing biodiversity protection. The Habitats Directive requires national governments to designate parts of their territory as 'special areas of conservation', protected areas that together constitute the EU's Natura 2000 network. Article 6(3) of the Habitats Directive requires special impact assessment procedures for projects likely to impact protected areas. While this provision has led to many conflicts over compliance, the Dutch 'nitrate crisis' is particularly intricate. Despite its limited size, the Netherlands is one of the world's largest exporters of agricultural products. Agricultural production releases large amounts of nitrogen into surface waters, leading to deteriorating water quality. Eutrophication through nitrogen deposits impacts numerous Dutch Natura 2000 sites (Van den Burg, 2019, pp. 112–113). Conflicts ensued over whether Dutch authorities would need to restrict agricultural activity where the risk of eutrophication was high. The Dutch government in 2015 devised a large-scale authorization scheme ('Programma Aanpak Stikstof'), which allowed authorities to offset current nitrogen deposition caused by economic activity against future, yet-to-be-implemented plans to reduce such deposits and other conservation measures (Squintani, 2019, p. 380). Several Dutch environmental ENGOs initiated litigation against this authorization scheme. In 2017, the Dutch Council of State (the highest administrative court) referred two cases initiated by the ENGOs 'Mobilization for the Environment' and 'Vereniging Leefmilieu' to the CJEU. In 2018, the CJEU ruled, first, that the operation of grazing cattle and the application of fertilizers falls under the Habitat Directive's requirement for public authorization and impact assessment if it takes place in the vicinity of Natura 2000 sites. Second, the assessment and authorization procedure must not take into account measures that lie in the future and whose off-setting impact cannot be assessed with certainty (*Mobilisation for the Environment*, joined cases C-293/17 and C-294/17, 2018). In response, the Council of State in 2019 declared the government's permitting scheme incompatible with the Habitats Directive. This led to significant problems, as the scheme encompassed not only agricultural activity but any economic activity that results in nitrogen deposits: first and foremost construction (Squintani, 2019, p. 381).

The government's attempts to establish an alternative authorization scheme that would meet nature conservation obligations caused intense conflict. One proposed measure, the massive buyout and closing of agricultural businesses in the vicinity of Natura 2000 sites, led to wide-spread protests by Dutch farmers lasting from 2019 into 2020 (Mathiesen, 2023). Out of the farmers' protests arose a new political party, the 'Farmer Citizen Movement' ('Boer Burger Beweging'), which did well in 2022 provincial elections and in 2024 entered a coalition supporting the Dutch government. Meanwhile, Dutch ENGOs have continued to litigate against permitting decisions. Such litigation has at times targeted grazing and fertilization permits to specific agricultural businesses, creating distinct clashes between economic livelihood and nature conservation (Mathiesen, 2023). In the wake of their intermittent success, the Dutch parliament has debated restricting the traditionally liberal standing rights for nongovernmental organizations (NGOs) in administrative procedures. In 2022, a parliamentary majority passed a nonbinding motion calling for requirements regarding representativity (Stolk, 2023, p. 1064).

Nature conservation in Sweden

Litigation in conflicts about nature conservation in Sweden demonstrates the effect of EU law largely outside of any CJEU involvement. One prominent conflict over compliance in Sweden concerns the return of wolves to areas of mid-Sweden where the species had been extinct for almost a century. The Habitats Directive contains a list of species, including the wolf, which Member States have a duty to protect. The Habitats Directive prohibits killing such animals except under limited circumstances. Like in many areas throughout Europe, the wolf's return to Sweden has led to conflicts. In Sweden, such conflicts have revived a dormant political cleavage between the urban center of Stockholm and the rural periphery (Berg and Solevid, 2015). Particularly in rural areas affected by the ongoing withdrawal of public services, the return of the wolf was seen as adding insult to injury. An aspect of this conflict that differentiates the Swedish case from the continent is the strong role of the hunting lobby. Swedish hunters worry about the impact of wolves on the elk population. Elk hunting is a popular pastime in rural Sweden, and hunters are an important constituency for mainstream political parties. The sale of hunting licenses for elk hunts is also an important income source for forests owners (Westlund, 2016).

In this context, the Swedish parliament decided in 2009 to cap the wolf population at 210 individuals (Alarik, 2016, p. 4). To manage this cap, the government authorized the issuance of hunting licenses for wolves. ENGOs strongly opposed this move. However, under restrictive standing rights for associations in Swedish administrative law, ENGOs were unable to challenge the first round of hunting authorizations in 2010 (Alarik, 2016, p. 5). This changed in 2012, after the ENGO Swedish Society for Nature Conservation (Naturskyddsföreningen) successfully argued before the Swedish Supreme Administrative Court that associations should have legal standing to challenge hunting authorizations following the CJEU's case law on the Aarhus Convention. The Supreme Administrative Court granted standing without sending a reference to Luxemburg (Alarik, 2016, p. 9). ENGOs were subsequently successful in challenging hunting authorizations for many years (Alarik, 2016, pp. 11–24). This changed in 2016 when the government changed the jurisdiction of courts that could hear legal challenges to hunting decisions. Rather than leaving jurisdiction to local courts, challenges to administrative decisions under hunting law would only be heard by the administrative court in Sweden's northernmost county of Norrbotten. Judges there proved largely unreceptive to the ENGO arguments (Darpö, 2018, p. 6). The Commission, for its part, had initiated an infringement procedure against Sweden in 2011, which remained open for the entirety of this period but, as of June 2025, has not progressed beyond the reasoned opinion stage (European Commission, 2011).[3]

In other areas of nature conservation, too, the Swedish government resorted to extraordinary measures to avoid costs imposed by environmental obligations. In a series of cases regarding limestone quarrying, ENGOs successfully challenged quarrying permits in various locations throughout Sweden. Limestone is a central component of cement and therefore an important resource. The largest limestone deposits in Sweden, however, are also home to sensitive habitat protected by Natura 2000 sites. All legal challenges to quarrying permits were based on the potential negative impact on nearby Natura 2000 sites. Following a successful legal challenge to a quarrying permit in Slite on the island of Gotland, the Swedish government intervened, citing a concern for the supply of cement for the Swedish building sector. It introduced a special law that allowed for an expedited permitting procedure with special exemptions from environmental impact assessment (Dahlen and Enkvist, 2024, pp. 32–33).

6 Conclusions

Our overview of different sources of data on compliance with EU environmental law indicates that conflicts over compliance are shifting to national legal systems. The number of infringement cases pursued by the Commission has declined since the Barroso I Commission. This partially reflects the improved performance of Member State in notifying transposition measures. However, this improvement is often formal rather than substantive, as timely transposition may mask compliance issues. Notably, discretionary infringement cases, focusing on incorrect transposition or bad application, have remained steady over the last 15 years, suggesting limited improvement in deeper compliance. An important trend in Commission enforcement is a shift in geographic focus from southern Europe to central and eastern Europe. Decentral enforcement, as measured by the number of preliminary reference cases, has meanwhile increased and now surpasses infringement cases. These references often originate from Western

3 The infringement case number for this proceeding is INFR(2010)4200.

Member States with strong civil society engagement, revealing compliance issues that central enforcement overlooked or ignored. The case studies demonstrate that many conflicts over compliance, even when they are severe, play out without the involvement of EU institutions—sometimes even without the CJEU. They also highlight serious compliance deficits in countries traditionally held as leaders in environmental protection. National and local governments in Germany, the Netherlands and Sweden take extraordinary measures to avoid costs for important constituencies. These include interference with ordinary jurisdiction, challenges to ENGO standing and special laws to circumvent outcomes of the legal process.

The empirical focus on the politics of compliance offers several avenues for future research. First, it calls for a broader understanding of compliance with EU environmental law that moves beyond simplistic categorizations. Second, we need more systematic data on national conflicts over compliance. Third, comparative studies should seek to identify and categorize different types of conflict and mitigation strategies, exploring potential links.

References

Alarik, O. (2016) *Rättsfallen om licensjakt efter varg i Sverige—bakgrund och kronologi.* Stockholm: Naturskyddsföreningen.

Alter, K.J. (2001) *Establishing the supremacy of European law.* Oxford: Oxford University Press.

Berg, L. and Solevid, M. (2015) 'Tracing a political cleavage: The wolf issue in Sweden', *European Politics and Society,* 16(4), pp. 488 – 522.

Börzel, T.A. (2003) *Environmental leaders andlLaggards in Europe.* Aldershot: Ashgate.

Börzel, T.A. (2006) 'Participation through law enforcement: The case of the European Union', *Comparative Political Studies,* 39(1), pp. 128 – 152.

Börzel, T.A. (2021a) 'Berlin infringement database'. Version 2021.1. Berlin: Freie Universität Berlin.

Börzel, T.A. (2021b) *Why noncompliance. The politics of law in the European Union.* Ithaca: Cornell University Press.

Börzel, T.A. and Buzogány, A. (2019) 'Compliance with EU environmental law', *Environmental Politics,* 28(2), pp. 315 – 341.

Börzel, T.A., Hofmann, T., Panke, D. and Sprungk, C. (2010) 'Obstinate and inefficient: Why Member States do not comply with European law', *Comparative Political Studies,* 43(11), pp. 1363 – 1390.

Bothner, F., Töller, A.E. and Schnase, P.P. (2022) 'Do lawsuits by ENGOs improve environmental quality?', *Sustainability,* 14(11), pp. 65 – 92.

Brekke, S.A., Fjelstul, J.C., Hermansen, S.S.L. and Naurin, D. (2023) 'The CJEU database platform: Decisions and decision-makers', *Journal of Law and Courts,* 11(2), pp. 1 – 22.

Chayes, A. and Chayes, A.H. (1993) 'On compliance', *International Organization,* 47(2), pp. 175 – 205.

Checkel, J.T. (2001) 'Why comply?', *International Organization,* 55(3), pp. 553 – 588.

Conant, L. (2002) *Justice contained.* Ithaca: Cornell University Press.

Conant, L., Hofmann, A., Soennecken, D. and Vanhala, L. (2018) 'Mobilizing European law', *Journal of European Public Policy,* 25(9), pp. 1376 – 1389.

Dahlen, M. and Enkvist, V. (2024) 'Regeringsformens natur och naturens rättigheter', in: Jonsson Cornell, A., Ruotsi, M., Taube, C. and Wilske, O. (eds.) *De lege. Regeringsformen 50 år 1974 – 2024.* Uppsala: Iustus, pp. 23 – 42.

Darpö, J. (2018) *Gabriel och vargen.* Available at: http://jandarpo.se/wp-content/uploads/2021/10/2018-Varg-till-Gabriel.pdf (Accessed: 15 February 2025).

Downs, G.W., Rocke, D.M. and Barsoom, P.N. (1996) 'Is the good news about compliance good news about cooperation?', *International Organization,* 50(3), pp. 379 – 406.

Duina, F.G. (1997) 'Explaining legal implementation in the European Union', *International Journal of the Sociology of Law,* 25(2), pp. 155 – 179.

Dyevre, A. and Lampach, N. (2021) 'Subnational disparities in EU law use', *Journal of European Public Policy,* 28(4), pp. 615 – 631.

Egeberg, M. (1999) 'The impact of bureaucratic structure on policy making', *Public Administration,* 77(1), pp. 155 – 170.

European Commission (2007) 'Communication from the commission: A Europe of results: Applying community law', *COM*(2007) 502 final. Available at: https://eur-lex.europa.eu/legal-content/EN/TXT/?uri=celex:52007DC0502 (Accessed: 14 June 2025).

European Commission (2011) 'Press release: Commission urges Sweden to respect EU nature legislation and protect endangered wolves', 16.6.2011. Available at: https://ec.europa.eu/commission/presscorner/detail/en/ip_11_732 (Accessed: 14 June 2025).

European Commission (2023) 'Stocktaking report on the Commission working methods for monitoring the application of EU law', *SWD*(2023) 254 final. Available at: https://commission.europa.eu/publications/stocktaking-report-commission-working-methods-monitoring-application-eu-law_en (Accessed: 14 June 2025).

European Union (1980) 'Council Directive 80/779/EEC on air quality limit values and guide values for sulphur dioxide and suspended particulate', *Official Journal* L 229, 30.8.1980, pp. 30 – 48.

European Commission (1985) 'Council Directive 85/203/EEC on air quality standards for nitrogen dioxide', *Official Journal L* 328, 06/12/2008, pp. 28 – 37.

European Commission (1992) 'Council Directive 92/43/EEC on the conservation of natural habitats and of wild fauna and flora', *Official Journal L 206, 22.7.1992, pp. 7 – 50.*

European Commission (1996) 'Council Directive 96/62/EC on ambient air quality assessment and management', *Official Journal L* 296, 21.11.1996, pp. 55 – 63.

European Commission (2008) 'Directive 2008/50/EC of the European Parliament and of the Council on ambient air quality and cleaner air for Europe', *Official Journal L* 152, 11.06.2008, pp. 1 – 44.

European Commission (2009) 'Directive 2009/147/EC of the European Parliament and of the Council on the conservation of wild birds', *Official Journal L* 20, 26.1.2010, pp. 7 – 25.

Falkner, G. (2018) 'A causal loop? The Commission's new enforcement approach in the context of non-compliance with EU law even after CJEU judgments', *Journal of European Integration,* 40(6), pp. 769 – 784.

Falkner, G., Treib, O., Hartlapp, M. and Leiber, S. (2005) *Complying with Europe.* Cambridge: Cambridge University Press.

Falkner, G., Treib, O. and Holzleitner, E. (2008) *Compliance in the European Union.* Aldershot: Ashgate.

Fjelstul, J., Naurin, D., Brekke, S.A., and Hermansen, S.S.L. (2024) 'The IUROPA CJEU Database Platform (v2.00.00)', in: Lindholm, J. et al. (eds.) *The Court of Justice of the European Union (CJEU) Database.* Available at: https://www.iuropa.pol.gu.se (Accessed: 14 June 2025).

Hartlapp, M. and Falkner, G. (2009) 'Problems of operationalisation and data in EU compliance research', *European Union Politics,* 10(2), pp. 281 – 304.

Haverland, M. and Romeijn, M. (2007) 'Do Member States make European policies work?', *Public Administration,* 85(3), pp. 757 – 778.

Hofmann, A. (2019) 'Left to interest groups? On the prospects for enforcing environmental law in the European Union', *Environmental Politics,* 28(2), pp. 342 – 364.

Kaeding, M. (2006) 'Determinants of transposition delay in the European Union', *Journal of Public Policy,* 26(3), pp. 229 – 253.

Kelemen, R.D. and Pavone, T. (2016) 'Mapping European law', *Journal of European Public Policy*, 23(8), pp. 1118 – 1138.

Kelemen, R.D. and Pavone, T. (2023) 'Where have the guardians gone', *World Politics*, 75(4), pp. 779 – 825.

Knill, C. (1998) 'Implementing European policies: The impact of national administrative Traditions', *Journal of Public Policy*, 18(1), pp. 1 – 28.

König, T. and Mäder, L. (2014) 'The strategic nature of compliance', *American Journal of Political Science*, 58(1), pp. 246 – 263.

Linos, K. (2007) 'How can international organizations shape national welfare states?', *Comparative Political Studies*, 40(5), pp. 547 – 5470.

Mastenbroek, E. (2003) 'Surviving the deadline: The Transposition of EU directives in the Netherlands', *European Union Politics*, 4(4), pp. 371 – 396.

Mathiesen, K. (2023) 'Protecting nature, destroying lives', *Politico.eu*, 9.3.2023. Available at: https://www.politico.eu/article/johan-vollenbroek-netherlands-nitrogen-pollution-climate-change-farming (Accessed: 13 February 2025).

Mbaye, H.A.D. (2001) 'Why national states comply with supranational law', *European Union Politics*, 2(3), pp. 259 – 281.

Pavone, T. (2024) 'Making the European Court work: Nicola Catalano and the origins of European legal integration', in: Gallo, D., Nicola, R.M.G. and Cecchetti, L. (eds.) *The Italian Influence on European Law: Judges and Advocates General (1952 – 2000).* London: Hart Publishing.

Raustiala, K. and Slaughter, A.-M. (2002) 'International law and compliance', in: Carlsnaes, W. Risse, T. and Simmons, B. (eds.) *Handbook of international relations.* London: Sage, pp. 538 – 558.

Simmons, B.A. (1998) 'Compliance with international agreements', *Annual Review of Political Science*, 1(1), pp. 75 – 93.

Squintani, L. (2019) 'G. The Netherlands', *Yearbook of International Environmental Law*, 30(1), pp. 379 – 384.

Steunenberg, B. and Toshkov, D. (2009) 'Comparing transposition in 27 Member States of the EU', *Journal of European Public Policy*, 16(7), pp. 951 – 970.

Stolk, R. (2023) 'De algemeenbelangactie in strijd met het algemeen belang?', *Nederlands Juristenblad*, 98(14), pp. 1064 – 1071.

Süddeutsche Zeitung (2019) 'Streit um Luftreinhaltung: Bund und Land sehen keine Grundlage für Zwangshaft', Available at: https://www.sueddeutsche.de/muenchen/muenchen-luftreinhaltung-eugh-duh-soeder-zwangshaft-1.4586297 (Accessed: 14 June 2025).

Sverdrup, U. (2004) 'Compliance and conflict management in the European Union', *Scandinavian Political Studies*, 27(1), pp. 23 – 43.

Tallberg, J. (2002) 'Paths to compliance: Enforcement, management, and the European Union', *International Organization*, 56(3), pp. 609 – 643.

Thomson, R. (2007) 'Time to comply. National responses to six EU labour market directives Revisited', *West European Politics*, 30(5), pp. 987 – 1008.

Töller, A.E. (2021) 'Driving bans for diesel cars in German cities', *European Policy Analysis*, 7(2), pp. 486 – 507.

Van den Burg, A. (2019) 'Blijft de rekening van stikstofemissie nu nog bij de natuur liggen?', *Milieu & Recht*, 46(2/3), pp. 112 – 116.

Weiler, J.H.H. (1981) 'The community system: The dual character of supranationalism', *Yearbook of European Law*, 1, pp. 268 – 306.

Westlund, B. (2016) Älgjakten riskerar ställas in i Värmland. *Svensk Jakt*, 5.2.2016. Available at: https://svenskjakt.se/start/nyhet/algjakten-i-varmland-riskerar-bli-installd (Accessed: 13 February 2025).

Wurzel, R.K.W., Liefferink, D. and Di Lullo, M. (2019) 'The European Council, the Council and the Member States', *Environmental Politics*, 28(2), pp. 248 – 270.

Zhang, Y. (2022) 'Limits of law in the multilevel system', *Journal of Common Market Studies*, 60(4), pp. 1001 – 1018.

Zhelyazkova, A., Kaya, C. and Schrama, R. (2016) 'Decoupling practical and legal compliance', *European Journal of Political Research*, 55(4), pp. 827 – 846.

Zhelyazkova, A., Kaya, C. and Schrama, R. (2017) 'Notified and substantive compliance with EU law in enlarged Europe', *Journal of European Public Policy*, 24(2), pp. 216 – 238.

Zhelyazkova, A. and Yordanova, N. (2015) 'Signalling "compliance"', *European Union Politics*, 16(3), pp. 408 – 428.

Jeroen van der Heijden

European Union urban environmental and climate policy

Abstract: Europe is highly urbanized, with most Europeans living in cities. The quality of life in these areas is closely tied to local environmental conditions and global climate change impacts, including air and water quality, access to natural spaces, noise pollution and rising temperatures. Cities consume significant resources and face many environmental challenges, but they also offer opportunities for solutions. Urban areas enable efficient resource management by reducing reliance on private transportation and promoting energy-efficient buildings. Recognizing this, the European Union (EU) emphasizes the role of cities in achieving climate change goals through initiatives like the European Green Deal. EU cities and local governments are crucial in implementing pollution-related laws, policies and programs. This chapter provides an overview of EU urban environmental and climate policies, especially after the 2015 Paris Agreement, using theories and concepts from urban environmental and climate policy literature.

Keywords: Urban governance; cities; urbanization; climate policy; local policy

1 Introduction

Cities[1] have long been considered primary victims of environmental harm and climate change *and* point sources for their causes (van der Heijden, 2018). Since the 1990s, cities consequently have been positioned as crucial in fighting climate change, offering opportunities for implementing and scaling regenerative, sustainable and resilient practices. However, current environmental and climate initiatives by cities and city-networks have proven insufficient for achieving a timely and just transition toward environmentally sustainable and climate-resilient cities (Acuto and Leffel, 2021; Burley Farr et al., 2023).

This situation persists in Europe, where approximately 75 percent of the population resides in cities and urban areas, accounting for approximately 80 percent of Europe's total energy consumption and more than 70 percent of its CO_2 emissions (European Commission, 2019b; European Commission, 2023). While cities across Europe have made significant strides in reducing negative impacts on the natural environ-

1 Unfortunately, no agreed upon definition of "city" or "urban area" currently exists. The European Commission advocates for: "[A]n urban centre consists of contiguous grid cells with a density of at least 1,500 inhabitants per km^2 and a total population of at least 50,000; An urban cluster consists of contiguous grid cells with a density of at least 300 inhabitants per km^2 and a total population of at least 5,000" (European Commission, 2019b, p. 20).

https://doi.org/10.1515/9783111321523-018

ment, including CO_2 emission reductions, they collectively lack a trajectory to achieve carbon neutrality by 2050. The European Commission (EC) recognizes that achieving environmentally sustainable and zero-carbon cities in a socially inclusive manner requires substantial systemic changes (European Commission, 2021a).

Notably, although the urban environmental and climate policy and governance literature has highlighted the slow pace of urban environmental and climate transitions since at least the turn of the millennium (Bulkeley and Betsill, 2003), it was only after the 2015 Paris Agreement and the New Urban Agenda in 2016 that the EC began to focus on cities as focal points for its environmental and climate ambitions. Until 2020, generally cities and urban areas were not specifically addressed in European Union (EU) environmental and climate policies, including those concerning water and biodiversity (de Luca et al., 2021).

This situation has, however, changed significantly with the introduction of the European Green Deal (European Commission, 2019a), the New European Bauhaus (European Commission, 2021b) and the Urban Agenda for the EU (European Commission, 2021e)—all briefly explained in Section 3 of this chapter. Indeed, since the 2020s, there has been a surge in EU-level environmental and climate policies, programs and initiatives targeting cities (Eurocities, 2023). However, will they be sufficient for a just transition to carbon-neutral cities in Europe by 2050?

This chapter addresses that question as a starting point. In what follows, Section 2 briefly reviews the broad urban climate policy and governance literature, while Section 3 summarizes the proliferation of EU-level urban environmental and climate policies, programs and initiatives. Subsequently, Section 4 evaluates these policies, programs and initiatives through the research lens presented in Section 2. Section 5 discusses the challenges facing today's EU-level urban environmental and climate policy and governance, while Section 6 examines the limitations of current urban and climate policy and governance theories and concepts to address efforts at the EU level. Finally, Section 7 proposes future alternative approaches to study and improve EU-level urban environmental and climate policy and governance and Section 8 concludes.

2 Historical and intellectual development of urban environmental and climate policy

As mentioned above, dedicated urban environmental and climate policies at the EU-level have only emerged since the early 2020s. Of course, examples do predate this period, such as the Covenant of Mayors (CoM) launched by the EC in 2008 (Croci et al., 2017), but they are exceptions. Also, the CoM can in the context of this handbook best be understood as an ex-post EU policy, which at the time of its launch endorsed and supported existing environmental and climate efforts deployed by city governments. Consequently, there is not much of a policy record or academic literature to delve into regarding EU-level urban environmental and climate developments before the mid-2010s. However, significant progress has occurred at the local, national and international levels, upon which this section will focus. What follows is a high-level discussion of the extant literature from the last three decades.

From the Local Agenda 21 (UNCED, 1992) to recent global climate summits, cities have been recognized as crucial for environmental and climate action. In the mid-2010s, alongside the Paris Conference of the Parties (COP) in 2015, a Climate Summit for Local Leaders emphasized urban leadership in climate initiatives. This event garnered significant attention and influence in shaping the Paris Agreement (United Nations, 2015). Cities also feature prominently in the United Nations' Sustainable Development Goals of 2015, underscoring their importance in global sustainability efforts (UNDP, 2015). Additionally, the New Urban Agenda from the 2016 HABITAT Conference strongly emphasizes cities' roles in both climate change mitigation and adaptation (United Nations, 2016).

When examining these advances, one might assume cities have become integral to global climate governance. However, the reality is less optimistic (Westman et al., 2022). Cities, while sites and actors in climate action, still struggle for formal recognition in international policymaking. They face institutional barriers to being heard in climate negotiations and acknowledged in agreements. Side-events at COPs remain separate from formal negotiations, and initiatives like the Sustainable Development Goals are not directly referenced in the Paris Agreement. Moreover, the Paris Agreement does not explicitly recognize cities or urban areas as actors in climate governance, emphasizing "country-driven" processes instead (United Nations, 2015, Articles 7, 9 and 11). Despite international discourse on urban climate governance's importance, still not enough is done to empower cities as active participants—within the EU and beyond. Additionally, there is a lack of coordination between international fora on how cities should contribute to climate action (Kern, 2023).

Similarly, at the national level, city policy and governance structures often impede cities' ability to enact meaningful environmental and climate actions (Burley Farr et al., 2023). Cities frequently lack the authority to enforce specific environmental and climate standards with their citizens and businesses. While they can develop and implement zoning and planning legislation, they typically lack the authority to regulate the performance of buildings, roads, transportation and energy usage within their boundaries. This regulatory power rests with regional and/or national governments (van der Heijden, 2014). However, national governments have been slow to strengthen building codes and vehicle emission regulations, for example, despite these being critical areas where significant urban environmental and climate progress is achievable (Rosenzweig et al., 2018).

For these reasons, cities around the world, including in Europe, have begun seeking alternative environmental and climate policies, governance programs and initiatives. For example, globally cities are actively engaging in innovative governance processes to tackle local and trans-local climate challenges through experimental governance. This approach involves iterative testing of governance instruments within specific jurisdictions or populations to adapt and potentially scale them up (Bulkeley, 2023). Hundreds of urban climate governance experiments, ranging from the local to the international scale, have been initiated to address barriers to effective climate action, such as political, financial, technological and social challenges (Eisenack and Roggero, 2022).

These experiments signify more than local government-led problem-solving; they involve formal collaborations between local governments, private actors and civil society to develop and trial new forms of governance (Patterson and Huitema, 2022). Stakeholders are optimistic about drawing lessons from experiments and scaling them up across cities and countries. Motivations for cities to experiment with innovative governance instruments vary, from adapting to structural changes in governance to actively involving stakeholders in collaborative processes (Westman and Castán Broto, 2018). Expectations include developing smarter instruments through stakeholder involvement, increasing instrument acceptance and compliance, and moving toward positive incentives rather than punitive measures (see also Chapter 32).

Another area of activity can be found in regional, national and international city networks, such as ICLEI—Local Governments for Sustainability, the C40 Cities Climate Leadership Group and the Covenant of Mayors for Climate and Energy (Smeds and Acuto, 2018). These networks facilitate knowledge exchange, joint experimentation and governance solutions for urban climate challenges, often bypassing national governments in international arenas (Cortes Berrueta et al., 2022). They assist cities in overcoming regional and national barriers to climate governance by providing information and resources for member cities, something particularly beneficial for smaller municipalities that lack institutional capital.

3 EU-level urban environmental and climate policy since adoption of the Paris Agreement

While the EC has a long history of developing and implementing environmental and climate policies (see for example Chapters 20, 32 and 34), these policies have not typically included an explicit focus on cities (de Luca et al., 2021; Kemmerzell, 2022). This has changed with the adoption of the Urban Agenda for the EU (UAEU), launched in 2016, and the New European Bauhaus (NEB), adopted in 2020. It is for this reason that this section only engages with EU-level urban environmental and climate policy since the adoption of the Paris Agreement.

The UAEU aims to address the complexities and challenges faced in EU urban areas by focusing on "better regulation", "better funding" and "better knowledge". It recognizes that EU legislation directly affects urban authorities and aims to anticipate and simplify its implementation at the local level. Similarly, it seeks to streamline access to EU funding and enhance coordination among urban authorities. Moreover, the UAEU emphasizes the importance of sharing successful urban development experiences and improving the urban policy knowledge base. It advocates for a balanced, sustainable and integrated approach to urban challenges. This entails involving all levels of government, promoting policy complementarity and respecting subsidiarity principles (NLU, 2016).

The UAEU promotes multilevel and multi-stakeholder cooperation to strengthen the urban dimension in EU policy and encourages collaboration between urban authorities, local communities, civil society, businesses and knowledge institutions to drive sustainable development. It recognizes the diversity of urban areas across the EU and the need for cooperation within functional urban areas and with surrounding regions to address local challenges and promote wider territorial benefits. The UAEU, through its partnerships and frameworks, aims to create more resilient, inclusive and sustainable urban environments across the EU (European Commission, 2021e).

The NEB links the European Green Deal (European Commission, 2019a) to the everyday lives and habitats of European citizens (see Chapter 20). It invites all Europeans to collectively envision and construct a sustainable and inclusive future that is "beautiful, sustainable, and inclusive" (European Commission, 2021b, p. 2). EC President von der Leyen announced the initiative in September 2020. The NEB is described as a "think-do tank", bringing together concepts of action labs, city-networks and accelerators. The initiative is presented as highly innovative, as it has been co-created with citizens, non-governmental organizations, education institutions, research and technology organizations, firms and others; bridges design, arts, science, technology and culture; and seeks to steer societal transformation along the values of (environmental) sustainability, aesthetics and inclusion.

The UAEU, the NEB and the European Green Deal have spurred a string of EU-level urban environmental and climate policies, programs and initiatives, which can only be discussed in general terms here. These include, but are not limited to, a class of endeavors that largely seeks to experiment with new urban environment and climate actions, create knowledge about these experiments and disseminate that knowledge across European cities. Examples include the European Urban Initiative (European Urban Initiative, 2022), the NetZeroCities initiative (European Commission, 2021a), the Renovation Wave Initiative (European Commission, 2020c), the Territorial Agenda 2023 (European Commission, 2020d) and URBACT IV (URBACT, 2023). URBACT IV is an initiative targeting a range of urban themes, including environmental sustainability and climate change.

Another class of endeavors provides cities with platforms to network, share ideas and collaborate. These include the Circular Cities and Regions Initiative (European Commission, 2020b), the European Climate-ADAPT platform (European Commission, 2019b), the Green City Accord (European Commission, 2021c), the Milan Urban Food Policy Pact (European Commission, 2019b) and the Urban Nature Platform (European Commission, 2022b). Last but not least, another class of endeavors mainly seeks to highlight best practices and reward cities that have taken the lead in urban environmental and climate policies, programs and initiatives, such as the Green Capital

Awards and the Green Leaf Awards (European Commission, 2021a; European Union, 2024) and the Intelligent Cities Challenge Initiative (European Commission, 2020b).

Crucially, all of these endeavors rely on voluntary participation from cities and other stakeholders. Just as cities have limited power to mandate improved environmental and climate behavior of their citizens, so too the EC has limited power to mandate actions and initiatives toward more environmentally sustainable and carbon neutral cities. Among the few mandatory urban environment and climate policy requirements at the EU level are the energy efficiency codes set in the Energy Performance of Buildings Directive (European Union, 2018) and the construction products rules set in the European Construction Product Regulation (European Commission, 2023).

4 An evaluation of EU-level urban environmental and climate policy

At the writing of this chapter, the urban environmental and climate policies at the EU level have not been in force long enough to be evaluated in the academic literature. However, the EC and related stakeholders have conducted some initial assessments that merit consideration.

Among the EU-level initiatives discussed earlier, the UAEU stands out with the longest history since the adoption of the Paris Agreement. The EC's evaluation indicates positive progress, with eighty-five actions underway by 2021, thirty-nine of which were completed (European Union, 2021). For instance, the Urban Agenda Partnership for Circular Economy, involving six urban authorities, five EC departments and five stakeholders, operated from 2018 to 2021, implementing twelve actions aimed at fostering knowledge on urban circular economy development (European Commission, 2021d) (see Chapter 36). Outputs mainly consist of knowledge documents like case studies, position papers and handbooks (for an example, see European Commission, 2020a).

While the quantity of outputs from the UAEU is impressive, questions linger about their quality and utility, especially for cities and stakeholders not directly involved in the partnerships (Eurocities, 2023). Reported concerns include uncertainty in action implementation, uneven stakeholder engagement, ineffective governance mechanisms and limited outreach beyond direct participants. Additionally, internal coherence and communication challenges exist within the UAEU (European Commission, 2021e).

Similar patterns emerge in the evaluations of other EU-level urban environmental and climate initiatives. Many are self-evaluated by the EU, often portraying progress in positive terms without substantial evidence. For instance, in a self-evaluation by the EC, NEB is lauded for significant progress, but details on this progress remain scarce (European Commission, 2021b). Similarly, while the Green Cities Accord receives praise in another EC self-evaluation (European Commission, 2022a), tangible outcomes beyond a booklet highlighting a handful of best practices are limited since its launch in 2020.

Moreover, publicly available information on some initiatives raises concerns about their effectiveness. For example, evaluations of the Construction Product Regulation in 2019 barely addressed the environmental sustainability of construction products (European Commission, 2019c). Subsequent documents like the 2023 Roadmap for its implementation failed to outline strategies for improving environmental sustainability in Europe's construction sector (European Commission, 2023). Similarly, the EU Strategy for a Sustainable Built Environment, launched in 2021, has already seen partial transfer to the Recovery and Resilience Facility and the Renovation Wave for Europe initiative (European Parliament, 2022), with limited updates on its performance or future commitments in recent documents from the EC and European Parliament (EP) (European Parliament, 2024).

5 Challenges with EU-level urban environmental and climate policy

Taking a step back and examining EU-level urban environmental and climate policy through the theories and concepts provided by the broader academic literature on this topic, several challenges are identified. The initial lack of focus on "the urban" in EU environmental and climate policy and the current proliferation of endeavors in this context fit a broader trend of increasing maturity but also future uncertainty within EU environmental policy (Zito, Burns and Lenschow, 2019). While the policies, programs and initiatives discussed in this chapter provide a rich and diverse landscape of possibilities and actions, a first set of challenges lies in their sector-driven nature (i. e., their focus on energy, urban green or circular economy but without a holistic view), a lack of clarity about the role and relevance of the different initiatives and programs and significant fragmentation and possibly competition among them (Eurocities, 2023). Lacking a focus on holistic approaches, the current EC endeavors in this context run the risk of fizzling out rather than achieving something larger than the sum of the individual policies, programs and initiatives (Westman et al., 2022).

A related challenge of these endeavors is their voluntary and experimental nature. Following the broader EU environmental and climate policy literature, it is warranted to question whether the current "soft governance" approach chosen by the EC is forceful enough to ensure that all European cities achieve carbon neutrality by 2050 (Schoenefeld and Jordan, 2020). Likewise, the central operational model of these endeavors—policy experiments—could be troublesome in the long run. Decades of urban environmental and climate policy experimentation have indicated that lessons from these efforts are not always transferable to other contexts, and that a willingness to make an urban policy experiment succeed in its experimental setting may backfire once it is implemented under "normal" conditions, which could include a lack of political will, leadership or resources (Bulkeley, 2023). Moreover, the endeavors typically engage with leading cities and leading urban actors in Europe, and it remains questionable if the majority of cities and actors consider them as equal peers they can and wish to learn from (van der Heijden, 2017).

Finally, it is not always clear (to say the least) how the policies, programs and initiatives aim to achieve urban environmental and climate transitions in Europe in a just and equal manner. While many explicitly express a desire to achieve "climate just" urban transitions, their focus is often on overcoming technical, financial and regulatory barriers rather than addressing existing inequalities or those that may result from such transitions—a typical challenge in this context (Hughes and Hoffmann, 2020; Pedersen Zari et al., 2022). This particular challenge may be addressed through the Territorial Agenda 2030, which was launched in 2020 to address growing inequalities between places and people in Europe and to address unsustainable development in Europe. In other words, it aims to achieve a double mission of a "just Europe" and a "green Europe" (European Commission, 2020d). In addition, questions about climate justice and equity questions only become more important if one looks beyond the EU and considers Global South countries and cities. Moreover, the first evaluation of the Agenda was only available by November 2024 (Espon, 2024), by which time many of the other endeavors were well underway and may have lacked further opportunities to adjust their environmental and climate justice focus (cf. Fitzgerald, 2022; Krueger et al., 2022). The evaluation found that, although the priorities and principles of the Territorial Agenda are widely applied across the EU, there is still room to enhance their implementation and raise their visibility (Espon, 2024).

6 Limitations of urban environmental and climate policy theories and concepts to address efforts at the EU-level

Related to the above, it may be difficult to study the development, implementation and performance of EU-level urban environmental and climate policy through theories and concepts provided by the broader academic literature on this topic. They have typically not been developed to assess policy interventions at the administrative level occupied by the EC. Rather, these theories and concepts have largely been developed to assess (individual) environmental and climate policies and actions at the city level (or even lower levels such as the neighborhood, street, or even building level) or at the country level (Castán Broto and Westman, 2020; van der Heijden, 2019). This raises several challenges, explored below.

The first challenge is the complexity and multilevel nature of EU policymaking, including supranational, national and subnational levels. This complexity makes it difficult to apply urban theories and concepts developed for single-level policy systems (Corrêa do Lago, Sánchez Chaparro and Lumbreras, 2023). While the notion of "multilevel governance" increasingly features in the academic literature on urban environmental and climate policy (Betsil and Bulkeley, 2021), its current operationalization may not fully capture the dynamics at play in the EU context (Pierre, 2019). This challenge is amplified by the criticism that the EC and EP often face for their perceived democratic deficit and lack of legitimacy (Bürgin, 2023). Studying multilevel urban governance and policymaking may require the modification of theories so that they address these concerns in the EU context.

A second challenge involves the institutional dynamics of the EU's institutional framework (including the EC, the EP and the Council of the European Union), which operates differently from traditional national or local institutions. Theories and concepts that have resulted from urban environmental and climate policy at the national or local level may be too limited to capture the complex dynamics of and within the EU's institutional framework (Kern, 2023). Additionally, such theories and concepts may also be too limited to capture the diversity of EU Member States, which involves a variety of political systems, cultures and socioeconomic conditions (Ehnert et al., 2018) (see also Chapter 14).

A third challenge concerns the difficulty of implementing and enforcing EU urban environmental and climate policies across Member States. EU institutions may lack the formal power or capacity to ensure that Member States abide by EU policies, or they may have to rely on implementation and compliance information self-provided by Member States (van der Heijden and Van Bueren, 2013). This, combined with the geographical distance between Brussels and the diverse (national and local) contexts, may result in situations where much non-implementation or noncompliance goes unnoticed (Shabb and McCormick, 2023; see also Chapter 34).

A different challenge posed for existing theories and concepts in studying EU-level urban environmental and climate policy is that notions of environmental and climate justice and equity are only now beginning to become mainstream in the literature (Branny et al., 2023; Burch, 2021). Also, increasingly scholars argue that urban environmental and climate change challenges cannot (and should not) be overcome in isolation as they are deeply intertwined with challenges related to social justice, equality, fairness and inclusion (Bai et al., 2024). However, the existing literature on urban environmental and climate policy, emerging around sectors such as urban energy, urban green and urban social disparities, is still relatively siloed (Vogel, 2024).

7 Future alternative approaches to study and improve EU-level urban environmental and climate policy and governance

Future research into EU-level urban environmental and climate policy may aim to address the challenges discussed earlier. One approach could involve increasing critical research into the gap between EU policy rhetoric and action on the ground. Many of the EU's urban environmental and climate policies, programs and initiatives are still too "young" to demonstrate their effects and effectiveness. However, studying them in real-time could offer a counternarrative to the possibly overly positive EC self-evaluations.

It is essential, also, to critically understand which cities are participating in and benefiting from EU urban environmental and climate endeavors and why. There is a risk that these efforts primarily attract and support the "usual suspect cities", like Amsterdam and Malmo, and are unable to engage with the "nonleading" cities. Additionally, some cities may participate not out of alignment with the endeavor's spirit, but simply for access to financing or positive international exposure.

This calls for a stronger empirical understanding of how the EC and the EP develop and implement policies and create a narrative of success, and how cities interpret and implement them and create their own narratives of success. One central risk to explore is a bias to only highlight major successes by the EC and cities, overlooking failures or situations of lesser success. While a focus on major successes may reveal factors that aid cities in becoming more environmentally sustainable, resilient to climate risks and socially just, it is unlikely to explain minor successes or failures (and misses the dynamic of learning from failures) due to the complexity of EU-level urban environmental and climate policy.

To understand the complexity surrounding EU-level climate policies, methods such as process tracing, Qualitative Comparative Analysis, cluster analysis and realist evaluation could help trace pathways of interacting factors and outcomes. This may help, for example, in identifying essential configurations (small clusters of factors) that hold across a range of geographies, or, instead, different context-specific pathways for effective urban climate governance across EU regions (Byrne and Callaghan, 2014; Varone, Jacob and Bundi, 2023).

Such methods also help to address an increasing understanding that there is no single "best practice" route to low-carbon, climate-resilient or climate-just cities. The broader literature suggests many potential pathways for urban environmental and climate transitions. With that in mind, questions arise regarding the EC's predominant approach of voluntary city participation in knowledge generation endeavors (van der Heijden, 2023) and whether urban transitions unfold in manageable patterns or in messy, unmanageable manners (Bulkeley et al., 2013). To address such questions, traditional theories of the policy process (Weible, 2023) and of the broader context of EU environmental and climate policymaking may prove useful (Rayner et al., 2023), all the more so when complemented with critical urban theory (Castán Broto and Robin, 2020).

8 Conclusion

By evaluating EU policies through the lens of the broader urban environmental and climate policy literature, the chapter has explored the limitations of studying EU environmental and climate policies in the future. What becomes apparent from this chapter is the lack of a strong policy record or academic literature on EU urban environmental and climate policy pre-2015. Dedicated EU-level urban environmental and climate policies, programs and initiatives have proliferated since the adoption of the Paris Agreement and, logically, have only received academic interest recently. That being said, assessing the current variety of EU endeavors, one may find it challenging to see the forest for the trees. This poses a significant challenge for the EC and EP, necessitating robust future scholarship on the opportunities and constraints of these endeavors.

On a personal note, my optimism wanes when considering the wide array of EU urban environmental and climate policies, programs and initiatives. They lack coherence; their sheer quantity suggests they may be spread too thin; and they rely on a potentially misguided assumption that once "leading" cities develop knowledge and take voluntary action, "lagging" cities will follow suit. Due to the lack of an overarching approach to monitor and guide these EU endeavors, coupled with a reliance on what, in effect, are voluntary experiments, Europe may not achieve regenerative, sustainable, resilient and just cities by 2050. I remain hopeful, nevertheless, that future research in this area will prove me wrong.

References

Acuto, M. and Leffel, B. (2021) 'Understanding the global ecosystem of city networks', *Urban Studies*, 58(9), pp. 1758–1774.

Bai, X. et al. (2024) 'Translating Earth system boundaries for cities and businesses', *Nature Sustainability*, 7(1), pp. 108–119.

Betsil, M. and Bulkeley, H. (2021) 'Cities and the multilevel governance of global climate change', in: Mills, K. and Stiles, K. (eds.) *Understanding global cooperation*. Leiden: Brill, pp. 45–67.

Branny, A. et al. (2023) 'Smarter greener cities through a social-ecological-technological systems approach', *Current Opinion in Environmental Sustainability*, 55(April), pp. 1–23.

Bulkeley, H. (2023) 'The condition of urban climate experimentation', *Sustainability: Science, Practice and Policy*, 19(1), pp. 1–14.

Bulkeley, H. and Betsill, M. (2003) *Cities and climate change*. London: Routledge.

Bulkeley, H., Castán Broto, V., Hodson, M. and Marvin, S. (eds.) (2013) *Cities and low carbon transitions*. London: Routledge.

Burch, S. (2021) *Accelerating a just transition to smart, sustainable cities*. Waterloo: Centre for International Governance Innovation.

Bürgin, A. (2023) 'The European Commission', in: Rayner, T., Szulecki, K., Jordan, A. and Oberthur, S. (eds.) *Handbook on European Union climate change policy and politics*. Cheltenham: Edward Elgar, pp. 134–155.

Burley Farr, K. et al. (2023) 'Cities and regions tackle climate change mitigation but often focus on less effective solutions', *Communications Earth & Environment*, 4(439), pp. 1–12.

Byrne, D. and Callaghan, G. (eds.) (2014) *Complexity theory and the social sciences*. New York: Routledge.

Castán Broto, V. and Robin, E. (2021) 'Climate urbanism as critical urban theory', *Urban Geography*, 42(6), pp. 715–720.

Castán Broto, V. and Westman, L. (2020) 'Ten years after Copenhagen', *WIREs Climate Change*, 11(4), pp. 1 – 22.

Corrêa Do Lago, A., Sánchez Chaparro, T. and Lumbreras, J. (2023) 'A decade of climate action and the mission towards climate neutrality and adaptation in European cities', *Sustainability*, 14(su152416665), pp. 1 – 13.

Cortes Berrueta, S., van Der Heijden, J., Bush, S. and Boas, I. (2022) 'Unpacking the heterogeneity of climate city networks', *Cities*, 121(103512), pp. 1 – 9.

Croci, E. et al. (2017) 'Urban CO_2 mitigation strategies under the Covenant of Mayors', *Journal of Cleaner Production*, 169(December), pp. 161 – 177.

de Luca, C., Naumann, S., McKenna, D. and Simona, T. (2021) 'Nature-based solutions and sustainable urban planning in the European environmental policy framework', *Sustainability*, 13(5021), pp. 1 – 22.

Ehnert, F. et al. (2018) 'Urban sustainability transitions in a context of multi-level governance', *Environmental Innovation and Societal Transitions*, 26(March), pp. 101 – 116.

Eisenack, K. and Roggero, M. (2022) 'Many roads to Paris', *Global Environmental Change*, 72(January), 102439.

Epson (2024) *Stocktaking review of the Territorial Agenda 2030.* Brussels: EPSON 2030.

Eurocities (2023) *How the EU can work better with cities.* Available at: https://eurocities.eu/resources/how-the-eu-can-work-better-with-cities/ (Accessed: 26 June 2025).

European Commission (2019a) 'The European Green Deal', *COM*(2019) 640 final. Available at: https://eur-lex.europa.eu/legal-content/EN/TXT/?uri=celex:52019DC0640 (Accessed: 26 June 2025).

European Commission (2019b) *The future of cities.* Ispra: European Commission. Available at: https://publications.jrc.ec.europa.eu/repository/bitstream/JRC116711/the-future-of-cities_online.pdf (Accessed: 26 June 2025).

European Commission (2019c) 'Evaluation of regulation (EU) No 305/2011 laying down harmonised conditions for the marketing of construction products. Executive summary', *SWD*(2019) 1771 final.

European Commission (2020a) *Better regulation for a circular economy.* Available at: https://ec.europa.eu/futurium/en/system/files/ged/7012_europa_decentraal_sv-b5_en_web_spreads_v2.pdf (Accessed: 26 June 2025).

European Commission (2020b) *Circular economy action plan.* Brussels: European Commission. Available at: https://eur-lex.europa.eu/legal-content/EN/TXT/?qid=1583933814386&uri=COM:2020:98:FIN (Accessed: 26 June 2025).

European Commission (2020c) 'Support from the EU budget to unlock investment into building renovation under the renovation qave', *SWD*(2020) 550 final. Available at: https://eur-lex.europa.eu/legal-content/EN/TXT/?qid=1603122391413&uri=CELEX:52020SC0550 (Accessed: 26 June 2025).

European Commission (2020d) *Territorial Agenda 2030.* Brussels: European Commission. Available at: https://territorialagenda.eu/wp-content/uploads/TA2030_jun2021_en.pdf (Accessed: 26 June 2025).

European Commission (2021a) *100 climate-neutral and smart cities by 2030.* Brussels: European Commission.
https://research-and-innovation.ec.europa.eu/system/files/2021 – 09/cities_mission_implementation_plan.pdf (Accessed: 26 June 2025).

European Commission (2021b) 'New European Bauhaus', *COM*(2021) 573 final. Available at: https://eur-lex.europa.eu/legal-content/EN/TXT/?uri=CELEX%3A52021DC0573 (Accessed: 26 June 2025).

European Commission (2021c) *Press kit—information on the Green City Accord for media.* Brussels: European Commission. Available at:
https://environment.ec.europa.eu/system/files/2023 – 06/EGCEGL-Presskit-including-winners-2023.pdf (Accessed: 26 June 2025).

European Commission (2021d) *Final report: Urban agenda for the EU on circular economy.* Available at: https://futurium.ec.europa.eu/sites/default/files/2021-07/Urban%20Agenda%20for%20the%20EU%20%20Circular%20Economy%20-%20Final%20report.pdf (Accessed: 26 June 2025).

European Commission (2021e) *Urban agenda for the EU: Multi-level governance in action—2021 update.* Brussels: European Commission. Available at: https://ec.europa.eu/regional_policy/en/information/publications/brochures/2021/updated-version-2021-urban-agenda-for-the-eu-multi-level-governance-in-action (Accessed: 26 June 2025).

European Commission (2022a) *Green city accord: Best practices.* Brussels: European Commission. Available at: https://environment.ec.europa.eu/document/download/52f23571-579b-4bca-94ea-4e932cf7ec6b_en?filename=Green%20City%20Accord%20Best%20Practice%20Collection.pdf (Accessed: 26 June 2025).

European Commission (2022b) *Urban greening plans: Guidance for cities to help prepare an urban greening plan—DRAFT.* Brussels: European Commission. Available at: https://environment.ec.europa.eu/topics/urban-environment/urban-nature-platform_en (Accessed: 13 August 2024).

European Commission (2023) *Roadmap for the implementation of the construction products regulation.* Brussels: European Commission. Available at: https://ec.europa.eu/docsroom/documents/57514 (Accessed: 26 June 2025).

European Parliament (2022) *Legislative train 06.2022: Strategy for a sustainable built environment.* Brussels: European Parliament. Available at: https://www.europarl.europa.eu/legislative-train/carriage/strategy-for-a-sustainable-built-environment/report?sid=6001 (Accessed: 26 June 2025).

European Commission (2024) *Legislative train 03.2024: Strategy for a sustainable built environment.* Brussels: European Parliament. Available at: https://www.europarl.europa.eu/legislative-train/carriage/strategy-for-a-sustainable-built-environment/report?sid=7901 (Accessed: 26 June 2025).

European Union (2018) 'Directive 2010/31/EU of the European Parliament and of the Council of 19 May 2010 on the energy performance of buildings (recast)', *Official Journal of the European Union L* 153/13. Available at: https://eur-lex.europa.eu/eli/dir/2010/31/oj/eng (Accessed: 26 June 2025).

European Union (2021) *Review of the contributions of the urban agenda for the EU to the implementation of the new urban agenda.* Brussels: European Union. Available at: https://www.urbanagenda.urban-initiative.eu/sites/default/files/2022-12/Review%20of%20the%20UAEU%20contributions%20to%20the%20NUA%20-%20Final%20report.pdf (Accessed: 26 June 2025).

European Union (2024) *EU missions: 100 climate-neutral and smart cities.* Brussels: European Union. Available at: https://research-and-innovation.ec.europa.eu/funding/funding-opportunities/funding-programmes-and-open-calls/horizon-europe/eu-missions-horizon-europe/climate-neutral-and-smart-cities_en (Accessed: 26 June 2025).

European Urban Initiative (2022) *European urban initiative: Innovative actions guidance.* Brussels: European Union/Région Hauts-de-France. Available at: https://www.urban-initiative.eu/sites/default/files/2023-05/EUI-IA%20GUIDANCE_7X2022.pdf (Accessed: 26 June 2025).

Fitzgerald, J. (2022) 'Transitioning from urban climate action to climate equity', *Journal of the American Planning Association*, 88, pp. 508–523.

Hughes, S. and Hoffmann, M. (2020) 'Just urban transitions', *WIREs Climate Change*, 11(3), pp. 1–11.

Kemmerzell, J. (2022) 'Cities in European energy and climate governance', in: Knodt, M. and Kemmerzell, J. (eds.) *Handbook of energy governance in Europe.* Cham: Springer, pp. 298–316.

Kern, K. (2023) 'Cities in EU multilevel climate policy', in: Rayner, T., Kacper, S., Jordan, A. and Oberthur, S. (eds.) *Handbook on European Union climate change policy and politics.* Cheltenham: Edward Elgar, pp. 176–197.

Krueger, E. et al. (2022) 'Governing sustainable transformations of urban social-ecological-technological systems', *Nature Urban Sustainability*, 2(art.10), pp. 1–14.

NLU (2016) *Urban agenda for the EU.* Amsterdam: Netherlands Presidency of the Council of the European Union.

Patterson, J. and Huitema, D. (2022) 'Institutional innovation in urban governance', *Journal of Planning Literature*, 37(1), pp. 374–398.

Pedersen Zari, M., Mackinnon, M., Varshney, K. and Bakshi, N. (2022) 'Regenerative living cities and the urban climate–biodiversity–wellbeing nexus', *Nature Climate Change*, 12(July), pp. 601–603.

Pierre, J. (2019) 'Multilevel governance as a strategy to build capacity in cities: Evidence from Sweden', *Journal of Urban Affairs*, 41(1), pp. 103–116.

Rayner, T., Szulecki, K., Jordan, A. and Oberthur, S. (2023) 'The global importance of EU climate policy: An introduction', in: Rayner, T., Szulecki, K., Jordan, A. and Oberthur, S. (eds.) *Handbook on European Union climate change policy and politics*. Cheltenham: Edward Elgar, pp. 1-21.

Rosenzweig, C. et al. (2018) *Climate change and cities.* Cambridge: Cambridge University Press.

Schoenefeld, J. and Jordan, A. (2020) 'Towards harder soft governance?', *Journal of Environmental Policy & Planning*, 22(6), pp. 774–786.

Shabb, K. and McCormick, K. (2023) 'Achieving 100 climate neutral cities in Europe', *npj Climate Action*, 2(6), pp. 1–10.

Smeds, E. and Acuto, M. (2018) 'Networking cities after Paris', *Global Policy*, 9(4), pp. 549–559.

UNCED (1992) *Agenda 21.* Rio de Janeiro: United Nations.

UNDP (2015) *Sustainable development goals.* New York: UNDP.

United Nations (2015) *Paris agreement.* Paris: United Nations Treaty Collection.

United Nations (2016) *New urban agenda.* Quito: United Nations General Assembly.

URBACT (2023) *URBACT IV Programme manual.* Brussels: URBACT.

van der Heijden, J. (2014) *Governance for urban sustainability and resilience.* Cheltenham: Edward Elgar.

van der Heijden, J. (2017) *Innovations in urban climate governance.* Cambridge: Cambridge University Press.

van der Heijden, J. (2018) 'Cities and sub-national governance', in: Jordan, A. and Huitema, D. (eds.) *Polycentricity in action.* Oxford: Oxford University Press, pp. 97–115.

van der Heijden, J. (2019) 'Studying urban climate governance', *Earth System Governance*, 1(1), article 100005.

van der Heijden, J. (2023) 'Towards a science of scaling for urban climate action and governance', *European Journal of Risk Regulation*, 14(3), pp. 513–525.

van der Heijden, J. and Van Bueren, E. (2013) 'Regulating sustainable construction in Europe', *International Journal of Law in the Built Environment*, 5(1), pp. 5–20.

Varone, F., Jacob, S. and Bundi, P. (eds.) (2023) *Handbook of public policy evaluation.* Cheltenham: Edward Elgar.

Vogel, R. (ed.) (2024) *Handbook of urban politics and policy.* Cheltenham: Edward Elgar.

Weible, C. (ed.) (2023) *Theories of the policy process, fifth edition.* London: Routledge.

Westman, L. and Castán Broto, V. (2018) 'Climate governance through partnerships', *Global Environmental Change*, 50(May), pp. 212–221.

Westman, L. et al. (2022) 'Compound urban crises', *AMBIO*, 51(6), pp. 1402–1415.

Zito, A., Burns, C. and Lenschow, A. (2019) 'Is the trajectory of European Union environmental policy less certain?', *Environmental Politics*, 28(2), pp. 187–207.

Thibaut Joltreau and Andy Smith

Business, environmental policy and the European Union: Deep politics with major impacts

Abstract: Within the European Union (EU), the depiction of 'business' as uniformly opposed to environmental policy oversimplifies a complex landscape of economic actors and activities. This chapter explores corporate engagement in EU environmental policymaking, highlighting firms and interest groups as significant *policy actors*. It reviews the literature on business strategies toward policy and the role of institutional contexts as political opportunity structures. Such research shows the influence of business on environmental policy through long-term relationships with EU administrations and politicians, including interactions with the Commission, European Parliament and national governments. However, we argue that the influence of firms and their representatives on European environmental policy can be more finely assessed by focusing on specific industries, their respective political economies and how their institutions and organizations frame 'the environment' at different stages along the value chain.

Keywords: Business; environmental policy; climate policy; interest groups; industry regulation

1 Introduction: Business, environmental policy and the European Union

'Business' is often depicted in public discourse as simply being against environmental policy. While sometimes true, such claims are excessively sweeping, failing to grasp the fundamental variety of economic actors together with their often deep linkages to the political realm. Fortunately, recent publishing in the field of environmental and climate policymaking has accumulated robust research on both this variety and these linkages at the European Union (EU) scale. Indeed, our systematic literature review shows (see Box 1) a more accurate and stimulating picture of how businesses have reacted economically and politically to environmental and climatic issues. Moreover, by utilizing strong generic theories and methodologies, this research offers vital insight to the analysis both of the EU itself and of environmental regulation at varying scales.

Nevertheless, we contend that three important knowledge and analytical gaps remain. The first concerns temporality. We argue that firms and their interest groups should be viewed as *policy actors* constantly engaged in co-constructing policy through long-term, embedded relationships with their counterparts from the European Com-

https://doi.org/10.1515/9783111321523-019

mission (EC), the European Parliament (EP) and national governments. Indeed, one finding is that relatively few academic publications actually target the EU-business-environmental policy relationship over time. The second knowledge gap stems from the focus of most studies on readily visible policymaking instead of the political economies which structure it. Here, alongside much other research, we contend that the influence of firms on European environmental policy is generally high but not always decisive (Rosendal, 2005; Dür, Bernhagen and Marshall, 2015; Vormedal, 2017; Vormedal, Gulbrandsen and Skjærseth, 2020). Moreover, this influence is best assessed through research focused on the regulation of specific industries, the institutions that underpin them, together with the power relations that make and, generally, reproduce them. Finally, research needs to better acknowledge that business success with regard to EU environmental policymaking stems not only from the political resources of firms themselves but also from the inability of their opponents, in particular environmentalist nongovernmental organizations (NGOs), to counter arguments framed as 'economic', and therefore 'necessary' (see also Chapter 7). As Colin Hay (2016) underlines, the economic is fundamentally political because it is contingent. Consequently, analysis must theorize that the EU-business-environmental policy linkage could have been constructed otherwise—and still could be.

Box 1: The sources and methodology of our literature review

To review the literature on the relationship between business, environmental policy and the EU, we selected eleven social sciences academic journals that cover these topics. For each, we searched for the following keywords in the published articles' titles: 'environmental policy', 'EU environmental policy', 'business' and 'business power'. In total, seventy-two articles were collected and reviewed, the oldest dating back to 1997.

The journals scrutinized:

Journal of European Public Policy
Journal of Environmental Policy & Planning
Organization & Environment
Sustainability
New Political Economy
Environmental Politics
Global Environmental Politics
Review of International Political Economy
Environmental Innovation and Societal Transitions
Environmental Policy and Governance
Business and Politics

2 Leading interpretations of the EU-business-environment relationship

The most compelling analyses of this relationship fall into two categories. The first groups together research focused on the strategies adopted by the businesses or interest groups studied. The second targets the institutions that structure such lines of attack.

Business strategies to build key alliances and frame issues

Research tracking business influence via its strategies also has two sub-sets, one emphasizing the impact of each actor's relational resources, the other centered instead on businesses' capacity to define issues to their advantage.

Within EU studies, both neofunctionalists (Haas, 1958) and intergovernmentalists (Hoffmann, 1966) first implicitly used the relational approach to stress how business representatives worked to support the EC, their respective national governments or sometimes both. It was only in the 1990s, when EU studies came to use policy analysis more systematically, that such claims were investigated within research focused directly on business-public authority relations. For example, David Coen (1997) generated data from which he theorized the EU as a case of 'elite pluralism'. This posited that large firms have a built-in advantage over smaller ones when accessing policymakers. Similarly, Justin Greenwood mapped business-EU public authority relations in his first book (Greenwood, 1997) and three updated editions. Significantly, as early as the 2003 edition, Greenwood highlighted that "there can also be found degrees of collaboration between business and 'light green' interest groups, such as WWF and the European Environmental Bureau" (2003, p. 188). He extended these findings more recently by examining decision-making within EU 'trilogues' (Greenwood and Roederer-Rynning, 2021).

However, Coen's contention that big businesses are systematically advantaged within EU decision-making has not only been rendered more nuanced in general terms (Eising, 2007; Dür, Bernhagen and Marshall, 2015), but also through environmental policy research. Adriana Bunea (2013) exemplifies this approach, defining 'lobbying success' as 'preference attainment'. Two of her findings are particularly noteworthy. First, she concludes that business has more power "over outcomes in a policy area where higher levels of regulation bring about concentrated costs on specific economic agents such as car producers or airlines operators" (p. 567). Second, "organizations representing 'diffuse interests', such as environmental NGOs and local authorities, perform significantly worse in achieving preferences than main business groups, representing 'concentrated interests'" (p. 567). Hence, it is vital to distinguish between the political activities of individual businesses and those of interest groups, then to unveil empirically the inner workings of business associations to assess the degree to which they actually represent and aggregate sectoral interests. Similarly, Meckling and Hughes's (2018) analysis of solar panel imports from China emphasizes the strategic dimension of firms both cultivating relationships with public actors and of uniting amongst themselves across the EU. This is demonstrated by analyzing how intra-business divisions between solar power proponents, in particular regarding global value chains, 'confused' decision-making within the EC, the EP and the Council. More generally, the structural heterogeneity of business representation within and across Member States clearly affects how EU and national policies are made.

Meckling (2015) tackles this business heterogeneity when studying the EU's emission trading scheme. Specifically, he seeks to explain variations in how firms engage with environmental politics within sectors, across sectors and institutional contexts and over the policy cycle. He finds "four ideal-type political strategies in environmental politics: *opposition*-firms trying to veto a regulatory initiative; *hedging*-firms seeking to minimize compliance costs across a global industry; *support*-firms aiming to create or expand markets for environmental products and services; and *non-participation*" (pp. 19–20). He concludes that hedging has become dominant and that research should therefore "focus on the role of corporate influence in instrument choice and policy design instead of a binary analytic lens of corporate support versus opposition" for environmental policy (p. 20). Finally, within relational approaches to business strategies that target environmental policy, our analysis also includes more sociological approaches that explore the foundations of the relationships in question. Laurens (2018) proposes both a history and a sociology of affinities and linkages between business associations' employees based among Brussels and EC officials. Indeed, Laurens' rich empirical findings underscore a compelling political economy argument: the need to go beyond ideational arguments that often overstate the performativity of liberal ideology. Instead, Laurens advocates examining how affinities among the business community's staff illuminate the tangible social dynamics which underpin the functioning of European capitalism.

The second subset of research on business-environmental policy relations at the EU scale centered on actors' resources and concerns their ability to 'frame' issues in ways that fit their respective perceptions, value systems and preferences. Compatible with constructivist theory in EU studies (Checkel, 1999; Parsons, 2003), the framing concept was developed from sociological research (Goffman, 1974) into questions of how issues become 'public problems' or not (Gusfield, 1981), and thence orient policy-making. It has been deployed effectively to analyze overall business-public authority relations in the EU by Boräng and Naurin (2015), then by Keller (2018). The former conclude for example that, "when competition is low, and a few business actors get to dominate the [policy] process and the media", the odds even out between businesses and civil society NGOs (p. 513). Keller's analysis goes a stage further by underlining that, contrary to popular and academic expectations, during framing at the EU scale, business engages in *both* 'quiet politics' (i. e., the technicizing of issues; Culpepper, 2010) and 'noisy politics' (i. e., politicization).

More generally, framing analysis concerning environmental policy is particularly well applied by Sandra Eckert (2021) in her analysis of the varieties of ways 'the circular economy' and 'the bioeconomy' have been given institutionalized definitions at the EU scale. Her analysis shows that private companies have 'proactively engaged' in framing these notions and that consequently they have largely set the parameters of policy in both the issue areas concerned (p. 190). However, to do so, such companies engaged in policymaking in different ways. More generally, she concludes that businesses are frequently involved in 'framing competition' (p. 191), the outcomes of which affect policy outcomes in varying, and sometimes counter-intuitive, ways. Pollex and Lenschow (2020) also pursue this argument by analyzing how business interest representation has worked to 'dismantle' EU environmental legislation. Focusing on post-legislative implementation measures, such as setting product specifications, these authors analyze how 'the intensity' of a policy can be diluted or even result in "a regulatory agency giving away enforcement powers" (2020, p. 21). They conclude that when businesses succeed in obtaining 'self-regulation' during implementation, this often means that norms are diluted, or are never actually adopted (e.g., for 'ecodesign', or some 'ecolabels'). Similarly, Boasson, Burns and Pulver (2023) analyze the role played by 'business organizations' not only over framing, but as implementors of technologies and standards such as building codes (pp. 519–20). They notably conclude that more research is needed on the small and medium-sized companies (SMEs) that also implement EU policy and not just on the large and most obviously involved corporations (p. 521).

In summary, research on framing sometimes also targets how actors simultaneously build up their relations with others, and vice versa. However, this is not always the case. Instead, a focus on one type of resource (be it relational or a capacity to frame) rather than both is frequently stressed, sometimes leading analysis to become unidirectional, thus neglecting the interplay between framing and power relations (Joltreau, 2025). Partly for this reason, other researchers adopt a more institution-focused line of analysis.

The inertia of policymaking: When institutions favor business access and interests

A second strand of the literature has examined the role of institutional settings in determining the opportunities available for business to influence policymaking. In his 'elite pluralism' approach, Coen (1997, p. 92) already concluded that "the bargaining strength of each actor can be seen as a function of policy domains, economic conditions and institutional arrangements". More recently, Meckling (2015) also argues that business 'strategy formation' strongly relies on 'institutional environments'. A political system's characteristics, along with its power structure and decision-making mechanisms, have been shown to play a significant role in shaping how interests are represented. Specifically, political and institutional arrangements constrain business influence strategies, which are contingent upon the 'political opportunity structure' accessible to them (Kitschelt, 1986; Tarrow, 1996). Institutional arrangements therefore have structural and formative roles within public policies in establishing an 'incentive structure' (North, 1990) that dictates avenues for accessing and intermediating public and private interests. Studies of corporate political lobbying have thus revealed that fragmented political systems typically facilitate easy access for interest groups, whereas centralized systems often pose initial access challenges but yield greater efficacy once established (Beyers, 2004; Grossman and Saurugger, 2012; Choi, Jia and Lu, 2015; Ehrlich and Jones, 2016).

In the EU case, the variety of interest representations is reflected in the numerous channels available for engagement with EU institutions and more generally within the EU's pluralist political system, which fosters consultation with private interests and civil society. Business lobbying efforts particularly target the EC, whose openness correlates primarily with its legislative initiation function (Nugent, 1995; Bouwen, 2009). Given its involvement in decision-making at all levels and possession of diverse resources over policy instruments design, the EC is a focal point for business representatives. Similarly, the EP attracts business actors' lobbying efforts, who particularly target committee rapporteurs (Eising, 2007). Economic sector representatives may also engage with the Council, although its fragmented intergovernmental structure poses challenges for gaining access (Hayes-Renshaw, 2009). Lastly, well-organized interest groups with substantial financial resources can, to some extent, advocate before the Court of Justice of the European Union (CJEU) (Alter and Vargas, 2000; Conant, 2002). Bouwen and McCown (2007) have also demonstrated the widespread use of recourse to the CJEU by individual businesses.

In summary, the literature has shown that the EU is an open institutional setting concerning interest representation. The extent of business access to EU institutions thus involves a combination of institutional openness and business resources, such as the production of private expertise, which constitutes a prerequisite for being seen as legitimate (Beyers, 2002, 2004; Princen and Kerremans, 2008). Pieter Bouwen (2004) has thus notably conceptualized interest group access to EU institutions as a reciprocal exchange which involves three 'access goods': expert knowledge, information about the European general interest and information about national-level interests. This production of knowledge and information generates symbolic resources that can be accumulated via interactions developed with policymakers (see Chapter 5).

This creates self-reinforcing mechanisms favoring already well-endowed firms. In institutionalist terms, these routinized interactions, themselves facilitated by institutional arrangements, generate long-term path dependence and lock-in effects within policymaking processes. There is indeed a long tradition of research adopting a 'lock-in perspective' to study reinforcing mechanisms that drive stabilization and resistance within *national* policy systems (Pierson, 1993). The argument is that past institutional choices generate normative and interest-driven commitments that shape the very possibilities of future policymaking (Pierson, 2000). These institutional legacies foster a positive feedback loop that reduces the feasibility of change for subsequent policies and serves to reinforce the status quo (Howlett, 2009). Institutionalist approaches have notably examined institutionalized barriers to environmental policy change at the national level (Groen et al., 2023). Similarly, the EU institutional evolution as a polity and integrated market, and the growing importance of environmental discourse, has involved changing 'political opportunity structures' for businesses.

Institutional arrangements can thus be studied concurrently with change in 'institutional context' and 'exogenous shocks' that often prompt shifts within it. Initially, in the 1970s "the path dependent linkage of environmental policy to single market dynamics [...] meant that the imperatives of the single market framing also featured in environmental policy" (Zito, Burns and Lenschow, 2019, p. 196). This concretely implied that businesses in their framing practices could play on ambiguity between environmental and market imperatives. In the 1980s and 1990s, the Single European Act and the growing idea of sustainable development, although increasingly structuring the EU's environmental policy (Zito, Burns and Lenschow, 2019, p. 197), did not fundamentally alter this original tension between economic and environmental objectives, and thus the political opportunity structure for businesses. In the 2000s, although environmental policy objectives remained, the framing of 'competitiveness' gained prominence within EU policy processes (Zito, Burns and Lenschow, 2019). The 'polycrisis' of the 2010s (sovereign debt, migration, Brexit), which created institutional instability in the intergovernmental system, likewise did not favor new avenues for environmental policy reframing. Research has subsequently suggested that, while the EU may not be actively dismantling its environmental policy, this polycrisis has created an increasing emphasis on combatting bureaucratic obstacles and tempering environmental objectives (Burns and Tobin, 2016; Gravey and Jordan, 2016; Steinebach and Knill, 2017).

Within this ideational context, Amanda Machin (2019) has shown that the ecological modernization paradigm has thrived in EU policymaking circles, with strong depoliticizing effects (see also Chapter 3). According to her analysis, the dominant framing of market rationality, one which prevents a democratic debate of alternative political goals and standpoints, constrains EU environmental policymaking. Similarly, ecological modernization discourse in the agricultural sector has only been applied to legitimizing existing practices, thus reproducing low environmental policy integration within the Common Agricultural Policy (Alons, 2017). Lastly, the 'circular economy narrative' that now predominates within EU institutions has also resulted from a coalition of business representatives and policymakers, one which has ultimately reproduced the ecological modernization paradigm: "As soon as the new EU Commission under President Jean-Claude Juncker assumed office, it built a 'status quo coalition' with established business stakeholders and tried to dismantle the [circular economy] narrative by withdrawing [the] Zero Waste [program]" (Leipold, 2021, pp. 1049–1050). Juncker's leadership "created a 'joint coalition' of environmental and business voices within the Commission and reshaped the initial narrative" to reprioritize economic growth and international competitiveness over environmental concerns (pp. 1049–1050). In summary, as *policy actors*, business representatives can take advantage of the political opportunity structures of both existing EU institutional arrangements and dominant economic paradigms to sway the environmental policymaking process.

Some analytical limitations: Too micro but also too macro?

Despite its many qualities, the literature reviewed above has two main limitations flagged here, then another explored in more depth in section 3. The first is that business lobbying practices are often considered to affect policy too narrowly, thus reducing the co-constructive dimension of much policymaking. In the EU, where 'consulting with stakeholders' has become a standard practice, a sociological study of this process necessitates examining the full spectrum of actors involved (firms, policymakers, NGOs, think tanks, etc.) and requires analyzing their resources and relative power, as well as how their political work influences, and is influenced by, institutions.

Indeed, a second limitation of the literature concerns analysis of the impact of institutional arrangements upon political opportunity structures. When over-emphasized, a focus on path dependence and lock-in effects can obscure the fierce framing conflicts and the plurality of competing interests at work. When one posits from the outset an impact of existing institutional arrangements, the role of agency and actors' interactions is often downplayed. It is therefore important to conceptualize self-reinforcing institutional dynamics as the result of the agency of the actors involved, be they public or private, and how they have worked politically to reproduce institutions. Accordingly, Galik and Chelbi (2021) have distinguished between passive stability, active stability, intended inaction and failed action to identify more precisely the relational processes at work leading to institutional stasis. Passive stability involves the reinforcement of existing institutions through norm-induced behaviors and the continuation of established practices, thus constraining institutional change. Active stability emphasizes purposeful actions by established interests to maintain existing frames, while intended inaction involves the deliberate avoidance of actions that could lead to change. Failed action occurs when efforts to foster institutional change are unsuccessful, often caused by the work of dominant actors.

These limitations can be overcome by studying the interrelations between EU environmental governance and business power at the industry level, i. e., at a 'meso-' level which encompasses both 'sectoral' governance and the political economy of specific productive systems. This approach enables researchers to move beyond a narrow focus on the explicitly political activities of individual firms and their interest groups. Instead, it encompasses key dimensions of the economic activity itself, enabling examination of the causes and effects of its specific regulatory institutions on EU environmental policymaking. This involves analyzing the interplay between industry-specific governance structures and policy processes. By doing so, researchers can understand comprehensively the long-term effects of an industry's institutions upon EU environmental policymaking, while also exploring the sociology of actor relations operating within institutional reproduction or change.

3 Going further: Generating comprehensive research on EU environmental regulation and business power at the level of industries

More specifically, our proposition is to focus on the regulation of distinct industries to generate pertinent data through multiple, comparable case studies. To do so, we have built a theoretical framework drawing on regulationist economics (Boyer and Saillard, 2002) that considers both the influence of institutions and the political work of a wide range of actors to reproduce or change them. Among the institutions in question, four key elements that structure the 'life of industries' always need distinguishing: finance, sourcing, employment and market access (Jullien and Smith, 2014). Empirical studies need to unveil how various actors, such as business groups, but also public actors (bureaucratic agents, parliament representatives) and civil society representatives (associations, NGOs) *work politically* to reproduce or change certain sets of institutions related to each of these elements, in accordance with their perceived 'interests' (Jullien and Smith, 2011). This approach enables research to generate empirical results on the regulation of economic activity and its environmental impact, but also to evaluate the degree of business influence within that process. Comparative analysis across different industries demonstrates that the regulation of each one is both contingent and structured by its respective institutions (Jullien and Smith, 2014). In each case, research also needs to examine the alternative problem framings and policy instruments which could have been developed in the past and logically could still be.

Additionally, concerning the environmental regulation of economic activities, Nina Kelsey (2018) contends that categorizing industries in terms of what their actors think will be gained or lost as a result of prioritizing environmental policy within them can enhance our comprehension of the likelihood of industry-policy feedback that leads to increasing, long-run environmental policy success. Kelsey identifies four categories as ideal types: Winner industries that directly benefit from environmental policy; Loser industries, for whom environmental regulation represents an existential threat to their business model; Convertible industries that have the capability to switch to nonpolluting products; and Management industries, which only *use* polluting goods as inputs rather than *making* them, or generate pollutants only as waste. Kelsey argues that each of these categories is characterized by differing potential responses to policy controls on pollutants they produce or consume, and that these differing responses mediate the potential for policy feedback. Empirically, Kelsey shows that Convertible industries are the most interesting for policymakers to target, since they "allow for the rapid addition of large, mature industry groups and coalitions to support policymaking" (p. 637). For example, from the angle of decarbonization, public utilities and auto manufacturers can be viewed as Convertible industries. These initially produce carbon-emitting products, but their core competencies are transferable to closely related non-emitting or low-emitting alternatives. Such a transition incurs costs, such as investing in new production facilities. However, once the transition is made, these companies undergo a fundamental shift in their material interests: they transition from opposing pollution controls to supporting them to help foster markets for the nonpolluting substitutes they have invested in. Additionally, Winner industries such as renewable energy industries "matter most to outcomes when they can scale quickly" (p. 637), especially those with "low capital intensity, rapid production timelines, and the ability to scale to many stakeholders quickly" (p. 638).

In summary, we call for more empirical research at an industry level that targets the issue-framing and alliance-building of public and private actors to shape regulatory institutions that have an impact on environmental regulation and, more fundamentally, meso-political economies (Joltreau, 2025). If this approach considers business actors to be policy actors, we also emphasize that the former rarely constitute a homogeneous group. Our politics-of-industry approach thus cumulatively draws upon the results from the literatures presented in this chapter with regard to both relational and framing analysis and institutional analysis, but also seeks to integrate them within a dynamic and actionable framework for political economy analysis centered on the level of specific industries and their value chains.

4 Conclusion and future challenges for policymakers and research

The need to politically articulate business and environmental policy has clearly become one of the key challenges not just for the EU but for humankind. Driven by climate change, biodiversity loss and other effects of pollution from socioeconomic activity, this challenge will only increase in the coming years. As this chapter has mapped out, social science has already generated robust and convincing analyses of the generally conflictual processes and suboptimal outcomes of how environmental policy has been made to fit the way the economy has been regulated at the EU scale. Stimulating theories have been developed and, increasingly, a wide range of tested methods has been applied during data collection and analysis. Nonetheless, much more still needs to be done in and outside of social science to render its results in this domain compelling and audible, particularly to policymakers, both at this scale and at others (particularly the local and global) with which it overlaps. In fact, industry regulation is fundamentally multilevel, considering the interplay between global, EU and national institutions (Oberthür and Gehring, 2006) and the role of territorially embedded institutional arrangements (Joltreau, 2024).

For future research, we thus suggest examining the multilevel interaction between business political activities and EU environmental policy within specific industries, thereby embracing their unique political economies and value chains. Each case can be analyzed by tracing the business impact on environmental policy all along value chains, from resource extraction and sourcing activities to the production and selling of goods and services, together with how policy regulates pollution and its equivalents at each stage. By mapping these dynamics onto policy subfields like waste management, air pollution and energy usage, research can elucidate the long-term links between business operations and environmental concerns within policy frameworks.

Our own academic community needs to push even harder to isolate what precisely has driven the current (mis)fit between socioeconomic, environmental and political domains. Beyond academia, much more must be done to convince a variety of policymakers that social science can help them go beyond the dead end of considering all economic activity to be necessary and therefore trumping environmental protection. As contemporary political economy shows clearly (Hay, 2016; Smith, 2016), human agency largely structures the economy through political processes, therefore both economic structures and their relationship to the environment are highly contingent. Just as this relationship could have been otherwise in the past, if certain conditions already identified by our sciences are met, it still could be in the future. For example, within the agri-food industry, climate objectives will only ever be met if policymaking is made more pluralistic, transition pathways backed by massive public funding are institutionalized, and those who fail to take such paths are strongly penalized. As the immediate post–World War II period clearly demonstrated, transitioning economic activity is achievable but only through strong institutional steering underpinned by galvanizing political discourse that has genuine social meaning.

References

Alons, G. (2017) 'Environmental policy integration in the EU's common agricultural policy: greening or greenwashing?', *Journal of European Public Policy*, 24(11), pp. 1604 – 1622.

Alter, K.J. and Vargas, J. (2000) 'Explaining variation in the use of European litigation strategies: European Community law and British gender equality policy', *Comparative Political Studies*, 33(4), pp. 452 – 482.

Beyers, J. (2002) 'Gaining and seeking access: The European adaptation of domestic interest associations', *European Journal of Political Research*, 41(5), pp. 585 – 612.

Beyers, J. (2004) 'Voice and access: Political practices of European interest associations', *European Union Politics*, 5(2), pp. 211 – 240.

Boasson, E.L., Burns, C. and Pulver, S. (2023) 'The politics of domestic climate governance: Making sense of complex participation patterns', *Journal of European Public Policy*, 30(3), pp. 513 – 536.

Borăng, F. and Naurin, D. (2015) '"Try to see it my way!" Frame congruence between lobbyists and European Commission officials', *Journal of European Public Policy*, 22(4), pp. 499 – 515.

Bouwen, P. (2004) 'Exchanging access goods for access: A comparative study of business lobbying in the European Union institutions', *European Journal of Political Research*, 43(3), pp. 337 – 369.

Bouwen, P. (2009) 'The European Commission', in Coen, D. and Richardson, J. (eds.) *Lobbying the European Union: Institutions, actors, and issues.* David and Jeremy Richardson. Oxford: Oxford University Press, pp. 19 – 38.

Bouwen, P. and McCown, M. (2007) 'Lobbying versus litigation: Political and legal strategies of interest representation in the European Union', *Journal of European Public Policy*, 14(3), pp. 422 – 443.

Boyer, R. and Saillard, Y. (eds.) (2002) *Regulation theory: The State of the art.* Updated ed. London: Routledge.

Bunea, A. (2013) 'Issues, preferences and ties: Determinants of interest groups' preference attainment in the EU environmental policy', *Journal of European Public Policy*, 20(4), pp. 552–570.

Burns, C. and Tobin, P. (2016) 'The impact of the economic crisis on European Union environmental policy', *JCMS: Journal of Common Market Studies*, 54(6), pp. 1485–1494.

Checkel, J.T. (1999) 'Social construction and integration', *Journal of European Public Policy*, 6(4), pp. 545–560.

Choi, S.-J., Jia, N. and Lu, J. (2015) 'The structure of political institutions and effectiveness of corporate political lobbying', *Organization Science*, 26(1), pp. 158–179.

Coen, D. (1997) 'The evolution of the large firm as a political actor in the European Union', *Journal of European Public Policy*, 4(1), pp. 91–108.

Conant, L.J. (2002) *Justice contained: Law and politics in the European Union.* Ithaca, New York: Cornell University Press.

Culpepper, P.D. (2010) *Quiet politics and business power: Corporate control in Europe and Japan.* New York: Cambridge University Press.

Dür, A., Bernhagen, P. and Marshall, D. (2015) 'Interest group success in the European Union: When (and why) does business lose?', *Comparative Political Studies*, 48(8), pp. 951–983.

Eckert, S. (2021) 'Varieties of framing the circular economy and the bioeconomy: Unpacking business interests in European policymaking', *Journal of Environmental Policy & Planning*, 23(2), pp. 181–193.

Ehrlich, S.D. and Jones, E. (2016) 'Whom do European corporations lobby? The domestic institutional determinants of interest group activity in the European Union', *Business and Politics*, 18(4), pp. 467–488.

Eising, R. (2007) 'The access of business interests to EU institutions: Towards élite pluralism?', *Journal of European Public Policy*, 14(3), pp. 384–403.

Galik, C.S. and Chelbi, L. (2021) 'Revisiting institutional stability: A systematic review and distillations of dominant modes', *Environmental Policy and Governance*, 31(5), pp. 463–473.

Goffman, E. (1974) *Frame analysis: An essay on the organization of experience.* Boston: Northeastern University Press.

Gravey, V. and Jordan, A. (2016) 'Does the European Union have a reverse gear? Policy dismantling in a hyperconsensual polity', *Journal of European Public Policy*, 23(8), pp. 1180–1198.

Greenwood, J. (1997) *Representing Interests in the European Union.* London: Macmillan Education UK.

Greenwood, J. (2003) *Interest representation in the European Union.* New York, Palgrave Macmillan, 2003.

Greenwood, J. and Roederer-Rynning, C. (2021) 'Organized interests and trilogues in a post-regulatory era of EU policy-making', *Journal of European Public Policy*, 28(1), pp. 112–131.

Groen, L. et al. (2023) 'Re-examining policy stability in climate adaptation through a lock-in perspective', *Journal of European Public Policy*, 30(3), pp. 488–512.

Grossman, E. and Saurugger, S. (2012) *Les groupes d'intérêt: Action collective et stratégies de représentation.* Second Edition. Paris: A. Colin.

Gusfield, J.R. (1981) *The culture of public problems: Drinking-driving and the symbolic order.* Chicago: University of Chicago Press.

Haas, E.B. (1958) *The uniting of Europe: Political, social, and economic forces 1950–1957.* Stanford: Stanford University Press.

Hay, C. (2016) 'Good in a crisis: The ontological institutionalism of social constructivism', *New Political Economy*, 21(6), pp. 520–535.

Hayes-Renshaw, F. (2009) 'Least accessible but not inaccessible: Lobbying the Council and the European Council', in: Coen, D. and Richardson, J. (eds.) *Lobbying the European Union: Institutions, Actors, and Issues.* Oxford: Oxford University Press, pp. 70–88.

Hoffmann, S. (1966) 'Obstinate or obsolete? The fate of the nation-state and the case of Western Europe', *Daedalus*, 95, pp. 862–916.

Howlett, M. (2009) 'Process sequencing policy dynamics: Beyond homeostasis and path dependency', *Journal of Public Policy*, 29(3), pp. 241–262.

Joltreau, T. (2024) 'The politics of agro-industrial greening: Policy processes, market institutions and local power relations in the sugarcane sector of French overseas departments', *Journal of Environmental Policy & Planning*, 26(5), pp. 487–501.

Joltreau, T. (2025) 'Subsidizing unprofitable industries: The political determinants of agro-industrial policy in French overseas departments', *Regulation & Governance* [online preprint], https://doi.org/10.1111/rego.12657

Jullien, B. and Smith, A. (2011) 'Conceptualizing the role of politics in the economy: Industries and their institutionalizations', *Review of International Political Economy*, 18(3), pp. 358–383.

Jullien, B. and Smith, A. (eds.) (2014) *The EU's government of industries: Markets, institutions and politics.* Abingdon: Routledge.

Keller, E. (2018) 'Noisy business politics: Lobbying strategies and business influence after the financial crisis', *Journal of European Public Policy*, 25(3), pp. 287–306.

Kelsey, N. (2018) 'Industry type and environmental policy: Industry characteristics shape the potential for policymaking success in energy and the environment', *Business and Politics*, 20(4), pp. 615–642.

Kitschelt, H.P. (1986) 'Political opportunity structures and political protest: Anti-nuclear movements in four democracies', *British Journal of Political Science*, 16(1), pp. 57–85.

Laurens, S. (2018) *Lobbyists and bureaucrats in Brussels: Capitalism's brokers.* London: Routledge.

Leipold, S. (2021) 'Transforming ecological modernization "from within" or perpetuating it? The circular economy as EU environmental policy narrative', *Environmental Politics*, 30(6), pp. 1045–1067.

Machin, A. (2019) 'Changing the story? The discourse of ecological modernisation in the European Union', *Environmental Politics*, 28(2), pp. 208–227.

Meckling, J. (2015) 'Oppose, support, or hedge? Distributional effects, regulatory pressure, and business strategy in environmental politics', *Global Environmental Politics*, 15(2), pp. 19–37.

Meckling, J. and Hughes, L. (2018) 'Protecting solar: Global supply chains and business power', *New Political Economy*, 23(1), pp. 88–104.

North, D.C. (1990) *Institutions, institutional change and economic performance.* Cambridge: Cambridge University Press.

Nugent, N. (1995) 'The leadership capacity of the European Commission', *Journal of European Public Policy*, 2(4), pp. 603–623.

Oberthür, S. and Gehring, T. (eds.) (2006) *Institutional interaction in global environmental governance: Synergy and conflict among international and EU policies.* Cambridge, Massachusetts: The MIT Press.

Parsons, C. (2003) *A certain idea of Europe.* Ithaca/London: Cornell University Press.

Pierson, P. (1993) 'When effect becomes cause: Policy feedback and political change', *World Politics*, 45(4), pp. 595–628.

Pierson, P. (2000) 'Increasing returns, path dependence, and the study of politics', *American Political Science Review*, 94(2), pp. 251–267.

Pollex, J. and Lenschow, A. (2020) 'Many faces of dismantling: Hiding policy change in non-legislative acts in EU environmental policy', *Journal of European Public Policy*, 27(1), pp. 20–40.

Princen, S. and Kerremans, B. (2008) 'Opportunity structures in the EU multi-level system', *West European Politics*, 31(6), pp. 1129–1146.

Rosendal, G.K. (2005) 'Governing GMOs in the EU: A deviant case of environmental policy-making?', *Global Environmental Politics*, 5(1), pp. 82–104.

Smith, A. (2016) *The politics of economic activity.* First edition. Oxford, United Kingdom: Oxford University Press.

Steinebach, Y. and Knill, C. (2017) 'Still an entrepreneur? The changing role of the European Commission in EU environmental policy-making', *Journal of European Public Policy*, 24(3), pp. 429–446.

Tarrow, S. (1996) 'States and opportunities: The political structuring of social movements', in: McAdam, D., McCarthy, J.D. and Zald, M.N. (eds.) *Comparative perspectives on social movements: Political opportunities, mobilizing structures, and cultural framings.* Cambridge: Cambridge University Press, pp. 41 – 61.

Vormedal, I. (2017) 'Corporate strategies in environmental governance: Marine harvest and regulatory change for sustainable aquaculture', *Environmental Policy and Governance*, 27(1), pp. 45 – 58.

Vormedal, I., Gulbrandsen, L.H. and Skjærseth, J.B. (2020) 'Big oil and climate regulation: Business as usual or a changing business?', *Global Environmental Politics*, 20(4), pp. 143 – 166.

Zito, A.R., Burns, C. and Lenschow, A. (2019) 'Is the trajectory of European Union environmental policy less certain?', *Environmental Politics*, 28(2), pp. 187 – 207.

Nathalie Berny

Advocating for the environment in Brussels

Abstract: The European Union's environmental legislation has fostered the creation of European networks of environmental nongovernmental organizations and the restructuration of existing international environmental organizations. In parallel, the multiplication of organizations deprived of members' support, such as foundations, particularly in the field of climate change policy has altered the landscape of organizations advocating for the environment in Brussels. Interest group and social movement scholars have neglected this diversity and the underlying organizational questions. This chapter outlines the distinctive logics of mobilization, maintenance and decision-maker access of these diverse organizations. We suggest examining both the internal dimension of organizations' management and the external dimension of advocacy strategies to stress how such organizations can shape EU policies and respond to normative democratic issues.

Keywords: Nongovernmental organizations; think tanks; foundations; lobbying; organizational maintenance

1 Introduction

This chapter considers a variety of organizations that advocate for the environment in the European Union (EU). Numerous environmental nongovernmental organizations (ENGOs), think tanks and foundations, all with operating offices in Brussels, fall into this category; some have played critical roles in this policy domain. Advocacy refers to the diverse modes of action that interest groups usually deploy to shape public policies and set the agenda on potentially overlooked issues. It corresponds with an extensive understanding of lobbying activities encompassing direct relationships with decision-makers but also grassroots mobilization, public communication and research (Baumgartner and Leech, 1998). Interestingly, organizations that hold primary aims separate from influencing public decisions (which defines per se interest groups) have developed a large, similar range of activities.

Organizational aims, functioning and, to some extent, funding logics differ greatly. *Environmental nongovernmental organizations* are the institutionalized component of environmental movements (Dalton, 1994). ENGOs gained in professional expertise by hiring staff while relying on membership support to pressure public authorities and shape their decisions. *Think tanks* are private research institutes that provide policy-relevant knowledge to decision-makers and the public to foster policy advice and public debate. *Foundations* are grant-making organizations that support the initiatives of the other two. All these organizations are nonprofit and defend a collective cause rather than specific constituency interests. While constituencies refer to the publics

https://doi.org/10.1515/9783111321523-020

affected by their interventions, only ENGOs can claim a membership of individuals or of grassroots organizations, as frequently is the case at the EU level.

Different academic literatures have scrutinized these three organizational types. Knowledge about ENGOs active in Brussels is mainly limited to individual case studies on public policies or cross-sectoral comparative interest group studies that address their role in shaping political decisions. Research is scarce on environmental think tanks and foundations operating at the EU level. Considered a separate category of policy players, the latter sometimes are merged with nongovernmental organizations (NGOs) as part of the civil society sector across sectoral studies on interest groups or policies (Berkhout et al., 2018).

Questioning actual differences between the aforementioned organizations offers a vantage point to grasp the constraints on actors striving to promote the environment and the dynamics structuring the relationships between policy actors in this field. The European Commission (EC) needs expertise and "sound information and advice" (Mazey and Richardson, 1992, p. 110) but also support from the publics concerned to design and facilitate the implementation of new policies (see Chapters 5, 32 and 34). In Brussels and elsewhere, environmental policy collides with the status quo that prevails in policy sectors organized around producer interests, such as energy, transport or agriculture. Environmental administrations have traditionally relied on ENGOs' support and critical pressure to balance the weight of sectoral interests (McFarland, 1987). Considering how pro-environmental forces, beyond ENGOs, get organized and achieve success is valuable, especially in times of environment and climate emergency.

This chapter stresses two key analytical dimensions: 'mobilization' and 'influence' (Berkhout et al., 2018). The first section explains how the different environmental organizations came into existence and established themselves over time. We then examine their potential influence in this policy field by focusing on their joint action and distinctive ways of mobilizing expertise and social pressure. This two-fold approach offers complementary perspectives for comparing the three types of pro-environment actors and thus insight into related knowledge gaps.

2 Mobilization: Entrepreneurship and institutional patronage

Because collective action has costs (i. e. time, efforts and resources) for those willing to join, not all interests or collective causes get represented (Olson, 1965). Two mechanisms contribute to the 'mobilization of interests', namely the formation and the maintenance of new organizations (Walker, 1991). Some *entrepreneurs* are ready to bear the cost of the group's initial activities by offering incentives to potential members. If successful, member support will sustain the collective's activities (Salisbury, 1969). *Patrons* may also be willing to support materially the creation of new groups. They might be private, such as foundations or corporations, or public, such as agencies, cities or universities (Walker, 1991). Especially useful for explaining the interest group boom in the United States (US) context since the 1960s, these two mechanisms are also observable in Brussels. They are relevant for mapping the characteristics and potential relationships between the three organizational types.

NGOs: supporting environmental policy development

The first associations created in Brussels emerged during the environmental mobilizations of the 1960s–1970s. They initially relied exclusively on the good will and time of national activists. A mix of entrepreneurship and institutional patronage explains their growth. Indeed, the EC initially encouraged the formation of European associations collecting the views of national constituencies across policy sectors (Greenwood, 2017).

Belgian activists and their counterparts from other European countries created the European Environmental Bureau (EEB) in 1974, a federation gathering national organizations. The EC welcomed the initiative, providing initial funding for the Bureau's conferences and workshops. The EEB was often a formative experience for the (new) environmental groups that joined and were being organized at both national and international levels (Lowe and Goyder, 1983; Dalton, 1994). Included in the latter were Friends of the Earth (FoE) activists who created their own network in 1985. They realized the value of a European office to gain precious information and potential leverage on political processes shaping policies at home (Berny, 2008). Existing international ENGOs followed this precedent. Based on the one organization member per country principle, the World Wildlife Fund (WWF), Greenpeace and Birdlife International established a Brussels office in the 1990s. They formalized a European entity, more or less independent from the international one, that consisted of European national groups participating in its activities (Berny, 2008).

During the 1990s, the aforementioned organizations proved their value for the EC units beyond the Directorate-General for Environment in sectoral policies such as agriculture and regional development (Long, 1995). The EC institutional patronage evolved into a competitive funding stream for environmental groups with an EU scope, either research- or advocacy-oriented (by Council Decision 97/872/EC). As in national contexts, pluriannual grants provided precious support for developing ENGO organizational-strategic capacities in the longer run (Berny, 2013a). NGOs have also developed the competence necessary to obtain and manage LIFE project grants across Europe, engaging public and private partners and stakeholders. These funding opportunities incentivized newcomers to establish a Brussels presence from the 2000s onwards. Entrepreneurs, coming sometimes from ENGOs, or international organizations, such as Climate Action Network, contributed to a renewal, reflecting the breadth of the EU environmental legislation and its international leadership. Additionally, other nonprofit sectors started addressing sustainability or climate issues, for instance Oxfam concerning development aid.

Today's picture features organizations varied in size, topics and shades of green (e.g., calling for more/less radical socioeconomic change, as illustrated by organizations renting at the Mundo-B NGO hub building). Like for any interest group, the Brussels staff usually monitor EU policy developments, relay information to their network, coordinate positions and organize advocacy. National organizations may have direct interactions with EU decision-makers and sometimes via their Brussels offices (e.g., NABU, the German partner of Birdlife International).

Think tanks: providing evidence-based policy recommendations

Think tanks inform decision-makers and the public, by providing "research, analysis, and advice on public policy on an independent basis" (Marybel Perez as quoted by Rastrick, 2017, p. 13). Although their credibility implies a certain level of neutrality, they have a value-oriented agenda in terms of priorities and solutions.

The literature on US think tanks is considerably larger than the EU subfield. The first Brussels-based organizations emerged in the 1980s (Rastrick, 2017). Across European countries, foundations, political parties or public authorities had previously offered patronage to such organizations (Plehwe, 2021). In Brussels, European parties may have their own foundation since the EU Regulation 1524/2004, while the EC has its in-house think tank since 2014. Over the 2000s, well-established think tanks, such as the European Policy Centre, or more recently Europe Jacques Delors, have addressed issues related to climate change and sustainability. Indeed, their work program tends to align with the agenda of EU institutions, with certain topics deemed essential to get the latter's attention.

For the far fewer think tanks whose primary *raison d'être* is EU-level environmental policy, the formation has depended on the initiative of a few supported by external funding. The Brussels-based *Institute for European Environmental Policy* (IEEP) was established in 1974, initially in Bonn with offices in Paris and London, to provide education to the public and decision-makers on European environmental problems. After the initial funding from the European Cultural Foundation, the EC and Member States commissioned its work (Weill, 2021). Likewise, a US environmental lawyer, with the support of the McIntosh Foundation, initiated the 2007 creation of ClientEarth, which specializes in litigation and now has several branches in Europe. ClientEarth's legal team has filled a competence gap in Brussels since 2009, where NGOs had lamented their lack of legal capacity (Goodman and Connelly, 2018). By developing advocacy, supporting public causes and ENGOs, ClientEarth follows the action template of US public interest law firms and is thus difficult to categorize. Its funding stems from foundations, to a lesser extent the public and, increasingly, individual donors.

Some green think tanks originating in Member States have been significantly active at the EU level, such as Ecologic (Öko-Institut) in Germany or E3G (based in the United Kingdom but with a Brussels office). The Green Tank, founded in Greece, is a 2018 addition.

Foundations and philanthropy: Funding collective action and projects

Foundations are the "organizational form through which private wealth is funnelled to public goals" (Betsill et al., 2022, p. 686). They might be corporate or private (e.g., associated with a wealthy family or donors); some become more independent in terms of governance and funding from this initial support (Cracknell, Khan and Lombardi, 2023). Environmental foundations based in Member States have supported the ENGO sector in Brussels; one example is Heinrich Böll, a foundation linked to the German Green Party (Berny, 2013a). Foundations operating in Brussels with European outreach appear to be rare and relatively new. Research remains scarce on environmental foundations (Betsill et al., 2022, Plehwe, 2021), particularly in the EU context. Compared to EU institutional funding (Crepaz and Hanegraaff, 2020; Sanchez Salgado, 2014), foundation patronage in the growth of the Brussels NGO sector has not been as well studied.

Research on climate philanthropy nevertheless provides insights on its deployment in Europe. The US foundations that played a key part in the emergence of environmental groups and collective causes at home in the 1960s (Jenkins et al., 2017) have grappled with the climate change issue since the 1980s to better coordinate their international level efforts. They developed a strategic approach over time that focused on awareness-raising, supporting advocacy groups through capacity-building and more specific priorities by pooling grant-making efforts (Morena, 2017). This resulted in the 2008 creation of Climate Works and of regional offices, including the European Climate Foundation (ECF), one year later, all operating as regranting foundations.

Climate Works' objective is to expand fundraising and operations to shape the most crucial rounds of climate negotiations, as corporate foundations have massively invested in think tanks and public communication to prevent progress at the international level and in several key countries (Plehwe, 2021). The ECF, which pursues this objective at the EU level, has also become more strategic, developing public communication strategies in addition to lobbying (Morena, 2017). Unlike the US, the EU does not ban foundations from lobbying. Among the mostly US foundations that foster climate philanthropy, the Oak Foundation stands out because of its European reach and support for broader environmental issues, but it operates no Brussels office. By contrast, the ECF declared in 2024 the equivalent of fifteen full-time staff undertaking lobbying activities in the EU transparency register. The ECF has become a key funding partner for many ENGOs in Brussels but has also developed its own advocacy team.

Interorganizational links and persisting differences

Interest groups and social movement scholars have traditionally highlighted the importance of material support from existing organizations, including ENGOs and foundations, to create collective action voicing environmental concerns (Dalton, 1994; Jenkins et al., 2017). In EU studies, the questions of formation and maintenance nevertheless lost their salience among interest group scholars, while think tanks and foundations have remained understudied.

However, several trends in the Brussels ENGO sector beg for studies of both organizational aspects, as a growing number of diverse organizations operate under the broader sustainability label. Little is known about interorganizational links and group formation. Newcomers, such as the ECF, have undoubtedly transformed the ENGO funding landscape and probably their advocacy. A new wave of climate activists has pressed decision-makers for adopting bold climate action across Europe since 2018 (Parks, Oberthür and Maarov, 2023). Interestingly, research on young activists and climate mobilizations rarely addresses the organizational infrastructure of these movements or differentiates the genuinely new groups, such as Fridays for Future, from the youth branch of existing NGOs (Orsini and Kang, 2023).

The different possible sources of income mentioned in the literature also suggest interorganizational and possibly transnational links (cf. Figure 1). NGOs' and think tanks' activities may be funded by public authorities, other NGOs and foundations, either based in Member States or at the EU level. Political parties may support foundations or think tanks. For instance, the IEEP was commissioned over time by the EC, the European Parliament, several Member States, international and national NGOs.

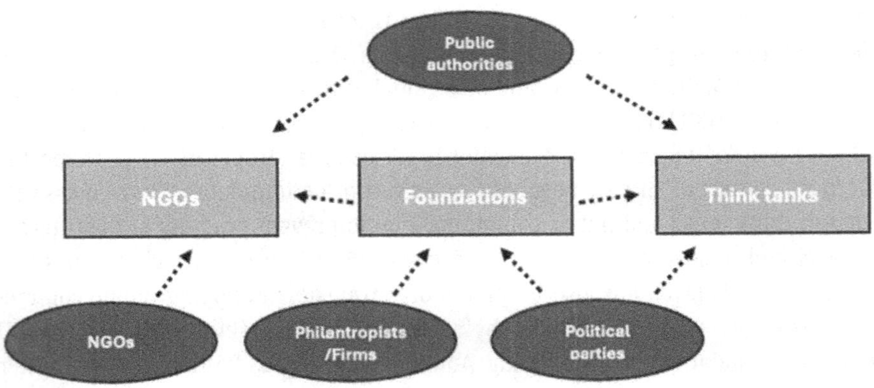

Figure 1: Possible sources of funding at the EU and domestic levels.

Finally, the comparison between the three types of organizations indicates some convergence in terms of activities. The case of the ECF illustrates the blurring lines between NGOs, think tanks and foundations. All the organizations mentioned above claim expertise on policy problems and their context, whether they provide it in-house or commission research to obtain it. They also engage with the public debate by convening meetings with decision-makers and the media, and utilizing social media. They often share the same legal status; for instance, Greenpeace and the ECF are both foundations registered in the Netherlands, while the EEB and ClientEarth in Brussels are associations registered under Belgian law. Indeed, the legal framework for nonprofit organizations and related obligations varies from one European country to another, offering different comparative advantages.

Although all three organization types strive for the attention of EU decision-makers and (to a lesser extent) the public, critical differences persist. ENGOs have, in theory, the moral and material support of a membership, even if other income sources eventually prevail. Income diversification through public grants and foundation funding is often needed to expand their activities, especially in Brussels, where they rely on organizations' rather than individual membership. NGOs are supposed to represent their members and be accountable for their activities. Conversely, anybody with enough money can start a think tank or a foundation (Plehwe, 2021). The world of foundations and think tanks is notoriously opaque concerning funding. Environmental foundations rarely disclose fully the allocation and origins of their funding, explaining partly the lack of research on the subject (Lee and Abbot, 2024). The next section investigates how organizations' constitutive differences might influence the role they play in the policy process.

3 Influence: Collective action across Europe and in Brussels

The exchange-resource model, which assumes a mutual dependency regarding information and support between interest groups and EU decision-makers, has been mainstream in EU studies (Mazey and Richardson, 1992; Greenwood, 2017; Pakull, Marshall and Bernhagen, 2020). The concept of access—the frequency of their interactions—has been used as a proxy to deduce influence. Large-scale comparison between different interest groups has questioned whether 'interest groups' characteristics, such as sectional *versus* diffuse interests or EU *versus* domestic, determine their capacity to match EU decision-makers' expectations (Pakull, Marshall and Bernhagen, 2020). More fine-grained analyses of organizations' strategies and individual decisions are required to balance such generalization and differentiate between ENGOs, think tanks and foundations. Drawing on ENGOs research, I focus on two important levers for environmental policy influence: the mobilization of their membership or constituencies across multiple decision-making levels and coalition politics in Brussels.

Taking advantage of multilevel policymaking

Expertise and knowledge about Member States' contexts are key EU policy resources. While environmental think tanks and foundations sometimes have offices in European countries, the ENGOs' membership, made of national voluntary organizations, is precious for providing knowledge on both policy problems and processes in Member States. Moreover, it constitutes potential leverage for garnering broader social support for EU policies or exerting pressure on national and European authorities. However, playing the 'Brussels game' (Mazey and Richardson, 1992) notoriously drives ENGOs toward 'inside' rather than 'outside strategies' (Walker, 1991), targeting decision-makers or the public, respectively (Rucht, 1997; Parks, 2015). Consequently, earlier studies criticized ENGO activities on normative grounds, questioning the effective participation of ENGOs' membership and whether the logics of compromise necessarily shaped their strategies. However, research on Europeanization revealed a complex picture of cooperation and joint action between a mix of different organizations beyond formal membership.

Effective membership participation in the staff decisions of the Brussels-based ENGOs is challenging (Rucht, 1997; Warleigh, 2001; Kröger, 2016). Lobbying at the EU level is resource- and time-consuming for national organizations, while gains in influence and credit with their constituencies are uncertain (Berny, 2013a; Rucht, 1997). Although European ENGOs assist them in engaging with EU policy processes and issues, not all members have the capacity to contribute to their agenda or even respond to joint action. By mobilizing the network's competences and views at different policy stages, working groups prove the mutual benefits of cooperation. National members may bring new issues to the EU level, such as the shale gas ban or maritime safety (Berny, 2008), while the European offices invite them to share their knowledge at the EU level. For instance, the WWF Europe documented the ecological impact of austerity policies in Greece thanks to its national branch and Greek ENGO partners. Finally, ENGOs such as Birdlife International and FoE Europe invest in capacity-building in their respective networks, expecting collective returns from stronger national organizations (Berny, 2013a).

Research on the Europeanization of environmental groups—the process where EU integration shapes domestic actors' priorities and modes of action—shows that EU-level ENGOs helped establish 'transnational NGO networks' in Central and Eastern European countries. EU NGOs have successfully used pre-accession funding to coordinate the national NGOs and get them involved in establishing the Natura 2000 network under the Habitats Directive (Börzel and Buzogány, 2010; Andonova and Tuta, 2014). National organizations have become more professionalized and dependent on external funding, prompting criticism of 'NGOization' and 'westernization' (Fagan and Buzogány, 2022). Given the potential of energy transition policies in Eastern Europe, questioning the EU's East/West divide is urgent, but studies offer a more nuanced picture of the dynamics and strategic challenges involved.

The transnational mobilizations around the river Loire in France in the 1980s (Mermet, 2018) and the Białowieża forest in Poland (Szulecka and Szulecki, 2022) in the late 2010s (respectively coined the last wild river and last primitive forest of Europe), illustrate the dual strategies involving participation in consultative procedures, lobbying, grassroots mobilizations and radical activism enabled by a mix of groups. Indeed, ENGOs often deploy blame and encouragement, pressure and support, when engaging public authorities. The value of transnational cooperation must be assessed from the organizations' standpoint. Europeanization does not necessarily divert national groups from their mission or deplete their resources, provided they arbitrate with their own organizational imperatives (Berny, 2013b; Kröger, 2016). Looking at the black box of organizations illuminates genuine learning processes about EU opportunities (Andonova and Tuta, 2014; Berny, 2013b; Börzel and Buzogány, 2010).

For think tanks, playing the multilevel game involves two key strategic decisions: concluding partnerships with think tanks based in other countries and the iteration of national offices across Europe (Rastrick, 2017). This is the case also in the environmental sector. The IEEP has concentrated its activities in Brussels since 2001, while working with other pro-environment think tanks across Europe that have strong expertise in EU affairs. In 2019, IEEP started a membership organization (Think Sustainable Europe) to join efforts of environmental think tanks active in the Member States or across Europe (sixteen in 2024). Along with creating a multistakeholder platform, the initiative has monitored the implementation of the European Green Deal (EGD). Enhancing implementation is crucial to an organization such as ClientEarth, whose mission is to exploit or even create opportunities of litigation at EU and Member State levels (Berny, 2026). ClientEarth in Brussels has been coordinating litigation targeting Member States' strategies across Europe with its European offices and other NGOs. ClientEarth also provides reports, training and policy advice to NGOs, judges and decision-makers. As a foundation, the ECF has directed funding toward capacity-building in Brussels and Member States. The ECF has participated in climate litigation projects and establishing citizen assemblies (Lee and Abbott, 2024). Recent studies reflect the proliferation of such initiatives in Brussels and beyond (Colli, 2024).

Beyond the membership of NGOs and projects, multiple links between organizations delineate a community where trust and mutual recognition are conducive to further cooperation, alongside with competition for access, resources and taking credit for collective action. This also applies to the coalition-building logics observable in Brussels.

Coalition politics and mutual recognition

Coalition politics reflects the importance of expertise and public support to access decision-makers. The European Commission has encouraged the creation of coalitions to facilitate its consultations (Greenwood, 2017). While an alliance implies sharing a common stance on a given policy issue, a coalition implies a more longstanding cooperation, where resources are pooled and decisions are binding for its members (Wilson, 1995). Some organizations might invest more resources to maintain a coalition. The number of participants and their reputation (their reliability in providing expertise and conveying members' views; see Mazey and Richardson, 1992) strengthen collective stances. Interwoven links exist between ENGOs and other organizations through overlapping membership—for instance, ClientEarth joined the EEB's EU-level organizations' memberships, all providing information and networking resources crucial to induce collective action (Berny, 2008).

The Green 10 (G10) is the most high-profile environmental coalition. The first ENGOs settled in Brussels formed it to meet regularly with the EC Directorate-General and gain more credibility together *vis-à-vis* other institutions. During the 2019–2024 mandate of the von der Leyen Commission, they often met Commission Vice President Timmermans, responsible for the European Green Deal. The G10 members can share common concerns and react swiftly together, including when collective approval is not met. For example, six of them, more supportive of the EGD, launched a communication campaign for the hearing of the 2024–2029 Commissioners, asking them to respond to nineteen priorities. G10 members, with other NGOs, think tanks and unions, participated in various efforts to monitor and advocate for the alignment of the Recovery and Resilience Fund in Member States with the EGD priorities (EEB, 2021). This illustrates the web of connections between various organizations active at the EU or Member State levels. From the 2021 CAP reform to the negotiation of the Nature Restoration Law, coalition politics is an ever-present reality and, at different stages of a policy process, enables a mix of strategies.

The diversity and number of coalition members enhance coalition credibility, but they might also imply building alliances with policy actors beyond the environment (Bocse, 2021). Critical battles, such as the adoption of the Registration, Evaluation, Authorization and Restriction of Chemicals (REACH) Regulation, involved an alliance between the NGO sector, consumer organizations and small firms (see Chapter 27). A common narrative voiced by different interests on a highly public salient issue does not always bring success. Coalition politics and outsider strategies are not exclusively used by less-resourced actors such as pro-environmental actors (Bocse, 2021). Research on interest groups highlights the importance of public attention, confirming the necessity to combine lobbying with public communication strategies (Parks, 2015).

Field builders or gatekeepers?

Mapping the multiple links organizations active in environmental advocacy have when it comes to collective action remains challenging but worth considering in view of two competing assumptions found in research into foundations and interest groups. The foundations play the role of a 'field builder'. They facilitate collective action (Betsill et al., 2022) but also channel and thus may constrain the issues to be covered, the narratives told, and modes of action taken (Jenkins et al., 2017). Similarly, the part played by the most prominent ENGOs in terms of competence and organizational capacity can be questioned as brokers or gatekeepers for the rest of the environmental organizations to access EU processes. Moreover, professionalized organizations more successful in attracting their funding would also be prone to compromise on stances (Jenkins et al., 2017).

Research on foundations, think tanks, ENGOs and their links is needed to address this debate. These questions delineate the strategic dilemma for ENGOs and their activities, from funding to advocacy, that depend on various publics. However, the margin of autonomy in terms of agenda and resources is not alike for all organizations. We suggest looking more thoroughly at what ENGOs do (together) and the resulting public environmental decisions (Mermet, 2018).

In this respect, Brussels-based ENGOs are policy players. They can play the long game in Brussels: pushing for policy solutions when the context is favorable and fighting against the dismantling of existing legislation when it is not. The 2019–2024 sequence of the European Green Deal is enlightening in this respect. ENGOs actively participated in building proposals upon previous initiatives, such as the former Soil Directive, and monitoring the progress of related policymaking. The recent backlash by the right-wing Members of European Parliament to prevent the LIFE operating grant from funding ENGOs' advocacy activities suggests that, indeed, ENGOs matter in EU policymaking (Gros et al., 2025). Additionally, the supposed collusion between the main field players, ENGOs and foundations needs cautious appraisal. ENGOs have been increasingly dealing with project-oriented funding. Consequences include: constrained time spans of action, scaled-up pooled grants that complicate applications and reporting burdens with tight deadlines. While not publicly vocal, ENGOS sometimes sound critical of foundations that compete with them for access without showing the same democratic credentials, namely the support of a membership.

4 Conclusion

Setting up collective action to support the preservation of public goods, such as the environment, is notoriously challenging. This chapter explored the diversity of involved organizations through the lens of two key dimensions, namely mobilization and influence. Insights from organizational theory in EU studies have mainly contributed large-scale comparisons of interest groups at the expense of the logics sustaining individual organizations and their activities in relationship with potential allies. Think tanks and foundations are often conflated with ENGOs. Confusion still prevails because the existing EU registers (the transparency register, the EC meeting register, and advisory committee registers) use different criteria in this regard, while the registered self-proclaimed environmental credentials are sometimes dubious (Nosko and Ušiak, 2023).

ENGOs, think tanks and foundations have nevertheless distinct logics of mobilization and influence. They do not operate with the same constraints. The grant-making organizations undertaking advocacy activities, such as the ECF, have financial security and thus stability and strategic foresight (Morena, 2017). By contrast, ENGOs and independent think tanks often operate with limited resources and critical allocation choices. All compete for public attention and access to decision-makers without showing the same democratic credentials. The lack of disclosure of foundations' funding and activities is especially problematic. Conversely, the Green 10 members in coalition with other NGO sectors have committed to full disclosure of funding and activities in the transparency register to set an example against corporate interests (Berny, 2014).

Research centered on organizations and transnational cooperation shows that not all organizations are alike when dealing with organizational imperatives and advocacy. Collective logics for the environment at the EU level justify institutional patronage but also new forms of access to ensure plural voices are heard (Parks, Oberthür and Maarov, 2023). Among the diversity of organizations advocating for the environment in Brussels, several have more established presence and access to decision-makers within specific policies because of their expertise and involvement over time. For instance, only a few think tanks, ENGOs and the ECF participate in the meetings with the numerous industry representatives in European climate and energy policy (Nosko and Ušiak, 2023).

By differentiating ENGOs, think tanks and foundations, social network analysis (Bocse, 2021) could help document the links within the environmental advocacy community in terms of funding and cooperation to determine whether the main policy players effectively prevent or allow outsiders to voice concerns. Similarly, a population ecology approach that involves mapping population dynamics could prove useful to document convergence in organizational forms, division of labor and chance of survival (Berkhout et al., 2018). A better knowledge of the environmental advocacy community, attuned to their diversity and needs, is strategically valuable for pro-environmental forces. Private funding (corporate or individual) for the environment remains marginal compared to other public causes (Cracknell, Khan and Lombardi, 2023), hardly competing with the gigantic fossil fuel industry investment in attacking environmental ambitions (Brulle and Downie, 2022).

References

Andonova, L.B. and Tuta, I.A. (2014) 'Transnational networks and paths to EU environmental compliance: Evidence from new Member States', *Journal of Common Market Studies,* 52(4), pp. 775 – 793.

Baumgartner, F. and Leech, B. (1998) *Basic interests. The importance of groups in politics and political science.* Princeton, NJ: Princeton University Press.

Berkhout, J. et al. (2018) 'Making inference across mobilisation and influence research: Comparing top-down and bottom-up mapping of interest systems', *Political Studies,* 66(1), pp. 43 – 62.

Berny, N. (2008) 'Le lobbying des ONG internationales d'environnement à Bruxelles : Les ressources de réseau et d'information, conditions et facteurs de changement de l'action collective', *Revue française de science politique,* 58(1), pp. 93 – 116.

Berny, N. (2013a) 'Building the capacity to play on multilevel policy processes: French environmental movement organisations and the European Union', *Social Movement Studies,* 12(3), 298 – 315.

Berny, N. (2013b) 'Europeanization as organizational learning: When French ENGOs play the EU multilevel policy game', *French Politics,* 11(3), pp. 217 – 240.

Berny, N. (2026). 'Under normative pressure: the European Union at odds with the Aarhus Convention', *Journal of European Integration,* 48(1), pp. 97 – 118.

Betsill, M.M., Enrici, A., Le Cornu, E. and Gruby, R.L. (2022) 'Philanthropic foundations as agents of environmental governance: A research agenda', *Environmental Politics,* 31(4), pp. 684 – 705.

Bocse, A.M. (2021) 'Relational power, brokers and influence: A study on the controversial issue of fracking in the European Union', *Journal of Common Market Studies,* 59(5), pp. 1267 – 1283.

Börzel, T. and Buzogány, A. (2010) 'Environmental organisations and the Europeanisation of public policy in Central and Eastern Europe: The case of biodiversity governance', *Environmental Politics*, 19(5), 708 – 735.

Brulle, R. and Downie, C. (2022) 'Following the money: Trade associations, political activity and climate change', *Climatic change*, 175(3 – 4), p. 11.

Colli, F. (2024) 'Legal opportunity structures: social movements in the European courts'. In: Delplano, R., Gentile, G., Lonardo, L. and Nowak, T. (ed.) *Interdisciplinary research methods in EU law: A handbook*. Cheltenham: Edward Elgar Publishing, pp. 97 – 115.

Cracknell, J., Khan, H. and Lombardi, G. (2023) *Environmental funding by European foundations*. Brussels: European Environmental Funders Group (Philea).

Crepaz, M. and Hanegraaff, M. (2020) 'The funding of interest groups in the EU: Are the rich getting richer?', *Journal of European Public Policy*, 27(1), pp. 102 – 121.

Dalton, R.J. (1994) *The green rainbow: Environmental groups in Western Europe*. New Haven (CT), London: Yale University Press.

EEB (2021) *National recovery and resilience plans (NRRPs): Boost for long-term sustainability or missed opportunity?*. Position paper, 31 March. Available at: https://eeb.org/wp-content/uploads/2021/04/EEB-paper-NRRPs-April-21.pdf (Accessed: 26 July 2024).

Fagan, A. and Buzogány, A. (2022) 'Beyond Europeanization: Political ecology and environmentalism in Central and Eastern Europe', *Environmental Politics*, 31(7), pp. 1203 – 1213.

Goodman, M. and Connelly, J. (2018) 'The public interest environmental law group: From USA to Europe', *Environmental Politics*, 27(6), pp. 1014 – 1032.

Greenwood, J. (2017) *Interest representation in the European Union*. Basingstoke: Macmillan.

Gros, M., Guillot L. and Coi, G. (2025) EPP's war on NGOs is driving a wedge through Europe's political center, *Politico Europe*, 5 May. Available at: https://www.politico.eu/article/european-peoples-party-epp-ngo-funding-civil-society-far-right/

Jenkins, J.C., Carmichael, J.T., Brulle, R.J. and Boughton, H. (2017) 'Foundation funding of the environmental movement', *American Behavioral Scientist*, 61(13), pp. 1640 – 1657.

Kröger, S. (2016) *Europeanised or European? Representation by civil society organisations in EU policy making*. Colchester: ECPR Press.

Lee, M. and Abbot, C. (2024) 'Philanthropy and environmental law', *Journal of Law and Society*, 51(3), pp. 413 – 434.

Long, T. (1995) 'Shaping public policy in the European Union: A case study of the Structural Funds', *Journal of European Public Policy*, 2(14), pp. 672 – 679.

Lowe, P. and Goyder, J. (1983) *Environmental groups in politics*. London: George Allen and Unwin.

Mazey, S. and Richardson, J.J. (1992) 'Environmental groups and the European Community: Challenges and opportunity', *Environmental Politics*, 1(4), pp. 109 – 128.

McFarland, A.S. (1987) 'Interest groups and theories of power in America', *British Journal of Political Science*, 17(2), pp. 129 – 147.

Mermet, L. (2018) 'Pro-environmental strategies in search of an actor: A strategic environmental management perspective on environmental NGOs', *Environmental Politics*, 27(6), pp. 1146 – 1165.

Morena, E. (2017) 'Follow the money: Climate philanthropy from Kyoto to Paris'. In: Aykut, S., Foyer, J. and Morena, E. (eds.) *Globalising the Climate: COP21 and the Climatisation of Global Debates*. London: Routledge, pp. 95 – 115.

Nosko, A. and Ušiak, J. (2023) 'Effects of COVID-19 on civil society voices in European energy and climate policy', *Energy Policy*, 174, 113421.

Olson, M. (1965). *The logic of collective action : Public goods and the theory of groups*. Cambridge: Harvard University Press.

Orsini, A.J. and Kang, Y.H. (2023) 'European leadership and European youth in the climate change regime complex', *Politics and Governance*, 11(2), pp. 84 – 96.

Pakull, D., Marshall, D. and Bernhagen, P. (2020) 'Shop till you drop? Venue choices of business and non-business interests in the European Union', *Interest Groups & Advocacy*, 9(4), pp. 520–540.

Parks, L. (2015) *Social movement campaigns on EU policy: In the corridors and in the streets.* New York: Springer.

Parks, L., Oberthür, S. and Maarov, T. (2023) *Contemporary climate activism and EU climate policy: Societal engagement as public participation*, GreenDeal-NET.

Plehwe, D. (2021) 'Think tanks and the politics of climate change'. In: Abelson, D.E. and Rastrick, C.J. (eds.) *Handbook on think tanks in public policy.* Cheltenham: Edward Elgar Publishing, pp. 150–165.

Rastrick, C.J. (2017) *Think tanks in the US and EU : The role of policy institutes in Washington and Brussels.* London: Routledge.

Rucht, D. (1997) 'Limits to mobilization: Environmental policy for the European Union'. In: Smith, J., Chatfield, C. and Pagnucco, R. (eds.) *Transnational social movements and global politics: Solidarity beyond the state.* Syracuse, NY: Syracuse University Press, pp. 195–213.

Salisbury, R.H. (1969) 'An exchange theory of interest groups', *Midwest Journal of Political Science*, 13(1), pp. 1–32.

Sanchez Salgado, R. (2014) 'Rebalancing EU interest representation? Associative democracy and EU funding of civil society organizations', *Journal of Common Market Studies*, 52(2), pp. 337–353.

Szulecka, J. and Szulecki, K. (2022) 'Between domestic politics and ecological crises: (De)legitimization of Polish environmentalism', *Environmental Politics*, 31(7), pp. 1214–1243.

Walker, J.L. (1991) *Mobilizing interest groups in America: Patrons, professions, and social movements.* Ann Arbor: University of Michigan Press.

Warleigh, A. (2001) '"Europeanizing" civil society: NGOs as agents of political socialization', *Journal of Common Market Studies*, 39(4), pp. 619–639.

Weill, C. (2021) *Petite et grande histoire de l'environnement, Konrad von Moltke (1941–2005).* Paris: Museo éditions.

Wilson, J.K. (1995) *Political organizations.* Princeton: Princeton University Press.

Amanda Machin

Becoming the green citizen in Europe? Discipline, dissent and critical acts

Abstract: The European Green Deal (EGD) refers to citizens as the 'driving force' of the transition to a greener economy. Citizens are expected to change their behavior and also contribute creatively to agenda setting, data gathering and policy implementation. This apparently makes environmental policy more inclusive, democratic and legitimate. Yet, Europeans do not exactly fulfil these demands; their practices often fall short or exceed the conduct expected of them. This chapter considers the disciplining of citizens through European Union environmental policy, resistance to such disciplining and the forging of new identities and pathways through such resistance. Drawing on Isin's 'acts of citizenship', I argue that Europeans can be active claimants of a European citizenship that they enact through their creative dissent against what is regarded as unjust environmental policy. Dissent does not necessarily support sustainability, but through critical acts citizens can highlight inequalities and inadequacies in EU environmental strategy and substantiate the meaning of European citizenship.

Keywords: European politics; European Green Deal; Climate Pact; Critical Acts of Citizenship; environmental movements.

> Tens of thousands of children are school striking for the climate on the streets of Brussels. Hundreds of thousands are doing the same all over the world. We are school striking because we have done our homework [...] We know that most politicians don't want to talk to us. Good. We don't want to talk to them either [...] We need new politics [...] We need a whole new way of thinking [...] our political leaders have wasted decades through denial and inaction. And since our time is running out, we have decided to take action. (EESC, 2019)
>
> —Greta Thunberg, at the EESC event 'Civil Society for rEUnaissance', 21 February 2019

1 Introduction: European citizenship and environmental policy

What does it mean to be a citizen of the European Union (EU) at a time when both environmental concerns and environmental policies are attracting acute attention? How are EU citizens positioned within environmental policy initiatives, practices and discourses? Is the EU citizen an object of concern or protected by certain environmental rights and awarded particular duties? Or are EU citizens actually involved in the policymaking itself as active political subjects of the sustainability transition—as 'citizen scientists' and 'co-creators' of environmental policy for example? In the latter case, what does active participation consist of and what motivates it? Could active

https://doi.org/10.1515/9783111321523-021

resistance and dissent *against* EU environmental policy also count as a right and duty of European citizens?

The answers given to these questions depend substantially on the particular understanding, or 'political imaginary', of citizenship held by those providing them. A political imaginary is a background understanding that is partly constitutive of political activities in any society (Adams, Smith and Straume, 2012). For democracy to function, for example, there must be a widely shared imaginary of democracy that guides the behavior and interactions of political actors and informs their ideas about what is legitimate, feasible and valuable—and what is not (Machin, 2022). Different imaginaries of citizenship offer distinct, and sometimes competing, expectations about what it means to be a citizen; the shifts in the dominant imaginaries of citizenship have huge repercussions for the self-understandings of democratic subjects. In this chapter, I offer a typology of imaginaries of citizenship and their implications for environmental policymaking and democratic politics in Europe. As I explain, conventionally, *liberal citizenship*, which emphasizes rights and negative freedoms of individuals, has been distinguished from both *communitarian citizenship*, which focuses on the common good, and from *civic republicanism citizenship*, which allocates active duties and positive freedom. All three indubitably highlight important dimensions of belonging to a polity at a time of pressing environmental crises. Nevertheless, these imaginaries have been criticized—by environmentalists among others—for failing to fully incorporate the rich character of citizenship in a liberal democracy. Indeed, I argue that the three dominant imaginaries of citizenship omit the role of critical acts through which citizens enact their identity and *become* citizens. Such critical acts can be detected as arising around climate change and climate policy, for example, in the protests and speeches of Greta Thunberg and her fellow climate strikers.

For this reason, I advance an alternative imaginary that I refer to as *critical green citizenship*. In this imaginary, dissenting and disagreeing Europeans act critically and creatively for or against what they regard as (un)just and (in)effective environmental policy and by so doing *become* citizens. Such performativity—through which citizens become citizens and sculpt the meaning of political belonging by performing political acts—is particularly relevant for those who are interested in European politics and environmental policy for two reasons. First, because the implication that citizenship is a work-in-progress could have significance for the strengthening of a EU identity and community. Debates have long circulated around whether European citizenship is "a purely decorative institution" or, on the contrary, should not be underestimated as "the engine for creating a political community" (Kostakopoulou, 2008, p. 286). For some, European citizenship is insubstantial and lacking any concomitant duties and strong sense of identity or "emotional attachment" (Shore, 2004, p. 26) that certainly seem to be key features for citizenship of the nation-state. However, Dora Kostakopoulou (2007, p. 642), for example, has reversed this argument, claiming that EU citizenship can be regarded as an important experiment that itself works as a catalyst for a post-national community. Critical acts of citizens in relation to environmental issues can tentatively be understood as relevant in underpinning a nascent EU identity and a lively democratic European politics—although they might also expose its exclusions and divisions (Machin and Tan, 2022).

Relatedly, the other reason that critical acts of citizens are pertinent is precisely because environmental problems such as climate change demand a supranational conception of citizenship that moves beyond, or away from, its connection with the state (Latta, 2013; Dobson, 2003). In his work on the changing spatiality and configuration of citizenship, Alex Latta (2013, p. 566) poses a question that has long occupied scholars of environmental politics and policy: "if political subjects are constituted within states, how might citizens respond to ecological crises that overflow sovereign territorial jurisdictions?" And yet, as he warns, disentangling citizenship from the state is hardly an easy matter (see also Isin and Turner, 2007). In the imaginary of critical green citizenship, dissenting citizens demand more radical environmental politics at the EU as well as state level, while they simultaneously challenge and even extend constituency boundaries. Of course, dissent does not necessarily work in the service of sustainability, but it is nevertheless through critical acts that citizens can become political subjects and are able to highlight the inequalities and inadequacies in EU environmental strategy and substantiate the meaning and identity of EU citizenship, in a marked contradiction to its current formal circumscribed application.

I start this chapter reflecting on previous research on citizenship and environmental policy and its relevance for Europe. Second, I specify a typology of imaginaries of citizenships and their implications for EU environmental policy. Here, drawing on a previous conceptualization of Green European Citizenship undertaken with Evrim Tan (Machin and Tan, 2022) and on Engin Isin's work on "acts of citizenship" (Isin, 2013; Isin and Nielsen, 2008), I develop further a conception of critical green citizenship, defined as a form of identification and belonging that is performatively constructed through acts of protest and prefiguration around environmental matters. Third, I give some examples of the acts of critical green citizens responding to the EU environmental policy before concluding by considering policy implications and pathways for future research.

2 Why does citizenship matter?

Citizenship has long been a concern for those worried about the environment. Conscious of the problem of relying on technologies that have not yet been developed and the limits of market instruments to change long-term behavior, scholars and policymakers have suggested that citizens play a significant role in the transformation or transition toward a more sustainable economy and society (Dobson and Bell, 2006, p. 3). As Ralph Horne and colleagues (2016, p. 1) put it, "Many purely market-based solutions to climate change are simplistic, have proved unsuccessful and are likely to exaggerate the power of drivers and processes that have led to run-away carbon emissions, rather than unifying stakeholders holistically in the practice of multiple strategies". In contrast to the widespread tendency to emphasize the efforts of individual consumers to switch to more environmentally friendly products and practices—which constitutes what Michael Maniates calls "the individualization of responsibility" (2001, p. 33)—the call to 'green citizens' is a demand for a more far-reaching and wider political and institutional change that harnesses the power of the collective (Maniates, 2001; Machin, 2012).

Numerous proposals have been made to reconfigure citizenship in response to ecological awareness and threat; some promote a form of 'environmental citizenship' (Bell, 2005; Hailwood, 2005), others a more radical 'ecological citizenship' (Dobson, 2003; MacGregor, 2006; Hayward, 2006; Smith, 1998; Smith and Pangsapa, 2008; Wolf, Brown and Conway, 2009). Additionally, 'sustainability citizenship' (Barry, 2006; Horne et al., 2016), 'sustainable citizenship' (Jaufar, 2021; Micheletti and Stolle, 2012), 'energy citizenship' (Lennon et al., 2020), and 'climate citizenship' (Vihersalo, 2017) have been offered as alternatives for imagining the shifting character of political belonging. In this chapter I use the term 'green citizenship' as an umbrella term that encompasses the different terminology, concepts and imaginaries (Gabrielson, 2008; Machin, 2012; Machin and Tan, 2022).

As the number of different labels indicates, there is no consensus on how exactly citizenship should be reimagined, *yet* all these different accounts emphasize that a transformation toward more sustainable ways of life demands more than the summary of individual efforts; a substantive change involves a collective effort that engages with citizens as the members of communities that are either affected by environmental change or responsible for it. One other key idea across the different conceptions is that the general aim is not to apply dominant ideas of citizenship to particular environmental concerns but to actually transform those ideas of citizenship and of environmental politics more broadly. Teena Gabrielson (2008, p. 430) has argued for bringing together green thinking with theories of citizenship, because this would advance both bodies of literature. Further reflection on green citizenship in Europe can also contribute to our understanding of European environmental politics and EU environmental policy. As stated above, if green citizenship can contribute to the emergence of a vibrant European democratic politics, then it has intriguing, if unpredictable, implications for European integration and policymaking.

In the next section I construct a heuristic typology of imaginaries of green citizenship. Imaginaries are background understandings that influence the way that political actors visualize the world around them, how they anticipate the future and how they interact with others. Imaginaries are stable but not fixed; they shift over time in relation to material, economic and socio-political changes while themselves playing a central role in both social continuity and change (Adams et al., 2015, p. 19). The different imaginaries of citizenship highlight the components of citizenship (rights, virtue, duties and acts) and arenas of citizenship (private and public) to varying degrees (see Table 1).

3 Imaginaries of green citizenship

Liberal citizens as environmental rights bearers

Many scholars have argued that, despite its reputation as shoring up rampant capitalism, liberalism does not have to be irreconcilable with care for nonhuman nature (Wissenburg, 1998). The insight that liberalism can, and should, be 'greened' has informed conceptions of 'liberal environmental citizenship' that acknowledge the severity of environmental challenges and, equally, the importance of liberal values that command widespread loyalty and give legitimacy to any citizenship regime (Bell, 2005; Hailwood, 2005). According to Derek Bell, while a commitment to the environment contradicts the traditional liberal idea that the environment should be regarded as 'property' (2005, p. 180), that idea can be revised with no break with liberalism. Liberal citizens, he explains, should be regarded as "citizens of an environment" (2005, p. 182), and he argues that the essential role of the environment in supplying basic needs implies that "the liberal commitment to environmental sustainability should trump property rights to (parts of) the physical environment" (2005, p. 183).

Liberal environmental citizenship is mainly (although not entirely) preoccupied with the freedom and rights of the individual. Departing from T. H. Marshall's delineation of civil, political, and social rights (1950), liberal environmentalists propose the introduction of a new set of constitutional 'environmental rights' (Hayward, 2005), which emerge in two different ways. First, existing constitutional rights to clean air and water should be respected and secured and, if necessary, expanded to ensure the fulfilment of citizens' basic environmental needs and their protection against environmental harms, such as pollution. Since the actual content of those rights is likely to be disputed, liberal green citizens also have the procedural rights to participate in decisions about the content of environmental policy (Bell, 2005, p. 187). Second, and more controversially, rights are extended to nonhuman nature and future generations in order to automatically ensure that long-term environmental concerns are considered (Hooley, 2018; Smith, 2020). As Gabrielson (2008, p. 431) summarizes, the liberal approach to green citizenship tackles "the substantive content of social rights historically considered critical in liberal democracies" as well as "the appropriate range of subjects to whom the rights and duties of citizenship apply".

Communitarian virtues and good green citizens?

Alongside an attention to rights, numerous accounts of green citizenship emphasize that citizenship implies a set of *virtues* (Barry, 1999, 2006; Connelly, 2006; Hayward, 2006; Smith and Pangsapa, 2008). Virtues can be defined as character traits that a citizen needs in order to realize environmental ends (Connelly, 2006, p.51). Discussions in these accounts invoke the idea of a 'good citizen' who displays frugalness, care and compassion (Connelly, 2006) as well as discipline, loyalty, courage, perseverance, commitment, tolerance and knowledge (Barry, 2006, p. 35). In contrast to the 'green consumer' who might choose 'local' and 'eco' products to buy, the 'good green citizen' attempts to reduce their overall consumption and will "demonstrate a connection to nature" (Guckian, De Young and Harbo, 2017, p. 74). According to Tim Hayward, the most important virtue of citizenship is *resourcefulness*, which entails a lower impact on natural resources and human flourishing. As he explains, "If a major vice of environmentally harmful practices is the profligate use of resources, and rendering into 'mere resources' items which should be considered to be of inherent value, then the countervailing virtue can be characterised as 'resourcefulness'" (Hayward, 2006, p. 442).

But where and how do advocates of resourcefulness and other 'eco-virtues' expect these character traits to be learned and practiced? As far as the EU is concerned, virtues might be cultivated through the creation and dissemination of programs, such as the European Climate Pact. The European Commission launched this initiative in 2020 with the aim of spreading information, facilitating local discussion, encouraging lifestyle change and inspiring communities to find solutions (European Commission, 2024a). The Pact states that it will promote and support the development of 'green skills' and 'educational and training institutions' that will allow citizens to take advantage of job opportunities in the green economy (European Commission, 2020, p. 14). Despite this emphasis on the economic self-interest of individuals, it also pledges that it will "engage with different stakeholders and civil society with the aim to commit them to climate action and more sustainable behaviour" and "offer support for a European climate movement to grow and consolidate" (2020, p. 3). Citizens are invited to volunteer to become 'European Climate Pact ambassadors' and to 'lead by example' (European Commission, 2020; Tosun, Pollex and Crumbie, 2023) or to register a pledge to respect the six values laid out in the pact, which include responsibility and commitment, transparency, no greenwashing, ambition, local specificity and diversity (European Commission, 2020, p. 6). Such volunteers surely epitomize the imaginary of the 'good green citizen', who is not only demonstrating responsiveness to nature but also a responsibility to their communities.

Republican citizens as active participants in green politics

The liberal imaginary of citizenship is often contrasted to the republican imaginary, which places special value on the shared duties or responsibilities that are seen as inseparable from the status of membership in a political community (Dagger, 1997, p. 12). According to republicanism these duties do not conflict with freedom, but are on the contrary essential to achieving it, because the citizen who does not help to determine the society they live in is ultimately subservient to the will of others (Oldfield, 1990, p. 181). In the republican imaginary, the duties of a citizen go beyond the remit of individual behavior and extend to their active participation in policymaking itself. Citizenship duties in relation to climate change, therefore, are not discharged by fulfilling predetermined tasks (such as recycling waste, using public transport or reducing energy use) or by pledging to respect predefined values but by actually participating in decisions about the nature and number of those tasks and values.

It is clear why the model of republicanism has appealed to environmentalists. Scholars such as John Barry have proposed models of 'green republicanism' that demand that citizens actively contribute to political discussions around environmental issues such as climate change (Barry, 1999, 2006; Fremaux, 2019). Green republican citizens, Barry emphasizes, do not necessarily have to conform to one understanding of 'the common good' but are, on the contrary, expected to engage in debates over the meaning of that 'common good'. That said, the 'common good' is understood by green republicans in the non-anthropocentric terms of the natural environment and sustainability (Fremaux, 2019, p. 9). For Barry "one does not just have the right to demand changes to create a more sustainable society, but one has the obligation to do so" (Barry, 2006, p. 33). Deliberative forums such as climate citizens assemblies and European Citizens' Panels can be seen as the arenas in which Europeans are able to fulfil their obligations to participate in environmental politics. These forums select participants through sortition and invite them, along with experts, to discuss pressing issues such as climate change (see European Commission, n.d.).

Climate citizens assemblies, however, have been accused of being oriented toward reaching consensus on predefined topics, rather than highlighting reasons for disagreement (Machin, 2023). The question that irresistibly arises here, then, is whether this obligation to actively participate might involve *challenging and criticizing* the very institutions that provide environmental rights and policy and circumscribe the arenas in which Europeans can deliberate on these policies. This question is raised by Barry (2006) but intriguingly is left undeveloped. It is the importance of 'critical acts' that can be seen as part of what I formulate next as a distinct, albeit only nascent, imaginary of 'critical green citizenship'.

Green citizenship and critical acts?

Green citizenship can also be imagined as a *practice* (Wolf, Brown and Conway, 2009). As Isin (2013) explains, this understanding entails approaching citizenship not as a passive status but as a matter of acting in a way that actually brings a political subject into being. This imaginary of citizenship moves away from the idea that the political subject already exists with a set of preassigned and predetermined rights and duties. Instead, it suggests that it is through struggles against unfairness, exclusion and inadequate policy that a political subject emerges to claim their rights and become citizens. These deeds may be pleasurable or painful, emotional or somber, collective or individual, but they all "break with repetition of the same" to create anew (Isin and Nielsen, 2008, p. 2). Although people do not necessarily see their activities in these terms, what they do when they demonstrate against certain laws or programs or when they call for better provision of services, is to perform "their right to have rights" as a citizen (Isin, 2013, p. 22). As this reminds us, citizenship rights have very often emerged as a result of the struggle of social movements (Turner, 1990, p. 199).

For Isin, "Citizenship is performed in the sense that it involves being and acting with others, negotiating different situations and identities, articulating ourselves as distinct yet similar to others in our everyday lives, asking questions of right and wrong and acting as citizens" (Isin, 2013, p. 22; see also Isin and Nielsen, 2008). The emergence of a new political subject through such 'being and acting with others' is precisely what can be observed in the climate movement, and its struggle with or against dominant approaches to demand more just, inclusive and adequate responses to urgent and severe environmental concerns.

In contrast to the three imaginaries above, the imaginary of critical green citizenship I promote here emphasizes the 'acts of citizenship' that enact a political subject and challenge environmental policy in different ways. These acts of citizenship might involve protesting either for (or against) bolder action on climate change, to promote (or dissent) from particular technologies for renewable energy or strategies for decarbonization. They might entail performing strategies for sustainability that mobilize concerned individuals and politicize young people through 'bottom up' civil society led movements, from 350.org to Fridays for Future to Extinction Rebellion and Letzte Generation to the Yellow Vests. They might offer a glimpse of new possibilities through practices of prefiguration which attempt to "realize a radically alternative future in the present" (Schiller-Merkens, 2022, p. 68). These innovations will of course not produce straightforward solutions to a problem such as climate change or biodiversity loss; struggles against institutions and structures and attempts to prefigure the future will undoubtably encounter numerous challenges (Schiller-Merkens and Machin, 2023) and uncover the complexities of tackling a global environmental problem that evades techno-fixes and dodges silver bullets. Yet grass-roots activism, if well organized, can play a key role in pushing for change (Gunningham, 2018).

Critical Green Citizenship is an imaginary in which identification and belonging is performatively constructed through acts of protest and prefiguration around environmental matters. This resonates with Gabrielson's pleas for an emphasis on critical reflectiveness in accounts of green citizenship "greens ought to leaven the focus on guilt, responsibility, and burden with larger measures of critical reflectiveness, agency, hope, and opportunity" (Gabrielson, 2008, p. 441).

4 Critical green citizenship in Europe?

Which of these imaginaries is most prominent in the EU environmental policy arena? Previous analysis of EU climate policy has shown that it has constructed the role of citizens in sustainability transition as a matter of lifestyle change in the private sphere in terms of a rather 'thin' 'environmental-lite' citizenship (Vihersalo, 2017). This analysis fits with Isin's observation that, although the EU has played a key role in con-

Table 1: Comparison of imaginaries of citizenship.

Imaginary of Citizenship	Characterization of the Citizen	Primary Component	Main Arena	Implications for European policy and politics	Instruments
Liberal	Individual rights bearers	Rights	Domestic and market	Protection and expansion of rights	Constitutional and legal
Communitarian	Good green citizens	Virtues	Domestic and community	Education and enlightenment	European Climate Pact
Civic republican	Active participants	Duties	Public, deliberative forums	Expansion of opportunities for deliberation and involvement in environmental policymaking	Climate citizens assemblies; Citizens' panels; Citizens' engagement platform
Critical green	Critical actors	Identity	Public, civil society, streets	'Bottom-up' critical engagement, protest	Demonstrations, environmental movements

structing the European citizen (Isin, 2013, p. 19), this citizen is often constructed as a passive bearer of *already* existing rights (2013, p. 20).

The European Green Deal (EGD), however, has emphasized the *active* involvement of citizens in the sustainability transition as its "driving force of the transition" (European Commission, 2019; see also Machin and Tan, 2022). Arguably, within the environmental policy of the EU is circulating a more communitarian imaginary in which citizens are encouraged to change their behavior and display the virtues of a 'good green citizen' by, for example, joining the European Climate Pact and becoming ambassadors for more sustainable lifestyles. The recent implementation of European Citizens' Panels and the online Citizens' Engagement Platform, as "your dedicated space to engage and debate on EU policies that affect us all" (European Commission, 2024b), indicates, too, the growing relevance of the republican imaginary, in which citizens are not only expected to adopt sustainable behavior by using greener forms of transport and reducing carbon footprints but also to participate in political discussions on selected topics such as energy efficiency.

Is it also possible that European subjects are performing critical acts of citizenship in relation to climate change and environmental policy, in a way that resonates with the imaginary of Critical Green Citizenship? This possibility would suggest that not only are challenges being made to EU environmental policy and commitments, but that European citizenship is itself being enacted and reimagined.

Scholars of citizenship have argued that while it is important to note that citizenship is originally tightly tied to the nation state, it might be helpful to consider citizenship beyond the state. As Isin and Bryan Turner (2007, p. 14) point out, "no state exists in a social, political or economic isolation" but are themselves are interconnected in international regimes, meaning that citizens are entrenched within a "complex web of rights and responsibilities". According to Smith and Pangsapa citizenship "is no longer fixated on membership of a particular nation-state legally defining the rights and duties of individuals but acts as a contested space for a variety of identity construction projects" (2008, p. 27). It is interesting, then, to consider the possibilities of EU citizenship and how this form of citizenship might be reconfigured in relation to environmental policy to contest both the current content of existing citizenship status, rights and responsibilities but also the current scope of their allocation to some subjects and not others (Machin and Tan, 2022).

Isin (2013, pp. 26–27) explains that the subjects of European citizenship are not only those who legally hold citizenship status in a Member State but those, such as migrants, refugees and aliens, who constitute themselves with 'the right to claim rights' (see also Rojas, 2013). "European citizenship is not only membership in a state. It is a relationship that governs the conduct of the (subject) positions that constitute it" (Isin, 2013, p. 27). Isin discusses sex-workers and Roma, but more relevant for my argument here are climate protestors based in the EU such as Greta Thunberg who has derided the EGD for its lack of ambition. The movement Fridays for Future, started and led by Thunberg, can legitimately be criticized for its failure to strongly contest mainstream narratives (Marquardt, 2020). For all its lack of radicality however, Fridays for Future illustrates in thick brush strokes the frustration of young people about the lack of ambitious EU policy on climate change, and it has also allowed them to actively constitute themselves *as citizens.* Many Fridays for Future activists are below the (current) voting age, yet they nevertheless performed, and thus produced, their right to have a say about their future.

Critical acts of citizenship are performed in various ways and with different agendas against the dominant regimes, strategies, mechanisms and narratives. These acts may not be directly aimed at advancing or strengthening environmental policy; for example, the Yellow Vest movement (Mouvement des gilet jaunes) emerged in France in 2018 in opposition to a universal rise in fuel taxes and its disproportionate impact on low and middle-class citizens (Bejar-Garcia, 2020). Many of the Yellow Vests had not previously taken part in collective action and importantly avoided discussing or declaring views on institutional politics, yet they were mobilized around environmental policy and therefore politicized (Reungoat, Buton and Jouhanneau, 2022). Although they had an entirely different aim from Fridays for Future, the participants in both movements *performed* citizenship and *became* citizens. It might be precisely the struggles and disagreements over and around the EU and its environmental policies that mobilizes political subjects, provokes their imagination, deepens the salience of identifications with Europe and revitalizes its political landscape (Isin, 2013, p. 19; see also Tambakaki, 2011, p. 581).

5 Conclusion

Different models of citizenship proffer distinct imaginaries of the environmental citizen which appear within policy strategies and discipline the population of Europe. I have presented (and promoted) an imaginary of citizenship in which Europeans resist and contest environmental policy to *become* citizens while at the same time enacting EU citizenship anew. This implies, for example, the EGD as a key strategy of the European Commission for tackling climate change should not be passively supported by environmentally concerned citizens; it should be critically assessed and frequently challenged. It is crucial to open EU environmental policy strategy to the challenges of those who disagree with its aims and assumptions.

Is the request for the Commission to open up the EGD to criticism from the public too ambitious and unrealistic a demand? Perhaps. But then it is all the more important to ensure that citizens have the right to protest on the streets of Europe so that dissenting voices are heard, even when they are not welcomed. The right to protest is a fundamental right of Critical Green Citizenship, just as the duty to demonstrate against an unconscionable governmental policy is one of its central responsibilities. On a continent faced with interconnecting environmental hazards and contradictory political demands, Critical Green Citizenship certainly does not hold all the answers, it only sparks new questions. More research is needed on the implications, problems and limits of Critical Green Citizenship, the possibilities, values and dangers of fomenting critical capacities, the mechanisms that might expand European imagination with regards to the solutions to environmental problems, the problems that need addressing and, finally, the meaning of citizenship and belonging in the EU and beyond.

References

Adams, S., Smith, J.C.A. and Straume, I.S. (2012) 'Political imaginaries in question', *Critical Horizons*, 13(1), pp. 5–11.

Adams, S., Blokker, P., Doyle, N.J., Krummel, J.W.M. and Smith J.C.A. (2015) 'Social imaginaries in debate', *Social Imaginaries*, 1(2), pp. 15–52.

Barry, J. (1999) *Rethinking green politics: Nature, virtue and progress.* London: Sage.

Barry, J. (2006) 'Resistance is fertile: From environmental to sustainability citizenship'. In: Dobson, A. and Bell, D. (eds.) *Environmental citizenship.* MIT Press, pp. 21–48.

Bejar-Garcia, C. (2020) 'France's Yellow Vest movement and the global debate on climate change', *Harvard International Review.* Available at: https://hir.harvard.edu/frances-yellow-vest-movement-and-the-global-debate-on-climate-change/ (Accessed: 25 June 2025).

Bell, D.R. (2005) 'Liberal environmental citizenship', *Environmental Politics*, 14(2), pp. 179–194.

Connelly, J. (2006) 'The virtues of environmental citizenship'. In: Dobson, A. and Bell, D. (eds.) *Environmental Citizenship.* MIT Press, pp. 49–73.

Dagger, R. (1997) *Civic virtues: Rights, citizenship, and republican liberalism.* Oxford: Oxford University Press.

Dobson, A. (2003) *Citizenship and the environment.* Oxford: Oxford University Press.

Dobson, A. and Bell, D. (2006) 'Introduction'. In: Dobson, A. and Bell, D. (eds.) *Environmental citizenship.* Cambridge, London: MIT Press, pp. 1–17.
EESC (2019) '"You're acting like spoiled irresponsible children":Speech by Greta Thunberg, climate activist'. European Economic and Social Committee. Available at: https://www.eesc.europa.eu/en/news-media/videos/youre-acting-spoiled-irresponsible-children-speech-greta-thunberg-climate-activist#:~:text=And%20I%20am%20sorry%2C%20but,acting%20like%20spoiled%20irresponsible%20children (Accessed: 21 June 2024).
European Commission (2019) 'The European Green Deal', *COM*(2019) 640 final. Available at: https://eur-lex.europa.eu/legal-content/EN/TXT/?qid=1576150542719&uri=COM%3A2019%3A640%3AFIN (Accessed: 23 September 2024).
European Commission (2020) 'European Climate Pact', *COM*(2020) 788 final. Available at: https://eur-lex.europa.eu/legal-content/EN/TXT/?uri=COM%3A2020%3A788%3AFIN (Accessed: 23 September 2024).
European Commission (2024a) *What is the European Climate Pact?* Available at: https://climate-pact.europa.eu/get-inspired/resources/what-european-climate-pact_en (Accessed: 23 September 2024).
European Commission (2024b) 'Citizens' Engagement Platform—Your space to participate in European policymaking'. Available at: https://citizens.ec.europa.eu/index_en (Accessed: 25 June 2025).
European Commission (n.d.) *European Citizens' Panels: A new phase of citizen engagement.* Available at https://citizens.ec.europa.eu/european-citizens-panels_en. (Accessed: 25 June 2025).
Fremaux, A. (2019) *After the Anthropocene: Green republicanism in a post-capitalist world.* Cham: Springer.
Guckian, M., De Young, R. and Harbo, S. (2017) 'Beyond green consumerism: Uncovering the motivations of green citizenship', *Michigan Journal of Sustainability,* 5(1), pp. 73–94.
Gabrielson, T. (2008) 'Green citizenship: A review and critique', *Citizenship Studies*, 12(4), pp. 429–446.
Gunningham, N. (2018) 'Mobilising civil society: Can the climate movement achieve transformational social change?', *Interface: a journal for and about social movements*, 10(1–2), pp. 149–169.
Hailwood, S. (2005) 'Environmental citizenship as reasonable citizenship', *Environmental Politics*, 14(2), pp. 195–210.
Hayward, T. (2005) *Constitutional environmental rights.* Oxford: Oxford University Press.
Hayward, T. (2006) 'Ecological citizenship: Justice, rights and the virtue of resourcefulness', *Environmental Politics*, 15(3), pp. 435–446.
Hooley, D. (2018) 'Political agency, citizenship, and non-human animals', *Res Publica*, 24, pp. 509–530.
Horne, R., Fien, J., Beza, B. and Nelson, A. (eds.) (2016) *Sustainability citizenship in cities: Theory and practice.* London and New York: Routledge.
Isin, E.F. (2013) 'Claiming European Citizenship'. In: Isin, E.F. and Saward, M. (eds.) *Enacting European Citizenship.* Cambridge University Press.
Isin, E.F. and Nielsen, G.M. (2008) 'Introduction: Acts of Citizenship'. In: Isin, E.F. and Nielsen, G.M. (eds.) *Acts of Citizenship.* London and New York: Zed Books.
Isin, E.F. and Turner, B.S. (2007) 'Investigating citizenship: An agenda for citizenship studies', *Citizenship Studies*, 1(1), pp. 5–17.
Jaufar, S. (2021) 'Shaping of sustainable citizenship among young people of Kulhudhuffushi, Maldives and Hamilton, New Zealand: Context, conditions and experiences', *Sustainable Earth*, 4(1).
Kostakopoulou, D. (2007) 'European Union citizenship: Writing the future?', *European Law Journal*, 13(5), pp. 623–646.
Kostakopoulou, D. (2008) 'The evolution of European Union citizenship', *European Political Science*, 7(3), pp. 285–295.
Latta, A. (2013) 'Locating nature's citizens: Latin American ecologies of political space', *Citizenship Studies*, 17(5), pp. 566–580.
Lennon, B. et al. (2020) 'Citizen or consumer? Reconsidering energy citizenship', *Journal of Environmental Policy & Planning*, 22(2), pp. 184–197.
MacGregor, S. (2006) *Beyond Mothering Earth: Ecological Citizenship and the Politics of Care.* Vancouver and Toronto: UBC Press.

Machin, A. (2012) 'Decisions, disagreement and responsibility: Towards an agonistic green citizenship', *Environmental Politics*, 21(6), pp. 847–863.
Machin, A. (2022) 'Climate Democracy: Sceptical, Rational and Radical Imaginaries', *WIRES Climate Change*, 13(4), e774.
Machin, A. (2023) 'Democracy, Agony, and Rupture: A Critique of Climate Citizens' Assemblies', *Politische Vierteljahresschrift*, 64, pp. 845–864.
Machin, A. and Tan, E. (2022) 'Green European Citizenship? Rights, Duties, Virtues, Practices and the European Green Deal', *European Politics and Society*, 25(1), pp. 152–167.
Maniates, M. F. (2001) 'Individualization: Plant a Tree, Buy a Bike, Save the World?', *Global Environmental Politics*, 1(3), pp. 31–52.
Marquardt, J. (2020) 'Fridays for Future's Disruptive Potential: And Convenient Youth Between Moderate and Radical Ideas', *Frontiers in Communication*, 5. Available at: https://doi.org/10.3389/fcomm.2020.00048.
Marshall, T.H. (1950) *Citizenship and social class and other essays*. Cambridge: Cambridge University Press.
Micheletti, M. and Stolle, D. (2012) 'Sustainable citizenship and the new politics of consumption', *The ANNALS of the American Academy of Political and Social Science*, 644(1), pp. 88–120.
Oldfield, A. (1990) *Citizenship and Community: Civic Republicanism and the Modern World*. London: Routledge.
Reungoat, E., Buton, F. and Jouhanneau, C. (2022) 'Becoming political while avoiding politics: A study of Yellow Vests first-timers', *French Politics*, 20, pp. 395–419.
Rojas, C. (2013) 'Acts of indigenship: Historical struggles for equality and colonial difference in Bolivia', *Citizenship Studies*, 17(5), pp. 581–595.
Schiller-Merkens, S. (2022) 'Social transformation through prefiguration? A multi-political approach of prefiguring alternative infrastructures', *Historical Social Research / Historische Sozialforschung*, 47(4), pp. 66–90.
Schiller-Merkens, S. and Machin, A. (2023) 'Knowing food: Food policy councils and the challenges of co-producing knowledge', *International Journal of Politics, Culture and Society*. 36(3), pp. 297–309.
Shore, C. (2004) 'Whither European citizenship? Eros and civilization revisited', *European Journal of Social Theory*, 7(1), pp. 27–44.
Smith, G. (2020) 'Enhancing the legitimacy of offices for future generations: The case for public participation', *Political Studies*, 68(4), pp. 996–1013.
Smith, M.J. (1998) *Ecologism: Towards ecological citizenship*. Buckingham: Open University Press.
Smith, M.J. and Pangsapa, P. (2008) *Environment and citizenship: Integrating justice, responsibility and civic engagement*. London and New York: Zed Books.
Tambakaki, P. (2011) 'Agonism and the reconception of European citizenship', *British Journal of Politics and International Relations*, 13(4), pp. 567–585.
Tosun, J., Pollex, J. and Crumbie, L. (2023) 'European climate pact citizen volunteers: Strategies for deepening engagement and impact', *Policy Design and Practice*, 6(3), pp. 344–356.
Turner, B. S. (1990) 'Outline of a theory of citizenship', *Sociology*, 24(2), pp. 189–217.
Vihersalo, M. (2017) 'Climate citizenship in the European Union: Environmental citizenship as an analytical concept', *Environmental Politics*, 26(2), pp. 343–360.
Wissenburg, M. (1998) *Green liberalism: The free and green society*. London: UCL Press.
Wolf, J., Brown, K. and Conway, D. (2009) 'Ecological citizenship and climate change: Perceptions and practice', *Environmental Politics*, 18(4), pp. 503–521.

Eze Paez and Núria Almiron

The neglected majority: Nonhuman animals as legitimate European Union environmental policy stakeholders

Abstract: This chapter argues that nonhuman animals are legitimate stakeholders whose interests should be given priority in drafting European Union (EU) environmental policy. So far, however, EU policy in this regard has been informed by an environmentalist approach that fails to give full consideration to individual animals' interests, leading to wrongful interventions such as culling, support for insect farming or certain forms of rewilding. In contrast, we advance an alternative environmental policy framework that takes seriously animals' interests, creating new regulatory opportunities for animal farming and environmental management. The proposed framework also calls for the creation of new EU institutions with the brief of identifying and representing animals' best interests. To be successful, this framework has to overcome a series of challenges—such as how to institutionalize animals' interests as stakeholders, how to gather in an ethical way the evidence necessary for drafting sound policies or how to identify the criteria for the ethical management of human-nonhuman animal conflicts. We provide some policy examples that may fit our framework and some that are excluded by it.

Keywords: Animals as stakeholders; farming; environmental policies; moral and political considerability of animals; speciesism

1 Introduction

Only human beings can deliberate about the policies their communities implement. Nevertheless, they are not the only ones who are affected by human policy decisions. Nonhuman animals are also affected. This is particularly true of environmental policy, i.e., how governments manage ecosystems and the animal populations that inhabit them, fight against pollution and climate change and attempt to build more sustainable food systems.

These policy decisions have a major impact on nonhuman animals living in nature. Yet urban greening practices or attempts at controlling their populations will affect liminal animals (those inhabiting urban and peri-urban zones) sometimes through lethal methods. Similarly, animal farming is a major pollutant and climate change contributor. Whatever we decide about this industry, it will greatly affect the animals that are exploited for food. Still, the greatest number of animals that are affected, for good or ill, by our policy choices are those yet unborn: i. e., the individuals belonging to future animal generations.

https://doi.org/10.1515/9783111321523-022

This chapter assesses how the European Union's (EU) environmental policies have worked for animals. All polities, not just the EU, have a moral duty to take nonhuman animals seriously and without discrimination. We have two main reasons to focus on the EU. First, it has tried to build a reputation as a global leader of progressive policies concerning animal rights and welfare, and, indeed, it is more advanced in this respect that other Global North regions. Second, its decisions have a strong global impact on nonhuman animals, directly and indirectly.

Still, EU environmental policy has failed to accord sentient animals the robust consideration that is their due. We start with an initial justification of this negative evaluation (Section 2). As animal ethicists have argued convincingly, sentient nonhuman animals deserve full moral and political consideration. They should be regarded as legitimate political stakeholders on a par with human beings. Nevertheless, after analyzing some major EU environmental policy measures, we show how the Union does not consider protecting animals important for its own sake (Section 3). EU policies on the management of so-called 'invasive' species, nature restoration and food system sustainability are crucial evidence (Section 4). As remedies, we offer proposals for meaningful reform while admitting that their implementation presents serious challenges (Section 5). We acknowledge that our assessment of how the EU works for animals is bleak, but reform is possible and must be pursued (Section 6).

2 The moral and political consideration of animals

Academic criticism of EU environmental policy from the animal rights standpoint is rare (e.g., Platvoet, 2023). Fortunately, there is abundant work in animal ethics and political philosophy that can tackle this problem.[1] This section reviews this literature's main arguments asserting that sentient nonhuman animals deserve full moral and political consideration, which implies that they are legitimate stakeholders in the political decision-making process.

Why and how nonhuman animals matter

Human societies, particularly in the Western tradition, have often regarded nonhuman animals' interests as negligible compared to human interests. This perspective is evident in both individual attitudes and the social, political and economic systems that humans have created, and to which nonhuman animals are subjected. In stark contrast to humans, who enjoy comprehensive rights as citizens in liberal democracies, nonhuman animals are treated as property, expendable for purposes such as production, entertainment and biomedicine.

1 The most influential treatises in animal ethics are arguably Singer (2023) and Regan (2004 [1983]).

During the last fifty years, however, many moral and political philosophers have argued convincingly that this disadvantageous differential treatment of nonhuman animals is just another instance of unjustified discrimination: *speciesism*, akin to sexism, homophobia, transphobia or racism. Species membership, as a taxonomic category defined by humans, cannot justifiably determine moral relevance, since it does not correlate inherently with other morally relevant traits. Arguments that humans deserve greater moral consideration based on superior cognitive abilities fail to account for significant variations within humans themselves, such as in young children, cognitively disabled individuals or those affected by old age (Horta, 2014). Using cognitive capacity as a criterion for moral considerability could undermine the principle of human equality fundamental to our political systems.

Moreover, moral deliberation should consider the impact of our choices on all affected entities, regardless of species membership or cognitive capacities (Horta, 2018). Sentience, or the ability to experience pleasure and pain, makes an entity susceptible to being positively or negatively affected by events. Therefore, if there is evidence of an entity's sentience, their wellbeing should be factored into our moral decisions. Ignoring this in moral deliberation unjustifiably excludes potential harms or benefits to them.

This emphasis on sentience is paramount because many animals subjected to our political institutions are sentient individuals. In 2024, scholars from different backgrounds published the 'New York Declaration on Animal Consciousness', stating their points of agreement in light of recent advances in animal cognition and behavioural science (The New York Declaration on Animal Consciousness, 2024). There is strong scientific evidence supporting the subjective experiences of mammals and birds and at least the realistic possibility of such experiences in all vertebrates (including reptiles, amphibians or fish) and many invertebrates, like cephalopods, and crustaceans and even some insects. Consequently, it is crucial to consider the potential consciousness of these animals in moral and policy decisions. Policymakers are urged to mitigate welfare risks for these animals as research continues to expand our understanding of their experiences (Andrews et al., 2024).

Many nonhuman animals are likely sentient, and our individual choices and policies should respect their interests in living good lives with minimal suffering and abundant positive experiences. Various normative theories including consequentialist (e.g., de Lazari-Radek and Singer, 2014), deontological (e.g., Korsgaard, 2019) and character-based (e.g., Hursthouse, 2000) approaches support ethical obligations to nonhuman animals. We are morally obligated to avoid inflicting harm on animals. This involves experimentation or uses for trivial human benefits, such as those found in the animal-based food and clothing industries, or in entertainment and sport. Additionally, we should assist animals in distress in situations where we find it impermissible to avoid helping humans facing similar risks.

In the past fifteen years, the 'political turn' in animal ethics, led by several scholars, has emphasized the significant political implications of recognizing sentient nonhuman animals as morally considerable and of opposing speciesism. Notably, Donaldson and Kymlicka (2011) have argued for granting at least domesticated animals a form of citizenship status, which others argue should be extended to all sentient animals (Cochrane, 2018). This does not imply voting rights but suggests their interests are a part of the common good and should be represented in democratic processes. Even without full acceptance of animal citizenship, the rejection of speciesism leads to the conclusion that animal interests must be seriously considered in democratic decision-making, akin to how institutions protect the fundamental interests of noncitizens. This calls for robust institutional protections and rights for animals, treating their interests as those of legitimate stakeholders in policy decisions.

Different environmental approaches and nonhuman animals

Some versions of environmentalism, like anthropocentric speciesism, lie at the root of wrongful attitudes towards nonhuman animals. For instance, in the rhetoric of European environmental policy, nature is valued anthropocentrically because it is recognized, in the light of the best scientific evidence, that its preservation is necessary for the wellbeing of present and future human generations (see also Chapter 3). A second kind of environmentalism values inherently non-sentient nature (Leopold, 1949; Taylor, 1986; Callicott, 1989). It must be preserved as it stands even if it is incompatible with the wellbeing of sentient nonhuman individuals. These views fail to fully encompass the interests of the other animals and must therefore be rejected.

A third kind of environmentalism considers natural entities and processes to matter because of how they can impact positively or negatively the lives of sentient beings. Unlike anthropocentric environmentalism, it stresses consideration of the long-term interests of nonhuman animals, both present and future, in our policy design. This sentientist form of environmentalism tasks us with crafting institutions and policies centered on the wellbeing of all sentient individuals, whatever their species (see Section 5).

3 How EU environmental policy unjustifiably neglects nonhuman animals

The European Union's mandate to draft and implement environmental policy is found in Article 191 Treaty on the Functioning of the European Union (TFEU) (European Union, 2016). According to this legal provision, European environmental policy must contribute to pursuing the protection of the environment and human health, the rational use of natural resources and international cooperation to deal with environmental problems, especially climate change. The foundation of European environmental policy is, thus, anthropocentric. Its main aim is, either directly or indirectly, protecting human interests. The protection of animal rights and welfare is completely absent. Indeed, animals are not mentioned at all.

Nonhuman animals do feature in EU treaty law. Article 13 TFEU recognizes that animals are sentient beings, identifying animal sentience as the grounds for the EU's legal obligation to "pay full regard to the welfare requirements of animals" in "formulating and implementing" certain policies, including agriculture, fisheries, transport, internal market, research and technological development or space. Noticeably, though, environmental policy is absent. This legal requirement of full regard to animal welfare, as established by Art. 13 TFEU, is not absolute, being limited by a further duty to respect "the legislative or administrative provisions and customs of the Member States relating in particular to religious rites, cultural traditions and regional heritage". Member State provisions may validly trump animal welfare considerations. That would be considered completely unacceptable if human wellbeing was at stake.

These treaty law provisions inform derived EU law and policy. Consider the European Green Deal (EGD), which since 2019 constitutes the most important EU environmental policy framework (European Commission, 2019). It is presented as 'a new growth strategy' for fairness and prosperity, with the aims of achieving net-zero emissions of greenhouse gasses (i. e., climate neutrality) by 2050, decoupling economic growth from resource use, preserving Europe's natural capital and protecting "the health and well-being of citizens from environment-related risks and impacts" (European Commission, 2019, p. 2).

Given our purposes, we shall focus on two core EGD strategies. The first is the Biodiversity Strategy 2030 (see also Chapter 23; European Commission, 2020a). It is a plan for protecting and restoring nature in Europe so that European biodiversity is on the path to recovery by 2030 (European Commission, 2020a, p. 3). The justification for this policy is defined exclusively in terms of human interests, being presented as necessary for human wellbeing, the economy, the prevention of new pandemics and combating climate change (European Commission, 2020a, pp. 2–3).

Building on the EGD, the EU later approved the Eighth Environment Action Program (EAP) as part of its new environmental strategy (European Union, 2022). The Eighth EAP aims at climate neutrality, a zero-waste economy, regenerative growth, inequality reduction, biodiversity conservation and nature restoration. The long-term goal of these policy priorities, however, is expressed in the anthropocentric environmentalism discussed in Section 2, as "ensuring the prosperity of present and future generations globally, guided by intergenerational responsibility" (Art. 2.1). In considering how to achieve these objectives, EU policymakers were keen on ensuring "a just transition that leaves no one behind" (Art. 2.2 a). In this sense, the Eighth EAP requires policy measures to be carried out "in a socially fair and inclusive way" (Art. 3 f) and authorities are required to incorporate a gender perspective at all policymaking stages (Art. 3 g). This is a commendable concern for justice, albeit restricted exclusively to human beings.

A second major EGD initiative is the Farm to Fork Strategy (European Commission, 2020b), which has the overarching aim "to reduce the environmental and climate footprint of the EU food system and strengthen its resilience" as well as "ensuring food security in the face of climate change and biodiversity loss" (European Commission, 2020b, p. 6). Unlike in the biodiversity roadmap, animal 'health and welfare' are mentioned in this strategy's outline. It appears, however, alongside the protection of 'land, soil, water, air' and plant health and welfare as part of the effort to reduce the EU's environmental footprint, as distinct from the related efforts of guaranteeing food security and affordability (see also Chapter 28). Thus, individual nonhuman animals are classified as merely a part of the natural environment (alongside soil, water or air). The implementation of a food system that takes their interests seriously is never articulated as a separate policy aim of equal importance to the rest. Certainly, the Eighth EAP appears to be more amicable to nonhuman animal interests when discussing the future of the EU's food system. It requires authorities to transform it in a way that "ensures a high level of animal welfare" (Art. 3 n). Nevertheless, as we will see in Section 4, the specifics of the Farm to Fork Strategy clarify that European policymakers consider the basic interests of farmed animals' not to die or suffer to matter less than the interests of European producers and consumers.

4 Wrongful practices in EU environmental policy

The anthropocentric views informing EU environmental policy cause serious harm to nonhuman animals. This section highlights a series of such wrongful practices. It is beyond the scope of this chapter to provide an exhaustive listing of objectionable policies. Instead, we focus on three major examples: the management of so-called 'invasive species', nature restoration initiatives, and the encouragement of certain forms of animal farming as part of the effort to create a sustainable European food system.

Managing 'invasive species'

As part of its Biodiversity Strategy 2030, the European Commission called for 'stepping up' the implementation of the EU Invasive Species Regulation (European Union, 2014) with the aim of halving the number of threatened endangered species (see European Commission, 2020a, p. 14). This law's purpose is to establish a framework for managing 'invasive alien species', defined as species "outside their natural range" "whose introduction or spread has been found to threaten or adversely impact biodiversity and related ecosystem services" (Art. 3, letters 1, 2 and 6). Member States must prevent the introduction of species of EU concern in European territory. If already present, states are legally required to implement lethal and nonlethal population control measures. For the sake of human wellbeing and biodiversity conservation, animals that arrive from outside Union territory must be controlled, contained and, if deemed necessary, eradicated.

Interpreted in its best light, this regulation is admittedly identifying a real problem. The presence in a territory of newly arrived individuals from a certain nonhuman animal species might threaten local human beings with harm. Likewise, it might threaten other nonhuman animals long established in the area. Sometimes, both as individuals and as policymakers, we are confronted with human-nonhuman animal conflicts of interest, just as we might have to solve similar conflicts between human beings or between different nonhuman animals. These conflicts must be managed in an ethically appropriate way. This requires us to take into account the interests of all those individuals affected, giving them impartial consideration. That precludes excluding the interests of some individuals or assigning them less importance, simply because of their species.

EU law does not comply with this requirement. When determining whether a species poses sufficient risk to warrant classification as of EU concern, institutions are required to make a cost-benefit analysis (Art. 5). They must consider the costs of the damage it may cause to biodiversity, native species and human beings. They also must take into account the known uses for the species and evaluate social and economic benefits deriving from those uses. This risk assessment procedure is unjustifiably speciesist. It excludes from the cost-benefit analysis the benefit which so-called invasive species might derive from inhabiting their new ecosystem. These animals are sentient individuals whose interests matter as much as the similar interests of human beings and of members of native nonhuman species. The law, as it stands, empowers the Commission not to include in the list of Union concern those non-Union species whose presence might not be detrimental overall (or even potentially beneficial) for human beings and native nonhuman animals. Likewise, the law should allow institutions to exclude from the list those non-EU species that derive a greater benefit from being in EU territory than the harm they cause to humans and other animals.

Neglect of non-EU species' interests also features in the provisions that regulate their eradication and management. Member States have a duty to eradicate individuals from recently introduced species which are not yet widely spread (Art. 17). Yet states are also exempt from this obligation if the long-term costs of eradication are "exceptionally high and disproportionate to the benefits" (Art. 18.1 b) or "have very serious adverse impact on human health, the environment or other species" (Art. 18.1 c). For European lawmakers, what ultimately matters is human wellbeing or the protection of native species. The wellbeing of animals of non-Union species is deemed entirely unimportant. A non-speciesist perspective, however, finds this morally unjustifiable. There might be eradication attempts that cause more harm to non-Union nonhuman animals than benefits to humans and native animal species. In these cases, eradication should be prohibited rather than legally required.

Finally, consider the population management measures which Member States are required to undertake once a non-Union species is already widespread. These must be proportionate, based again on a cost-benefit analysis and prioritized according to risk evaluation and cost-effectiveness (Art. 18.1). Yet, as before, policymakers are not obligated to take into account the wellbeing of animals of non-Union species. A systematic interpretation of the law might argue that, as in previous cases, they are required only to take into account human wellbeing and possible harm to native animals. If so, excluding the interests of non-EU animal species is unwarranted.

At the implementation level, the law requires policymakers to consider the wellbeing of 'invasive' animals, ensuring they are spared avoidable pain without compromising the effectiveness of management measures (Art. 18.3). The targeted animals must be spared unnecessary suffering, but serious suffering is permitted if less harmful methods are ineffective. Thus, non-EU animals' wellbeing is always subordinate to human interests and biodiversity conservation.

Nature restoration initiatives

The Biodiversity Strategy 2030 called for a revamping of existing EU legislation on nature restoration. Several EU laws already require Member States to restore, or reestablish, certain natural habitats and ecosystems (European Union, 1992, Art. 3; European Union, 2000, Art. 4; European Union, 2008, Art. 1; European Union, 2009, Art. 3). To that end, a new Nature Restoration Law has been enacted (European Union, 2024). The law's purpose is to contribute to "the continuous, long-term and sustained recovery of biodiverse and resilient nature [...] through the restoration of ecosystems", achieving the EU's goals concerning climate change and enhancing food security (Art. 1). Again, the lawmakers' intent is mainly anthropocentric. This is evidenced in the obligation that Member States' national restoration plans "aim at optimising the ecological, economic and social functions of ecosystems as well as their contribution to the sustainable development of the relevant regions and communities" (Art. 14.16 b).

This legislative proposal unjustifiably fails to treat individual nonhuman animals as fully morally considerable individuals. Adequate ecosystems and natural habitats are necessary for the existence, and flourishing, of human communities—but also for the animal communities inhabiting those ecosystems. To the extent that they are sentient, nonhuman animal interests should be considered in policy decisions about which natural spaces should be restored, how and with what urgency. Furthermore, the number of sentient animals living in nature vastly exceeds the number of both human beings and domesticated animals (Tomasik, 2009). This suggests that their interests should be given priority in ecosystem management. Thus, a non-speciesist piece of legislation should require Member States to draft restoration plans that aim at optimizing ecosystem functions primarily for the benefit of their nonhuman animal inhabitants.

Annex VII of the law lists examples of restoration measures which Member States may make use of (Art.14.16 a). One example is the removal and control of 'invasive alien' species. As Section 4 explained, the mere fact that an individual belonging to a non-EU species is considered threatening to human wellbeing or native animal species is insufficient justification for its eradication, containment and control. Furthermore, national restoration plans must take into account old Habitats Directive measures (Art. 14.14 a). These include the reintroduction of species that previously inhabited an area as part of restoration efforts (Art. 22). Member States must study the desirability of reintroducing certain species (such as the gray wolf, the Iberian lynx, or the brown bear) that were native to their territory. This is subject to two conditions, namely, that there is sufficient evidence that reintroduction contributes to the targeted species' favorable conservation status and adequate public consultation.

However, policymakers are not required to consider the impact which the reintroduction of a certain species might have on the wellbeing of the individual nonhuman animals *themselves* who might be introduced and on the wellbeing of the other nonhuman animals affected by reintroduction. It might be the case that the relocation of some individuals to a habitat where conspecifics (i. e., members of the same species) had been present makes the species more resilient. However, the individuals introduced in the new habitat might have *worse* lives there than in their previous area of abode. Taking the interests of animals seriously commits us to considering these possible harms and accepting that, at least in some cases, they might tip the balance of reasons against reintroduction measures in particular, or restoration efforts in general, whatever the benefits for human beings.

The food system: Greater sustainability in exchange for more suffering

We finish this overview of wrongful practices with a closer look at the Farm to Fork Strategy (European Commission, 2020b). A just food system involves much more than sustainability, security and affordability (see Section 2). Fully considering the interests of nonhuman animals requires us to transition to food production methods that are free from animal exploitation.

The future envisioned by EU institutions falls far short of that ideal. New ways of profiting from already existing animal-derived products are proposed for the sake of greater sustainability. For instance, farmers are encouraged to obtain new sources of revenue by investing in biogas production from manure, thereby contributing to the reduction of methane emitted by their farm animals (p. 8). Member States are encouraged to promote farmed fish and marine invertebrates since aquaculture allegedly has a lower carbon footprint than land animal farming (p. 11). This ignores the strong evidence that fishes and other sea animals, like octopuses, crabs or shrimps, are sentient individuals. Being smaller than most exploited land animals, the suggested substitution may only increase the overall number of exploited animals and the amount of suffering we cause them.

Much more worrisome is the Commission's encouragement of insect food (for humans) and feed (for animals under exploitation) (p. 16). We cannot rule out the possibility that many insects are sentient. Moreover, given their small size, an extraordinary amount of them must be farmed to produce and sell their protein. The EU envisions insect feed as a partial substitute for soya-derived products. A system in which insect-feed has replaced plant-based alternatives amounts to a system in which exploitation has been compounded: the exploitation of insects enables the exploitation of other sentient animals, to which they are fed.

5 Towards a Union more respectful of nonhuman animals

The creation of a non-speciesist community in which animals are treated as equal fellow members of our society requires radical change. We will advance more modestly a series of proposals that may instigate a EU that is better for sentient animals and outline likely challenges to be overcome.

Proposals for a Europe that works for nonhuman animals

A short-term step may consist in changing the status of animals in EU law, following a trend currently underway in some Member States.[2] At the treaty level, a specific provision should be enacted defining the legal nature of animals as sentient individuals with a wellbeing, and interests, of their own. Such a provision should also give EU institutions a mandate to enact EU-wide regulations that would define a new legal regime for nonhuman animals. Thus far, other animals have traditionally been considered goods over which human beings have property rights. The EU needs a new regulatory framework in which animals are no longer property but legal persons with basic rights. Progress may be quicker for certain animals, like companion animals or great apes, where there are less entrenched economic interests and more compassionate societal attitudes. Successful steps to change the legal nature of these individual animals may accelerate reforms for other animals.

At a more specific policy level, the foundations of the EU environmental approach require an overhaul. Their focus should be the protection of individual sentient animals in nature on a par with the protection human wellbeing. That requires a new model of ecosystem management. It must eschew the traditional conservationist approach (see Section 2.2.) that subordinates the interests of sentient nonhuman animals to the preservation of species, habitats and ecosystems. The movement for compassionate conservation must be lauded for recognizing that respect for sentient animal interests imposes moral side-constraints on conservationist strategies (Bekoff and Pierce, 2017). Still, from a non-speciesist approach, it is insufficient. Respect for sentient beings must be its main goal, not a side-constraint to conservation efforts. This

2 See, for instance, the Civil Codes of France (Art. 515–15), Portugal (Art. 201ª-B), or Spain (Art. 333). Beyond the EU, see also the United Kingdom's Animal Welfare (Sentience) Act. Available at: https://www.legislation.gov.uk/ukpga/2022/22/enacted (Accessed: 25 November 2024).

is the core idea behind the emerging field of welfare biology (Faria and Horta, 2019), which calls for environmental management policies that improve the wellbeing of animals living in nature.

Some challenges to meaningful reform

If we consider nonhuman animals to be legitimate stakeholders in EU policy, on a par with human beings, then that status must be institutionalized. The challenge is how to robustly entrench animals' interests in EU institutions, without rendering their consideration dependent on the arbitrary will of contingent office-holders. This is an issue that has recently garnered attention in the literature on the political status of animals (for instance, Smith, 2012; Hooley, 2018; Vink, 2020; Magaña, 2022).

One first, easy step would be the creation of a European Commissioner for Animal Rights and Welfare. More ambitiously, taking inspiration from the European Environment Agency, it would be necessary to establish an EU-wide animal protection agency. Additionally, an independent animal ombudsman, responsible before the European Parliament, could be created. Nevertheless, such changes alone are insufficient. It is necessary to ensure that Parliament itself is required to track the interests of animals, perhaps by reserving seats to Members of European Parliament dedicated to representing animals.

A further difficulty consists in obtaining the relevant evidence to devise sound policies. If we want to draft policies with an acceptably low risk of counterproductive results, there is much we still need to know. The EU should use its financial power to push research institutions into devoting more resources to this field. There is presently very little investment in research that takes animal wellbeing into account (cf. UPF-CAE, 2022). This funding should be allocated to noninvasive, non-anthropocentric research, primarily devoted to gathering scientific evidence to improve the wellbeing of individual animals living in nature.

The primary challenge to animal policy reform is conflicting human interests. Policies prioritizing animal interests can clash with the economic objectives of stakeholders like agribusinesses, which may face higher costs from stringent welfare laws or reduced market shares due to alternatives. Traditional elites and rural groups involved in hunting may oppose new legal statuses for animals that restrict such activities. Conservationist sectors might also resist changes if these policies conflict with established practices in nature restoration and species management.

Consequently, the success of the proposed reforms must involve a shift in societal values. Those willing to effect change must have greater political influence than those willing to prevent it. In this sense, advocates for animals should not only engage in institutional politics but also work to expand our societies' moral circle (Anthis and Paez, 2021).

6 A bleak assessment of the past and a call for action for the future

There is much to criticize about how the European Union has approached, so far, its mandate on the environment. At a treaty level, the protection of individual sentient animals is not a mandatory goal of European environmental policy (Art. 191 TFEU). Nature restoration and species reintroduction initiatives can be designed and implemented without considering their overall impact on nonhuman animal wellbeing. It is legally permissible to opt for the eradication, containment and control of animals labeled as 'invasive', including lethal methods. Green and climate-friendly rhetoric is employed in ways that support and encourage the expansion of animal exploitation industries, like aquaculture or the production of insect food and feed.

Until fundamental societal change comes, there are some feasible reforms worth trying. Treaty law and lower-level legislation should abolish the property status of sentient animals, elevating them to the status of rightsholders. This would establish the necessary legal foundations for more robust animal protection laws. Further research is needed on the emerging discipline of welfare biology, which offers more ethical grounds for a new environmental management regulatory framework benefitting present and future animals. Research on institutional design will help identify reforms that ensure animals' interests are taken into consideration in the political decision-making process. A Commissioner for Animal Rights and Welfare, a European animal protection agency, an ombudsman for animals or dedicated animal representatives in the European Parliament would constitute decisive steps in the right direction.

EU policy needs to move beyond anthropocentric environmentalism to include the interests of nonhuman animals, both present and future. Stakeholders with conflicting interests who can exert great influence on the development of public policy will resist this move. Nevertheless, change is not only morally imperative for animals' sake but also pragmatically beneficial for the environment and for human wellbeing.

References

Andrews, K., Birch, J., Sebo, J. and Sims, T. (2024) 'Background to the New York Declaration on Animal Consciousness'. Available at: https://sites.google.com/nyu.edu/nydeclaration/background?authuser=0 (Accessed: 25 November 2024).

Anthis, J. R. and Paez, E. (2021) 'Moral circle expansion: A promising strategy to impact the far future', *Futures*, 130, 102756.

Bekoff, M., and Pierce, J. (2017) *The animal's agenda: Freedom, compassion, and coexistence in the human age.* Boston, MA: Beacon Press.

Callicott, J. B. (1989) *In defense of the land ethic: Essays in environmental philosophy.* Albany: State University of New York Press.

Cochrane, A. (2018) *Sentientist politics. A theory of global inter-species justice.* Oxford: Oxford University Press.

De Lazari-Radek, K. and Singer, P. (2014) *The point of view of the universe: Sidgwick and contemporary ethics.* Oxford: Oxford University Press.

Donaldson, S. and Kymlicka, W. (2011) *Zoopolis: A political theory of animal rights.* Oxford: Oxford University Press.

European Commission (2019) 'The European Green Deal', *COM*(2019) 640 final. Available at: https://eur-lex.europa.eu/legal-content/EN/TXT/?uri=COM:2019:640:FIN (Accessed: 19 June 2025).

European Commission (2020a) 'EU biodiversity strategy for 2030: Bringing nature back into our lives', COM(2020) 380 final. Available at: https://eur-lex.europa.eu/legal-content/EN/TXT/?uri=celex%3A52020DC0380 (Accessed: 25 November 2024).

European Commission (2020b) 'A Farm to Fork Strategy: For a fair, healthy and environmentally-friendly food system', *COM*(2020) 381 final. Available at: https://eur-lex.europa.eu/legal-content/EN/TXT/?uri=CELEX:52020DC0381 (Accessed: 25 November 2024).

European Union (2009) Directive 2009/147/EC of the European Parliament and of the Council of 30 November 2009 on the conservation of wild birds (codified version), Art. 3. Available at: https://eur-lex.europa.eu/legal-content/EN/TXT/?uri=CELEX%3A02009L0147-20190626 (Accessed: 25 November 2024).

European Commission (1992) 'Council Directive 92/43/EEC of 21 May 1992 on the conservation of natural habitats and of wild fauna and flora, Art. 3'. Available at: http://data.europa.eu/eli/dir/1992/43/2013-07-01 (Accessed: 25 November 2024).

European Commission (2000) 'Directive 2000/60/EC of the European Parliament and of the Council of 23 October 2000 establishing a framework for Community action in the field of water policy, Art. 4'. Available at: http://data.europa.eu/eli/dir/2000/60/2014-11-20 (Accessed: 25 November 2024).

European Commission (2008) 'Directive 2008/56/EC of the European Parliament and of the Council of 17 June 2008 establishing a framework for community action in the field of marine environmental, Art. 1'. Available at: http://data.europa.eu/eli/dir/2008/56/2017-06-07 (Accessed: 25 November 2024).

European Commission (2014) 'Regulation (EU) No 1143/2014 of the European Parliament and of the Council of 22 October 2014 on the prevention and management of the introduction and spread of invasive alien species'. Available at: http://data.europa.eu/eli/reg/2014/1143/2019-12-14 (Accessed: 25 November 2024).

European Commission (2016) *Treaty on the functioning of the European Union.* Available at: https://eur-lex.europa.eu/legal-content/EN/TXT/?uri=celex%3A12016ME%2FTXT (Accessed: 19 June 2025).

European Commission (2022) 'Decision (EU) 2022/591 of the European Parliament and of the Council of 6 April 2022 on a General Union Environment Action Programme to 2030'. Available at: http://data.europa.eu/eli/dec/2022/591/oj (Accessed: 25 November 2024).

European Commission (2024) 'Proposal for a Regulation (EU) 2024/1991 of the European Parliament and of the Council of 24 June 2024 on nature restoration and amending Regulation (EU) 2022/869'. Available at: http://data.europa.eu/eli/reg/2024/1991/oj (Accessed: 25 November 2024).

Faria, C. and Horta, O. (2019) 'Welfare biology', in: Fischer, B. (ed.) *The Routledge handbook of animal ethics.* New York: Routledge, pp. 455–466.

Hooley, D. (2018) *The political status of nonhuman animals.* PhD Thesis. University of Toronto.

Horta, O. (2014) 'The scope of the argument from species overlap'. *Journal of Applied Philosophy*, 31(2), pp. 142–154.

Horta, O. (2018) 'Moral considerability and the argument from relevance', *Journal of Agricultural and Environmental Ethics*, 31, pp- 369–388.

Hursthouse, R. (2000) *Ethics, humans, and other animals: An introduction with readings.* New York: Routledge.

Korsgaard, C.M. (2018) *Fellow creatures: Our obligations to the other animals.* New York: Oxford University Press.

Leopold, A. (1949) *A Sand County almanac and sketches here and there.* New York: Oxford University Press.

Magaña, P. (2022) 'The political representation of nonhuman animals', *Social Theory and Practice,* 48(4), pp. 665 – 680.

Platvoet, V. (2023) 'Wild things: Animal rights in EU conservation law,' *Journal of International Wildlife Law & Policy,* 26 (2), pp. 79 – 103.

Regan, T. (2004 [1983]). *The case for animal rights.* Berkeley: University of California Press.

Singer, P. (2023) *Animal liberation Now.* London: The Bodley Head.

Smith, K. (2012) *Governing animals: Animal welfare and the liberal state.* New York: Oxford University Press.

Taylor, P.W. (1986) *Respect for nature: A theory of environmental ethics.* Princeton: Princeton University Press.

The New York Declaration on Animal Consciousness (2024) *The New York declaration on animal consciousness.* Available at: https://sites.google.com/nyu.edu/nydeclaration/declaration?authuser=0 (Accessed: 25 November 2024).

Tomasik, B. (2009) 'How many wild animals are there?', in *Essays on reducing suffering.* Available at: https://reducing-suffering.org/how-many-wild-animals-are-there/ (Accessed: 25 November 2024).

UPF-Centre for Animal Ethics (UPF-CAE) (2022) *EU research & animal suffering. scrutinizing the Horizon 2020 programme.* Barcelona: UPF-Centre for Animal Ethics.

Vink, J. (2020) *The open society and its animals.* Basingstoke: Palgrave Macmillan

Section C **Policies**

Introduction: Policies

This section offers a comprehensive overview of how environmental goals, principles and concerns have evolved not only within the confines of environmental policy but also across a variety of policy domains increasingly affected by environmental costs and risks. The first three chapters focus on the expanding scope of the European Union (EU) climate agenda.

The chapter by **Jørgen Wettestad** and **Lars H. Gulbrandsen** traces the consolidation of climate mitigation policies from the first Climate and Energy Package approved in the beginning of 2000 to the 'Fit for 55' package adopted in 2023. Identifying four distinct phases of policy development, their chapter analyzes key features such as ambition, coherence and sectoral coverage. The authors demonstrate how the policy trajectory has been shaped by both internal dynamics and external influences, including the roles of key institutional actors. **Tim Rayner** and **Lisanne Groen** explore the evolution of the EU's climate adaptation agenda over the past two decades. Their chapter illustrates how adaptation has gained increasing prominence within the EU's climate and environmental policy framework, cutting across multiple sectors. They highlight the political and scientific challenges associated with the current emphasis on 'transformative' adaptation and shift the analytical lens towards experimentalist and political economy approaches.

The complex and underexplored nexus between climate, migration and security is addressed by **Julia M. Blocher, Diogo Andreolla Serraglio** and **Annabel Beckmann.** Their chapter reviews the EU's evolving response to climate-induced migration, emphasizing a persistent tension between securitization and adaptation. Their analysis shows that, despite efforts by the European Commission, a coherent EU policy framework in this area remains elusive, hindered by divergent national interests and political sensitivities. The authors nonetheless argue that the EU has unique potential to lead in global climate migration governance, positioning migration as a tool for climate adaptation and sustainable development.

The section then turns to the three traditional pillars of environmental policy: biodiversity, water and waste, each of which face both enduring and emerging challenges. In his chapter on biodiversity, **Raoul Beunen** reflects on key policy milestones from the Bern Convention and Birds Directive (1979) to the Habitats Directive (1992), examining their role in the Europeanization of biodiversity policy. **Beunen** highlights the importance of stakeholder involvement and calls for greater attention to policy failure, resistance and backlash—especially in the context of misinformation, polarization and populism, which are increasingly shaping sustainability debates. The chapter on water policy by **Burcin Demirbilek, David Benson** and **Oliver Fritsch** underscores the growing complexity of water governance and the need for greater integration and coordination. After reviewing the evolution of EU water policy, the authors discuss current and emerging challenges—particularly those linked to climate change, biodiversity loss and unsustainable consumption patterns. Their chapter

https://doi.org/10.1515/9783111321523-023

also calls for new theoretical and analytical approaches to better understand these trends and inform future policy learning. **Anna Broka** examines waste policy and governance, focusing on legislative developments at the EU level and implementation challenges at the local level. Adopting a multilevel governance perspective, her chapter analyzes the interplay between EU directives, national priorities and local capacities. **Broka** highlights how the success of EU waste policy is contingent on both domestic political will and community-level pro-environmental behaviors.

Acknowledging the importance of other EU policy priorities and sectors in shaping EU environmental policy, the section ends with three economic production sectors that are highly interdependent with environmental policy problems: energy, chemicals and food policies. The greening of EU energy policy is analyzed by **Andrea Prontera** and **Ekaterina Domorenok**, who chart the transformation of energy policy instruments to incorporate environmental considerations. Their chapter shows how traditional regulatory tools have increasingly been supplemented by financial and coordination instruments, strengthening the environmental dimension of energy policy and aligning it more closely with climate goals.

The emerging environmental focus in chemicals and food policy is scrutinized in the chapters by **Emanuela Bozzini** and **Giulia Bazzan**, respectively. Although these two policy domains have evolved along different trajectories, both are characterized by persistent gaps and inconsistencies that have hindered their environmental integration. Both authors call for a more coherent and integrated approach to green policymaking in these sectors and underscore the need for further research to understand the evolving risks, challenges and drivers of policy outcomes.

Lastly, the external dimension of EU environmental policy is comprehensively examined by **Tom Delreux. Delreux** analyzes how the EU promotes environmental objectives internationally, focusing on four key avenues: enlargement, internal policies with external spillover effects, sustainability clauses in trade agreements and international dialogue mechanisms. His analysis shows how the EU has shaped global environmental governance and positioned itself as a leader in multilateral negotiations. His chapter concludes with reflections on the geopolitical significance of the EU's external environmental agenda and the mainstreaming of environmental objectives into EU foreign policy.

Jørgen Wettestad and Lars H. Gulbrandsen

The steady ratcheting up of European Union climate mitigation policy: Phases and driving factors

Abstract: This chapter outlines the development of European Union (EU) climate policy over time, divided into four main phases, with particular attention to the period from the first climate and energy package adopted in 2009 up to the 'Fit for 55' package adopted in 2023. Focused design dimensions of this analysis are the fundamental ambitiousness of policy; the coverage of sectors and activities; and the coherence of policies. For each phase we assess how policy and ratcheting up has been shaped by central actors and factors both inside and outside of the EU—i. e., the European Commission; the European Parliament; the Council of Ministers/Member States; and developments in the EU-external environment. Finally, we summarize six main trends in the policy development and related central challenges ahead. Although significant emissions cuts have been achieved and the most recent Fit for 55 package means further ratcheting up, there is still a gap to what scientific bodies deem necessary to comply with the 'well below 2 degrees' target in the Paris Agreement. Furthermore, although EU climate policy has become more coherent over time; more knowledge is needed.

Keywords: European Union climate mitigation policy; climate change; European Green Deal; Fit for 55; policy design

1 Introduction

This chapter first outlines the development of European Union (EU) climate policy over time, divided into phases; we focus on the period from the first climate and energy package adopted in 2009 up to the 'Fit for 55' (FF55) package adopted in 2023. Focused design dimensions of this analysis are the fundamental policy *ambitiousness* (mainly the degree of greenhouse gas (GHG) emissions reductions agreed on), the *coverage* of sectors and activities (as GHG emissions stem from numerous differing activities, and effective policies need to cover all or most of these activities), and the policy *coherence* (to enhance synergies and avoid incompatible or conflicting policies that could generate implementation failures). For each phase we survey how central actors and factors both inside and outside of the EU (i. e., the European Commission; the European Parliament (EP); the Council of Ministers/Member States; and critical EU-external environment developments) have shaped policy and ratcheting up. The role of these institutions, actors and forces has changed over time, and we summarize evolving knowledge about this development. Finally, we evaluate main development trends and identify central challenges, both for research and practice. The FF55 climate pack-

https://doi.org/10.1515/9783111321523-024

age represents a significant ratcheting up of EU climate policy in terms of ambitiousness, coverage and possibly also coherence. However, assessing policy coherence stands out as challenging and a central issue for future research. Furthermore, recent EU level and Member State political developments are likely to create turbulence (see Chapter 4), possibly leading to a climate policy backlash in the implementation phase toward 2030.

2 The evolution of EU climate policy

Initial EU climate policy dates to the late 1980s, with the first EU climate policy package launched in 1990. A key element was a carbon tax proposal. However, due to the opposition of the United Kingdom (UK) and others (taxation requiring unanimity for adoption), this proposal was abandoned in the mid-1990s. Under the auspices of the United Nations Framework Convention on Climate Change (UNFCCC), the Kyoto Protocol was then adopted in 1997, which included a target for the EU to cut its emissions by eight percent in the 2008–2012 period from a 1990 baseline. The Protocol also established three flexible mechanisms: international emissions trading; joint implementation (with specific relevance for Russia and the Eastern European countries), and a clean development mechanism (primarily projects in developing countries).

At this stage the EU possessed no forceful common policy. Although the EU had been skeptical about flexible mechanisms leading up to the Kyoto Protocol, a small group of entrepreneurial economists in the Directorate-General (DG) for Environment managed to convince first the rest of the Commission and subsequently the whole EU about the need to develop an EU Emissions Trading System (ETS) (Skjærseth and Wettestad, 2008). This effort achieved success in 2003 with the first ETS Directive adoption. A pilot phase for 2005–2007 was decided on, followed by the Kyoto commitment phase from 2008–2012. As the EU then was a global ETS frontrunner, industry and Member States were uncertain about this new instrument, leading both to a decentralized initial design where Member States decided how many credits (allowances) were handed out. Allowances were also given out for free. Other EU climate policy elements at this stage were nonbinding renewables targets to be achieved by 2010, energy efficiency measures, and car emissions standards.

The ETS pilot phase did not develop very well, with too many allowances being handed out and a carbon price sinking toward zero in 2007. Simultaneously, climate change was climbing the European political agenda; the Commission started developing a new, broader policy package for 2008 (Oberthür and Pallemaerts, 2010; Jordan et al., 2011; Boasson and Wettestad, 2013).

The next sections examine EU climate policies in three distinct policy phases: (1) 2005–2009: creating the 2020 targets and the first climate and energy package, (2) 2010–2018: developments leading to the first 2030 package, and (3) 2019–2023: the ratcheting up of the 2030 package. For each phase, we assess outcomes in terms of ambitiousness, coverage and coherence, and examine driving factors and actors.

The 2020 targets and the first climate and energy package (2005 – 2009)

A first linking of climate and energy policy

Beginning with ambitiousness, the 2008 package, often referred to as the '20/20/20' package, set a 1990 baseline and emissions reduction targets of 20 percent by 2020 (and the ETS emissions by 21 percent compared to 2005) and the increase of renewables and energy efficiency by 20 percent. The central previous target was the EU's Kyoto Protocol target of an 8 percent reduction by 2008–2012. Hence, the 20 percent target represented increasing ambitiousness, however only loosely grounded in climate science at the time. It instead primarily expressed what was seen as politically feasible (Boasson and Wettestad, 2013).

Concerning the EU ETS, setting the 21 percent cap reflected expectations of continuing economic growth and related emissions development. When the financial crisis hit the EU beginning in 2009, these expectations proved wrong, strongly contributing to an accumulating allowance surplus and a long period of low carbon prices (i. e., around EUR 5 or less) (Skovgaard, 2013; Wettestad and Jevnaker, 2016).

Turning to coverage, the 2008 package combined several policies not previously seen in combination. The package contained four main elements: a significant tightening of the EU ETS (for the 2013–2020 phase), covering power companies and energy-intensive industries; an Effort-Sharing Regulation (ESR) establishing national targets for emissions the ETS did not cover (i. e., transport, agriculture, buildings, waste); a Renewables Directive; and a Carbon Capture and Storage (CCS) Directive.

EU climate policies included other policies, such as a car emissions regulation, a fuel quality directive, an energy efficiency directive, and an energy performance of buildings directive. However, the UN system and elsewhere, rather than the EU, debated other significant emissions and activities, including both airlines (discussed in the International Civil Aviation Organization) and shipping (discussed in the International Maritime Organization) emissions. Similarly, the UNFCCC contained emissions from Land Use, Land Use Change and Forestry (LULUCF) as a reporting requirement, whereas the EU climate policy framework items had no specific focus on these emissions (Romppanen, 2020).

Regarding policy coherence, an early significant linking of climate and energy policies occurred (Boasson and Wettestad, 2013; Delbeke and Vis, 2016; Skjærseth et al., 2016). Although key possible policy interactions were identified in Impact Assessments and other documents in the policy preparation phase and a certain degree of horse-trading happened between the dossiers in the final decision-making stages (Gulbrandsen and Christensen, 2014, p. 517; Skjærseth et al., 2016), climate policy coherence was moderate. Policies were mainly developed individually, with limited attention to developing coherent policies.

Driving actors and factors

Climate change attention and concern among the public and voters in the EU Member States grew in the 2000s. Germany and the UK were particularly important in the new climate policy drive's early phase from 2005 to 2007/2008. February 2005, when the Kyoto Protocol entered into force, marks this period's beginning. Symbolizing the EU's assumption of unilateral climate policy leadership, the Commission adopted the Communication 'Winning the Battle against Global Climate Change' the same month (European Commission, 2005).

A mainly eastward EU enlargement happened one year earlier, with ten countries joining. This had significant consequences for subsequent policy developments. Due not least to their dependence on Russian gas, these countries contributed to an increasing weight given to energy security and the necessity of viewing climate and energy policy in combination. This EU enlargement had also incorporated Member States heavily dependent on coal in their energy systems, leading them to regard potentially costly climate policies with significant skepticism. Poland especially stood out as a political heavyweight, with almost as many votes in the Council as Germany or the UK. Poland emerged as a foot-dragger in the 2008 negotiations and subsequent policy processes.

The Commission sought to strengthen its policy leadership position through a Climate Change Program, with the ETS as the new policy cornerstone. Commission President Barroso did not join the 'climate train' until 2007. Barroso, a shrewd political player, sensed that the 'political climate for climate' was changing in key Member States and that he would need a response to secure himself a second presidential term.

Turning to the EP, the United States (US) had withdrawn from the Kyoto Protocol in 2001. This contributed to greater EU-internal unity, reducing EP climate criticism and activism. Moreover, its formal decision-making role and weight had increased since the Amsterdam Treaty entered into force (May, 1999). This meant a further extension and simplification of the co-decision procedure. Nevertheless, in key processes, notably the ETS decision-making, the Parliament failed to markedly affect the outcome, although it actively sought to introduce more auctioning, market streamlining and centralized control than the Commission was proposing.

Also, the increasing climate concern in Europe and the wish to show EU climate leadership before the international climate negotiations in Copenhagen in December 2009 influenced the EP. Generally, the Parliament supported the new EU climate policy drive and played particularly interesting roles in the cases of CCS and renewables.

Setting the sails for 2030: The 2018 policies (2010–2018)

Increasing policy scope

Although the financial crisis hampered EU climate policy from 2010 onward, thinking about post-2020 policy soon became essential. A central process milestone was the European Council 2014 meeting (European Council, 2014). Here Member States unanimously adopted overall guidelines for a 2030 package. These were further elaborated and specified in decisions taken in 2018: reduce 'domestic' emissions by 'at least' 40 percent compared to 1990, with the ETS as the main instrument. The overall target entailed a 43 percent cut (compared to 2005) for the ETS sectors, and a higher annual linear reduction factor (2.2 percent from 2021 onwards). Industries exposed to carbon leakage would remain shielded; an 'innovation fund' would also support low-carbon innovation in industrial sectors. As Central and Eastern Member States had lower Gross Domestic Product and high shares of coal in their energy mix, solidarity provisions for low-income Member States were added, including a specific 'modernization fund'.

Important reform of the carbon market reform was secured in 2015, with the adoption of the Market Stability Reserve, an automatic 'market thermostat' to start reducing the allowances surplus from 2019 onwards. Initially, 12 percent of the surplus was to be withdrawn. This withdrawal rate doubled in the 2018 decisions (Wettestad and Jevnaker, 2016, 2019). The 2018 Effort-Sharing Regulation established an EU-wide target of 30 percent emissions reduction compared to 2005 levels in the following sectors: domestic transport (excluding aviation), buildings, agriculture, waste and small industry. Each Member State was allocated national targets to collectively contribute to the overall EU emission reduction target (Romppanen, 2023). The revised Renewable Energy Directive set an overarching European renewable energy target of 32 percent by 2030. The Directive included rules ensuring renewables uptake in the transport sector and in heating and cooling.

As a third climate policy pillar, the EU added the LULUCF sector to the 2018 climate package. Even before adopting the Paris Agreement, the EU decided to include the LULUCF sector in its climate policy framework to achieve the economy-wide emissions reduction target for 2021–2030 (Savaresi, Perugini and Chiriaco, 2020). In 2015, the EU had ruled out including the LULUCF sector in the EU ETS. Accordingly, the two options were including LULUCF in the ESR scope or developing a separate EU climate policy pillar. Eventually the latter approach was taken, but the LULUCF pillar was connected to the ESR pillar through flexibility mechanisms allowing credit/debit exchanges (Romppanen, 2020). The binding target for the LULUCF sector was the so-called 'no-debit rule': i. e., each EU Member State shall ensure that at least an equivalent amount of accounted removals compensates for accounted emissions from land use in the period 2021–2030.

The 2018 package of measures was not adopted in a single, major round like the 2008 package. Instead, finalization occurred in several trilogues, with representatives from the Commission, EP and Member States. Through impact assessments and policy design, the Commission sought coherence among the key package elements in the initiation phase, resulting in a fairly coherent policy package.

Driving actors and factors

An important initial background factor in this case was the financial crisis which influenced the EU from 2008 onwards and reduced the general climate policy drive for some years: for instance, contributing to a lowering of the carbon price (Skovgaard, 2013). However, by 2015–2018, increasing popular concern about climate change was notable, e. g., in the youth protest movements in Germany and elsewhere.

The Member States reflected a clear East-West divide in this period, e. g., Poland in 2011 blocking the energy roadmap for 2050 (Wurzel, Di Lullo and Liefferink, 2023). The 2016 UK decision to leave the EU had clear, short-term impacts, but Brexit did not significantly weaken the climate policy pacesetting coalition of Member States (Moore, 2023).

The Commission established a new DG Climate Action in 2010, symbolizing climate change's growing importance in EU politics (Bürgin, 2023). Jean-Claude Juncker succeeded Barroso as Commission President in 2014. The Second Barroso Commission and Juncker Commission had some ambition and determination in developing climate and energy policies (e. g., the ETS reform and the initial 2030 framework) but launched few other grand new initiatives in this area. One exception was the Juncker Commission initiating the Energy Union process in 2016 (Szulecki et al., 2016). This led subsequently to the 2018 Governance Regulation and its request for detailed National Energy and Climate Plans (Knodt, 2023).

The EP has a mixed record in this period (Burns, 2012, 2019; Buzogany and Cetkovic, 2021; Wendler, 2019; Petri, Zapletalova and Biedenkopf, 2023). Some green activism did occur. However, the EP created a crisis concerning the EU ETS in the spring of 2013 by rejecting a moderate ETS reform (i. e., postponing the auctioning of some allowances, called 'backloading') (Wettestad, 2014). Nevertheless, the EP reversed rather quickly. The 2014 elections witnessed an increase of green representatives, but also a further right-wing influx.

The EU-external environment saw several important regional and international developments, partly with lagging effects. Regionally, there was Russian aggression against Ukraine in 2014, with a related gas supply crisis and increased energy prices. The Paris Agreement (a new, 'bottom-up' global United Nations (UN) climate agreement) was adopted in December 2015. It stressed regular ratcheting up of national policies and plans, with the overall goal of keeping global warming beneath 2 degrees and toward 1.5 degrees (Dimitrov, 2016). In the US, Donald Trump became president in 2016 and declared the intention to withdraw the US from the Paris Agreement. Hence, the EU was facing various 'turbulence' (see Chapter Gravey; Dupont and Torney, 2021).

Making the FF55 package (2019 – 2023)

Larger policy scope

Incoming Commission President Ursula von der Leyen's 2019 program signaled a European Green Deal, including both a broadening of the ETS to include shipping, new carbon pricing for the transport and buildings sectors, and a carbon border tax. This was further specified into a 'Fit for 55' package. Despite the Covid-19 challenge, which started in the winter of 2020, the Commission launched the package in July 2021. The FF55 package was adopted in 2023 and signified further ratcheting up of the 2030 framework. Beyond further tightening of existing policies, several new elements are included:

- The gradual incorporation of shipping into the ETS from 2024 to 2026—i. e., emissions from all intra EU voyages and 50 percent of voyages in and out (Earsom and Delreux, 2021; Wettestad and Gulbrandsen, 2022);
- New carbon pricing for the transport and buildings sectors (Leenders, Smeets and Liefferink, 2024; Wettestad, 2024a);
- The phasing in of a Carbon Border Adjustment Mechanism (CBAM) from 2026 onwards that will require importers with more lenient domestic carbon pricing to buy certificates mirroring EU carbon prices, leveling the regulatory playing field (Smith Overland and Szulecki, 2023; Wettestad, 2024b).

Ambitiousness has also increased. The ETS target adopted in April 2023 was a 62 percent reduction by 2030. Linked to the CBAM's introduction, the phasing out of free allowances from 2026 onwards increases the speed of this transition to auctioning and a more direct exposure to the carbon price, for these sectors.

The overall ESR target was hiked up to 40 percent. The national targets set differing annual emission limits for each Member State calculated using a trajectory system leading to the 2030 emission reduction targets. The new ETS for transport and buildings (an ETS2) from 2027 onward, in combination with the ESR targets, represents increasing regulatory challenges for these two sectors which constitute central ESR parts.

The Renewables Directive became significantly more ambitious. Following the 2022 Russian invasion of Ukraine, the EP and the Council compromised on a provisional agreement for a binding target for 2030 of at least 42.5 percent, with an aim to reach 45 percent, as part of the REPowerEU response (European Commission, 2022). The revised 2023 LULUCF Regulation increased the ambition for the land use sector significantly, with a net carbon removal target of 310 million tons CO_2 equivalents (CO_2e) by 2030.

The revised LULUCF regulation involves two phases. From 2021 to 2025, the regulation does not affect the current 'no-debit' rule. From 2026 to 2030, the EU-wide target of 310 million tons CO_2e net removal by 2030 applies, representing roughly a 15 percent increase in the EU's net removals compared to current levels. This phase also enlarges the regulation's terrestrial scope to include wetland management activities and effectively all managed land. An important change in this phase is abandoning the accounting categories and the Forest Reference Levels from the first phase and getting closer in approach to the UNFCCC accounting rules (Gulbrandsen, 2024).

A further development was the 2021 adoption of the European Climate Law, codifying both the 2030 target and a net-zero 2050 target. The Climate Law also established the European Scientific Advisory Board on Climate Change.

Finally, although knowledge so far is limited, the complex and broad FF55 package has been characterized as more coherent than earlier EU climate policy packages (Oberthür and von Homeyer, 2023). First, the Commission rhetoric of an 'integrated package' was strong and persistent. For instance, the ETS Directive Impact Assessment emphasized a general coherence with the remainder of the 2030 framework. Second, the policy preparation and Impact Assessments carried out elaborate cross-policy analyses. For example, the LULUCF Assessment discussed the relationship to the ESR quite extensively—and the reverse. Third, three to five trilogue meetings occurred (the exact number varyied between the dossiers), involving representatives of the Commission, EP and Member States discussing and horse-trading across a few key dossiers, such as the ETS, the ETS2 and the CBAM. These meetings facilitated a final coordination of key dossiers. However, questions of coherence need further research clarification.

Driving actors and factors

First, the von der Leyen Commission arguably has exerted strong leadership, tackling both the Covid and Ukraine challenges, and performing well overall compared to previous Commission leadership (Dupont, Oberthür and von Homeyer, 2020; Bürgin, 2023). Furthermore, this Commission has carried out positive reorganization. The Juncker Commission merged the energy and climate portfolios. Von der Leyen reversed this, allocating the climate portfolio to first executive Vice-President Frans Timmermans who was also given responsibility for the Green Deal package (Bürgin, 2023). Several contextual conditions have been conducive for the present Commission's climate policy entrepreneurship, including climate policy's high salience (Bürgin, 2023, p. 34).

The Commission was the architect behind more ambitious FF55 targets, including renewable energy and, subsequently, the noted REPowerEU plan (European Commission, 2022). Overall, comparing 2023 outcomes with the 2021 Commission proposals, it is striking that the decision-making process retained a main part of the Commission's proposed policy architecture.

As to the EP, the strengthening of green forces continued in the 2019 elections; much of the design of von der Leyen's summer 2019 political program can be seen as consciously catering to central EP priorities (Petri, Zapletalova and Biedenkopf, 2023).

In the FF55 decision-making process the EP pushed somewhat more ambitious proposals than the Commission's initial ones, such as seeking a 63 percent ETS cap and 4.6 percent Linear Reduction Factor (LRF) near 2030 and reduced flexibilities in the ESR. By contrast, the EP was very divided on the ETS2 process and ended up pushing for several 'brakes', such as a price ceiling and exemption for private actors until 2029 (Leenders, Smeets and Liefferink, 2024; Wettestad, 2024a). The EP achieved some victories, particularly concerning the CBAM with a somewhat quicker phasing out of free allowances and system phasing in, and a broader range of sectors included. The EP supported the Commission's LULUCF proposal for a more demanding net removal target. Overall, the EP has contributed to increased final ambitiousness of the FF55 package somewhat, but outcomes do not differ substantially from the Commission proposals.

In the FF55 process, entrepreneurship from strong Member States and issue-specific coalitions has occurred. A good example is France's role in the CBAM process. France set the carbon border tax ball in motion in 2007, with repeated (but also failed) efforts in 2012. However, France persisted and in the FF55 process managed to build a Member State coalition positive about the CBAM idea, helped by 'conducive developments' both within and outside the EU (Wettestad, 2024b).

By comparison, Germany was rather lukewarm to CBAM but was central in establishing the ETS2 for transport and buildings. Germany's position was likely related to the 2019 adoption of a domestic ETS2. Germany struggled quite a long time to build a pro-ETS2 Member State coalition, with France on the reluctant side.

The Council supported most of the Commission's proposal for FF55. Compared to the EP, the Council generally pushed for more flexibility in achieving the targets. For example, whereas the EP proposed reducing some of the ESR flexibility thresholds, the Council proposed increasing them. The trilogue outcomes were rather similar to the Commission proposal, with only minor adjustments.

Focusing on decision-making procedures, the European Council adopted by unanimity the 2020 package in December 2008. The finalization processes of both the 2018 package and the FF55 package were clearly different. First, as discussed above, the main finalizing negotiations involved a series of trilogue meetings. Second, Council final round decisions in April 2023 were taken by qualified majority, meaning that Polish and Hungarian votes against the ETS files (including CBAM) made no difference.

Regarding the EU-external development, the Green Deal's launch must be seen as part of the EU response to the 2015 Paris Agreement. Actors in all the EU institutions strengthened their argumentative power by referencing this Agreement and the need to better align EU policy with the 1.5 degrees temperature goal. From a multilevel perspective, significant nongovernmental organization (NGO) pressure 'from below', such as the Fridays for Future movement in Germany, pushed the Member States and EU institutions.

Another such rippling effect was the EU's response to the Trump Presidency and his administration's increasingly isolationist and anti-climate policy. This policy angered EP actors, among others, and contributed to the drive to establish an EU carbon border tax (i. e., the CBAM).

The Covid-19 pandemic followed the 'Trump challenge'; afterwards came the Russian February 2022 attack on Ukraine. Common to both challenges was that they could easily have provided climate policy laggards with a window of opportunity for slowing, halting or even reversing EU climate policy development. Countries such as Poland and Hungary tried this, but with little success (e. g., Buzogány, Ćetković and Maltby, 2023; Skjærseth, 2023).

3 Concluding reflections

EU climate policy has developed considerably over time, arguably speeding up further after the 2019 launch of the European Green Deal. At least six main trends are identifiable, with related challenges for both further research and policy practice.

Increasing ambitiousness but a gap remains

EU climate policy ambitiousness has increased considerably over time, not least with the FF55. The 2009 targets were only very loosely based on climate science; the 20/20/20 targets mainly reflected what was regarded as politically feasible. Later targets have been gradually increasingly aligned with developing climate science, as communicated by the Intergovernmental Panel on Climate Change. Emissions have also been reduced significantly—by 32.5 percent in 2022 (compared to a 1990 baseline).

However, the European Scientific Advisory Board on Climate Change (established in 2021) has pointed to the continuing gap between EU policy and what climate science says needs to be done (The European Scientific Advisory Board on Climate Change, 2024). Several challenges for further research exist here: how different EU political actors use climate science in internal policy processes (cf., Boasson and Wettestad, 2013); and how several recent institutional developments, such as the establishment of the European Climate Law and the noted European Scientific Advisory Board on Climate Change, function and help remind policymakers about the relationship to climate science.

The EU ETS as a 'cornerstone': Will it last?

Shifting to instrument development, the initial EU ETS has finally come to function as the policy cornerstone it was intended to be. In the wake of the 2018 reforms, the carbon price started to increase and peaked above EUR 100 in February 2023. It has since dropped to a level of around EUR 70 in 2024. Nonetheless, price analysts forecast that the price will increase steadily in the second half of the 2020s and into the 2030s, with also possibilities of prices in the new ETS2 quickly surpassing prices in the ETS.

However, there are several uncertainties related, for example, to the flexibility mechanisms' functioning in the case of the ETS2. Furthermore, and this holds for several points discussed here, if energy prices go high and also push carbon prices, a political backlash might occur tthat can also generate pressure to change the ETS architecture. If the policy architecture remains as agreed so far, there will be no new allowances handed out in the ETS after 2039.

More climate policy instruments means increasing coherence challenges

As noted above, the sheer *number* of policies has increased significantly over time (Jordan and Moore, 2022; Dupont et al., 2023). In the 1990s, the EU was desperately seeking effective common policies after the carbon tax was blocked. Presently, policies exist covering most of the comprehensive sources of GHG emissions, from industry to transport and, to some extent, agriculture. Furthermore, links have increasingly been made between climate policy and other policies, such as trade, social justice and food (Dupont et al., 2023). This impressive development also means increasing coherence challenges, i. e., policies in one area/issue working well with and not contradicting policies in other areas. This includes not least the relationship to land use and forestry—the LULUCF sector—as discussed below.

Assessing coherence is substantially more challenging than assessing ambitiousness and coverage. Our knowledge of EU climate policy coherence is limited and much remains to be seen in the implementation of policies. As coverage has increased even more in the FF55 round of reform, the need to address this research gap becomes more pressing.

The trajectory of the 'LULUCF sector'

As shown above, the LULUCF sector has developed from being more of a separate pillar and UNFCCC reporting obligation to becoming one of the three main EU climate policy pillars. Increasing integration of this sector may allow the EU to move quicker toward closing the gap discussed above. However, analysts and environmental NGOs have warned that including this sector can lead to a watering down of climate policy and a relaxation of the drive to cut emissions in other sectors. Such a development may occur because the revised LULUCF Regulation (2023) and the FF55 framework allow some net carbon removals in the LULUCF sector in each Member State to count toward the overall 55 percent emissions reduction target for 2030. If this policy continues in future EU climate policy packages, some environmental NGOs and observers fear that the LULUCF sector may be a loophole to avoid emission cuts in some countries or reduce EU ambitiousness (CAN Europe, 2021; Ursin, 2023).

Implications of increasing use of policy packaging and trilogues

Section 2 noted several important institutional developments, including the increasing tendency to launch new policies in linked packages and the finalization of decision-making processes in the more intimate but less transparent trilogue processes. This possibly increased the Commission's importance in the final decision-making round, as the Commission has several interinstitutional advantages. In both the CBAM and ETS2 processes, "the package protected the policies" (e.g., Wettestad, 2024a). We need to know more about policy packaging and the use of linking in different ways. We also need more knowledge on the inter-institutional dynamics in trilogues. Research so far seems to focus on the EP role.

The pacesetting role of the Parliament

As indicated above, the EP powers have increased with each treaty change, and co-decision-making has become the default procedure. The EP's perceived role as a 'green pacesetter' has been challenged, especially by internal divisions and the influx of right-wing representatives since the 2009 elections (see Chapter 11).

Green forces also strengthened their position in the 2013 and 2019 elections. As section 2 indicates, it is reasonable to see von der Leyen's initial talk about a Green Deal as part of an effort to cater to EP greens. Although the 2024 EP elections saw a certain strengthening of right-wing and climate-skeptical forces and a weakening of the Greens, the main picture is one of likely overall continuity in the EP role rather than a drastic change.

References

Boasson, E.L. and Wettestad, J. (2013) *EU climate policy: Industry, policy interaction and external environment.* Farnham: Ashgate.

Bürgin, A. (2023) 'The European Commission: A climate policy entrepreneur', in: Rayner, T., Szulecki, K., Jordan, A. and Oberthür, S. (eds.) *Handbook on European Union climate change policy and politics.* Cheltenham: Edward Elgar, pp.23–38.

Burns, C. (2012) 'The European Parliament: Still the EU's environmental champion?', in: Jordan, A. and Adelle, C. (eds.) *Environmental policy in the European Union.* Abingdon: Routledge, pp. 132–152.

Burns, C. (2019) 'In the eye of the storm? The European Parliament, the environment and the EU's crises', *Journal of European Integration*, 41(3), pp. 311–327.

Buzogány, A. and Ćetković, S. (2021) 'Fractionalized but ambitious? Voting on energy and climate policy in the European Parliament', *Journal of European Public Policy*, 28(7), pp. 1038–1056.

Buzogány, A., Ćetković, S. and Maltby, T. (2023) 'EU renewable energy governance and the Ukraine War: Moving ahead through strategic flexibility?', *Politics and Governance*, 11(4), pp. 263–274.

CAN Europe (2021) *Position paper on the revision of the EU LULUCF regulation.* Available at: https://caneurope.org/position-paper-on-the-revision-of-the-eu-lulucf-regulation/ (Accessed: October 2024).

Delbeke, J. and Vis, P. (2016) *EU climate policy explained.* London: Routledge.

Dimitrov, R. (2016) 'The Paris Agreement on climate change: Behind closed doors', *Global Environmental Politics*, 16(3), pp. 1–10.

Dupont, C. and Torney, D. (2021) 'Climate governance and the European Green Deal in turbulent times', *Politics and Governance*, 9(3), pp. 312–315.

Dupont, C., Oberthür, S. and von Homeyer, I. (2020) 'The Covid-19 crisis: A critical juncture for EU climate policy development?', *Journal of European Integration*, 42(8), pp. 1095–1110.

Dupont, C. et al. (2023) 'Three decades of EU climate policy: Racing towards climate neutrality?', *WIREs climate change.* Available at: https://doi.org/10.1002/wcc.86E.

Earsom, J. and Delreux, T. (2021) 'A nice tailwind: The EU's goal achievement at the IMO initial strategy', *Politics and Governance*, 9(3), pp. 401–411.

European Commission (2005) *Winning the battle against global climate change.* COM(2005) 35 final. Available at: https://eur-lex.europa.eu/legal-content/EN/TXT/PDF/?uri=CELEX:52005DC0035&from=EN (Accessed: October 2024).

European Commission (2022) *REPowerEU plan.* COM(2022) 230 final. Available at: https://eur-lex.europa.eu/legal-content/EN/TXT/?uri=COM%3A2022%3A230%3AFIN (Accessed: October 0000).

European Council (2014) *Conclusions.* ST 169/2014 INIT. Available at: https://data.consilium.europa.eu/doc/document/ST-169-2014-INIT/en/pdf (Accessed: October 2024).

Gulbrandsen, L.H. and Christensen, A.R. (2014) 'EU legislation to reduce carbon emissions from cars: Intergovernmental or supranational policy-making?', *Review of Policy Research*, 31(6), pp. 503–528.

Gulbrandsen, L.H. (2024) 'Implementing the EU LULUCF regulation in Norway: Short-term and long-term policy coherence challenges', *Forest Policy and Economics*, 166, 103270.

Jordan, A. et al. (2011) *Climate change policy in the European Union.* Cambridge: Cambridge University Press.

Jordan, A. and Moore, B. (2022) 'The durability-flexibility dialectic: The evolution of decarbonisation policies in the European Union', *Journal of European Public Policy*, 30(3), pp. 425–444. https://doi.org/10.1080/13501763.2022.2042721

Knodt, M. (2023) 'Instruments and modes of governance in EU climate and energy policy: From energy union to the European Green Deal', in: Rayner, T., Szulecki, K., Jordan, A. and Oberthür, S. (eds.) *Handbook on European Union Climate Change Policy and Politics.* Cheltenham: Edward Elgar, pp. 202–216.

Leenders, E., Smeets, S. and Liefferink, D. (2024) 'Leadership in EU policy-making: A deep dive into leadership in the extension of the EU emissions trading system', *Journal of European Public Policy*, pp. 1–23.

Moore, B. (2023) 'Brexit: Weighing the implications for EU and UK climate governance', in: Rayner, T., Szulecki, K., Jordan, A. and Oberthür, S. (eds.) *Handbook on European Union climate change policy and politics.* Cheltenham: Edward Elgar, pp. 337–350.

Oberthür, S. and Pallemaerts, M. (2010) *The new climate policies of the European Union: internal legislation and climate diplomacy.* Brussels: VUB Press.

Oberthür, S. and von Homeyer, I. (2023) 'From emissions trading to the European Green Deal: The evolution of the climate policy mix and climate policy integration in the EU', *Journal of European Public Policy*, 30(3), pp. 445–468.

Petri, F., Zapletalova, V. and Biedenkopf, K. (2023) 'The European Parliament: A strong internal actor with external ambitions', in Rayner, T., Szulecki, K., Jordan, A. and Oberthür, S. (eds.) *Handbook on European Union climate change policy and politics.* Cheltenham: Edward Elgar, pp. 53–68.

Romppanen, S. (2020) 'The LULUCF regulation: The new role of land and forests in the EU climate and policy framework', *Journal of Energy & Natural Resources Law*, 38(3), pp. 261 – 287.

Romppanen, S. (2023) 'Targets, timetables and effort sharing as governance tools: emergence, scope and ambition', in Rayner, T., Szulecki, K., Jordan, A. and Oberthür, S. (eds.) *Handbook on European Union climate change policy and politics.* Edward Elgar.

Savaresi, A., Perugini, L. and Chiriaco, M.V. (2020) 'Making sense of the LULUCF regulation: Much ado about nothing?', *Review of European, Comparative & International Environmental Law*, 29, pp. 212 – 220.

Skjærseth, J.B. (2023) 'The war in Ukraine and EU climate leadership', *Czech Journal of International Relations*, 58(2), pp. 93 – 106.

Skjærseth, J.B. and Wettestad, J. (2008) *EU emissions trading: Initiation, decision-making and implementation.* Farnham: Ashgate.

Skjærseth, J.B., Eikeland, P.O., Gulbrandsen, L.H. and Jevnaker, T. (2016) *Linking EU climate and energy policies: Decision-making, implementation and reform.* Cheltenham: Edward Elgar.

Skovgaard, J. (2013) 'EU climate policy after the crisis', *Environmental Politics*, 23(1), pp. 1 – 17.

Szulecki, K., Fischer, S., Gullberg, A.T. and Sartori, O. (2016) 'Shaping the Energy Union: Between national positions and governance innovation in EU energy and climate policy', *Climate Policy*. 16(5), 548 – 567.

Smith, I.D., Overland, I. and Szulecki, K. (2023) 'The EU's CBAM and its "significant others": Three perspectives on the political fallout from Europe's unilateral climate policy initiative', *Journal of Common Market Studies*, 62(2), pp. 603 – 618.

The European Scientific Advisory Board on Climate Change (2024) *Towards EU climate neutrality: Progress, policy gaps and opportunities.* Available at: https://europa.eu/ (Accessed: October 2024).

Ursin, L. (2023) 'We can't hide behind the land sink', *Energi og Klima.* Available at: https://www.energiogklima.no/to-grader/innsikt/we-cant-hide-behind-the-land-sink (Accessed: October 2024).

Wendler, F. (2019) 'The European Parliament as an arena and agent in the politics of climate change: comparing the external and internal dimension', *Politics and Governance*, 7(3), pp. 327 – 338.

Wettestad, J. (2014) 'Rescuing EU emissions trading: Mission impossible?', *Global Environmental Politics*, 14(2), pp. 64 – 81.

Wettestad, J. (2024a) 'EU emissions trading for transport and buildings: Saved by synergistic institutional interaction?', *Journal of Common Market Studies.* Available at: https://doi.org/10.1111/jcms.13671.

Wettestad, J. (2024b) 'The EU's carbon border adjustment mechanism: Shaped and saved by shifting multi-level reinforcement?', *Review of Policy Research.* Available at: https://doi.org/10.1111/ropr.12597.

Wettestad, J. and Gulbrandsen, L.H. (2022) 'On the process of including shipping in EU emissions trading', *Politics and Governance*, 10(1), pp. 246 – 255.

Wettestad, J. and Jevnaker, T. (2016) *Rescuing EU emissions trading: The climate policy flagship.* Basingstoke: Palgrave.

Wettestad, J. and Jevnaker, T. (2019) 'Smokescreen politics? Ratcheting up EU emissions trading in 2017', *Review of Policy Research*, 36(5), pp. 635 – 659.

Wurzel, R., Di Lullo, M. and Liefferink, D. (2023) 'The European Council, Council and Member States: Jostling for influence', in: Rayner, T., Szulecki, K., Jordan, A. and Oberthür, S. (eds.) *Handbook on European Union climate change policy and politics.* Cheltenham: Edward Elgar, pp. 38 – 53.

Tim Rayner and Lisanne Groen

Enhancing resilience, or continuing complacency? The (constrained) development of European Union adaptation policy

Abstract: From tentative beginnings two decades ago, adaptation now occupies an increasingly important position in the overall European Union (EU) climate (and environmental) policy portfolio, impinging upon multiple policy sectors. Attaining this prominence has required careful policy framing to overcome several constraints but has been helped by a supportive global institutional context. Latterly, a shift in both policy and academic research has seen more 'transformative' types of adaptation increasingly advocated. But whether the EU is capable of delivering sufficiently transformational policy reforms to match the seriousness of the climate crisis remains debatable. In the research literature on EU adaptation policy, multilevel policy diffusion and sectoral mainstreaming have received particular attention, with other angles relatively neglected. In an emerging era of 'Mission-led governance' and increasingly costly extreme weather events, future research could usefully turn to concepts of experimentalist governance and political economy to analyze progress in EU adaptation policy.

Keywords: European Union, adaptation, Mission-led governance, transformational policy

1 Introduction

After some reluctance to acknowledge its importance, particularly in the Global North, adaptation to climate impacts has gained an increasingly high policy profile. No matter how successful mitigation measures may be in reducing emissions, some degree of climate change is widely recognized as inevitable (IPCC, 2022). Bowing to this inevitability, the global climate regime, including the United Nations Framework Convention on Climate Change (UNFCCC) and Paris Agreement (Lesnikowski et al., 2017), now recognizes adaptation's policy importance alongside longer-established mitigation concerns.

In Europe, the world's fastest warming continent (WMO, 2023),[1] European Union (EU) institutions have recognized the need for a more prominent supranational role, noting that, like mitigation, policies can be more effective if responsibility is shared between different governance levels (Biesbroek and Swart, 2019). Since 2019, 'climate

1 Key climate change impacts in Europe can be broadly classified by biogeographical region, albeit with considerable intraregional variation. See Figure 1, reproduced as online material with permission.

https://doi.org/10.1515/9783111321523-025

resilience' has joined climate neutrality as a high-level policy goal for the European Green Deal (EGD), with the Commission pledging that by 2050 the EU will be "fully adapted to the unavoidable impacts of climate change" (European Commission, 2021a, p. 22). As with mitigation, policy effectiveness is increasingly seen to depend on a 'whole-of-government' response, raising potentially profound questions of key, established policy sectors. Compared to mitigation, progress is harder to monitor and evaluate (Biesbroek and Lesnikowski, 2018). Political and policy sciences research has typically framed the EU response in terms of its multilevel governance, policy co-ordination and intergovernmental aspects, but it has also begun to reflect more on themes of social justice and political economy.

This chapter highlights how EU policy has come further than many expected, given significant constraints, but also how much more concerted effort is still required given worsening climate impacts, hitting southern (and south-eastern) Member States in particular. Arguably, the EU's long-term resilience as a stable political and economic entity depends significantly on how effectively its multiple governance levels respond to current and future climate risks and coordinate in increasingly 'transformational' ways (Rayner, 2023). As the EU struggles to ensure its own resilience from worsening climate impacts, both those making and implementing policy and those analyzing these efforts must adjust their approaches accordingly (Rayner, 2023).

2 Emerging EU policy responses: Rationales and sensitivities

Historic emergence of adaptation policy

The language articulating adaptation policy reflects the history of scientific work captured in regular Intergovernmental Panel on Climate Change (IPCC) reports, and specifically its Working Group II on Impacts, Adaptation and Vulnerability. Many of the key terms appear regularly in EU-level documents and are also reflected in new organizational arrangements, though often without much explicit definition. Climate change adaptation is a "process of adjustment to actual or expected climate and its effects" (IPCC, 2022, p. 2898). Adaptation planning and implementation can reduce climate risk vulnerability and provide wider co-benefits for other policy goals, e.g., poverty reduction and job creation. It may be undertaken ad hoc by affected stakeholders as autonomous adaptation or be more consciously planned. Actions range from structural (e.g., dykes that reduce exposure to flooding), nonstructural (e.g., improved early warning systems and emergency preparedness) to economic instruments (e.g. insurance). Ecosystem-based adaptation, such as expanding wetlands as green infrastructure to mitigate flooding or tree cover to cool cities, is increasingly advocated as a response that enables co-benefits under the banner of nature-based solutions (Calliari et al., 2022).

In some cases, problems can be made unintentionally worse, or new ones created, by pursuing pathways that either shift vulnerabilities, reinforce social inequalities or produce significant problems for future generations; outcomes typically labeled 'maladaptation'. Actions that increase greenhouse gas emissions are a further variant of maladaptation. With continued reliance on incremental adaptation (extensions of actions and behaviors that already reduce the losses or enhance the benefits of natural variations in extreme weather/climate events) seen as increasingly inadequate, deliberate transformational adaptation involving "a profound shift towards sustainability [...] facilitated by changes in individual and collective values and behaviours, and a fairer balance of political, cultural and institutional power in society" (IPCC, 2022, p. 2925) is increasingly advocated. Such transformation would tackle underlying causes of vulnerability and promote 'just resilience' (Lager et al., 2023).

Given wide geographical variation in the challenges, the locus of adaptation policy, in contrast to mitigation policy, is often assumed to be local. As well as their responsibility for detailed spatial planning and proximity to vulnerable populations and territories, local and regional authorities are seen as offering appropriate venues for the experimentation and networking judged critical in polycentric approaches to climate governance (Biesbroek and Lesnikowski, 2018); many have adopted this role enthusiastically (Eurocities, 2021; Kern, 2023). Local- or regional-level actors also have the capacity to develop transnational networks and thereby catalyze more effective global-level action (Setzer et al., 2020). Simultaneously, the important role of national governments to set conducive frameworks and ensure adequate action has also been increasingly accepted (Clar and Steurer, 2019).

Adaptation arrives on the EU agenda

Given the logic of local action and the EU's abiding constitutional concern for 'subsidiarity' (see Chapter 1), the fundamental question that has exercised EU policymakers is what roles can most usefully and legitimately be performed at the supranational level? How to construct a policy framework that is flexible enough to allow Member State sovereignty to implement policies suitable for local contexts while simultaneously meeting overall continent-wide resilience objectives?

Schoenefeld, Schulze and Bruch (2022) note that, in principle, adaptation policies might spread through various 'diffusion mechanisms', including learning, competition, coercion, and emulation. Diffusion can occur horizontally—among jurisdictions at the same level, such as municipalities—but also vertically: either top-down, from international or national to lower levels, or bottom-up, whereby national or local action might trigger action at international/supranational scale. The initial emergence of EU-level action stemmed in large degree from bottom-up demands (Rayner and Jordan, 2010), as policy entrepreneurs at local/ city-level, and some early-moving Member States encouraged Commission action. Ever since, local authorities' support for EU-level action has been consistent, partly to secure more reliable support for their efforts from their own national governments. By contrast, support from Member States to the EU's first steps was qualified, as it has been ever since, by wariness about extending Commission competence, particularly into matters of land-use planning (Biesbroek and Swart, 2019; Rayner and Jordan, 2010).

Even before consultations began on a formal adaptation policy response, the earliest EU-level moves occurred reactively: after high-profile and large-scale 'focusing events' in various 'cognate sectors', particularly the 2002 Central European floods and the 2003 heatwave (Rayner and Jordan, 2010). A 2002 'flood summit' decided to offer affected Member States assistance to tackle damage totaling over EUR 15 billion. Establishing the EU Solidarity Fund as a new instrument to mobilize emergency financial assistance to respond to natural disasters (excluding drought) and noninsured damage exceeding a certain threshold, received unanimous support from Member States and the European Parliament. The 2007 Floods Directive also originated from this sequence of events. The idea of pooling resources to enable timely and decisive interventions to avoid substantial damages and loss of life into a permanent rapid reaction force to tackle regular forest fires in Southern Europe also took root in advance of more formal EU adaptation policy, under the auspices of the EU Civil Protection Mechanism. This prioritizes prevention and preparedness, as well as response (Lenaerts, Tagliapietra and Wolff, 2022).

Beyond solidarity, periodic consultation exercises since 2005 have expressed a series of rationales to legitimize EU-level adaptation policy (most recently in European Commission, 2021b). These include: scale benefits from jointly developing scientific knowledge on current and future climate impacts to inform better decisions (the Copernicus Climate Change Service offering one example) and increased budgets allocated to adaptation under the Horizon Europe Research and Innovation program (discussed in the context of development cooperation and migration, see Chapter 22). The need to manage cross-border spillovers resulting from adaptive actions (or absence thereof) undertaken unilaterally by individual Member States is also accepted in principle, while both policy documents and academic literature highlight the need for coordination or mutual adjustment between strategies emanating from different governance levels (Clar, 2019).

Mainstreaming adaptation concerns in sectors with already well-established EU competence was uncontroversial with Member States (Rayner and Jordan, 2010). The rationale that, without adaptation, the effectiveness of EU spending on agriculture and regional development may be compromised, along with the smooth functioning of the single market with its extensive international supply chains, has galvanized policy action (Lenaerts, Tagliapietra and Wolff, 2022). Accordingly, the Commission has, since 2014, followed a more coercive approach to diffusion in cohesion and to some extent agricultural policy, using ex ante conditionality/enabling conditions. Similarly, InvestEU has provisions on sustainability-proofing all financing and investment operations above a certain size. The European Investment Bank has similar commitments and pledged 15 percent of its overall climate finance for adaptation by 2025 (Harding, Nauwelaers and Haegeman, 2024).

A further rationale for EU-level action involved increasing recognition that the success of emission reduction (mitigation) efforts depends partly on resilience to climate impacts, including protection of carbon sinks (such as forests at risk from drought and wildfires), and adequate water supplies for a decarbonized power sector. Such concerns have raised interest in nature-based solutions to mitigate and adapt to climate change simultaneously (Calliari et al., 2022).

The 2021 adaptation strategy

The Commission expressed these rationales for supranational involvement in its revamped 2021 EU adaptation strategy (European Commission, 2021a), which replaced the less formalized, less ambitious 2013 version, and in its parallel moves to enhance civil protection/ disaster-response capacity (European Commission, n.d. a). The revised strategy (part of the EGD) pursues a more 'whole-of-government' approach to make adaptation 'smarter, faster and more systemic' while also minimizing the risks to EU countries from climate impacts occurring beyond European borders. In support of the strategy, the 2021 European Climate Law called for action whereby:

> Member States shall [...] ensure that policies on adaptation in the Union and in Member States are coherent, mutually supportive, provide co-benefits for sectoral policies, and work towards better integration of adaptation to climate change in a consistent manner in all policy areas, including relevant socioeconomic and environmental policies and actions, where appropriate, as well as in the Union's external action. (European Union, 2021, Art. 5(2))

National adaptation strategies and plans must be updated and communicated biennially in dedicated reports, enabling the Commission to assess collective progress every five years. By 2023, all Member States had plans in place; ten reported having adopted dedicated national climate laws that included adaptation aspects (European Environment Agency, 2023).[2] Similarly, the trend toward more legally binding approaches is also visible in the adoption of a legislative framework for nature protection that further incentivizes adopting nature-based (adaptation) solutions, which culminated in the 2024 Nature Restoration Law (see Calliari et al., 2022). These developments notwithstanding, the Commission still lacks capacity compared to areas of greater competence to force Member State action (Buser, 2023).

While it has at times hinted that it could adopt a more regulatory approach to spur action, especially from the more laggardly Member States (Biesbroek and Swart, 2019), in its 2021 strategy the Commission preferred not to risk provoking national governments. Instead, it encouraged regional/local level progress through an innovative new approach: the EU Mission on Adaptation (European Commission, n.d. b). The Mission is one of five of its kind (including one for Climate Neutral Cities), that

2 Figure 2 (reproduced with permission as online material) depicts the variety of policy approaches.

together constitute a novel EU Research and Innovation (R&I) policy direction and is inspired by economist Marianna Mazzucato's (2019) conceptualization and a number of pioneering attempts to deliver more transformative, place-based adaptation (Rayner, 2023). Parallel EU initiatives are also underway to better understand how 'Transformative Innovation' can more systemically tackle wider societal challenges, recognizing that entire socio-technical systems need to change (Harding, Nauwelaers and Haegeman, 2024).

The Mission is intended to support at least 150 European regions and communities in developing visions of a climate-resilient future and the innovation pathways to reach them, as well as in testing solutions and "preparing the ground for deep-rooted systemic change" (Directorate-General R&I, 2021, p. 15). By 2030, seventy-five "large-scale demonstrations of systemic transformations to climate resilience across European regions and communities" (Directorate General R&I, p.2) are intended to inspire others.[3] As well as this ambition for diffusion by emulation or learning (see Schoenefeld, Schulze and Bruch, 2022), the new Mission also tries to develop hitherto absent cross-domain synergies (Harding, Nauwelaers and Haegeman 2024).

Broadly in line with IPCC (2022) terminology and frequent promotion of 'transformative' adaptation, the 2021 EU Adaptation Strategy's phrase 'just resilience' speaks partially to the sense that adaptation measures need carrying out in a manner equivalent to 'just transition' in climate change mitigation, and "a concern for the uneven burdens imposed by climate impacts and risks, due to unequal exposure to hazard, pre-existing inequalities and differences in adaptive capacities and capabilities (including, e.g., socioeconomic, historical and intersectional injustice)" (Lager et al., 2023, p. 12).

The international dimension

Concerning external action, the EU is a significant aid donor for adaptation. Alongside the United Nations, the EU is one of the main funders of climate action, especially in poorer countries, channeling aid through development cooperation policy and to a lesser extent trade and neighborhood policies (for how this relates to migration, see Chapter 22). The main aim is to promote sustainable economic growth, in line with the existing multilateral legal framework centering around the UNFCCC (Pérez de las Heras, 2015), which the EU has consistently championed. EU aid includes support for developing nationally determined contributions and national adaptation plans (European Environment Agency, 2024). However, at UNFCCC Conference of the Parties 27, the EU missed the opportunity to address disaster-induced displacement, its policy-

3 Table 1, as online material with permission, shows provisional indicators for the EU Mission on Adaptation (European Commission et al., 2024).

making hampered by insufficient exchange and coordination among EU institutions (see Chapter 22).

To fulfil its commitment to mainstream climate change adaptation (and mitigation) in its development cooperation, in 2007 the EU founded the Global Climate Change Alliance (GCCA, becoming the GCCA+ flagship initiative in 2014). This promotes dialogue, technical and financial adaptation support, especially to poorer small island states. The climate mainstreaming goal required both adaptation and mitigation implementation through procedures and adjustments in EU delegations' organization. The growing political salience of the mainstreaming agenda is one key driver of the EU's commitment, resulting in a degree of top-down political will and resource reallocation (De Roeck, Orbie and Delputte, 2018; De Roeck, 2019).

3 EU adaptation policy scholarship

Of the academic research focusing on EU adaptation policy since its inception, much has concentrated on Member State efforts, comparing the coverage of their national adaptation plans and strategies, and preferred instrument mixes (see e.g., Biesbroek and Delaney, 2020; Pietrapertosa et al., 2018). Typically, these contributions highlight selectivity in coverage and limitations in ambition or the Commission's inability to 'coerce' (e.g., Russel et al., 2020). Official evaluations have likewise found design and implementation of Member State adaptation strategies to be too fragmented and that, while countries have increasingly mainstreamed adaptation concerns in key areas where direct climate impacts are more readily visible (such as agriculture or water management), progress has lagged in many other policy domains whose importance will grow as impacts worsen.

Another well-ploughed furrow has been to identify the cities in EU countries that have made the most progress (Reckien et al., 2023) and the reasons underpinning their relative success. Given that local and regional authorities implement an estimated 90 percent of adaptation policies in the EU, this focus is not unreasonable (Committee of the Regions, 2020). Studies find that the limited range of responsibilities and corresponding powers of local authorities often undermines ambitious place-based adaptation strategies. Reckien et al. (2023) found that although half of EU cities have an adaptation plan, with many significantly improved over time, monitoring, evaluation, participation (especially by marginalized and vulnerable groups) and plan consistency remain particularly weak.

Rather less has been written on EU-level adaptation policy, much of it taking the form of book chapters which note that, without a more developed competence, the Commission is reliant on an 'Open Method of Coordination' governance approach (Biesboek and Swart, 2019; Rayner and Jordan, 2010). When explicitly addressing the EU level, the limited journal scholarship typically mirrors the Commission's own research focus (as reflected in, e.g., its impact assessments) in explaining increased EU policy involvement in particular realms, referencing the need to 'climate-proof' EU spending, ensure single market functioning, avoid transboundary spill-overs, express intra-EU solidarity etc. (Hochrainer-Stigler, Linnerooth-Bayer and Lorant, 2017). Researchers have studied the extent to which the objectives of adaptation policy mainstreaming (or integration) are being achieved (e.g., Brouwer, Rayner and Huitema, 2013; Buser, 2023; Russel et al, 2018). Some literature also proposes more ambitious policy framework extensions or revisions (e.g., Lenaerts, Tagliapietra and Wolff, et al., 2022; Hochrainer-Stigler et al., 2017, 2023). Some recent contributions have assessed growing systemic economic risks to the EU posed by increasingly costly extreme weather events, focusing on the Solidarity Fund's adequacy (Hochrainer-Stigler et al., 2023).

The literature also addresses the apparent limits to EU adaptation policy involvement, focusing on the lack of explicit competence and respect for subsidiarity (e.g., Biesbroek and Swart, 2019; Rayner and Jordan, 2010, 2013). Member State opposition sometimes reflects 'high politics' considerations regarding sensitive issues, such as migration (Blocher, 2016). Where the EU does have competence, temporal mismatches between policy cycles and institutional dynamics within the Commission, including a degree of rivalry over internal divisions of responsibility (Candel, Princen and Biesbroek, 2021) that limit coordination, may slow policy progress. Budgetary cycles are seen to be particularly influential in this respect, setting allocations to a domain for a certain period and thereby hampering possibilities for intermediate reforms (Candel, Princen and Biesbroek, 2021). Moreover, certain Commission Directorate-Generals (DGs) have been identified as preferring lower levels of adaptation policy ambition (Russel et al., 2018), in particular DG Agriculture, which is backed by one of the EU's most influential producer lobbies with the ear of numerous Member State governments (Candel, Princen and Biesbroek, 2021, p. 110). A technocratic unwillingness to 'politicize' issues and call into question neoliberal ideological assumptions has also been identified (Remling, 2018), a tendency which some associate with mainstream civil society actors at the city level as well (De Rosa, de Moor and Dabaieh, 2022).

Research has highlighted differing incentives for adaptation policy compared to mitigation, with the former lacking the clearer energy security co-benefits, shorter-term profitability, regulation or generous incentives to opening new and large markets characteristic of the latter (Harding, Nauwelaers and Haegeman, 2024). Before the 2015 Paris Agreement, adaptation investments were seen by EU policy makers as detracting from higher priority mitigation goals (Candel, Princen and Biesbroek, 2021, p. 110).

Given growing climate impacts, research has questioned the viability of continuing reliance on incrementalism generally and mainstreaming specifically (Rayner and Jordan, 2013). Scholars do, however, continue to see value in improving the approach to studying the effectiveness of mainstreaming; Runhaar et al. (2018), for example, conclude that future research syntheses and well-informed policy recommendations require more explicit definitions and unified frameworks. Nature-based solutions are attracting significant research attention, with findings suggesting, inter alia, the need for stronger target-led governance (Calliari et al., 2022).

Meanwhile, a limited internationally focused literature has appeared, with the GCCA as a particular focus. Efforts to mainstream adaptation in EU development co-operation are seen as inadequate (De Roeck, Orbie and Delputte, 2018; De Roeck, 2019). Scholars are also exploring the power dynamics operating in the EU's climate-development policy interactions with Global South countries, including adaptation from a justice perspective (von Lucke et al., 2021), concluding that the EU offers only a limited form of 'damage control'.

4 Limitations in current scholarship

Schoenefeld, Schulze and Bruch (2022, p. 9) have noted that, despite substantial evidence of the diffusion of adaptation policy *outputs*, evidence of effective implementation *outcomes* "remains limited, sporadic and inconclusive". This reflects a wider monitoring and evaluation problem for adaptation policy, wherever it is delivered, partially related to unclear metrics and indicators and the need for time to pass before judging newly adopted instruments' effectiveness. Moreover, Schoenefeld, Schulze and Bruch highlight a chronic lack of longitudinal data on adaptation policy change, especially comparative data, that hampers study of diffusion processes. Data collection through such initiatives as the Global Adaptation Mapping Initiative[4] promises more comprehensive assessments of whether and how policy diffusion can advance adaptation.

Another aspect of the literature where dissatisfaction has been expressed is the repeated identification of 'barriers' to progress, instead of moving further to uncover deeper dynamics to help identify better means to achieve adaptation goals. Calls for more sophisticated conceptualization of the underlying dynamics constituting 'lock-ins' are one response (Groen et al., 2022).

More specifically in terms of EU-level policy literature, Remling (2018) has been among the most critical, identifying the absence of more critical discourse analysis, of the kind able to identify unspoken ideological policymaking assumptions. Remling offers a potential new political-economic direction for more critical scholars to identify how dominant neoliberal policy framings limit conceptualization of EU adaptation responses, potentially at the expense of the most vulnerable.

Finally, the volume of literature on the global dimension of EU adaptation efforts compares unfavorably to that covering EU external climate policy more broadly. Scholars criticize the EU's efforts as a global actor *in general*, beyond climate change, especially what is seen as hypocritical window-dressing of itself as a normative and ethical power.

4 See https://globaladaptation.github.io/.

5 Confronting new realities

The inaugural EU Climate Risk Assessment (European Environment Agency, 2024), required by the 2021 Adaptation Strategy, identifies areas urgently in demand of more ambitious policy. Thirty-six key risks are identified; several, including, inter alia, coastal and marine ecosystems and wildfire risk to biodiversity and carbon sinks, are already said to be at critical levels and highly urgent.[5] It also highlights how the EU Solidarity Fund was exhausted for three years running from 2021–2023. In light of this work, and our own wider reading, further specific criticisms of the existing literature can be offered.

Firstly, research (both academic and by public institutions) has arguably been focused too heavily on individual sectors to appreciate adequately the systemic nature of the challenges facing the EU (and wider world). It needs greater orientation to 'problem domains' (Groen et al., 2022) and systems (Harding, Nauwelaers and Haegeman, 2024, p. 34; Rietig and Dupont, 2023). Secondly, research has been slow to recognize the major macroeconomic, fiscal and financial risk aspects of climate change, and the policy response required from institutions hitherto receiving little attention, including the European Central Bank. These aspects, and related questions of political economy, are crucial to the EU's success in enhancing its own resilience more systemically in terms of both vulnerability to 'shocks' from extreme events such as flooding and ensuring adequate public spending on adaptation in a restrictive fiscal climate (Palagi et al., 2023). This fits with a wider criticism that the rhetoric (in academic and policy circles) demanding transformational policy change is still to be matched by concrete analysis of what that means and what it would involve for the EU.

6 Challenges and opportunities for EU research

For policy diffusion to be effective in governing adaptation, understanding the conditions under which it produces desirable or undesirable (i. e., maladaptive) outcomes is essential. We follow Schoenefeld, Schulze and Bruch (2022) in calling for the evaluation of adaptation policy diffusion processes and outcomes (not just outputs) to be a core priority for future research.

As part of this, as Rayner (2023) highlights, the new 'Missions' offer an important new focus for EU-based research. Whether insights from Transformative Innovation approaches (as noted above) can make adaptation strategies more effective and systemically oriented in their conceptualization and implementation, is one opportunity for research (Harding, Nauwelaers and Haegeman, 2024). A similarly important avenue is the extent to which the Missions' participatory ideals can be delivered in practice and, in

5 Table 2 (online) presents risk assessment for thirty-six major climate risks, reproduced with permission from the European Environment Agency (2024).

turn, how far they can allow more transformative concepts, including 'just resilience', to win approval in the face of inertia or opposition (De Rosa, de Moor and Dabaieh, 2022). While some research (Cattino and Reckien, 2021) has suggested that wide participation is more likely to deliver transformative solutions in cases of adaptation planning processes compared to mitigation ones, this finding requires additional case evidence. How will 'just' resilience be interpreted? Moreover, what difference does this entail for the outputs, outcomes and ultimate impacts in the regions and communities concerned?

Beyond the effectiveness of Mission-related activity within the relevant localities, there are wider questions for EU governance scholars (Rayner 2023). The Mission follows a bottom-up governance model, so coordination mechanisms between the separate/neighboring regional initiatives are necessary. Will such tools be robust enough to secure coherent outcomes across subnational and also national boundaries? Will national governments support improved cross-national coordination—an identified weakness of EU strategy to date (European Commission, 2018)? How far will Member State governments include emerging Mission-derived outputs in their own national adaptation plans?

Many questions crop up regarding wider policy coherence. To what degree will Missions-related planning contribute to fostering synergies and coherence across economic, social and environmental policy siloes and across mitigation and adaptation strategies in the same locality (given that a separate EU Mission covers Climate Neutral Cities)? What happens if the Mission areas generate transformative proposals that clash with often static assumptions underpinning existing national and/or EU level environmental policies?

If fiscal policies constraining Member State public spending remain tight, how much scope will private sector actors and public authorities have to build new partnerships that stimulate the development, financing and delivery of new visions, covering aspects that the private sector has previously not viewed as part of its remit?

The field could also benefit from longer-term study of the consequences of 'laggard' regions choosing not to work with the Mission(s). Will they lag further behind or raise their ambitions? Emulating or learning from others requires sufficient resources to absorb information or even become aware of others' actions (Schoenefeld, Schulze and Bruch, 2022). Several EU municipal networks still primarily attract larger, wealthier and, in other ways, well-connected cities (Kern, 2023). If this continues, then the potential of municipal networks to spread adaptation policies more widely and toward more vulnerable communities will be compromised.

Conceiving this Mission-led era theoretically, insights from experimentalist governance literature (see, e.g., De Búrca, Keohane and Sabel, 2014) may be helpful. This pictures the policy process in terms of:

(1) setting framework goals and establishing metrics in an open process involving broad stakeholder participation;
(2) decentralized implementation;
(3) monitoring and reporting, including peer review; and
(4) evaluation and revision of the goals in light of experiences.

Polycentric theory (Jordan et al., 2018) usually assumes that (3) and (4) will necessarily happen, but whether they actually do is an empirical question. An experimental governance perspective might suggest tracking the extent to which criteria 3 and 4 are present and happening in a concerted way in the EU.

Beyond the place-based adaptation networks embodied in the Mission, and their effects at the EU level, further key research agendas need development. These include how the EU's external role might develop and translate 'just resilience' into more global terms. Internally, how might policy processes reflect major emerging risks and political economic challenges linked to climate impacts, particularly concerning macro-fiscal planning? How will divisions between Northern Member States and more heavily climate-impact damaged Southern counterparts be handled? Whether 'burden sharing' on such questions will receive an equivalent degree of political attention and negotiation as it does for mitigation policy, and how this occurs, will be important to watch.

References

Biesbroek, R. and Delaney, A. (2020) 'Mapping the evidence of climate change adaptation policy instruments in Europe', *Environmental Research Letters*, 15, 083005.

Biesbroek, R. and Lesnikowski, A. (2018) 'Adaptation: The neglected dimension of polycentric climate governance', in: Jordan, A., Huitema, D., Van Asselt, H. and Forster, J. (eds.) *Governing climate change: Polycentricity in action?* Cambridge: Cambridge University Press, pp. 303 – 319.

Biesbroek, R. and Swart, R. (2019) 'Adaptation policy at supranational level? Evidence from the European Union', in: Keskitalo, E.C.H., and Preston, B.L. (eds.) *Research handbook on climate change adaptation policy*. Cheltenham: Edward Elgar, pp. 194 – 211.

Blocher, J. (2016) 'Climate change and environment related migration in European Union policy', in: Rosenow-Williams, K. and Gemenne, F. (eds.) *Organizational perspectives on environmental migration*. London: Routledge, pp.38 – 56.

Brouwer, S., Rayner, T. and Huitema, D. (2013) 'Mainstreaming climate policy: The case of climate adaptation and the implementation of EU water policy', *Environment and Planning* (C), 31, pp. 134 – 153.

Buser, A. (2023) 'Towards a Climate Resilient European Union? Prospects and Limitations of a General EU Climate Adaption Law', *Journal for European Environmental & Planning Law*, 20, pp. 127 – 144.

Calliari, E., et al. (2022) 'Building climate resilience through nature-based solutions in Europe: A review of enabling knowledge, finance and governance frameworks', *Climate Risk Management*, 37, 100450.

Candel, J.J.L., Princen, S. and Biesbroek, R. (2021) 'Patterns of coordination in the European Commission', *Journal of European Public Policy*, 30(1), pp. 104 – 127.

Cattino, M. and Reckien, D. (2021) 'Does public participation lead to more ambitious and transformative local climate change planning?', *Current Opinion in Environmental Sustainability*, 52, pp. 100 – 110.

Clar, C. (2019) 'Coordinating climate change adaptation across levels of government', *Journal of Environmental Planning and Management*, 62(12), pp. 2166 – 2185.

Clar, C. and Steurer, R. (2019) 'Climate change adaptation strategies at different levels of government', in: Keskitalo, E.C.H. and Preston, B.L. (eds.) *Research handbook on climate change adaptation policy*. Cheltenham: Edward Elgar, pp. 310 – 326.

Committee of the Regions (2020) *Resolution of the European Committee of the Regions: The Green Deal in partnership with local and regional authorities.* 2020/C 79/01. Available at: https://eur-lex.europa.eu/legal-content/EN/TXT/PDF/?uri=CELEX:52019XR4351 (Accessed: 4 March 2025).

De Búrca, G., Keohane, R.O. and Sabel, C. (2014) 'Global experimentalist governance', *British Journal of Political Science*, 44(3), pp. 477 – 486.

De Roeck, F., Orbie, J. and Delputte, S. (2018) 'Mainstreaming climate change adaptation into the European Union's development assistance', *Environmental Science & Policy*, 81, pp. 36 – 45.

De Roeck, F. (2019) 'Governmentality and the climate-development nexus: The case of the EU Global Climate Change Alliance', *Global Environmental Change*, 55, pp. 160 – 167.

De Rosa, S.P., de Moor, J. and Dabaieh, M. (2022) 'Vulnerability and activism in urban climate politics', *Cities*, 130, 103848.

Directorate General R&I (2021) *EU Mission adaptation to climate change implementation plan.* Available at: https://research-and-innovation.ec.europa.eu/system/files/2021-09/climatmissionimplementationplanfinalforpublication.pdf (Accessed: 26 November 2024).

Eurocities (2021) *A mayors alliance for the European Green Deal.* Available at: https://eurocities.eu/latest/a-mayors-alliance-for-the-european-green-deal/ (Accessed: 26 November 2024).

European Commission (2018) 'Evaluation of the EU strategy on adaptation to climate change', *SWD*/2018/461 final. Available at: https://eur-lex.europa.eu/legal-content/EN/TXT/?uri=celex:52018SC0461 (Accessed: 4 March 2025).

European Commission (2021a) 'Forging a climate-resilient Europe: The new EU strategy on adaptation to climate change', *COM*(2021) 82 final. Available at: https://eur-lex.europa.eu/legal-content/EN/TXT/?uri=celex:52021DC0082 (Accessed: 4 March 2025).

European Commission (2021b) 'Impact assessment report accompanying the communication from the Commission to the European Parliament, the Council, the Economic and Social Committee and the Committee of the Regions: Forging a climate-resilient Europe—The new EU Strategy on adaptation to climate change', *SWD*(2021) 25 final. Available at: https://eur-lex.europa.eu/legal-content/EN/TXT/?uri=SWD:2021:25:FIN (Accessed: 4 March 2025).

European Commission (n.d. a). *EU civil protection mechanism.* Available at: https://civil-protectionhumanitarian-aid.ec.europa.eu/what/civil-protection/eu-civil-protectionmechanism_en (Accessed: 26 November 2024).

European Commission (n.d. b) *EU Mission: Adaptation to climate change.* Available at: https://research-and-innovation.ec.europa.eu/funding/funding-opportunities/funding-programmes-and-open-calls/horizon-europe/eu-missions-horizon-europe/adaptation-climate-change (undated). (Accessed: 26 November 2024).

European Environment Agency (2022) *Report 11/2022 – Advancing towards climate resilience in Europe.* Available at: https://www.eea.europa.eu/publications/advancing-towards-climate-resilience-in-europe (Accessed: 26 November 2024).

European Environment Agency (2024) *European climate risk assessment.* ISSN 1977 – 8449. Available at: https://www.eea.europa.eu/publications/european-climate-risk-assessment (Accessed: 26 November 2024).

European Union (2021) 'Regulation (EU) 2021/1119 of the European Parliament and of the Council of 30 June 2021 Establishing the Framework for Achieving Climate Neutrality and Amending Regulations (EC) No 401/2009 and (EU) 2018/1999' ('European Climate Law'). *Official Journal of the European Union L* 243/1. Available at: https://eur-lex.europa.eu/eli/reg/2021/1119/oj/eng (Accessed: 4 March 2025).

Groen, L. et al. (2022) 'Re-examining policy stability in climate adaptation through a lock-in perspective', *Journal of European Public Policy*, 30(3), pp. 488 – 512.

Harding, R., Nauwelaers, C. and Haegeman, K. (2024) *Transformative innovation for climate change adaptation: A mapping-based framework for territories.* Carat, G. and Gnamus, A. (eds.), Luxembourg: Publications Office of the European Union, https://data.europa.eu/doi/10.2760/319559, JRC137300.

Hochrainer-Stigler, S., Linnerooth-Bayer, J. and Lorant, A. (2017) 'The European Union Solidarity Fund: an assessment of its recent reforms', *Mitigation and Adaptation Strategies for Global Change*, 22(4), pp. 547 – 563.

Hochrainer-Stigler, S., Zhu, Q., Reiter, K. and Ciullo, A. (2023) 'Challenges of instruments that should tackle multi-hazard and multi-risk situations', *Mitigation and Adaptation Strategies for Global Change*, 28(8), e41.

IPCC (2022) *Annex II: Glossary*, in: Pörtner, H.-O., et al. (eds.) *Climate change 2022: Impacts, adaptation and vulnerability. Contribution of Working Group II to the Sixth Assessment Report of the Intergovernmental Panel on Climate Change.* Cambridge: Cambridge University Press, pp. 2897 – 2930.

Jordan, A., Huitema, D., Van Asselt, H. and Forster, J. (eds.) *Governing climate change: Polycentricity in action?* Cambridge: Cambridge University Press.

Kern, K. (2023) 'Cities in EU multilevel climate policy', in: Rayner, T., Szulecki, K., Jordan, A. and Oberthür, S. (eds.) *Handbook on European Union climate change policy and politics.* Cheltenham: Edward Elgar, pp. 113 – 128.

Lager, F., et al. (2023) *Just resilience for Europe: Towards measuring justice in climate change adaptation.* ETC CA. Available at: https://doi.org/10.25424/CMCC-BATP-3M95.

Lenaerts, K., Tagliapietra, S. and Wolff, G.B. (2022) 'How can the European Union adapt to climate change?', *Intereconomics*, 57, pp. 314 – 321.

Lesnikowski, A. et al. (2016) 'What does the Paris Agreement mean for adaptation?', *Climate Policy*, 17, pp. 825 – 831.

Mazzucato, M. (2019). *Governing Missions in the European Union.* Brussels: European Commission Directorate-General for Research and Innovation. Available at: https://research-and-innovation.ec.europa.eu/knowledge-publications-tools-and-data/publications/all-publications/governing-missions-european-union_en (Accessed: 4 March 2025).

Palagi, E., Guzzardi, D., Faccio, T. and Roventini, A. (2023) 'In search of lost time: An ensemble of policies to restore fiscal progressivity and address the climate challenge', in: Cerniglia, F., Saraceno, F. and Watt, A. (eds.) *Financing investment in times of high public debt: 2023 European public investment outlook.* Cambridge: Open Book Publishers, pp. 169 – 190.

Pérez de las Heras, B. (2015) 'Adaptation to climate change in the European Union: Between supranational action and state reluctance', *IUCNAEL EJournal.* Available at: https://www.iucnael.org/en/documents/1263-adaptation-to-climate-change (Accessed: 29 November 2024).

Pietrapertosa, F., Khokhlov, V., Salvia, M. and Cosmi, C. (2018) 'Climate change adaptation policies and plans: A survey in 11 South East European countries', *Renewable and Sustainable Energy Reviews*, 81(2), pp. 3041 – 3050.

Rayner, T. and Jordan, A. (2010) 'Adapting to a changing climate: An emerging European Union policy?', in: Jordan, A. et al. (eds.) *Climate Change Policy in the European Union.* Cambridge: Cambridge University Press, pp. 145 – 166.

Rayner, T. and Jordan, A. (2013) 'The European Union: The polycentric climate policy leader?', *WIRES Interdisciplinary Reviews: Climate Change*, 4(2), pp. 75 – 90.

Rayner, T. (2023) 'Adaptation to climate change: EU policy on a Mission towards transformation?', *npj Climate Action*, 2(36).

Reckien, D., et al. (2023) 'Quality of urban climate adaptation plans over time', *npj Urban Sustainability*, 3(13).

Remling, E. (2018) 'Depoliticizing adaptation: A critical analysis of EU climate adaptation policy', *Environmental Politics* 27(3), pp. 477 – 497.

Rietig, K. and Dupont, C. (2023) 'Climate policy integration and climate mainstreaming in the EU budget', in: Rayner, T., Szulecki, K., Jordan, A. and Oberthür, S. (eds.) *Handbook on European Union climate change policy and politics.* Cheltenham: Edward Elgar, pp. 246 – 258.

Runhaar, H. et al. (2018) 'Mainstreaming climate adaptation: Taking stock about what works from empirical research worldwide', *Regional Environmental Change*, 18, pp. 1201 – 1210.

Russel, D., den Uyl, R. and de Vito, L. (2018) 'Understanding policy integration in the EU—Insights from a multi-level lens on climate adaptation and the EU's coastal and marine policy', *Environmental Science & Policy*, 82, pp. 44 – 51.

Russel, D., et al. (2020) 'Policy coordination for national climate change adaptation in Europe: all process, but little power', *Sustainability*, 12(13), 5393.

Schoenefeld, J., Schulze, K. and Bruch, N, (2022) 'The diffusion of climate change adaptation policy', *WIREs Climate Change*, 13(3), e775.

Setzer J. et al. (2020) 'Transnationalization of climate adaptation by regional governments and the RegionsAdapt initiative', *Global Sustainability*, 3, e10, pp. 1 – 10.

von Lucke, F., Diez, T., Aamodt, S. and Ahrens, B. (2021) *The EU and global climate justice.* London: Routledge.

WMO (2023) *State of the climate in Europe 2022.* World Meteorological Organization. Available at: https://wmo.int/publication-series/state-of-climate-europe-2022 (Accessed: 26 November 2024).

Julia M. Blocher, Diogo Andreolla Serraglio, Annabel Beckmann

The rambling construction of climate-migration-security nexus in the European Union

Abstract: This chapter examines the European Union's (EU) evolving approach to climate change-induced migration. It describes the shift from a security-centric perspective to a development-oriented approach emphasizing adaptation and resilience-building in the Global South, highlighting a persistent tension between security and adaptation or development narratives, in which different actors and narratives have variably pushed forward and retreated. A review of official and unofficial EU communications and discursive tools tracks the history of human mobility approaches in the EU, demonstrating points at which political sensitivities and uneven national interests have hindered the establishment of a cohesive policy framework. Despite Commission-led efforts, concrete measures to manage climate-induced migration remain limited. Reactive crisis management rather than proactive policy development often characterized EU efforts. The chapter underscores the EU's unique potential to lead global climate migration governance, calling for more integrated policy responses to respond to human mobility more generally and to specifically harness migration as a strategy for climate change adaptation and sustainable development.

Keywords: European Union; climate migration; climate adaptation; securitization; disaster displacement

1 Introduction

Over the years, policymakers and scholars have emphasized the necessity of international cooperation in global migration governance to facilitate smooth movement and enhance the role of migration in global sustainable development. More recently, attention has shifted toward exploring the role of migration in climate change adaptation, although empirical studies on the topic exhibit gaps in theoretical and empirical understandings (Black et al., 2011; Vinke et al., 2020; Piguet, 2022). These discussions feed a renewed euphoria about the potential for labor migration to contribute to resilience-building, echoing (yet largely disconnected from) a large body of older neoliberal economic research on migration and development (Bettini and Gioli, 2016). The discourse on 'migration as adaptation' celebrated the positive contributions of mobile people to origin, transit, and destination areas. This research stream, closely linked to international development practice, may have suffered from confirmation bias due to policy approval in some international circles, e. g., the 2030 Agenda for Sustainable Development and the 2018 Global Compact for Safe, Orderly and Regular Migration (UNGA, 2018).

https://doi.org/10.1515/9783111321523-026

Part of the international research and practitioner community has recently recognized its own failure to deliver on the promise of adaptive migration, indicated by a more moderated tone in the United Nations Framework Convention on Climate Change (UNFCCC) discussions on disaster displacement, habitability, and noneconomic loss and damage.[1] Gaps in climate migration-related mobility research, which has historically focused on isolated instances of movement rather than incremental migratory patterns, contribute to the lack of effective international and regional policy documents. Moreover, political will has been a significant barrier: these topics are highly politically sensitive due to concerns over human agency and national sovereignty in migration regimes. Moreover, public sentiment in many Western countries has also turned further against migration, partly fueled by alarmist media reports of climate displacement en masse (Moran, 2022; Sullivan and Townsend, 2022).

The trajectory of the European Union's (EU's) commitment to integrating climate-related migration and mobility has tracked these challenges. Yet, the EU only referred to the issue of climate-induced migration relatively late; it still lacks a comprehensive policy framework addressing the topic (Kraler Katsiaficas and Wagner, 2020).

This chapter considers the EU's approach to environment and migration issues, as the EU's regional governance structure and geopolitical power as an agenda-setting body uniquely positions it to drive state cooperation on climate change-induced migration. Its significant capacities to adopt a common migration and asylum policy and to influence neighboring and non-Member States are core to this potential (Geddes and Somerville, 2012). However, the EU's institutional and political specificities have also hindered meaningful advances in climate-related mobility.

This chapter argues that the institutional focus on environmental migration has shifted from its earlier position rooted in 'climate security' to one emphasizing technical and financial support for climate change adaptation and development cooperation. We review relevant official EU strategies, laws, policies, and communications referencing climate mobility in different forms, together with gray literature and insights from interviews with policy experts.

We focus on the European Commission as the engine of EU policies and of European integration: it proposes laws, makes sure EU laws are properly applied and manages EU spending programs. States' delegation of power to the Commission—alongside the Court of Justice and, to a lesser extent, the Parliament (Wennerhed, 2019; Serraglio and Schraven, 2021)—is intended to reduce the transaction costs of policymaking (Pollack, 2003). This is particularly relevant for the historically sensitive area of migration and asylum policies, as the Commission was deliberately designed to be a technocratic body removed from sovereignist politics (Mérand and Selmayr, 2021).

The Commission's treatment of the topic has generally been threefold: formulating and implementing asylum and migration policies, including environmental con-

1 Encompassing climate harms that cannot be mitigated or adapted to, and displacement is itself defined as such a loss (Serdeczny, Waters and Chan, 2016).

cerns for about a decade; promoting environmental protection and climate action; and foreign policy and external cooperation, for example, supporting negotiations toward a Global Compact for Migration (GCM). While this chapter cannot address all three of these points comprehensively, it analyses the main developments that are indicative of the EU's overall approach in official and unofficial (discursive) communications.

Each of these three main policy areas reveals the challenges to furthering a policy agenda on human mobility. Our approach contributes to existing policy analyses by examining organizational developments and practical actions, such as implementing existing instruments and allocating research funds to address environmental migration.

2 The evolution of environment- and climate-related mobility: From securitization to adaptation

The emergence of migration and displacement in EU policy agendas

Movement of people is essential to European integration, impacting economic, political, and cultural ties across the EU. The EU has historically stood out among supranational organizations for its free movement policies and efforts to enhance international cooperation on migration.

However, migration and asylum policies developed remarkably slowly compared to other policy areas (Popp, 2014). This stems from the EU's initial reluctance to delve into politically sensitive areas and varying national interests (Geddes and Somerville, 2012). Initially, the EU's migration model left the entry and integration of non-EU migrants to bilateral discussions between the sending and receiving countries. Differences among Member States, with some favoring restrictive approaches and others more open policies, has hindered progress on internal and external migration policies (Castles, 2009).

The 1997 Treaty of Amsterdam addressed migration from outside the EU, introducing joint policies for twenty-five states by May 2004. This included managing migration flows, common asylum standards, partnerships with origin countries and integration of non-EU nationals. Although the Treaty brought these issues into a common EU framework, it did not establish a comprehensive migration policy. Moreover, several countries, such as the United Kingdom (UK), Ireland, and Denmark opted out of common asylum and migration policies. This set the EU on a long path toward an uneven migration governance system. Any external approaches tended to focus on undocumented migration and internal security, such as an October 2005 informal meeting of EU Heads of State (UK Parliament Press Office, 2005). This led to the communication on the 'global approach to migration' (GAM), which the Justice and Home Affairs Council later presented and endorsed (Council of the European Union, 2006).

Initially, such as through discussions in the EU Council, environmental migration was primarily viewed through the lens of asylum and refugee issues: whether persons affected by environmental factors qualify for subsidiary protection (McAdam, 2012). Consensus was elusive and debates on this topic were politically unpopular in several Western Member States and among some humanitarian actors. Early strategic documents on climate change in development cooperation did not consider migrants or displaced people arriving in the EU, focusing instead on potential conflicts and food insecurity in partner countries plus possible spillover (European Commission, 2003, p. 11). A tendency to view mobility as a challenge to be managed rather than a development opportunity or a human right (Hakli, Kudžmaite and Kallio, 2024) persisted for some time.

The emergence and securitization of climate-related mobility

Between 2004 and 2009, the EU began connecting environmental and climatic changes and migration. A dominant—if not exclusive—framing of environment- and climate-related mobility was cemented in European policy circles many years (Blocher, 2016). This narrative presents migration as an unavoidable climate change outcome, and mass migratory flows toward Europe and migration-related threats are explicitly or implicitly presented as inevitable eventualities in order to create a sense of insecurity and unease (Barnett and Adger, 2007; Reuveny, 2007; Trombetta, 2014). Treatment of climate-related mobility reflected a trend toward securitization of climate change more broadly, for which scholars and policy actors interpret climate change as a matter for traditional means of security policy (Brzoska, 2009; Oels, 2012; Boas, 2015). This securitized framing reflects the 'fortress Europe' mentality (Yavuz, 2024), focusing on measures to prevent and contain migration rather than strengthening coordinated and human-centered solutions (Stepka, 2022; Yavuz, 2024).

The first explicit mention of the climate-mobility nexus came in 'Adapting to Climate Change in Europe' (European Commission, 2007), which emphasized the EU's role in averting climate change impacts (for more on the development of EU adaptation policy, see Chapter 21). Specifically, it highlighted the imperative to enhance the EU's capacity to mitigate and manage conflicts potentially exacerbated by "forced migration and internal displacement of individuals" (European Commission, 2007, p. 20).

This perspective prompted the Council to commission the 2008 'Joint Paper on Climate Change and International Security.' It framed climate change as a threat that exacerbated existing tensions and insecurity (European Commission, 2008, p. 2). This marks the first documented push to consider climate-induced migration as a by-product of climate-induced instability in the formulation of a European migration policy. In 2009, the Commission launched a White Paper on 'Adapting to climate change: Towards a European framework for Action.' It briefly touched on security and migration issues related to climate change (European Commission, 2009, p. 15). The title notwithstanding, it does not make central the adaptation of people when referring to mobility. As the 1951 Refugee Convention does not cover environmental factors, the paper recommended integrating climate adaptation measures into all of the EU's foreign policy activities. It is notable that these documents focus on the security implications of climate-induced migration—especially the cross-border movements that are of most concern to EU security actors—rather than on the formulation of appropriate responses (Blocher, 2016). Migration is included in a securitizing process of climate change (Wennerhed, 2019, p. 60).

For example, also in 2009, the Stockholm Program (the EU's five-year plan for internal security policy spanning 2010–2014) referred to climate change as a driver of security-relevant migratory flows and accordingly requested that the Commission evaluate the impacts of climate change on population movements toward Europe (Council of the European Union, 2010). Hence, the Commission issued the 2013 communication 'Climate Change, Environmental Degradation, and Migration'. It stressed that climate-induced migration should be better integrated into international policy dialogue and cooperation efforts, with the EU's global approach to migration and mobility (GAMM; see below) cited as an example (European Commission, 2013).

The resistance of some actors to adopting broader migration policies that could also address climate-induced migration was supported by a renewed emphasis on more traditional security concerns (Blocher, 2016). A key indicator is that, driven by the agenda of the more politically conservative Juncker Commission that entered office in 2014, the Directorate-General (DG) for Home Affairs was renamed as Migration and Home Affairs. This change again demonstrated that the issues of internal security around migration and asylum still determine responsibilities in the migration area (Collett, 2015). An alternative would have been to create a separate department for the field of migration, which would have allowed space for emerging mobility topics like environmental and development issues.

Arguably, the removal of environmental factors from protection discussions enabled security actors to deemphasize climate in their own discussions and focus on 'traditional' security issues related to more immediate crises in Syria and Crimea as well as turmoil in Egypt and Libya (Youngs, 2014; Blocher, 2016; Beckmann, 2023). Wennerhed (2019, p. 2). This underlines an "increasingly alarmist discursive construction" of climate-induced migration within EU policy circles, which became more pronounced due to the impacts of the Syrian refugee crisis and tensions with Russia. While the 2015 European Migration Agenda lists climate change alongside civil war, persecution, and poverty as one of the main causes of irregular migration and displacement (European Commission, 2015), the Commission's focus shifted primarily due to other political and security crises—noticeably away from climate change (Pérez, 2020).

The shift to development cooperation

The EU's work on climate-induced migration and displacement evolved from a security-centric to a development-oriented approach from 2010–2011 onwards, supplemented by human-centered approaches, such as those outlined by a European Parliament study (Kraler, Katsiaficas and Wagner, 2020). This shift occurred both in discourse and in institutional structures and priorities, as noted below in various key moments in this evolution.

Research on the climate-mobility nexus grew rapidly since 2011, fueled by publications by the Intergovernmental Panel on Climate Change (Solomon et al., 2007), Stern (2007) and the UK Foresight Office (Foresight, 2011) as well as the publication of many pieces of 'gray' literature from nongovernmental organizations and United Nations (UN) agencies (Piguet, 2022). Academics were critical of the security framing (Nordås and Gleditsch, 2007; Bettini, 2013; Gleditsch and Nordås, 2014; Boas, 2015). The narrative shifted in some degree toward framing migration as a positive force for climate change adaptation, recognizing that the income from remittances, as well as other benefits of migration, can help people affected by climate change to cope (Gemenne and Blocher, 2017). The migration scholarly community was also eager to center the agency and positive contributions of migrants (Ransan-Cooper et al., 2015). This discourse was supported by migration practitioners, especially from the International Organization for Migration, which benefits strategically and materially from escaping the constraints of a crisis-focused and humanitarian framing of this topic (Hall, 2015; Schriever, 2024). The international development community agreed and understood the potential to link funding for climate projects back to migration and development, such as the inclusion of human mobility in National Adaptation Plans.

Together, these changes pushed debates on climate-related movements away from deterministic and natural-science based projections of cross-border movements (in which persons were commodified as potential future arrivals on Western doorsteps) toward approaches that focused more on migrant sending areas and the fate of the migrants (and their families). A researcher-practitioner community coalesced, developing collaborations such as the Advisory Group on Human Mobility and Climate, a group comprised of researchers and UN agencies that seeks to inform policy processes (Advisory Group on Human Mobility and Climate, 2015). The EU, especially the Commission, emerged as an agenda-setter in this space. The EU strengthened its funding of watershed research projects,[2] advocacy for positive framings of (regular) migration with third country partners and promotion of dialogue on these topics in key international forums.

2 Between 2010 and 2014, the EU funded 'Environmental Change and Forced Migration Scenarios', 'Migration, Environment and Climate Change: Evidence for Policy', 'High-End Climate Impacts and Extremes' and more.

Even as more nuanced framings bubbled up through the researcher-practitioner community as alternatives to the security framing, these were not reflected in official EU documents until 2013–2014. A key milestone was the 2013 UN High-Level Dialogue on Migration and Development (Mayrhofer and Ammer, 2014). EU representatives reiterated the need to further explore how environmental changes drive population movements (European Commission, 2013). The document highlighted that climate and environmental degradation are already having a growing impact on migration and mobility and advocated for a more detailed examination and appropriate responses to the human mobility–climate change nexus, especially within the realms of development cooperation, foreign policy and humanitarian assistance (European Commission, 2013). The Commission's documents adopted a perspective built upon development cooperation, suggesting that migration due to environmental drivers can contribute to regional growth (Mayrhofer and Ammer, 2014).

The demise of a common EU approach to migration and mobility

The discursive shift described above lent itself to another important development in the EU, namely: the feeble release of the Global Approach to Migration and Mobility and the stagnating work toward a common EU approach to migration that persists to today. The EU's migration policies have been implemented through bilateral cooperation frameworks, such as mobility partnerships and common agendas for migration and mobility (CAMMs). These initiatives focus on visa liberalization, remittances and skilled worker migration, generally overlooking climate change's impact on migration profiles. Identifying a need for entry points into international policy cooperation on migration (Serraglio and Schraven, 2021), the GAMM, building on the 2005 GAM, was released in 2011 as a nonbinding communication (European Commission, 2011a). The GAMM is the EU's external migration policy framework; it concentrates on issues of (ir)regular migration, human trafficking, refugee protection and migrant rights, thereby fostering the linkages between migration and development (European Commission, 2011a.). While the GAMM leans heavily into development framings, it lacks specific provisions to tackle the climate-mobility nexus (Blocher, 2016). For example, no harmonized legal protection for cross-border disaster displacement is offered. In parallel, a planned official communication that would focus on climate change and migration was delayed; it eventually emerged in 2013 as a Staff Working Document (European Commission, 2013). Where the GAMM addresses migration and climate change (European Commission, 2011b, pp. 6–7), it emphasizes adaptation and resilience-building in the Global South, as do other strategic documents (European Commission, 2011b, 2013).

The weaknesses of the GAMM are largely the result of a preexisting issue: lack of political will to jointly address migration, traditionally a matter of national sovereignty. Most of its efforts lack concrete and meaningful steps to enhance migration opportunities or legal provisions. It proved to be too difficult for the Commission to implement the GAMM in a tangible manner because the relevant tools, including how many migrants were allowed in, still constituted a Member State competence. This situation was unlikely to change (House of Lords European Union Committee, 2012). The voluntary nature of implementing the GAM (see above) and the GAMM hampered the Commission and External Action Service's efforts to promote cooperative, migrant-centered policies (Blocher, 2016). Instead, joint EU efforts emphasize reducing migratory pressures and irregular migration flows. Moreover, the CAMM dialogues and EU engagement in international development forums often focus on addressing specific labor market needs. The thematic programs, for example, are limited to funding thematic projects and resilience-building efforts.

Some areas of external policies on migration and forced displacement, especially those exemplified in the adaptation and development foci of the GAMM, found their way into DG Development and Cooperation-EuropeAid (DEVCO) between 2011 and 2014. This built the foundation for more fruitful engagements on migration cooperation with third countries, linking human mobility with climate change adaptation in a way that was shielded somewhat (and siloed) from the national security and humanitarian foci of DG Migration and Home Affairs.

3 The European Commission from 2016 to today

Climate and environment engagements

In its role as an agenda setter, the EU has pursued opportunities to show leadership on climate-related human mobility and development or climate change adaptation, especially in developing countries (for a broader analytical context, see Chapter 29). The EU's work toward global agreements on migration cooperation since 2015–2016 has been managed by DG International Partnerships, formerly DG DEVCO, which manages the EU's engagements with key climate-human mobility forums like the Platform on Disaster Displacement (PDD).

The Commission has encouraged and supported workshops and discussions on this topic in diverse forums, especially in the UNFCCC, often highlighting the research that it has funded via the Research and Innovation Programs (see examples illustrated in Chapter 21). The Commission communicates its stances in convening spaces it helps to fund, like the UN Advisory Group on Human Mobility or the PDD, which typically circulate common messaging ahead of UNFCCC meetings like the annual Conference of the Parties (COP) (for example, on loss and damage; PDD et al., 2022).

In addressing noneconomic loss and damage, including displacement, the EU has exerted leadership. At COP27 in 2022, the EU helped launch a new global fund on loss and damage. At COP28, the EU and its Member States pledged over EUR 400 million, more than half of initial pledges.

Despite these promises, the incoherence in the EU's approach to climate change and to human mobility are noteworthy; dialogue on the latter, which has tended to focused on migration origin areas, is quite disconnected from the EU Member States' historical responsibility for climate change impacts and resulting displacement.

'Safe' international arenas to discuss migration

Beside the array of EU initiatives described above, the realm of global migration governance has experienced a proliferation of both formal and informal institutions operating across multilateral, regional and bilateral spheres. While a degree of fragmentation is likely to persist, enhanced coordination and organization among these entities is possible.

The EU and individual states have pushed for positive framings and multilateral cooperation on climate-related mobility in different forums, not least the Global Forum on Migration and Development and the UNFCCC. However, the 2018 Global Compact for Safe, Orderly and Regular Migration (GCM) is the first global agreement of its kind on *migration* through formal UN processes, achieving what discussions via development and environment-focused forums could not.

Three of the twenty-three goals of the GCM mention climate change and disaster risk (Warner, 2022). In Objective 2, signatory states committed to mitigating the adverse effects of climate change and environmental degradation, which serve as underlying migration drivers. Objective 5 underscored the imperative to devise viable solutions for migrants grappling with slow-onset natural disasters, even when the prospect of adjustment or return becomes untenable. These solutions encompass organized relocation initiatives and the provision of specialized visa options. Finally, in Objective 23, nations pledged to bolster cooperation to expedite the implementation of the 2030 Sustainable Development Agenda in regions characterized by persistent irregular migration, influenced by climate change, disasters and other contributing factors (UNGA, 2018).

The GCM is a significant milestone, offering a structured platform for UN member countries to discuss climate induced migration. The 2022 International Migration Review Forum, which marked the GCM's first comprehensive assessment since its adoption, saw an increased focus on the relationship between climate change, migration and displacement (Huckstep and Dempster, 2022). The GCM fails to adequately address the implications of climate change on return migration and the associated challenges. The absence of explicit guidelines regarding return migration may deter states from endorsing regular migration initiatives, including hosting refugees. Furthermore, uncertainties persist regarding the willingness of states with established border control and return policies to broaden legal pathways to safe routes in the absence of regulation for remigration. This ambiguity observed in the GCM negotiations raises questions about the expansion of legal migration pathways in such contexts (Warner, 2022).

Co-chair of PDD

The EU has been present in the Nansen Initiative. Initially launched in October 2012 by the governments of Norway and Switzerland, it aimed for a protection agenda for cross-border displaced persons in the context of disasters and climate change and the resulting Platform on Disaster Displacement. The EU served as PDD Chair from July 2022 to December 2023 (PDD, 2023) and in this context emphasized the need to integrate global frameworks, closing protection gaps, exchanging knowledge, strengthening data and improving communication. This role requires enhanced collaboration with Global South countries to develop effective measures (PDD, 2021). Therefore, the EU intends to present recommendations to enhance the PDD's role as a platform to "[...] becoming more operational by, for example, facilitating access to funding. Others relate to supporting research and data dissemination and giving topics such as the climate-migration-conflict nexus and planned relocations more visibility through effective agenda-setting" (Hahn and Fessler, 2023, p. 12). Despite the EU holding the PDD chair at that time, its stance at COP27 failed to address migration or displacement, marking a 'missed opportunity' to connect climate initiatives with disaster-induced displacement (Hahn and Fessler, 2023).

4 Discussion and conclusion

This chapter emphasizes the ongoing challenges the EU faces in effectively incorporating environmental factors into its migration and asylum policies while balancing national interests, security concerns and the broader goals of sustainable development and climate change adaptation. The evolution of EU policy development on climate-related mobility reveals a persistent tension between security and adaptation or development narratives, in which different actors and narratives have variably been introduced and retreated.

A functionalist perspective suggests that the EU's effort to set a positive agenda on environment- and climate-related mobility is intended to trigger further cooperation between states on migration and asylum questions. As with other cross-border environmental concerns, these are traditional areas of common ground (Blocher, 2016). The potential for positive 'spillover' into more sensitive issues areas is a main added value of intergovernmental and supranational organizations on this issue (Hall, 2013) and would lead to an overall expansion of the human rights environment for migrants.

Nevertheless, critiques persist regarding the EU's underlying motivations. Beckmann (2023) notes that the EU's focus on development cooperation in the period between 2011 and today serves to advance its own interests, particularly in reducing irregular migration flows from the Global South. By framing migration as a development issue, the EU not only reinforces this strategic objective but also shifts the responsibility for managing climate-induced migration onto countries of origin, thereby avoiding the need for broader policy reforms that would be essential to effectively address the complex challenges of climate induced migration.

A persistent challenge in the EU and a fundamental reason for the relatively reserved work on human mobility, including in the context of climate change, is the lack of political will to cede sovereignty on domestic migration policies. European states are increasingly restrictive and opposed to immigration, questioning the effectiveness of potential new conventions and institutions (Kolmannskog and Trebbi, 2010). European perspectives are extremely Eurocentric, as they often ignore Europe's responsibility for numerous causes of forced migration (Nash, 2023). Despite the numerous public acknowledgements of the need for improved coordination, some of which are referenced above, policymaking in this realm remains hindered by a dearth of structured exchange and coordination among EU institutions (for more on international obligations and relationships, see Chapter 21). This is due to inadequate political prioritization, reluctance to transcend security-centric approaches and a deficiency in long-term strategic planning (Hahn and Fessler, 2023). This combines with a trend of political parties in Europe adopting populist and anti-migration positions—which are fueled, partly, by alarmist narratives and securitizing acts described above (Trombetta, 2014; Moran, 2022; Sullivan and Townsend, 2022).

This chapter argues that a security approach to climate mobility not only limits the scope for meaningful policy interventions but also puts at risk the very people it seeks to address. The EU has yet to implement comprehensive strategies to address the topic adequately and further explore the role of migration in climate change adaptation measures. The policy framework needed to harness the potential of migration is still lacking (Gemenne and Blocher, 2017). The EU's approaches to addressing climate-induced migration have predominantly been reactive rather than proactive, mostly focused on short-term crisis management strategies with gaps in both humanitarian and development spending (Blocher, 2016; Hahn and Fessler, 2023). Moreover, the EU's thematic funding for addressing the climate change–human mobility nexus has been insufficient (Blocher, 2016). All of this led to missed opportunities to develop adequate and forward-looking approaches and suggests that climate-induced migration continues to occupy a relatively low position on the EU policy agenda.

Even if the Commission has made efforts to address climate change and migration, the overall advancement of EU migration and asylum integration has stalled. As the EU moves forward, it can confront the contradictions in its migration governance, particularly by shifting away from security-driven speeches and toward more holistic, human-centered approaches that recognize the complex realities of climate-related mobility. The climate mobility topic provides a 'safe' space to test integrative policies, as have other areas of environmental cooperation. Balancing this opportunity with the deep-rooted political challenges will be essential for the EU to develop a comprehensive approach to human mobility, climate change and development cooperation that avoids the current policy incoherence between those three issue areas. The construction of the EU broadly and the Commission specifically provides a unique opportunity to make meaningful policy advances on this topic—not only in less developed countries, but within the EU itself.

References

Advisory Group on Human Mobility and Climate (2015) 'Human mobility in the context of climate change'. Available at: https://publications.iom.int/books/human-mobility-context-climate-change (Accessed: 6 September 2024).

Barnett, J. and Adger, W.N. (2007) 'Climate change, human security and violent conflict', *Political Geography*, 26(6), pp. 639–655.

Beckmann, A. (2023) *EU responses to human mobility in a changing climate: A multi-layered analysis related to EU policy on environmentally-induced displacement outside of Europe.* Unpublished Master's thesis. Management Center Innsbruck.

Bettini, G. (2013) 'Climate barbarians at the gate? A critique of apocalyptic narratives on "climate refugees"', *Geoforum*, 45, pp. 63–72.

Bettini, G. and Gioli, G. (2016) 'Waltz with development: Insights on the developmentalization of climate-induced migration', *Migration and Development*, 5(2), pp. 171–189.

Black, R., Bennett, S., Thomas, S. and Beddington, J. (2011) 'Migration as adaptation', *Nature*, 478, pp. 447–449.

Blocher, J. (2016) 'Climate change and environment related migration in the European Union Policy: An organizational shift towards adaptation and development', in: Gemenne, F. and Rosenow-Williams, K. (eds.) *Organizational perspectives on environmental migration.* London: Routledge, pp. 38–56.

Boas, I. (2015) *Climate migration and security: Securitisation as a strategy in climate change politics.* London: Routledge. Available at: https://www.earthsystemgovernance.org/publication/climate-migration-and-security-securitisation-as-a-strategy-in-climate-change-politics/ (Accessed: 4 October 2024).

Brzoska, M. (2009) 'The securitization of climate change and the power of conceptions of security', *Sicherheit & Frieden*, 27(3), pp. 137–145.

Castles, S. (2009) 'Development and migration—migration and development: What comes first? Global perspective and African experiences', *Theoria: A Journal of Social and Political Theory*, 56(121), pp. 1–31.

Collett, E. (2015) *The development of EU policy on immigration and asylum: Rethinking coordination and leadership.* Washington, D.C.: Migration Policy Institute (MPI). Available at: https://www.migrationpolicy.org/research/development-eu-policy-immigration-and-asylum-rethinking-coordination-and-leadership (Accessed: 5 September 2024).

Council of the European Union (2006) *Presidency conclusions.* Available at: www.consilium.europa.eu/ueDocs/cms_Data/docs/pressData/en/ec/87642.pdf (Accessed: 4 October 2024).

Council of the European Union (2010) *The Stockholm Programme: An open and secure Europe serving and protecting citizens.* 2010/C 115/01. Available at: https://eur-lex.europa.eu/legal-content/EN/TXT/?uri=uriserv%3AOJ.C_.2010.115.01.0001.01.ENG&toc=OJ%3AC%3A2010%3A115%3ATOC (Accessed: 4 October 2024).

European Commission (2003) 'Communication from the Commission to the Council and the European Parliament—Climate change in the context of development cooperation', *COM*(2003) 85 final. Available at: http://eur-lex.europa.eu/legal-content/EN/TXT/?uri=CELEX:52003DC0085 (Accessed: 10 July 2014).

European Commission (2007) 'Adapting to Climate Change in Europe', *COM*(2007) 354 final. Available at: https://eur-lex.europa.eu/legal-content/EN/TXT/?uri=celex%3A52007DC0354 (Accessed: 10 July 2014).

European Commission (2008) *Climate change and international security: Paper from the high representative and the European Commission to the European Council.* Available at: https://www.consilium.europa.eu/ueDocs/cms_Data/docs/pressdata/EN/reports/99387.pdf (Accessed: 19 March 2022).

European Commission (2009) *Adapting to climate change: Towards a European framework for action. COM*(2009) 147 final, White Paper. Available at: https://eur-lex.europa.eu/LexUriServ/LexUriServ.do?uri=COM:2009:0147:FIN:EN:PDF (Accessed: 10 July 2014).

European Commission (2011a) 'The global approach to migration and mobility', *COM*(2011) 743 final. Available at: https://eur-lex.europa.eu/legal-content/EN/TXT/?uri=CELEX%3 A52011DC0743 (Accessed: 6 September 2024).

European Commission (2011b) *With third countries in the areas of migration and asylum, 2011–2013 multi-annual strategy paper.* Available at: https://ec.europa.eu/europeaid/thematic-programme-cooperation-third-countries-areas-migration-and-asylum-2011–2013-multi-annual_en (Accessed: 10 December 2014).

European Commission (2013) 'Climate change, environmental degradation, and migration', *SWD*(2013) 138 final. Available at: https://eur-lex.europa.eu/legal-content/EN/TXT/PDF/?uri=CELEX:52013SC0138 (Accessed: 10 July 2014).

European Commission (2015) 'A European agenda on migration', *COM*(2015) 240 final. Available at: https://eur-lex.europa.eu/legal-content/EN/TXT/?uri=CELEX:52015DC0240 (Accessed: 10 July 2014).

Foresight (2011) *Migration and global environmental change: Future challenges and opportunities.* Final Project Report. London: The Government Office for Science.

Geddes, A. and Somerville, W. (2012) 'Migration and environmental change in international governance: The case of the European Union', *Environment and Planning C: Government and Policy*, 30(6), pp. 1015–1028.

Gemenne, F. and Blocher, J. (2017) 'How can migration serve adaptation to climate change? Challenges to fleshing out a policy ideal', *The Geographical Journal*, 183(4), pp. 336–347.

Gleditsch, N.P. and Nordås, R. (2014) 'Conflicting messages? The IPCC on conflict and human security', *Political Geography*, 43, pp. 82–90.

Hahn, H. and Fessler, M. (2023) *The EU's approach to climate mobility: Which way forward?* Brussels: European Policy Centre. Available at: https://www.epc.eu/en/Publications/The-EUs-approach-to-climate-mobility-Which-way-forward~553098 (Accessed: 4 October 2024).

Hakli, J., Kudžmaite, G. and Kallio, K.P. (2024) 'Devaluing personhood: The framing of migrants in the EU's new pact on migration and asylum', *Transactions of the Institute of British Geographers* [Preprint]. Available at: https://doi.org/10.1111/tran.12676.

Hall, N. (2013) *Moving beyond their mandates? How international organizations are responding to climate change.* Oxford: University of Oxford.

Hall, N. (2015) 'Money or mandate? Why international organizations engage with the climate change regime', *Global Environmental Politics*, 15(2), pp. 79–97.

House of Lords European Union Committee (2012) *The EU's Global Approach to Migration and Mobility.* 8th Report of Session 2012–13 HL Paper 91. London: Her Majesty's Stationary Office. Available at: https://www.google.com/url?sa=t&source=web&rct=j&opi=89978449&url=https://secure.ipex.eu/IPEXL-WEB/download/file/082dbcc53b70d1c2013bada727292289/FINAL%2BGAMM%2BReport.pdf&ved=2ahUKEwiLr9fg3K6IAxU7ygIHHd2tIl4QFnoECBQQAQ&usg=AOvVaw02zFWLWLHH7BMHB7PenyLZ (Accessed: 10 October 2024).

Huckstep, S. and Dempster, H. (2022) 'Climate migration at the 2022 International Migration Review Forum', *Center for Global Development.* Available at: https://www.cgdev.org/blog/climate-migration-2022-international-migration-review-forum (Accessed: 30 October 2023).

Kolmannskog, V. and Trebbi, L. (2010) 'Climate change, natural disasters and displacement: A multi-track approach to filling the protection gaps', *International Review of the Red Cross*, 92(879), pp. 713–730,

Kraler, A., Katsiaficas, C. and Wagner, M. (2020) *Climate change and migration: Legal and policy challenges and responses to environmentally induced migration.* Brussels: European Parliament. Available at: https://www.europarl.europa.eu/RegData/etudes/STUD/2020/655591/IPOL_STU(2020)655591_EN.pdf (Accessed: 5 September 2024).

Mayrhofer, M. and Ammer, M. (2014) 'People moving in the context of environmental change: The cautious approach of the European Union', *European Journal of Migration and Law*, 16(3), pp. 389–429.

McAdam, J. (2012) *Climate change, forced migration, and international law.* Oxford: Oxford University Press.

Mérand, F. and Selmayr, M. (2021) 'The European Commission as a political engine of European Integration: In conversation with Martin Selmayr'. *Groupe d'études géopolitiques.* Available at: https://geopolitique.eu/en/2021/04/27/the-european-commission-as-a-political-engine-of-european-integration-in-conversation-with-martin-selmayr/ (Accessed: 4 October 2024).

Moran, J. (2022) 'Climate, conflict, and migration: Europe's next frontier of populism', *European Center for Populism Studies*, 7 December. Available at: https://www.populismstudies.org/climate-conflict-and-migration-europes-next-frontier-of-populism/ (Accessed: 10 February 2024).

Nash, S.L. (2023) 'The view from the fortress: European governance perspectives on climate change and migration', in: Nicholson, C.T.M. and Mayer, B. (eds.) *Climate migration: Critical perspectives for law, policy, and research.* Oxford: Hart Publishing, pp. 131–149.

Nordås, R. and Gleditsch, N.P. (2007) 'Climate change and conflict', *Political Geography*, 26(6), pp. 627–638.

Oels, A. (2012) 'From "securitization" of climate change to "climatization" of the security field: Comparing three theoretical perspectives', in: Scheffran, J., et al. (eds.) *Climate change, human security and violent conflict: Challenges for societal stability.* Berlin: Springer, pp. 185–205.

PDD (2021) *Platform on disaster displacement (PDD) strategy 2019–2022. Annex I: Workplan.* Available at: https://disasterdisplacement.org/wp-content/uploads/2021/07/20052021-Annex-I-Revised-PDD-Workplan-2019–2022-FINAL.pdf (Accessed: 9 June 2023).

PDD (2023) 'Platform on Disaster Displacement'. Steering Group. Available at: https://disasterdisplacement.org/about-us/the-steering-group/ (Accessed: 7 October 2024).

PDD, International Organization for Migration (IOM), and Internal Displacement Monitoring Centre (IDMC) (2022) '15 Observations on disaster displacement as loss and damage', *Disaster Displacement*, 2 November. Available at: https://disasterdisplacement.org/portfolio-item/15-observations-on-disaster-displacement-as-loss-and-damage/ (Accessed: 28 October 2023).

Pérez, B.F. (2020) 'El papel del sector privado europeo ante las migraciones climáticas: una propuesta de debida diligencia', in: *Fundación Ecología y Desarrollo (ECODES).* Available at: https://migracionesclimaticas.org/wp-content/uploads/2020/11/Informe_El_Papel_del_Sector_Privado_Europeo_ante_las_Migraciones_Climaticas-ECODES_2020.pdf (Accessed: 10 July 2024).

Piguet, E. (2022) 'Linking climate change, environmental degradation, and migration: An update after 10 years', *WIREs Climate Change*, 13(1), e746.

Pollack, M.A. (2003) 'Delegation, agency, and agenda setting in the European Union', in: Pollack, M.A. (ed.) *The engines of European integration: Delegation, agency, and agenda Setting in the EU.* Oxford: Oxford University Press, pp. 19–72.

Popp, K. (2014) 'Regional policy perspectives', in: Piguet, E. and Laczko, F. (eds.) *People on the move in a changing climate: The regional impact of environmental change on migration.* Dordrecht: Springer, pp. 229–253.

Ransan-Cooper, H. et al. (2015) 'Being(s) framed: The means and ends of framing environmental migrants', *Global Environmental Change*, 35, pp. 106 – 115.

Reuveny, R. (2007) 'Climate change-induced migration and violent conflict', *Political Geography*, 26(6), pp. 656 – 673.

Schriever, S. (2024) 'Framing migration as adaptation: IOM's aspirations to manage climate migration', *Geopolitics*, pp. 1 – 29. Available at: https://doi.org/10.1080/14650045.2024.2368624.

Serdeczny, O., Waters, E. and Chan, S. (2016) *Non-economic loss and damage in the context of climate change: Understanding the challenges.* Working Paper 3/2016. Discussion Paper. Available at: https://www.econstor.eu/handle/10419/199466 (Accessed: 3 October 2024).

Serraglio, D.A. and Schraven, B. (2021) 'Rechtliche und politische Perspektiven zum Stand der globalen Governance hinsichtlich klimabezogener Mobilität', Bonn: Expertise im Auftrag des Sachverständigenrats für Integration und Migration (SVR) Available at: https://www.svr-migration.de/wp-content/uploads/2023/05/SVR_Expertise_Klimabezogene-Mobilitaet-2021_Serraglio-Schraven.pdf (Accessed: 10 July 2024).

Solomon, S. et al. (eds.) (2007) *Climate change 2007: The physical science basis. Contribution of Working Group I to the Fourth Assessment Report of the Intergovernmental Panel on Climate Change.* IPCC. Cambridge: Cambridge University Press.

Stepka, M. (2022) 'The Copenhagen School and beyond: A closer look at securitisation theory', *IMISCOE Research Series*, pp. 17 – 31. Available at: https://doi.org/10.1007/978-3-030-93035-6_2.

Stern, N. (2007) *The economics of climate change: The Stern review.* Cambridge: Cambridge University Press. Available at: https://www.cambridge.org/us/academic/subjects/earth-and-environmental-science/climatology-and-climate-change/economics-climate-change-stern-review (Accessed: 6 September 2024).

Sullivan, J.P. and Townsend, K. (2022) 'Climate migration: Adding fuel to the ethnocentric fire', *Terrorism and Political Violence*, 34(5), pp. 914 – 925.

Trombetta, M.J. (2014) 'Linking climate-induced migration and security within the EU: Insights from the securitization debate', *Critical Studies on Security*, 2(2), pp. 131 – 147.

UK Parliament Press Office (2005). *Report on informal heads of state/government meeting.* https://publications.parliament.uk/pa/ld200506/ldhansrd/vo051114/text/51114 – 54.htm

UNGA (2018) 'Global Compact for Migration: A/RES/73/195, Resolution adopted by the General Assembly on 19 December 2018'. New York: United Nations General Assembly.

Vinke, K., et al. (2020) 'Migration as adaptation?', *Migration Studies*, 8(4), pp. 626 – 634.

Warner, K. (2022) 'Risk, climate change and human mobility in international policy',I n: Preuß, H.-J., Beier, C. and Messner, D. (eds.) *Forced displacement and migration: Approaches and programmes of international cooperation.* Wiesbaden: Springer Fachmedien, pp. 147 – 159.

Wennerhed, F.M. (2019) *The discursive construction of climate migration in the EU: A critical discourse analysis of climate migration in EU legislative institutions.* Published Master's thesis. Wageningen University, Environmental Policy Group. Available at: https://edepot.wur.nl/504774 (Accessed: 24 June 2025)

Yavuz, F.G. (2024) *Securitizing migration: An analysis of European Union's asylum and migration policies in response to climate-induced migration.* Published Master's thesis. Middle East Technical University, Department of European Studies.

Youngs, R. (2014) *Climate change and European security.* Oxford: Routledge.

Raoul Beunen

The evolution of European Union biodiversity policy: Shifting debates and new challenges

Abstract: The European Union (EU) has a long history of biodiversity policy aimed at protecting and restoring the natural heritage of its Member States. This chapter will elaborate on the most important policy developments since the introduction of the Bern Convention and the Birds Directives in 1979 and the Habitats Directive in 1992 and the way in which the scientific literature has discussed these. It reflects on the role of biodiversity policy in the processes of Europeanization, the fit and misfit between the Birds and Habitats Directives and national policies and practices, the growing attention for stakeholder involvement and the need to better understand policy failure, backlash and opposition. Over the decades EU biodiversity policy has brought many benefits, but many challenges remain. The rise of post-truth society and the effects of misinformation, polarization and populism that have become much more visible in recent years, deserve more attention in the scientific research on biodiversity and related sustainability challenges.

Keywords: Biodiversity policy; Natura 2000; Nature Restoration Law; institutional change; sustainability challenges

1 Introduction

The European Union (EU) has a long history of biodiversity policy, aimed at protecting and restoring the natural heritage of its Member States. At the core of EU biodiversity policy are the Birds and Habitats Directives, the EU Biodiversity Strategy, the Natura Restoration Law and Natura 2000, a network of protected areas established to conserve and restore species and their natural habitats. The Natura 2000 network encompasses over 27,000 sites across Europe, including both terrestrial and marine areas and covers approximately 19 percent of the land area and about 9 percent or the marine and coastal territory (European Environment Agency, n.d.). Despite many conservation successes, some profound challenges for bending the curve of biodiversity loss remain (Brondizio et al., 2019; Campagnaro et al., 2019; European Commission, 2016; Engelhardt, Bowler and Hof 2023; Hermoso et al., 2022; Princé et al., 2021). Given the ongoing decline of certain species, the further deterioration of natural habitats and the growing climate change impact, it is worrisome that the adoption of the Nature Restoration Law clearly showed that formulating ambitious policies has become much more difficult (Cliquet et al., 2024; Pe'er et al., 2023). Although EU biodiversity has been effective in many regards, it also has become clear that the implementation is facing major challenges and needs to be enhanced to actually halt biodiversity decline and restore natural ecosystems and the many benefits these bring to society. This

https://doi.org/10.1515/9783111321523-027

chapter will place recent events in a historical perspective and reflect on the most important policy developments since the introduction of the Bern Convention and the Birds Directives in 1979 as well as on the main policy challenges that EU biodiversity currently faces.

2 Policy formulation and implementation

Already in the 1970s, the EU recognized the need for coordinated action to address environmental issues. Over the years, this recognition led to the adoption of the Birds Directive (European Communities, 1979) in 1979 and the Habitats Directive (European Communities, 1992) in 1992. Together these directives aim to protect species and their natural habitats across Europe. The directives require Member States to designate protected areas (the Natura 2000 sites) and to adopt their legal framework to ensure the appropriate management and restoration of sites and the protection of a wide range of species and natural habitats. The first decades of EU biodiversity policy were marked by processes of agenda setting, discussions on policy design and the negotiations necessary to get the Birds and Habitats Directives adopted by all Member States (Evans, 2012; Fairbrass and Jordan, 2001; Jongman, 1995). Various authors have reflected on these processes by which biodiversity gradually became an important EU domain (Evans, 2012; Meyer, 2010). Important drivers for the development and adaption of EU biodiversity policy were the increasing societal concerns about the decline of biodiversity as well as the growing awareness that action is needed on all levels, including the international level (Ferranti et al., 2013; Meyer, 2011). Ambitions to harmonize policies between different EU members and creating a level playing between countries also played a role. The various agreements about nature conservation and the gradual development of EU biodiversity policy gave an important impulse to the development of knowledge on biodiversity within the EU and about possibilities for policy design.

Ecologists from various countries were involved in the discussions on the organization of protection and restoration of EU biodiversity. Discussions focused on technical details on policy design, the selection of species and habitats that deserve protection and on the relation with the Bern Convention that was agreed in 1979. The Bern Convention and the Birds Directives were in the beginning two different processes, clearly distinguishing between national responsibilities and joint action at the EU level, but over the decades EU biodiversity policy became increasingly the main approach to translate ambitions from the Bern Convention and other international agreements on biodiversity into actions. The Habitats Directives, for example, represents a clear commitment from the EU to the ambition to bend the curve of biodiversity decline. The network concept that gained prominence in ecological studies and biodiversity policy was also integrated into EU policy, and the label Natura 2000 was coined to refer to the European network of sites protected under the Birds and Habitats Directives (Evans, 2012; Jongman, 1995).

In the 1990s and the first years of the 21st century most attention in policy practices and scientific reflections focused on Member State implementation of the directives, the selection and designation of Natura 2000 sites and the translation of the EU directives into national policy and management approaches (Ledoux et al., 2000; Pinton, 2001; Popescu et al., 2014). The scientific literature focused on the differences in pace in which the Birds and Habitats Directives were transposed into national policies and on the factors that could explain the differences between frontrunners and laggards. Attention was, for example, given to the extent to which national institutions and practices fit with the requirements of the Birds and Habitats Directives (Bouwma et al., 2016) and to differences in policy styles in political cultures (Fairbrass and Jordan, 2002). The need for institutional change and the extent to which EU requirements differed from existing national frameworks and from current practices within the Member States were seen as important factors that explained implementation differences (Alphandéry and Fortier, 2001; Bouwma, Arts and Liefferink, 2017; Ferranti, Beunen and Speranza, 2010). It was particularly interesting to observe that countries with a long tradition of nature conservation faced more difficulties in transposing the Birds and Habitats Directives then some of the new EU members (Beunen, 2006; Ledoux et al., 2000).

In hindsight it is interesting to observe that a fair amount of the literature is characterized by the underlying, often explicit, assumptions that Member States were actually very committed to implement the EU directives in the best possible way and that transposition of these directives into national law and policy will be done in ways that help in working toward achieving the agreed upon ambitions. The experiences in, for example, the Netherlands showed that a lot of effort was taken to delay the process and to circumvent legal requirements from the Habitats Directive (Beunen and Kole, 2021). Although many studies demonstrated that the transposition and implementation of EU biodiversity policy was a very slow and difficult process, the scientific literature paid relatively little attention to the purposive actions of Member States and other actors in delaying the process of implementation and in findings ways to weaken or circumvent the requirements they agreed upon. Europeanization was an important discourse in much of the literature, and something like a Brexit or institutional capture by a selected group of interest groups was hardly considered by those analyzing the implementation of EU biodiversity policy.

3 Ecological impact and effectiveness

A substantial part of the literature focuses on the effectiveness and ecological impact of the Birds and Habitats Directives. Many authors have studied to what extent the Natura 2000 network and its legal requirements cover all aspects of biodiversity (Davis et al., 2014; Popescu et al., 2014). Several studies show that certain species groups or certain types of habitats are poorly covered (Morán-López et al., 2020). Although the Birds and Habitats Directives target a large selection of species and habitats, their actual impact on species and places that are not part of the Natura 2000 network depend on the way Member States selected sites and organized national conservation policy. In theory, many species not explicitly mentioned in the directives could benefit from the protection of the areas that they depend on. Furthermore, both directives also require the protection of species, particularly birds, outside protected areas.

The Birds and Habitats Directives stimulated nature conservation in many European countries, strengthening national, regional and local conservation efforts (European Commission, 2016; Ferranti et al., 2019). Some countries, such as the Netherlands, however, opted to limit the legal protection of species and their habitats to the requirements of the Birds and Habitats Directives (Beunen and Kole, 2021), even though more action is clearly needed to realize the conservation goals as formulated by the Birds and Habitats Directive. Such an approach to EU policy is also reflected in the discourse on 'gold plating' (Morris, 2011). The term gold plating refers to claims that national regulation is stricter than EU directives require (Squintani, 2019). It is a business-oriented frame that sees EU directives mostly as obstacle for economic activities (Ferranti et al., 2019). It is part of a broader discourse that criticizes European policy, the EU, or 'Brussels', in general, and it drives a form of implementation aimed at minimalizing and delaying actions and diluting conservation ambitions (Chapron et al., 2017). In the Netherlands, this discourse was reflected in the decision to limit the number of Natura 2000 sites, to annul the legal protection of nature areas not designated as Natura 2000 sites, and various attempt to circumvent the legal requirements of the Habitats Directive in order to facilitate the expansion of livestock farming (Beunen and Kole, 2021). This discourse in which the Birds and Habitats Directives is mainly seen as an obstacle created several of the implementation failures that have been reported (Beunen, Van Assche and Duineveld, 2013; European Commission, 2016).

Notwithstanding the reported implementation problems, various studies have shown that the Birds and Habitats Directives did contribute enormously to the conservation of species and habitats in Europe (Beresford et al., 2016; Donald et al., 2007; Princé et al., 2021). Without EU biodiversity policy the ecological situation would certainly have been much worse. Nonetheless, many studies show that the designation of Natura 2000 sites and formalizing legal protection by itself are insufficient to halt biodiversity loss (Engelhardt, Bowler and Hof, 2023; Spiliopoulou et al., 2023; van der Sluis et al., 2016). More efforts are needed to actually halt biodiversity decline, to transform practices and activities that put biodiversity at risk and to restore ecosystems and species' populations.

These findings are also reflected in the formal evaluation of the Birds and Habitats Directives published in 2016 (European Commission, 2016). The Fitness Check concluded that the directives "are fit for purpose but fully achieving their objectives and realizing their full potential will depend on substantial improvement in their implementation [...]" (2016, p. 8). This Fitness Check was a key event in the evolution of EU biodiversity policy, as it led to the conclusions that the Birds and Habitats Directives are useful and effective (and do not require revision) and that more efforts are necessary to realize the ambitions and goals of both directives. These conclusions were strongly supported by scientific evidence but were not obvious given the substantial number of critiques and the serious attempts to revise and weaken the directives (Ferranti et al., 2019).

4 Stakeholder involvement

Stakeholder engagement is an important topic in both policy and management practices as well as in the scientific literature on Natura 2000. Various studies have explored how various stakeholders have been involved in the site selection and development or adaption of management practices, showing both the good examples as well as some of the main challenges (Blondet et al., 2017; Ferranti et al., 2013; Gallo et al., 2018; Hiedanpää, 2002; Krott et al., 2000; Maczka et al., 2019; Stoll-Kleemann, 2001). Studies on stakeholder involvement in Natura 2000 reflect the wider insights in the scientific literature that the practices of stakeholder involvement are very diverse, leading to both positive and negative outcomes. The effects of stakeholder involvement on conservation goals are less often studied and mostly only within very particular cases. Understanding the impact of stakeholder involvement beyond the specific still proves to be challenging and cannot be fully understood without accounting for the changing societal perspectives on biodiversity and biodiversity policy and on government and governance more generally. This is also reflected in studies on public support for biodiversity conservation that find support in general to be high but might be less visible in debates in the political domain or in the perspective stakeholders offer in particular cases.

An interesting observation is that in general the scientific studies seem to give more attention to those stakeholders that are critical or even skeptical about nature conservation because of fears concerning restrictions for their own activities, like famers, foresters and hunters (Hiedanpää, 2002; Krott et al., 2000), than to those who support conservation actions or benefit from them, like environmental nongovernmental organizations (ENGOs), certain entrepreneurs and the wider public. A main challenge that characterizes biodiversity policy is that it aims to protect and even restore certain habitats, and this might imply restrictions for human activities and in some cases even a change of current, harmful practices. These restrictions and the need to adapt current practices are key issues in debates with stakeholders and one of the main reasons why developing and implementing solutions can be difficult. Nevertheless, many cases show that sustainable solutions are possible, and that stakeholder involvement is key to finding these solutions and ensuring societal support (Blondet et al., 2017). More generally, the studies point to the importance of awareness and the need to ensure that the implementation of EU biodiversity policy is inclusive (Kokkoris et al., 2023).

5 The Fitness Check of the Birds and Habitats Directives

A key event in the evolution of EU biodiversity policy was the Fitness Check of the Birds and Habitats Directives (Santos, 2009). In December 2016, the European Commission (EC) presented the results of the formal evaluation of the Birds and Habitats Directives. This evaluation paid attention to relevance, efficiency, effectiveness, coherence with other EU policies and the EU added value. The main conclusion stated that the directives are fit for purpose but that their implementation needs improvement. It showed that, despite the overall success of improving conservation practices throughout the EU, many challenges remain. The Fitness Check combined scientific evidence about the implementation of the Birds and Habitats Directives with stakeholder views. A study of the different views put forward by Member States, interest groups and nongovernmental organizations showed that in general three different perspectives on EU biodiversity policy are distinguishable (Ferranti et al., 2019). The first perspective focuses on problems that governments and certain stakeholders experience and argues that legislative drawbacks in the directives cause these problems. It is a perspective that sees EU biodiversity policy mostly as a barrier for economic development. This perspective was for example reflected in views from governmental organizations in Germany, the Netherlands and Bulgaria and interest groups from the industry, agriculture and fishery sectors. The second perspective holds that many of the problems that mark the implementation processes are generated by improper Member State implementation. It was reflected in the views of governmental organizations from, for example, Germany, Greece and Finland but also in the views brought forward by ENGOs. The third perspective commends the benefits of the directives in face of the existing implementation problems. It highlights the added value of EU biodiversity policy in terms of novel conservation approaches, advanced knowledge and financial means that became available. This perspective was brought to the fore by many governmental organizations, for example, from Germany, Spain, Sweden and Slovakia, by most of the ENGOs that submitted their view to the European Commission's and by some interest groups, for example, those representing the tourism sector.

The overview shows that Member States voice different views, but also that views within a Member State governmental organizations can clearly differ. In Germany, for example, the Federal Ministry for the Environment, Nature Conservation emphasizes the benefits of the directives, whereas the Federal Ministry of Transport and Digital Infrastructure + Federal Road Administration complains about legislative drawback and the Gemeinde- und Städtebund Rheinland-Pfalz about inadequate national implementation. The different perspectives are also reflected in ongoing debates regarding positive and negative aspects of EU biodiversity policy and show that nature conservation is also a competition between different views, each pushing for a different framing and for different policies and implementation practices. These varying views were, for example, clearly visible in the political and societal debates about the Nature Restoration Law adopted in 2024.

6 The rise, near fall, and adoption of the Nature Restoration Law

In 2020, the EC published the EU Biodiversity Strategy for 2030 (European Commission, 2020). This strategy is part of the European Green Deal (EGD) and sets ambitious goals to protect and restore biodiversity. The strategy aims to put Europe on a path to ecological recovery by protecting at least 30 percent of EU land and sea areas, promoting nature-based solutions and addressing the main drivers of biodiversity loss. It clearly states that relying on only (legal) nature protection is insufficient and that additional efforts are needed to restore nature, to realize ecological corridors between nature areas and to effectively manage protected areas. The strategy links biodiversity to other societal challenges like the need to reduce greenhouse gas emissions, adapt to climate change, ensure food security and sustain vital ecosystem services like drinking water, fertile soils, and pollination. It therefore promotes the integration of biodiversity in other policy domains like agriculture, forestry, urban planning, energy, and climate.

The EU Biodiversity Strategy also addresses some of the shortcoming of the Birds and Habitats Directives, more specifically the need for legal requirements concerning the development and implementation of nature restoration plans. Whereas the Birds and Habitats Directives are aimed at restoring nature, these directives put forward neither specific requirements nor clear deadlines for achieving a sustainable conservation status for species and habitats. This allowed Member States to be inactive. In many Member States even the minimal requirement of preventing (further) deterioration was not always met. Recognizing these failures in the implementation and enforcement of the Birds and Habitats Directives, the EC proposed a legally binding approach in the form of the Nature Restoration Law.

The proposal for the Nature Restoration Law was developed with input from a public consultation and five stakeholder workshops. Overall, there seemed to be a broad support for the law and when the EC published the first proposal in June 2022; it did not gain significant attention or criticism. It was only when the European Parliament debated the law at the end of 2023 that it suddenly faced fierce critiques from right-wing parties and lobby groups representing the agricultural sector. Although the critiques were largely based on unjustified claims about consequences for food security and economic development (Pe'er et al., 2023), they had a severe impact on the proposal. In February 2024, the European Parliament adopted a weakened version and only after many of the initial conservation requirements were diluted or cancelled (Cliquet et al., 2024).

The final Member State approval was the last step that remained. This step became at risk after the Dutch government suddenly changed its position, stating it would vote against the Nature Restoration Law. This would mean that the majority of votes needed for adoption was lost and hence the proposal was taken from the agenda. It was put back on the agenda after Austria's Environment Minister Leonore Gewessler stated that she would vote in favor of the Nature Restoration Law, therewith securing the required majority for the approval. The Nature Restoration Law was formally adopted in June 2024. In the same time period, ambitious proposals to reduce pesticide use (Candel, Pe'er and Finger, 2023) and to green the Common Agricultural Policy (Guyomard et al., 2023) were cancelled, partly based on critiques also voiced against the Nature Restoration Law (see Chapter 4).

The developments around the adoption of the Nature Restoration Law and related environmental policies show that the formulation and implementation of ambitious environmental policies have become much more difficult. They also show that, to understand policy processes, one should study the strategies that certain actors use to create doubt, distribute disinformation and obstruct environmental policy and sustainability transitions. These strategies certainly deserve much more attention than they currently get in the literature on EU policy (cf. Oreskes and Conway, 2011). Recent developments also raise the question whether the earlier critiques on the implementation of the Birds and Habitats Directives reported in several scientific publications were based on legitimate claims or also on strategic attempts to delay or weaken the implementation of EU biodiversity policy.

7 Reflections

The evolution of EU nature conservation policy illustrates the challenge of formulating, implementing and adapting ambitious policies in a complex and continuously changing context. For a long time, the evolution was characterized by optimistic perspectives about Europeanization and sustainable development. More recently, it has become clearer that policies can create backlash (see Chapter 37), that implementation experiences differ and can in different ways impact implementation practices and policy processes (see Chapter 9) and that societal and political changes occurring outside the specific biodiversity domain can have a profound impact on policy processes within that domain. In the context of EU biodiversity policy this means that the opposition against EU environmental policy has grown, that critical and anti-environment discourses have become more pronounced and more influential, and that policymaking for sustainability has become much more difficult. The opposition against environmental policy is not only visible in the biodiversity domain, but also in debates about water quality (e. g., Chapter 24; Wiering, Liefferink and Beijen, 2018), agriculture (Chapter 28; van der Ploeg, 2020) and climate (Lamb et al., 2020; Stoddard et al., 2021). These strategies not only obstruct environmental policy and sustainability transitions, but they also disrupt society and its governance as they feed processes like populism

(Ofstehage, Wolford and Borras Jr, 2022; van der Ploeg, 2020), polarization, and regulatory capture (Saltelli et al., 2022). It reflects a larger trend that shows that formulating and implementing ambitious environmental policy have become much more difficult.

A second reflection concerns the role and impact of power dynamics in implementation studies. The numerous studies on the implementation of EU biodiversity policy show that policy implementation and policy evaluation are political process strongly influenced by the same power struggles that mark the formulation and adoption of these policies. These power struggles are partly addressed in the scientific literature but deserve more attention. From a power/knowledge perspective it is interesting to observe that at least some part of the scientific literature tends to reproduce frames in which EU environmental policy is presented as a technocratic and top-down approach and as a barrier for economic development. It would scientifically be more relevant and interesting to reflect on how such frames emerge, who is pushing them and how they impact policy formation and implementation.

Third, the number of scientific studies reflecting on implementation failures, on the factors that explain the lack of implementation and on the difficulties in actually halting biodiversity loss and achieving nature restoration is relatively low, particularly compared to the number of studies focusing on ecological aspects (Blicharska et al., 2016; Popescu et al., 2014). The fact that the main environmental policy challenges are found in the social domain warrants a call for a more prominent role of social sciences and for the development of approaches, perspectives and methodologies that help to grasp power/knowledge dynamics, different forms of obstruction and actions needed to sustain environmental ambitions and democratic ideals.

8 Future challenges

Major challenges for EU biodiversity policy are the growing opposition against environmental policy and the political struggles to uphold current policies. This is, for example, witnessed in the serious attempts to dilute the EGD ambitions (Brulle, Roberts and Spencer, 2024; Ofstehage, Wolford and Borras Jr, 2022). Recent political developments in various Member States have shown that discussions and contestation go beyond the more traditional differences between stakeholders and between different political parties. The post-truth era presents a whole new set of challenges for politics, policy and policy research and for the actors involved in these processes. The rise of populism, both on the national and the European level, and the growing use of misinformation and alternative facts within policy processes put enormous pressure on the formulation and implementation of environmental policies. In terms of research, more attention is needed for the actions and strategies by which policies and governance get undermined, as well as for those that are necessary for institutional maintenance. Such actions might include awareness raising, enforcement and providing sound evidence for political debates, but also studying and exposing the strategies that some actors use to undermine governance. These studies might help to make governance systems more resilient to processes of obstruction, and they are an indispensable part of the ongoing research about sustainability transformations.

References

Alphandéry, P. and Fortier, A. (2001) 'Can a territorial policy be based on science alone? The system for creating the Natura 2000 Network in France', *Sociologia Ruralis*, 41(3), pp. 311 – 328.

Beresford, A.E. et al. (2016) 'The contributions of the EU nature directives to the CBD and other multilateral environmental agreements', *Conservation Letters*, 9(6), pp. 479 – 488.

Beunen, R. (2006) 'European nature conservation legislation and spatial planning: For better or for worse?', *Journal of Environmental Planning and Management*, 49(4), pp. 605 – 619.

Beunen, R. and Kole, S. (2021) 'Institutional innovation in conservation law: Experiences from the implementation of the Birds and Habitats Directives in the Netherlands', *Land Use Policy*, 108, 105566.

Beunen, R., Van Assche, K. and Duineveld, M. (2013) 'Performing failure in conservation policy: The implementation of European Union directives in the Netherlands', *Land Use Policy*, 31, pp. 280 – 288.

Blicharska, M., Orlikowska, E.H., Roberge, J.-M. and Grodzinska-Jurczak, M. (2016) 'Contribution of social science to large scale biodiversity conservation: A review of research about the Natura 2000 network', *Biological conservation*, 199, pp. 110 – 122.

Blondet, M. et al. (2017) 'Participation in the implementation of Natura 2000: A comparative study of six EU Member States', *Land Use Policy*, 66, pp. 346 – 355.

Bouwma, I., Arts, B. and Liefferink, D. (2017) 'Cause, catalyst or conjunction? The influence of the Habitats Directive on policy instrument choice in Member States', *Journal of Environmental Planning and Management*, 60(6), pp. 977 – 996.

Bouwma, I., Liefferink, D., Van Apeldoorn, R. and Arts, B. (2016) 'Following old paths or shaping new ones in Natura 2000 implementation? Mapping path dependency in instrument choice', *Journal of Environmental Policy and Planning*, 18(2), pp. 214 – 233.

Brondizio, E.S., Settele, J., Díaz, S. and Ngo, H. (2019) *Global assessment report on biodiversity and ecosystem services of the intergovernmental science-policy platform on biodiversity and ecosystem services*. Bonn: IPBES Secretariat.

Brulle, R.J., Roberts, J.T. and Spencer, M.C. (2024) *Climate obstruction across Europe*. Oxford: Oxford University Press.

Campagnaro, T. et al. (2019) 'Half earth or whole earth: What can Natura 2000 teach us?', *BioScience*, 69(2), pp. 117 – 124.

Candel, J., Pe'er, G. and Finger, R. (2023) 'Science calls for ambitious European pesticide policies', *Nature Food*, 4(4), pp. 272 – 272.

Chapron, G., Epstein, Y., Trouwborst, A. and López-Bao, J.V. (2017) 'Bolster legal boundaries to stay within planetary boundaries', *Nature Ecology and Evolution*, 1, 0086.

Cliquet, A. et al. (2024) 'The negotiation process of the EU Nature Restoration Law proposal: Bringing nature back in Europe against the backdrop of political turmoil?', *Restoration Ecology*, e14158.

Davis, M. et al. (2014) 'Literature review: The ecological effectiveness of the Natura 2000 Network'. ETC/BD report to the EEA. European Environment Agency. Available at: https://www.eionet.europa.eu/etcs/etc-bd/products/etc-bd-reports/the_ecological_effectiveness_of_the_natura_2000_network/ (Accessed: 25 June 2025).

Donald, P.F. et al. (2007) 'International conservation policy delivers benefits for birds in Europe', *Science*, 317(5839), pp. 810 – 813.

European Commission (2016) 'Fitness Check of the EU nature legislation (birds and habitats directives) Directive 2009/147/EC of the European Parliament and of the Council of 30 November 2009 on the Conservation of Wild Birds and Council Directive 92/43/EEC of 21 May 1992 on the Conservation of Natural Habitats and of Wild Fauna and Flora'. *SWD*(2016) 472 final. Available at: https://commission.europa.eu/system/files/2017-01/swd-2016-472-final_en.pdf (Accessed: 24 June 2025).

European Commission (2020) 'EU Biodiversity Strategy for 2030. Bringing Nature Back into Our Lives'. *COM*(2020) 380 final. Available at: https://eur-lex.europa.eu/legal-content/EN/TXT/?uri=celex:52020DC0380 (Accessed: 25 June 2025).

European Communities (1979) 'Council Directive 79/409/EEC of 2 April 1979 on the conservation of wild birds'. *Official Journal of the European Commission.* L 103. Available at: https://eur-lex.europa.eu/legal-content/EN/ALL/?uri=CELEX:31979L0409 (Accessed: 4 September 2024).

European Communities (1992) 'Council Directive 92/43/EEC of 21 May 1992 on the conservation of natural habitats and of wild fauna and flora'. *Official Journal of the EC.* L 206, p.7. Available at: https://eur-lex.europa.eu/eli/dir/1992/43/oj/eng (Accessed: 4 September 2024).

European Environment Agency (n.d.) *Natura 2000 barometer.* Available at: https://www.eea.europa.eu/data-and-maps/dashboards/natura-2000-barometer (Accessed: 4 September 2024).

Engelhardt, E.K., Bowler, D. E. and Hof, C. (2023) 'European Habitats Directive has fostered monitoring but not prevented species declines', *Conservation Letters,* 16(3), e12948.

Evans, D. (2012) 'Building the European Union's Natura 2000 network', *Nature Conservation*, 1, pp. 11–26.

Fairbrass, J. and Jordan, A. (2001) 'Protecting biodiversity in the European Union: National barriers and European opportunities?', *Journal of European Public Policy,* 8(4), pp. 499–518.

Fairbrass, J. and Jordan, A. (2002) 'Biodiversity policy: The Birds and Habitats Directives', in: Jordan, A. (ed.) *The Europeanisation of British environmental policy: A departmental perspective.* Basingstoke: Palgrave.

Ferranti, F., Beunen, R. and Speranza, M. (2010) 'Natura 2000 Network: A comparison of the Italian and Dutch implementation experiences', *Journal of Environmental Policy and Planning,* 12(3), pp. 293–314.

Ferranti, F., Beunen, R., Vericat, P. and Geitzenauer, M. (2019) 'The Fitness Check of the Birds and Habitats Directives: A discourse analysis of stakeholders' perspectives', *Journal for Nature Conservation,* 47, pp. 103–109.

Ferranti, F., Turnhout, E., Beunen, R. and Behagel, J.H. (2013) 'Shifting nature conservation approaches in Natura 2000 and the implications for the roles of stakeholders', *Journal of Environmental Planning and Management*, pp. 1–16.

Gallo, M. et al. (2018) 'Collaboration and conflicts between stakeholders in drafting the Natura 2000 Management Programme (2015–2020) in Slovenia', *Journal for Nature Conservation,* 42, pp. 36–44.

Guyomard, H. et al. (2023) 'How the green architecture of the 2023–2027 Common Agricultural Policy could have been greener', *Ambio,* 52(8), pp. 1327–1338.

Hermoso, V. et al. (2022) 'The EU Biodiversity Strategy for 2030: Opportunities and challenges on the path towards biodiversity recovery', *Environmental Science and Policy,* 127, pp. 263–271.

Hiedanpää, J. (2002) 'European-wide conservation versus local well-being: The reception of the Natura 2000 Reserve Network in Kaarvia, SW-Finland', *Landscape and Urban Planning,* 61, pp. 113–123.

Jongman, R.H. (1995) 'Nature conservation planning in Europe: Developing ecological networks', *Landscape and urban planning,* 32(3), pp. 169–183.

Kokkoris, I.P. et al. (2023) 'Natura 2000 public awareness in EU: A prerequisite for successful conservation policy', *Land Use Policy,* 125, 106482.

Krott, M. et al. (2000) 'Voicing Interests and ConcErns: NATURA 2000: An ecological network in conflict with people', *Forest Policy and Economics,* 1, pp. 357–366.

Lamb, W.F. et al. (2020) 'Discourses of climate delay', *Global Sustainability,* 3, e17.

Ledoux, L., Crooks, S., Jordan, A. and Kerry Turner, R. (2000) 'Implementing EU biodiversity policy: UK experiences', *Land Use Policy*, 17, pp. 257–268.
Maczka, K. et al. (2019) 'The ecosystem services concept as a tool for public participation in management of Poland's Natura 2000 network', *Ecosystem Services*, 35, pp. 173–183.
Meyer, J.-H. (2010) 'Saving migrants: A transnational network supporting supranational bird protection policy', in: Kaiser, W., Leucht, B. and Gehler, M. (eds.) *Transnational networks in regional integration: Governing Europe 1945–83.* Basingstoke: Palgrave, pp. 176–198.
Meyer, J.-H. (2011) 'Green Activism: The European Parliament's Environmental Committee promoting a European environmental policy in the 1970s', *JEIH Journal of European Integration History*, 17(1), pp. 73–86.
Morán-López, R., Cortés Gañán, E., Uceda Tolosa, O. and Sánchez Guzmán, J. (2020) 'The umbrella effect of Natura 2000 annex species spreads over multiple taxonomic groups, conservation attributes and organizational levels', *Animal Conservation*, 23(4), pp. 407–419.
Morris, R.K. (2011) 'The application of the Habitats Directive in the UK: Compliance or gold plating?', *Land Use Policy*, 28(1), pp. 361–369.
Ofstehage, A., Wolford, W. and Borras Jr, S.M. (2022) 'Contemporary populism and the environment', *Annual Review of Environment and Resources*, 47(1), pp. 671–696.
Oreskes, N., and Conway, E.M. (2011) *Merchants of doubt: How a handful of scientists obscured the truth on issues from tobacco smoke to global warming.* London: Bloomsbury Publishing.
Pe'er, G. et al. (2023) *Scientists support the EU's Green Deal and reject the unjustified argumentation against the Sustainable Use Regulation and the Nature Restoration Law. Open letter (Full Version, 9.7.2023).* Available at: https://helda.helsinki.fi/server/api/core/bitstreams/485e28d0-58a7-48c3-ba38-09e354b75fc0/content (Accessed: 24 June 2025).
Pinton, F. (2001) 'Conservation of biodiversity as a European directive: The challenge for france', *Sociologia Rurales*, 41(3), pp. 329–342.
Popescu, V.D. et al. (2014) 'Species, habitats, society: An evaluation of research supporting EU's Natura 2000 network', *PloS ONE*, 9(11), e113648.
Princé, K. et al. (2021) 'Long-term effectiveness of Natura 2000 network to protect biodiversity: A hint of optimism for common birds', *Biological conservation*, 253, 108871.
Saltelli, A. et al. (2022) 'Science, the endless frontier of regulatory capture', *Futures*, 135, 102860.
Santos, E. B. (2009) *Ecotoxicology research developments.* New York: Nova Biomedical Books.
Spiliopoulou, K. et al. (2023) 'Protected areas and the ranges of threatened species: Towards the EU Biodiversity Strategy 2030', *Biological conservation*, 284, 110166.
Squintani, L. (2019) 'Gold-Plating: A misleading overarching concept', in: *Beyond minimum harmonisation: Gold-plating and green-plating of European environmental law.* Cambridge: Cambridge University Press, pp. 13–77.
Stoddard, I. et al. (2021) 'Three decades of climate mitigation: Why haven't we bent the global emissions curve?' *Annual Review of Environment and Resources*, 46(1), pp. 653–689.
Stoll-Kleemann, S. (2001) 'Opposition to the designation of protected areas in Germany', *Journal of Environmental Planning and Management*, 44(1), pp. 109–128.
van der Ploeg, J. D. (2020) 'Farmers' upheaval, climate crisis and populism', *The Journal of Peasant Studies*, 47(3), pp. 1–17.
van der Sluis, T. et al. (2016) *How much biodiversity is in Natura 2000? The "umbrella effect" of the European Natura 2000 Protected Area Network: Technical report* (Alterra-rapport; No. 2738). Wageningen: Alterra.
Wiering, M., Liefferink, D. and Beijen, B. (2018) 'The internal and external face of Dutch environmental policy: A case of fading environmental leadership?', *Environmental Science and Policy*, 81, pp. 18–25.

Burcin Demirbilek, David Benson and Oliver Fritsch

European Union water policy: Still incrementally evolving, not yet through

Abstract: Water policy is one of the central components of the European Union's (EU) environmental *acquis communautaire*. Evolution of this policy sector, however, has been far from trouble free, with incrementalism characterizing policy expansion since the early 1970s. Academic attempts to interpret this evolution have proved similarly disjointed, with different theoretical perspectives mapping onto broader trends in the European integration, public policy and environmental governance literatures. As water policy continues evolving, it faces new challenges both within and outside the EU, primarily related to the globalization of environmental risks from climate change, biodiversity loss and unsustainable consumption. Consequently, water policy is entering a new evolutionary phase involving further institutional innovation alongside its internationalization through water diplomacy, norm diffusion and policy transfer. New opportunities are emerging for researchers to conceptualize, theorize and empirically analyze these evolutionary trends to inform future policy learning.

Keywords: European Union water policy; policy expansion; incrementalism; internationalization; decolonization.

1 Introduction

Policy expansion is often subject to incrementalism, what Charles Lindblom (1979, p. 517; Jordan et al., 2003) memorably called 'muddling through', whereby policy change occurs slowly and unevenly as opposed to radically and at a fast pace. This feature is certainly evident in the European Union's (EU) water policy sector, which has evolved through successive regulatory interventions to become an important component of the environmental *acquis communautaire* (Benson and Jordan, 2010a). Here, European institutions have gradually adopted measures to regulate qualitative and quantitative aspects of inland, coastal and marine waters. An epistemologically and theoretically diverse literature, which itself is still developing, has studied this evolution. Yet, as EU water policy matures, it currently faces significant challenges, primarily linked to the increasing globalization of environmental risks, such as climate change, biodiversity loss and unstainable consumption. In responding to these threats, the EU is once again engaging in policy innovation, creating new opportunities for analysis.

As EU water policy enters its sixth decade, this chapter has several aims, each linked to its historical evolution. First, it examines the genesis of water policy in the early 1970s, along with its gradual expansion via three main phases up to the 2000s, focusing primarily on inland and coastal water management. Second, the chapter dis-

https://doi.org/10.1515/9783111321523-028

cusses how scholars have interpreted this evolutionary process through different theoretical perspectives. Third, the chapter identifies current challenges to EU water policy along with recent innovative responses, including amendments to existing policies and novel regulatory measures. One significant development also discussed is a shift in EU priorities toward achieving greater internationalization of the water *acquis* through policy transfer and water diplomacy. What becomes apparent is that, while the velocity of policy innovation measurably declined after 2000, the sector is—to paraphrase Lindblom (1979)—still incrementally evolving, not yet through. Finally, the chapter outlines related avenues for future water policy research agendas.

2 Genesis and evolution

Previous studies have charted EU water policy expansion across several sequential stages or phases (for example, Aubin and Varone, 2004; Benson and Jordan, 2008). The first dimension encompasses the mid-1970s until the late 1980s. By the late 1960s, chronic transboundary pollution of rivers such as the Rhine had become politically significant across Western Europe, prompting the then European Economic Community (EEC) to intervene through European Parliament (EP) reports, resolutions and communications plus Council recommendations (Commission of the European Communities, 1971, 1973). The EEC also identified land-based pollution threats to the Mediterranean as particularly pressing (Wurzel, 2002). European Commission (EC) scientific experts started investigating these pollution risks prior to the 1972 European Council Paris Summit, where national governments endorsed proposals for adopting an EEC environment policy (Wurzel, 2002; Benson, 2007). The Commission consequently identified water pollution controls as a central objective of its First Environment Action Program (EAP) 1973 (Commission of the European Communities, 1973). The EAP determined that marine pollution from land-based and other sources required joint action by national governments and the EEC. It also outlined water pollution issues in the Rhine basin, with the Commission stating that it would "make appropriate proposals in this important sector" (Commission of the European Communities, 1973, p. 28).

Following from the EAP commitments, initial policy expansion involved adopting several 'command and control' directives aimed at reducing water pollution, featuring ambient environmental quality standards, exposure standards and emission limit values (Haigh, 2003; see also Chapter 32). Given the concerns over pollution threats to marine and freshwater resources specifically, earlier directives imposed quality standards for shellfisheries, freshwater fisheries, inland and coastal bathing water and surface waters for drinking. Additional directives then followed for setting drinking water standards, protecting groundwater, controlling dangerous substances in waters and preventing titanium dioxide pollution.

Implementing these first-generation water directives proved problematic for Member States. Several countries failed to properly transpose these measures into national legislation, while their costs and harmonized standards became intervening factors in uneven implementation. For example, the Bathing Water Directive (76/160/EEC), which set standards for pollution levels in bathing water, was politically contentious for the United Kingdom (UK) and West Germany since it required significant public investment in wastewater treatment infrastructure (Wurzel, 2002). Another problem for the UK, which had traditionally relied upon regulatory flexibility involving water pollution objectives set according to local receiving waters, was the EEC's harmonized regulatory approach. Nonetheless, Directive 76/464/EEC aimed at preventing the discharge of dangerous substances into waters provided a 'parallel' approach allowing both forms of control (Haigh, 2003, pp. 4.2–1). Another evident deficiency with these early water directives was their standard setting based upon end-water use and limited targeting of point and non-point source polluters, particularly agriculture and wastewater treatment plants.

The second phase of water *acquis* evolution therefore confronted specific polluters. This changed approach began in the late 1980s, mainly in response to the Oslo and Paris conventions on preventing waste dumping at sea, dissatisfaction with the 'end-use' approach of initial water directives and, critically, the availability of European structural funding for wastewater infrastructure (Weale et al., 2000, p. 361). Governments previously resistant to further European water legislation shifted their positions to support such change. The 1988 Frankfurt meeting of European government ministers consequently reached agreement, allowing adoption of the Urban Waste Water Treatment Directive (91/271/EEC). It compelled all municipalities over a certain population size to apply secondary treatment to sewage discharges. Another measure, Directive 91/676/EEC, introduced what Haigh (2003, pp. 4.2–2) calls a 'preventative approach' to eutrophication, requiring Member States to designate so-called nitrate vulnerable zones where application of inorganic and organic fertilizers would be restricted.

Greater integration of water management through the development of the Water Framework Directive (WFD) characterized EU water policy's third phase (Chave, 2001; Kaika, 2003). The Council and EP rejected Commission attempts in 1993 to replace earlier water directives and introduce a new directive on the ecological quality of surface waters (Haigh, 2003). The EP's Environment Committee then lobbied for the introduction of a new directive based upon integrated water management, reflecting the principles established at the Dublin International Conference on Water and the Environment 1992. Finally adopted in 2000, Directive 2000/60/EC addressed water pollution through requiring Member States to designate river basin districts within their territories, develop river basin management plans (RBMPs) for each district, implement programs of measures to achieve 'good' ecological status of waters, monitor water quality and report findings. Adaptive management was also compelled through requiring multi-annual reviews and revision of RBMPs. The subsequent 2007 Floods Directive (2007/60/EC) and 2008 Marine Strategy Framework Directive (2008/56/EC) also reflected WFD's integrated approach, featuring integrated regional planning for controlling flood risks and protecting marine ecosystems respectively.

The EU has since mainly focused on revising preexisting directives, marking a visible slowdown in the velocity of water policy expansion. A new Directive (2006/7/EC) replaced the Bathing Water Directive in 2006, containing updated implementation criteria (Benson and Jordan, 2010b). Revised Drinking Water Directives were adopted in 1998 (Directive 98/83/EC) and 2020 (Directive (EU) 2020/2184). The Commission launched a consultation on amending the Urban Waste Water Treatment Directive in 2018, publishing a proposal for its revision in 2022 (European Commission, 2022). Finally, the EU's Zero Pollution Action Plan for Water, Air and Soil (European Commission, 2021, 2023), discussed below, proposes further changes to water policies.

3 Academic interpretations: trends in integration theorizing

European integration theorizing has also evolved via several interconnected phases (Rosamond, 2000). While 'grand theories' such as neofunctionalism (Haas, 1958) and intergovernmentalism (Hoffmann, 1966) initially explored why and how steps toward integration are taken, later mid-range political theories examined how an integrated EU functions, relying on ideas borrowed from legal studies, governance and public policy (see Chapter 2). Several theoretical paradigm shifts are discernible as academic fashions shift over time, influencing EU water policy analysis.

Legal scholars first analyzed specific EEC water policy instruments and their implementation. Nagel (1977), for example, examined the implementation of early water directives to show how the EEC's mandatory uniform approach to water quality standards caused significant compliance problems for states such as the United Kingdom and West Germany. Integration scholars also utilized the public policy literature to analyze this sector. Richardson (1994) examined actor coalitions within EU water policy process via network analysis. Wurzel (2002) deployed neo-pluralist policy network analysis, which examines how public actors (governments, EU institutions) undertake governance steering in coordination with private interests, to research EU water policymaking. Others employed new institutionalist theories to understand water policy development (Jordan, 1999). Multilevel governance theory was also used to analyze early EU water directives (Benson, 2007).

Several other perspectives feature in the sector analysis, reflecting their popularity within integration studies. Europeanization, in which Member States seek to influence EU policymaking and institutions and adapt to them in their domestic context, became a significant focus of integration studies from the 1990s onwards (Radaelli, 2003). Europeanization theories were subsequently employed to analyze EU environmental policy (Knill and Lehmkuhl, 2002; Jordan and Liefferink, 2004) and the water sector specifically (Jordan, 1998; Jordan, 2002). A 'renaissance' in federalism thinking, following the European Constitution political debate, also saw federal theory applied to EU water policy (Benson and Jordan, 2008). More recently, the EU water policy process, primarily WFD implementation, has become increasingly subject to post-decisional theoretical interpretations drawn from the wider environmental governance literature, for example regarding its public participation or economic valuation requirements (Kochskämper et al., 2016; Boeuf and Fritsch, 2016). Nonetheless, contemporary research still incorporates integration studies, particularly through investigations into the external Europeanization of EU water policy (Demirbilek, 2023).

4 Toward environmental policy integration

The World Economic Forum, in its Global Risks Report 2023, argues that the world faces interconnected, interacting risks, including climate change, biodiversity loss and natural resource depletion, that collectively present a 'polycrisis' imperiling our planetary future (World Economic Forum, 2023). Threats to global water resources include shifting precipitation patterns, aquatic biodiversity loss, ecosystem health impacts and ecosystem services provision, over-abstraction of surface and ground waters and water pollution (United Nations, 2018). These trends raise questions over how to devise water policy measures in conjunction with, if not fully integrated into, political action in environmental policy areas such as biodiversity, climate and energy (see Chapter 33). Such questions hold even greater significance since the United Nations' (UN) adoption of its Sustainable Development Goal (SDG) 6 targets for ensuring access to clean water and sanitation by 2030 (United Nations, 2015), thereby extending the scope of water policy integration to nonenvironmental policy areas, including human rights, land use and public health.

The increasing complexity of risks to water resources has led to EU institutional innovation via new policy instruments. They include 'soft' laws, which enables locally specific, information-driven and adaptive policy responses, but also new regulatory measures and the strategic 'packaging' of water policy instruments as part of the European Green Deal (EGD) that integrate aquatic resources management with action in the fields of biodiversity, climate and energy.

Recent EU water policy innovation has included soft policy amendments to existing measures. Soft policy instruments can include government information and advice, issued to modify societal and individual behavior (Wurzel, Zito and Jordan, 2013). The mainstreaming of climate change objectives into the WFD is one such institutional innovation. A 2009 guidance document had this specific purpose (European Commission, 2009). Although the WFD is primarily concerned with maintaining water quality, the guidance advised national implementers on how to integrate climate change in RBMP through conducting a 'climate check' of programs of measures (European Commission, 2009). A methodology for assessing these measures was also provided.

One new 'hard' policy innovation adopted responding to water scarcity, climate change and over-abstraction is Regulation (EU) 2020/741 on minimum requirements for water reuse. As water resources competition increases across the EU, wastewater recycling for non-domestic uses is receiving wider political and public acceptance as a management practice. To govern such activities, the Regulation sets harmonized quality standards for urban wastewater reuse for agricultural irrigation in Member States, which link to the EU's circular economy policy and objectives for integrated water management under the WFD. The circular economy (see Chapter 36) refers to an economic system characterized by minimizing wastes through the reduction, reuse, recycling and resource recovery (Fitch-Roy, Benson and Monciardini, 2020).

Other recent EU water policy innovation has come through the strategic 'packaging' of water-management policies, linking to the revision of preexisting instruments and new measures in other environmental policy areas. The EGD is an overarching meta-policy for economic growth designed to ensure a climate-neutral, clean and circular economy (European Commission, 2019). Its main implementing measures are contained in sectoral strategy documents that bundle different policies together in 'packages' or 'portfolios' (Howlett and Rayner, 2013). One EGD objective is achieving 'zero pollution' by meeting targets such as reducing plastics pollution of marine and inland waters by 50 percent by 2030. In addition to establishing a Zero Pollution Stakeholder Platform for disseminating information, the Commission has published three sectoral policy packages: the Chemical Strategy for Sustainability; the Zero Pollution Action Plan for Water, Air and Soil; and an initiative to revise industrial emissions legislation (European Commission, 2021). To meet EGD pollution targets, the 2021 Zero Pollution Action Plan for example proposes revising the Drinking and Bathing Water Directives to provide greater health protection from plastics pollution, along with amending other water and maritime laws (European Commission, 2021). Consequently, current proposals for amending the WFD, Groundwater Directive and Environmental Quality Standards Directive reflect the Plan objectives (European Commission, 2023).

5 Internationalization of EU water policy

We label another significant area of recent EU water policy innovation 'internationalization', highlighting two major dynamics: external Europeanization through direct policy transfer and indirect normative diffusion processes, including EU water diplomacy. Policy transfer involves the deliberate transposition, partially or in its entirety, of a policy developed in one political context to another (Benson and Jordan, 2011). Moreover, policy learning can occur indirectly through diffusion processes, as policy knowledge is communicated between political actors. Mechanisms for policy diffusion between countries can include learning through regional proximity, leader-laggard and other dynamics (Berry and Berry, 2018).

Attempts to diffuse EU water policy principles reflect its ambition for recognition as a trustworthy global environmental policy entrepreneur (see Chapter 29). However, the EU's policy transfer agenda reflects its relationship to its direct and indirect neighborhood, which creates interdependencies that can be shaped proactively and constructively for mutual benefit. As part of its enlargement dynamics, the EU has exported water policy beyond its borders through direct transfer. Under a process of external Europeanization, the EU requires accession states to assimilate the environmental *acquis* into their national legal frameworks to meet the Copenhagen Criteria for Union membership (Börzel and Risse, 2012). Since the last significant enlargement rounds in 2004 and 2007, such legal conditionality has led to the ongoing transfer of EU water policy instruments such as the WFD to several candidate states. These 'importer' countries include Türkiye (Demirbilek et al., 2020), despite its stalled accession process, Serbia (Takić et al., 2017) and other Balkan states (Kaštelan-Macan et al., 2007; Baraj et al., 2017).

As Börzel and Risse (2012, p. 291) show, this top-down Europeanization argument for external policy change is less sustainable the further away one is geopolitically from the EU's 'shadow of conditionality'. They suggest that 'transnational diffusion' provides a better theoretical lens "to capture the more indirect ways in which the EU may affect domestic or regional institutional change" beyond its borders (Börzel and Risse, 2012, p. 291). Accordingly, EU water policy has diffused externally to non-EU states, for instance via the voluntary adoption of EU water policy norms in regionally proximate states such as Norway, which implements the WFD with Sweden (Hovik and Hanssen, 2016) and Iceland within the European Economic Area (Gunnarsdottir, Gardarsson and Bartram, 2015). Switzerland supports EU states in implementing the WFD through transboundary cooperation in managing river basins (Federal Office for the Environment, 2022).

Another increasingly important vehicle for water policy diffusion is EU water diplomacy. Reflecting observations on the growing normative power of Europe (Manners, 2002) and EU external governance (Lavenex and Schimmelfennig, 2013), the EU has increasingly promoted its environmental policy norms globally through its nascent foreign policy (Adelle, Biedenkopf and Torney, 2017). A critical mechanism in this respect is water diplomacy, defined as developing "joint water governance arrangements by applying foreign policy means" (Sehring et al., 2022, p. 200). Key water diplomacy aspects include preventive diplomacy for reducing tensions between riparian countries, integrating stakeholders in the water diplomacy process, cooperation for water allocation and equitable use of shared waters, producing technical knowledge and, finally, supporting political interaction between stakeholders (Keskinen, Salminen and Haapala, 2021, p. 3). This agenda has increased in tandem with growing EU external action powers, particularly after the Lisbon Treaty. Schunz and Topcuoglu (2023, pp. 24–26) describe how the EU's water diplomacy takes four main forms, depending upon which European Commission actor (i. e., Directorate-General (DG)) is responsible for its promotion. The European External Action Service uses water policy as an instrument for peacebuilding and conflict reduction in non-EU states by implementing the Common Foreign and Security Policy (Schunz and Topcuoglu, 2023, pp. 24–26; Tomalová and Ullrichová, 2021). Meanwhile, DG for International Partnerships utilizes water diplomacy for international development assistance; the DG for

Environment employs it to promote its water protection policies externally (Schunz and Topcuoglu, 2023).

One significant example of the latter diplomacy is the EU Water Initiative (EUWI), which originally was a partnership mechanism for supporting implementation of the UN Millennium Development Goals in Africa (Partzsch, 2008). Agreed upon at the World Summit on Sustainable Development 2002, the EU-Africa Strategic Partnership on Water Affairs and Sanitation established an African Working Group. Two other regional partnerships were adopted at the summit: Eastern Europe, Caucasus and Central Asia; and Latin America. Another partnership for the Mediterranean region was then developed. The EUWI subsequently morphed into Commission-steered regionally focused governance networks designed ostensibly for diffusing WFD norms to non-EU states (Fritsch et al., 2017, 2020). While its success was limited, primarily due to misfits between the WFD model and institutional contexts in importer countries (Fritsch et al., 2017, 2020), the Initiative nonetheless survives in reduced form, supplemented by two additional institutional innovations, the India-EU Water Partnership and the China Europe Water Platform. The former has a formal Memorandum of Understanding for collaboration on water management issues between India and the EU, while the latter supports high-level policy dialogue, academic research and business cooperation between China and the EU (India-EU Water Partnership, 2023; China Europe Water Platform, 2023). This collaborative approach to water diplomacy emphasizes diffusing knowledge around management best practice rather than transferring specific water policy instruments (Fritsch et al., 2020). Accordingly, the EU, along with Member States such as the Netherlands, also now operate what Bilgen and Mukhtarov (2024) term a "hydrohub", by strategically promoting itself as global source of water management knowledge. However, the influence of EU water diplomacy is questionable, particularly given its neocolonial nature as discussed below.

Although the EU is an active exporter of water policy norms, it also 'downloads' water policy from the international level. One recent example is EU commitments to the UN's Water Action Agenda. A 2023 UN Water Conference outcome, the Agenda has resulted in several hundred voluntary commitments from state and nonstate actors worldwide for action on water problems (United Nations, 2023). For the EU's contribution, the Council of the EU has pledged thirty-three main commitments for achievement by 2030, based around themes that include water as a human right, water for health, water for peace and security, climate adaptation and restoring biodiversity (General Secretariat of the Council, 2023). Pledges include, for example, improving EU citizen's access to clean water and sanitation.

6 Research agendas

Recent developments in the EU's water policy lend themselves to potentially innovative research agendas, thereby providing a renewed role for scholars in conceptual and theoretical development, empirical analysis and normative policy work. Here, we focus on three main areas: to researching policy innovation and internationalization processes outlined above, we add a decolonization perspective with a view to refocusing external EU policy away from its current 'water coloniality' toward supporting indigenous knowledge, marginalized groups and local ecosystem-based approaches through greater consideration of justice. From this perspective, colonialism has caused environmental injustice by ignoring local knowledge and indigenous rights to water and land (Bray, 2021; Hartwig et al., 2022). Indigenous people should have self-determination and water rights to ensure fair participation in environmental decision-making and provide justice and equality (Mathur and Mulwafu, 2018).

Policy innovation

One evolving EU water policy issue that requires additional investigation is the shift from producing single policy outputs to the strategic packaging of water policy instruments. Scholars have already started to investigate how complex, cross-cutting environmental issues, such as the circular economy, are being governed through EU policy innovation (for example, Fitch-Roy, Benson and Monciardini, 2020). However, more research is required, particularly regarding the content and effectiveness of water policy packaging, along with its integration with other strategic objectives and legal measures. For example, the Zero Pollution Action Plan (European Commission, 2021, 2023) relies so far on reviewing and amending existing legal measures to prevent plastics pollution rather than adopting entirely new policy measures. This raft of strategic policy innovation may be less innovative in tackling water pollution than previously assumed. Therefore, a new, dedicated research agenda based on conceptualizing water policy packaging, theorizing how packaging occurs in practice and empirically analyzing its outputs and outcomes appears timely. Particularly interesting for understanding water policy innovation is whether such interventions result in effective controls on water pollution, given the implementation issues evident since the 1970s. Equally worth studying is the coherence of individually packaged instruments in meeting EU water policy objectives.

Internationalization

Internationalization also creates further research opportunities. While scholars have provisionally mapped out the conceptual parameters of EU water diplomacy (Fritsch et al., 2017, 2020; Ruiz, 2020; Tomalova and Ullrichova, 2021; Schunz and Topcuoglu, 2023), such studies remain under-theorized, particularly from European integration, public policy and international relations perspectives. For example, public policy scholars have generated an extensive theoretical toolbox for understanding policy transfer and diffusion mechanisms (Benson and Jordan, 2011; Berry and Berry, 2018). Others have developed theory around the role of transfer agents and expert networks that can be productively applied to analyzing how actors undertake EU water diplomacy (Demirbilek et al., 2020). Integration theorists meanwhile might draw upon existing Europeanization arguments to explain EU water diplomacy's domestic impact in importer states.

Decolonization

Research agendas could additionally focus on developing approaches to reversing the 'coloniality' (Sultana, 2022) of EU water diplomacy, which represents an attempt to impose a hegemonic knowledge system on global water management by promoting incompatible European-centric norms in the Global South. Critical scholars have noted how hierarchical North-South power relations, established under past colonial eras, are replicated through the dominance of knowledge systems curated by Western countries (Sultana, 2022). In water management, 'best practice' concepts, theories and models developed in these contexts are propagated to Southern countries through such 'diplomatic' means, regardless of their appropriateness. For example, the Council of the EU (2021), in its Conclusions on Water in the EU's External Action, prioritizes achieving UN SDG 6 targets on access to clean water and sanitation through EU water diplomacy but also emphasizes a critical role for integrated water resources management (IWRM) and water nexus concepts. However, EUWI's relative failure in achieving diffusion of the WFD—a variant of IWRM—to Africa, Latin America and Central Asian states due to its technical, economic and political incompatibility (Fritsch et al., 2017, 2020) highlights the need to rethink the promotion of such concepts within EU water diplomacy. Indeed, Partzsch (2008; see also Fritsch, Adelle and Benson, 2017) argues that European state actors dominated the EUWI process, with only limited consideration of the partner countries' views. Decolonizing the EU's external water policy to ensure greater justice could then involve it recognizing indigenous knowledge, traditional management practices and belief systems rather than propagating a continued emphasis on inflexible Western-supplied 'solutions' that, at best, lack contextual empathy or, at worst, force an epistemological hegemony alongside technical dependency on importer countries.

7 Conclusions

Although the velocity of EU water policy expansion has slowed markedly since the early 2000s, it is by no means finished. Many of the pollution problems the water *acquis* was originally adopted to address are still evident, while 'new' risks such as climate change, biodiversity loss and overconsumption necessitate further policy innovation. The EU's drive to act as a global water policy entrepreneur has also expanded water diplomacy, making it an increasingly significant component of the Union's external action. Consequently, this renewed policy activism presents opportunities for scholars to conceptualize, theorize and empirically evaluate it for future learning. More specifically, researchers could productively focus on examining the effectiveness of water policy innovation resulting from the packaging of instruments, particularly in countering water pollution, the internationalization of EU water policy through direct transfer and norm diffusion, along with the impacts of water coloniality as a precursor that would inform decolonization of the Union's water diplomacy. Like the water *acquis* itself, our knowledge of this important policy sector—to paraphrase Lindblom (1979)—is still incrementally evolving, not yet through.

References

Adelle, C., Biedenkopf, K. and Torney, D. (eds.) (2017) *European Union external environmental policy: Rules, regulation and governance beyond borders.* Basingstoke: Palgrave Macmillan.

Aubin, D. and Varone, F. (2004) 'The evolution of European water policy', in: Kissling-Näf, I. and Kuks, S. (eds.) *The evolution of national water regimes in Europe.* Dordrecht: Springer, pp. 49 – 86.

Baraj, E., Gjoka, A., Lilo, R. and Allabashi, R. (2017) 'Assessment of water monitoring system in Albania under the perspective of EU legislation and Austrian practice', *Albanian Journal of Agricultural Sciences,* pp. 155 – 164.

Benson, D. (2007) *Task allocation in the European Union: Testing the explanatory value of federal theories.* Unpublished doctoral thesis. Norwich: University of East Anglia.

Benson, D. and Jordan, A. (2008) 'Understanding task allocation in the European Union: Exploring the value of federal theory', *Journal of European Public Policy,* 15(1), pp. 78 – 97.

Benson, D. and Jordan, A. (2010a) 'Environmental policy', in: Cini, M. (ed.) *European Union politics.* Oxford: Oxford University Press, pp. 358 – 376.

Benson, D. and Jordan, A. (2010b) 'The scaling of water governance tasks: A comparative federal analysis of the European Union and Australia', *Environmental Management,* 46, pp. 7 – 16.

Benson, D. and Jordan, A. (2011) 'What have we learned from policy transfer research? Dolowitz and Marsh revisited', *Political Studies Review,* 9(3), pp. 366 – 378.

Berry, F.S. and Berry, W.D. (2018) 'Innovation and diffusion models in policy research', in: Weible, C. and Sabatier, P.A. (eds.) *Theories of the policy process.* London: Routledge, pp. 253 – 297.

Bilgen, A. and Mukhtarov, F. (2024) 'Selling excellence: Hydrohubs and policy mobility in a neo-liberal world order', in: Fritsch, O. and Benson, D. (eds.) *Handbook on the governance and politics of water resources.* Cheltenham: Edward Elgar, pp.332 – 357.

Boeuf, B. and Fritsch, O. (2016) 'Studying the implementation of the Water Framework Directive in Europe: A meta-analysis of 89 journal articles', *Ecology and Society,* 21(2), pp. 19.

Börzel, T.A. and Risse, T. (2012) 'From Europeanization to diffusion', in: Risse, T. (ed.) *Domestic politics and norm diffusion in international relations.* London: Routledge, pp. 290 – 307.

Bray, L.A. (2021) 'Settler colonialism and rural environmental injustice: Water inequality on the Navajo Nation', *Rural Sociology,* 86(3), pp. 586 – 610.

Chave, P. (2001) *The EU Water Framework Directive.* London: IWA Publishing.

China Europe Water Platform (CEWP) (2023) *China Europe water platform.* Available at: https://www.cewp.eu (Accessed: 21 December 2023).

Commission of the European Communities (1971) *First communication of the Commission about the Community's policy on the environment.* Brussels: Commission of the European Communities. Available at: https://aei.pitt.edu/3126 (Accessed: 21 June 2025)

Commission of the European Communities (1973) *Programme of action of the European Communities on the environment.* Brussels: Commission of the European Communities. Available at: https://cordis.europa.eu/programme/id/ENV-ENVAP-1C (Accessed: 21 June 2025)

Council of the European Union (2021) *Council conclusions on water in the EU's external action.* Brussels: Council of the European Union. Available at: https://data.consilium.europa.eu/doc/document/ST-14108-2021-INIT/en/pdf/ (Accessed: 21 June 2025)

Demirbilek, B. (2023) *Europeanisation in Turkish water management policy: A sociological institutionalism perspective.* Lanham: Lexington Books.

Demirbilek, B., Fitch-Roy, O., Benson, D. and Fairbrass, J. (2020) 'Going "off script": The influence of instrument constituencies on the Europeanisation of Turkish water policy', *Water Alternatives,* 13(3), pp. 691–708.

European Commission (2009) *Common implementation strategy for the Water Framework Directive. Guidance document no. 24: River basin management in a changing climate.* Brussels: European Commission. Available at: https://circabc.europa.eu/sd/a/a88369ef-df4d-43b1-8c8c-306ac7c2d6e1/Guidance%2520document%2520n%252024%2520-%2520River%2520Basin%2520Management%2520in%2520a%2520Changing%2520Climate_FINAL.pdf (Accessed: 21 June 2025)

European Commission (2019) 'The European Green Deal', *COM*(2019) 640 final. Available at: https://eur-lex.europa.eu/legal-content/EN/TXT/?uri=celex:52019DC0640 (Accessed: 21 June 2025).

European Commission (2021) *Pathway to a healthy planet for all: EU Action Plan: Towards zero pollution for air, water and soil.* Brussels: European Commission. Available at: https://eur-lex.europa.eu/legal-content/EN/TXT/?uri=celex:52021DC0400 (Accessed: 21 June 2025)

European Commission (2022) *Proposal for a directive of the European Parliament and the Council concerning urban wastewater treatment (recast).* Brussels: European Commission. Available at: https://eur-lex.europa.eu/legal-content/EN/TXT/?uri=celex:52022PC0541 (Accessed: 21 June 2025)

European Commission (2023) *Zero pollution action plan.* Brussels: European Commission. Available at: https://environment.ec.europa.eu/strategy/zero-pollution-action-plan_en (Accessed: 21 June 2025)

Federal Office for the Environment (2022) *Water: In brief.* Bern: FOEN. Available at: https://www.bafu.admin.ch/bafu/en/home/topics/water/in-brief.html (Accessed: 14 January 2024).

Fitch-Roy, O., Benson, D. and Monciardini, D. (2020) 'Going around in circles? Conceptual recycling, patching and policy layering in the EU circular economy package', *Environmental Politics,* 29(6), pp. 983–1003.

Fritsch, O., Adelle, C. and Benson, D. (2017) 'The EU Water Initiative at 15: Origins, processes and assessment', *Water International,* 42(4), pp. 425–442.

Fritsch, O., Benson, D., Adelle, C. and Massot, A. (2020) 'Three faces of the European Union Water Initiative: promoting the Water Framework Directive or sustainable development?', *Water Alternatives,* 13(3), pp. 709–730.

General Secretariat of the Council (2023) *List of voluntary commitments for the Water Action Agenda to be presented by the European Union for the UN 2023 Water Conference.* Brussels: Council of the European Union. Available at: https://data.consilium.europa.eu/doc/document/ST-7443-2023-INIT/en/pdf&ved=2ahUKEwjRnNbWy4KOAxVkZmwGHcNZNe0QFnoECAkQAQ&usg=AOvVaw1SqjhfJKOLJhCOvEpQKSRf (Accessed: 21 June 2025).

Gunnarsdottir, M.J., Gardarsson, S.M. and Bartram, J. (2015) 'Developing a national framework for safe drinking water—Case study from Iceland', *International Journal of Hygiene and Environmental Health,* 218(2), pp. 196–202.

Haas, E.B. (1958) *The uniting of Europe: Political, social and economic forces, 1950–1957.* Stanford: Stanford University Press.

Haigh, N. (2003) *Manual of environmental policy: The EU and Britain.* Leeds: Maney Publishing and Institute for European Environmental Policy (IEEP).

Hartwig, L.D., Jackson, S., Markham, F. and Osborne, N. (2022) 'Water colonialism and Indigenous water justice in south-eastern Australia', *International Journal of Water Resources Development*, 38(1), pp. 30 – 63.

Hoffmann, S. 1966. 'Obstinate or obsolete? The fate of the nation-state and the case of Western Europe', *Daedalus*, 95(3), pp. 862 – 915.

Hovik, S. and Hanssen, G.S. (2016) 'Implementing the EU Water Framework Directive in Norway: Bridging the gap between water management networks and elected councils?', *Journal of Environmental Policy & Planning*, 18(4), pp. 535 – 555.

Howlett, M. and Rayner, J. (2013) 'Patching vs. packaging in policy formulation: Assessing policy portfolio design', *Politics and Governance*, 1(2), pp. 170 – 182.

India-EU Water Partnership (2023) *India-EU water partnership*. Available at: https://www.iewp.eu (Accessed: 21 December 2023).

Jordan, A. (1998) 'Private affluence and public squalor'? The Europeanisation of British coastal bathing water policy', *Policy & Politics*, 26(1), pp. 33 – 54.

Jordan, A. (1999) 'European Community water policy standards: Locked in or watered down?', *Journal of Common Market Studies*, 37(1), pp. 13 – 37.

Jordan, A. (2002) *The Europeanization of British environmental policy: A departmental perspective.* Basingstoke: Palgrave Macmillan.

Jordan, A., Wurzel, R.K.W., Zito, A.R. and Brückner, L. (2003) 'Policy innovation or "muddling through"? "New" environmental policy instruments in the United Kingdom', *Environmental Politics*, 12(1), pp. 179 – 200.

Jordan, A. and Liefferink, D. (2004) *Environmental policy in Europe: The Europeanization of national environmental policy.* London: Routledge.

Kaika, M. (2003) 'The Water Framework Directive: A new directive for a changing social, political and economic European framework', *European Planning Studies*, 11(3), pp. 299 – 316.

Kaštelan-Macan, M. et al. (2007) 'Water resources and waste water management in Bosnia and Herzegovina, Croatia and the State Union of Serbia and Montenegro', *Water Policy*, 9(3), pp. 319 – 343.

Keskinen, M., Salminen, E. and Haapala, J. (2021) 'Water diplomacy paths: An approach to recognise water diplomacy actions in shared waters', *Journal of Hydrology*, 602, 126737.

Knill, C. and Lehmkuhl, D. (2002) 'The national impact of European Union regulatory policy: Three Europeanization mechanisms', *European Journal of Political Research*, 41(2), pp. 255 – 280.

Kochskämper, E., Challies, E., Newig, J. and Jager, N.W. (2016) 'Participation for effective environmental governance? Evidence from Water Framework Directive implementation in Germany, Spain and the United Kingdom', *Journal of Environmental Management*, 181, pp. 737 – 748.

Lavenex, S. and Schimmelfennig, F. (eds.) (2013) *EU external governance: Projecting EU rules beyond membership.* London: Routledge.

Lindblom, C.E. (1979) 'Still muddling, not yet through', *Public Administration Review*, 39(6), pp. 517 – 526.

Manners, I. (2002) 'Normative power Europe: A contradiction in terms?', *Journal of Common Market Studies*, 40(2), pp. 235 – 258.

Mathur, C. and Mulwafu, W. (2018) 'Colonialism and its legacies, as reflected in water, incorporating a view from Malawi', *Wiley Interdisciplinary Reviews: Water*, 5(4), e1287.

Nagel, S. (1977) 'Proposed EEC directives: Member states balk', *Environmental Policy and Law*, 3, pp. 175 – 177.

Partzsch, L. (2008) 'EU Water Initiative—A (non-) innovative form of development cooperation', in: Scheumann, W., Neubert, S. and Kipping, M. (eds.) *Water politics and development cooperation: Local power plays and global governance.* Berlin, Heidelberg: Springer, pp. 379 – 400.

Radaelli, C.M. (2003) 'The Europeanization of public policy', in: Featherstone, K. and Radaelli, C. (eds.) *The politics of Europeanization.* Oxford: Oxford University Press, pp. 27 – 56.

Richardson, J. (1994) 'EU water policy: Uncertain agendas, shifting networks and complex coalitions', *Environmental Politics*, 3(4), pp. 139–167.
Rosamond, B. (2000) *Theories of European integration.* Basingstoke: Palgrave.
Ruiz, C.M. (2020) 'EU water diplomacy', *International Journal of Water Management and Diplomacy*, 1(1), pp. 1–9.
Schunz, S. and Topcuoglu, E. (2023) 'A European Union 'water diplomacy'? Frames of water in EU external action', *The Hague Journal of Diplomacy*, 19(2), pp. 340–375.
Sehring, J. et al. (2022) 'Diving into water diplomacy: Exploring the emergence of a concept', *Diplomatica*, 4(2), pp. 200–221.
Sultana, F. (2022) 'The unbearable heaviness of climate coloniality', *Political Geography*, 99, 102638.
Takić, L., Mladenović-Ranisavljević, I., Vasović, D. and Đorđević, L. (2017) 'The assessment of the Danube River water pollution in Serbia', *Water, Air, & Soil Pollution*, 228, pp. 1–9.
Tomalová, E. and Ullrichová, E. (2021) 'Water diplomacy: The new modus operandi of EU diplomacy? Innovative methods in diplomatic practice', *The Hague Journal of Diplomacy*, 16(4), pp. 471–492.
United Nations (2015) *Sustainable development goals.* New York: United Nations.
United Nations (2018) *The United Nations world water development report 2018: Nature-based solutions for water.* Paris: UNESCO.
United Nations (2023) *Summary of proceedings: UN 2023 Water Conference.* New York: UN General Assembly.
Weale, A. et al. (2000) *Environmental governance in Europe: An ever closer ecological union?* Oxford: Oxford University Press.
World Economic Forum (2023) *The global risks report 2023: 18th edition.* Geneva: World Economic Forum.
Wurzel, R.K.W. (2002) *Environmental policy-making in Britain, Germany and the European Union: The Europeanisation of air and water pollution control.* Manchester: Manchester University Press.
Wurzel, R.K.W., Zito, A.R. and Jordan, A. (2013) 'From government towards governance? Exploring the role of soft policy instruments', *German Policy Studies/Politikfeldanalyse*, 9(2), pp. 21–48.

Anna Broka

The waste management policy in the European Union: One framework with different local practices

Abstract: This study examines waste management policies and governance within the European Union's multilevel framework, assessing the effectiveness of policy interventions in promoting pro-environmental behavior. Through a comparative qualitative analysis of Austria, Sweden, Latvia and Spain, it explores economic measures, regulations and public engagement. Findings highlight diverse local adaptations within the common Waste Framework Directive.

Keywords: Waste Management Directive; European Union, multilevel governance; pro-environmental behavior

1 Introduction

Waste policy management has been a major topic of debate in the global (United Nations (UN)), regional (European Union (EU), Organization for Economic Co-operation and Development (OECD)) and local arenas for decades. Member State governments are under pressure to comply with the 2008 EU-level Waste Framework Directive (WsFD) (European Environment Agency, 2013) and its consolidated version.

The WsFD defines the hierarchy for waste management policies at national and local levels: prevention, preparing for reuse, recycling, energy recovery and disposal. Several important principles are included from the outset. Despite the significance of this policy and its implementation, academic research in this area remains limited and somewhat outdated. Existing literature has explored key issues, including the EU's definition of waste (Zito, 2000), priority management responses (Fischer, 2011), stakeholder participation in waste management (Weale et al., 2000; Challies et al., 2017) and the role of economic instruments (Bailey, 2003). However, contemporary challenges and developments in waste management have been largely overlooked, with greater emphasis placed on life cycle analysis.

This chapter addresses this gap by examining the current EU waste management multilevel governance framework, focusing on the needs of local governments and pro-environmental behavior (PEB).

First, the Waste Management Action Program (WMAP) was originally developed as a unique framework for cooperation and integration, aiming to coordinate efforts globally (at the UN and OECD levels) and regionally (among European Economic Community (EEC)/EU Member States and third countries). Second, it emphasized integrating environmental policy with other sectoral policies (such as social affairs and agriculture) to comprehensively address household waste management practices. Finally,

https://doi.org/10.1515/9783111321523-029

waste management issues and actions were recognized as complex problems, many of which were local challenges. Consequently, municipalities were identified as key actors in searching for solutions (European Economic Community, 1973, Chapters 1 and 7).

This chapter focuses on the intricate nature of waste management governance and the effectiveness of EU policy interventions in alignment with the principles of PEB (European Union, 2008). Evidence from EU waste management within a multilevel governance framework (see also Chapters 2 and 13) prompts an examination of how strict centralized regulations versus more flexible, locally tailored and individual behavioral approaches influence local recovery and utilization rates. Furthermore, the importance of environmental protection should not be addressed solely from a global- or macro-regional perspective; it should also incorporate locally grounded knowledge that reflects both diversity and innovation in waste management practices. Official data on municipal waste management in the EU and national fact sheets highlight the heterogeneity among countries, with pressures on economic efficiency and the evolving behaviors in reuse and recycling (Eurostat, 2024; European Environment Agency, 2023a, 2024). Our focal question is to explore how diverse local waste management policies and practices contribute to the EU multilevel governance waste management ecosystem.

This chapter employs a macro-level comparative qualitative analysis to explore local waste management and household practices related to PEB. Four EU countries —Austria, Sweden, Latvia and Spain—are selected to represent typical cases from continental, Scandinavian, eastern and southern Europe, respectively. The analysis utilizes an environmental policy framework encompassing (1) economic measures (e.g., taxes and pricing structures), (2) direct local policy regulations, (3) recycling, reuse and repair schemes and (4) public information and education campaigns (OECD, 2008).

The study makes three key contributions. First, it extensively explores the flexibility of the EU-level waste management hierarchy, including the use of economic instruments, the quality and availability of treatment facilities and the diversification of waste management initiatives. Second, this comparative data analysis offers new perspectives on a common EU framework, highlighting the convergence of local-level policies in the selected cases. Finally, it presents evidence of four distinct local-level waste management policy approaches aligning with a common WsFD framework.

2 EU waste management policy as a multilevel governance standard

The 1973 WMAP asserted that waste management issues must be addressed at the local level and involve local solutions, since most emerging problems were inherently local (European Economic Community, 1973). Today, the EU-level waste management policy follows a unique structure of multilevel governance, combining cooperation and the integration of standards, underpinned by consistent environmental protection principles. The Waste Framework Directive 2008/98/EC (European Union, 2008) is a key framework defining the EU waste hierarchy (European Union, 2018). This framework necessitates the further development of national waste strategies, setting of clear objectives in national disposal plans and implementation of accompanying actions with delineated responsibilities among various stakeholders. Since the 1990s, the evolution of European Commission rules involving directives and regulations has provided operational and managerial control over waste disposal in the EU. Most recently, the WsFD introduced new incremental targets for municipal waste reuse and recycling —up to 50 percent by 2020 and 65 percent by 2035 (European Commission, 2023). The evolution of the waste management system since the 1990s aligns with EU environmental strategies and is primarily regulated through directives on urban waste, packaging, landfills, electronic equipment, plastics and hazardous materials. A more intensive phase began in 2010 with the EU WsFD and its amendments. The latest shift is linked to the European Climate Law (European Union, 2021), which aims for climate neutrality by 2050, promoting multilevel dialogue with local authorities, businesses, investors, civil society and the public (Figure 1).

There is a clear knowledge gap about the diversity of multilevel governance policies and their interplay with national-level, case-specific and overarching EU legislation. Local practices largely shape the implementation of waste management policies, necessitating broad participation from various stakeholders. However, local politicians, concerned over potential voter backlash, frequently undermine EU-level waste management policies due to pressures from local businesses and other actors (see also Chapter 34).

One example highlights this challenge in the implementation of municipal waste treatment in accordance with the WsFD and Landfill Directives. Mature welfare states such as Austria, Belgium, Germany, Finland, Luxembourg, the Netherlands, Sweden and the United Kingdom have demonstrated robust waste management practices, consistently performing above average across various criteria. The second group of countries—Spain, Hungary, Ireland, Portugal and Slovenia—exhibits a moderate deficit, performing below average across several dimensions. Finally, countries such as Bulgaria, Cyprus, Estonia, Greece, Italy, Lithuania, Malta, Poland and Slovakia face the most significant implementation gaps and severe deficits across most criteria, including waste-prevention policies. Simultaneously, ensuring sufficient capacity for waste generation, recycling and treatment and adherence to nonhazardous landfill quality standards, form significant challenges for many countries (BiPRO, 2012).

More recent analysis (Castillo-Giménez, Montañés and Picazo-Tadeo, 2019) of the EU-28 countries identifies Denmark, Austria, the Netherlands, Luxembourg, Germany and France as the top municipal waste management performers. Conversely, Central and Eastern European (CEE) countries Bulgaria, Hungary, Estonia, Slovenia, Latvia, the Czech Republic, Poland and Romania and southern EU countries such as Cyprus and Greece rank among the poorest performers. Better performance is observed in coun-

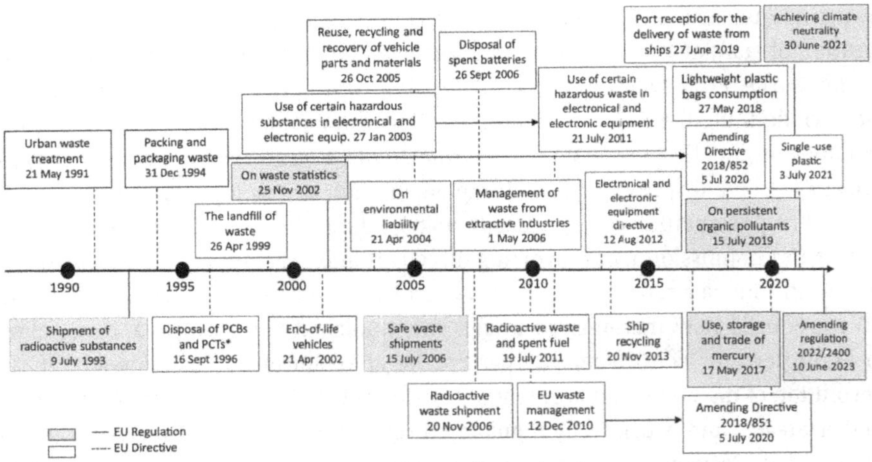

Figure 1: Timeline of key EU regulations and directives related to waste management from 1991 to 2023. Source: Author's own analysis based on a review of European Union laws and regulations on the waste management system, using data from EUR-Lex (European Union, n.d.). *Disposal of polychlorinated biphenyls (PCBs) and polychlorinated terphenyls (PCTs).

tries such as Sweden, Italy and Slovenia, which manage larger quantities of waste per capita primarily through recycling, composting and digestion activities. In contrast, most Eastern European countries, along with Greece and Malta, handle smaller amounts of waste, predominantly relying on landfilling. These CEE countries are also among the most heavily penalized when assessing municipal waste management scenarios, particularly in terms of the quantities of waste per capita processed through each of the four treatment options. Overall, it is noteworthy that most European citizens reside in countries demonstrating medium-to-low performance levels in municipal waste treatment.

Local authorities often experience pressure from higher governmental authorities and the media, leading them to seek alternative solutions that deviate from established practices. This occurs despite EU waste management policies assigning significant responsibilities to local governments for managing municipal waste (Andersson and Stage, 2018; Botelho, 2012; Alacevich, Bonev and Söderberg, 2021).

Between 2014 and 2020, seventeen EU Member States[1] utilized EUR 4.9 billion in funding allocated for household waste management projects, which included initiatives such as waste minimization and various treatment methods, including biological, thermal, incineration and landfill treatment. In 2017, an additional EUR 5.9 billion in funding became available to support total investments in household waste management. However, eleven Member States did not incorporate this funding into their pol-

1 Belgium, Bulgaria, Cyprus, Czech Republic, Spain, France, Croatia, Hungary, Italy, Lithuania, Latvia, Malta, Poland, Romania, Slovakia.

icy planning. Although overall resources were almost evenly divided between preventive measures (46 percent) and treatment measures (54 percent), the allocation varied across countries. For example, countries such as Belgium, Bulgaria and Slovakia prioritized preventive measures, dedicating over 50 percent of their resources to these initiatives. In contrast, countries including Cyprus, France and Romania placed greater emphasis on waste treatment measures (European Commission, 2019).

The most recent scholarly research demonstrates the positive impact of EU legislation on policy convergence, although considerable variation in performance still exists among the EU-27 countries (Ríos and Picazo-Tadeo, 2021; Callao, Latorre and Martinez-Nuñez, 2021; Callao, Martínez-Nuñez and Latorre, 2019; Castillo-Giménez, Montañés and Picazo-Tadeo, 2019; Kong, Phillips and Sul, 2019, etc.). At the national level, the definition of household waste varies across countries, which complicates policy implementation, underscoring the multilevel governance complexities. Consumer behavior, the scope and quality of recycling activities and the promotion of sustainable consumption and production practices significantly influence the effectiveness of governmental policies aimed at reducing or minimizing household waste (Berglund, 2005; Minelgaitė and Liobikienė, 2019).

Waste-prevention programs have been in place for more than a decade (since December 2013, under Article 29 of the WsFD), but waste treatment remains the predominant municipal waste management approach. The local components of reducing, reusing and recycling are still limited in PEB behavior practices at the individual level. Consequently, broader societal and economic changes driving shifts in attitudes, behavior, social norms, policies and regulations require more responsive institutional structures to support PEB behavior practices. Technological advancements and improved value chains can further these changes (Peura, Voutilainen and Kantola, 2022; Savastano, Belcastro and Dentale, 2019). Closer examination of national systems reveals that some countries are able to take their own initiative and push EU policies forward while others rely on EU-level efforts made to advance local environmental policies (Zito, 2000).

Analyzing local waste management policy practices at the household level provides insights into the distributional effects, including who bears the costs and how shared responsibility is implemented in practice. Although the EU exerts political pressure, the effectiveness of national and local waste reduction and minimization efforts largely depends on consumer behavior. Consequently, recycling activities, consumer practices and the promotion of sustainable consumption and production are essential components of a cohesive, multilevel waste management system (Berglund, 2005; Minelgaitė and Liobikienė, 2019). The complexities of multilevel governance raise concerns regarding the integration of local waste management practices and PEB behavior into broader democratic processes and societal values, particularly when such practices are not yet established.

3 Data

This case study examines EU waste management practices, focusing on waste prevention and generation systems at both the municipal and household levels. The policy document analysis incorporates strategies such as nudging, labeling and various informational campaigns. Of particular significance is the direct link between PEB behavior and preventive waste policy measures, which warrants further clarification.

The analytical framework includes two key dimensions of waste management policy: (1) the *waste-prevention system*, extending from the national to the municipal level and (2) *household-level waste-prevention behavior*. The comparative dataset on waste management in the EU-27, based on Eurostat data from 2014 and updated thereafter, includes national expenditures on environmental protection, reflecting the resources allocated to safeguarding the natural environment. Notably, the analysis also incorporates domestic material consumption (DMC), which reveals considerable variation among EU-27 Member States. These differences in material categories stem from disparities in sectors such as industry, construction, transportation and other major economic activities. DMC's complex composition and distribution are closely linked to PEB and consumption-related household behaviors. Municipal waste accounts for approximately 10 percent of the total waste generated within the EU. Variations in municipal waste generation and treatment can be attributed to differences in consumption patterns, economic wealth and the methodologies employed in municipal waste collection and management. The Classification of Individual Consumption by Purpose, expressed in purchasing power standards, encompasses categories such as food and beverages, clothing and footwear, housing, water, electricity and fuels, furnishings, household maintenance, health, transport, education, communication, leisure, cultural activities and miscellaneous goods and services. Household-generated waste is defined as any substance or object discarded by a household, in accordance with the Waste Framework Directive (WsFD) treatment types. This is reported at the local household level and weighted per capita. Prevention measures include recycling operations and municipal waste that is prepared for reuse (See Table 2 in the Appendix at the end of the chapter.). This data analysis, which focuses on municipal waste-prevention management strategies and household prevention behaviors, highlights systemic differences among EU countries. Additionally, a document analysis of policy planning and legislation, along with a content analysis of policies in four case countries—Austria, Latvia, Sweden and Spain—was conducted.

4 Municipal waste-prevention systems and household waste performance

Since 2014, household-level waste generation has shown an increasing trend in most EU countries. However, Belgium, Bulgaria, Greece, Italy, Latvia and Luxembourg reveal a decreasing trend (Eurostat, 2023). Figure 2 maps out the different performances in four different clusters in terms of performance of municipal-level waste management versus household waste behavior. A Cluster (1) comprising mature EU welfare states (Austria, Denmark, Cyprus, Finland, Germany, Greece, Luxemburg, Malta, Portugal and Sweden), with well-established waste-prevention management systems operating across EU, national and local levels, is identifiable in the bottom left-hand quarter of Figure 2. Significant government and nonprofit institutional expenditure on environmental protection serving households, low municipal waste generation with high rates of treatment, low DMC per capita and high recycling rates for packaging waste characterize these systems. On the household-level waste-prevention behavior dimension, these countries perform well. They demonstrate lower household consumption expenditure, low levels of household waste generation and strong municipal waste recycling performance. These indicators highlight the effectiveness of EU multilevel integrated waste-prevention and management approaches.

Figure 2 reveals in the bottom right quarter a Cluster (2) consisting of countries (Estonia, Latvia, Hungary, Romania, Spain and Ireland) that exhibit relatively strong performance in municipal level waste management systems but perform less effectively at the household level compared to Cluster 1. Furthermore, only a few have established operational systems for preparing waste for reuse. These countries represent well-performing regulated waste management systems at the municipal (local) level, but their flexibility in involving different stakeholders at the household level often results in low PEB in household waste-prevention systems.

In the top left corner of Figure 2, Cluster 3 encompasses countries (Belgium, Italy, France, the Netherlands, Czech Republic and Lithuania) that demonstrate lower performance in waste-prevention management systems at the municipal level but relatively strong performance in PEB systems at the household level. While the municipal-level waste-prevention management systems are relatively flexible, they are less effective compared to those in Clusters 1 and 2. However, the household-level PEB systems in these countries deliver good results, showcasing strengths in well-established and functioning household waste operation systems. Information campaigns, labeling initiatives and other promotional efforts that effectively influence behavioral change may further support this success.

Finally, Cluster 4 in the top right corner of Figure 2 encompasses the remaining CEE EU countries (Bulgaria, Hungary, Poland, Slovakia and Slovenia), which exhibit lower waste management performance. While these systems may be relatively flexible compared to those in Clusters 1 and 2, their effectiveness is limited. Additionally, these countries demonstrate low performance in PEB *waste-prevention systems* at the household level. This analysis confirms that the CEE EU group employs diverse waste management and household PEB waste-prevention strategies. At the household level, PEB policy strategies lack sufficient actions to drive substantive progress both for those older and new EU countries. Notably, despite being wealthier, EU nations with a longstanding history of developed EU- and national-level regulated waste management systems, these countries demonstrate comparatively weaker systemic perfor-

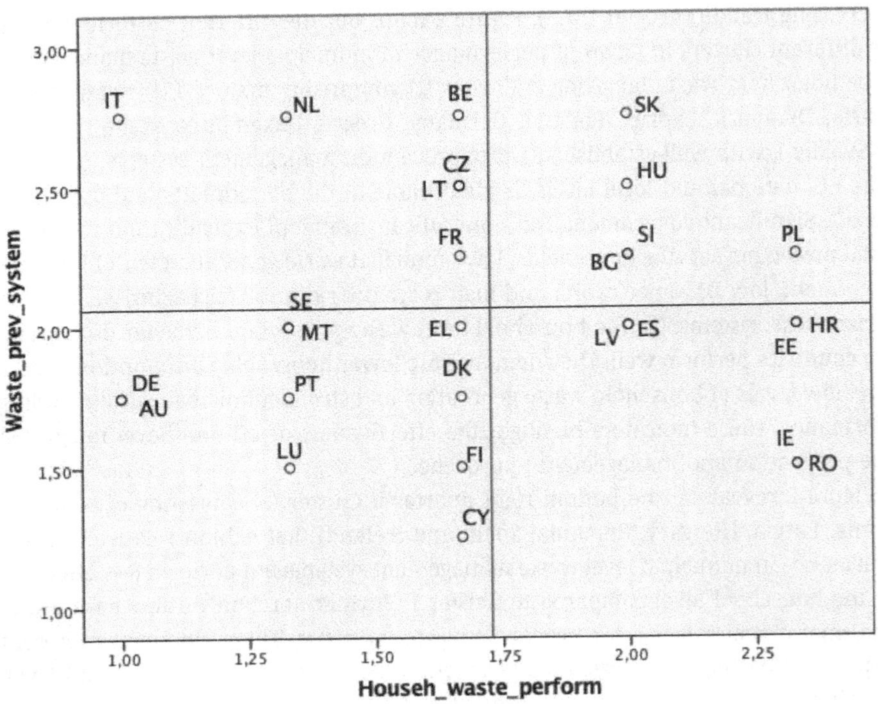

Figure 2: Performance of municipal level waste-prevention management versus household waste behavior. Source: Author's own compilation based on Eurostat data (see online for Table 1).

mance at the municipal and household levels, although they may perform well at the national level.

Case analysis

Austria is a strong performer in both *regulated waste-prevention management systems* and household waste-prevention behavior. Although Austria's expenditure on environmental protection as a percentage of GDP is the highest among EU countries at 3.3 percent, only 0.5 percent is attributed to household-level environmental protection. This analysis suggests that Austria's waste management system is primarily coordinated through a centralized approach that states that waste prevention is a top priority. Austria's shift from landfill dependency to highly efficient recycling practices has led to consistently strong performance since 1989, supported by the Contaminated Sites Remediation Act (*Altlastensanierungsgesetz*) and the Waste Management Act (*Abfallwirtschaftsgesetz*), along with regulations implemented at the federal state level (Federal Ministry—Republic of Austria, n.d.; Bundeskanzleramt der Republik Österreich, 2025a; Bundeskanzleramt der Republik Österreich, 2025b). Austria's waste and resource management policies align with the EU Circular Economy (2018) principles and WsFD, encompassing waste collection and management. Responsibility for municipal waste is shared among provincial (state) governments (*Bundesländer*) in nine regions, leading to variations in waste treatment and prevention performance. The responsibilities include strategic planning and regulation of regional management plans according to the Waste Management Act, coordination of waste treatment facilities, environmental monitoring and compliance and hazardous waste management (Government of Austria, n.d.; European Environment Agency, 2023b).

The collection of waste is regulated by the individual or waste management laws. The organization of the collection of municipal waste is the responsibility of the individual municipalities (*Gemeinden*) or municipal associations handling household waste collection and local waste services. The information on how waste collection is organized, what requirements are obligated i.e., waste separation and the costings on municipal level. The main duties are to organize household waste collection, including separate collection of recyclable materials such as paper, glass, plastic and organic waste, organization of local recycling centers and organization of public awareness and education campaigns and setting and managing waste collection fees to finance local waste services (European Environment Agency, 2023b; Federal Ministry—Republic of Austria, n.d.).

Austria boasts the highest recycling rate for municipal waste (58.7%) among EU Member States. At the household level, citizens are required to sort and dispose of waste according to municipal or waste management association guidelines. The Austrian Waste Prevention and Recovery Strategy (2006–2011) and Waste Prevention Program 2023 (WPP) is a framework to foster public engagement, promoting practices such as household composting and providing guidelines for hiring, repairing and reselling products. The fields of action are construction, plastic and packaging, food, textiles, reuse and repair, households, businesses and organizations. WPP clearly defines the continuity to implement the prevention measures, i.e., promotion of sustainable consumption models, manufacturing and use of resource-efficient, durable, reparable and reusable products, prevention of critical raw materials waste, encouragement of repair and reuse activities on different levels, reduction of waste generation, including food waste. National regulations obligate households to adopt responsible practices, supported by well-established local structures and public initiatives. For instance, since 2013, the initiative Food is Precious! by the Federal Ministry for Climate Action, Environment, Energy, Mobility, Innovation and Technology, in close cooperation with businesses, federal states, municipalities, municipal waste management associations, employees, consumers and social institutions, exemplifies a formal organizational framework that is hierarchically structured and aligned with the EU WsFD. In this framework, the state plays a significant role in ensuring compliance through robust institutional multilevel governance mechanisms (European Environment Agency, 2023b; see more in appendix Table 1).

Sweden also performs well, with national waste management actions dating back to the 1998 Environmental Code. Local waste management plans must include regulations defining the handling of municipal waste (Riksdagsförvaltningen, 1998). Sweden has a National Waste Management Plan and Waste Prevention Program for the period 2018–2023. Under this framework, all 290 municipalities are required to develop local waste management plans, with some municipalities collaborating to create regional waste management plans (European Environment Agency, 2022a).

Two important municipal policy instruments for waste management include: the tariff schedule for waste management and special systems for the separate collection of food waste. It means that the municipal waste management fee covers costs related to containers, collection, transport, treatment, recycling centers, information, planning and administration. This fee structure incentivizes waste reduction and proper sorting by households. For the food separation, municipalities provide infrastructure and services to facilitate the segregation of food waste from other household waste, promoting its treatment through anaerobic digestion or composting. This initiative aligns with national environmental goals and contributes to sustainable waste management practices (Avfall Sverige, 2023).

Both the direct and indirect effects of waste management policies are important to consider. Municipalities are responsible for waste management and prevention, aligning their actions with national objectives, strategies and policies. Even for measures beyond their direct responsibility, municipalities must integrate relevant objectives and actions into their plans, monitored through local or regional waste plans (European Environment Agency, 2022a). A 'pay-as-you-throw' system, where residents are charged based on the waste they dispose of, has positively impacted recycling and PEB. Some municipalities use weight-based tariff systems, where residents pay per kilogram of waste (e.g., forty municipalities in 2014, decreasing to thirty-three by 2019), with separate fees for biowaste. Additionally, the introduction of weight-based tariffs has been associated with increased recycling rates, as residents are incentivized to sort their waste to reduce disposal costs (Andersson and Stage, 2018; Dahlén and Lagerkvist, 2010; European Environment Agency, 2022a). However, this system remains weaker than volume-based schemes because the economic incentives are less visible. Food waste collection is widely available, with door-to-door services covering up to 85 percent of households, including high-rise buildings. Economic incentives often focus on container volume and collection frequency fees (European Environment Agency, 2022a). Variations in waste collection systems across municipalities reflect the freedom municipalities have in implementing their systems. Waste fees are structured to encourage recycling, with municipalities legally required to provide services at cost-recovery prices. Most waste production is managed by those responsible for generating it, supported by extended producer responsibility schemes, including a mandatory deposit-return system for plastic beverage bottles and metal cans (Avfal Sverige, 2023; Appendix Table 1).

Municipal waste policies play a vital role in helping Swedish households move up the waste management hierarchy. However, the impact of the measures under the 2013 waste-prevention program cannot be fully observed through municipal solid waste statistics alone. Waste generation correlates closely with household expenditure and consumption patterns, and Sweden's per capita household expenditure has risen annually since 2012. This has resulted in a slight decoupling effect, where waste generation outpaces household PEB improvements. Sweden's waste-prevention goals are integrated into broader environmental quality objectives, targeting private enterprises, public organizations and consumers. Policies promote sustainable consumption, production and efficient raw material use. Measures include reduced Value Added Tax for repairing household appliances, bicycles, textiles and information and communications technology, alongside government support for collection facilities and recycling centers to encourage reuse. Initiatives like food donation, eco-design and public information campaigns aim to prevent waste and reduce littering. Households are legally required to sort waste (Avfall Sverige, 2023; see Appendix Table 1). Sweden exemplifies *a regulated waste-prevention system* with a strong collective national commitment to environmental protection, emphasizing producer responsibility, mandatory waste sorting and flexible waste operation choices.

Latvia has developed strongly performing waste-prevention management systems at the municipal level since the 1990s. The most recent national Waste Management Plan for 2021–2028 prioritizes waste prevention for the first time, aligning with the EU WsFD (Cabinet of Ministers, 2021). Latvia's regulatory framework consists of the Waste Management Law (Saeima, 2010, last amended in 2020) sets targets for Municipal Solid Waste recycling and outlines the responsibilities of the Ministry of Environmental Protection and Regional development, the municipalities and waste management companies (European Environment Agency, 2022b). The plan targets all sectors, including the public, industry and households. However, it does not include specific government measures to promote resource-efficient, durable, reparable, or reusable practices, relying heavily instead on local-level capacity.

For instance, reuse activities introduced in 2020 remain limited and depend purely on consumer-related actions such as donations and the repair of textiles and shoes. The separation of biowaste, which constitutes nearly half of municipal waste, has been mandatory only since 2021, and until 2022 this was a voluntary initiative for producers and remains voluntary for households, reflecting highly flexible choices. Provided measures include the prevention of packaging waste and the introduction of a deposit system for beverage packaging in the national territory (from 2022). Food disposal activities are strictly regulated, while taxation is the primary instrument used to reduce municipal waste disposal. Latvia's municipal waste management system can be characterized as relatively regulated but highly individualized and flexible at the household level (European Environment Agency, 2022b). The strong focus on waste treatment rather than waste prevention, unlike wealthier countries hinders the country's waste management system. A lack of hierarchical clarity and collective waste management traditions affects the weak national and municipal level performance. Recent reforms have divided municipal administrative territories into household regional waste management zones (Cabinet of Ministers, 2023). However, as early as 2016, the absence of a strategic framework for green infrastructure policy development and a lack of awareness at the municipal level were identified as barriers to public participation (OECD, 2019). Waste collection is managed by private companies or municipalities, operating alongside packaging and hazardous waste collection schemes, which vary by municipality. Insufficient recycling performance can be attributed to shortcomings in existing separate collection systems. The European Environment Agency (2022a) report indicates that Latvia's municipal waste generation per capita increased from 410 kg/person in 2016 to 478 kg/person in 2020. Despite this increase, the country continues to rely heavily on landfilling, suggesting that improvements in separate collection systems are necessary to enhance recycling rates. Latvia exemplifies a relatively well-regulated municipal waste management system that is still transitioning toward a waste-prevention model. However, overly flexible household-level waste management options result in low PEB performance (Melece, Brizga and Ernšgteins, 2018) (see Appendix Table 1).

Spain operates with shared responsibilities between regional and national authorities. Regional waste plans are divided among autonomous regions, while municipalities conduct local-level waste management. A volume-based tariff system predominates, supplemented by a collection point system for mixed waste, glass, paper and other packaging materials. Subscriptions are available for the separate collection of biowaste, and in some regions, biowaste is prioritized over packaging, with composting options available following presorting (European Environment Agency, 2023c).

Civic amenity sites collect recyclables, including plastics, metals, garden and wood waste, construction and demolition waste and items for reuse or preparation, such as clothing, furniture, lumber, electrical and electronic waste and hazardous waste. Flexible and individual eco-social innovations are accelerating recycling efforts. The State Program for Waste Prevention (2014–2020) was Spain's first national-level program, assigning responsibility to producers, distribution and service sectors, consumers, end users and public administration. Specific measures include education and awareness campaigns, product reuse and repair and the promotion of secondhand shops for furniture, toys and books (European Environment Agency, 2023c). In Spain, waste management practices vary across municipalities, with some opting to collect biowaste separately from packaging waste. This approach often involves presorting, where residents separate organic waste from other materials before collection. The separated biowaste is then directed to composting facilities, facilitating the production of compost for agricultural use. For instance, the Waste Agency of Catalonia (*Agència de Residus de Catalunya*) has been at the forefront of biowaste management since 1993, mandating biowaste separation in municipalities with over 5,000 inhabitants. Later, 'Law 9/2008, of 10 July', amending 'Law 6/1993 of 15 July', extended this requirement to all towns and villages across Catalonia. At the regional level, the Waste Agency of Catalonia plays a central role in supervising, promoting and improving biowaste collection across the region (Jourdan and Favoino, 2024).

Thus, in Spain environmental attitudes are positively associated with five reported waste-related behaviors: buying minimally packaged products, using reusable packaging and separating glass, plastic and paper. Demographics (e.g., gender, race, socioeconomic status) and cultural participation are also indicative factors in influencing behavior. The three Rs of sustainability—reduce, reuse and recycle—are frequently observed at the individual behavior scale (Escario, Rodríguez-Sánchez and Casaló, 2020; Minelgaitė and Liobikienė, 2019; Crociata and Mattoscio, 2016, see Appendix Table 1).

Spain shares similarities with Latvia in adopting a relatively flexible approach that does not perform strongly on household prevention behavior. At the waste management level, waste treatment remains the dominant strategy and Spain is transitioning to a comprehensive preventive waste management system at the local level. This system is regulated by regional (autonomous) rules, civic amenity sites and bottom-up eco-social cooperative systems, with relatively high waste collection costs (since 1985). The system involves multiple actors and flexible household-level actions.

5 Conclusion

The analysis of waste management performance across EU countries highlights distinct clusters with varying effectiveness at municipal and household levels. While some nations, such as those in Cluster 1, exemplify well-established, multilevel waste-prevention systems with strong household engagement, others, like those in Cluster 4, continue to struggle with both municipal and household waste-prevention efforts. The findings suggest that highly regulated waste management frameworks, combined with policies promoting household pro-environmental behavior, contribute to more effective waste prevention. However, flexibility in municipal systems does not always translate into strong household-level engagement, as seen in Clusters 2 and 3. This underscores the need for integrated strategies that bridge municipal-level waste management with household behavioral incentives to enhance overall waste prevention and recycling performance across the EU.

Austria and Sweden exemplify strong, well-regulated waste-prevention systems, integrating municipal and household-level strategies with national policies. Austria's centralized approach and emphasis on recycling have resulted in high performance, while Sweden's municipal-level flexibility and financial incentives encourage household waste reduction. Latvia, despite a well-regulated municipal system, faces challenges due to flexible household waste management policies and limited prevention measures. Spain's decentralized approach allows regional variations, with initiatives promoting recycling and reuse. These cases highlight the importance of multilevel governance, public engagement and economic incentives in achieving effective waste prevention and management.

This case study illustrates a strong commitment to the EU's multilevel governance in the waste management policies in Austria and Sweden, while also highlighting the persistence of distinct national and local collective interests. At the individual level, there is a tension between environmental responsibilities and personal freedom, as reflected in Swedish environmental policy and legislation. Environmental norms in both countries are clearly articulated in official policy documents, which assert that environmentally preferable behaviors and even lifestyles should take precedence over individual preferences, placing collective needs above individual ones.

However, the analysis suggests that the potential conflict between environmental obligations and the pursuit of individual life projects is largely mitigated in wealthier countries by framing environmental responsibility within the context of consumer behavior in economic markets. More efforts are needed to promote PEB behavior in wealthier nations, as consumer responsibility, recycling and reuse still lag. This contrasts with countries like Latvia and Spain, where environmental responsibility is not as deeply embedded in the roles of citizens within the democratic framework and collective responsibility within the local preventive waste management system. The results do not contradict the previously mentioned analysis but rather specifically address municipal waste management and household-level PEB, which is the focus of this chapter.

Funding details: This work was supported by the Latvian Council of Sciences, project 'Nudging for behavioral change to improve households' waste management' project No. lzp-2020/1–0303.

References

Alacevich, C., Bonev, P. and Söderberg, M. (2021) 'Pro-environmental interventions and behavioural spillovers: Evidence from organic waste sorting in Sweden', *Journal of Environmental Economics and Management*, 108, 102470.

Andersson, C. and Stage, J. (2018) 'Direct and indirect effects of waste management policies on household waste behaviour: The case of Sweden', *Waste Management, Working Paper No. 148.* Stockholm: The National Institute of Economic Research (NIER).

Avfall Sverige [Swedish Waste Management Association] (2023) *Swedish Waste Management.* Available at: https://www.avfallsverige.se/in-english/ (Accessed: 22 November 2024).

Bailey, I. (2003) *New environmental policy instruments in the European Union: Politics, economics, and the implementation of the Packaging Waste Directive.* Farnham: Ashgate Publishing.

Berglund, C. (2005) 'Economic efficiency issues with respect to recycling behaviour and waste management policy', *International Journal of Sustainable Development.* Available at: https://doi.org/10.1504/IJSD.2005.008892

BiPRO (2012) *Screening of waste management performance of EU Member States.* Report prepared for the European Commission, DG Environment, July 2012. Available at: https://ec.europa.eu/environment/pdf/waste/studies/Screening_report.pdf (Accessed: 2 February 2022).

Botelho, A. (2012) 'The impact of education and training on compliance behaviour and waste generation in European private healthcare facilities', *Journal of Environmental Management*, 98, pp. 5–10.

Bundeskanzleramt der Republik Österreich (2025a) *Bundesrecht konsolidiert: Gesamte Rechtsvorschrift für Abfallwirtschaftsgesetz 2002 [Waste Management Act 2002].* Available at: https://www.ris.bka.gv.at/GeltendeFassung.wxe?Abfrage=Bundesnormen&Gesetzesnummer=20002086 (Accessed: 20 February 2023).

Bundeskanzleramt der Republik Österreich (2025b) *Bundesrecht konsolidiert: Gesamte Rechtsvorschrift für Deponieverordnung 2008 [Landfill Ordinance 2008].* Available at: https://www.ris.bka.gv.at/GeltendeFassung.wxe?Abfrage=Bundesnormen&Gesetzesnummer=20005653 (Accessed: 10 June 2022).

Cabinet of Ministers (2021) *Ministru kabineta 2021. gada 22. janvāra rīkojums Nr. 45 'Par Atkritumu apsaimniekošanas valsts plānu 2021.–2028. gadam'*. Available at: https://likumi.lv/ta/id/320476 (Accessed: 21 February 2025).

Cabinet of Ministers (2023) *Noteikumi par atkritumu apsaimniekošanas reģioniem.* Regulations No. 301, 13 June 2023. Available at: https://likumi.lv/ta/id/342688 (Accessed: 21 February 2025).

Callao, C., Latorre, M.P. and Martinez-Nuñez, M. (2021) 'Understanding hazardous waste exports for disposal in Europe: A contribution to sustainable development', *Sustainability*, 13(16), 8905.

Callao, C., Martínez-Nuñez, M. and Latorre, P. (2019) 'European countries: Does common legislation guarantee better hazardous waste performance for European Union member states?', *Waste Management*, 84, pp. 147 – 157.

Castillo-Giménez, J., Montañés, A. and Picazo-Tadeo, A.J. (2019) 'Performance in the treatment of municipal waste: Are European Union member states so different?', *Science of the Total Environment*, 687, pp. 1305 – 1314.

Challies, E., Newig, J., Kochskämper, E. and Jager, N.W. (2017) 'Governance change and governance learning in Europe: Stakeholder participation in environmental policy implementation', *Policy and Society*, 36(2), pp. 288 – 303.

Crociata, A. and Mattoscio, N. (2016). 'Output-oriented data envelopment analysis for measuring recycling efficiency: An application at the Italian regional level', *Environmental Education Research*, 22(4), pp. 551 – 570.

Dahlén, L. and Lagerkvist, A. (2010) 'Pay as you throw: Strengths and weaknesses of weight-based billing in household waste collection systems in Sweden', *Waste Management*, 30(1), pp. 23 – 31.

European Commission (2019) *Study on investment needs in the waste sector and on the financing of municipal waste management in Member States.* Available at: https://data.europa.eu/doi/10.2779/769124; https://op.europa.eu/en/publication-detail/-/publication/4d5f8355-bcad-11e9-9d01-01aa75ed71a1 (Accessed: 23 January 2025).

European Commission (2023) 'Proposal for a targeted revision of the Waste Framework Directive'. Available at: https://environment.ec.europa.eu/publications/proposal-targeted-revision-waste-framework-directive_en (Accessed: 1 March 2024).

European Economic Community (1973) *Declaration of the Council of the European Communities and of the Representatives of the Governments of the Member States meeting in the Council of 22 November 1973 on the Programme of Action of the European Communities on the Environment.* Official Journal of the European Communities, No. C 112/1. Available at: https://eur-lex.europa.eu/legal-content/EN/TXT/PDF/?uri=CELEX:41973X1220 (Accessed: 21 February 2025).

European Environment Agency (2013) *Towards a green economy in Europe: EU environmental policy targets and objectives 2010 – 2050.* Report 8/2013. Copenhagen: European Environment Agency.

European Environment Agency (2022a) *Early warning assessment related to the 2025 targets for municipal waste and packaging waste. Country profile. Sweden.* Available at: https://www.eea.europa.eu/publications/many-eu-member-states/early-warning-assessment-related-to (Accessed: 2 November 2024).

European Environment Agency (2022b) *Early warning assessment related to the 2025 targets for municipal waste and packaging waste. Country profile. Latvia.* Available at: https://www.eea.europa.eu/publications/many-eu-member-states/latvia (Accessed: 31 June 2023).

European Environment Agency (2023a) *2023 waste prevention country fact sheets.* Available at: https://www.eea.europa.eu/themes/waste/waste-prevention/countries/2023-waste-prevention-country-fact-sheets (Accessed: 2 November 2024).

European Environment Agency (2023b) *Waste prevention country profile. Austria.* Available at: https://www.eea.europa.eu/themes/waste/waste-prevention/countries/2023-waste-prevention-country-fact-sheets/austria_waste_prevention_2023/view (Accessed: 21 March 2024).

European Environment Agency (2023c) *Waste prevention country profile. Spain.* https://www.eea.europa.eu/themes/waste/waste-prevention/countries/2023-waste-prevention-country-fact-sheets/spain_waste_prevention_2023/view (Accessed: 21 March 2024).

European Environment Agency (2024) *Country reports and fact sheets.* Available at: https://www.eea.europa.eu/publications/municipal-waste-management-across-european-countries/copy_of_municipal-waste-management-across-european-countries (Accessed: 2 November 2024).

European Union (2008) 'Directive 2008/98/EC of the European Parliament and of the Council of 19 November 2008 on waste and repealing certain directives,' L 312/3. Available at: https://eur-lex.europa.eu/legal-content/EN/TXT/?uri=CELEX:32008L0098 (Accessed: 2 November 2022).

European Union (2018) 'Directive (EU) 2018/851 of the European Parliament and of the Council of 30 May 2018 amending Directive 2008/98/EC on waste', L 150/109. Available at: https://eur-lex.europa.eu/legal-content/EN/TXT/?uri=celex%3A32018L0851 (Accessed: 21 February 2025).

European Union (2021) 'Regulation (EU) 2021/1119 of the European Parliament and of the Council of 30 June 2021 establishing the framework for achieving climate neutrality and amending Regulations (EC) No 401/2009 and (EU) 2018/1999 ('European Climate Law')', Available at: https://eur-lex.europa.eu/legal-content/EN/TXT/?uri=celex%3A32021R1119) (Accessed: 12 February 2025).

European Union (n.d) *Environment and climate change.* Available at: https://eur-lex.europa.eu/summary/chapter/20.html (accessed: 28 December 2024).

Eurostat (2024) *Municipal waste by waste management operations.* Available at: https://doi.org/10.2908/ENV_WASMUN (Accessed: 1 February 2024).

European Union (2023) *EU's domestic material consumption remained stable in 2022.* Available at: https://ec.europa.eu/eurostat/web/products-eurostat-news/w/ddn-20230731-1 (Accessed: 31 June 2023).

Escario, J.-J., Rodríguez-Sánchez, C. and Casaló, L.V. (2020) 'The influence of environmental attitudes and perceived effectiveness on recycling, reducing, and reusing packaging materials in Spain', *Waste Management*, 113, pp. 251–260.

Federal Ministry—Republic of Austria (n.d.) *History and principles.* Available at: https://www.bmk.gv.at/en/topics/climate-environment/waste-resource-management/hap.html (Accessed: 20 December 2024).

Fischer, C. (2011) 'The development and achievements of EU waste policy', *Journal of Material Cycles and Waste Management*, 13, pp. 2–9.

Government of Austria (n.d.) *Waste.* Available at: https://www.oesterreich.gv.at/en/themen/bauen_und_wohnen/abfall.html (Accessed: 10 April 2024).

Jourdan, M. and Favoino, E. (2024) *LIFE BIOBEST D3.4 – Factsheets on the analysis of best practices in communications and engagement.* Available at: https://zerowasteeurope.eu/wp-content/uploads/2024/06/LIFE-BIOBEST-Country-Factsheets-Waste-Agency-of-Catalonia.pdf?utm (Accessed: 20 February 2025).

Kong, J., Phillips, P.C.B. and Sul, D. (2019) 'Weak convergence: Theory and application', *Journal of Econometrics*, 209(2), pp. 185–207.

Lundmark, C., Matti, S. and Michanek, G. (2010) 'The Swedish environmental norm: Balancing environmental obligations and the pursuit of individual lifestyles', in: Soderhölm, P. (ed.) *Environmental policy and household behaviour: Sustainability and everyday life.* London: Routledge, pp. 175–192.

Melece, L., Brizga, J. and Ernšgteins, R. (2018) 'Municipal waste management issues', *Conference paper: 17th International Scientific Conference Engineering for Rural Development*, Jelgava. Available at: DOI: 10.22616/ERDev2018.17.N474.

Minelgaitė, A. and Liobikienė, G. (2019) 'Waste problem in the European Union and its influence on waste management behaviours', *Science of the Total Environment*, 667, pp. 86–93.

OECD (2008) *Environmental policy frameworks: A review of OECD work.* Organization for Economic Co-operation and Development. Available at: https://doi.org/10.1787/9789264041234-en (Accessed: 1 February 2022).

OECD (2019) *OECD environmental performance reviews: Latvia 2019.* Organization for Economic Co-operation and Development. Available at: https://www.oecd.org/environment/country-reviews/OECD-Environmental-Performance-Reviews-Latvia-2019-9789264312551-en.htm (Accessed: 10 March 2022).

Peura, P., Voutilainen, O. and Kantola, J. (2022) 'From garbage to product and service systems: A longitudinal Finnish case', *Waste Management*, 140, pp. 143–153.

Riksdagsförvaltningen (1998) *Miljöbalken (1998:808), 15 kap. 41 §.* Stockholm: Sveriges Riksdag. Available at: https://www.riksdagen.se/sv/dokument-och-lagar/dokument/svensk-forfattningssamling/miljobalk-1998808_sfs-1998-808/ (Accessed: 2 April 2022).

Ríos, A. and Picazo-Tadeo, A.J. (2021) 'Measuring environmental performance in the treatment of municipal solid waste: The case of the European Union-28', *Ecological Indicators*, 123, 107328.

Saeima (2010) *The Waste management law.* Available at: https://likumi.lv/ta/en/en/id/221378-waste-management-law (Accessed: 21 February 2025).

Savastano, M., Belcastro, M. and Dentale, F. (2019) 'The role of waste collection centres in a circular economy scenario: An empirical study of citizens' perception', *Environmental Engineering & Management Journal*, 18(10), pp. 2181–2192.

Weale, A., Pridham, G., Cini, M., Konstadakopulos, D., Porter, M. and Flynn, B.. (2002) *Environmental governance in Europe: An ever closer ecological union?* Oxford: Oxford University Press.

Zito, A. (2000) *Creating environmental policy in the European Union.* Houndmills, Basingstoke: Macmillan Press.

Appendix

Table 1: Local waste management ecosystems.

	Sweden	Austria	Latvia	Spain
A volume-based tariff system (mostly)	The municipalities are responsible for the collection and treatment of municipal waste as well as for monitoring waste streams and reporting waste collection and treatment data to the Swedish EPA.	Split between the provincial governments (9); specific waste streams, separate collection system.	The local government is responsible for municipal waste, the state waste management plan and regional plans (Law 2010).	Shared between local, regional and national authorities; Regional waste plans (autonomous regions); local-level management of municipal waste from households.
PAYT system	A weight-based tariff: Some municipalities pay for each kg they throw (40 in 2014; 33 in 2019); the waste fee is differentiated to motivate recycling.	Legislation to divert biodegradable municipal waste from landfills—long history.	A weight-based tariff with flexibility some flexibility	A collection point system for mixed waste, glass, paper and packaging other than glass.

Table 1 *(Continued)*

	Sweden	Austria	Latvia	Spain
Food waste collection	Variation: non-system, system for single special bags/ containers or special market segments (190 in 2014). Food waste is the only fraction which is widely separately, collected through door-to-door collection. Up to 85 percent of the municipalities offer door-to-door collection of food waste to some extent, including for high-rise buildings (Swedish EPA, 2021b).	The separate collection of biogenic waste; biologically treated residues and compost waste (e. g., quality requirements and standardized, nationwide rules for compost from waste).	Variation between municipalities in application of different solutions (size of containers, payment etc.)	Subsidies to enhance separate collection of biowaste; few municipalities in other regions; biowaste is collected instead of packaging waste; composting with presorting.
Curbside collection of packaging and other sorting options	Variation in availability and sorting types (multi-compartment containers); centralized, households are required by law to sort.	Separate collection, large part destined for recycling or special treatment; preparation for reuse and recycling (paper, metal, plastic and glass) from households and possibly from other origins.	Plastic waste deposit system; Multi-compartment containers (households are required to deposit the waste by the law).	Civic amenity sites are used for collecting recyclables including plastics, metals, garden and wood waste, construction and demolition waste for reuse or preparation such as clothes, furniture, lumber, waste electrical and electronic equipment (WEEE) and hazardous waste.

Table 1 *(Continued)*

	Sweden	Austria	Latvia	Spain
Other disposal options	Biological recovery, throw household waste outdoors or incinerate it themselves, door-to-door services.	Broad scope of options including regional–municipal level public service providers and associations handling household waste collection	Special bags in most municipalities (seasonal); collection of recycling materials.	Eco-social innovations, speeding up efforts in recycling.

Note: The Table 1 compares local waste management systems in four EU countries—Sweden, Austria, Latvia and Spain—across five dimensions: tariff systems, PAYT (pay-as-you-throw) schemes, food waste collection, curbside sorting and other disposal options. The table highlights the diverse institutional arrangements and municipal responsibilities, reflecting differing levels of policy integration, financial incentives and infrastructure development.
Data source: country reports on waste management and official government level reports, regulations.

Table 2: EU local level waste management strategies and practices at the household level.

The EU-27 (from 2020)	Expend. on environ. protection as % of GDP (a) households and (b) nonprofit institutions serving households (1)	Munici-pal waste (a) genera-tion and (b) treat-ment kg per capi-ta (2)		Domestic material consumption (DMC) tonnes per capita (3)	Recycling of packaging waste for monitoring compliance with policy targets (4)	Mean consumption expenditure per household by COICOP consumption purpose in PPS annual (5)	Waste generated by households, billions tonnes (6)	Municipal waste recycling operations, kg per capita (7)	Municipal waste preparing for reuse (8) (Yes=1)
Belgium (BE)	1.53	518	517	12,656	82,2	32 916	5,10	279	1
Bulgaria (BG)	1.16	448	437	20,814	61,7	12 849	2,70	136	
Czech Republic (CZ)	1.50	445	440	15,673	71,6	16 094	4,61	155	
Denmark (DK)	1.00	814	806	23,765	69,7	30 192	3,49	396	1
Germany (DE)	0.83	626	626	14,828	68,7	31 405	37,28	424	1
Estonia (EE)	0.95	379	346	28,007	63,4	17 033	0,52	112	1
Ireland (IE)	0.63	595	582	23,769	64,2	33 655	1,68	235	1
Greece (EL)	1.23	503	503	12,005	58,8	23 359	4,48	91	
Spain (ES)	0.84	463	463	8,934	69,1	28 953	22,15	167	
France (FR)	1.29	544	538	11,419	64,8	29 315	31,09	223	1
Croatia (HR)	1.31	432	402	10,53	53,9	21 034	1,21	112	
Italy (IT)	1.22	494	451	8,165	69,1	28 467	29,59	240	

Table 2 *(Continued)*

The EU-27 (from 2020)	Expend. on environ. protection as % of GDP (a) households and (b) nonprofit institutions serving households (1)	Munici-pal waste (a) genera-tion and (b) treat-ment kg per capi-ta (2)		Domestic material consumption (DMC) tonnes per capita (3)	Recycling of packaging waste for monitoring compliance with policy targets (4)	Mean consumption expenditure per household by COICOP consumption purpose in PPS annual (5)	Waste generated by households, billions tonnes (6)	Municipal waste recycling operations, kg per capita (7)	Municipal waste preparing for reuse (8) (Yes=1)
Cyprus (CY)	0.58	647	557	17,342	64,4	34 879	0,37	104	1
Latvia (LV)	0.83	426	406	14,036	58,5	15 503	0,70	148	1
Lithuania (LT)	1.29	459	435	17,876	61,4	16 852	1,30	204	1
Luxembourg (LU)	0.51	749	749	23,538	69,7	49 680	0,22	379	
Hungary (HU)	0.93	393	393	14,002	48,3	18 968	3,64	134	
Malta (MT)	1.83	647	630	12,186	36,9	27 197	0,18	74	1
The Netherlands (NL)	1.63	514	514	10,25	75,7	32 878	8,68	283	
Austria (AU)	0.48	655	648	17,805	65,9	34 611	4,39	390	1
Poland (PL)	1.04	325	325	17,554	57,0	17 807	10,90	115	
Portugal (PT)	0.70	490	487	15,962	59,9	24 670	5,08	144	
Romania (RO)	0.98	275	253	24,74	51,5	13 024	4,17	34	
Slovenia (SI)	0.84	476	381	13,576	66,4	25 958	0,63	268	1

Table 2 *(Continued)*

The EU-27 (from 2020)	Expend. on environ. protection as % of GDP (a) households and (b) nonprofit institutions serving households (1)	Munici-pal waste (a) genera-tion and (b) treat-ment kg per capi-ta (2)		Domestic material consumption (DMC) tonnes per capita (3)	Recycling of packaging waste for monitoring compliance with policy targets (4)	Mean consumption expenditure per household by COICOP consumption purpose in PPS annual (5)	Waste generated by households, billions tonnes (6)	Municipal waste recycling operations, kg per capita (7)	Municipal waste preparing for reuse (8) (Yes=1)
Slovakia (SK)	1.33	407	397	12,355	68,0	17 516	2,17	143	
Finland (FI)	0.82	542	542	44,133	67,6	29 802	1,92	221	1
Sweden (SE)	1.09	437	435	24,163	66,5	28 257	4,41	195	

Note: This text outlines key local-level indicators used to assess waste management and environmental protection efforts across EU countries. It describes eight columns of data, including household spending on environmental services, government and nonprofit involvement, domestic material consumption, municipal waste generation and treatment and the recycling of packaging and household waste. Indicators also link household waste to consumption patterns and track progress in circular economy practices such as recycling and reuse. Due to data limitations, reuse data at the household level is only available for select countries. The dataset provides a macro-level view of national waste policies and performance.

Source: Eurostat database: https://ec.europa.eu/eurostat/data/database (1; 2;) National expenditure on environmental protection by institutional sector [env_ac_ep-neis1__custom_9136699] percentage of gross domestic product (GDP), average; (2) Waste generated by households by year and waste category [ten00110] (a) and municipal waste treatment (b) by waste management operations [env_wasmun__custom_14028495] kg per capita; (3) Domestic material consumption per capita [ten00137]; (4) Recycling rates of packaging waste (..); [env_waspacr__custom_14046174]; (5) Mean consumption expenditure per household with expenditure greater than zero by COICOP consumption purpose [hbs_exp_t123a__custom_9132967]; (6) Waste generated by households [ten00110]; (7) Municipal waste—recycling, kg per capita [env_wasmun__custom_14028495]. Data selected from 2014 to most recent 2020–2022. (8) Municipal waste –preparing for reuse [env_wasmun__custom_14028495].

Andrea Prontera and Ekaterina Domorenok

Greening European Union energy policy: Reconciling sustainability, industrial development and security

Abstract: This chapter provides a concise overview of how the green dimension of European Union (EU) energy policy has consolidated and expanded while at the same time progressively intersecting with other policy sectors, including research and innovation, industrial development and circular economy, to mention a few. The analysis focuses specifically on the nature of energy policy instruments, reflecting on how they have transformed over time to incorporate environmental objectives and concerns. We identify and outline four main phases of the aforementioned processes, illustrating the evolving link between energy and environmental policy domains. Drawing on the longstanding debate on the limitations of the so-called "regulatory state" as the dominant model of policymaking in the EU, we demonstrate how this rationale in the energy sector has progressively been complemented by the use of an increasing number of financial and coordination instruments, which have strengthened the green dimension of EU energy policy.

Keywords: Green energy; environmental policy; regulatory state; catalytic state; policy instruments

1 Introduction

The environmental footprint of the energy sector remains one of the main concerns of the European Union (EU), despite the recognition back in the 1970s of the need to take into consideration environmental concerns by adopting the principle of environmental policy integration (Solorio and Morata, 2012, p. 6). As studies have shown, the progress and outcome of these policy efforts have so far been mixed (Dupont and Oberthür, 2012), even if the number and intensity of the energy policy instruments that incorporated environmental and climate goals have significantly increased over time.

The consolidation of the green pillar within the EU energy policy has evolved along the following four directions: i) growing political commitment to climate mitigation and decarbonization goals; ii) introduction of specific green energy targets to be achieved; iii) introduction of dedicated policy instruments aimed at reducing emissions and expanding the share of the clean energy production and consumption; and iv) establishment of a longer-term agenda to ensure continuity and strategic vision (Kettner and Kletzan-Slamanig, 2020).

This chapter focuses on charting the way in which EU energy policy has incorporated environmental and climate priorities by focusing on the main phases in the development of those policy instruments enacted for its 'greening'. Taking stock of exist-

https://doi.org/10.1515/9783111321523-030

ing scholarship on the topic (Kettner and Kletzan-Slamanig, 2020; Oberthür and von Homeyer, 2022), we explore the scope and nature of the energy-environmental link, illustrating how the breadth and intensity of the EU's approach in this area have increased over time. We identify four phases, from the European Economic Community founding Treaty to the most recent development within the European Green Deal (EGD) through which the energy-environmental nexus has evolved: i) 1957–1991, origins and early steps; ii) 1992–2008, consolidating the energy-environmental linkage; iii) 2009–2018, the green industrial shift; and iv) 2019–2024, decarbonization, resource efficiency and security.

When analyzing the key developments in each phase, we focus on the evolving goals of the EU in this field as well as on the set of policy instruments deployed to achieve them. Therefore, we adopt a three-fold analytical framework that distinguishes between the different types of resources the EU, as a 'stylized' state form (Caporaso 1996, p. 29), can mobilize to support the greening of the energy sector. Specifically, we show how the reliance on regulation associated with the so-called 'regulatory state (Majone, 1994, 1997) has progressively been coupled with other forms of EU intervention. These latter do not involve public ownership, planning or the large budgetary appropriation associated with the 'positive state'. Rather, they are based on information, networking and financial tools for mobilizing private resources, which are associated with the 'catalytic state' conceptualization (Prontera and Quitzow 2022; Prontera, 2024). This conceptualization emphasizes a facilitative or catalytic role for the EU, and particularly for the European Commission, in encouraging network building and public-private collaboration for green energy development. Finally, we highlight that recent trends in the EU green energy policy include an emerging focus on critical raw materials, which strengthens the links between the EU's internal and external green actions.

2 Origins and early steps: 1957–1991

As is well known, energy played a central role in European integration after the Second World War. The first steps included the creation of the European Coal and Steel Community (1951) and the European Atomic Energy Community (1957), covering both the primary energy source of the time (coal) and the most promising one (nuclear energy). In the 1960s, however, the rapid diffusion of oil into the continent decoupled energy issues from the integration process until the late 1980s, when the European Commission launched the internal energy market project under the Single European Act (SEA). The project aimed to liberalize Member States' electricity and gas sectors to lower prices and enhance the security of the supply. It also envisaged the creation of a new common regulatory framework for these sectors at the European level. This idea challenged the traditional organization of national energy policy, which was based on direct forms of state interventionism in line with the positive state perspective. Between the late 1970s and 1980s, several European Commission communications and

Council resolutions were issued, addressing environmental concerns while establishing common energy policy objectives (Collier, 2002). Notable among these are the 1973 guidelines and priority actions for Community energy measures; the 1977 Council recommendation on the rational use of energy in industrial undertakings and the 1986 Council resolution, which identified the promotion of renewable energy as one of the Community's key energy objectives.

Despite the opposition from several Member States and energy companies, the internal energy market project began to take shape in the early 1990s. This process coincided with an increasing awareness about the energy sector's environmental impacts and the growing recognition of the need to adopt the environmental policy integration (EPI) principle in this field. In fact, several legislative acts underpinned by the EPI principle were adopted in the beginning of 1980s, largely shaped by a regulatory rationale.

The European Commission made an explicit commitment to include environmental aspects in energy policymaking in the Fourth Action Program (1987–1992), which was approved shortly after the SEA, paving the way for emerging EU environmental policy to be largely driven by the regulatory state logic (see Chapter 1 for more details).

3 Consolidating the energy-environmental linkage: 1992–2008

Since the beginning of the 1990s, the EU's climate agenda has become the main driver of the nascent EU green energy policy (e.g., Jordan et al., 2010; Wurzel and Connelly, 2010). Building on its environmental competences, the EU increasingly prioritized climate change in the aftermath of the 1992 Rio Summit. In that period, however, the EU's approach to greening energy policy was based largely on soft coordination of Member States' research and development (R&D) policies. The environmental component of energy policy was further strengthened following the 1992 signing of the Maastricht Treaty, which established the obligation to integrate the environmental requirements into the definition and implementation of EU policies and activities (Art. 6, Treaty Establishing the European Community; Art. 11, The Treaty on the Functioning of the European Union). However, no specific provisions regarding the energy sector were introduced. During the negotiations preceding the signature of the Maastricht Treaty, the inclusion of an "energy chapter" was proposed to extend EU competences beyond a predominant market focus, but this suggestion was not accepted by the Member States (Schubert, Pollak and Kreutler, 2016). In the following years, the EU's energy policies progressed in line with the regulatory state logic, which, as Chapter 31 illustrates, underpinned the consolidation and expansion of the environmental dimension of the single market. Within this logic, regulation has been conceived of as an effective tool of policy steering and control, given the limited amount of budgetary appropriation the EU could count on. The integration of the environmental dimension into EU energy policy has largely taken shape in response to growing concerns about climate change. An important step in this direction was the Commission's 1990 'Communication to the Council on Energy and the Environment', followed by the publication of its proposed climate change strategy. These initiatives paved the way for the development of an energy efficiency program (SAVE) and a renewable energy program (ALTENER), although the implementation of both proved challenging (Collier, 2002).

The promotion of renewable energy, which was considered among the main means of combating climate change, gained momentum in the early 2000s. In that period, the EU's green energy policy quickly expanded, leading to a gradual "greening" of the EU regulatory state: i. e., the introduction of regulations, targets and market-based instruments for climate, renewables and energy efficiency into the EU regulatory and policy framework (Figure 1). This trend originated from the European Climate Change Program adopted by the European Commission to implement the Kyoto targets. Within this framework, the first binding legislative acts strengthening the environmental dimension of energy policy were approved, promoting renewable energy in the electricity sector ('Directive 2001/77/EC' or 'RES Directive') and increasing standards for energy efficiency ('Energy Performance of Buildings Directive'). Along with the aforementioned regulatory instruments, the Emissions Trading System (ETS) ('Directive 2003/87/EC' or 'ETS Directive') was introduced (see Chapter 20). This instrument soon became a cornerstone of EU climate policy, putting a price on carbon for large industrial and power plants. Its scope was first extended in 2008 to include domestic aviation and later in 2023 to cover buildings, road transport and small emitting industry.

In the mid-2000s, renewable energy continued to rise on the EU policy agenda due to internal and international developments (Solorio and Bocquillon, 2017). After the 2004 Eastern enlargement, the EU's dependence on fossil fuel imports increased, a trend expected to continue due to declining domestic fossil fuel production. The 2006 gas crisis between Ukraine and Russia raised concerns about energy security, especially as Russia started pursuing a more assertive foreign policy in the post-Soviet region. In its 2007 Communication 'An Energy Policy for Europe', the Commission emphasized the importance of renewables for both climate mitigation and energy security (European Commission, 2007). At the end of 2008 during the first Barroso Commission, the EU reached a consensus on the 2020 Climate and Energy Package, in the midst of international climate negotiations focused on a post-Kyoto agreement. This package strengthened the integration of climate and energy policies, along the lines traced in the Green Paper 'A European Strategy for Sustainable, Competitive and Secure Energy' (European Commission, 2006). The package included a series of legislative measures that set out the main EU regulatory and policy framework for 2020 and consolidated the greening of the EU regulatory state (Figure 1). In particular, the Renewable Energy Directive (RED) ('Directive 2009/28/EC', or 'RED I Directive') established a common framework for promoting renewables not only in the electricity sector but also in the transport, heating and cooling sectors, setting an overall EU target of 2 percent by 2020. The 2020 Climate and Energy Package also included a revision of the ETS, a decision on sharing the efforts among Member States to reduce greenhouse gas emissions not covered by the ETS mechanism and a new directive on energy efficiency. The latter upgraded the previous directives' ambition, establishing a common regulatory framework for the promotion of energy efficiency to ensure the achievement of a new target of energy savings of 20 percent or more by 2020. Importantly, as the Commission requested, the 'RED I Directive' provided for mandatory targets for Member States in terms of overall share of renewables in gross final energy consumption. However, due to the resistance of some Member States, the Commission failed in its attempts to harmonize the national support schemes for renewables in the electricity sector according to the tradable green certificates model. Germany and Spain, which had very successfully expanded the deployment of renewables due to feed-in tariffs, particularly opposed this proposal, which would limit their positive state's green developmental strategies based on large subsides and direct spending.

4 An industrial shift in EU green energy policy: 2009 – 2019

In 2009, the Lisbon Treaty entered into force. It finally included a specific chapter on energy, explicitly mentioning the development of renewable energy sources among the EU's objectives, along with security of supply, energy efficiency, market integration and energy networks. This chapter did not change the nature of the EU's competences on energy matters, which are shared with the Member States. It did, however, strengthen the role of EU institutions in energy policymaking. This period has also been characterized by the repercussions of the 2008 global financial crisis. The crisis strongly affected state-market relations in Europe, leading to the emergence of a more interventionist approach by the EU beyond its traditional regulatory state focus in energy policy. The EU gradually abandoned its previous policies based on liberalization and market-oriented (horizontal) policies, which focused on creating enabling conditions for market actors and stimulating R&D, in favor of a more targeted action to supporting strategic economic sectors. These trends marked the origins of an EU industrial policy, which was subsequently strengthened following a new consensus between France and Germany (Di Carlo and Schmitz, 2023). This shift has been particularly evident in the green energy policy field, where the nucleus of an EU catalytic state, with its essence illustrated below, began to emerge, having energy networks and low-carbon technologies at its core (Prontera and Quitzow, 2022). These technologies were considered not only as essential ingredients for mitigating climate change and reducing the EU's dependence on fossil fuels but also as a means of revitalizing European economic development in the face of an increasingly competitive global environment.

The catalytic state perspective (Prontera and Quitzow, 2022; Prontera, 2024) recognizes that, as a green industrial policy actor, the EU has specific features due to its very limited budget and independent revenue-raising capabilities and its partial competences in the areas of energy, industrial and innovation policy. These constraints

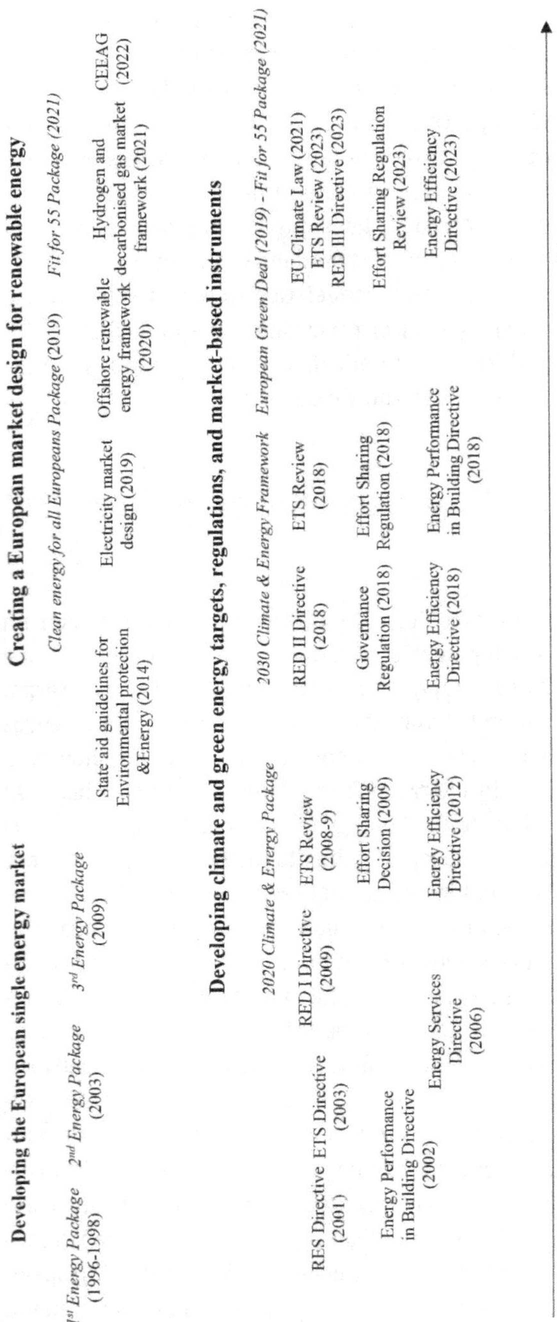

Figure 1: The greening of the EU regulatory state in the field of energy policy.
Sources: adapted and updated from Prontera and Quitzow (2022).

are an obstacle to the adoption of the more direct means of intervention traditionally associated with the positive state (Majone, 1997). Consequently, the EU has sought to steer and enhance its green industrial and technological capacity and promote energy networks in a more indirect way and with fewer resources. The Commission has acted as a catalyst and facilitator of investment projects by deploying nodality (i. e., centrality and visibility in information network) and treasury-based tools (Hood, 1983). With the former policy tools, governmental agents can exploit their nodal position to promote networks and shape the structuring of these networks, and they can use their information and knowledge resources to influence actors' behavior within these networks. More specifically, the Commission has promoted the creation of multi-stakeholder platforms, public-private partnerships and pan-European industry alliances (e. g., the European Battery Alliance, the European Raw Materials Alliance, the Clean Hydrogen Alliance, the Solar PV Alliance) to improve coordination between industrial actors and R&D agencies at the EU and national level in order to achieve its goals. With regard to treasury-based policy tools, being constrained by its limited budget, the EU has used innovative financial mechanisms such as blending and guarantees to enhance the impact of its green investment agenda. Blending is the strategic use of a small contribution from the EU budget (e. g., in the form of grants) to leverage additional funding from partner financial institutions and the private sector. For implementing these mechanisms, the EU has also increasingly mobilized the European development banks—both the European Investment Bank and the European Bank for Reconstruction and Development—to catalyze investments in strategic projects, often in cooperation with the national development banks of EU Member States (e. g., Mertens and Thiemann, 2019).

The rise of the EU catalytic state in the green energy sector was initiated under the second Barroso Commission (Figure 2). In this period, EU policymakers recognized that the traditional regulatory state approach was insufficient to achieve ambitious energy and climate objectives in the face of a more challenging external environment. Between 2008 and 2013, the EU launched the European Economic Recovery Plan (EERP) along with other policy measures that targeted energy infrastructure, such as the Trans-European Networks for Energy and the Connecting Europe Facility for Energy (Figure 2; Table 2). These were supplemented by further initiatives to promote low-carbon innovations, combining financial assistance, public-private partnerships and multi-stakeholder platforms (e. g., SET Plan, NER 300, FP7-JUs, EIT-InnoEnergy) (Figure 2; Table 2). While the EU had already implemented programs for energy R&D and infrastructure in previous years, the scale, scope and green focus of these actions had significantly expanded subsequently.

The catalytic state in the green realm was consolidated further under the Juncker Commission, which launched the Investment Plan for Europe and the European Fund for Strategic Investments (EFSI)—the so-called Juncker Plan in 2014–2015 in response to the slow recovery after the crisis and increasing geopolitical (Russia) and geoeconomic (China) challenges (Figure 2). While the EERP focused on EUR 5 billion in direct spending on infrastructure and an additional EUR 15 billion in European Investment

Bank funding, the Juncker Plan aimed to leverage EUR 315 billion in investment, mainly through the strongly expanded use of guarantees and blending. Later, in 2018, the Juncker Commission launched the InvestEU program to further expand the Investment Plan, bringing the investment target to EUR 500 billion, and to create a single governance framework for the EFSI and several other financial instruments. These additional means have shown a significantly increased ambition of the EU's green energy investment agenda, expanding the use of new forms of financial support that involved EU development banks and private-public partnerships to promote low-carbon technology and energy networks. In parallel, several other initiatives for innovation and deployment developed, increasingly targeting renewables and low-carbon technology, such as solar photovoltaic (PV) systems, offshore wind and batteries (Figure 2; Table 2). To encourage investment in cross-national strategic projects, the Commission created the Important Projects of Common European Interest (IPCEI) in 2014. This new measure has also allowed Member States to use state aid in a targeted way to foster industrial development, thus overcoming an important constraint that had traditionally limited more proactive industrial policies across Europe.

Figure 2: The rise of the EU catalytic state for low-carbon technology and energy networks.
Sources: adapted and updated from Prontera and Quitzow (2022).

The EU green industrial shift that evolved within the catalytic state framework did not replace the efforts to green the EU regulatory state, which continued also during the Junker Commission (Figure 1). In 2014, the EU enacted new guidelines on state aid for environmental protection and energy, which prescribed that feed-in tariffs were no longer regarded as permissible state aid. These incentive mechanisms had to be gradually replaced by tools that granted more relevance to market-oriented dynamics, such as feed-in-premiums and tradable green certificate schemes. Promoting a more ambitious green agenda in the post-crisis period was challenging, especially in view of increasing internal opposition to stringent climate policy from Central and Eastern EU Member States (Skovgaard, 2014). However, in the run up to the Conference of the Parties 21, which resulted in the Paris Agreement, the EU agreed on the 2030 Climate and Energy Framework to upgrade the previous package with new targets for 2030. The concrete measures for implementing this framework, however, were introduced only in 2018.

Table 1: Main climate and green energy targets and achievements in the EU.

	2020 Climate and Energy Package	Achieved in 2020	2030 Climate and Energy Framework	European Green Deal/ European Climate Law
Climate	20 % reduction in GHG emissions from 1990 levels by 2020	24 % (*)	40 % reduction in GHG emissions from 1990 levels by 2030	55 % reduction in GHG emissions from 1990 levels by 2030 Climate neutrality by 2050
Renewable energy	20 % of renewables in the EU final energy consumption by 2020	22 %	32 % of renewables in the EU final energy consumption by 2030	Fit for 55 Package 2021: 40 % of renewables in the EU final energy consumption by 2030 RED III directive 2023: 42,5 % of renewables in the EU final energy consumption by 2030 (***)
Energy efficiency	20 % reduction in the EU's primary and final energy consumption by 2020	Achieved (**)	32.5 % of energy savings, compared to projections of the expected energy use in 2030	Reducing EU final energy consumption by 11.7 % by 2030, compared to the projected energy use for 2030 ()

Source: author's elaboration. Notes (*) = this data is from 2019, as the data for 2020 is affected by the consequences of the COVID-19 crisis (EEA 2021); (**) = see European Commission (2022); (***) = another 2.5 % can be achieved through voluntary contributions by the member states or through pan-European measures (45 % by 2030 was the overall target proposed by the Commission in the 2022 REPowerEU Plan); () = this target translates into a primary energy consumption target of 992.5 million tonnes of oil equivalent and a final energy consumption target of 763 Mtoe (the previous targets were 1128 million tonnes of oil equivalent for primary energy and 846 million tonnes of oil equivalent for final energy).

5 Broadening the scope of the energy-environmental link: 2019 – 2024

Both the EU catalytic state and the greening of the EU regulatory state further expanded under the von der Leyen Commission and the EGD (Figure 1). The latter provided several important novelties in the EU's green energy agenda. First, a Green Deal Investment Plan was launched, which was instituted following the Russian invasion of Ukraine as part of the launch of the REPowerEU Plan. With this plan the Commission fostered the integration of the EU industrial, energy and climate policy, as exemplified by the 2023 'Green Deal Industrial Plan' (European Commission 2023a) and related initiatives such as the Net-Zero Industry Act (NZIA) and the Critical Raw Materials Act (European Commission 2023b, 2023c). The NZIA was also a response to the challenge the United States Inflation Reduction Act posed to the European green industry. It aims to expand industrial capacity in several low-carbon technologies (e. g., solar and wind equipment, batteries, electrolysers and fuel cells and grid technology) by leveraging private resources and increasing public-private collaborations with initiative like the Net-Zero Strategic Projects, the Net-Zero Europe Platform and the Net-Zero Industry Group (Table 2).

Furthermore, in 2019, the Commission launched the "Clean Energy for All Europeans" Package aimed at reforming the electricity market design to better enable the diffusion of renewable energy in the continent. The package intervened in the design of the EU electricity market, allowing more flexibility to accommodate an increasing share of renewable energy in the grid. In its turn, the 2030 Climate and Energy Framework provided for a further revision of the ETS, an effort-sharing regulation, a new directive on renewables, the 'RED II' ('Directive EU 2018/2001') and energy efficiency. These directives established EU level targets by 2030—at least a 32 percent share for renewable energy at the EU level and at least 32.5 percent of energy savings (compared to projections of the expected energy use in 2030)—but without nationally binding objectives.

Earlier in 2018, the EU enacted the so-called Governance Regulation ('Regulation 2018/1999'), which required Member States to draft National Energy and Climate Plans and submit their progress reports every two years. The European Commission is responsible for assessing and monitoring national strategies, as well as providing recommendations and guidance on the implementation of Member States' energy policies (Knodt, Ringel and Müller, 2020). Consistent with the above, between 2020 and 2021 the Commission launched the framework for offshore renewable energy and for hydrogen and decarbonized gas; these strategies, finalized in 2023, were intended to foster creation of a European market design for green energy. In 2022, the Commission approved the new Guidelines on State Aid for Climate, Environmental Protection and Energy (CEEAG), which expanded the possibility for Member States to support investments in all the low-carbon technology that could assist in achieving the EGD objectives. The aforementioned measures, together with the European Climate Law and the provisions included in the Fit for 55 (FF55) package (of particular note are the reform of the ETS, a new effort-sharing system, the 'RED III Directive', the revision of the 'Energy Efficiency Directive' and an additional reform of the electricity market design —all finalized in 2023) further upgraded the EU climate and green energy ambition and targets (Figure 1; Table 1).

Building on the REPowerEU Plan framework advanced earlier in the 2022, the 'RED III Directive' increased the 2030 target for renewables from 32 to 42.5 percent (Table 1). To achieve the new target, the EU will have to install more than 100 gigawatts of new wind and solar capacity every year. To facilitate this huge expansion, the 'RED III Directive' introduced new common rules to accelerate approval procedures for the installation of renewables. It also set more ambitious targets in the area of green hydrogen (in industry), as well as regulatory provisions to facilitate cross-border cooperation projects involving more Member States (e.g., joint offshore wind projects).

Table 2: The policy tools of the EU catalytic state in the green sector (selection).

Year	Measure	Notes
2008	Strategic Energy Technology Plan (SET Plan) and NER 300	Support for low-carbon innovation with financial assistance and multi stakeholder platforms
2009	European Energy Programme for Recovery (EEPR)	Financial assistance to energy networks and offshore wind projects
2009	7th Framework Programme-Joint Undertakings (FP7-JUs)	Research funding and public-private partnerships in low-carbon technology fields (upgraded in 2014 with Horizon 2020 and, in 2021, with Horizon Europe)
2010	European Institute of Innovation and Technology (EIT)	It works in coordination with Horizon programmes supporting research, innovation and promoting industrial partnerships. It focuses on different sectors, including renewable energy (InnoEnergy) and raw materials (EIT Raw material)
2013	Trans European Energy Networks for Energy (TEN-E)	Governance framework for planning and supporting cross-national energy networks, the so-called Projects of Common Interest (PCIs)
2013	Connecting Europe Facility for Energy (CEF-E)	CEF-E works in coordination with TEN-E offering financial support to cross-national energy networks
2014	Important Project of Common European Interests (IPCEI)	Tool to support cross-national investment projects combining state aid and private capital (e.g. IPCEI batteries, IPCEI hydrogen)
2015	SET-Plan review	Upgrading of the SET-Plan, better focus on renewable energy technology (e.g. PV, wind, batteries) in line with the 2015 Energy Union Strategy
2017	EFSI 2.0	Upgrading of the EFSI, better focus on green and climate projects
2018	European Innovation Council (EIC)/ EIC Fund	Support for research and innovation for the green and digital transition
2018	European Battery Alliance	Pan-European industry alliances that brings together EU and national authorities, regions, industry, research institutes and other stakeholders in the battery value chain
2019	Innovation Fund	Upgrading of NER 300 for supporting low-carbon technology
2020	European Raw Material Alliance	Pan-European industry alliances that brings together EU and national authorities, regions, industry, research institutes and other stakeholders in the raw materials value chain. Its goal is to reduce Europe's dependency on those raw materials critical for the green and digital transitions
2020	European Clean Hydrogen Alliance	Pan-European industry alliances that brings together EU and national authorities, regions, industry, research institutes and other stakeholders in the clean hydrogen value chain. Its goal is to support the large-scale deployment of clean hydrogen technologies

Table 2 *(Continued)*

Year	Measure	Notes
2021	InvestEU	Successor and upgrading of EFSI. It aims to support investment in innovation and industrial capacity through guarantees and cooperation with the European Investment Bank and national development banks (linked to the Green Deal Investment Plan)
2022	TEN-E Review	Revision of the previous 2013 TEN-E scheme, focus on electricity networks, wind offshore corridors and hydrogen corridors
2022	CEF-E Review	Revision of the previous 2013 CEF-E scheme, focus on electricity and cross-border renewable energy projects
2022	Solar PV Alliance	Pan-European industry alliances that brings together EU and national authorities, regions, industry, research institutes and other stakeholders. Its goal is to build resilience and strategic autonomy for Europe's solar photovoltaic (PV) value chain
2023	NZIA	The Net-Zero Europe Platform includes representatives from the Commission and the member states. It monitors progress towards the NZIA objectives and increases coordination among the actors involved in strategic projects. The Net-Zero Industry Group supports the Net-Zero Europe Platform and facilitates the involvement of industrial actors

Source: author's elaboration.

Another important dimension of the evolving green pillar of EU energy policy is the EU's strategy on critical raw materials (CRM). In 2020, the Commission issued the related Action Plan, which updated and improved the past EU strategy that dated back to 2011. The new plan introduced measures to improve the diversification and resilience of critical supply chains, driven by the concern which emerged during the Covid-19 pandemic that showed the EU's vulnerability to external supply shocks and shortages. Notably, the Action Plan focused on minerals such as lithium, cobalt, nickel and rare earth elements (REEs), which were fundamental to the EU's green industrial turn. The plan aimed to ensure "resilience through a secure and sustainable supply of critical raw materials" (European Commission, 2020, p. 2) by pursuing developing resilient value chains for EU industrial ecosystems, reducing dependence on primary CRM through circular use of resources, sustainable products and innovation, strengthening domestic sourcing of raw materials and diversifying sourcing from third countries. Regarding the latter objective, the EU has started to develop a raw materials diplomacy that targets resource-rich countries in several regions of the world since 2021 (Table 3), as the EU is not endowed with significant CRM resources and is largely dependent on imports to meet its needs. However, supply chains serving Europe are highly concentrated in a few geographic areas, with China the leading supplier of several CRMs. This condition is increasingly perceived as a potential risk due to growing geopolitical tensions. To address this issue, the Commission's 2023 Communication on a Green Deal Industrial Plan for the Net-Zero Age proposed to draft specific legislation on CRM—the Critical Raw Material Act (CRMA), which was finally enacted in 2024 with 'Regulation 2024/1252'.

The starting point of the CRMA was the recognition that the EU will never be self-sufficient in the supply of many materials critical to the energy transition; it will continue to rely on imports for the majority of its consumption, but these should be reduced and diversified. The CRMA therefore provided for regulatory measures and domestic targets for a CRM list, as well as foreign policy measures. The domestic targets (by 2030) relate to the proportion of extraction (10 percent), processing (40 percent) and recycling (25 percent) of critical minerals and materials (e.g., cobalt, copper, lithium, nickel, REEs and graphite products) that should take place in the EU, as well as a threshold (65 percent) for the maximum annual consumption at each stage of production and processing that can come from a single third country. The CRMA, however, did not foresee new EU-level funding. Instead, it introduced provisions on supply chain monitoring, stockpiling, coordination between Member States and improving recyclability. In addition, to facilitate capacity expansion within the EU, it provided for a simplified regulatory framework for permits and access to funding for so-called Strategic Projects, i.e., projects that contribute to capacity expansion and involve Member States and private actors. The CRMA also focused on sustainability criteria for CRM supply chains in terms of circularity and recyclability and environmental footprint. It also provided for the inclusion of similar criteria in the EU's external relations by promoting sustainable and circular economy practices, decent working conditions and respect for human rights in third countries alongside their raw material value chains. This new focus on sustainability was included subsequently in the new bilateral strategic partnerships signed by the EU with third countries in 2023 and 2024 (Table 3).

Alongside this renewed bilateral resource diplomacy, the CRMA proposed using EU trade agreements to improve supply chain diversification. It also envisaged the establishment of a Joint Purchasing Mechanism to aggregate demand for CRMs at the European level and better negotiate with producer countries and the creation of a Critical Raw Materials Club with like-minded countries willing to strengthen global supply chains and follow EU standards and practices on sustainability. In this vein, the EU seeks to leverage the access to its internal market to promote its preferred green rules and principles globally. This approach represents the "external face" of the EU regulatory state, which exemplifies the bloc's ability to deploy regulatory power to pursue foreign policy objectives (e.g., Goldthau and Sitter, 2015; Prontera, 2024). At the same time, the EU also seeks to externalize its catalytic state approach: it has mobilized the investment agenda of the EU Global Gateway Strategy to promote CRM projects abroad (e.g., strategic projects under the CRMA can also be located in third countries).

Table 3: EU bilateral dialogues and partnerships on CRM supply chains (2021–2024).

Year	Initiative
2021	EU-Canada Strategic Partnership on Raw Materials
2021	EU-Ukraine Strategic Partnership on Raw Materials and Batteries
2022	EU-Kazakhstan Strategic Partnership on Raw Materials, Batteries and Renewable Hydrogen
2022	EU-Namibia Partnership on Raw Materials and Renewable Hydrogen
2023	EU-Argentina Strategic Partnership on Sustainable Raw Materials Value Chain
2023	EU-Chile Strategic Partnership on Sustainable Raw Materials Value Chain
2023	EU-Zambia Strategic Partnership on Sustainable Raw Materials Value Chain
2023	EU-Democratic Republic of Congo partnership on Critical and Strategic Raw Materials Value Chains
2023	EU-Greenland Strategic Partnership on Sustainable Raw Materials Value Chain
2024	EU-Rwanda Strategic Partnership on Sustainable Raw Materials Value Chain
2024	EU-Norway Strategic Partnership on Sustainable Raw Material Value Chains and Battery Value Chains
2024	EU-Uzbekistan Strategic Partnership on Sustainable Raw Materials Value Chain
2024	EU-Australia Strategic Partnership on Sustainable Critical and Strategic Minerals
2024	EU-Serbia Strategic Partnership on Sustainable Raw Materials, Battery Value Chains and Electric Vehicles

Sources: author's elaboration.

6 Conclusions

The analysis conducted in this chapter illustrates the progressive strengthening and broadening of the intersection between EU energy and environmental policy agendas. In this evolution, the EU has expanded its policy toolbox far beyond that expected by a regulatory state. However, because of its (institutionally) constrained nature as a quasi-state, the EU has not shifted towards the direct means of intervention associated with the positive state. Instead, it developed catalytic state capabilities to achieve its policy objectives through network-building and public-private cooperation. These catalytic state capabilities have gradually been institutionalized alongside the EU's regulatory core, which has also been stretched to achieve more challenging and diversified goals. However, further research is needed to understand if the criticism and concerns expressed in existing studies regarding the ambition and consistency of the EU's action aimed at the greening of the energy sector (Kettner and Kletzan-Slamaning, 2018; Dupont and Oberthür, 2012) have been overcome by the legislative upgrading enacted by the EGD and the deployment of a more composite set of policy tools. Likewise, the scope and speed of climate policy integration, which asymmetrically involved the different sectors, remain to be researched. Also, a more nuanced reflection on the outcomes of the shift from the principle of environmental policy integration to climate policy integration (see Chapters 20 and 33) is needed, given the relevance of the latter for the linkage between energy policies, research and development, green investments and a circular economy. Another important future research trajectory is the implementation progress of the legislative acts included in the EGD and, especially, in its FF55 package, which links the green energy agenda to other strategic sectors including transport, infrastructure, agriculture and land use, and just transition. Last but not least, the green energy pillar is central to the EU new industrial policy, though a clear picture is needed of how its different components of internal and external energy policies can combine and work in synergy in the years to come.

References

Caporaso, J. (1996) 'The European Union and forms of state: Westphalian, regulatory or post-modern?', *Journal of Common Market Studies*, 34(1), pp. 29 – 52.

Collier, U. (2002) 'European Union Energy Policy in a Changing Climate', in: Lenschow A. (ed.) *Environmental policy integration: Greening sectoral policies in Europea*. London: Earthscan.

Di Carlo, D. and Schmitz, L. (2023) 'Europe first? The rise of EU industrial policy promoting and protecting the single market', *Journal of European Public Policy*, 30(10), pp. 2063 – 2096.

Dupont, C. and Oberthür, S. (2012) 'Insufficient climate policy integration in EU energy policy: The importance of the long-term perspective', *Journal of Contemporary European Research*, 8(2), pp. 228 – 247.

European Commission (2006) 'A European strategy for sustainable, competitive and secure energy', *COM*(2006) 105 final. Available at: https://eur-lex.europa.eu/legal-content/EN/TXT/PDF/?uri=CELEX:52006DC0105 (Accessed: 21 June 2025).

European Commission (2007) 'An energy policy for Europe', *COM*(2007) 1 final. Available at: https://eur-lex.europa.eu/legal-content/EN/TXT/PDF/?uri=CELEX:52007DC0001 (Accessed: 22 June 2025).

European Commission (2020) 'Critical raw materials resilience: Charting a path towards greater security and sustainability', *COM*(2020) 474 final. Available at: https://eur-lex.europa.eu/legal-content/EN/TXT/PDF/?uri=CELEX:52020DC0474 (Accessed: 18 June 2025).

European Commission (2023a) 'A Green Deal industrial plan for the net-zero age'. *COM*(2023) 62 final. Available at: https://eur-lex.europa.eu/legal-content/EN/TXT/PDF/?uri=CELEX:52023DC0062 (Accessed: 15 June 2025).

European Commission (2023b) 'Proposal for a regulation of the European Parliament and of the Council on establishing a framework of measures for strengthening Europe's net-zero technology products manufacturing ecosystem (Net Zero Industry Act)', *COM*(2023) 161 final. Available at: https://eur-lex.europa.eu/resource.html?uri=cellar:6448c360-c4dd-11ed-a05c-01aa75ed71a1.0001.02/DOC_1&format=PDF (Accessed: 12 June 2025).

European Commission (2023c) 'Proposal for a regulation of the European Parliament and of the Council establishing a framework for ensuring a secure and sustainable supply of critical raw materials and amending Regulations (EU) 168/2013, (EU) 2018/858, 2018/1724 and (EU) 2019/1020', *COM*(2023) 160 final. Available at: https://eur-lex.europa.eu/resource.html?uri=cellar:903d35cc-c4a2-11ed-a05c-01aa75ed71a1.0001.02/DOC_1&format=PDF (Accessed: 3 June 2025).

Goldthau, A. and Sitter, N. (2015) *A liberal actor in a realist world: The European Union regulatory state and the global political economy of energy*. Oxford: Oxford University Press.

Hood, C. (1983) *Tools of government*. London: Macmillan International Higher Education.

Jordan, A. et al. (eds.) (2010) *Climate change policy in the European Union*. Cambridge: Cambridge University Press.

Kettner, C. and Kletzan-Slamanig, D. (2020) 'Is there climate policy integration in European Union energy efficiency and renewable energy policies? Yes, no, maybe', *Environmental Policy and Governance*, 30(3), pp. 141 – 150.

Knodt, M., Ringel, M. and Müller, R. (2020) '"Harder" soft governance in the European Energy Union', *Journal of Environmental Policy & Planning*, 22(6), pp. 787 – 800.

Majone, G. (1994) 'The rise of the regulatory state in Europe', *Western European Politics*, 17(3), pp. 77 – 101.

Majone, G. (1997) 'From the positive to the regulatory state: Causes and consequences of changes in the mode of governance', *Journal of Public Policy*, 17(2), pp. 139 – 167.

Mertens, D. and Thiemann, M. (2019) 'Building a hidden investment state? The European investment bank, national developments banks and European economic governance', *Journal of European Public Policy*, 26(1), pp. 23 – 43.

Oberthür, S. and von Homeyer, I. (2022) 'From emissions trading to the European Green Deal: The evolution of the climate policy mix and climate policy integration in the EU', *Journal of European Public Policy*, 30(3), pp. 445 – 468.

Prontera, A. (2024) *Green superpowers: China, the European Union, and the United States in the global energy transition*. Oxford: Oxford University Press.

Prontera, A. and Quitzow, R. (2022) 'The EU as catalytic state? Rethinking European climate and energy governance', *New Political Economy*, 27(3), pp. 517 – 531.

Schubert, S.R., Pollak, J. and Kreutler, M. (2016) *Energy policy of the European Union*. London: Palgrave Macmillan.

Skovgaard, J. (2014) 'EU climate policy after the crisis', *Environmental Politics*, 23(1), pp. 1 – 17.

Solorio, I. and Bocquillon, P. (2017) 'EU Renewable Energy Policy: A Brief Overview of Its History and Evolution', in: Solorio, I. and Jorgens, H. (eds.) *A guide to EU renewable energy policy: Comparing Europeanization and domestic policy change in EU Member States*. Cheltenham: Edward Elgar, pp. 23 – 42.

Solorio, I. and Morata, F. (2012) 'Introduction: The Re-evolution of Energy Policy in Europe', in: Solorio, I. and Jorgens, H. (eds.) *A guide to EU renewable energy policy: Comparing Europeanization and domestic policy change in EU member states*. Cheltenham: Edward Elgar, pp. 1 – 22.

Wurzel, R.K. and Connelly, J. (eds.) (2010) *The European Union as a leader in international climate change politics*. London: Routledge.

Emanuela Bozzini

The European Union regime for chemicals: Toxic and regulatory ignorance

Abstract: This chapter examines the European Union's (EU) regulatory regime for chemicals highlighting the issue of 'toxic ignorance'. Significant uncertainties persist regarding the number of chemicals in circulation, their environmental contamination and their impacts on human health. The literature on regulatory issues is similarly limited. The extant literature asserts that the EU's chemical regime, while ambitious, is marked by regulatory gaps and inconsistencies, particularly in chemical testing and evaluation. The chapter highlights the fragmented nature of EU chemical regulations, the slow pace of developing regulatory guidelines and the challenges of applying the precautionary and substitution principles effectively. It calls for a more integrated and coherent approach to chemical regulation and a stronger academic focus on understanding and addressing the regulatory and policy issues surrounding EU chemical safety.

Keywords: Chemical policy; REACH; toxic ignorance; EU regulation; public health

1 Introduction

If we summarize the current understanding of chemicals' presence in everyday life, the term 'toxic ignorance' (Environmental Defense Fund, 1997; Vaughan, 2015) is apt. This notion encompasses three dimensions. Firstly, there is uncertainty surrounding the exact number of chemical substances circulating in regional and global markets. On the basis of Chemical Abstracts Service (CAS) numbers, the United Nations Environment Program (UNEP) (2019) estimated a total of around 140,000 substances. Yet, CAS numbers primarily indicate chemical circulation in Western and Organization for Economic Cooperation and Development (OECD) countries, neglecting emerging markets which now represent 40 percent of global turnover. More comprehensive estimates suggest the number of substances could be as high as 350,000 (Wang et al., 2020).

Secondly, we lack precise knowledge about the extent of chemical contamination in water, air and soil. It is noteworthy that whereas planetary boundaries for climate change, biodiversity loss and other stressors were calculated in 2009 (Rockström et al., 2009), the estimations of a planetary boundary for chemical pollution remained unquantified until 2022 because of methodological difficulties and data gaps (Persson et al., 2022). Partly this is because chemical pollution can be seen as a negative externality of a vast range of activities, including agricultural, mining and industrial production practices. The use of pesticides and fertilizers in intensive farming contributes to long-term soil and water pollution and biodiversity degradation (European Environ-

https://doi.org/10.1515/9783111321523-031

ment Agency, 2022). Heavy metals and other pollutants have been discovered in thousands of active and abandoned industrial sites across the European Union (EU) (Payá Pérez and Rodríguez Eugenio, 2018). Other significant pollution sources include leakages from waste disposal and industrial accidents.[1] Cribb (2017) characterizes this as a 'chemical avalanche', and estimations are that at the global level approximately 220 billion tonnes of chemicals are released into the environment each year (Naidu et al., 2021). Further, transboundary effects are evident, with EU chemical emissions detected in polar regions (Stokes and Vaughan, 2013) and persistent, bioaccumulative chemicals found in remote, pristine environments (Gruber, 2018). In short, while indicators hint at significant contamination levels, the full scope remains unclear.

Thirdly, Vaughan (2015, p. 41) points to a severe knowledge gap regarding chemical impact on human health and the environment persisting over the years. This includes uncertainties about toxicity, persistence, bioaccumulation and biomagnification properties. One primary reason for this knowledge gap is the limited number of substances tested for safety (Muir et al., 2023). A second is the time lag between developments in regulatory ecotoxicology and progress in science that incrementally expands the knowledge and evidence-base of harmful effects.

This chapter argues that the notion of toxic ignorance should be extended to encompass not only ignorance of the number, presence and toxic effects of chemicals but also of regulatory and policy issues surrounding them. While EU environmental policy developments have been extensively analyzed, as this handbook demonstrates, initiatives to protect public health and the environment from chemical pollution have not received sustained attention. As the following sections will clarify, our knowledge of the main chemical-related policy initiatives of the EU, like Registration, Evaluation, Authorization and Restriction of Chemicals (REACH) and pesticides and biocides regulations are incomplete. The pervasive presence of chemical substances in our environment warrants a more systematic scholarly effort to better understand the outputs, outcomes and impacts of EU chemical policy. This chapter is structured into five main sections. The following one surveys existing literature on EU chemical policies and maps areas of scholarly focus. Sections three, four and five discuss existing scholarly work on EU chemical policy, supplemented by references to policy debates and official reports published by the European Commission, the European Chemicals Agency (ECHA) and stakeholders. The concluding section identifies key areas and questions that merit prioritization in future research agendas.

1 Some major accidents have gained notoriety, such as the Seveso disaster in Italy in 1976 and the 1986 fire at the Sandoz plant in Basel. Thousands of minor accidents often go unreported, making it challenging to assess the overall chemical contamination resulting from such incidents.

2 The literature on EU chemical policy: a map

The literature on chemical policy, both generally and within the EU context, is sparse and lacks comprehensive sectoral coverage, making the regulation of chemicals "a relatively uncharted territory" (Eriksson, Gilek and Rudén, 2010, p. 167). The reasons for this neglect are unclear, although Vaughan (2015, p. 22) suggests that "chemical regulation may appear dull and impenetrable" and "convoluted" in the words of Bergkamp and Herbatschek (2014, p. 222). Alternatively, one might hypothesize that prioritization of climate change–related issues in policy and academic debates has somewhat overshadowed interest in 'old-style' chemical pollution (see Tosun chapter).

This literature review reveals that scholarly attention to policy processes in the chemical sector has been cyclical and fragmented. The 2006 adoption of REACH prompted the publication of significant analysis of the policy formulation phase of what EU policymakers and scholars alike considered as one of the most ambitious initiatives in world chemical regulation (Coria, 2018) and the "most controversial" (Fisher, 2008). Stokes and Vaughan (2013) provide a detailed EU chemical policy history; Bergkamp (2013) and Vaughan (2015) have described its features. More specific studies have focused on coalition dynamics (Selin, 2007), the structure of conflicts around territorial and ideological cleavages (Lindgren and Persson, 2008), the role of environmental leaders in advocating for ambitious policies (Selin, 2007) and the role of European Parliament rapporteurs in shaping legislative proposals (Thierse, 2019). Some scholarly interest also exists in comparative policy analysis, focusing on convergences and divergences with the United State (US) regime (Applegate, 2008; Botos, Graham and Illés, 2019; Larson and Jordan, 2019).

Research on the subsequent implementation of REACH is patchy. Studies have addressed the functioning of some of the most complicated or controversial sections, such as the inclusion of chemicals in the list of substances of very high concern (Alaranta and Turunen, 2021; Coria, Kristiansson and Gustavsson, 2022; Klika, 2015b, 2015a), persisting gaps and delays in evaluating the toxic properties of substances (Bozzini, 2017; Paleari, 2016) and the application of the precautionary and substitution principles (Abelkop and Graham, 2014; Hansen, Carlsen and Tickner, 2007; Lofstedt, 2014).

Similar gaps exist in the analysis of other legislative initiatives. Available studies illustrate some of the most relevant chemical-related legislation, e. g., pesticides (Bozzini, 2017) and cosmetics (Ferreira et al., 2022). Nanomaterials have also attracted consistent interest while others are rather neglected, e. g., biocides and toys. Overall, the academic understanding of the scope and effectiveness of regulatory regimes in terms of environmental and public health protection remains incomplete.

3 Main features of the EU chemical regulatory regime

The development of the EU chemical regime follows a well-known pattern that is typical of EU environmental policy. Legislation on chemicals was initially introduced in the late 1960s to address the marketing and use of substances across the then six Member States. Notably, the recognition that differences in national provisions directly affected the establishment and functioning of the common market primarily drove one of the first legislative initiatives, Directive 67/548/EEC, on the classification, packaging and labeling of dangerous substances (Preamble). Since the early 1970s, the need to address the adverse effects of transboundary chemical pollution has constituted an additional strong justification for adopting common regulatory provisions. Consequently, environmental and public health protection goals have been integrated into chemical legislation since the mid-1970s. Directive 76/769/EEC on the marketing and use of certain dangerous substances and preparations, a precursor to REACH, foresaw restrictions to protect public health and the environment.

Subsequently, there has been a rapid expansion of chemical-related legislation, following various criteria and resulting in a highly complex regulatory regime. Today, key provisions relevant to the entire chemical sector include the REACH regime adopted in 2007 and the 2008 regulation on classification, labeling and packaging that harmonize EU substances classifications with the United Nations' Globally Harmonized System. Further transversal norms are those on Good Laboratory Practice, which regulate standards for laboratory testing procedures.

Additionally, the EU chemical regime includes provisions addressing the presence of toxic substances in environmental media (air, water and to a lesser extent, soil), specific substances like lead, sulphur, mercury, polychlorinated biphenyls, perfluoroalkyl and polyfluoroalkyl substances (PFAS), and categories of products like pesticides, fertilizers, cosmetics, toys, detergents and pharmaceuticals. Relevant provisions are also found in waste legislation, regulation of industrial processes and provisions on workplace chemical exposure.

While each piece of legislation plays a crucial role in the EU's chemical regulatory framework, delving into the specifics of individual laws is beyond the scope of this paper. However, using available analyses, this section will identify some trends and policy developments that appear common to the main chemicals-related legislation, thereby characterizing the EU chemical regime.

First, all chemical regulations revised, reformed or adopted in the 2000s are similarly informed by policy principles at the core of EU environmental policy, in particular the 'polluter pays' principle and the precautionary principle. Writing about REACH, Fisher (2008) noted that it represents an application of the sustainable development concept, aiming to promote a more efficient, innovative and competitive marketplace while achieving a higher level of health and environmental protection. This theme of reconciling economic and environmental goals also informs other chemical regulations on pesticides, biocides and cosmetics. Also common in all EU chemical regulations is a reference to the substitution principle. This is specific to chemical policy and prescribes the phasing out of hazardous substances and their substitution with safer alternatives (Lofstedt, 2014). Finally, the 'one substance one assessment' principle informs the EU chemical policy, ideally aiming for each molecule to be tested and classified for its intrinsic hazardous properties only once.

However, while the various chemical-related acts share a general orientation, a closer examination of regulatory details reveals significant differences in requirements, evaluation criteria and methodologies. A joint statement by ECHA and the European Food Safety Authority (EFSA) highlighted that "currently, risk assessment and risk management of the same chemical is carried out at different times for different uses by different bodies, under different legislation, often using different data and potentially leading to seemingly different outcomes" (ECHA and EFSA, 2020, p. 1).

A useful illustration involves looking at differences in authorization requirements. REACH specifies rules for substances that are manufactured or imported for quantities above 1 tonne a year. Some classes of chemicals are exempted: pesticides, biocides, pharmaceuticals (on the ground that have a separate regulatory regime) and, more puzzlingly, polymers. Consequently, only around 45,000 out of the 105,000 substances that are estimated to be on the EU market are subject to REACH and require data generation. In the cosmetics field, the evaluation assesses the safety of products, which can be placed on the market only if a 'responsible person' for safety is designated and submits information to the cosmetic products notification portal. All molecules to be employed as biocides and pesticides are subject to a dual system of premarket authorization: first, active substances, i. e., molecules active against pests, are evaluated at the EU level and (if considered safe) granted an EU-wide approval. Second, plant protection products (specific commercial formulations containing an active substance as an ingredient) are evaluated at the national level to take into account specific agronomic conditions and uses.

In short, the incremental development of regulatory provisions for different substances and products has resulted in a compartmentalized and fragmented regime that presents different levels of stringency, tends to duplicate efforts and lacks internal coherence.

A second feature of the EU chemical regime is the persisting presence of data gaps, with many existing chemicals still largely untested. Historically, the EU lacked regulatory controls for chemicals, allowing them to enter and circulate in the European market without limitations. In 1979, Directive 67/548/EEC was amended to introduce requirements for submitting dossiers on the toxicity and related risks of substances, which may pose threats to human health and the environment (Article 6). However, these requirements applied only to 'new chemicals'—those entering the European single market from September 1981 onwards—while 'existing substances' were exempt. According to the European Commission (2001, p. 6), these new chemicals constituted only 1 percent of the substances on the market. In 1993, a program was initiated to evaluate 141 'existing substances', marking the first effort to systematically assess thousands of chemicals already in use (Hertel, 1996).[2] National competent authorities were in charge of these assessments, but the procedures were "lengthy and cumbersome" (Renn and Elliott, 2011, p. 236). After ten years, Member States had only completed assessments for an initial group of forty-one chemicals, revealing a lack of administrative capacity that seriously affects the working of the EU regime. A decisive step was taken with the adoption of REACH, which is based on the principle of 'no data, no market'. REACH extends testing obligations and shifts the burden of proof to manufacturers, requiring them to submit data proving that the substances they market are safe. Despite this, challenges in keeping up with market dynamics persist. As of the time of writing, the REACH database includes entries for around 27,000 substances, out of the 45,000 substances for which data are required.

A third EU chemical regime characteristic is the difficulty in finalizing regulatory guidelines to provide standards for data collection and evaluation. Since the 1980s, a clear trend toward the standardization of laboratory practices, protocols for testing and classification of substances have characterized the regulatory regime. Lacking an overarching legal framework for chemical management at the global level, states and stakeholders have engaged in voluntary programs to facilitate coordination, disseminate knowledge and define guidelines for assessing the most significant adverse environmental and public health effects (Selin, 2013). The EU and national authorities actively cooperate in international forums such as the Strategic Approach to International Chemicals Management, its recent successor, the Global Framework on Chemicals, the OECD and, in the pesticide sector, the European and Mediterranean Plant Protection Organization and US agencies. Concerning testing guidelines, it is notable that some, such as the Ames test for carcinogenicity, have been in place since the 1970s.

However, the development and validation of testing protocols have struggled to keep pace with rapid advancements in toxicology and endocrinology, which over time have revealed new and unanticipated adverse effects of chemical exposure. EU legislators have been relatively quick to introduce new testing obligations in regulations, generally mandating the Commission and/or ECHA to develop appropriate guidelines within a limited timeframe. For example, the 2009 pesticides regulation requires substances to be tested for their endocrine-disrupting properties but does not provide criteria for assessment and demands that guidance be adopted within two years. Unfortunately, there has been a systematic underestimation of the difficulties in defining evaluation standards and translating toxicology and ecotoxicology principles into workable regulatory testing protocols. Notably, the guidelines on endocrine disruption have been approved in ECHA and EFSA in 2018 (ECHA and EFSA, 2018). Similar delays occurred in the risk assessment of chemical mixtures, nanochemicals or in the screening of PFAS. Furthermore, it is important to note that there are still gaps in areas related to the environmental impact, fate and behavior of chemicals. These delays in the adoption of guidelines and the existence of gaps have resulted in inconsis-

2 Council Regulation (EEC) No 793/93, also known as the Existing Substances Regulation.

tencies and delays in risk assessment (Bodar et al., 2003; Bozzini, 2017; Paleari, 2016) and seriously calls into question the overall stringency of the EU chemical regime.

4 Regulatory controversies

Chemical regulation is inherently controversial, since it "gives rise to a politics fuelled not only by competing values and scientific uncertainty but also by debates over the way in which risks are distributed, managed and regulated by a state" (Fisher, 2008, pp. 542–543). Such competing views and interests have been evident during the policy formulation stage of chemical-related legislative acts (Bozzini, 2017; Vaughan, 2015). As Selin (2007, p. 64) summarized in his analysis of REACH, it "was created despite intense resistance from influential and well-organized industry interests, and outspoken suspicion from leading European politicians and national industry and trade ministers", as well as from US stakeholders and institutions who strongly opposed key provisions informed by a precautionary approach. The final text was adopted thanks to the advocacy of Sweden and other northern Member States, Directorate-General for Environment, Green Members of European Parliament and environmental and public health public interest groups that managed to secure agreement on a diluted version of the original Commission proposal (Selin, 2007; Stokes and Vaughan, 2013).

Controversies have continued in the last decade of policy implementation, shedding light on critical characteristics of the EU chemicals regulatory regime. First, the exact application of the precautionary principle to the regulation of certain chemicals where safety has been questioned, such as bisphenol A, glyphosate and neonicotinoids, has been subjected to extended debate (Alemanno, 2010; Arcuri and Hendlin, 2019; Bozzini, 2020). More specific to the chemical sector is the application of the substitution principle. Critics argue that substitution "is a blunt and imprecise regulatory instrument and should be used with care and most certainly on a case-by-case basis" (Lofstedt, 2014, p. 555). First, difficulties arise because rarely is one active substance better than another across all relevant health and environmental profiles. For example, chemicals that are less persistent in the environment can have higher toxicity. Second, there are dilemmas regarding the application modalities of the principle. According to the European Chemical Industry Council (CEFIC), the leading organization representing European chemical industries, "substitution is the replacement of one substance with another with the aim of achieving a lower level of risk" (CEFIC, 2005, p. 1). In other words, it involves substituting one chemical with another. A broader approach, often referred to as 'functional substitution', includes both chemical and nonchemical solutions. This approach seeks a less hazardous substance, product or process that provides functionality equivalent to the original substance. As a result of such ambiguities in the conception of substitution, its application on biocides and pesticides and in the context of REACH remains marginal (Coria, Kristiansson and Gustavsson, 2022; Klika, 2015a).

A second relevant line of controversy centers around the issue of conflict of interest. As briefly mentioned above, REACH and all other chemical-related acts put the burden of proof on manufacturers and importers. This is the object of fierce criticism. First, industry representatives have complained about the amount and costs of testing, which they believe exceed safety needs and hinder innovation (Bozzini, 2018). From a different angle, critics observe that it makes the entire risk assessment system dependent upon data generated (and paid for) by industry, and thus biased (Pesticides Action Network, 2014). This is a big issue for REACH, since, as Elizabeth Fisher (2008) noted, 95 percent of dossiers submitted to ECHA do not undergo any process of quality control beyond an initial completeness check. Controversies have arisen also in sub-sectors like pesticide and biocides where national and EU agencies are obliged to evaluate dossiers submitted by manufacturers (Corporate Europe Observatory, 2017; EFSA, 2017). The controversy over the evaluation of the carcinogenicity of the herbicide glyphosate—highlighted by environmental nongovernmental organizations' conclusion that "it appears that EFSA's conclusions may have been unduly influenced by Monsanto" (Pesticides Action Network, 2017 p. 21)—is a clear example of this problem.

Finally, it is worth mentioning the ongoing debate about the use of animal testing for the safety of substances. European citizens have expressed concerns over animal welfare on various occasions, most recently in the 2023 European citizens' initiative Save Cruelty Free Cosmetics. In policy and scientific circles, ethical considerations have been widely discussed under the label '3R Principle', which aims to Replace animal experiments altogether, Reduce the number of animals used and Refine protocols to avoid suffering. Since 2013, animal tests for cosmetic products have been banned. In other sub-sectors, there are restrictions. For example, Article 62 of the Biocide Regulation mandates data-sharing among manufacturers on vertebrate animal tests and prohibits the duplication of such tests. Reliance on animal testing is problematic not only from an ethical standpoint but also due to questions about the reliability of results, especially regarding the extrapolation of findings from animals to humans (see Almiron/Paez Chapter). As the field of regulatory toxicology evolves, there is a growing recognition of the need for alternative testing methods that better reflect human physiology and responses.

5 Comparative perspectives

The European Commission often describes the EU chemical regulatory regime as 'the strictest in the world'. Scholars working on comparative policy analysis tend to agree with this statement. Papers comparing EU REACH and the US Toxic Substances Control Act (TSCA) tend to highlight that EU provisions are more precautionary, more centralized and (contrary to US regulations) put the burden of proof on manufacturers (Applegate, 2008; Botos, Graham and Illés, 2019; Renn and Elliott, 2011). A similar argument can be made for the regulation of pesticides (Bozzini, 2017) and cosmetics

(Cribb, 2017).[3] Taking a long-term perspective, Vogel (2012) showed that the EU regulatory regime for hazardous chemical substances has become increasingly stringent over time in response to public concerns about public health and environmental safety and the adoption of the precautionary approach.

Despite some criticisms that REACH has not fully achieved its initial ambitions (Stokes and Vaughan, 2013), it remains a potentially influential model for chemical regulation globally (Heyen, 2013). Notably, some scholars suggested that other countries might look to REACH as a blueprint for their regulatory reforms. Cha and Koo (2021) show that most of the seventy countries in their analysis have adapted their domestic regulations to align with REACH in order to overcome technical barriers to trade. More detailed case studies support this conclusion. For example, the analysis of Liu (2016) suggests that reforms of the Taiwanese chemical regime have been directly informed by developments in EU REACH, while the 2011 reform of the Chinese chemical legislation is known as "China REACH" (Sun, 2019). By contrast, the EU influences on Japanese and US legislation appear limited (Naiki 2010). Indeed, there was considerable anticipation among scholars that the expected reform of US chemical legislation would align more closely with European principles and approaches. However, when US legislators reformed the TSCA in 2016, this expectation did not materialize, reflecting a persisting divergence in regulatory philosophies between the two jurisdictions (Vogel, 2012).

Finally and importantly, in recent years scholars have pointed out that the protection of environment and public health in the EU is not aligned with policy toward third countries. Pesticides banned for utilization in the EU are still produced for export to third countries (Sarkar et al., 2021). *Public Eye* (2020) published a journalistic investigation highlighting that big EU-based agrochemicals companies like Syngenta, Bayer and Basf sell tonnes of products containing highly hazardous substances like atrazine and paraquat to countries like Brazil. The European Commission addressed the issue in 2023 (European Commission 2023d). A decision on the proposed provisions is pending at the time of writing.

6 Future developments in policy and research

The EU chemicals regulatory framework is both complex and highly ambitious due to its stringent regulatory criteria. However, it faces significant challenges that need to be addressed to ensure effectiveness. One major shortcoming is the protracted pace of evaluations, which leaves thousands of untested chemicals on the market and undermines the 'no data, no market' principle that is supposed to inform REACH and other

3 For example, the US has authorized the use of around 1,500 substances for use as pesticides, while the EU authorizes 450. In the field of cosmetics, the US Food and Drug Administration has banned 11 substances, the EU over 1,300.

chemical-related regulations. Additionally, the framework heavily relies on data generated by the chemical industry itself. This dependency raises significant concerns about potential conflicts of interest, possibly undermining public trust in the objectivity and reliability of the evaluations and the overall legitimacy of the EU regime (Klika, 2015b).

The stringency of the EU framework is also questioned due to slow development (or lack) of detailed regulatory guidelines to specify procedures for conducting public health and environmental evaluations. While scientific understanding of the adverse effects of chemicals on the environment and public health is advancing rapidly, regulators struggle to keep pace and update risk assessment criteria. Without clear and timely guidelines, the effectiveness and consistency of the EU's regulatory regime are compromised, leaving the public and the environment exposed to undetected chemical risks.

Since the adoption of the European Green Deal (EGD), the 2020 Chemical Strategy for Sustainability the Zero Pollution Action Plan, and the so-called "Omnibus VI" package, the Commission has addressed some of the most pressing issues, particularly by streamlining evaluations through better enforcement of the 'one substance, one assessment' principle and promoting coordination among relevant agencies.[4] However, as with other environmental proposals in the EGD context (see Gravey Chapter), the actual adoption of reforms remains an open question.

In this rapidly evolving context, academic research could play a vital role in analyzing and enhancing the EU's chemical regulatory framework. Significant knowledge gaps need to be addressed to overcome the 'regulatory ignorance' that currently characterizes the field. In particular, comparative analysis of different chemical sub-sectors is largely neglected. Such analysis could be instrumental in assessing the coherence and coordination among various regulatory provisions. By examining how different sub-sectors are regulated and how they interact, researchers can provide valuable insights into the outputs, outcomes and impacts of the EU regulatory regime. Furthermore, systematic academic research can help identify best practices and areas for improvement, contributing to more informed policymaking. Addressing these gaps neglected by policymakers and academics is urgent, as chemical pollution poses an immediate and escalating threat to both public health and the environment.

References

Abelkop, A.D.K. and Graham, J.D. (2014) 'Principles and tools of chemical regulation: A comment on "the substitution principle in chemical regulation: a constructive critique"', *Journal of Risk Research*, 17(5), pp. 581–586.

4 The European Commission published three legislative initiatives on streamline assessments of chemicals across EU legislation, improve the knowledge base on chemicals and allocate tasks among EU agencies , and simplification (European Commission 2023b, 2023a, 2023c, 2025).

Alaranta, J. and Turunen, T. (2021) 'How to reach a safe Circular Economy? Perspectives on reconciling the waste, product and chemicals regulation', *Journal of Environmental Law,* 33(1), pp. 113 – 136.

Alemanno, A. (2010), 'The fabulous destiny of bisphenol A (BPA)', *European Journal of Risk Regulation,* 1(4), pp. 397 – 400.

Applegate, J.S. (2008) 'Synthesizing TSCA and REACH: Practical principles for chemical regulation reform', *Ecology Law Quarterly,* 35(4), pp. 721 – 769.

Arcuri, A. and Hendlin, Y.H. (2019) 'The chemical Anthropocene: Glyphosate as a case study of pesticide exposures', *King's Law Journal,* 30(2), pp. 234 – 253.

Bergkamp, L. (ed.) (2013) *The European Union REACH regulation for chemicals: Law and practice.* Oxford: Oxford University Press.

Bergkamp, L. and Herbatschek, N. (2014) 'Regulating chemical substances under REACH: The choice between authorization and restriction and the case of dipolar aprotic solvents', *Review of European, Comparative & International Environmental Law,* 23(2), pp. 221 – 245.

Bodar, C.W.M. et al. (2003) 'Evaluation of EU risk assessments existing chemicals (EC Regulation 793/93)', *Chemosphere,* 53(8), pp. 1039 – 1047.

Botos, Á., Graham, J.D. and Illés, Z. (2019) 'Industrial chemical regulation in the European Union and the United States: A comparison of REACH and the amended TSCA', *Journal of Risk Research,* 22(10), pp. 1187 – 1204.

Bozzini, E. (2017) *Pesticide policy and politics in the European Union: Regulatory assessment, implementation and enforcement.* London: Palgrave Macmillan.

Bozzini, E. (2018) *Assessing criteria and capacity for reliable and harmonised 'hazard identification' of active substances.* Brussels: European Parliamentary Research Service.

Bozzini, E. (2020) 'Contrasting norms on the use of evidence in risk assessment: The controversy surrounding the carcinogenicity of glyphosate', *Health, Risk & Society,* 22(3 – 4), pp. 197 – 213.

CEFIC (2005) *CEFIC Paper on substitution and authorisation under REACH.* Brussels: CEFIC.

Cha, Y. and Koo, M.G. (2021) 'Who embraces technical barriers to trade? The case of European REACH regulations', *World Trade Review,* 20(1), pp. 25 – 39.

Coria, J. (2018) 'The economics of toxic substance control and the REACH Directive', *Review of Environmental Economics and Policy,* 12(2), pp. 342 – 358.

Coria, J., Kristiansson, E. and Gustavsson, M. (2022) 'Economic interests cloud hazard reductions in the European regulation of substances of very high concern', *Nature Communications,* 13(1), 6686.

Corporate Europe Observatory (2017) 'Monsanto papers hearing at EU Parliament to lift lid on flawed EU pesticide approval process'. Available at: https://corporateeurope.org/pressreleases/2017/10/monsanto-papers-hearing-eu-parliament-lift-lid-flawed-eu-pesticide-approval (Accessed: 25 March 2025).

Cribb, J. (2017), *Surviving the 21st century: Humanity's ten great challenges and how we can overcome them.* Cham: Springer.

ECHA and EFSA, with the technical support of the JRC (2018) 'Guidance for the identification of endocrine disruptors in the context of regulations (EU) 528/2012 and (EC) 1107/2009', *EFSA Journal,* 16(6). Available at: https://doi.org/10.2903/j.efsa.2018.5311.

ECHA and EFSA (2020) 'In support of the EU chemicals strategy for sustainability: One substance—one assessment'. Available at: https://www.efsa.europa.eu/en/corporate/pub/osoa (Accessed: 25 March 2025)

EFSA (2017) 'EFSA statement addressing stakeholder concerns related to the EU assessment of glyphosate and the "Monsanto Papers"'. Available at: http://www.efsa.europa.eu/sites/default/files/170523-efsa-statement-glyphosate.pdf (Accessed: 11 July 2025).

Environmental Defense Fund (1997) *Toxic Ignorance. The Continuing Absence of Basic Health Testing for Top-selling Chemicals in the United States.* New York: EDF.

Eriksson, J., Gilek, M. and Rudén, C. (eds.) (2010) *Regulating Chemical Risks: European and Global Challenges.* Dordrecht: Springer.

European Commission (2001) *White Paper. Strategy for a Future Chemicals Policy.* COM(2001) 88 final. Available at: https://eur-lex.europa.eu/legal-content/EN/TXT/?uri=celex:52001DC0088 (Accessed: 25 March 2025).

European Commission (2023a) *Proposal for a REGULATION OF THE EUROPEAN PARLIAMENT AND OF THE COUNCIL amending Regulations (EC) No 178/2002, (EC) No 401/2009, (EU) 2017/745 and (EU) 2019/1021 of the European Parliament and of the Council as regards the re-attribution of scientific and technical tasks and improving cooperation among Union agencies in the area of chemicals.* COM(2023) 783 final. Available at: https://eur-lex.europa.eu/legal-content/EN/TXT/?uri=celex:52023PC0783 (Accessed: 25 March 2025).

European Commission (2023b) *Proposal for a DIRECTIVE OF THE EUROPEAN PARLIAMENT AND OF THE COUNCIL amending Directive 2011/65/EU of the European Parliament and of the Council as regards the re-attribution of scientific and technical tasks to the European Chemicals Agency.* COM(2023) 781 final. Available at: https://eur-lex.europa.eu/legal-content/EN/TXT/?uri=celex:52023PC0781 (Accessed: 25 March 2025).

European Commission (2023c) *Proposal for a REGULATION OF THE EUROPEAN PARLIAMENT AND OF THE COUNCIL establishing a common data platform on chemicals, laying down rules to ensure that the data contained in it are findable, accessible, interoperable and reusable and establishing a monitoring and outlook framework for chemicals.* COM(2023) 779 final. Available at: https://eur-lex.europa.eu/legal-content/EN/TXT/?uri=celex:52023PC0779 (Accessed: 25 March 2025).

European Commission (2023d) 'Hazardous chemicals—prohibiting production for export of chemicals banned in the European Union'. Available at: https://ec.europa.eu/info/law/better-regulation/have-your-say/initiatives/13750-Hazardous-chemicals-prohibiting-production-for-export-of-chemicals-banned-in-the-European-Union_en (Accessed: 11 July 2025).

European Commission (2025) Proposal for a REGULATION OF THE EUROPEAN PARLIAMENT AND OF THE COUNCIL amending Regulations (EC) No 1272/2008, (EC) No 1223/2009 and (EU) 2019/1009 as regards simplification of certain requirements and procedures for chemical products. COM(2025) 531 final. Available at https://data.consilium.europa.eu/doc/document/ST-11433-2025-INIT/en/pdf (Accessed: 30 December 2025)

European Environment Agency (2022) *Zero Pollution Monitoring Assessment.* Copenhagen: EEA.

Ferreira, M. et al. (2022), 'Overview of cosmetic regulatory frameworks around the world', *Cosmetics,* 9(4), 72.

Fisher, E. (2008) 'The "perfect storm" of REACH: charting regulatory controversy in the age of information, sustainable development, and globalization", *Journal of Risk Research,* 11(4), pp. 541–563.

Gruber, K. (2018) 'Cleaning up our future health', *Nature,* 555(7695), pp. S20–S22.

Hansen, S.F., Carlsen, L. and Tickner, J.A. (2007) 'Chemicals regulation and precaution: does REACH really incorporate the precautionary principle', *Environmental Science & Policy,* 10(5), pp. 395–404.

Hertel, R.F. (1996) 'Outline on risk assessment programme of existing substances in the European Union', *Environmental Toxicology and Pharmacology,* 2(2), pp. 93–96.

Heyen, D.A. (2013) 'Influence of the EU chemicals regulation on the US policy reform debate: is a "California effect" within REACH?', *Transnational Environmental Law,* 2(1), pp. 95–115.

Klika, C. (2015a) 'Risk and the Precautionary Principle in the implementation of Reach: the inclusion of Substances of Very High Concern in the Candidate List', *European Journal of Risk Regulation,* 6(1), pp. 111–120.

Klika (2015b) 'The implementation of the REACH authorisation procedure on chemical substances of concern: what kind of legitimacy?', *Politics and Governance,* 3(1), pp. 128–138.

Larson, D.B. and Jordan, S.R. (2019) 'Playing it safe: toy safety and conformity assessment in Europe and the United States', *International Review of Administrative Sciences,* 85(4), 763–779.

Lindgren, K.O. and Persson, T. (2008) 'The structure of conflict over EU chemicals policy', *European Union Politics,* 9(1), pp. 31–58.

Liu, R.H. (2016) 'A review and discussion of EU Regulation (EC) No 1907/2006 concerning the Registration, Evaluation, Authorisation and Restriction of Chemicals (REACH) -and the latest developments of the Taiwan Toxic Chemical Substances Control Law', *Euramerica,* 46(2), pp. 243 – 304.

Lofstedt, R. (2014) 'The substitution principle in chemical regulation: a constructive critique', *Journal of Risk Research,* 17(5), pp. 543 – 564.

Muir, D.C.G., Getzinger, G.J., McBride, M. and Ferguson, P.L. (2023) 'How many chemicals in commerce have been analyzed in environmental media? A 50 year bibliometric analysis', *Environmental Science & Technology,* 57(25), pp. 9119 – 9129.

Naidu, R. et al. (2021) 'Chemical pollution: A growing peril and potential catastrophic risk to humanity', *Environment International,* 156, 106616.

Naiki, Y. (2010) 'Assessing policy reach: Japan's chemical policy reform in response to the EU's REACH regulation', *Journal of Environmental Law,* 22(2), pp. 171 – 195.

Paleari, S. (2016) 'Managing chemicals under REACH 'hybridity': Progress and problems in the implementation process', *Review of European, Comparative and International Environmental Law,* 25(3), pp. 307 – 316.

Payá Pérez, A. and Rodríguez Eugenio, N. (2018) 'Status of local soil contamination in Europe: Revision of the indicator "Progress in the management contaminated sites in Europe"', *JRC Technical Reports.* Varese: Joint Research Centre.

Persson, L. et al. (2022), 'Outside the safe operating space of the planetary boundary for novel entities', *Environmental Science & Technology,* 56 (3), pp. 1510 – 1521.

Pesticides Action Network (2014) *Missed and dismissed: Pesticide regulators ignore the legal obligation to use independent science for deriving safe exposure levels.* Brussels: PAN Europe, https://www.pan-europe.info/sites/pan-europe.info/files/public/resources/reports/pane-2014-missed-and-dismissed.pdf (Accessed: 25 March 2025).

Pesticides Action Network (2017) *Glyphosate and cancer: Authorities systematically breach regulations.* Brussels: PAN Europe. Available at: https://www.pan-europe.info/sites/pan-europe.info/files/public/resources/reports/20170713_Glyphosate_Report_Global2000_EN.pdf (Accessed: 25 March 2025).

Public Eye (2020) *Banned in Europe: How the EU exports pesticides too dangerous for use in Europe.* Available at: https://www.publiceye.ch/en/topics/pesticides/banned-in-europe (Accessed: 25 March 2025).

Renn, O. and Elliott, D. (2011) 'Chemicals', in: Wiener, J.B., Rogers, M.D., Hammett, J.K. and Sand, P.H. (eds.) *The reality of precaution: Comparing risk regulation in the United States and Europe.* Washington DC: RFF Press, pp. 223 – 256

Rockström, J. et al. (2009) 'Planetary boundaries: Exploring the safe operating space for humanity', *Ecology and Society,* 14(2), 32.

Sarkar, S. et al. (2021) *The use of pesticides in developing countries and their impact on health and the right to food.* Brussels: European Parliament. Available at: https://doi.org/10.2861/28995.

Selin, H. (2007) 'Coalition politics and chemicals management in a regulatory ambitious Europe', *Global Environmental Politics,* 7(3), pp. 63 – 93.

Stokes, E. and Vaughan, S. (2013), 'Great expectations: Reviewing 50 years of chemicals legislation in the EU', *Journal of Environmental Law,* 25(3), pp. 411 – 435.

Sun, S. (2019) 'Chemical regulations in China: An overview', *IRCL,* 2, 75.

Thierse, S. (2019) 'Policy entrepreneurship in the European Parliament: Reconsidering the influence of rapporteurs', *Journal of European Public Policy,* 26(2), pp. 267 – 285.

UNEP (2019) *Global chemicals outlook II: From legacies to innovative solutions: Implementing the 2030 Agenda for Sustainable Development—Synthesis report.* Geneva: United Nations Environment Programme.

Vaughan, S. (2015) *EU chemicals regulation: New governance, hybridity and REACH.* Cheltenham: Edward Elgar Publishing.

Vogel, D. (2012) *The politics of precaution: Regulating health, safety, and environmental risks in Europe and the United States.* Princeton: Princeton University Press.
Wang, Z., Walker, G.W., Muir, D.C.G. and Nagatani-Yoshida, K. (2020) 'Toward a global understanding of chemical pollution: A first comprehensive analysis of national and regional chemical inventories', *Environmental Science and Technology*, 54(5), pp. 2575–2584.

Giulia Bazzan

Unravelling complexity: Challenges in shaping European Union sustainable food policies

Abstract: This chapter delves into the European Union's (EU) food policy within the broader context of EU environmental policy, highlighting the historical evolution, current dynamics and future vision for a sustainable food system. It underscores the EU's significant initiatives, such as the Farm to Fork and Biodiversity strategies under the Green Deal, which aim to align food safety, sustainability and environmental conservation. The analysis employs theoretical frameworks like policy networks, neo-institutionalism, policy learning and policy integration frameworks to dissect the complexities of EU food policy. Additionally, it addresses current governance challenges, emphasizing the need for improved coordination, equitable food access and sustainable practices. The chapter also explores future prospects, advocating for configurational comparative analysis to better understand the intricate factors influencing policy outcomes. This comprehensive exploration provides a nuanced understanding of the EU's role in shaping sustainable global food systems amidst evolving environmental and socioeconomic landscapes.

Keywords: European Union food policy; sustainability transition; food safety; environmental conservation; policy integration

1 Introduction

The European Union (EU) has long recognized the intricate link between food policy and environmental objectives. Facing the urgent challenges of climate change, biodiversity loss and sustainable resource management, the EU's food policy is pivotal to its comprehensive environmental strategy. This chapter critically examines the EU's integrated approach to food policy, particularly the Farm to Fork and Biodiversity strategies under the European Green Deal (EGD), arguing that, despite significant steps towards sustainability, substantial barriers remain. By examining historical evolutions, current dynamics and theoretical frameworks, it underscores the EU's role in global food governance and identifies key drivers, obstacles and solutions for future policy development.

EU food policy is not an isolated domain but an integral part of EU environmental policy (Alemanno and Gabbi, 2016; Alemanno, 2016). This integration is reflected in regulatory frameworks harmonizing the goals of food safety, sustainability and environmental conservation. The EGD, with its Farm to Fork and Biodiversity strategies, exemplifies the EU's commitment to transforming its food system into a model of sustainability and resilience (Bazzan, Daugbjerg and Tosun, 2023). However, the imple-

https://doi.org/10.1515/9783111321523-032

mentation of these strategies has faced significant political and stakeholder resistance, raising questions as to the extent of their transformative impact.

Central to the EU food policy are several key themes addressing the multifaceted nature of food systems. The sustainability transition focuses on reducing the environmental footprint from production to consumption (De Schutter, Jacobs and Clément, 2020; Galli et al., 2020), aiming to lower greenhouse gas emissions, enhance soil health and minimize water use, all while ensuring economic viability for farmers and food producers. Yet, progress is uneven across Member States, and the effectiveness of the Common Agricultural Policy's (CAP) greening payments is questionable (Alons, 2019; Daugbjerg and Feindt, 2017; Zwaan, Alons and van Voorst, 2022).

Food safety and quality are pivotal in EU food policy (Alemanno, 2015; Bazzan, 2017; Bazzan, 2021), with rigorous standards to ensure food safety and nutritional value, protecting consumer health and bolstering trust in the EU's food system, enhancing its global competitiveness. Nonetheless, enforcement and consistency across Member States remain challenges (Bazzan, 2021;Bazzan and Vogeler, 2025; Bazzan, Kuenzler and Vogeler, 2025).

Biodiversity and environmental conservation are linked to sustainable food systems (see Chapter 23). EU policies aim to protect habitats, preserve genetic diversity and support sustainable farming (Bazzan, Candel and Daugbjerg, 2023; Bazzan, Daugbjerg and Tosun, 2023). The decline in biodiversity threatens food security, necessitating integrated land and resource management. Food security is critical amid a growing population and climate change (Candel and Biesbroek, 2018; Matthews, 2015; Moragues-Faus, Sonnino and Marsden, 2017; Righettini, 2025). The EU aims to ensure a stable food supply, reduce import dependency and support agricultural innovation. However, geopolitical tensions and global disruptions expose supply chain vulnerabilities.

Health and nutrition are increasingly prominent in EU food policy that addresses obesity, malnutrition and noncommunicable diseases. The EU promotes balanced diets and healthy lifestyles through food labeling, reduced sugar and fat content and increased fruit and vegetable consumption. Achieving widespread behavioral change remains challenging, however.

Lastly, animal welfare is essential in EU food policy (Di Concetto, 2024; Vogeler, Hornung and Bandelow, 2020; Vogeler 2019). The EU has pioneered high standards for animal treatment, acknowledging the crucial role of ethical considerations and consumer expectations in shaping food production practices (for a critical perspective on the EU approach, see Chapter 19). However, a persistent debate exists over balancing animal welfare standards with the economic pressures on farmers. These standards often escalate costs for farmers due to the need for improved housing, feed, veterinary care and overall management practices. Furthermore, EU farmers are at a competitive disadvantage against countries with lower animal welfare standards, impacting production costs and market prices. Lastly, the implementation and enforcement of these standards vary across Member States, resulting in inconsistencies (Bazzan and Vogeler, 2025).

EU food policy seeks to balance people, planet and prosperity through regulatory measures, incentives and nodality. The transition to a sustainable, safe and equitable food system faces political resistance, stakeholder conflicts and agricultural exceptionalism. This chapter explores these themes, providing an overview of challenges and opportunities in shaping sustainable EU food policies. It uses policy networks, policy learning and policy integration frameworks to examine the EU's proactive measures addressing challenges and opportunities for transformative change. It highlights persistent challenges, stressing the need for coordination, equitable food access and sustainable practices. This chapter outlines the challenges and prospects for researchers in EU food policy, emphasizing configurational comparative analysis methods to provide insights into policy complexity and outcomes.

2 Historical evolution of EU food policy

The EU has navigated a complex trajectory in shaping its food policy, marked by transformative shifts in governance, regulatory frameworks and socioeconomic objectives. Initially, the CAP was established post-war to secure food supplies and stabilize agricultural markets, with a focus on boosting productivity and ensuring farmers' livelihoods through extensive subsidies and market interventions.

However, these subsidies soon led to overproduction and environmental degradation. By the 1980s and 1990s, the unsustainable nature of these policies became evident, prompting reforms like the 1992 MacSharry reforms, which introduced environmental considerations into the CAP and shifted from production-focused subsidies to environmentally sustainable support mechanisms (Daugbjerg, 2003).

In the early 2000s, the EU incorporated broader sustainability goals, influenced by the Lisbon Strategy and the Europe 2020 strategy, advocating for sustainable agricultural practices and biodiversity conservation. A key milestone was the introduction of 'Regulation 178/2002', the General Food Law, in response to the Bovine Spongiform Encephalopathy crisis, which established a comprehensive approach to food safety and created the European Food Safety Authority (EFSA). The EFSA's establishment was crucial in restoring consumer confidence and ensuring high levels of food safety, public health and environmental sustainability. Further measures included enhancing food traceability, improving crisis management and increasing transparency, culminating in 'Regulation (EU) 2019/1381' on food safety governance. The EGD, with the Farm to Fork (F2F) and Biodiversity strategies it introduced in 2020, has signified a paradigmatic shift towards an integrated approach to food systems, aiming to reduce reliance on pesticides and antimicrobials, boost organic farming and strengthen food system resilience. However, these ambitious goals have faced significant challenges and resistance.

In December 2021, the European Commission (EC) proposed a legislative framework for sustainable food systems and new regulations on the Sustainable Use of Plant Protection Products, targeting a 50 percent reduction in chemical pesticide use by 2030. Yet, in March 2024, the Commission withdrew the proposal due to a lack of agreement within the Council and European Parliament. The F2F strategy continues to encounter political and stakeholder resistance, with farmers protesting the economic impacts of reduced pesticide use and increased organic farming; internal disagreements within the Commission further complicate reforms.

Since 2019, the EU's efforts to transition towards a sustainable food system through the Green Deal and F2F strategy have been substantial, but they have been met with resistance, particularly from the agricultural sector. This has led to political pushback and delays in implementation, exemplified by the withdrawal of the pesticide regulation proposal in 2024, highlighting the struggle to balance environmental goals with practical and economic considerations.

3 Theoretical developments and research contributions

The area of EU food policy and its governance have generated an extensive body of research, drawing the attention of scholars from a wide range of disciplines and perspectives. Over the years, policy and governance scholars have studied EU food and agriculture policymaking as a generative empirical example in the theoretical development of policy and governance studies (Daugbjerg and Feindt, 2017, p. 1566). These studies (Alemanno, 2015; Alons, 2019; Bazzan, 2021; Bazzan, Daugbjerg and Tosun, 2023; Becker, 2023; Biesbroek and Candel, 2020; Candel and Biesbroek, 2018; Coleman, Skogstad and Atkinson, 1996; Coleman and Grant, 1998; Daugbjerg, 2003; Daugbjerg and Feindt, 2017, 2019; Daugbjerg and Swinbank, 2012, 2015, 2016; Feindt, 2010, 2018; Feindt and Flynn, 2009; Greer, 2017; Grohmann and Feindt, 2024; Havinga, Casey and van Waarden, 2015; Jackson and Deeg, 2012; Jordan, Maloney and McLaughlin, 1994; Kay, 2005; Lowe, Feindt and Vihinen, 2010; Marek and Tosun, 2023; Popp, Feindt and Daedlow, 2021; Schebesta and Candel, 2020; Skogstad, 1998, 2008; Termeer, Biesbroek and van den Brink, 2012; Termeer, Dewulf and Biesbroek, 2019; Thomann, 2018) have contributed to theoretical developments in public policy and governance within a number of research fields concerned with the explanation of policy outcomes, policy stability and policy change (Candel and Daugbjerg, 2020; Daugbjerg and Feindt, 2017).

One of the significant theoretical contributions in EU food policy research has been the exploration of policy networks and paradigm shifts (see Chapters 2 and 3). Coleman, Skogstad and Atkinson (1996) and Coleman and Grant (1998) examined the dynamics of policy networks and their impact on agricultural policymaking. Their work highlighted how the interaction between various stakeholders within these networks leads to cumulative policy changes. This approach aligns with the concept of policy feedback, as Daugbjerg (2003) discussed, where past policy decisions shape future policy developments through established networks and paradigms.

Skogstad (1998, 2008) further elaborated on the notion of paradigm shifts, investigating the persistence of agricultural exceptionalism in the EU and the United States, providing insights into how deeply ingrained paradigms can influence policy continuity and resistance to change, even in the face of globalization and international pressures. However, there is a need for more research on how these networks adapt to changing policy environments and how they impact policy coherence. Understanding these processes is essential for addressing issues such as food safety, sustainability and agricultural practices.

Candel and Biesbroek (2016, 2018) have significantly contributed to understanding policy integration within the EU food policy context. Their research focuses on the mechanisms that facilitate or hinder the integration of various policy domains, such as food security and climate change adaptation. This processual understanding of policy integration is crucial for addressing complex, cross-cutting issues in EU governance. The integration of new policy instruments (see Chapter 22), as explored by Bazzan, Daugbjerg and Tosun (2023), underscores the EU's efforts to achieve policy coherence through initiatives like the F2F strategy, illustrating how innovative policy tools can enhance policy integration and lead to more effective governance outcomes. However, achieving effective integration remains a significant challenge, requiring more empirical studies to identify successful practices for achieving policy coherence across different domains.

Feindt and Flynn (2009) and Daugbjerg and Swinbank (2012, 2015, 2016) have examined the concepts of institutional layering and policy change within the EU's agricultural policy. Their work demonstrates how incremental changes and the addition of new policy layers can lead to substantial transformations over time, providing a nuanced perspective on the evolution of the CAP and the incorporation of sustainability criteria for biofuels. Despite recent reforms aimed at integrating environmental sustainability into the CAP, an exceptionalist legacy remains. Future research should explore how new institutional arrangements can overcome path dependencies and drive policy innovation. Similarly, Feindt (2010), Termeer, Biesbroek and van den Brink (20129, Termeer, Dewulf and Biesbroek (2019) and Grohmann and Feindt (2024) highlight the importance of policy learning and adaptation in the context of environmental policy integration. Feindt's study on policy learning within the CAP provides valuable insights into how policymakers incorporate environmental considerations into agricultural policy, while Termeer and colleagues' work on adaptation strategies emphasizes the need for flexible and adaptive governance structures to address climate change challenges. More studies are needed on integrating policy learning into the design and implementation processes to enhance the effectiveness of EU food policies (Dunlop and Radaelli, 2019).

The exploration by Alemanno (2015) and Bazzan (2021) of governance frameworks for food safety and risk regulation provides critical insights into the regulatory mechanisms ensuring food safety in the EU. Alemanno's critical analysis of the multilateral governance framework offers a normative perspective on food safety regulations, while Bazzan's examination of governance designs highlights the role of rules in ensuring effective food safety regulation. Becker (2023) examines how the EC, despite facing challenges in legislative influence, effectively utilized its implementation powers to align the CAP with the EGD, showcasing its ability to act as a policy entrepreneur by blending hard and soft law to pressure Member States into compliance.

While the literature on EU food policy and governance is robust, several gaps remain. There is a limited focus on how policies are implemented and enforced in practice, with most studies concentrating on policy design, agenda setting and formulation. This leaves a gap in understanding the practical challenges and dynamics involved in executing and monitoring policies effectively. Additionally, the impact of digitalization, artificial intelligence and other emerging technologies on food policy and governance is underexplored, highlighting a need for research on how these innovations could transform policy processes and outcomes. Comparative studies examining the differentiated implementation of EU food policies across Member States, considering their unique political, economic and cultural contexts, are also scarce (for a general overview of Member State contexts, see Chapter 14). Such research could reveal important variations and contribute to more tailored and effective policy recommendations. Moreover, there is a need for longitudinal studies that track the long-term impacts of specific food policies to evaluate their sustained effectiveness.

The study of the EU's efforts to shape sustainable food policies requires a balanced assessment of achievements and ongoing challenges. For instance, while the F2F strategy introduced new sustainability goals, it faced significant political and stakeholder resistance, leading to the watering down of some proposals. It is important to discuss the resilience of agricultural exceptionalism in the face of new policy initiatives and the implications for future policy development, including the need for deeper reforms to meet sustainability expectations and address systemic challenges (Greer, 2017).

4 Current challenges in EU food governance

EU food policy faces several significant governance challenges in the current landscape. These challenges are multifaceted and stem from the need to balance various priorities and interests while ensuring the sustainability and resilience of the food system.

Achieving sustainability within the EU's food policy framework is complex, requiring the reconciliation of food production needs with environmental sustainability. Agriculture, a significant contributor to climate change due to greenhouse gas emissions from livestock, fertilizers and deforestation, is also highly vulnerable to the impacts of climate change, such as altered precipitation patterns and extreme weather events, which threaten crop yields and food security. Furthermore, intensive farming practices have led to habitat destruction and a significant decline in biodiversity.

Several underlying issues exacerbate the complexity of these sustainability challenges. Economic pressures on farmers often lead to prioritizing short-term financial gains over long-term sustainability. This includes the reliance on subsidies that do not adequately promote environmental objectives. Additionally, there is significant disparity in the implementation and enforcement of policies across Member States, leading to uneven progress (see Chapters 14 and 34). Conflicting interests among stakeholders, including industry, environmental groups and policymakers, create blockages in advancing comprehensive reforms. These intertwined factors collectively contribute to the slow and uneven progress observed in achieving sustainability in the EU's food policy. For example, the CAP's eco-schemes introduced in the 2023–2027 reform aim to incentivize sustainable practices, but their uptake has varied widely across Member States due to diverging national priorities and administrative capacities.

Despite the EU's commitment to reducing greenhouse gas emissions and promoting sustainable agricultural practices through initiatives like the Green Deal and the F2F strategy, progress has been slow and uneven across Member States. The CAP, for instance, has faced criticism for its limited environmental impact, despite the introduction of measures like cross-compliance and greening payments. Its traditional focus on income support for farmers has often overshadowed environmental objectives. Although reforms have introduced environmental requirements, these measures have frequently been seen as inadequate. For example, the effectiveness of greening payments has been questioned, with critics arguing that they primarily serve as income support rather than genuinely promoting sustainable practices. EU policies must promote agricultural practices that protect and enhance biodiversity, such as crop diversification and organic farming. Sustainable management of water and soil resources is equally essential, as over-extraction of water for irrigation and soil degradation through erosion, contamination and loss of fertility pose long-term threats to food production. Policies must incentivize practices that conserve these critical resources. An illustrative case is the limited success of crop diversification measures under greening requirements, where studies found negligible biodiversity benefits due to weak enforcement and flexibility in implementation.

Ensuring a stable and secure food supply is fundamental, particularly in light of global disruptions. Events like the Covid-19 pandemic and geopolitical tensions have highlighted the fragility of global supply chains, leading to food shortages and price volatility. Strengthening the resilience of these supply chains is paramount. The EU's reliance on imports for certain food products makes it susceptible to external market fluctuations and trade policies. Reducing this dependency through local production and diversification of import sources is crucial. For example, the European Commission's 2022 Communication on Safeguarding Food Security introduced measures to boost EU-grown protein crops like legumes, aiming to reduce dependence on imported animal feed, particularly soy from South America. Developing robust contingency plans to maintain food supplies during crises is essential, including strategic reserves and policies that ensure continued access to essential foodstuffs. These challenges in food security and supply chain resilience stem from several critical areas. The volatility of global markets significantly impacts the EU's food supply, while the lack of robust contingency planning exacerbates vulnerabilities during crises. Additionally, local production limitations and over-reliance on a few import sources increase susceptibility to external shocks.

Health and nutrition are also vital components of the EU's food policy. Rising rates of obesity and related diseases, such as diabetes and cardiovascular conditions, necessitate policies that encourage healthier eating habits. This involves improving the nutritional quality of food and promoting lifestyle changes. Ensuring the safety and quality of food products through stringent standards and effective monitoring systems is critical, and the EU must continue to uphold high food safety standards to protect consumers. Increasing public awareness about nutrition and promoting healthier food choices is essential, with education campaigns and clear labeling to help consumers make informed decisions. Insufficient public awareness about nutrition stems from deeper societal factors, including the pervasive influence of advertising, consumer markets that prioritize convenience and highly processed products and inconsistent media messaging on health. Additionally, socioeconomic disparities limit access to nutritious foods and healthy lifestyle options, further exacerbating these issues. Therefore, addressing these barriers requires a more integrated approach, involving not only consumer education but also structural changes in food marketing and greater support for equitable food access. For instance, the 2022 revision of the EU School Scheme increased funding for fruit, vegetables and milk distribution in schools, which promoted healthier eating habits among children.

Supporting the economic sustainability of the agricultural sector while ensuring fair competition and market access is a persistent challenge. Many farmers face low incomes and high operational costs, and policies must ensure fair pricing, adequate subsidies and financial support to sustain farmers' livelihoods. Ensuring that small and medium-sized farms can compete in the market and access new technologies and innovations is crucial, and policies should support market diversification and the adoption of sustainable practices. Investing in rural areas to prevent depopulation and ensure the viability of farming communities is essential, including improving infrastructure, services and economic opportunities in rural regions.

The global nature of food systems introduces another layer of complexity to EU food governance. The EU is both a major importer and exporter of food, which means its policies have far-reaching impacts beyond its borders (see Chapter 29). International trade agreements and global market dynamics can undermine EU sustainability efforts if not aligned with its environmental goals. For instance, trade policies that prioritize economic gains over environmental protections can lead to increased imports of products with lower environmental standards, thus negating the benefits of domestic sustainability measures. Moreover, international cooperation is crucial for addressing transboundary environmental issues such as biodiversity loss, climate change and pollution. The EU's role in international organizations and its ability to influence global food governance frameworks are vital for promoting sustainability. However, achieving cohesive international policies is challenging due to differing national interests and regulatory standards. This involves both splits over national interests within the EU and negotiations with third-party countries. Aligning these interests requires diplomatic engagement and leveraging the EU's influence to push for global standards that support sustainability. A key example is the EU-Mercosur trade agreement, which has been criticized for potentially undermining the EU's environmental standards by allowing the import of products linked to deforestation.

Several driving forces compound the complexity of global food systems governance. Conflicting national interests within the EU and with third-party countries during negotiations create significant challenges. Additionally, international trade agreements that prioritize economic gains over environmental protections can undermine sustainability efforts. The need for international co-operation to address transboundary environmental issues further complicates policy coherence. The EU's Sustainability Impact Assessments (SIAs) attempt to preempt these tensions by evaluating environmental and social effects of trade agreements, such as those with India, Philippines and Malaysia.

Ensuring coherent and effective implementation of food policies across diverse Member States poses significant governance challenges. Achieving policy coherence is essential for the effectiveness of food governance, as differing national priorities and regulations complicate the alignment of food policies with related policies, such as trade, health and environment. Guaranteeing consistent enforcement of EU regulations across Member States is challenging though necessary, as disparities in compliance can lead to market distortions and undermine policy effectiveness. Effective coordination among various stakeholders, including governments, industry and civil society, is needed to ensure broad support and successful implementation of food policies. Integrated governance approaches can facilitate this coordination. The difficulties in ensuring policy coherence and effective implementation arise from several key factors. Strengthening monitoring and enforcement mechanisms is likewise crucial. The EU's 2021 reform of the CAP included a new performance-based delivery model, requiring Member States to submit Strategic Plans, yet initial evaluations revealed discrepancies in environmental ambition.

Addressing the aforementioned policy and governance challenges requires a multifaceted approach involving collaboration across sectors and levels of governance, innovation in sustainable practices and a commitment to protecting both people and the planet. For instance, promoting sustainable practices can unlock governance challenges by reducing environmental impacts and ensuring long-term food security. Strengthening supply chain resilience through local production and diversified import sources can mitigate the risks of global disruptions. Enhancing health and nutrition through stringent standards and public awareness campaigns can improve public health outcomes and reduce healthcare costs. Supporting the economic sustainability of farmers through fair pricing, subsidies and access to technology can ensure the viability of the agricultural sector and rural communities. Furthermore, international co-operation and alignment of policies can amplify the EU's influence in global food governance, promoting sustainability on a broader scale.

5 Future prospects and research directions

As the EU continues to navigate the complexities of sustainable food policy, a valuable avenue for future research would build on and further expand the existing theoretical contributions to address evolving challenges. Configurational comparative approaches emerge as crucial tools for understanding the intricate interactions within policy environments. These methods allow for a nuanced analysis of how specific institutional configurations, stakeholder engagements and governance practices combine to produce effective policy outcomes (Bazzan et al., 2023; Engeli, Rihoux and Allison, 2014; Rihoux and Ragin, 2009).

Comparative research highlights the necessity of tailoring policies to local contexts. By examining how different Member States implement EU food policies, researchers can uncover variations that lead to more successful outcomes (Bazzan, 2021; Havinga et al., Casey and van Waarden, 2015; Thomann, 2018). This approach can provide valuable lessons on the conditions under which policies achieve their intended goals, particularly in addressing sustainability and resilience.

Future studies should continue to explore the dynamics of multilevel governance, emphasizing how decisions at local, national and supranational levels interact to shape food policy outcomes. Understanding these interactions can help identify best practices for policy coordination and integration, essential for addressing cross-cutting issues like climate change and food security (Biesbroek and Candel, 2020; Candel and Biesbroek, 2018). Additionally, policy integration remains critical, and studies should explore how to better align food policies with broader environmental, health and economic objectives (Candel and Biesbroek, 2018).

The role of policy networks in facilitating effective governance cannot be overstated. Future research should focus on how these networks can be optimized to enhance collaboration among stakeholders, ensuring that diverse perspectives and expertise contribute to policy development and implementation (Coleman and Grant, 1998; Marsh and Smith, 2000). This can lead to more robust and inclusive food policies that better meet the needs of various actors.

Building on neo-institutionalism, future research should investigate how institutional reforms can overcome path dependencies and foster innovation (Kay, 2005; Daugbjerg, 2003). For instance, reforming the CAP to support agroecology could break away from traditional monoculture-focused subsidies and promote more sustainable farming. This includes exploring new governance structures that support adaptive and resilient policy frameworks capable of responding to emerging challenges and technological advancements (Grohmann and Feindt, 2024).

Policy learning must be integrated into the fabric of EU food policy to ensure continuous improvement. Future research should focus on mechanisms for systematic learning from past policy experiences which has shown the benefits of integrated pest management in reducing environmental damage, such as the overuse of chemical pesticides, while maintaining yields. This will enable the design of more effective interventions (Feindt, 2010; Dunlop and Radaelli, 2019).

Emerging technological innovations present new opportunities and challenges for EU food policy. Future research should examine how these technologies can transform policy processes and outcomes, for example, by using artificial intelligence to monitor food supply chains and predict demand, thus reducing waste and optimizing resource use.

In conclusion, advancing EU food policy research requires a commitment to building on established theoretical frameworks while embracing innovative approaches. By leveraging configurational comparative analysis, researchers can develop insights that drive more effective and sustainable food policies. Addressing the multifaceted challenges of food governance demands a holistic and adaptive approach, ensuring that EU food policy evolves to meet the needs of a changing world.

References

Alemanno, A. (2015) 'The multilateral governance framework for food safety: A critical and normative overview', in: Hammoudi, A., Grazia, C., Surry, Y., Traversac, JB. (eds.) *Food safety, market organization, trade and development.* Springer, Cham, pp. 9–43.

Alemanno, A. (2016) 'Foundations of EU food law and policy', in: Alemanno, A. and Gabbi, S. (eds.) *Foundations of EU food law and policy.* London Routledge, pp. 1–14.

Alemanno, A. and Gabbi, S. (eds.) (2016) *Foundations of EU food law and policy: Ten years of the European food safety authority.* London: Routledge.

Alons, G. (2019) 'Environmental policy integration in the EU's common agricultural policy: Greening or greenwashing?', in: Daugbjerg, C. and Feindt, P. (eds.) *Transforming food and agricultural policy.* London: Routledge, pp. 40–58.

Bazzan, G. (2017) 'Effective governance of food safety regulation across EU Member States: Towards operationalization', *European Journal of Risk Regulation*, 8(3), pp. 565–572.

Bazzan, G. (2021) *Effective governance designs of food safety regulation in the EU: Do rules make the difference?* Cham: Palgrave Macmillan.

Bazzan, G., Candel, J. and Daugbjerg, C. (2023) 'Designing successful agri-environmental schemes: A mechanistic analysis of a collective scheme for eco-system services in the Netherlands', *Environmental Science and Policy*, 146, pp. 123–132.

Bazzan, G., Candel, J., Daugbjerg, C. and Pecurul, M. (2023) 'Identifying institutional configurations for policy outcomes: A comparison of ecosystem services delivery', *Policy Studies Journal*, 51(3), pp. 501–527.

Bazzan, G., Daugbjerg, C. and Tosun, J. (2023) 'Attaining policy integration through the integration of new policy instruments: The case of the Farm to Fork Strategy', *Applied Economic Perspectives and Policy*, 45(2), pp. 803–818.

Bazzan, G. and Vogeler, C. S. (2025) Differentiated policy implementation in food safety and animal welfare policymaking, *European Policy Analysis*, 1–21.

Bazzan, G., Kuenzler, J. and Vogeler, C. S. (2025) Conditions favoring the reduction of pesticides: A qualitative comparative analysis of EU member states, *Review of Policy Research*, 42(6), 1480–1495.

Becker, S. (2023) 'Supranational entrepreneurship through the administrative backdoor: The Commission, the Green Deal and the CAP 2023–2027', *Journal of Common Market Studies*, 62(3), pp. 688–704.

Biesbroek, R. and Candel, J.J.L. (2020) 'Mechanisms for policy (dis)integration: Explaining food policy and climate change adaptation policy in the Netherlands', *Policy Sciences*, 53(1), pp. 61 – 84.

Candel, J.J.L. and Biesbroek, R. (2016) 'Toward a processual understanding of policy integration', *Policy Sciences*, 49(1), pp. 211 – 231.

Candel, J.J.L. and Biesbroek, R. (2018) 'Policy integration in the EU governance of global food security', *Food Security*, 10(1), pp. 195 – 209.

Candel, J., & Daugbjerg, C. (2020). 'Overcoming the dependent variable problem in studying food policy'. *Food Security, 12*(1), pp. 169 – 178.

Coleman, W. and Grant, W. P. (1998) 'Policy convergence and policy feedback: agricultural finance policies in a globalizing era', *European Journal of Political Research*, 34(2), pp. 225 – 247.

Coleman, W., Skogstad, G. and Atkinson, M. (1996) 'Paradigm shifts and policy networks: Cumulative change in agriculture', *Journal of Public Policy*, 16(3), pp. 273 – 301.

Daugbjerg, C. (2003) 'Policy feedback and paradigm shift in EU agricultural policy: The effects of the MacSharry reform on future reform', *Journal of European Public Policy*, 10(3), pp. 421 – 437.

Daugbjerg, C., Farsund, A.A. and Langhelle, O. (2019) 'The resilience of paradigm mixes: Food security in a post-exceptionalist trade regime',I n: Daugbjerg, C. and Feindt, P.H. (eds.) *Transforming food and agricultural policy*. London: Routledge, pp. 134 – 151.

Daugbjerg, C. and Feindt, P.H. (2017) 'Post-exceptionalism in public policy: Transforming food and agricultural policy', *Journal of European Public Policy*, 24(11), pp. 1565 – 1584.

Daugbjerg, C. and Feindt, P.H. (eds.) (2019) *Transforming food and agricultural policy: Post-exceptionalism in public policy*. London: Routledge.

Daugbjerg, C. and Swinbank, A. (2012) 'An introduction to the "new" politics of agriculture and food', *Policy and Society*, 31(4), pp. 259 – 270.

Daugbjerg, C. and Swinbank, A. (2015) 'Globalization and new policy concerns: the WTO and the EU's sustainability criteria for biofuels', *Journal of European Public Policy*, 22(3), pp. 429 – 446.

Daugbjerg, C. and Swinbank, A. (2016) 'Three decades of policy layering and politically sustainable reform in the European Union's Agricultural Policy: Policy layering and politically sustainable reform', *Governance*, 29(2), pp. 265 – 280.

De Schutter, O., Jacobs, N. and Clément, C. (2020) 'A "Common Food Policy" for Europe: how governance reforms can spark a shift to healthy diets and sustainable food systems', *Food Policy*, 96, 101849.

Di Concetto, A. (2024) 'Farm animal welfare and food information for European Union consumers: Harmonising the regulatory framework for more policy coherence', *European Journal of Risk Regulation*, 15(1), pp. 122 – 136.

Dunlop, C.A. and Radaelli, C.M. (2019) 'Policy instruments, policy learning and politics: Impact assessment in the European Union', in: Capano, G., Howlett, M., Ramesh, M. and Virani, A. (eds.) *Making policies work*. Cheltenham: Edward Elgar Publishing, pp. 115 – 136.

Engeli, I., Rihoux, B. and Allison, C.R. (2014) 'Intermediate-N comparison: Configurational comparative methods', in: Engeli, I. and Rothmayr, C. (eds.) *Comparative policy studies: Conceptual and methodological challenges*. London: Palgrave Macmillan, pp. 85 – 107.

Feindt, P.H. (2010) 'Policy learning and environmental policy integration in the Common Agricultural Policy, 1973 – 2003', *Public Administration*, 88(2), pp. 296 – 314.

Feindt, P.H. (2018) 'EU agricultural policy', in: Heinelt, H. and Münch, S. (eds.) *Handbook of European policies*. Cheltenham: Edward Elgar Publishing, pp. 115 – 133.

Feindt, P.H. and Flynn, A. (2009) 'Policy stretching and institutional layering: British food policy between security, safety, quality, health and climate change', *British Politics*, 4(3), pp. 386 – 414.

Galli, F. et al. (2020) 'How can policy processes remove barriers to sustainable food systems in Europe? Contributing to a policy framework for agri-food transitions', *Food Policy*, 96, 101871.

Greer, A. (2017) *Agricultural policy in Europe*. Manchester: Manchester University Press.

Grohmann, P. and Feindt, P.H. (2024) 'The importance of calibration in policy mixes: Environmental policy integration in the implementation of the European Union's Common Agricultural Policy in Germany (2014 – 2022)', *Environmental Policy and Governance*, 34(1), pp. 16 – 30.

Havinga, T., Casey, D. and van Waarden, F. (2015) 'Changing regulatory arrangements in food governance', in: Havinga, T., van Waarden, F. and Casey, D (eds.) *The changing landscape of food governance.* Cheltenham: Edward Elgar Publishing, pp. 3 – 18.

Jackson, G. and Deeg, R. (2012) 'The long-term trajectories of institutional change in European capitalism', *Journal of European Public Policy*, 19(8), pp. 1109 – 1125.

Jordan, G., Maloney, W.A. and McLaughlin, A.M. (1994) 'Characterizing agricultural policy-making', *Public Administration*, 72(4), pp. 505 – 526.

Kay, A. (2005) 'A critique of the use of path dependency in policy studies', *Public Administration*, 83(3), pp. 553 – 571.

Lowe, P., Feindt, P.H. and Vihinen, H. (2010) 'Introduction: Greening the countryside? Changing frameworks of EU agricultural policy', *Public Administration*, 88(2), pp. 287 – 295.

Marek, C. and Tosun, J. (2023) 'Tackling the environmental and climate footprint of food systems: How "transformative" is the EU's Farm to Fork strategy?', in: Edmondson, B. (ed.) *Sustainability transformations, social transitions and environmental accountabilities.* Cham: Springer International Publishing, pp. 265 – 297.

Marsh, D. and Smith, M. (2000) 'Understanding policy networks: Towards a dialectical approach', *Political Studies*, 48(1), pp. 4 – 21.

Matthews, A. (2015) 'Food security as a driver of integration in Europe', in: Brennan, L. and Murray, P. (eds.) *Drivers of integration and regionalism in Europe and Asia.* London: Routledge, pp. 180 – 195.

Moragues-Faus, A., Sonnino, R. and Marsden, T. (2017) 'Exploring European food system vulnerabilities: Towards integrated food security governance', *Environmental Science and Policy*, 75, pp. 184 – 215.

Popp, T.R., Feindt, P.H. and Daedlow, K. (2021) 'Policy feedback and lock-in effects of new agricultural policy instruments: A qualitative comparative analysis of support for financial risk management tools in OECD countries', *Land Use Policy*, 103, 105313.

Righettini, M. S. (2025) The Governance of Food Security in Europe: Collaborative Street-Level Bureaucracies and Learning in Turbulent Times. Cham: Springer Nature Switzerland. https://doi.org/10.1007/978-3-031-98083-1

Rihoux, B. and Ragin, C.C. (eds.) (2009) *Configurational comparative methods: Qualitative comparative analysis (QCA) and related techniques.* Thousand Oaks: Sage.

Schebesta, H. and Candel, J. (2020) 'Legal and regulatory frameworks in achieving policy integration: The case of EU food policy', *Journal of European Public Policy*, 27(6), pp. 893 – 911.

Skogstad, G. (1998) 'Ideas, paradigms and institutions: Agricultural exceptionalism in the European Union and the United States', *Governance*, 11(4), pp. 463 – 490.

Skogstad, G. (2008) *Internationalization and Canadian agriculture: Policy and governing paradigms.* Toronto: University of Toronto Press.

Termeer, C.J.A.M., Biesbroek, R. and van den Brink, M. (2012) 'Institutions for adaptation to climate change: Comparing national adaptation strategies in Europe', *European Political Science*, 11(1), pp. 41 – 53.

Termeer, C.J.A.M., Dewulf, A. and Biesbroek, R. (2019) 'A critical assessment of the wicked problem concept: Relevance and usefulness for policy science and practice', *Policy and Society*, 38(2), pp. 167 – 179.

Thomann, E. (2018) 'Food safety policy: Transnational, hybrid, wicked', in: Thompson, W. (ed.) *Oxford research encyclopedia of politics.* Oxford: Oxford University Press.

Vogeler, C.S. (2019) 'Why do farm animal welfare regulations vary between EU member states? A comparative analysis of societal and party political determinants in France, Germany, Italy, Spain and the UK', *Journal of Common Market Studies*, 57(2), pp. 317 – 335.

Vogeler, C.S., Hornung, J. and Bandelow, N.C. (2020) 'Farm animal welfare policymaking in the European Parliament: A social identity perspective on voting behaviour', *Journal of Environmental Policy and Planning*, 22(4), pp. 518 – 530.

Zwaan, P., Alons, G. and van Voorst, S. (2022) 'Monitoring and evaluating the CAP: A (post-) exceptionalist policy arrangement?', *Journal of European Public Policy*, 30(12), pp. 1 – 24.

Tom Delreux

European Union external environmental policy: Engagement with third countries and international institutions

Abstract: This chapter examines the external dimension of European Union (EU) environmental policy by analyzing how the EU pursues environmental objectives toward third countries and international institutions. It explores four venues through which the EU conducts external environmental policy. First, via the enlargement venue the EU spreads its environmental regulatory framework toward candidate countries. Second, the unilateral venue consists of internal policies affecting third countries, either deliberately or unintentionally. Third, the bilateral venue contains sustainability clauses in trade agreements with third countries as well as dialogue mechanisms, capacity-building and diplomatic outreach. Fourth, at the multilateral level, the EU has co-shaped the global environmental governance architecture and presented itself as a leader in multilateral environmental negotiations. The chapter concludes by reflecting on the geopolitical relevance of the EU's external environmental policy and on the mainstreaming of environmental objectives in the EU's foreign policy.

Keywords: External climate policy; external environmental policy; extraterritorial effects; EU foreign policy; multilateral environmental agreements

1 Introduction

The European Union's (EU) environmental policies not only impact its Member States but also third countries and the wider world. As most environmental problems have a global dimension—or are even global problems in nature, such as climate change—it should not be a surprise that the EU aims to address environmental problems in the EU, but also beyond its borders. This chapter examines the external dimension of EU environmental policy, analyzing how the EU pursues environmental objectives toward third countries and international institutions. It argues that the EU conducts external environmental policy through four venues: enlargement, unilateral policies with an impact on third countries, bilateral relations and multilateral diplomacy. The chapter subsequently discusses the use of these four venues by the EU. It ends with a reflection on the mainstreaming of environmental objectives in the EU's foreign policy more broadly.

https://doi.org/10.1515/9783111321523-033

2 The enlargement venue

The first venue through which the EU has externalized its environmental policy toward a large part of the European continent is via its enlargement policy. Enlargement policy involves *ex ante* conditionality, which means that candidate countries—which are at that moment third countries for the EU and thus countries to which environmental policy can be externalized—must comply with certain conditions before they can join the EU (Schimmelfennig, 2008). One of these conditions is complying with the existing *acquis communautaire*, i. e., the EU legislation in force. This provides the EU with remarkable leverage over structural policy reforms in third countries in Europe (Keukeleire and Delreux, 2022). While this condition covers all EU policy fields, it is *a fortiori* applicable to environmental policies. Via the carrot of enlargement and the associated *ex ante* conditionality mechanism, the EU has managed to spread environmental standards in Europe.

The enlargement venue has particularly been important in the context of the 2004–2007 "Central and Eastern European" enlargement. The state of the environment in most of the countries joining the EU in that period was bad, particularly in areas such as water quality. Environmental standards were low or even nonexistent. The accession process has externalized the more stringent and ambitious standards to these countries. The enlargement venue is currently relevant for the EU's external environmental policies toward the Western Balkans countries and more recently also toward countries such as Ukraine, Georgia and Moldova, which were recognized as candidate countries after the Russian invasion in Ukraine. Indeed, as the 'enlargement fatigue' of the 2010s seems to be over because of geopolitical considerations, the EU's externalization of its environmental policy via the enlargement venue now affects these European-but-not-yet-EU countries.

3 The unilateral venue

Conducting external environmental policy through the unilateral venue refers to internal policies that have an extraterritorial effect on third countries. Two types of extraterritorial effect via unilateral environmental policies are distinguishable: those with a deliberate or primary effect on third countries and others with an unintentional or secondary external effect.

The first type of unilateral policies explicitly targets third countries. In the last decade, the EU is increasingly adopting such unilateral regulatory policies in the field of trade. These policies are unilateral in the sense that the EU adopts them without the formal involvement or approval of third countries. Yet, they are designed to have an external effect as they not only address trade-related practices of third countries but also aim to promote environmental objectives. In the context of the European Green Deal, a Regulation on Deforestation Free Products and a Directive on Corporate

Sustainability Due Diligence have been adopted. Aiming to achieve reductions of carbon emissions from the maritime sector, the EU has also adopted unilateral policies targeting regulatory addressees both in and beyond the EU, such as the Regulation on Monitoring, Reporting and Verification of CO_2 emissions and the Fuel EU Regulation. These legislative acts regulate emissions from ships 'regardless of their flag' and thus have extraterritorial effects (Abegón Novella, 2024).

Another example is the Carbon Border Adjustment Mechanism (CBAM) (Wettestad, 2023; see Chapter 20). CBAM is a climate-related unilateral trade instrument that has been in force since 2023 but will only be fully operational from 2034 onwards. It requires that third country exporters pay a carbon price at the EU border that corresponds to what European producers have to pay for an allowance under the EU's Emissions Trading System (ETS). It thereby aims to counter the risk of 'carbon leakage', i. e., the relocation of European industries to countries with less stringent climate policies, and to incentivize third countries to adopt more stringent climate policies in their jurisdiction. Although its scope might be extended in the future, CBAM currently only applies to imports from specific energy-intensive sectors.

A second type of internal, unilaterally adopted environmental policies is policies with unintentional external effects, or at least effects on third countries that are not the policy's primary purpose. The underlying rationale here is that the norms and standards that are determined in EU legislation are conditions that products and services have to comply with before they can be sold on the European market. This applies to all producers, irrespective of whether they are European or not. Through the so-called 'Brussels Effect', the EU has "unilateral power to regulate global markets" (Bradford, 2020, p. xiv). The EU's internally determined environmental standards become global standards because private corporations in third countries operating in the global market are incentivized to adhere to EU standards if they want to bring their products to the EU market. While the Brussels Effect has the potential to work in several policy fields, environmental policy is particularly suited for having such unintended external effects as it is a policy field in which the standards are determined in the jurisdiction where the products are sold. The Brussels Effect is observable for instance in the area of chemicals regulation, where many global producers of chemicals now comply with the EU's stringent standards and where third countries such as South Korea, Japan and China have adopted domestic legislation that is inspired by the EU's regulatory framework (Biedenkopf, 2018).

4 The bilateral venue

The third venue through which the externalization of EU environmental policy occurs is via bilateral relations between the EU and a third country. This can take different forms.

Since 2011, the EU systematically includes legally binding sustainability clauses in the bilateral free trade agreements with third countries. The free trade agreement with South Korea was the first agreement of a new generation of trade agreements with a systematic inclusion of such provisions. These clauses, usually referred to as 'trade and sustainable development' (TSD) chapters, cover both environmental and labor standards. Regarding environmental standards, they refer to the importance of the ratification and implementation of multilateral environmental agreements (MEAs) and mainly include references to climate change and biodiversity, although forest management or the sustainable use of marine resources are also often mentioned. Since 2016, a clause that commits third countries to ratify and effectively implement the Paris Agreement on climate change is also systematically included. Overall, the content and the scope of the TSD chapters largely vary from one bilateral trade agreement to another (Lamy et al., 2021). The EU does not employ a single template or a unified approach in its different bilateral trade agreements. Before 2011, the scope of environmental standards was smaller and these provisions were not legally binding (Postnikov, 2018). The TSD chapters also establish bilateral cooperation arrangements and institutional structures for future dialogue on environmental matters between the EU and its trading partner.

Using the attractiveness of its market, the EU thus tries to externalize regulatory policies, such as environmental standards (Damro, 2012). While the rationale is that the EU may reduce trade preferences if third countries do not fulfil the requirements of the sustainability clauses, this form of *ex post* conditionality is mostly not very effective. Indeed, there is little evidence that the sustainability clauses have systematically strengthened environmental protection in third countries. Successful implementation of these provisions often depends on domestic factors in the third country in question, such as administrative capacities. Moreover, the lack of systematic effectiveness is partly due to the relative vagueness of the provisions and to the rather soft enforcement procedures, which are based upon consultation and dialogue rather than hard sanctioning (Postnikov, 2018). The EU thus has a 'soft' or 'cooperative' approach to the enforcement of TSD chapters (Morin and Rochette, 2017). This has led to TSD chapters being criticized for "serving primarily the purpose of 'window dressing', and not bringing about positive change through rule exportation" (Nessel and Orbie, 2022, p. 198). In practice, the chapters thus favor commercial interests over environmental protection.

Ex post conditionality is also the mechanism behind the promotion of environmental policies in the context of the European Neighbourhood Policy (ENP), which is the EU's umbrella framework for strengthening its relations with the third countries in its eastern and southern neighborhood. Via the 'more for more' principle, the EU aims to achieve internal reforms in the ENP countries in exchange for market access, visa liberalization and financial support (Keukeleire and Delreux, 2022). This incentive of conditionality is complemented by the Commission publishing guides and recommendations to the ENP countries, encouraging them to converge their environmental policies with the EU's (Biedenkopf and Groen, 2021). The EU has also established transgovernmental networks and frameworks for cooperation to provide capacity-building and share best practices (Shyrokykh, 2022). The result is a patchwork of different cooperation patterns with several ENP countries, whereby these countries are incentivized and supported to engage in domestic policy reforms, but also in cooperating with EU bodies, such as the European Environment Agency. Although several requested internal reforms in the ENP countries deal with environmental policies, the environment is not among the most prioritized policy fields in the EU's relations with ENP countries (Buzogány, 2018).

Bilateral relations do not only take the form of agreements and conditionality. External environmental policy is also conducted bilaterally through capacity-building. Via financial support, technical assistance, training and personnel exchanges, the EU aims to assist third countries in designing, formulating and implementing domestic environmental policies, which are often based upon existing EU environmental policies (Biedenkopf and Groen, 2021). Policy learning and emulation—and hence no longer conditionality—are the underlying mechanisms here (see Chapter 2).

A prime climate policy example that the EU is actively promoting to be implemented in third country jurisdictions is emissions trading based upon the EU's own ETS design. The Commission has for instance organized training courses, study visits or workshops for experts and officials from third countries to support third countries in setting up national emission trading systems. The design of such policies and markets in, for example China and South Korea, is largely inspired by the EU example, demonstrating the relevance of such capacity-building efforts, which is less visible than the bilateral policies based on conditionality (Biedenkopf, Van Eynde and Walker, 2017). Likewise, in the run-up to the 2015 Paris climate conference, the EU helped developing countries to establish their national climate action plan (the so-called 'Intended Nationally Determined Contribution'), which was to be submitted to the United Nations Framework Convention on Climate Change (UNFCCC) and which was an essential element of the design—and success—of the Paris Agreement (Torney and Cross, 2018).

Finally, bilateral relations take the form of diplomacy and outreach. EU Delegations in third countries often play an important role (Biedenkopf and Petri, 2019). The EU conducts bilateral diplomacy to try to influence the domestic environmental policies of third countries, but also to try to convince third countries about the EU's positions and to try to gather intelligence about the positions of these countries in the context of multilateral environmental negotiations. Bilateral outreach has the potential to give the EU a better understanding of specific situations or constraints faced by third countries, which may be important during multilateral negotiations. Through the so-called 'Green Diplomacy Network' the EU and its Member States aim to coordinate their bilateral outreach and to integrate environmental concerns into the broader diplomatic relations with third countries (Torney and Cross, 2018; Bremberg and Michalski, 2024).

5 The multilateral venue

Global environmental governance, or conducting external environmental policy via the multilateral venue, has traditionally been an EU priority. Over recent decades, the EU has developed into a major player in global environmental governance on a wide range of environmental issues, including air, biodiversity, climate, chemicals, waste and ocean governance (Delreux, 2021). The EU and its Member States have been co-shapers of several multilateral environmental regimes and treaty frameworks (Kelemen and Vogel, 2010). The EU is a party to more than sixty MEAs and it has played a major role in the negotiation processes of these MEAs as well as in the subsequent follow-up negotiations (for instance, in the framework of Conferences of the Parties to the MEAs).

The EU presents itself as an 'environmental leader', and in the literature it is usually considered to be a leader in multilateral environmental negotiations (e.g., Zito, 2005). While several studies on the EU's role in global environmental governance have applied different conceptualizations of leadership (Liefferink and Wurzel, 2017; Tobin, Torney and Biedenkopf, 2023), EU leadership is generally understood as the EU advocating strong environmentally friendly measures at the international level. Although the EU indeed usually promotes relatively stringent environmental measures, there are a few issues on which the EU's positions are mostly less ambitious, such as technology transfer or new financial mechanisms, which are issues about which countries from the Global South are much more in a demanding position. Another qualification on the EU's leadership is a relative assessment: compared to other major powers and negotiation blocs, the EU is indeed usually among those that defend the most ambitious environmental positions (Delreux and Ohler, 2021). However, that level of leadership and ambition is often insufficient to achieve the goals of many MEAs—such as limiting global warming to the 2 degrees of the Paris Agreement or halting biodiversity loss per the Convention on Biological Diversity—let alone to effectively improve the state of the environment. Moreover, the EU's actual internal and external policies do not always fit with its leadership discourse and self-proclaimed objectives (Çelik, 2022).

The EU's multilateral leadership has primarily been studied in the field of international climate negotiations (e.g., Wurzel and Connelly, 2011; Parker, Karlsson and Hjerpe, 2017; Oberthür and Dupont, 2021; Schunz, 2022). The EU managed to lead in the 1990s when the Kyoto Protocol, a diplomatic success for the EU, was negotiated. The EU aimed to continue this leading role in the 2000s, advocating for ambitious climate agreements. However, the 2009 Copenhagen conference was a major failure for the EU. Here, the EU's leadership image was badly damaged, as the EU was sidelined from the endgame of the negotiations, and the outcome did not at all reflect the EU's preferences. Lessons were learned from the Copenhagen experience, and the EU modified its strategy. While maintaining its preferences for an ambitious climate agreement, the EU invested more in coalition- and bridge-building (Bäckstrand and Elgström, 2013). This more pragmatist, or even strategic, negotiation approach ultimately led to the EU's success during the negotiations on the 2015 Paris Agreement (Oberthür and Groen, 2018).

The leadership approach that the EU has mostly applied is 'leading by example', which refers to setting the example of ambitious environmental policies by adopting them in the EU (i. e., internal environmental policies) and convincing third countries of their feasibility and the fact that such policies can go hand in hand with economic growth. Leading by example aims to highlight the international credibility of the EU when it promotes ambitious environmental policies at the international level. It might also provide inspiration to third countries to adopt similar policies at their domestic level. For instance, in the run-up to two important climate change conferences —Copenhagen in 2009 and Paris in 2015—the EU tightened its internal emission reduction targets and a set of binding policies to implement these targets. These internal targets also sent a signal to the EU's external partners that the EU was serious about climate change 'at home' and trying to convince third countries of the EU's 'good example'.

The EU's enduring support of multilateral solutions to global environmental problems is a clear example of its preference for multilateralism in its foreign policy more broadly. While this preference has clearly shaped the EU's international identity and while it has contributed to the establishment and development of multilateral institutionalized structures (agreements, organizations), it is nowadays increasingly difficult for the EU to conduct external environmental policy via the multilateral venue. Multilateralism and the international rules-based order are increasingly contested. The increasing turbulence of the post–Paris Agreement period, with rising geopolitical and geo-economic tensions, populist governments in some of the world's major powers, a weakened belief in global governance institutions, have made the international context increasingly challenging for the EU to exert environmental leadership (Tobin, Torney and Biedenkopf., 2023; Bremberg and Michalski, 2024). Moreover, the EU's relative power in world politics and global governance is declining at the expense of emerging (or 'emerged') economies, which are now the major carbon emitters (Oberthür, 2016; Biedenkopf and Groen, 2021). This not only means that the high days of traditional multilateralism in environmental governance are probably over but also that the use of the venue that is closest to the EU's DNA is increasingly challenging for the EU.

Nonetheless, while the multilateral venue as such has become less evident for conducting EU external environmental policy, it has also become more diverse. Environmental issues—and particularly climate change—have become an issue in a range of multilateral fora that do not exclusively or primarily focus on the environment or climate. Indeed, climate change is today no longer only discussed in the framework of the UNFCCC but also in the Group of Seven/Twenty (G7/20), the International Maritime Organization (IMO), the International Civil Aviation Organization and many other formal and informal institutional arrangements, treaty frameworks and plurilateral initiatives. The EU's climate diplomacy has adapted to this changing international context, as it takes this 'international regime complex' increasingly into account by addressing climate issues in various international fora (Earsom and Delreux, 2021). The EU has also taken diplomatic initiatives to mobilize multilateral and plurilateral fora to heighten third countries' climate ambitions, such as the Global Methane Pledge (Earsom and Delreux, 2023).

6 Mainstreaming environmental objectives in EU foreign policy

The environment, and particularly climate change, has increasingly become a foreign policy issue as environmental objectives, such as the EU's 2050 climate neutrality target, require the transition toward sustainable economic and societal structures and systemic changes that not only extend beyond the borders of the EU but also beyond the environmental policy field. This is why environmental concerns are called to become more integrated—or mainstreamed—into other policy fields, such as foreign policy (see Chapter 33).

Moreover, environmental policy integration is a legal principle of EU environmental law, seeking a mainstreaming of environmental objectives in all other EU policies, including foreign policies. However, this legal principle is far from being fully implemented in the EU (Dupont and Jordan, 2021). The environmental policy integration principle has recently gained more political traction in the context of the 2019 European Green Deal. Calling for a systemic approach to achieve climate neutrality by 2050, the Green Deal explicitly calls for incorporating environmental policies in other EU external policies, leading to potential 'Green Deal diplomacy' (Fajardo des Castillo, 2024). In that sense, the Green Deal has an important external dimension and has an impact on the EU as an international actor in several fields.

Particularly climate change has increasingly become a driver of different foreign policy facets (Tocci, 2023; Youngs and Lazard, 2023; also see Chapter 30). Climate change has major security components, such as conflicts over scarce natural resources, which may have destabilizing effects and entail serious military, humanitarian or migration consequences (see Chapter 22). Despite the growing awareness of the so-called climate-security nexus in the EU's discourse, the actual foreign policies do not always sufficiently take into account these concerns (Bremberg, Sonnsjö and Mobjörk, 2019). The transition toward climate neutrality also alters the EU's relations with countries that export fossil energy (such as Russia or the Gulf states) as well as with countries that the EU relies on for critical raw materials that are needed for green energy technologies (such as China). The diversification of energy sources and the EU's 'new' dependence on other exporting markets indeed raise questions on the energy and raw material security of the EU, and they have shaped the debate on the EU's strategic autonomy.

Nonetheless, environment and climate change have been taken more seriously in EU foreign policy in the last decade. Not only are environmental provisions systematically included in bilateral trade agreements (see above), but climate conditionality is also increasingly characterizing the EU's development cooperation policy (Adelle et al., 2018). However, despite the strong discourse on environmental conditionality in trade and development cooperation policy, pure commercial interests—or other conditions, such as migration-related conditions—often still dominate.

Although climate change has become a high-politics issue with important foreign policy relevance, the EU has a tendency to approach it in a rather legalistic and technocratic way. A strategic approach that considers the external dimension of environmental and climate policy as a genuine foreign policy issue is still largely lacking (Schunz, 2019). As climate change becomes a geopolitical issue, the EU increasingly faces broader strategic challenges in this field. The current geopolitical situation, with great power rivalries and contested multilateralism, poses one of the main challenges for the EU as an international actor in the field of environmental and climate policy: i. e., how to "enhance its capacity for strategic action" (Oberthür and Dupont, 2021, p. 1096).

However, some recent moves indicate that the EU's external environmental policy is "in the process of becoming to a larger extent informed by geopolitics and strategic thinking" (Schunz, 2019, p. 351). Climate change is occasionally debated in the Foreign Affairs Council and the EU has adopted a number of Climate Diplomacy Action Plans, specifying the priorities of the EU's climate diplomacy, outlining opportunities for diplomatic outreach in non-climate related international fora and highlighting the links between climate and other facets of foreign policy (Delreux and Earsom, 2024; Torney and Cross, 2018). Such efforts also potentially lead to the involvement of policymakers from the foreign policy community in external environmental policymaking. Not only Member States' foreign affairs ministers (via the Foreign Affairs Council) but also the European External Action Service are gradually becoming important climate actors (Earsom and Delreux, 2023).

7 Conclusion

The EU's set of stringent internal environmental policies not only provide the EU with an incentive to externalize these rules and objectives beyond its borders, but they also provide a solid basis for such external engagement. This chapter has discussed the four venues via which the EU's external environmental policies are conducted: enlargement, internal policies with extraterritorial effects, bilateral relations and multilateral diplomacy. While taken together these four venues have allowed the EU to conduct external policies and to profile itself as an important—and often 'leading'—international actor in this field, the EU is currently also facing challenges in each of these four venues. Each of these challenges puts limits on the EU's ability to continue to export its environmental policies and to shape environmental governance externally.

The geographic reach of the enlargement venue is by definition limited to third countries in Europe that are not yet an EU Member State but aspire to become one. Moreover, there has been an 'enlargement fatigue' after the Central and Eastern European enlargement wave of 2004–2007, although enlargement has made a comeback on the political agenda since the 2022 Russian invasion in Ukraine. The unilateral venue, where internal environmental policies have extraterritorial effects, has recently become more important in the externalization of EU environmental policies. Although such policies are regularly an effective tool to externalize environmental standards, this approach is increasingly contested by third countries, both legally and diplomatically. With regard to the bilateral venue, the *ex post* conditionality behind environmental provisions in bilateral trade agreements are not always effective because of the soft approach behind their enforcement and because commercial interests seem to dominate when trade-offs between trade and the environment have to be made. Finally, while the multilateral venue has historically been the most prominent venue of the EU's external environmental policy, this venue is clearly under pressure—and thereby also the EU's capacity to conduct external environmental policy via multilateral agreements and institutions. The EU's—and even the West's—decreasing power, increasing geopolitical competition and the contestation of the international rules-based order and multilateral institutions make the strategy of pursuing environmental objectives via the venue that for a long time has been the EU's preferred one far less evident than before. Taken together, these challenges indeed show the need for the EU to develop a more strategic approach toward addressing environmental issues at the international level, in which environmental concerns go hand in hand with broader geopolitical considerations.

The literature on the EU's external environmental policies has evolved in parallel with the development of these policies. Reflecting the historical importance of the multilateral venue in the EU's external environmental policies, there is a comprehensive literature on the EU's role in global environmental governance and multilateral environmental negotiations. The bilateral venue mainly started to attract scholarly attention beginning in the 2010s, when TSD chapters become a more prominent part of the bilateral trade agreements and when the EU started to invest more in bilateral environmental—and mainly climate—outreach. Likewise, the more recent unilateral turn in trade policy and the growth of internal policies with extraterritorial effects have triggered attention to the unilateral venue.

While the literature is well-developed and offers a broad picture of the EU's external environmental policies, three avenues for future research can be identified. Each avenue starts from a question that the current state of the art has insufficiently addressed. First, external climate change policy gets a lot of attention, often at the expense of other external environmental policy fields, such as water, chemicals or biodiversity. Given the specificities of climate change, such as its high level of politicization and its explicit link with security, findings on EU external climate policy do not necessarily travel to external policies on other environmental issues, which should not disappear from the research agenda.

Second, the current literature offers a rather comprehensive picture of what the EU's external environmental policies look like and how the EU approaches third countries and international institutions in that regard. However, the literature is more limited on the questions on the EU's actual impact at the external scene. Such a research agenda comes with methodological challenges, such as how to measure impact and influence empirically? Nevertheless, future research should not avoid examining the EU's influence both on third-country policies and on the state of the environment outside Europe.

Third, most literature applies—often implicitly—a rather positive image of the EU. The fact that the EU is often portrayed as an 'environmental leader' is illustrative of this. However, future research could benefit from questioning the assumption that "the EU is good for the environment" and from employing more critical perspectives to the study of this field. For instance, incorporating analyses on the EU's historical responsibilities or the negative impact that other external policies of the EU (such as external fisheries policies or investment policies) might have on the external promotion of environmental objectives might qualify—and analytically strengthen—our understanding of the EU as an international actor in the environmental field.

References

Abegón Novella, M. (2024) 'EU regulatory action on maritime emissions. Unilaterally protecting the environment beyond IMO's global strategy', in: Campins Eritja, M. and Fernández-Pons, X. (eds.) *Deploying the European Green Deal: Protecting the environment beyond the EU borders*. Abingdon: Routledge, pp. 34–51.

Adelle, C., Delputte, S., De Roeck, F. and Nicholson, S. (2018) 'Environmental instruments in development cooperation: Promoting better development and environmental outcomes?, in: Adelle, C., Biedenkopf, K. and Torney, D. (eds.) *European Union external environmental policy: Rules, regulation and governance beyond borders*. London: Palgrave Macmillan, pp. 81–101.

Bäckstrand, K. and Elgström, O. (2013) 'The EU's role in climate change negotiations: From leader to "leadiator"', *Journal of European Public Policy*, 20(10), pp. 1369–1386.

Biedenkopf, K. (2018) 'Chemicals: Pioneering ambitions with external effects', in: Adelle, C., Biedenkopf, K. and Torney, D. (eds.) *European Union external environmental policy: Rules, regulation and governance beyond borders*. London: Palgrave Macmillan, pp. 189–208.

Biedenkopf, K. and Groen, L. (2021) 'External EU environmental policy', in: Jordan, A. and Gravey, V. (eds.) *Environmental policy in the EU: Actors, institutions and processes*. Fourth edition. Abingdon: Routledge, pp. 33–50.

Biedenkopf, K. and Petri, F. (2019) 'EU delegations in European Union climate diplomacy: The role of links to Brussels, individuals and country contexts', *Journal of European Integration*, 41(1), pp. 47–63.

Biedenkopf, K., Van Eynde, S. and Walker, H. (2017) 'Policy infusion through capacity building and project interaction: Greenhouse gas emissions trading in China', *Global Environmental Politics*, 17(3), pp. 91–114.

Bradford, A. (2020) *The Brussels effect: How the European Union rules the world*. Oxford: Oxford University Press.

Bremberg, N. and Michalski, A. (2024) 'The European Union climate diplomacy: Evolving practices in a changing geopoliticalcContext', *The Hague Journal of Diplomacy*, 19(3), 506 – 535.

Bremberg, N., Sonnsjö, H. and Mobjörk, M. (2019) 'The EU and climate-related security risks: A community of practice in the making?', *Journal of European Integration*, 41(5), pp. 623 – 639.

Buzogány, A. (2018) 'Neighbourhood countries: Promoting environmental protection close to home', in: Adelle, C., Biedenkopf, K. and Torney, D. (eds.) *European Union external environmental policy: Rules, regulation and governance beyond borders.* London: Palgrave Macmillan, pp. 233 – 252.

Çelik, F. (2022) 'The EU's different faces in climate diplomacy: Leadership, interest and responsibilities', *Journal of European Integration*, 44(8), pp. 1019 – 1039.

Damro, C. (2012) 'Market power Europe', *Journal of European Public Policy*, 19(5), pp. 682 – 699.

Delreux, T. (2021) 'The EU in international environmental negotiations', in: Jordan, A. and Gravey, V. (eds.) *Environmental policy in the EU: Actors, institutions and processes.* Fourth edition. Abingdon: Routledge, pp. 259 – 275.

Delreux, T. and Earsom, J. (2024) 'Missed opportunities: The impact of internal compartementalisation on EU diplomacy across the international regime complex on climate change', *Journal of European Public Policy*, 31(9), 2960 – 2985.

Delreux, T. and Ohler, F. (2021) 'Ego versus alter: Internal and external perceptions of the EU's role in global environmental negotiations', *Journal of Common Market Studies*, 59(5), pp. 1284 – 1302.

Dupont, C. and Jordan, A. (2021) 'Policy integration', in: Jordan, A. and Gravey, V. (eds.) *Environmental policy in the EU: Actors, institutions and processes.* Fourth edition. Abingdon: Routledge, pp. 203 – 219.

Earsom, J. and Delreux, T. (2021) 'Evaluating EU responsiveness to the evolution of the international regime complex on climate change', *International Environmental Agreements*, 21(4), pp. 711 – 728.

Earsom, J. and Delreux, T. (2023) 'A new kid in town? The evolution of the EEAS headquarters' involvement in EU climate diplomacy', *European Foreign Affairs Review*, 28(3), pp. 283 – 302.

Fajardo des Castillo, T. (2024) 'From climate diplomacy to Green Deal diplomacy', in: Campins Eritja, M. and Fernández-Pons, X. (eds.) *Deploying the European Green Deal: Protecting the environment beyond the EU borders.* Abingdon: Routledge, pp. 156 – 176.

Kelemen, D. and Vogel, D. (2010) 'Trading places: The role of the United States and the European Union in international environmental politics', *Comparative Political Studies*, 43(4), pp. 427 – 456.

Keukeleire, S. and Delreux, T. (2022) *The foreign Policy of the European Union.* Third Edition. London: Bloomsbury.

Lamy, P., Pons, G., Garzon, I. and Kauffmann, L. (2021) *Sustainable development in EU trade agreements: Much ado about nothing?.* Brussels: Europe Jacques Delors.

Liefferink, D. and Wurzel, R. (2017) 'Environmental leaders and pioneers: Agents of change?', *Journal of European Public Policy*, 24(7), pp. 951 – 968.

Morin, J. and Rochette, M. (2017) 'Transatlantic convergence of preferential trade agreements environmental clauses', *Business and Politics*, 19(4), pp. 621 – 658.

Nessel, C. and Orbie, J. (2022) 'Sustainable development in EU–Asia trade relations', in: Adriaensen, J. and Postnikov, E. (eds.) *A geo-economic turn in trade policy? EU trade agreements in the Asia-Pacific.* Cham: Palgrave Macmillan, pp. 197 – 221.

Oberthür, S. (2016) 'Where to go from Paris? The European Union in climate geopolitics', *Global Affairs*, 2(2), pp. 119 – 130.

Oberthür, S. and Dupont, C. (2021) 'The European Union's international climate leadership: Towards a grand climate strategy?', *Journal of European Public Policy*, 28(7), pp. 1095 – 1114.

Oberthür, S. and Groen, L. (2018) 'Explaining goal achievement in international negotiations: The EU and the Paris Agreement on climate change', *Journal of European Public Policy*, 25(5), pp. 708 – 727.

Parker, C., Karlsson, C. and Hjerpe, M. (2017) 'Assessing the European Union's global climate change leadership: From Copenhagen to the Paris Agreement', *Journal of European Integration*, 39(2), pp. 239 – 252.

Postnikov, E. (2018) 'Environmental instruments in trade agreements: Pushing the limits of the dialogue approach', in: Adelle, C., Biedenkopf, K. and Torney, D. (eds.) *European Union external environmental policy: Rules, regulation and governance beyond borders.* London: Palgrave Macmillan, pp. 59 – 79.
Schimmelfennig, F. (2008) 'EU political accession conditionality after the 2004 enlargement: Consistency and effectiveness', *Journal of European Public Policy*, 15(6), pp. 918 – 937.
Schunz, S. (2019) 'The European Union's environmental foreign policy: From planning to a strategy?', *International Politics*, 56(3), pp. 339 – 358.
Schunz, S. (2022) 'The European Union's roles in global atmospheric governance: Evolving towards a "pacifier"?', *Journal of European Integration*, 44(8), pp. 1161 – 1180.
Shyrokykh, K. (2022) 'Help your neighbor, help yourself: The drivers of European Union's climate cooperation in trans-governmental networks with its neighbors', *Governance*, 35(4), pp. 1095 – 1118.
Tobin, P., Torney, D. and Biedenkopf, K. (2023) 'EU climate leadership: Domestic and global dimensions', in: Rayner, T., Szulecki, K., Jordan, A. and Oberthür, S. (eds.) *Handbook on European Union climate change policy and politics.* Cheltenham: Edward Elgar Publishing, pp. 187 – 200.
Tocci, N. (2023) *A green and global Europe.* Cambridge: Polity Press.
Torney, D. and Cross, M. (2018) 'Environmental and climate diplomacy: Building coalitions through persuasion', in: Adelle, C., Biedenkopf, K. and Torney, D. (eds.) *European Union external environmental policy: Rules, regulation and governance beyond borders.* London: Palgrave Macmillan, pp. 39 – 58.
Wettestad, J. (2023) 'Proactive prevention of carbon leakage? The EU Carbon Border Adjustment Mechanism', in: Rayner, T., Szulecki, K., Jordan, A. and Oberthür, S. (eds.) *Handbook on European Union climate change policy and politics.* Cheltenham: Edward Elgar Publishing, pp. 231 – 245.
Wurzel, R. and Connelly, J. (eds.) (2011) *The European Union as a leader in international climate change politics.* Abingdon: Routledge.
Youngs, R. and Lazard, O. (2023) 'Climate, ecological and energy security challenges facing the EU: New and old dynamics', in: Rayner, T., Szulecki, K., Jordan, A. and Oberthür, S. (eds.) *Handbook on European Union climate change policy and politics.* Cheltenham: Edward Elgar Publishing, pp. 158 – 172.
Zito, A. (2005) 'The European Union as an environmental leader in a global environment', *Globalizations*, 2(3), pp. 363 – 375.

Section D **Policy pathways and dynamics**

Introduction: Policy dynamics and pathways

This section explores key policy dynamics and pathways in European Union (EU) environmental governance, focusing on the growing challenges posed by climate change, the tensions between environmental imperatives and socio-economic priorities and the urgent need for integrated, democratic and cross-sectoral policy responses. The contributions in this section highlight that certain policy dynamics continue to evolve but remain central: most emphatically, the importance of the common market, regulation as a policy tool and the efforts to enhance effective policy implementation with the Member States. While certain dynamics may indeed continue to be core to EU environmental governance questions, the EU continues to seek new approaches such as the European Green Deal (EGD) to address the complex challenges it faces.

Based on an analysis of European Council conclusions since 2015, the chapter by **Jale Tosun** shows how EU attention has progressively shifted from broader environmental concerns toward a stronger focus on climate change. However, **Tosun** argues that, with the introduction of the EGD, environmental issues have reemerged at the forefront, underscoring the importance of securing ambitious environmental commitments through climate policy channels.

The interplay between the EU single market and environmental policy is analyzed by **Henning Deters** and **Sebastian Heidebrecht.** Their chapter traces how the single market has alternately constrained and enabled environmental policy development. They reveal how austerity, deregulation and overlapping crises (polycrisis) have exerted downward pressure on environmental legislation, while the European Commission has increasingly resorted to delegated rule-making to sustain regulatory momentum. The chapter concludes by identifying the EGD as a catalyst for rethinking the environment–market nexus and a springboard for future research.

Another core element in EU environmental governance has been the role of the regulatory policy tool, which **Jan Pollex** and **Andrea Lenschow** assess in their chapter. They argue that the evolution of this EU environmental policy tool has been both hugely varying and constant. In contrast to some of the policymaker and scholarly emphases on alternative policy instruments, regulations continue to underpin EU environmental governance and serve as the key to understanding changes in EU environmental policy.

The next chapters in the section tackle some of the fundamental challenges that effective EU environmental policymaking faces. The evolution of integrated environmental policymaking is examined in the chapter by **Laura De Vito** and **Duncan Russel**, focusing on the 2024 Ambient Air Quality and Cleaner Air Directive and the 2000 Water Framework Directive. The chapter illustrates the EU's shift from tackling isolated pollution sources to adopting a more holistic and integrated approach that considers diffuse pollution, ecosystem interdependencies and cross-policy interactions. It emphasizes the need to further embed environmental policy integration principles to enhance governance capacity across multiple sectors and governance levels.

https://doi.org/10.1515/9783111321523-034

Policy integration raises the even wider issue of how the EU and its constituent actors implement environmental policy, which is the focus of the chapter by **Anthony Zito** and **Benedetta Cotta.** Their chapter explores how various EU actors have sought to focus on the key challenges to implementation and to overcome these barriers to policy delivery. They find that the policy response and academic focus have, over time, focused more on the barriers that have affected actor activity or inactivity rather than the ongoing problems posed by the nature of the policy problems and the design of the chosen solutions.

A vital element of any policy integration and policy delivery is the exercise of policy evaluation, which is tackled in the chapter by **Jonas Schoenefeld.** This chapter evaluates the actors that drive environmental policy evaluation and how they conduct and utilize this policy process. While arguing that environmental policy evaluation is increasing, **Schoenefeld** demonstrates that some fundamental hurdles exist in embedding evaluation in EU environmental governance, such as moving from a defensive to collaborative mindset among policy actors.

Moving toward strategies that might transform EU environmental governance, **Susanna Vanhamäki** examines how the concept of the circular economy has been integrated into EU environmental law and policy, particularly in relation to waste, energy and regional development. Her chapter outlines the evolution of circular economy thinking within EU frameworks and identifies several conceptual tensions and practical challenges that must be addressed to enable transformative economic, social, political and technological change.

The section concludes with the chapter by **Paul Tobin** and **Ebba Minas** that explores future EU direction ranging from the expansion to the outright termination of EU environmental policy. Their chapter explores four core possibilities: policy expansion, policy dismantling, policy termination and policy stasis. The authors highlight the conceptual ambiguity found in the academic approach toward understanding dismantling and the need for a nuanced approach to understanding policy change.

Jale Tosun

The rise of climate change and its implications for climate and environmental policy in the European Union

Abstract: The European Union (EU) has been proactive in addressing environmental degradation, resulting in a comprehensive body of environmental policy. As global attention has increasingly shifted to climate change, the EU has demonstrated its commitment to ambitious climate action both nationally and internationally. This chapter examines how the rise of climate change on the international political agenda has affected the EU's attention to climate and environmental issues. By analyzing European Council conclusions since 2015, we assess whether there has been a shift in EU political leaders' focus from environmental issues to climate change. Our empirical findings reveal that climate change has indeed dominated discussions at European Council meetings. However, the introduction of the European Green Deal has brought environmental issues back to the forefront of European leaders' political agendas, albeit with climate action still maintaining a dominant position.

Keywords: Agenda-setting; climate policy; environmental policy; European Green Deal; issue salience

1 Introduction

Traditionally, the European Union (EU) has been proactive in addressing environmental degradation, resulting in a comprehensive body of environmental policy. However, global attention has increasingly shifted to climate change, which has induced the EU to demonstrate its commitment to ambitious climate action. Despite the EU's commitment to both environmental and climate policies, the increasing international cooperation and public demand for climate action may have led to a prioritization of climate issues over broader environmental concerns. This chapter examines whether this shift in focus has indeed occurred, analyzing the balance between climate and environmental priorities in EU policymaking.

The development of European environmental policy began in 1972 with the adoption of the First Environmental Action Program (EAP). Covering a period from 1973 to 1976, the EAP was a response to the United Nations Conference on the Environment in 1972 and therefore reflected the growing international concern on environmental degradation.

The First EAP led to the creation of an organizational structure for environmental policy action in 1973: the Environmental Unit within the Directorate-General (DG) for industrial policies (Knill and Liefferink, 2007). This Unit evolved into a dedicated DG for environmental policies in 1981. As subsequent EAPs became more comprehensive

https://doi.org/10.1515/9783111321523-035

and ambitious, the areas of competence of DG Environment expanded correspondingly. The adoption of the environmental policy integration principle in 1999 marked a significant milestone, as it brought environmental policy into the mainstream of EU policymaking (Jordan and Lenschow, 2010).

Climate change has received enhanced attention since the late 1990s. Initially, DG Environment formulated the EU's climate policy. However, in 2010, this area was moved to a newly established DG for Climate Action. The creation of a dedicated DG Climate indicated this topic's increased political salience.

The coexistence of both DG Environment and DG Climate Action demonstrates the EU's commitment to environmental protection and climate action. This commitment is further reinforced by the Eighth EAP, which outlines the EU's environmental policy agenda from 2022 to 2030. Even more significantly, the European Green Deal (EGD), the EU's green growth strategy, encompasses goals related to both the environment and climate. Specifically, the EGD aims to achieve zero net emissions of greenhouse gases (GHGs) by 2050, decouple economic growth from resource use and ensure a just transition (Domorenok and Graziano, 2023; Tosun, 2023). Consequently, the policy actions proposed by the Commission within the EGD framework include both environmental and climate policies as well as initiatives targeting adjacent sectors such as energy, buildings and mobility (Oberthür and von Homeyer, 2023).

To assess whether climate and environmental action are given the same priority, this chapter examines the conclusions of the European Council meetings since 2015. The observation period for this study begins in 2015, coinciding with the signing of the Paris Agreement under the United Nations Framework Convention on Climate Change (UNFCCC). This agreement established a new regime for climate change governance, shifting focus toward national policymaking within individual UNFCCC Member States (Tobin, 2017). Consequently, we anticipate that 2015 marks a turning point when climate change became even more salient to the heads of state or government of EU Member States.

The chapter begins by explaining the concept of 'climatization', followed by a clarification of the empirical-analytical approach, which focuses on the European Council and the issues it highlights in its conclusions. The main findings of the empirical analysis are then presented, before being summarized and discussed in the concluding section.

2 The 'climatization' concept

Climate change is a global phenomenon and therefore extends beyond policymaking in the EU and its Member States, representing a key issue in global politics. As Aykut and Maertens (2021, p. 502) observe, 'climatization' is occurring, which they define as "a powerful yet uneven social process in which climate change increasingly becomes the frame of reference for the mediation and hierarchization of other global issues". They further explain that this process is not a top-down mechanism but rather the outcome of the collective mobilization of various actors and organizations engaged in climate action.

Three considerations suggest that it is plausible to expect a 'climatization' of EU policy. First, the EU has consistently sought to be recognized as a global leader in climate action (Oberthür and Roche Kelly, 2008; Tobin, Torney and Biedenkopf, 2023). One way to demonstrate leadership is by leading through example (Wurzel, Liefferink and Torney, 2019), specifically by adopting ambitious climate policies. The annual Conference of the Parties to the UNFCCC (COP) meetings provide the EU with opportunities to showcase its leadership ambitions by enacting such policies.

Second, there has been growing public demand for climate action from civil society actors within the EU, reaching a peak with the rise of the Fridays for Future movement in 2018/2019. Political figures, such as Members of the European Parliament, have responded to this movement and supported its calls for more ambitious climate policies (Pollex and Berker, 2024).

Third, environmental policy in the EU has existed since the 1970s, meaning the body of environmental policy is more developed and comprehensive than that of climate policy. This is particularly true for areas concerning environmental pollution control, which was one of the EU's earliest environmental policy areas (Knill and Liefferink, 2007). From this perspective, the EU needs to catch up in the realm of climate action, which is more recent and, therefore, less developed.

Given both external and internal pressures for climate action, it is reasonable to expect climate policy to feature more prominently on the EU's agenda than environmental policy. We anticipate that this prominence will increase as the salience of climate change continues to grow.

3 Agenda-setting in the EU

Formally, the European Commission holds a monopoly on legislative initiatives in the EU (see Chapter 10). However, the Commission does not operate in isolation; it has been receptive to proposals from other actors, primarily Member States, but also civil society organizations through mechanisms like the European Citizens' Initiative (Tosun, Béland and Papadopoulos, 2022). Whether the Commission puts forward a legislative initiative depends on agenda-setting processes, wherein policy actors strive to highlight the issues they prioritize as sufficiently important to warrant consideration for policy action (Alexandrova, Rasmussen and Toshkov, 2016; Alexandrova and Timmermans, 2015; Bocquillon, 2024; Knill and Liefferink, 2007; Princen, 2007).

In the EU, there exist two routes via which an issue can enter the political agenda: from below or from above, that is, via the 'low-politics' or 'high-politics' route (Princen, 2007). The low-politics route to agenda-setting is via experts and specialized bureaucrats in the EU organs, most notably the Commission, who become aware of an issue, gather information on it and develop a policy initiative. Low-politics agenda-setting corresponds to a routine activity and is relatively steady in terms of the topics that are incorporated into the political agenda (Alexandrova and Timmermans, 2015).

With the high politics route, problems enter the political agenda as matters of urgency and are formulated by political actors, most importantly EU's heads of state or government (Bocquillon, 2024). From this, it follows that agenda-setting via high politics is more dynamic, resulting in issues being placed on the agenda when they are perceived as salient or urgent and being excluded again when they are resolved or when policymakers realize that they are too hard to resolve to merit further attention at this point (Downs, 1998).

This chapter focuses on the high-politics route to agenda-setting and assesses how much attention the EU's heads of state and/or government, which come together in the European Council, dedicate to environmental issues relative to climate issues. Due to practical constraints, the European Council needs to be selective in the topics it handles. Therefore, it tends to focus on issues that are salient and/or urgent and require its members to show responsiveness (Alexandrova and Timmermans, 2015).

Thus, this chapter does not focus on the actual policy proposals made by the EU Commission or their adoption by the Council of the EU and the European Parliament. Instead, it centers on the attention European Council members give to environmental and climate issues. This research perspective aligns with the concept of 'climatization,' which refers to how actors frame issues (Aykut and Maertens, 2021): that is, how they present information in a particular way to influence how the audience perceives a given issue (see Chapter 2). Nevertheless, it is important to note that when issues are incorporated into the political agenda they are likely to be addressed through policy proposals and adoption. Therefore, indirectly, this chapter also touches on the policymaking process.

4 Database

The conclusions from European Council meetings have served as the primary data source for the Comparative Agendas Project, which has produced several publications demonstrating how the relative importance of different policy issues has evolved over time (Alexandrova, Rasmussen and Toshkov, 2016; Alexandrova and Timmermans, 2015).

Following the approach of the Comparative Agendas Project, this chapter analyzes the thirty-one conclusions from regular European Council meetings held between December 2015 and March 2024, as provided by a dedicated website (European Council, 2024). We examined these documents to identify statements referring to environmental issues or climate change. A distinction was made between mere references to these issues and the inclusion of dedicated chapters, with the latter indicating a higher level of responsiveness.

Table 1 below summarizes the empirical findings; it shows several references to both environmental issues and climate change. However, only climate change was consistently addressed with dedicated chapters in the conclusions, suggesting that it held greater salience than environmental issues during the period of investigation. Consequently, the European Council members responded to climate change more frequently and in a more visible manner.

5 Empirical insights

To provide a clearer overview of the empirical findings, we present the relevant statements from the European Council meeting conclusions in chronological order.

2015

The European Council meeting on December 17 and 18, 2015 was held only a few days after COP21. Consequently, the European Council welcomed the Paris Agreement and invited the Commission and the Council of the EU to assess its implications for the EU's 2030 Climate and Energy Framework by March 2016. As the 'remarks' column of Table 1 indicates, the conclusions very generally referred to sustainability in the chapter on the Economic and Monetary Union, but there was no mention of environmental issues *per se*.

2016

The European Council meeting on February 18 and 19, 2016 included an annex titled 'European Council Declaration on Competitiveness' in which the EU leaders committed themselves to high standards of environmental protection. The document contained no further reference to environmental policy or climate action. Likewise, we could not observe a single mention of climate change or environmental issues in the European Council meeting on 28 June 2016, in which migration was the main topic. It was also the meeting at which the United Kingdom's prime minister officially informed the EU Member States of the outcome of the Brexit referendum. There was also no mention of climate change or environmental issues in the European Council meeting held in December 2016.

However, climate change featured prominently in the conclusions of the European Council meeting of March 17 and 18, 2016. The European Council reiterated its support for the Paris Agreement and stated that it welcomed the Commission's communication titled 'Road from Paris'. It further reiterated its commitment to reduce greenhouse gas (GHG) GHG emissions, increase the share of renewable energies and improve energy efficiency as agreed upon by the European Council in October 2014. The EU leaders stressed that "adapting the legislation in order to implement this framework remains a priority" and that they invited the Commission to "rapidly present all the remaining relevant proposals to this end so as to swiftly engage the legislative process" (General Secretariat of the Council, 2016a, p. 5).

At its October meeting, the European Council welcomed the ratification of the Paris Agreement and stated that it would "keep under review the Energy Union, including all the elements of the 2030 climate and energy framework" as well as "continue to give strategic orientations on the related legislative proposals" (General Secretariat of the Council, 2016b, p. 6). It also referred to environmental protection in the context of EU's trade interests.

2017

At its meeting on June 22 and 23, 2017 the European Council affirmed its commitment to the highest environmental protection standards while promoting free trade. It dedicated an entire chapter to the Paris Agreement, strongly reaffirming its commitment and describing the agreement as a key element for modernizing the EU's industry and economy. In this chapter, as indicated in Table 1, EU leaders also referenced the 2030 Agenda for Sustainable Development and its seventeen Sustainable Development Goals (SDGs), viewing the Paris Agreement as crucial for implementing these goals.

At its October meeting, the European Council welcomed the launch of the European Fund for Sustainable Development and elaborated on sustainability, as Table 1 indicates. The document contained no other mentions of climate change or environmental issues.

The conclusions of the December meeting included a chapter dedicated to climate change. In it, the European Council welcomed the outcome of the One Planet Summit, which aimed to scale up public and private finance in support of climate action. The document also reaffirmed the EU's commitment to implementing the Paris Agreement and its aspiration to act as an international leader in combating climate change.

2018

The conclusions of the meeting of March 22, 2018 included a section on the Paris Agreement within the chapter on 'Other Items'. Therein, the European Council invited the Commission to present a proposal for a long-term EU GHG emissions reduction strategy by the first quarter of 2019. In the section on the single market, the European Council referred to sustainability in broad terms but without referring to environmental protection (see Table 1).

The Conclusions of the June meeting did not refer to either climate action or environmental policy. However, in the October meeting, climate change featured prominently, appearing in two sections under the chapter on external relations: In the first section, the European Council stated that it had taken note of the latest Intergovernmental Panel on Climate Change special report. In the second section, the EU leaders indicated their full support for Poland, which was responsible for organizing COP24. The European Council also stated that this event must "result in the adoption of ambitious and comprehensive implementing rules of the Paris Agreement" (General Secretariat of the Council, 2018, p. 5).

At the December meeting, the European Council welcomed the European Commission's (2018) communication 'A Clean Planet for all' and acknowledged the outcome of COP24. On that basis, it invited the Council of the EU to work together with the Commission to develop the communication further.

2019

The Conclusions of the first European Council meeting in 2019 dedicated an entire chapter to climate change, while environmental issues were only broadly referenced through mentions of sustainability, as Table 1 indicates. The climate change chapter focused primarily on the Paris Agreement. In this chapter, EU leaders emphasized the importance of the EU submitting an ambitious long-term strategy by 2020, called for the timely finalization of national long-term strategies and instructed the Council of the EU to begin work on a long-term climate strategy.

The Conclusions of the June meeting continued to give climate change prominence. The European Council welcomes the involvement of the European Commission and Member States in preparing the United Nations (UN) Secretary General's Climate Action Summit. The European Council invited the Council of the EU and the Commission to develop strategies for the transition to a climate-neutral EU and the European Investment Bank to intensify its activities in support of climate action. While environmental issues received no dedicated chapter, the European Council acknowledged them as one of multiple dimensions of a 'green transition' agenda. This corresponds to the logic of what the Commission would later launch as the EGD (European Commission, 2019). More precisely, it states that there is need to improve the quality of the environment and to fight loss of biodiversity and preserve environmental systems.

The European Council meetings in late 2019 continued to address climate change and environmental issues. The October 2019 meeting included a chapter on climate change, reflecting on the UN Climate Action Summit 2019. While the environment was not explicitly mentioned, it was inherent in the discussion of a green transition stated in the conclusions (see Table 1).

The December meeting featured an extensive chapter on climate change and acknowledged the European Commission's (2019) communication on the EGD. The conclusions also recognized environmental issues, stating, for example, that facilities of companies from the EU need to adhere to the highest international environmental and safety standards in third countries.

Throughout both meetings, climate change remained a prominent topic, and environmental concerns were increasingly integrated into broader policy discussions in relation to the EGD. The European Council demonstrated awareness of the need for global environmental responsibility among EU companies, reflecting a growing emphasis on sustainable practices beyond EU borders.

2020

The United Kingdom's departure from the EU and the Covid-19 pandemic marked this year. Consequently, several special European Council meetings were held, primarily dealing with containment of the spread of the Covid-19 virus. The online repository offers conclusions for only two regular meetings of the European Council that year.

The conclusions of the October meeting, despite the pandemic, included a dedicated chapter on climate change. In it, EU leaders emphasized the need to increase climate policy ambition, as discussed in the European Commission's (2020) communication on 'Stepping up Europe's 2030 climate ambition.' The European Council also acknowledged the EU's commitments to the Paris Agreement and the updating of 'Nationally Determined Contributions'. In the chapter on EU–Africa relations, the European Council referred to environmental protection.

The December meeting's Conclusions featured an even more extensive chapter on climate change, remarkably also engaging with environmental issues. The document highlighted the need to consider the environmental impacts of climate action, particularly potential positive environmental effects or co-benefits.

2021

The conclusions of the June meeting mentioned both climate change and environmental issues, though without dedicated chapters. The October meeting noted the COP26 on climate change and the 15th Conference of the Parties to the UN Convention on Biological Diversity (COP15) in its external relations section. This marked the first explicit mention of an international conference on environmental issues in the conclusions during the observation period. The European Council even called for establishing a framework on biodiversity protection.

The December meeting's conclusions barely mentioned climate change, only referring to it as a threat to be considered in EU–NATO cooperation. No environmental issues were mentioned in this document.

2022

The March meeting reflected the impact of Russia's invasion of Ukraine, with the agenda dominated by security issues, including energy supply security and prices. The European Council emphasized that energy security and climate neutrality could only be achieved through a well-functioning internal electricity market. They invited the Commission to improve the electricity markets' functioning. Environmental issues were indirectly addressed through references to green transition (see Table 1).

The June meeting focused on the implications of Russia's attack on Ukraine, not engaging with climate or environmental issues. In October, leaders reiterated their call for improved electricity market functioning to achieve energy sovereignty and climate neutrality. They also referenced COP27 on climate change and COP15 on biodiversity in external relations discussions. The December meeting stressed the need for investment in better energy technologies and infrastructure to end dependence on Russian fossil fuels, enhance energy security and accelerate green transition.

Overall, 2022 saw energy, security and defense as primary concerns for the European Council, marking a significant shift in the EU's policy priorities as leaders convened multiple emergency summits to address the unprecedented challenges facing the bloc's strategic autonomy and economic resilience (Oberthür and von Homeyer, 2023; Tosun, 2023).

2023

The March 2023 meeting concluded that more action was needed for the European economy's green transition, encompassing both climate and environmental aspects. Water security was introduced as an issue, with the Council welcoming the UN 2023 Water Conference. Russian aggression toward Ukraine remained prominent.

June's conclusions addressed environmental and climate issues in the context of EU industry policy, trade policy and external relations. Importantly, the leaders recognized climate change as one dimension of a broader global crisis including environmental degradation.

The October meeting referenced the upcoming COP28 on climate change and called for prompt agreement on the Critical Raw Materials Act, Net-Zero Industry Act and electricity market design reform. The December meeting focused on climate action, welcoming COP28 achievements, including agreements on emission reductions and transitioning away from fossil fuels.

2024

In March, the conclusions underlined the agricultural sector's importance in addressing environmental and climate challenges while acknowledging farmers' concerns. The European Council invited the Commission and Council to find solutions accommodating farmers' needs. While not explicitly requesting exemptions from environmental or climate policies, the Commission subsequently proposed loosening some climate and environmental measures as part of concessions to farmers (Tosun et al., 2024).

Table 1: Summary of the findings.

Date	Environmental Protection		Climate Action		Remarks
	Chapter	Reference	Chapter	Reference	
18/12/2015			■		Sustainability
19/02/2016		■			
18/03/2016			■		
28/06/2016					
21/10/2016		■		■	
15/12/2016					
23/06/2017		■	■		SDGs
19/10/2017					Sustainability
14/12/2017			■		
23/03/2018				■	Sustainability
28/06/2018					
18/10/2018				■	
14/12/2018				■	
22/03/2019			■		Sustainability
20/06/2019		■	■		
18/10/2019			■		Green transition
12/12/2019		■	■		European Green Deal
16/10/2020		■	■		
11/12/2020		■	■		
25/06/2021		■		■	
22/10/2021		■		■	
16/12/2021				■	
25/03/2022				■	Green transition
24/06/2022		■		■	
21/10/2022		■		■	
15/12/2022					Green transition
23/03/2023		■		■	
30/06/2023		■		■	
27/10/2023		■		■	
15/12/2023				■	
22/03/2024		■		■	

Notes: Author's elaboration. The dot indicates if the European Council conclusions have included environmental policy or climate policy. Dots in the 'reference' column indicate that the European Council made references to the policy in the conclusions. Dots in the 'chapter' column indicate dedicated chapters on the policy. The 'remarks' column specifies the concepts used in the documents consulted to refer to climate action and/or environmental protection.

Discussion

The analysis of the European Council conclusions has yielded several intriguing insights. Despite covering a relatively short period of nine years, we observed both stable and dynamic characteristics in the EU leaders' political agenda.

Climate change has consistently received greater emphasis than environmental issues, as evidenced by the frequent dedication to it through entire chapters, while environmental concerns were often mentioned elsewhere in the text without highlight. As explained in the conceptual considerations, the annual COPs on climate change have been a key factor in maintaining this continued attention. The EU leaders regularly referenced their positions in preparation for these COPs and responded to their outcomes, often including directives to other EU organs, particularly the Commission, to take action. Due to the COPs' significance, climate change was typically addressed either in dedicated chapters or as items in sections on EU external relations. In contrast, environmental issues were mentioned in the context of external relations only once, in reference to COP15 on biodiversity, which stands out as an event the European Council paid enhanced attention to (see also Tosun, 2023).

In the beginning, the European Council treated climate policy in tandem with energy issues, but then climate change became a stand-alone issue. A turning point was 2019, when climate change again became discussed in tandem with other topics and in the frame of green transition and the EGD. In 2022, the approach to climate change changed again in the wake of the Russian attack on Ukraine, when the security of energy supply and the question of affordable energy received attention. In this context, the European Council again discussed climate change together with energy security. However, the most recent conclusions also show that environmental issues have moved up on the political agenda. The documents do not include chapters on environmental policy, but they refer to concrete environmental issues and policy measures proposed in the frame of the EGD.

Overall, the empirical analysis supports the view that European environmental policy has experienced climatization. The European Council mentioned climate change more frequently and prominently than environmental policy. However, especially from 2019 onward it becomes clear that the EU leaders perceive climate policy and environmental policy to have the potential for generating synergies and co-benefits for citizens. Therefore, it is plausible to argue that climatization has created an opportunity for generating renewed attention to environmental policy. Interestingly, the joint recognition of climate and environmental policy was also visible in the conclusions of the March 2024 meeting of the European Council, which predominantly addressed measures in support of farmers.

Our interpretation of the data suggests that EU leaders conceive of climate and environmental policy as different policy fields. However, they are also aware of a need to coordinate and integrate measures targeting climate change and environmental degradation as well as additional policy measures necessary to achieve sustainable development.

6 Conclusion

The year 1992 marked a milestone in climate action. It was in that year that countries from all over the world joined the UNFCCC, a framework for international cooperation to combat climate change by limiting average global temperature increases and the resulting change to climate. Interestingly, the UNFCCC was signed at a time when global concern over environmental degradation was high. The annual COPs to the UNFCCC created repeated attention directed at climate change, which was particularly high, especially among EU leaders, when COP15 was held in Copenhagen and again on the occasion of COP21, which resulted in the signing of the Paris Agreement. COP15 was widely considered a failure because the national leaders could not agree on a regime for the period after the Kyoto Protocol (see Chapter 29; Dimitrov, 2010; Falkner, Stephan and Vogler, 2010).

The EU has been particularly keen on being perceived as an international leader in climate change governance (Oberthür and Roche Kelly, 2008; Tobin, Torney and Biedenkopf, 2023; Tosun, 2023; Wurzel, Liefferink and Torney, 2019). Given its commitment to fighting climate change and its aspiration to act as an international climate leader, the EU has directed considerable attention to this issue and has produced an extensive corpus of climate policies (Dupont et al., 2024), especially in the years between 2009 and 2015 (see Chapter 20).

Climate change has then gained even more traction by social mobilization, which started in 2018 but became more intense in 2019 with the diffusion of the Fridays for Future movement (Pollex and Berker, 2024). This, in turn, caused the formation of additional civil action groups with more radical demands. While it is notable that the EU's commitment to climate action has its origin in 1992 when environmental degradation was at the top of the global political agenda, so is the observation that environmental issues started to gain attention again in the wake of the mobilization for climate change.

As shown in this analysis, the EU leaders were aware of climate change and put it regularly on the political agenda while environmental issues received limited attention. This changed when the EU Commission proposed the EGD, which recognized the need for action in both climate and environmental policy (Tosun, 2023). Consequently, environmental issues have been given more prominence at the meetings of the European Council. Despite the visible increase in political attention to environmental issues, we could not observe a single instance when they dominated over climate change. Even when the EU leaders referred to the importance of the COP15 to the UN Framework Convention on Biodiversity, this event was co-mentioned with the COP to the UNFCCC.

Therefore, overall, we can conclude that climate change has become the main focus of the EU political leaders. This situation can create both a challenge and a chance for fighting environmental degradation. The challenge stems from the fact that drivers of environmental degradation and climate change are similar but not identical, entailing the need for distinct policy responses, which are ideally coordinated across the two sectors. Since climate change has gained currency, several civil society actors are redirecting their attention toward climate change, which potentially weakens their impact on environmental governance. This could be one reason why scholars have reported instances of environmental policy dismantling in the EU (Lenschow, Burns and Zito, 2020).

On the positive side, the continuously high levels of attention for climate change can help keep environmental degradation also on the political agenda. The UN Secretary-General António Guterres at the UN Environment meeting Stockholm+50 referred to climate change, air pollution and biodiversity loss as the most pressing issues facing humanity. He coined the term "triple planetary crisis" (see United Nations, 2024), which could be useful for securing attention to environmental issues via attention to climate change.

At a time when the EU has to deal with multiple crises at the same time, the delivery of the EGD sparks controversies. The voting of the member of the European People's Party in the European Parliament on elements of the EGD has demonstrated that EU Commission proposals do not automatically produce binding legislation. Moreover, when inspecting more closely which acts have been passed and which failed to do so, we can observe that climate-related proposals performed better than environmental ones (Tosun, 2023). Thus, even when moving from the agenda-setting stage to policy adoption, climate action seems to stand a better chance than policies that address environmental degradation.

This divergence in legislative success rates reflects deeper political and economic realities within the EU institutional framework. Climate policies, particularly those framed around carbon neutrality and energy transition, often align with broader economic competitiveness narratives and industrial transformation goals, making them more palatable to business-oriented political groups and economically focused member states. Climate policies also align better with the European Commission's shift from the EGD to the Clean Industrial Deal, which aims at strengthening the EU's industrial competitiveness and promoting decarbonization (European Commission, 2025). Environmental protection measures, by contrast, frequently encounter resistance when perceived as imposing immediate costs without clear economic returns, especially during periods of economic uncertainty or geopolitical tension. This economic framing proves critical even for climate policies: recent European Commission considerations to weaken the established 2035 ban on fossil-fuel vehicle sales demonstrate that even climate policy ambitions—despite their strategic alignment with industrial competitiveness—remain vulnerable to economic pressures and can be scaled back when the EU faces significant economic challenges.

The policy pattern also reveals how crisis contexts can reshape policy priorities, with climate action benefiting from its connection to energy security concerns heightened by geopolitical developments, while traditional environmental protection measures struggle to maintain political momentum. This trend suggests that successful environmental policy action may require stronger strategic framing that connects biodiversity protection, pollution reduction and ecosystem preservation to immediate economic and security interests.

All this calls for stimulating mobilization for environmental protection to ensure that it is indeed realized to the same degree as climate action, as foreseen by the EGD.

References

Alexandrova, P., Rasmussen, A. and Toshkov, D. (2016) 'Agenda responsiveness in the European Council: public Priorities, policy problems and political attention', *West European Politics*, 39(4), pp. 605 – 627.

Alexandrova, P. and Timmermans, A. (2015) 'Agenda dynamics on energy policy in the European Council', in: Tosun, J., Biesenbender, S. and Schulze, K. (eds.) *Lecture notes in energy: Energy policy making in the EU.* Volume 28. London: Springer, pp.41 – 61.

Aykut, S.C. and Maertens, L. (2021) 'The climatization of global politics: Introduction to the special issue', *International Politics*, 58(4), pp. 501 – 518.

Bocquillon, P. (2024) 'Setting the European agenda in hard times: The commission, the European Council and the EU polycrisis', *Journal of European Integration*, 46(4), pp. 567 – 574.

Dimitrov, R.S. (2010) 'Inside UN climate change negotiations: The Copenhagen Conference', *Review of Policy Research*, 27(6), pp. 795 – 821.

Domorenok, E. and Graziano, P. (2023) 'Understanding the European Green Deal: A narrative policy framework approach', *European Policy Analysis*, 9(1), pp. 9 – 29.

Downs, A. (1998) 'Up and Down with Ecology: The "issue-attention cycle"', in: Downs, A. (ed.) *Political theory and public choice.* Cheltenham: Edward Elgar Publishing, pp. 100 – 112.

Dupont, C. et al. (2024) 'Three decades of EU climate policy: Racing toward climate neutrality?', *WIREs Climate Change*, 15(1), e863.

European Commission (2018) 'A clean planet for all: A European strategic long-term vision for a prosperous, modern, competitive and climate neutral economy', *COM*(2018) 773 final. Available at: https://eur-lex.europa.eu/legal-content/EN/TXT/?uri=celex:52018DC0773 (Accessed: 15 July 2025).

European Commission (2019) 'The European Green Deal', *COM*(2019) 640 final. Available at: https://eur-lex.europa.eu/legal-content/EN/TXT/?uri=celex:52019DC0640 (Accessed: 15 July 2025)

European Commission (2020) 'Stepping up Europe's 2030 climate ambition: Investing in a climate-neutral future for the benefit of our people' *COM*(2020) 562 final. Available at: https://eur-lex.europa.eu/legal-content/EN/TXT/?uri=celex:52020DC0562 (Accessed: 15 July 2025).

European Commission (2025) 'The Clean Industrial Deal: A joint roadmap for competitiveness and decarbonisation', *COM*(2025) 85 final. Available at: https://eur-lex.europa.eu/legal-content/EN/TXT/?uri=celex:52025DC0085 (Accessed: 15 July 2025).

To European Council (2024) 'European Council conclusions'. Available at: https://www.consilium.europa.eu/en/documents-publications/public-register/euco-conclusions/ (Accessed: 20 November 2024).

Falkner, R., Stephan, H. and Vogler, J. (2010) 'International climate policy after Copenhagen: Towards a "building blocks" approach', *Global Policy*, 1(3), pp. 252 – 262.

General Secretariat of the Council (2016a) 'Conclusions', European Council meeting, 17 and 18 March 2016, Brussels.

General Secretariat of the Council (2016b) 'Conclusions', European Council meeting, 20 and 21 October 2016, Brussels.

General Secretariat of the Council (2018) 'Conclusions', European Council meeting, 18 October 2018, Brussels.

Jordan, A. and Lenschow, A. (2010) 'Environmental policy integration: a state of the art review', *Environmental Policy and Governance*, 20(3), pp. 147 – 158.

Knill, C. and Liefferink, D. (2007) *Environmental politics in the European Union: Policy-making, implementation and patterns of multi-level governance.* Manchester: Manchester University Press.

Lenschow, A., Burns, C. and Zito, A. (2020) 'Dismantling, disintegration or continuing stealthy integration in European Union environmental policy?', *Public Administration*, 98(2), pp. 340 – 348.

Oberthür, S. and von Homeyer, I. (2023) 'From emissions trading to the European Green Deal: The evolution of the climate policy mix and climate policy integration in the EU', *Journal of European Public Policy*, 30(3), pp. 445 – 468.

Oberthür, S. and Roche Kelly, C. (2008) 'EU leadership in international climate policy: Achievements and challenges', *The International Spectator*, 43(3), 35 – 50.

Pollex, J. and Berker, L.E. (2024) 'The European Parliament and Fridays for Future: Analysing reactions to a new environmental movement by Europe's climate policy champion', *Journal of European Integration*, 22(6), pp. 1 – 18.

Princen, S. (2007) 'Agenda-setting in the European Union: A theoretical exploration and agenda for research', *Journal of European Public Policy*, 14(1), pp. 21 – 38.

Tobin, P. (2017) 'Leaders and laggards: Climate policy ambition in developed states', *Global Environmental Politics*, 17(4), pp. 28 – 47.

Tobin, P., Torney, D. and Biedenkopf, K. (2023) 'EU climate leadership: Domestic and global dimensions', in: Rayner, T., Szulecki, K., Jordan, A. and Oberthür, S. (eds.) *Handbook on European Union climate change policy and politics.* Cheltenham: Edward Elgar Publishing, pp. 187 – 200.

Tosun, J. (2023) 'The European Union's climate and environmental policy in times of geopolitical crisis', *Journal of Common Market Studies*, 61(S1), pp. 147 – 156.

Tosun, J., Béland, D. and Papadopoulos, Y. (2022) 'The impact of direct democracy on policy change: Insights from European citizens' initiatives', *Policy & Politics*, 50(3), pp. 323 – 340.

Tosun, J. et al. (2024) 'Attributing responsibility to farmers for environmental protection and climate action: Insights from the European Union', *Journal of Environmental Studies and Sciences*, https://doi.org/10.1007/s13412-024-00981-7.

United Nations (2024) 'Guterres at Stockholm+50: "End the suicidal war against nature"', United Nations Regional Information Centre for Western Europe. Available at: https://unric.org/en/guterres-at-stockholm50-end-the-suicidal-war-against-nature/ (Accessed: 11 November 2024).

Wurzel, R.K.W., Liefferink, D. and Torney, D. (2019) 'Pioneers, leaders and followers in multilevel and polycentric climate governance', *Environmental Politics*, 28(1), pp. 1 – 21.

Henning Deters and Sebastian Heidebrecht

The single market and environmental policy: Catalysts and constraints

Abstract: This chapter examines the historical significance and ongoing impact of the single market on European Union (EU) environmental policy. As a dynamic and evolving area, environmental policy often functions separately from a purely market-liberal approach of deregulation or harmonization based on lowest common denominator solutions. While the single market has influenced environmental policy, it has never imposed firm constraints. Despite the reduction in the volume of environmental legislation following the 'polycrisis', there has been no systematic deregulation. In fact, the extent of delegated law-making by the European Commission has increased. With the 2019 European Green Deal, the Commission moreover proposed a package of ambitious environmental policy measures; in response to the Covid-19 pandemic, the EU took steps toward a 'green recovery' and increasingly leveraged access to the single market to promote environmental policy abroad.

Keywords: Environmental policy; single market; policy change; twin transition; Green Deal

1 Catalysts and Constraints

This chapter investigates the historical significance and enduring influence of the single market on European Union (EU) environmental policy. Our analysis focuses on the typical policymaking dynamics at the intersection of these areas rather than on the coherence between them (Chapters 7 and 33 cover the latter in depth). We argue that the single market is both a catalyst and a constraint. With changes in the larger economic and institutional context (see Chapter 4), one or the other dynamic dominates at different times, and the mechanisms by which the single market shapes environmental policy and politics change. We trace these dynamics from their early beginnings until the most recent developments during the 'polycrisis' (Zeitlin, Nicoli and Laffan, 2019). The emerging longer-term picture is that single market constraints can usually be overcome and that the single market often facilitates policy expansion and stringency. Yet environmental protection is far from a market integration side-effect. The catalyzing impacts are no substitute for political will and intergovernmental agreement.

These observations qualify two research traditions informing environmental policy scholarship (see Chapter 2). According to *liberal intergovernmentalism*, EU policy is determined by bargaining among governments with fixed preferences that are shaped by well-organized domestic interests (Moravcsik, 1993). Comparing the typical levels of intergovernmental conflict, market-making policy appears more amenable to integra-

https://doi.org/10.1515/9783111321523-036

tion than market-correcting environmental policy. Research in this tradition therefore emphasizes the constraining force of the single market. Simplifying slightly, the single market is efficient in the sense that in the long run all Member States benefit from transnational competition and trade. The challenge lies not so much in finding agreement but in averting free-riding, which is why the implementation of the four market freedoms and the Treaty's competition provisions were delegated to the European Commission and the Court of Justice of the EU (CJEU) (Pollack, 2003). By contrast, environmental protection is not primarily concerned with efficiency, and policy decisions depend on negotiations between the Member States. Although, as a regulatory policy, it rarely involves direct resource transfers but instead prescribes and prohibits certain activities (see Section 4 however), the redistributive implications of environmental policy are often salient and provoke controversy, especially between 'leader' and 'laggard' states. Even among the former, incompatible regulatory approaches can impose unequal adaptation costs that require hard compromise-building (Börzel, 2002; Chapter 14). Given the large and growing socioeconomic and institutional diversity among EU Member States, the threat of shallow compromises and deadlock looms large (Deters, 2019).

Neofunctionalism sees a greater potential for positive-sum interest constellations in environmental policy, especially when realizing the single market hinges on joint regulation. The core neofunctionalist idea is that European integration 'spills over' from areas where integration is relatively advanced into adjacent domains where it lags (Haas, 2004, p. 372; Niemann and Schmitter, 2009). Behind this are functional interdependencies that mobilize organized interests and policymakers who "discover that they cannot do A [...] without also doing B" (Lindberg and Scheingold, 1970, p. 117). Although attempts have been made to theorize integration bottlenecks and frustration ('spillback'; see Schmitter, 2004), spillover dynamics better account for the catalyzing effects of the single market than for its constraining impact. Spillover is most likely across 'low politics' domains characterized by relatively strong technicality and weak salience, for which the single market and the environment are prime examples (Weale, 1999). Divergent environmental provisions at the national level create non-tariff trade barriers that disturb free movement of goods and call for harmonization through EU-level environmental policymaking. Economies of scale further incentivize firms and trade organizations to seek uniform standards adopted at the higher governance level (Vogel, 1997). Even when diverging environmental regulations do not directly impede trade, the single market brings firms operating under different regimes into competition, with the more strictly regulated firms and environmental leader states consequently pushing for European environmental policy to 'level the playing field'.

The remainder of this chapter traces the single market's impact on the scope and stringency of environmental policy across three historical periods: the 'emergence' (1973–1986) of a European environmental policy; its 'expansion' and consolidation (1987–2008); and the most recent period of 'crises' (2009–2024). We demonstrate that over the last 50 years the single market has acted both as constraint and catalyst.

Initially, it catalyzed European environmental policymaking by creating demand for coordination, but it also prioritized market freedoms over conflicting environmental protection. From 1987 to 2008, new Treaty provisions and changes in single market jurisprudence mitigated the pro-market bias. The new settlement allowed an expansion and consolidation of environmental policy that grew independent of single-market forces. However, when in 2009 the EU plunged into the polycrisis, austerity and a broader deregulation agenda exerted downward pressure on environmental legislation, whereas the Commission increasingly turned to delegated environmental lawmaking behind the scenes. During the Covid-19 pandemic, the EU, rather than doubling down on deregulation, turned to a more protectionist industrial policy based on an extensive new fiscal capacity to promote a green recovery. The final section concludes by surveying what is known and still unknown about the environment-market nexus.

2 Emergence: 1973–1986

Historically, the single market precedes environmental protection as an EU policy field. The EU originally lacked jurisdiction over environmental policy, and the single market catalyzed the emergence of a European environmental policy by providing a substitute. While the founding Treaties of Paris and Rome empowered the EU institutions to integrate the national markets around the 'four freedoms' of goods, capital, services, and labor, they provided no explicit basis for environmental policy. The Commission therefore resorted to 'borrowing' the strong market provisions to regulate environmental matters (Knill and Liefferink, 2007, pp. 5–7; Rehbinder and Stewart, 1988, p. 15). Before the Single European Act (SEA), it based environmental legislation on Article 114,[1] which provided for the harmonization of laws that interfered with the single market, in addition to the so-called residual competence of Article 352 (Figure 1). The CJEU legally sanctioned this subterfuge (Rehbinder and Stewart, 1988, pp. 20–21).

Especially during this first period, the single market also catalyzed European environmental policymaking by creating demand for coordination. In the late 1970s, environmental movements and green parties emerged in many European countries. Governments, citizens and pressure groups became aware of ecological degradation (Weale et al., 2000, p. 246). Consequently, several Member States adopted domestic environmental policies, and those were often incompatible and interfered with the single market (Weale, 1999). Even when environmental issues did not transcend national borders, economic interactions created external effects that required managing. One important example was manufactured goods such as motor vehicles that posed environmental hazards. Although cars produce predominantly local pollution (except for climate emissions), a patchwork of national norms would have made it hard to

1 We use the most recent numbering in the Treaty on the Functioning of the EU (TFEU) rather than the historical equivalents. Unless specified differently, we always refer to the TFEU.

trade cars across borders (Rehbinder and Stewart, 1988, pp. 17, 76). The harmonization of product standards therefore became an early instance of environmental policymaking at the EU level (Gehring, 1997). 'Directive 70/220', which remains the basis for the Euro car emission norms to this day, responded to French and German domestic initiatives that threatened to fragment the European automobile market (Rehbinder and Stewart, 1988, pp. 16–17).

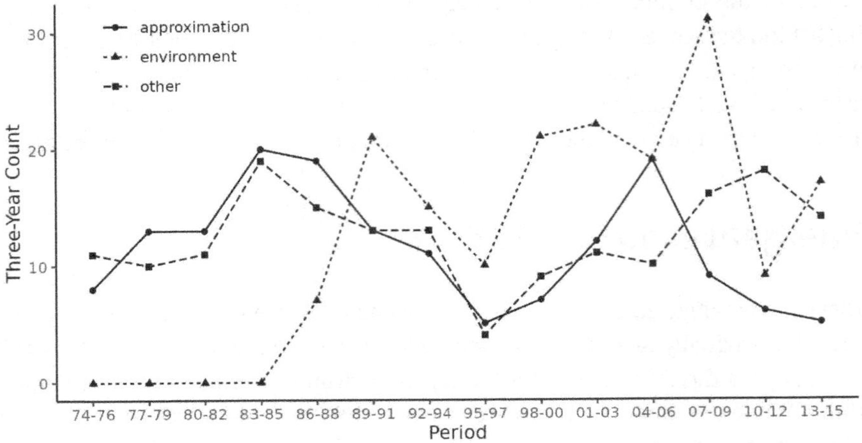

Figure 1: Use of single market and environment powers in environmental policymaking. Volume of secondary environmental law adopted in each three-year period (to smooth fluctuations) from one year after the First Environmental Action Programme until 2015. The data include all directives and regulations adopted by the EU Council and, if applicable, the European Parliament in environmental and animal protection (Eur-Lex directory codes 15.10 and 15.40). The use of the single market basis continues long after the introduction of a dedicated environment basis. Use of the environmental basis surpassed that of the former only with the move to majority voting in the early 1990s. Sources: Eur-Lex, compiled using eurlex (Ovádek, 2021) for secondary law, and EvoEU (Fjelstul, 2019) for Treaty bases.

The rise of domestic environmental regulation within the single market gave rise to "diagonal conflicts" (Joerges, 2007, p. 318) between the environmental and single market policy areas across governance levels. How they were resolved initially constrained environmental policymaking. From a legal perspective, the issue was whether the European market freedoms preempted market-restricting domestic regulation or whether trade interests should yield to environmental protection. At first, the CJEU favored trade. In the 1974 *Dassonville* decision, the Court notably read Article 30 as prohibiting national measures that could—even just potentially and without discriminating between foreign and domestic producers—restrict the free movement of goods.[2] In *Cassis* (1979), the CJEU moreover laid the ground for the principle of mutual recognition, according to which importing countries may not apply their product standards to

2 *Procureur du Roi v Benoît and Gustave Dassonville*, Case 8/74, 1974.

goods already regulated by equivalent foreign standards (Alter and Meunier-Aitsahalia, 1994).[3] Under Article 36, exceptions only hold when the restrictions were proportionate and so-called 'mandatory requirements' of public policy were defended. This raised the question of what counted as a mandatory requirement and how the Court would assess regulatory equivalence and proportionality (Holzinger, 2011, p. 120).

The legal uncertainty caused by *Dassonville* and *Cassis* constrained national product standards by dissuading Member States from regulating imports. Simultaneously, it encouraged them to promote EU level environmental policy to fill the ensuing regulatory gaps. The result was a remarkable production of European environmental law *avant la lettre*, based purely on single-market competencies and catalyzed by the need to coordinate domestic policy choices that could restrict market freedoms (Knill and Liefferink, 2007, pp. 9–10; Rehbinder and Stewart, 1988, p. 259). However, dependence on the single-market competences also forced the EU into a reactive role, whereas Member States had to provide the impetus and official rationale for harmonization by adopting national standards. Often, the Commission nevertheless took the lead by anticipating potential market restrictions (Holzinger, 1994, p. 68).

The market-liberal interpretation of the free movement of goods moreover constrained regulatory stringency by providing the least ambitious countries with a strong bargaining position. Since harmonization required unanimous agreement and since defaulting to domestic regulation meant risking judicial reversal, countries seeking harmonization to compensate for their constrained domestic leeway often had to accept shallow minimum compromises (Holzinger, 2011, p. 120; Knill and Liefferink, 2007, pp. 106–107; Scharpf, 1997).

Policymaking based on the single-market powers also constrained environmental regulation by introducing bias favoring market-making provisions. The lack of a dedicated competence limited the substance and scope of early environmental policy (Knill and Liefferink, 2007, p. 7), because all initiatives had to be framed as remedies against trade restrictions or distortions of competition. The EU did also adopt measures with rather perfunctory market rationales, such as 'Directive 76/160/EEC' concerning bathing water quality (Wurzel, 2006, p. 189) or 'Directive 79/409/EEC' on the conservation of wild birds (Rehbinder and Stewart, 1988, p. 102). Nevertheless, measures like nature conservation or quality standards for environmental media remained hard to justify. Because of the unsuitable legal basis, early environmental politics seemed obsessed with product standards despite there being no ecological reason for approaching environmental protection from this direction (Gehring, 1997).

---

3 *Rewe-Zentral AG v Bundesmonopolverwaltung für Branntwein*, Case 120/78, 1979.

3 Expansion: 1987 – 2008

In 1987, the SEA introduced a Treaty title dedicated to the environment. It mitigated the market-making bias by allowing the EU to adopt environmental policy under the new Article 192 without resorting to its single market powers and thus without feigning economic objectives. The single market nevertheless constrained environmental policymaking for some more years. As before under Articles 114 and 352, legislation based on Article 192 still required a unanimous Council. Finding agreement became even more difficult because the EU enlargements had doubled EU membership, increasing the economic divergence and the diversity of regulatory approaches (Deters, 2019). Accordingly, the situation might have been worse than before. However, the SEA subjected harmonization under Article 114 to the new cooperation procedure that allowed the Council to decide by a qualified majority and gave more power to the Commission and the European Parliament (EP) (see Chapter 11). The use of the single-market competences accorded with both actors' institutional interests, and the Commission also hoped to curb deviations from EU law. The result was a "treaty base game" (Rhodes, 1995), in which the supranational institutions pushed for the continued use of the single market powers (Holzinger, 2011, p. 119). The market-making bias thus remained until 1993, when the Maastricht Treaty extended the cooperation procedure to environmental legislation based on Article 192. Only from this point onwards was environmental policy adopted more often on a dedicated Treaty basis than by using the single-market competences (see Figure 1).

The SEA relaxed single-market constraints in another way. At the insistence of environmental pioneers Sweden and Denmark, an environmental guarantee (Article 114(5) TFEU) was introduced that allows the Member States to exceed harmonized environmental product standards (Liefferink and Andersen, 1998, p. 258). Such derogations, however, remain subject to conditions and the Commission must be notified of them (de Sadeleer, 2014, pp. 358 – 377). Developments of the free movement of goods jurisprudence also had a catalyzing effect on the stringency of product standards. In *Danish Bottles* (1988), the CJEU clarified that environmental protection was included in the category of mandatory requirements that justified exemptions from the prohibition of market restrictions.[4] Regulatory autonomy was thus returned to the Member States, and so the bargaining power in negotiations on product standards shifted in favor of the ambitious countries, who could now credibly threaten to limit access to their markets should harmonization not achieve their preferred level of stringency (Holzinger, 2011, p. 121; Scharpf, 1997). The result was a "trading up" dynamic (Vogel, 1997), wherein harmonization often approached the highest levels of extant domestic regulations.

Once a product regulation is harmonized, however, the trading-up dynamic stops and policy drift sets in. The market-making logic of harmonization deliberately cons-

---

4 *Commission of the European Communities v Kingdom of Denmark*, Case 302/86, 1988

trains domestic environmental policy by defining maximum product standards for imports that Member States may exceed only exceptionally and with Commission approval (de Sadeleer, 2014, pp. 358–377; Dougan, 2000). When new product standards are defined from scratch, policymakers negotiate against the backdrop of domestic regulatory autonomy. However, when harmonized rules are reformed, reflecting changing environmental conditions or technological progress, the existing EU policy becomes the default outcome, strengthening the least ambitious countries' bargaining position (Holzinger and Knill, 2004). Fritz Scharpf (1988, 2011) famously called this situation a "joint-decision trap". It arises when the distribution of veto power constrains joint decision-making at the EU level while EU law preempts unilateral action at the domestic level.

To an extent, delegation can overcome policy drift. Several 'tertiary' lawmaking procedures, including the original comitology (see Chapter 10) and the more recent delegated and implementing acts, empower the Commission to update policy settings in existing secondary law (Burns and Tobin, 2020). Depending on the procedure and scope of delegation, the Commission is subject to more or less control by the EP and Member States (Brandsma and Blom-Hansen, 2016). Since the Commission tends to push for stronger protection than the Council, and since the national experts in charge of controlling the Commission often form epistemic (expert) communities that are somewhat decoupled from domestic policy interests (Benz, 2009, pp. 142–143; Joerges and Neyer, 1997), delegation may compensate for the structural conservatism of harmonization (Deters, 2021, pp. 196–197). In quantitative terms, technocratic decisions adopted in this mode have become the dominant source of EU environmental law, surpassing political decision-making since the late 2000s (see Figure 2).

Process regulations, such as industrial emission ceilings, remain subject to lowest common denominator bargaining, as they were unaffected by the jurisprudential change discussed above (Knill and Liefferink, 2007, pp. 106–107). This is because diverging process regulations, unlike product standards, are of little direct concern for the single market. Since the Member States are not allowed to restrict the importation of goods and services or the outflow of investments based on their ecological production footprint, there is no need, from a market-making perspective, to bring diverging process regulations in line (Scharpf, 1997). The front-runner states may wish to 'level the playing field', but the single market prevents them from using market access for bargaining leverage. The laggard states can thus block joint policies that impair their competitive advantage. When EU environmental legislation depended on unanimous agreement, their veto could dictate the stringency of common process regulations. Since Maastricht, qualified majority voting has lowered the threshold, but with the heterogeneous enlarged EU it remains a tall hurdle. EU decision-making on process regulations is therefore often protracted, and various conflict-reducing mechanisms are deeply ingrained in EU policymaking (Deters, 2021, pp. 190–191; Falkner, 2011).

While they are prone to minimum compromises, environmental process regulations are, strictly speaking, not caught in joint-decision traps. EU process standards

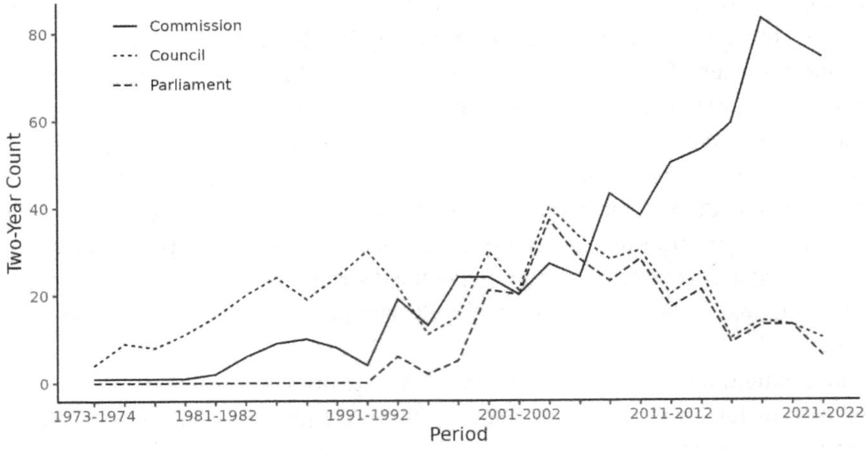

Figure 2: Distribution of environmental policy adopted by the main EU institutions 1973–2022. Volume of legal acts adopted by the European Commission, the Council of the EU, and the EP in each two-year period (to smooth fluctuations) since the first Environmental Action Programme. The data include implementing, delegated, and "regular" directives as well as implementing, delegated, and "regular" regulations in the areas of environment and animal protection (Eur-Lex directory codes 15.10 and 15.40). Apparent are the move to co-decision by the turn of the century, the declining legislative output in the last two decades, the recent signs of recovery, and the steady rise of Commission administrative policymaking. Source: Eur-Lex, compiled using eurlex (Ovádek, 2021).

lay down a minimum that Member States may exceed under the environmental guarantee. However, political-economic disincentives could militate against imposing stricter requirements on domestic firms than on their competitors abroad (Holzinger, Knill and Sommerer, 2008, p. 565). It is difficult to assess the extent to which market integration imposes such a chilling effect on domestic process regulation, but, while there are no signs of downward convergence (Holzinger, Knill and Sommerer, 2008; Holzinger and Sommerer, 2011; Jörgens, Lenschow and Liefferink, 2014), Member States at least sometimes 'gold-plate' environmental directives, exceeding their requirements during implementation (Jans et al., 2009; Thomson, Torenvlied and Judge, 2020).

4 Crises: 2008—Present

By the early 1990s, the relation between the single market and environmental policy was essentially settled. During the next fifteen years, the EU produced environmental legislation at an increasing rate (see Figure 2), relying mostly on Article 192 (Figure 1). However, starting with the 2008/09 global financial crisis, a series of external shocks led to a reevaluation of environmental market interventions and brought the constraining single-market logic to the fore (see Chapter 4). During the Euro crisis, the perceived need to promote a liberal single market posed constraints for environmental policy. While 'better regulation' had already been a rhetorical mainstay of the Lisbon Agenda (see Chapter 37), the Euro crisis amplified the discourse surrounding policy dismantling and the EU took the first steps toward action (Gravey and Jordan, 2016; Knill, Steinebach and Fernández-i-Marín, 2020). In December 2012, the Commission launched a Regulatory Fitness and Performance Program earmarking some major environmental policies for withdrawal (Gravey and Jordan, 2016, p. 1186). In 2010 and 2014, reorganizations of the environment and climate dossiers occurred within the Commission, weakening their standing (Gravey and Moore, 2019). Some observers regarded these developments as signaling a "post-austerity agenda to stabilize national economies and boost jobs growth and investment" (Čavoški, 2015, p. 501).

With the possible exception of climate policy (Burns and Tobin, 2020, p. 538), the environmental legislative output in fact decreased in the wake of the Euro crisis (Figure 2). In particular, the Commission almost wholly refrained from proposing new legislation on air and water protection between 2010 and 2014 (Steinebach and Knill, 2017, p. 430). In the short term, new proposals also became more lenient on average (Burns, Eckersley and Tobin, 2020, p. 9). Over the entire decade from 2007 to 2016, however, the stringency of environment-industry and air quality legislation remained stable, while climate policy even became stricter (Gravey and Moore, 2019, p. 25).[5] Furthermore, the feared large-scale dismantling of the existing environmental *acquis* did not come to pass, not even for pieces on the official 'hit-list' (Burns, Eckersley and Tobin, 2020, pp. 9–10; Gravey and Jordan, 2016; Knill Steinebach and Fernández-i-Marín, 2020).

In the crisis period, the Commission took ever more environmental policy decisions under administrative lawmaking procedures outside the legislative arena (Figure 2; Burns and Tobin, 2020). This might be seen as a venue shift toward "environmental policy by stealth" (Weale, 1999) to escape a constraining political-economic context (Deters, 2019). However, emerging research indicates that, despite increasing in quantity, administrative environmental lawmaking has become somewhat more lenient since 2009 (Burns and Tobin, 2020), and there are individual examples of administrative dismantling (Pollex and Lenschow, 2019).

In the early 2020s two global events once more threw the EU into crisis mode, but this time single-market principles were interpreted in a way that catalyzed environmental policy. From January 2020, the Covid-19 pandemic caused the biggest recession since the Second World War (Quaglia and Verdun, 2023, p. 635), and, two years later, the Russian invasion of Ukraine massively inflated energy prices (Goldthau and Youngs, 2023). Both events led to a comprehensive reevaluation of the EU's existing economic policy that—in its new emphasis on resilience and strategic autonomy and in its revival of ecological modernization—differed markedly from the austerity-focused Euro crisis response ten years before (Herranz-Surrallés, Damro and Eckert,

5 Examining a longer time frame, Burns and Tobin (2020, p. 536) find slightly lower climate policy stringency after the Euro crisis.

2024). The pandemic hit the EU shortly after the new von der Leyen Commission pushed the so-called European Green Deal (EGD) as the first priority of its working program. The EGD set an ambitious agenda, targeting climate neutrality by 2050 and a 55 percent reduction of net greenhouse gas emissions by 2030 compared to 1990 levels (see Chapter 20). So far, this agenda has resulted in a number of stringent policy proposals, in contrast to the restrained Commission activity during the Euro crisis (Pollex and Lenschow, 2025).

Another example of economic policy instruments used to promote environmental goals is the EU's Recovery and Resilience Facility (RRF), a EUR 672,5 billion fiscal instrument established to assist Member States in financial distress with loans and grants (Schoeller and Heidebrecht, 2024, p. 2511). The EGD reserves 37 percent of the facility's volume for financing the green transition and achieving climate targets (Di Carlo and Schmitz, 2023, p. 2079). This linkage marks a substantial departure from the predominantly regulatory environmental policy to one underpinned by significant fiscal capacities that far outstrip extant green funding instruments such as LIFE (EUR 6.5 billion from 1992 to 2020). The Commission recently also relaxed its application of the single-market provisions surrounding antitrust regulation and state aid, allowing the EU and its Member States to pursue more active industrial policies promoting the green transition (McNamara, 2024, p. 2380). On the EU-level, the Net-Zero Industry Act, an integral EGD element, sets a goal to produce at least 40 percent of the technology needed to achieve the 2030 targets domestically (Dimitrisina, 2023).

Finally, the EU began to use single-market access to leverage global environmental and climate politics while sheltering European firms against competition from less-regulated countries (see Chapter 29). An example is the 2023 Carbon Border Adjustment Mechanism ('Regulation 2023/956'). The Mechanism imposes a fee, to be paid by European importers, on certain carbon-intensive goods entering the EU. It is calculated according to the emissions embedded in the import product, matching the price of certificates under the EU's Emissions Trading System (Smith, Overland and Szulecki., 2024). Moreover, a 'Corporate Sustainability Due Diligence Directive' (2024/1760) was adopted in 2024 that requires companies operating in the single market to identify and mitigate adverse environmental and human rights impacts along their supply chains (Schilling-Vacaflor and Lenschow, 2023). To comply with global trade law, both instruments target foreign suppliers only indirectly via their European partners. These examples indicate that, in parallel with the most recent crises, the EU is moving toward an eco-protectionist approach that aims to prevent carbon leakage and uses the single market as a catalyst for climate and environmental protection abroad.

5 Outlook

The single market stood at the core of European integration from the beginning. Throughout its history, it interacted with the emergence and development of environmental policy in many ways. Starting from the assumption that environmental policymaking requires agreement among Member States with heterogeneous interests, research in the liberal intergovernmentalist tradition emphasized the constraints imposed by the single market, whereas scholars inspired by neofunctionalism were more optimistic and focused on its facilitating role. The long-term view adopted in this chapter unveils evidence of both dynamics, but, on balance, the single market has been a positive force. The emergence of environmental policy is partly due to spillover effects, yet the constitutional dominance of market freedoms and the lack of a proper Treaty basis also biased it toward market-making provisions and confined it to incremental change and lowest common denominator agreements. Institutional reforms and shifts in single-market jurisprudence later removed some of these constraints; environmental policy entered a dynamic phase of expansion and consolidation, driven in part by trading-up dynamics and in part by its decoupling from market considerations. When the current string of crises challenged the EU, it first seemed that a neoliberal vision of the single market would subject the environmental *acquis* to deregulation in the interest of a market-liberal recovery strategy. However, policy dismantling did not prevail over (limited) expansion. The response to the latest, pandemic-induced crisis episode envisions a green recovery based on a market-interventionist approach that combines active industrial policy, outward protectionism and an unprecedented fiscal capacity.

The dynamics at the intersection of the single market and EU environmental policy provide a long-running and fruitful research agenda. Today, the institutional balance between the policy areas can be regarded as settled, and some of the early academic debates have become stale, while others are more important and uncertain than ever. Among the more traditional questions remain the prevalence of regulatory competition and chilling effects. Since non-decisions and convergence via mutual adaptation rather than harmonization are hard to determine empirically, this issue calls for further methodological advances. Of more recent interest is the question of policy dismantling (see Chapter 37). So far it seems that the environmental *acquis* is quite resistant, but more encompassing empirical studies are needed to understand, in particular, the role of dismantling by stealth, especially given the latest turn to delegated law-making. The EGD offers another fertile research topic. At first blush, it heralds a shift of paradigmatic proportions, but European environmental politics is ripe with celebrated agendas that were squashed in subsequent policymaking and implementation.

References

Alter, K.J. and Meunier-Aitsahalia, S. (1994) 'Judicial politics in the European Community: European integration and the pathbreaking Cassis de Dijon decision', *Comparative Political Studies*, 26(4), pp. 535–561.

Benz, A. (2009) *Politik in Mehrebenensystemen.* Wiesbaden: VS Verlag.

Börzel, T.A. (2002) 'Pace-setting, foot-dragging, and fence-sitting: Member State responses to Europeanization', *Journal of Common Market Studies*, 40(2), pp. 193 – 214.
Brandsma, G.J. and Blom-Hansen, J. (2016) 'Controlling delegated powers in the post-Lisbon European Union', *Journal of European Public Policy*, 23(4), pp. 531 – 549.
Burns, C., Eckersley, P. and Tobin, P. (2020) 'EU environmental policy in times of crisis', *Journal of European Public Policy*, 27(1), pp. 1 – 19.
Burns, C. and Tobin, P. (2020) 'Crisis, climate change and comitology: Policy dismantling via the backdoor?', *Journal of Common Market Studies*, 58(3), pp. 527 – 544.
Čavoški, A. (2015) 'A post-austerity European Commission: No role for environmental policy?', *Environmental Politics*, 24(3), pp. 501 – 505.
de Sadeleer, N. (2014) *EU environmental law and the internal market*. Oxford, UK: Oxford University Press.
Deters, H. (2019) 'European environmental policy at 50: Five decades of escaping decision traps?', *Environmental policy and governance*, 29(5), pp. 315 – 325.
Deters, H. (2021) 'Policy making', in: Jordan, A. and Gravey, V. (eds.) *Environmental policy in the EU: Actors, institutions and processes*. Fourth edition. Oxon: Routledge, pp. 186 – 202.
Di Carlo, D. and Schmitz, L. (2023) 'Europe first? The rise of EU industrial policy promoting and protecting the single market', *Journal of European Public Policy*, 30(10), pp. 2063 – 2096.
Dimitrisina, R. (2023) *The key provisions in the EU's Net Zero Industry Act (Briefing note 'Decoding Brussels')*. Friedrich Ebert Stiftung. Available at: https://justclimate.fes.de/e/key-provisions-eus-net-zero-industry-act.html (Accessed: 15 January 2025).
Dougan, M. (2000) 'Minimum harmonization and the internal market', *Common Market Law Review*, 37(4), pp. 853 – 885.
Falkner, G. (2011) *The EU's decision traps: Comparing policies*. Oxford, UK: Oxford University Press.
Fjelstul, J.C. (2019) 'The evolution of European Union law: A new data set on the Acquis Communautaire', *European Union Politics*, 20(4), pp. 670 – 691.
Gehring, T. (1997) 'Governing in nested institutions: Environmental policy in the European Union and the case of packaging waste', *Journal of European Public Policy*, 4(3), pp. 337 – 354.
Goldthau, A.C. and Youngs, R. (2023) 'The EU energy crisis and a new geopolitics of climate transition', *Journal of Common Market Studies*, 61(S1), pp. 115 – 124.
Gravey, V. and Jordan, A. (2016) 'Does the European Union have a reverse gear? Policy dismantling in a hyperconsensual polity', *Journal of European Public Policy*, 23(8), pp. 1180 – 1198.
Gravey, V. and Moore, B. (2019) 'Full steam ahead or dead in the water? European Union environmental policy after the economic crisis', in: Burns, C., Tobin, P. and Sewerin, S. (eds.) *The impact of the economic crisis on European environmental policy*. Oxford, UK: Oxford University Press, pp. 19 – 42.
Haas, E.B. (2004) *The uniting of Europe: Political, social, and economical forces: 1950 – 1957*. Notre Dame, Indiana: University of Notre Dame Press.
Herranz-Surrallés, A., Damro, C. and Eckert, S. (2024) 'The geoeconomic turn of the single European market? Conceptual challenges and empirical trends', *Journal of Common Market Studies*, 62(4), pp. 919 – 937.
Holzinger, K. (1994) *Politik des kleinsten gemeinsamen Nenners? Umweltpolitische Entscheidungsprozesse in der EG am Beispiel der Einführung des Katalysatorautos*. Berlin: Edition Sigma.
Holzinger, K. (2011) 'Environmental policy in the joint-decision trap? The critical balance between "market-making" and "market-correcting"', in: Falkner, G. (ed.) *The EU's decision traps: Comparing policies*. Oxford, UK: Oxford University Press, pp. 111 – 127.
Holzinger, K. and Knill, C. (2004) 'Competition and cooperation in environmental policy: Individual and interaction effects', *Journal of Public Policy*, 24(1), pp. 25 – 47.
Holzinger, K., Knill, C. and Sommerer, T. (2008) 'Environmental policy convergence: The impact of international harmonization, transnational communication, and regulatory competition', *International Organization*, 62(4), pp. 553 – 587.

Holzinger, K. and Sommerer, T. (2011) '"Race to the bottom" or "race to Brussels"? Environmental competition in Europe', *Journal of Common Market Studies,* 49(2), pp. 315–339.

Jans, J.H. et al. (2009) '"Gold plating" of European environmental measures?', *Journal for European Environmental and Planning Law,* 6(4), pp. 417–435.

Joerges, C. (2007) 'Reconceptualizing the supremacy of European law: A plea for a supranational conflict of laws', in: Kohler-Koch, B. and Rittberger, B. (eds.) *Debating the democratic legitimacy of the European Union.* Lanham, MD: Rowman and Littlefield, pp. 311–328.

Joerges, C. and Neyer, J. (1997) 'Transforming strategic interaction into deliberative problem-solving: European comitology in the foodstuffs sector', *Journal of European Public Policy,* 4(4), pp. 609–625.

Jörgens, H., Lenschow, A. and Liefferink, D. (eds.) (2014) *Understanding environmental policy convergence: The power of words, rules and money.* First edition. Cambridge University Press.

Knill, C. and Liefferink, D. (2007) *Environmental politics in the European Union: Policy-making, implementation and patterns of multi-level governance.* Manchester: Manchester University Press.

Knill, C., Steinebach, Y. and Fernández-i-Marín, X. (2020) 'Hypocrisy as a crisis response? Assessing changes in talk, decisions, and actions of the European Commission in EU environmental policy', *Public Administration,* 98(2), pp. 363–377.

Liefferink, D. and Andersen, M.S. (1998) 'Strategies of the "green" member states in EU environmental policy-making', *Journal of European Public Policy,* 5(2), pp. 254–270.

Lindberg, L.N. and Scheingold, S.A. (1970) *Europe's would-be polity: Patterns of change in the European Community.* Englewood Cliffs, NJ: Prentice-Hall.

McNamara, K.R. (2024) 'Transforming Europe? The EU's industrial policy and geopolitical turn', *Journal of European Public Policy,* 31(9), pp. 2371–2396.

Moravcsik, A. (1993) 'Preferences and power in the European community: A liberal intergovernmentalist approach', *Journal of Common Market Studies,* 31(4), pp. 473–524.

Niemann, A. and Schmitter, P.C. (2009) 'Neofunctionalism', in: Wiener, A. and Diez, T. (eds.), *European integration theory.* Second Edition. Oxford, UK: Oxford University Press, pp. 45–66.

Ovádek, M. (2021) 'Facilitating access to data on European Union laws', *Political Research Exchange,* 3(1), 1870150.

Pollack, M.A. (2003) *The engines of European integration: Delegation, agency, and agenda setting in the EU.* Oxford, UK: Oxford University Press.

Pollex, J. and Lenschow, A. (2019) 'Many faces of dismantling: Hiding policy change in non-legislative acts in EU environmental policy', *Journal of European Public Policy,* 27(1), pp. 20–40.

Pollex, J. and Lenschow, A. (2025) 'When talk meets actions: Return to commission leadership in EU environmental policy-making with the European Green Deal', *Journal of European Public Policy,* 32 (9), pp. 2197–2222.

Quaglia, L. and Verdun, A. (2023) 'Explaining the response of the ECB to the COVID-19 related economic crisis: inter-crisis and intra-crisis learning', *Journal of European Public Policy,* 30(4), pp. 635–654.

Rehbinder, E. and Stewart, R. (1988) *Environmental protection policy.* New York: de Gruyter.

Rhodes, M. (1995) 'A regulatory conundrum: Industrial relations and the social dimension', in: Leibfried, S. and Pierson, P. (eds.), *European social policy: Between fragmentation and integration.* Washington, DC: Brookings Institution, pp. 78–122.

Scharpf, F.W. (1988) 'The joint-decision trap: Lessons from German federalism and European integration', *Public Administration,* 66(3), pp. 239–278.

Scharpf, F.W. (1997) 'The problem-solving capacity of multi-level governance', *Journal of European Public Policy,* 4(4), pp. 520–538.

Scharpf, F.W. (2011) 'The JDT model: Context and extensions', in: Falkner, G. (ed.) *The EU's decision traps: Comparing policies.* Oxford, UK: Oxford University Press, pp. 217–236.

Schilling-Vacaflor, A. and Lenschow, A. (2023) 'Hardening foreign corporate accountability through mandatory due diligence in the European Union? New trends and persisting challenges', *Regulation and Governance,* 17(3), pp. 677–693.

Schmitter, P.C. (2004) 'Neo-Neofunctionalism', in: Wiener, A. and Diez, T. (eds.) *European integration theory*. First Edition. Oxford, UK: Oxford University Press.

Schoeller, M.G. and Heidebrecht, S. (2024) 'Continuity despite crises: Germany's euro policy in the light of the pandemic, war and inflation', *Journal of European Public Policy*, 31(9), pp. 2509 – 2533.

Smith, I.D., Overland, I. and Szulecki, K. (2024) 'The EU's CBAM and its "significant others": Three perspectives on the political fallout from Europe's unilateral climate policy initiative', *Journal of Common Market Studies*, 62(2), pp. 603 – 618.

Steinebach, Y. and Knill, C. (2017) 'Still an entrepreneur? The changing role of the European Commission in EU environmental policy-making', *Journal of European Public Policy* 24(3), pp. 429 – 446.

Thomson, R., Torenvlied, R. and Judge, A. (2020) 'Incentives to comply: The impact of national governments' and stakeholders' preferences on compliance with EU laws', *Journal of European Public Policy*, 27(12), pp. 1801 – 1818.

Vogel, D. (1997) 'Trading up and governing across: Transnational governance and environmental protection', *Journal of European Public Policy*, 4(4), pp. 556 – 571.

Weale, A. (1999) 'European environmental policy by stealth: The dysfunctionality of functionalism?', *Environment and Planning C: Government and Policy*, 17(1), pp. 37 – 51.

Weale, A. et al. (2000) *Environmental governance in Europe: An ever closer ecological union?*. Oxford, UK: Oxford University Press.

Wurzel, R.K.W. (2006) *Environmental policy-making in Britain, Germany and the European Union*. Manchester: Manchester University Press.

Zeitlin, J., Nicoli, F. and Laffan, B. (2019) 'Introduction: The European Union beyond the polycrisis? Integration and politicization in an age of shifting cleavages', *Journal of European Public Policy*, 26(7), pp. 963 – 976.

Jan Pollex and Andrea Lenschow

European Union environmental regulation over time

Abstract: This chapter reflects on sixty years of European Union environmental regulation. It identifies five phases that explore different conceptions of the function of environmental regulatory activity and associated approaches. Each phase showcases key dynamics with references to policy examples. Despite a recurring 'back-and-forth' in regulatory ambition, the chapter concludes that path dependence secures environmental policy as a diverse but wide-ranging field of regulation.

Keywords: European Union; environmental policy; regulation; governance

1 Introduction

Our chapter title suggests an underlying assumption, namely that European Union (EU) environmental policy is of a regulatory nature. Second, it suggests that 'regulation' is not a fixed term but that 'regulation' comes in different 'shapes and colors', which may change over time. These assumptions invite us to reflect on the meaning of regulation briefly. Baldwin, Scott and Hood (1998) offered an influential distinction of three meanings of regulation: first, the narrowest definition refers to an "authoritative set of rules, accompanied by some mechanism [...] for monitoring and enforcement" (Baldwin, Scott and Hood, 1998, p. 3). Second, regulation involves "all efforts of state agencies to steer the economy" (Baldwin, Scott and Hood, 1998, p. 3), including taxation, subsidies, redistribution or public ownership. The third and broadest meaning includes all social control mechanisms with and without mechanisms of monitoring and enforcement and includes nonstate processes (Baldwin, Scott and Hood, 1998, p. 4). These three meanings imply a widening of perspective on the types of policy instruments that fit under the header of 'regulation' and in the range of actors involved in regulation. Although authoritative, that is legally binding, rules decided in EU legislative procedures dominate EU environmental policy; this chapter embraces broader meanings in tracing important developments of environmental regulatory instruments over time.

Another critical dimension is the relation between regulation and economic competition and the European market (see Chapter 31). The way this relationship is conceived has been one of the central struggles in European integration, with neoliberalists on the one side and advocates of regulated capitalism on the other side (Hooghe and Marks, 1997). This struggle generates different types of regulation. 'Neoliberals' favor deregulation and limited re-regulation *for* EU-level market creation. By contrast, 'regulated capitalism' calls for government/EU intervention in the market and thus the regulation *of* the market aiming at specific (sectoral) market designs, social welfare or

https://doi.org/10.1515/9783111321523-037

ecological objectives. This raises the question as to whether environmental regulation is instrumental in building a competitive European market or reflects priorities beyond the core market interests (see Chapter 7).

Finally, we examine changes in the regulatory process and the European Commission's (EC's) role in consulting with policy experts and stakeholders as "architects and defenders of regulatory objectives and rules" (Wallace and Reh, 2020, p. 96). This regulatory mode straddles often controversial legislative processes between the Council and European Parliament (EP) and relatively nontransparent, technocratic processes in committees or agencies preparing delegated and implementation acts.

This chapter suggests that the evolution of EU environmental policy touches on all three dimensions: the meaning of regulation, the relationship to the EU market and concerning the governance processes. We identify (partly overlapping) timelines and some key policy decisions for illustration:

- Phase 1: 'Market-Oriented, Top-Down Regulation' (late 1960s–1986)
- Phase 2: 'Expansion and Integration' (1987–1998)
- Phase 3: 'New Instruments and Better Regulation' (1993–2008)
- Phase 4: 'Dismantling Attempts after the Economic Crisis' (2009–2019)
- Phase 5: 'Revival of Top-Down Regulation with the Green Deal' (2019–2024)

These phases stand for specific regulatory features that emerged in response to changing political, economic and institutional framework conditions and associated conflicts: questions emerged regarding the appropriate regulatory style and policy instruments. In recent years, there have been debates about the need for deregulation to ease pressure on the economy versus the EU pushing for an ecological transformation of the economy.

Our suggested timelines should be understood as indicative rather than fixed: those processes shaping regulatory change rarely involved clear starting or end dates (Zito, Burns and Lenschow, 2019). That said, the treaty revisions mirroring the evolution of European integration as a whole have also been milestones impacting especially the earlier phases of EU environmental policy in delineating the scope of the policy field and its role in the overall European project (see Chapter 31; also Hildebrand, 1992; Knill and Liefferink, 2007, 2021). This chapter considers institutional and rhetorical changes at the treaty level as important framework conditions for the evolution of environmental policy. Still, it focuses on the regulatory features characterizing the policy field over time more than the causal dynamics behind the change.

The Eight Environmental Action Programs (EAPs) form an important source for tracing these regulatory features over time. Apart from highlighting the environmental problem areas to be addressed by EU policy, the EAPs have critically reflected on regulatory performance and frequently set the agenda for regulatory change (Machin, 2019). For instance, it was the Fifth EAP that prioritized the previously overlooked principle of environmental policy integration (EPI), thus questioning environmental policy being secondary to and largely instrumental for the EU market (see Chapter 33). While market creation is compatible with standards at the lowest common denominator, EPI is oriented at high levels of protection in all economic sectors. Similarly, while market creation calls for binding and preferably harmonized standards, EPI calls for wide stakeholder involvement to arrive at a shared commitment to environmental protection, inviting a broader set of policy instruments. Apart from EAPs, which started off as Commission strategy documents and transformed with the Seventh EAP into formal decisions of the European Parliament and the Council, our analysis utilizes core Commission documents that outline policy priorities (e.g., the European Green Deal, 2019) and similar European Council agenda-setting documents (sometimes overcoming log jams in the EU regulatory process). To match this largely declaratory level of policymaking with EU policy output, we picked single public policies that we consider exemplary for the regulatory features in the defined phases.

2 Phase 1: Establishment and early growth of largely market-oriented, top-down regulation

Despite not being a field of competency in the 1957 Treaty of Rome that established the European Economic Communities (EEC), the EEC passed a range of environmental regulations in the late 1960s, with the number increasing rapidly after 1973 and the First EAP. The logic of (early) environmental regulation was determined by the boundaries the Treaty imposed, primarily aiming to protect and enhance the common market. This common market, with anticipated positive effects for the standard of living, increasingly came under pressure due to the emergence of national environmental regulations, which, though focusing on problems of environmental protection, carried the potential of becoming barriers to trade (Weale et al., 2000). Therefore, these national environmental standards, especially those regulating tradeable products such as quality and emission standards, called for harmonization measures at the European level.

Two consequences follow in this early phase of development. First, regulation came in the form of binding legal acts (typically taking the form of directives) reflecting the narrow meaning of regulation. Broader meanings of regulation were not applicable, as the Commission was hindered from proposing, for instance, environmental subsidies, fees or taxes by the small Community budget and the Treaty. The Treaty furthermore determined the legal justification for these legal acts, namely the linkage of environmental policy to the common market. Knill and Liefferink (2021, p. 17) document the policy field's growth from 1970 to 1987; they show that only very few of the approximately 200 legal acts were passed solely based on Article 235, i.e., without explicit reference to the market. The common market's economic imperatives impacted not only the framing but also the expected depth of regulation as creating a level playing field for market actors clearly outscored the objective of achieving a high level of environmental protection (Rehbinder and Stewart, 1985). The impetus for EU regulations de facto came from Member States that, due to their national regulation, threatened to undermine the common market's functioning.

Given the above, two features of this early phase surprise: the impressive number of environmental regulatory acts and a regulatory level that frequently exceeded the lowest common denominator despite market framing and unanimity in the Council. In this early phase, three EAPs framed the continuous broadening of environmental objectives—covering the environmental media, water, and air and focusing on core areas linked to industrial production such as waste, noise, chemical and industrial emissions. The early Directives regulating car emissions were perfect examples of market integration in establishing minimum standards for motor vehicles to be traded freely on the European market (European Union, 1970). The Directive was adopted after France and Germany had adopted national standards, potentially hindering European trade (Arp, 1993).

Water regulation illustrates this early phase's surprising broadening and deepening of environmental regulation. Starting in the 1970s, several rather progressive quality standards were adopted concerning both water quality (e. g., surface freshwater for use as bathing water and drinking water) and the discharge of dangerous substances into water (e. g., groundwater, urban wastewater, nitrate). Arguably, many of these standards exceeded the requirements of mere market harmonization and generated significant costs for industry (having to install costly filtering and cleaning technologies) and national administrations charged with relevant data collection, measurement, authorization, monitoring and enforcement tasks (Knill, 2001). These directives followed environmental principles outlined in the EAPs, such as the high level of protection, prevention of harm and use of the best available technologies. References for setting high standards were taken from national pioneering states and international organizations, such as the World Health Organization, which the European regulators surpassed (Weale et al., 2000, p. 357). Many Member States and the affected industry during decision-making did not grasp the implementation costs, partly reflecting the complex, technical nature of the regulations. These costs became apparent later in complex and lengthy implementation battles fought between the Commission and many Member States, fueling future debates concerning EU environmental policy being overly ambitious, undermining European industrial competitiveness and violating the subsidiarity principle (see phase 3 below and Chapter 1).

3 Phase 2: Expansion and integration

The Single European Act marked a milestone in the evolution of European environmental policy, formally anchoring the policy in the Treaty as an autonomous competency of the Community while continuing to focus on eliminating non-trade barriers to national environmental policies. Phase 2 has two key features. First, the EU's body of environmental protection legislation expanded following both market-related and genuine environmental objectives. Second, a gradual commitment to environmental policy integration emerged in all policymaking (see Chapter 33).

With the rising awareness of environmental degradation and the challenges climate change poses, several EU Member States started setting environmental and climate standards. Such national regulations often sparked supranational responses. Whether national governments actively sought to trigger supranational policymaking by providing national rules (e. g., acting as a first mover, see Héritier, 1996) or whether they pursued environmental agendas without EU-wide rules in mind differs across cases (to examine the role of pioneer Member States, see Liefferink and Andersen, 1998; Liefferink and Wurzel, 2017). In many instances, the Commission used such national regulations to foster environmental policy and enlarge the supranational set of rules. Consequently, the EU, and particularly the Commission, expanded EU reach and relevance in this policy area. Overall, legally binding regulatory approaches and supranational standard setting characterize this period. Yet, softer forms of governance, addressing behavioral change more widely, also entered into the focus of environmental policymaking. The Fourth EAP highlights information instruments to increase public support for environmental protection and to change individual attitudes.

Second, with the expansion of EU environmental policy as (also) a market correcting policy, questions of how to best incorporate ecological protection not only at the 'end of pipe' but early on in economic activities and sectoral policies became more important. In the context of the so-called Brundtland report (1987), the need to integrate environmental concerns into domains such as energy or infrastructure policy became obvious to achieve objectives like sustainable development and healthy living conditions for EU citizens.

Although the conceptualization of EPI as giving 'principled priority' (Laverty and Hovden, 2003) to environmental protection did not take hold in the EU, several crucial steps marking the EU advancement of EPI occurred. For instance, after the Maastricht Treaty urged Member States to consider environmental impacts in their actions and adhere to the principle of sustainable development, the Amsterdam Treaty (1999) explicitly addressed EPI and, thus, the consideration of environmental impacts across all areas of policymaking. It made EPI a cornerstone of EU policymaking and gave it a quasi-constitutional status (Jordan and Lenschow, 2010). Over the past decades, mainstreaming environmental (and climate) protection objectives has remained an EU policymaking theme. However, with the changing impetus given to environmental protection overall (see below), EPI has experienced both periods of significant attention and times of relative neglect. Nevertheless, with the anchoring of the principle in EU Treaties and policymaking, consideration of environmental aspects has become a standard feature in policy formulation and design. One key example is the consideration of environmental consequences in impact assessments. Such assessments provide information on the economic, social and environmental impacts of proposed policies, outline conflicts between goals that need to be decided politically (e. g., Nollkämper, 1997, 2002) and are a crucial tool to realize EPI in everyday policymaking (Pollex, 2024; Adelle, Hertin and Jordan, 2006).

EU chemicals policy has been a critical field for EPI. EU activity in this area originated in the common market project and can be characterized as part of EU industrial policy. Due to the environmental and health impacts of chemicals, the EU began integrating such objectives into its chemical policy (see Chapter 27). For instance, Regulation 793/93 on substances of risk clearly addresses the potential environmental harms of chemical substances and demands manufacturers monitor substances closely, ensure environmental safety and report on potential exposures. A second example is the late 1980s integration of environmental objectives into the EU's cohesion policy, gearing supranational structural support toward sustainability (Lenschow and Baudner, 2016).

Overall, with the expansion of EU environmental policy, its quasi-constitutionalization and the integration of environmental objectives into other domains, the 1980s and early 1990s marked a peak for this policy area in terms of regulatory scope and overall standing as a core EU competence.

4 Phase 3: New instruments and better regulation

While phase two was characterized by the expansion of the environmental regulatory agenda and its diffusion into neighboring policy fields, phase three highlighted critical reflection. First, implementation problems of EU environmental policy began to overshadow the political agenda and were coupled with concerns over the effectiveness of EU regulation (see Chapter 34). In the Fifth EAP (1993–2000), the Commission announced greater emphasis on implementation, devoting an entire chapter to it. While the Maastricht Treaty followed suit with its Declaration on the Implementation of Community Law, the aftermath of the spring 1992 Danish referendum rejection shifted the debate effectively away from Member States' compliance with EU law to the principle of subsidiarity and the question whether Community institutions, most notably the Commission, tended to exceed the limits of their competencies. Criticisms suggested that certain areas could be handled (more) effectively by the Member States and that regulatory instruments left too little discretion to Member States and other competent parties. Thus, 'new environmental policy instruments' (NEPIs) and 'better regulation' became the keywords of this third phase.

These keywords resonated with a broader discourse at national as well as international levels. Toward the end of the 1980s, governments increasingly adopted 'new' instruments to encourage desired behaviors (Jordan et al., 2003). These instruments included economic instruments such as eco-taxes, emission fees, emission certificates, state subsidies and tradable permits, as well as context-oriented regulations, including procedural instruments, such as information and participation rights, as well as cooperative or voluntary agreements with (or among) private parties (Jordan, Wurzel and Zito, 2013). "Flexibility (not uniformity), participation (not top-down command), and learning (not sanctioning) are some keywords characterizing this new philosophy" (Lenschow, 2007, p. 421).

At the international level, the Organization for Economic Co-operation and Development (OECD) and several United Nations (UN) agencies (such as the UN Development Program and UN Environment Program) shaped a new 'governance' discourse and reflections on new and flexible instruments (e.g., UN, 1992; see also Giddings, Hopwood and O'Brien, 2002). Globalization, with its increasing international trade and interconnectedness, has pushed nation-states to the limits of their competencies and spheres of influence. Governing beyond the nation-state required international cooperation and the inclusion of nonstate actors to achieve objectives (Scharpf, 1999). This shift toward governance promoted forms of political steering that involved stakeholders in decision-making and instrument selection, providing them greater flexibility in achieving desired and context-sensitive outcomes.

Against this backdrop, the EU Commission emphasized a shift toward new instruments (European Commission, 1999). The shift toward more flexible instruments, which granted Member States, subnational entities, businesses, and public actors greater freedom to achieve agreed-upon objectives, coincided with a period of turbulence at the supranational level. After the rocky Maastricht Treaty ratification and the 1999 Santer Commission resignations, the new Commission president, Romano Prodi, was tasked with calming critics and increasing the EU's legitimacy in the eyes of its citizens (Radaelli, 2007; Pollex and van Voorst, 2024). The Prodi Commission's 'White Paper on Governance' further paved the way for a Better Regulation Agenda, focusing on more targeted and fit-for-purpose instruments, stakeholder involvement, evidence-based policymaking and evaluation and (ultimately) more effective regulation (Pollex and van Voorst, 2024).

One key example of this turn toward more flexible and voluntary approaches is the EU's eco-management and audit scheme (EMAS). It sought to nudge businesses to protect the environment, e.g., by revealing opportunities to cut costs by, for instance, reducing resource usage or energy consumption (European Union, 1993). Advocates for such schemes argue that, considering the highly diverse industry and business landscape in the EU, drafting binding top-down measures would prove highly difficult as they have to consider a plethora of specific circumstances or business models. In addition, they incentivized industries to develop their own ideas of how best to achieve environmental protection, thus overcoming complex compliance problems linked to top-down regulation (Franke and Wätzold, 1995). Accordingly, NEPIs and EMAS as representative cases correspond to a widening of the meaning of regulation; concerning their relationship to the market, they are ambiguous as their prime focus has become environmental protection through seeking 'win-win' effects for business actors.

Concerning the regulatory process, the EMAS case was interesting as the Commission's initial 1990 proposal envisaged a mandatory scheme obligating industry in the EU to participate in the scheme. However, Member States, particularly the United Kingdom, which had already introduced national schemes, pushed for a voluntary approach (Franke and Wätzold, 1995). In terms of implementation and effectiveness, despite its prominence, EMAS has not been a success story as the industry take-up stayed low. The number of registered companies even decreased over time due to competition with other international (ISO) and national schemes and inadequate consumer recognition (Knill and Lenschow, 1998; Daddi et al., 2018). The success of such schemes hinges on signatories' capacities to implement and revise their plans continuously, on governmental commitment and regulatory guidance and on public appreciation (Tröster and Hiete, 2018).

Though characteristic of the EU regulatory discourse in this third phase and leaving a mark on regulatory output, NEPIs never came to dominate EU regulatory policy (Holzinger, Knill and Lenschow, 2009). Only in the first generation of climate policies in the EU between 1990 and 1999, were NEPIs ever more than half of adopted instruments (cf. Moore et al., 2021, p. 307). Yet, although the NEPI proportion declined again in the 2000s, the EU remains committed to these new instruments, given the complexity and cross-cutting nature of environmental problems and the need to integrate private and societal actors in policymaking. Most recently, the EU has introduced the Climate Pact as a part of its Green Deal to "bring together regions, local communities, civil society, industry and schools. Together, they will design and commit to a set of pledges to bring about a change in behavior, from the individual to the largest multinational" (European Commission, 2020, p.1). Thus, flexible instruments building on (partial) self-regulation and stakeholder involvement have become a cornerstone of the EU's instrument portfolio and complement classical top-down regulatory approaches.

5 Phase 4: Dismantling attempts after the economic crisis

The 2008–2009 global economic crisis helped generate tensions between environmental protection attempts and economic priorities, which were not new in the evolution of EU environmental policy (see Chapter 7). The rhetoric of 'Better Regulation' (see above) had come along with Member States asking the Commission to devise a list of policies that could be scrapped. In these earlier periods, however, the Commission did not follow up on Member States' requests. Instead, it "made somewhat vague and symbolic promise to update rather than dismantle existing legislation" (Gravey and Jordan, 2020, p. 353). There is evidence that this changed in phase four, beginning with the Eurozone crisis and the Barroso II Commission (2009–2014) and lasting until the end of the Juncker Commission 2019 (see Chapter 37).

Thus, Commission activities in the 2010s differ from those in the 1990s: while the Santer and Prodi Commissions continued to focus on expanding supranational influence in environmental policy, Barroso and Juncker were open to engaging with attempts to reduce EU policies (see Chapter 10). With the Better Regulation Agenda and the Regulatory Fitness and Performance Program, both Commission Presidents fostered an agenda reflecting two aspects: first, environmental protection policy was framed as a burden on the economy. Consequently, to foster economic recovery, environmental policymaking was put on hold and attempts to dismantle particularly burdensome regulations were pursued. Second, when the Commission initiated policies, they lacked ambition (Steinebach and Knill, 2017; Burns, Eckersley and Tobin, 2020). Moreover, policy stopped even in the nonpoliticized dimensions of policy development, namely delegated and implementation acts in the hands of the Commission and regulatory committees. Several cases show that the Commission did not update existing policies to new circumstances or revise provisions to keep pace. Thus, research identified *dismantling by default* as a characteristic feature of this period (Pollex and Lenschow, 2020). This form of dismantling is "a subtle strategy by which a non-adjustment of, for example, standards, leads to a de-facto dismantling" (Pollex, 2022, p. 607; Bauer and Knill, 2012). Thus, instead of engaging in visible and active dismantling (i. e., noticeable and intentional actions to reduce or completely scrap existing policies), the Commission rather concealed its activities and did not publicly advertise its inactivity (and maintained the EU effort to be an international leader, see Chapter 29).

The EU's Ecodesign Directive ('2009/125/EC') is a key example to highlight developments. This framework policy provides the backdrop against which product-specific eco-design requirements for energy-related products are set. It allows the Commission to enact implementation measures for specific product groups, e. g., dishwashers or power transformers. With its entry into force, six regulations on product-specific requirements were introduced, and more were envisioned. In the following years, the Commission's inactivity shows with only a few new regulations being introduced (two in 2010 and only one in 2011).

Furthermore, the Directive reflected a turn to voluntary self-regulation as a faster and less costly alternative to mandatory requirements ('2009/125/EC, Art. 15/3b'). Compared to the initial framework, this implied dismantling, as industry interest in such voluntary agreements (VAs) was limited due to the coordination efforts required. Nevertheless, the three VAs proposed—for gaming consoles, imaging equipment (e. g., printers) and complex set-top boxes (e. g., TV receivers)—were less stringent than binding regulations and failed to address aspects like energy efficiency, recycling or consumer information. The Commission was not only proactive in promoting the establishment of VAs but was also in a crucial role in overseeing their implementation and ensuring their performance regarding environmental protection. The Commission defended using VAs against criticism from environmental nongovernmental organizations and some Member States (Pollex, 2022). This example illustrates how the Commission used its position in the EU's policymaking process to reduce activity, cap environmental ambition and even engage in non-visible forms of dismantling, e. g., by not adjusting standards or provisions (Steinebach and Knill, 2017; Burns and Tobin, 2020).

Overall, this period is characterized by a subtle dismantling of environmental regulation in its narrow meaning, in halting or loosening its built-in progressive mechanisms such as technological updates. Although we differentiate periods, this phase and previous developments, i. e., the turn to new and flexible instruments, are interlinked. Policymakers' intent in the 1990s and early 2000s to find new innovative instruments allowing for more flexibility paved the way for policy designs that the Commission later used to engage in dismantling. Member States' demands to reduce regulatory burdens, pursue more effective legislation and cut red tape contributed to the long-term development by which environmental provisions were framed as (potentially) disadvantageous to economic development. Phase 4 saw the Commission change its role in EU regulatory policymaking in both cutting back on its agenda-setting and (secondary) legislative functions. However, the EU quickly reversed course beginning in 2019.

6 Revival of top-down regulation?

The year 2019 marks a turn of events. When thousands of protesters mobilized by the Fridays for Future movement marched through the cities of Europe (and the world), demanding ambitious and immediate climate action, political actors responded (de Moor et al., 2021; Berker and Pollex, 2023). These protests also strengthened green parties in the European Parliamentary elections in May of 2019 and, overall, pushed environmental and climate policy to the top of agendas (see Chapter 11; Ripoll Servant, 2019). The European Parliament declared a climate emergency, and the incoming Commission President Ursula von der Leyen promised to answer the youths' demands. By introducing the European Green Deal (EGD), the Commission put environmental policy at the heart of its work.

Two developments characterize this period (see Chapter 20). First, the Commission ended a period of inactivity and proposed an extensive package of measures, ranging from flagship initiatives like the Climate Law to revisions of existing policy, e.g., a complete overhaul of the Ecodesign Directive, to new legislation like the Nature Restoration Law. Furthermore, first evidence suggests that the Commission also proposed far-reaching and ambitious measures (Pollex and Lenschow 2025). In various cases, the Commission proposed to move from a Directive (giving room for implementation to Member States) to binding Regulations, e.g., in the case of the battery and methane policy. Moreover, it expanded the scope of policies. Considering again the Ecodesign Directive, the Commission proposed to not just focus on energy-related products but to include "any physical goods that are placed on the market or put into service, including components and intermediate products" with the exception of foodstuff, medical products or products addressed by sector-specific policies, e.g., vehicles (European Union, 2024, Art. 1). Furthermore, this policy was also changed from a directive to a regulation. It now addresses not only energy usage but also aspects such as water usage and waste, e.g., prohibiting the destruction of unsold products.

Second, in addition to reinforcing top-down regulation in its narrow meaning, the EGD is also remarkable in its allocation of significant funds to the ecological transformation of the economy. Similar to the Cohesion Fund, which was widened in the late 1980s and early 1990s to support environmental investments in the new Mediterranean Member States and Ireland, the EGD was launched as the new growth strategy of the EU after the pandemic, with a view to promoting the transition to a climate-neutral economy by 2050. Thus, next to a wave of new legislative measures, the EGD aimed to mobilize funding worth at least EUR 1 trillion from the EU budget and other public and private sources until 2030 toward the objectives of a just transition to a climate-friendly economy. This plan significantly altered and ultimately widened the meaning of 'regulation' in the EU, assuming a steering role for a grand transformation. Also, it reversed the previous narrative of environmental regulation as a cost for business to one of environmental regulation and investment steering business toward a future-oriented economy.

The case of the Nature Restoration Law further illustrates these developments. Interestingly, as with the Climate Law, the Commission framed this policy as a 'law', which is not a usual or established designation of EU policies. The policy aims to protect EU biodiversity and ecosystems. Furthermore, the Commission notes that previous attempts under the Biodiversity Strategy for 2030 failed to achieve the necessary protection and restoration of ecosystems (see Chapter 23), with Member States not meeting existing voluntary targets (European Commission, 2022, p.3). In response, the Commission proposed a regulation establishing an overarching restoration target along with specific targets for particular ecosystems and species. This now allows the Commission to provide detailed requirements for ecosystem protection through delegated and implementing acts. The Commission sets detailed requirements for restoration and protection, minimizing Member State opportunities for adjustments. Additionally, environmental, climate and nature protection objectives were integrated into several EU programs. Most notably, supranational funding was tied to environmental objectives in the Next Generation EU program, which mobilized more than EUR 600 billion to foster recovery after the Covid-19 pandemic and establish a Recovery and Resilience Facility (Regulation 2021/241; European Union, 2021).

Overall, these developments mark a departure from previous patterns of the Commission's political steering. First, by opting for binding top-down measures, the Commission returns to approaches that dominated environmental policymaking in the 1970s and 1980s. It appears the Commission has shifted away from the regulatory restraint, focus on nonbinding instruments and periods of non-adjustment that characterized the past twenty-five to thirty years. Second, under the Commission's leadership, the EU widened its approach to regulating the economy by expanding its toolbox to 'state investments', potentially changing not only environmental policy but the overall EU polity. Third, apart from turning the relationship between economic policy and the economy on its head, there is a resurgence of intensive policymaking in classical areas of environmental protection sui generis, such as preserving and restoring ecosystems. While the Green Deal emphasizes industrial transformation and green growth, it prioritizes environmental protection, treating it as a central objective rather than a secondary concern supporting economic growth. This is particularly remarkable considering the turbulent times and ongoing crises (see Chapter 4). While previous Commissions abandoned environmental objectives in the face of downturns, the von der Leyen I Commission, with the backing of the European Parliament, remained steadfast in its commitment to these goals.

To summarize, the evolution of the EU's environmental regulation has been shaped by shifting policy dynamics combined with path dependencies, resulting in an extensive body of regulation, including hard and soft social control mechanisms. The past six decades saw alternating periods of ambitious, binding supranational measures and phases of reduced ambition, both in terms of breadth and depth of regulation. Despite this nonlinear trajectory, we see a building up of different regulatory instruments characterized by different scopes and intensities toward a coexistence of different governance approaches (cf. Héritier, 1996) rather than a fluctuation around a median line.

Recent events illustrate this intermittent pattern. The von der Leyen II Commission took office in a less favorable political climate, where right-wing populist parties, rather than the Greens, have shaped the European Parliament's position and influenced the Commission's composition and priorities. Given this shift, the previous ambitious and transformative agenda will not progress as initially planned. However, undoing the latest phase of EU environmental regulation would require active dismantling rather than a simple reversal. In light of past experience, we expect a change of gear, returning toward voluntary governance and moderate regulatory retrenchment rather than the undoing of the Green Deal. Future research will tell.

References

Adelle, C., Hertin, J. and Jordan, A. (2006) 'Sustainable development "outside" the European Union: What role for impact assessment?', *European Environment*, 16(2), pp. 57–72.

Arp, H. (1993) 'Technical Regulation and Politics: The Interplay between Economic Interests and Environmental Policy Goals in EC Car Emission Legislation', in: Liefferink, J.D., Lowe, P.D. and Mol, A.P.J. (eds.) *European integration and environmental policy*. London and New York: Belhaven Press, pp. 150–171.

Baldwin, R., Scott, C. and Hood, C. (1998) 'Introduction', in: Baldwin, R., Scott, C. and Hood, C. (eds.) *A reader on regulation*. Oxford: Oxford University Press, pp. 1–55.

Bauer, M.W. and Knill, C. (2012) 'Understanding policy dismantling: An analytical framework', in: Bauer, M.W., Jordan, A., Green-Pedersen, C. and Héritier, A. (eds.) *Dismantling public policy: Preferences, strategies, and effects*. Oxford: Oxford University Press, pp. 30–51.

Berker, L.E. and Pollex, J. (2023) 'Explaining differences in party reactions to the Fridays for Future-movement: A qualitative comparative analysis (QCA) of parties in three European countries', *Environmental Politics*, 32(5), pp. 755–792.

Burns, C. and Tobin, P. (2020) 'Crisis, climate change and comitology: Policy dismantling via the backdoor?', *JCMS: Journal of Common Market Studies*, 58(3), pp. 527–544.

Burns, C., Eckersley, P. and Tobin, P. (2020) 'EU environmental policy in times of crisis', *Journal of European Public Policy*, 27(1), pp. 1–19.

Brundtland, G.H. (1987) *Our common future: Report of the World Commission on Environment and Development*. Geneva: UN-Document A/42/427.

Daddi, T., De Giacomo, M.R., Frey, M. and Iraldo, F. (2018) 'Analysing the causes of environmental management and audit scheme (EMAS) decrease in Europe', *Journal of Environmental Planning and Management*, 61(13), pp. 2358–2377.

De Moor, J., De Vydt, M., Uba, K. and Wahlström, M. (2021) 'New kids on the block: Taking stock of the recent cycle of climate activism', *Social Movement Studies*, 20(5), pp. 619–625.

European Commission (1999) *Europe's environment: What directions for the future?, COM*(1999) 543 final. Available at: https://eur-lex.europa.eu/LexUriServ/LexUriServ.do?uri=COM:1999:0543:FIN:En:PDF (Accessed: *13 February 2025*).

European Commission (2020) *European Climate Pact, COM*(2020) 788 final. Available at: https://eur-lex.europa.eu/legal-content/EN/TXT/?uri=COM%3A2020%3A788%3AFIN (Accessed: *13 February 2025*).

European Commission (2022) 'Proposal for a Regulation of the European Parliament and of the Council on nature restoration, 22 June 2022'. Available at: https://eur-lex.europa.eu/legal-content/EN/TXT/?uri=celex%3A52022PC0304 (Accessed: 13 February 2025).

European Union (1970) 'Directive 70/220/EEC of 20 March 1970 on the Approximation of the Laws of the Member States Relating to Measures to Be Taken against Air Pollution by Emissions from Motor Vehicles', *Official Journal of the European Union L* 76. Available at: https://eur-lex.europa.eu/eli/dir/1970/220/oj/eng (Accessed: *13 February 2025*).

European Union (1993) 'Regulation (EEC) No 1836/93 of 29 June 1993 Allowing Voluntary Participation by Companies in the Industrial Sector in a Community Eco-management and Audit Scheme (EMAS)', *Official Journal of the European Union L* 168. Available at: https://eur-lex.europa.eu/eli/reg/1993/1836/oj/eng (Accessed: *13 February 2025*).

European Union (2021) 'Regulation (EU) 2021/241 of the European Parliament and of the Council of 12 February 2021 establishing the Recovery and Resilience Facility', *Official Journal of the European Union L 57. Available at:* https://eur-lex.europa.eu/legal-content/EN/ALL/?uri=CELEX:32021R0241 *(Accessed: 13 February 2025).*

European Union (2024) 'Regulation (EU) 2024/1781 of the European Parliament and of the Council of 13 June 2024 Establishing a Framework for the Setting of Ecodesign Requirements for Sustainable Products, Amending Directive (EU) 2020/1828 and Regulation (EU) 2023/1542 and Repealing Directive 2009/125/EC (Text with EEA relevance)', *Official Journal of the European Union.* Available at: https://eur-lex.europa.eu/eli/reg/2024/1781/oj/eng (Accessed: *13 February 2025*).

Franke, J. and Wätzold, F. (1995) 'Political evolution of EMAS: Perspectives from the EU, national governments and industrial groups', *European Environment*, 5(6), pp. 155–159.

Giddings, B., Hopwood, B. and O'Brien, G. (2002) 'Environment, economy and society: fitting them together into sustainable development', *Sustainable Development*, 10(4), pp. 187–196.

Gravey, V. and Jordan, A.J. (2020) 'Policy dismantling at EU level: Reaching the limits of "an ever-closer ecological union"?', *Public Administration*, 98(2), pp. 349–362.

Héritier, A. (1996) 'The accommodation of diversity in European policy-making and its outcomes: Regulatory policy as a patchwork', *Journal of European Public Policy*, 3(2), pp. 149–167.

Hildebrand, P. (1992) 'The European community's environmental policy, 1957 to '1992': From incidental measures to an international regime?', *Environmental Politics*, 1(4), pp. 297–315.

Holzinger, K., Knill, C. and Lenschow, A. (2009) 'Governance in EU environmental policy', in: Tömmel, I. and Verdun, A. (eds.) *Governance and policy-making in the EU.* Boulder: Lynne Rienner.

Hooghe, L. and Marks, G. (1997) 'The making of a polity: The struggle over European integration', *European Integration Online Papers* (EIoP), 1(4).

Jordan, A. and Lenschow, A. (2010) 'Environmental policy integration: A state of the art review', *Environmental Policy and Governance*, 20(3), pp. 147–158.

Jordan, A., Wurzel, R.K. and Zito, A.R. (2013) 'Still the century of 'new' environmental policy instruments? Exploring patterns of innovation and continuity', *Environmental Politics*, 22(1), pp. 155–173.

Jordan, A., Wurzel, R., Zito, A.R. and Brückner, L. (2003) 'European governance and the transfer of "new" environmental policy instruments (NEPIs) in the European Union', *Public Administration*, 81(3), pp. 555–574.
Knill C. (2001) *The Europeanization of national administrations: Patterns of institutional change and persistence.* Cambridge: Cambridge University Press.
Knill, C. and Lenschow, A. (1998) 'Coping with Europe: The implementation of EU environmental policy and administrative traditions in Britain and Germany', *Journal of European Public Policy*, 5(4), pp. 595–614.
Knill, C. and Liefferink, D. (2007) *Environmental politics in the European Union: Policy making, implementation and patterns of multi-level governance.* Manchester: Manchester University Press.
Knill, C. and Liefferink, D. (2021) 'The establishment of EU environmental policy', in: Jordan, A. and Gravey, V. (eds.) *Environmental policy in the EU: Actors, institutions and processes.* Fourth edition. Abingdon: Routledge, pp. 13–32.
Liefferink, D. and Andersen, M.S. (1998) 'Strategies of the "green" member states in EU environmental policy-making', *Journal of European Public Policy*, 5(2), pp. 254–270.
Liefferink, D. and Wurzel, R.K. (2017) 'Environmental leaders and pioneers: Agents of change?', *Journal of European Public Policy*, 24(7), pp. 951–968.
Lafferty, W. and Hovden, E. (2003) 'Environmental policy integration: Towards an analytical framework', *Environmental Politics*, 12(3), pp. 1–22.
Lenschow, A. (2007) 'Environmental policy in the European Union: Bridging policy, politics and polity dimensions', in: Jørgensen, K.E., Pollack, M. and Rosamond, B. (eds.) *Handbook of European Union politics.* London: Sage Publishing, pp. 413–431.
Lenschow, A. and Baudner, J. (2016) 'Cohesion policy and the green economy', in: Piattoni, S. and Polverari, L. (eds.) *Handbook on cohesion policy in the EU.* Cheltenham: Edward Elgar Publishing, pp. 369–383.
Machin, A. (2019) 'The more things change, the more they stay the same: the discourse ecological modernization in the European Union', *Environmental Politics*, 28(2), pp. 208–227.
Moore, B., Benson, D., Jordan, A., Wurzel, R.K., Zito, A.R. (2021) 'Governing with multiple policy instruments?', in: Jordan, A. and Gravey, V. (eds.) *Environmental policy in the EU: Actors, institutions and processes.* Fourth edition. Abingdon: Routledge, pp. 299–316.
Nollkämper, A. (1997) 'Habitat protection in European Community law: Evolving conceptions of a balance of interests', *Journal of Environmental Law*, 9(2), pp. 271–286.
Nollkämper, A. (2002) 'Three conceptions of the integration principle in international environmental law', in: Lenschow, A. (ed.) *Environmental policy integration: Greening sectoral policies in Europe.* London: Earthscan, pp. 22–32.
OECD (1997) *Evaluating economic instruments for environmental policy.* OECD: Paris.
Pollex, J. (2022) 'Simultaneous policy expansion and reduction? Tracing dismantling in the context of experimentalist governance in European Union environmental policy', *JCMS: Journal of Common Market Studies*, 60(3), pp. 604–633.
Pollex, J. (2024) 'Impact assessments', in: Brandsma, G.J. (ed.) *Handbook on European Union public administration.* Cheltenham: Edward Elgar Publishing, pp. 229–238.
Pollex, J. and Lenschow, A. (2020) 'Many faces of dismantling: Hiding policy change in non-legislative acts in EU environmental policy', *Journal of European Public Policy*, 27(1), pp. 20–40.
Pollex, J., and Lenschow, A. (2025) When talk meets actions–return to Commission leadership in EU environmental policy-making with the European Green Deal. *Journal of European Public Policy, 32*(9), 2197–2222.
Pollex, J. and van Voorst, S. (2024) 'Better Regulation', in: Brandsma, G.J. (ed.) *Handbook on European Union public administration.* Cheltenham: Edward Elgar Publishing, pp. 322–331.
Radaelli, C.M. (2007) 'Whither better regulation for the Lisbon agenda?' *Journal of European Public Policy*, 14(2), pp. 190–207.

Rehbinder, E. and Stewart, R. (1985) *Environmental protection policy, volume 2: Integration through law: Europe and the American federal experience.* Berlin: De Gruyter.

Ripoll Servent, A. (2019) 'The European Parliament after the 2019 elections: Testing the boundaries of the "cordon sanitaire"', *Journal of Contemporary European Research*, 15(4), pp. 331–342.

Scharpf, F.W. (1999) *Governing in Europe: Effective and democratic?* Oxford: Oxford University Press.

Steinebach, Y. and Knill, C. (2017) 'Still an entrepreneur? The changing role of the European Commission in EU environmental policy-making', *Journal of European Public Policy*, 24(3), pp. 429–446.

Tröster, R. and Hiete, M. (2018) 'Success of voluntary sustainability certification schemes: A comprehensive review', *Journal of Cleaner Production*, 196, pp. 1034–1043.

United Nations (1992) *Rio Declaration on Environment and Development.* Adopted at the United Nations Conference on Environment and Development, Rio de Janeiro, 3–14 June 1992. Available at: https://www.un.org/depts/german/conf/agenda21/rio.pdf (Accessed: 18 June 2025).

Wallace, H. and Reh, C. (2020) 'An institutional anatomy and five policy modes', in: Wallace, H., Pollack, M.A., Roederer-Rynning, C. and Young, A.R. (eds.) *Policy-making in the European Union.* Eighth edition. Oxford: Oxford University Press, pp. 67–105.

Weale, A. et al. (2000) *Environmental governance in Europe.* Oxford: Oxford University Press.

Zito, A.R., Burns, C. and Lenschow, A. (2019) 'Is the trajectory of European Union environmental policy less certain?', *Environmental Politics*, 28(2), pp. 187–207.

Laura De Vito and Duncan Russel

European Union integrated environmental policymaking: Sectoral analysis of water and air quality policy

Abstract: This chapter explores the evolution of more integrated environmental policymaking in the European Union (EU). While many studies have focused on broader administrative approaches the EU has adopted to drive integration across its environmental and climate policy portfolios, there are fewer insights into how environmental policy integration (EPI) principles have reached into the EU's sectoral policymaking. This chapter therefore focuses on two cases of flagship EU environmental directives, the 2024 Ambient Air Quality and Cleaner Air Directive and the 2000 Water Framework Directive, which both exemplify the shift from tackling specific pollution sources toward a more integrated approach that acknowledges diffuse sources, wider levels of environmental cycles and interactions with other policy priorities. We suggest that, although EPI principles are detectable in the two case studies, integration can be strengthened by setting up stronger enabling governance and policy mechanisms to govern cross-sectoral and multilevel interdependencies.

Keywords: Environmental policy integration; European Union environmental directives; air quality legislation; water quality legislation

1 Introduction

Environmental policy integration (EPI) is a mainstream principle in the European Union (EU). While enjoying wide support, it remains challenging to apply in practice, and it is difficult to identify the extent to which it shapes policymaking (see e.g., Jordan and Lenschow, 2010). So how does EPI get translated into European policymaking, and what does EPI require to drive the move toward more integrated EU policymaking to address the complexity and the interconnectedness of contemporary environmental challenges?

To answer these questions, we conduct a critical analysis of EPI provisions in EU water and air quality legislation. These are classic EU environmental policy areas. Because of their diffuse and evolving nature, both air and water pollution sources have posed significant challenges to EU environmental policy, and, despite significant progress, this has somewhat stalled in recent years. These are also areas with competing sectoral interests with different perspectives on the best approach (solutions) to the problem and levels of environmental ambition in relation to economic priorities. Furthermore, polluters are often dispersed, which makes implementation more challenging. EPI has the strong potential to unlock significant synergies because effective management of both air quality and water can help tackle other environmental challenges,

https://doi.org/10.1515/9783111321523-038

e.g., noise or climate change. These cases thus provide excellent examples of the challenges and opportunities facing policymakers in integrating EU environmental policy ambitions into sectoral policymaking.

In exploring EPI, the remainder of the chapter unfolds as follows. The next section outlines some of the historical context of EPI in the EU and examines some of the key conceptual themes in the relevant literature. Then we analyze EPI through the sectoral lenses of the 2024 Ambient Air Quality Directive and the Water Framework Directive. Finally, we explore the implications of the case study findings and suggest fruitful areas for future research.

2 EPI: Historical context and conceptual framing

By their functional nature, public administrations are geared toward creating clear lines of accountability, which has the knock-on effect of creating more siloed policymaking at the expense of cross-cutting objectives (Russel and Jordan, 2009; Jordan and Lenschow, 2008). This makes tackling environmental problems particularly difficult given that much environmental degradation is the result of activities across many policy sectors. EPI has been advocated as an approach to counteract this trend by placing environmental considerations at the heart of sectoral policymaking (Lenschow, 2002; Adelle and Russel, 2013).

The EU has been a frontrunner in terms of formalizing the EPI concept in the Commission and Member States (Dupont and Jordan, 2021). EPI was included in the 1986 Single European Act and was subsequently reinforced by Article 11 of the Treaty for the European Union, which stipulates that environmental protection is integrated into EU policymaking and implementation. Dupont and Jordan (2021, p. 204) suggest that this gives EPI a "constitutional-like status", which surpasses anywhere else in the world (also see Jordan and Lenschow, 2010). Various initiatives have reinforced this principled support for EPI. For example, the 1998 Cardiff Process incorporated environmental principles into all EU policies (see Jordan and Lenschow, 2008). Notably, despite the EPI being enshrined in key EU treaties and the setting up of initiatives to reinforce the concept, EPI implementation in the EU is said to be patchy (e.g., see Dupont and Jordan, 2021; Jordan and Lenschow, 2008). Moreover, since around 2010, the EU has tended to concentrate more exclusively on a narrower focus around climate policy integration (e.g., see Adelle and Russel, 2013; Adelle, Russel and Pallemaerts, 2012; Russel, Den Uyl and De Vito, 2018; Russel et al., 2020), which has sought to better align the EU's energy and climate targets (Dupont and Jordan, 2021) and to enhance the resilience of social, economic and environmental systems in the light of climate change impacts (Russel et al., 2020). Nonetheless, the EU's focus on a Green New Deal as a Covid-19 response has to some extent breathed new life into EPI as a strategy because of its requirement that all EU policies and actions should contribute toward the green growth agenda. However, optimism about the Green New Deal (e.g., see Dupont and Jordan, 2021) has quickly waned with, at the time of writing, strong push back against green targets by, for example, farming groups.

From an analytical perspective, there is a mature literature on EPI (e.g., Jordan and Lenschow, 2008, 2010; Knill, Steinbacher and Steinebach, 2020). These studies have tended to focus on horizontal integration, which looks at the alignment of environmental goals with sectoral policy interests (e.g., agriculture or transport) and is more concerned with how policies are formulated. However, to assess EPI's effectiveness in improving environmental outputs and outcomes, it is also important to consider a second dimension: vertical integration, which focuses on how EPI is applied during the policy implementation phase (Steinbacher, 2023). In multilevel governance systems, such as the EU, vertical integration approaches concern the extent to which the alignment between environmental and sectoral goals is followed through in the actions of different administrative tiers.

By analysing horizontal and vertical EPI provisions within flagship EU environmental directives, our analysis identifies the mechanisms (or lack thereof) that, theoretically, should promote integration of environmental principles (in this case related to air quality and water) in other policy areas. This Chapter is concerned with the outputs and outcomes side of EPI. We particularly wish to move beyond the meta-level assessments of the EU's EPI approach which have tended to focus on broader administrative mechanisms and processes (e.g., see Jordan and Lenschow, 2008; Persson et al., 2018) to specifically look at drivers for EPI in two critical EU policy sectors: air pollution (Chapter 32) and water quality (Chapter 24).

According to Adelle and Russel (2013), sector-level EPI can be analyzed through normative, procedural and substantive lenses. First, the normative lens of EPI considers whether the environment is a principal or secondary factor in sectoral policymaking (also see Lafferty and Hovedon, 2003). Second, the procedural lens sees EPI as a governing process that shapes day-to-day policymaking activities. Third, the substantive lens analyses EPI as an output by considering whether environmental considerations are embedded into sectoral policy (policy formulation), or whether the sectoral policy leads to improved environmental outcomes (policy implementation). In a similar vein, Dupont and Jordan (2021 say that EPI can encompass: 1) administrative integration processes to support policymaking, 2) policy outputs that coherently include environmental factors and 3) positive environmental outcomes.

Our definition of EPI broadly aligns with the principles outlined above. We focus on the environmental management principles expected to guide implementation processes across different governance tiers (Moss, 2004), administrative provisions or concrete measures to promote environmental standards, and whether these have led to environmental improvements. These analytical aims can be operationalized in EPI dimensions that relate to either or both the horizontal and vertical axes the literature identifies (see Table 1).

Table 1: EPI dimensions considered in the analysis (Authors).

EPI dimension		Observations
Horizontal integration	– Normative stance – Consideration of other policy sectors	– Are environmental objectives and risks identified and prioritized? – Are potential synergies and trade-offs between the environmental and other policy sectors recognized in principle?
Vertical integration	– Environmental management approaches	– Are environmental management approaches described that would support adoption of EPI by different governance tiers?
Horizontal/Vertical integration	– Administrative provision for integration and policymaking support – Environmental Policy Instruments – Environmental outcomes	– Are there administrative provisions that support development of more integrated policies? – Is reference made to classic environmental policy instruments to strengthen consideration of environmental principles in other areas and at different governance tiers? – Is there evidence of positive environmental outcomes?

3 Case study one: air quality

Policy context

Despite significant improvement, air pollution remains the single largest environmental risk to public health (European Environment Agency, 2023; Fuller et al., 2022). The historical evolution of air quality management in Europe, and globally, indicates that the focus of interventions and pollution control approaches has shifted between concerns regarding human health in urban areas and about the damage of pollution to agricultural crops, forests and ecosystems (Fowler et al., 2020). Since the 1990s and the early 2000s, public health considerations and health-based evidence, such as those outlined within the World Health Organization (WHO) global air quality guidelines, have informed air quality management approaches. Nonetheless, in the EU, the remit for managing air quality sits firmly within the environmental portfolio.

Historically, efforts to combat air pollution in the EU have been based on three pillars, focusing respectively on improving ambient air quality by reducing pollution concentrations ('Directive 2008/50/EC' and 'Directive 2004/107/EC', both substantially amended by 'Directive 2024/2881'), reducing emissions ('Directive 2016/2284') and setting emissions standards for key pollution sources.[1]

1 In air quality management, emissions, usually measured by weight over time, indicate pollutants

This analysis focuses primarily on the EU Ambient Air Quality and Cleaner Air Directive (AAQD) (European Union, 2024), the central EU regulatory tool in this sector with a focus on reducing concentrations to enhance public health and environmental protection (see also Chapter 32). The 2024 Directive reveals a stronger shift toward more integration.

The AAQD continues to set more stringent legal standards for harmful pollutants, strengthens the common monitoring and assessment framework and identifies a process to be rapidly activated if concentration levels are above the limits, with the aim of achieving compliance in the shortest time possible.

EPI analysis

Normative stance

The AAQD recognizes that air quality sits at the interface between public health and environmental protection. Its preamble references the Zero Pollution Action Plan as the document establishing the need to minimize the harmful effects of pollution on human health and the environment, thus indicating a move toward an integrated approach (European Union, 2024, p. 1). Theoretically, this should enhance consideration of the co-benefits of adopting an integrated normative stance; however, human health concerns heavily steer the main implementation drive.

Consideration of other policy sectors

Air quality plans and air quality roadmaps should ensure coherence with policy to reduce noise and emissions from industrial and agricultural sources. The directive also acknowledges the importance of ensuring consistencies with plans that have a significant impact on air quality: climate, biodiversity, transport, energy and agriculture legislation. The directive, however, does not provide for mechanisms to consider synergies and contradictions and ways to tackle these when they inevitably arise.

Environmental management approach

Zones and average exposure territorial units are the scale for air quality assessment and management. These are defined at the level of agglomerations—i. e., according to

leaving a source, whereas concentrations, measured by volume, indicate pollutants that are present in ambient air. The approach in the legislation reflects the fact that, although related, there is no linear relationship between emissions and concentrations. Therefore, the two measurements (and consequently the two legislative approaches) are not interchangeable.

the number of inhabitants and population density—and transcend administrative boundaries. These scales also dictate monitoring and assessment regimes and the development of action plans, which must be developed if exceedances are recorded within any of these areas. The European Environment Agency (EEA) reports that most air quality plans focus on health and target nitrogen dioxide (NO_2) and particulate matter (PM_{10}; $PM_{2.5}$), although there have been three plans in Spain, four in France and two in Italy that were developed specifically to protect vegetation.

Administrative provisions for integration and policymaking support

Because of air pollution's transboundary nature, international cooperation between Member States is explicitly addressed, with the Commission playing a supporting and coordinating role. Compared to the old version, the new AAQD emphasizes the importance of public participation with the expectations that Member States encourage the active involvement of all interested parties.

Despite the spatially integrated approach that should encourage sectoral and multilevel integration (Fremantle et al., 2022; Bondarouk and Liefferink, 2017; Barnes et al., 2018; Bondarouk and Mastenbroek, 2018), the directive does not identify mechanisms to achieve this.

Environmental policy instruments

Air quality standards represent the directive's central policy instrument driving its implementation, monitoring and assessment regime and incorporate health-based considerations. Notably, limit and target values are respectively not to be exceeded and to be attained where possible to protect human health. Member States shall also ensure compliance with critical levels, which indicate levels above which adverse effects for certain nonhuman receptors (e.g., trees) may occur.[2]

Environmental outcomes

Despite emissions reductions and a reported decoupling of economic activities and emissions, many Member States had not complied with the standards and have taken insufficient actions to minimize exceedances (European Parliament, 2021). This led the European Commission to issue a plan for revising the original AAQD to achieve a closer alignment to the WHO health-based recommendations. In October

2 The directive includes limits, targets, average exposure reduction obligations and concentration objectives, critical levels, alert and information thresholds, long-term objectives.

2024, the revised directive introduced stricter limits on $PM_{2.5}$ and PM_{10} and NO_2, albeit with the possibility for some regions to delay compliance. The new directive is geared toward greater participation and integration, at least in principle. However, as it will be reviewed in 2030, it is not yet possible to determine whether the new approach will improve environmental outcomes.

4 Case study two: water quality

Policy context

The water quality in freshwater bodies is fundamental to the health and functioning of ecological and human systems (see Chapter 24). Despite this, our freshwater systems are exposed to increased stress from agricultural runoff, sewerage system overflows during storm runoff events and over-extraction. Against this backdrop climate impacts in relation to unpredictable precipitation and extreme evaporation during summer heatwaves further fuel these stresses. As with air quality management, interventions to improve water quality in Europe and beyond have evolved from the perspective of human health to concerns about the damage degradation of freshwater systems causes to ecological systems. Since the early 2000s, there have also been concerns around the increased costs of cleaning up polluted water to make it fit for human consumption, fueling debates on the economic impact of freshwater pollution on consumers and the wider economy (Capodaglio and Callegari, 2018).

As with air quality, EU water quality firmly lies within the environmental portfolio of the Commission's Directorate-General Energy, Climate Change, Environment, with the EEA overseeing publication of data and information on water quality status. Also, as with air quality, water quality regulation sits on the interface of public and ecological health. There is a strong interdependency with agricultural policy, which has the most significant impact on water quality. It thus provides an interesting case study of policy integration at the health, environment and agriculture nexus.

This case study primarily focuses on the EU's flagship Water Framework Directive (WFD) as the primary piece of EU legislation relating to freshwater quality. It does so in the context of other major pieces of EU policy that interact with water policy, primarily the EU's Common Agriculture Policy, which forms the cornerstone of support for agricultural production while providing incentives for environmental improvements (Russel, 2016). According to the European Commission, the WFD focuses on ensuring good qualitative and quantitative health, i. e., on reducing and removing pollution and on ensuring that there is enough water to support wildlife at the same time as human needs (European Union, 2000). Broadly, the WFD follows a regulatory approach requiring Member States to establish, in relation to water freshwater pollution: 1) the best available techniques for emissions controls 2) emissions limits and 3) best environmental practice. Despite these ambitions, recent studies have shown that few water bodies have achieved good water status (De Vito, Fairbrother and Russel, 2020).

EPI analysis

Normative stance

There is an explicit recognition that agricultural and other economic activities impact freshwater quality with clear impacts on ecosystems. While human health impacts were at the forefront of the original intervention in this area, over time ecological health and water security have become the principal but not the exclusive objective. Unlike the AAQD, the WFD acknowledges water as a commercial product with unique heritage functions that require its protection. Moreover, it states: "Environmental objectives should be set to ensure that good status of surface water and groundwater is achieved throughout the Community and that deterioration in the status of waters is prevented at Community level" (European Union, 2000, 'Introduction', paragraph 26).

Consideration of other policy sectors

The WFD acknowledges the need to consider integration with other sectors beyond public health and environment, but with few specific details. Recent academic studies show how sectoral impacts on water quality may be quite extensive, with perceived conflicts between the WFD aims and those of the Habitats Directive, the Flood Directive, the Nitrates Directive, the Urban Waste Water Treatment Directive, to name but a few (Zingraff-Hamed, Serra-Llobet and Kondolf, 2022). EEA and European Commission-led reviews of the WFD have drawn on source-point pollution data from various sectors and evidence showing the impact of other economic activities (e. g., drainage works). Among these, the impacts of agricultural pollution receive particular attention.

Environmental Management approach

The principal WFD management approach is the requirement to produce a river basin management plan (RBMP) for every river basin in their territorial areas (Art. 4) (see Chapter 24). It also stipulates that the plans are produced on the back of stakeholder participation and engagement (Jager et al., 2016). In cases where a river basin cuts across Member State territories, Member States are required to coordinate to produce an RBMP. The RBMPs' purpose is to achieve good chemical and ecological status (against standards set by the WFD) through preservation and restoration of terrestrial water bodies and to prevent their deterioration. More detailed approaches that can target sub-basins or specific sectors can complement these plans.

Administrative provisions for integration and policymaking support

Policy integration is central to the WFD. Paragraph 16 in the introduction of the WFD ('Directive 2000/60/EC of the European Parliament and of the Council') stipulates the need for "further integration of protection and sustainable management of water into other policy areas such as energy, transport, agriculture, fisheries, regional policy and tourism is necessary". However, the WFD outlines few administrative measures for promoting such integration. Instead, it is envisaged that the policy integration occurs at the Member State level with the WFD acting as a catalyst. While the RBMPs are clear venues for greater policy integration and the inclusion of stakeholders, what can and cannot be done depends on the structural conditions provided by the broader policy environment at both Member State and EU levels.

Environmental policy instruments

As a framework directive, the WFD is a regulatory measure which sets common environmental quality standards based around permitted levels of a classified set of pollutant groups as a minimal set of standards. It also stipulates a combined approach incorporating at source control of pollution alongside the setting of emissions limit values and levels of environmental quality. However, the Members States' governments direct the precise means through which the states achieve these, with soft steering to highlight the importance of economic instruments and the 'polluter pays' principle to account for negative impacts on the aquatic environment. The WFD also stipulates mandatory public participation for producing river basin management plans.

Jager et al. (2016, p. 15) note that, while the WFD set common targets and timeframes, these were confronted by a "diversity of political-cultural contexts" operating at the Member State and substate levels of government. This, according to Jager et al. (2016), led to a degree of institutional adaptation that was particularly manifest in the diversity of approaches taken toward stakeholder participation in the basin management plans, with many Member States doing the bare minimum. Moreover, scholars argue that the formulation of RBMPs in some instances have been captured by vested interests, particularly agriculture and hydropower (Martínez-Fernández et al., 2020; cf. Voulvoulis, Arpon and Giakoumis, 2017). This situation paints a picture of incoherence rather than horizontal and vertical policy integration.

Environmental outcomes

Almost twenty-five years after its adoption, only around 40 percent of European water districts have achieved good ecological status (European Environment Agency, 2021) and only approximately 33 percent have achieved good chemical status (European Environment Agency, 2024). While a 2019 fitness check led by the European Commission (2019) concluded that the WFD is fit for purpose, it noted the need to do more to integrate water into other policies. The key findings show that the directives have led to a higher level of protection for water bodies and flood risk management than could have been expected without them.

Crucially, the lack of administrative mechanisms in the WFD, beyond the mandatory stakeholder participation within the RBMPs, has led to the inconsistencies between different governance levels and between competing sectoral interests, thus undermining the WFD objectives. The WFD's implementation has been undermined by integration problems, manifesting in a mismatch between the policy goals and the way they are implemented at the state and substate level, as is evidenced in studies of its effectiveness (e.g., De Vito, Fairbrother and Russel, 2020, Moss et al. 2020, Jager et al. 2016). Indeed, in their special issue on the WFD, Moss et al. (2020) note the WFD faced political resistance and governance bottlenecks due to, among other things, a lack of horizontal collaboration (also see Zingraff-Hamed, Serra-Llobet and Kondolf, 2022) and intersectoral conflicts (e.g., EU agricultural subsidies).

5 Discussion and directions for future research

Air and water legislation encompass many elements that constitute the reality of EU policy and regulation. The case studies feature some of the key principles that, in theory, should support both horizontal and vertical EPI from formulation to implementation in other policy areas. Our critical analysis of how these advanced cases of EU regulatory tools have included EPI provisions reveals both successful approaches and areas for improvement that generate broader lessons applicable to other policy areas. Table 2 summarizes the empirical findings.

There are three broad implications emerging from the two combined EPI analyses. Firstly, from a horizontal integration perspective, the two directives integrate environmental and public policy concerns, and they clearly identify environmental objectives and risks as a strong normative rationale for legislation, alongside public health. Moreover, despite progress toward more integration in the new AAQD, consideration of other policy sectors remains limited. This is somewhat unsurprising, as the directives do not directly control key levers that would in theory accelerate progress as there are key dependencies between environmental outcomes and policies developed within other sectors, such as agriculture for water or transport for air. Furthermore, there is a need to explicitly address synergies and especially tensions, con-

Table 2: EPI provisions in the AAQD and the WFD directives (Authors).

EPI dimension		Ambient Air Quality Directive	Water Framework Directive
Horizontal integration	Normative stance	Public health is the primary driver, but environmental protection is a core objective	Environmental protection is a core principle alongside protecting human health
	Consideration of other policy sector	Public Health, biodiversity, climate, transport, energy, agriculture	Public health and ecosystems
Vertical integration	Environmental management approaches	Spatially integrated zones and average exposure territorial units	Spatially integrated River Basin Management Plans
Horizontal/ vertical integration	Administrative provision for integration and policymaking support	Transboundary cooperation (joint short-term action plans); Ambient Air Quality Committee	Few measures outlined for promoting policy integration, including transboundary cooperation and public participation
	Environmental Policy Instrument	Air quality standards as principal policy instrument for protection of human health	Minimum environmental quality standards
	Environmental outcomes	Improvements on pollution concentrations have been recorded, but pollution from diffuse sources remains stubbornly high	Water quality improvements have been below expectations

tradictions and trade-offs that policy integration could help identify and that need open tackling.

Secondly, from a vertical integration perspective, in both examples spatially defined planning approaches reflect classic principles of environmental management that recognize the importance of going beyond administrative boundaries (Moss, 2004). These approaches are demanding from a governance perspective, as they may bring about conflicts and tensions not just between policy sectors but also between meso- and local-level authorities and new bodies that may be established (e.g., River Basin Management Authorities). Hence, careful consideration of governance arrangements that can minimize conflicts arising during vertical integration processes is critical.

Thirdly, some considerations apply to both horizontal and vertical integration. More emphasis on public participation is necessary as the success of environmental directives aiming to target diffuse pollution rely particularly on behavior change from critical groups (e.g., citizens, farmers). Public participation is valued under the WFD's RBM regime (Newig et al., 2014; Kochskämper et al. 2016). Yet, the directive prescribes information and consultation, while only encouraging involvement: this is a missed opportunity (Jager et al., 2016). Meaningful involvement receives a slightly stronger emphasis in the new AAQD. This could enrich policymaking with local knowledge and promote policy and social learning also regarding integration dynamics. Furthermore, alongside horizontal integration between sectors, vertical integration is affected by multilevel governance arrangements that distribute competences, powers and accountability appropriately and enable subnational actors to interact with other levels (Hooghe and Marks, 2001). The adoption of environmental standards as the main policy instrument leaves space for experimentation and iterative adjustments at lower governance tiers that can lead to tailored EPI in different contexts. In this regard, monitoring regimes could support this learning process as well as exerting their traditional regulatory function.

Despite some improvements, many Member States have historically struggled to meet environmental standards. Tackling diffuse pollution sources in an increasingly interconnected socioeconomic context requires synergistic approaches to European environmental policy. While challenging, this could strengthen the delivery of other strategic environmental objectives, e. g., biodiversity protection and climate change mitigation and adaptation.

Theories of policy integration can support this shift; our analysis has identified areas within the two directives where horizontal and vertical integration, which have so far been insufficient, can be enhanced. We have identified that a clear normative stance and consideration of other policy sectors in principle, and a spatially integrated management approaches can enable horizontal and vertical integration respectively. However, these are not sufficient and, so far, the inattention toward sector-level EPI has been a barrier to its full realization. EPI requires sector-level formal (and informal) governance and policy enablers guiding the day-to-day implementation phase, including through transboundary cooperation and environmental policy instruments that can act as EPI levers across sectors and at multiple levels of governance.

While there are few studies that drill down into the policy sectors as we have in this chapter, we can see indications that EPI has struggled to gain traction in other EU policies such as food, agriculture (Venghaus et al. 2019; Candel and Biesbroek, 2018) or climate adaptation (Russel et al., 2020). This suggests that, while the two cases are excellent exemplars of some of the challenges EPI faces, more empirical research could uncover how the implications from this study specifically apply to other EU environmental policies. This will be particularly important as our analysis did not go far enough to analyzing EPI in practice and in each directive's implementation settings.

Indeed, this analysis points to several promising governance and policy science research avenues. First, there is a pressing need to identify mechanisms for sectoral integration within multilevel governance settings, with due consideration of classic governance issues such as accountability and problem ownership. Additionally, policy studies could focus on advancing our understanding of successful EPI policymaking processes and outputs and on identifying the scope conditions under which they translate into desired environmental outcomes (Biesbroek, 2021; Russel et al., 2020). In so doing, however, governance and policy scholars should acknowledge the rapidly evolving nature of environmental challenges and emerging pollutants that might change perspectives on 'what' to integrate. Pursuing this research agenda would contribute to more meaningful integration and would provide EU environmental policy and legislation with appropriate levers to deliver stronger environmental outcomes alongside public health and other socioeconomic co-benefits.

References

Adelle, C. and Russel, D. (2013) 'Climate policy integration: A case of déjà vu?.', *Environmental Policy and Governance*, 23(1), pp. 1–12.

Adelle, C., Russel, D. and Pallemaerts, M. (2012) 'A "coordinated" European energy policy? The integration of EU energy and climate change policies', in: Francesc Morata, F. and Solorio Sandoval, I. (eds.) *European energy policy: An environmental approach.* Cheltenham: Edward Elgar, pp. 25–47.

Barnes, J.H., Hayes, E.T., Chatterton, T.J. and Longhurst, J.W. (2018) 'Policy disconnect: A critical review of UK air quality policy in relation to EU and LAQM responsibilities over the last 20 years', *Environmental Science and Policy*, 85, pp. 28–39.

Biesbroek, R. (2021) 'Policy integration and climate change adaptation', *Current Opinion in Environmental Sustainability*, 52, pp. 75–81.

Bondarouk, E. and Liefferink, D. (2017) 'Diversity in sub-national EU implementation: The pplication of the EU Ambient Air Quality Directive in 13 municipalities in The Netherlands', *Journal of Environmental Policy and Planning*, 19(6), pp. 733–753.

Bondarouk, E. and Mastenbroek, E. (2018) 'Reconsidering EU compliance: Implementation performance in the field of environmental policy', *Environmental Policy and Governance*, 28(1), pp. 15–27.

Candel, J.J. and Biesbroek, R. (2018). 'Policy integration in the EU governance of global food security.', *Food security*, 10, pp. 195–209.

Capodaglio, A.G. and Callegari, A. (2018) 'Can payment for ecosystem services schemes be an alternative solution to achieve sustainable environmental development? A critical comparison of implementation between Europe and China', *Resources*, *7(3)*, p. 40.

De Vito, L., Fairbrother, M. and Russel, D. (2020) 'Implementing the Water Framework Directive and tackling diffuse pollution from agriculture: Lessons from England and Scotland', *Water*, 12(1), p. 244.

Dupont, C. and Jordan, A. (2021) 'Policy integration', in: Jordan, A. and Gravey, V. (eds.) *Environmental policy in the EU.* Abingdon: Routledge, pp. 203–219.

European Commission (2019) 'Fitness check of the Water Framework Directive, Groundwater Directive, Environmental Quality Standards Directive and Flood Directive. Brussels, 10.12.2019', *SWD*(2019) 439 final. Available at: commission.europa.eu/system/files/2020–04/swd_2019_0439_en.pdf (Accessed: 26 June 2025).

European Environment Agency (2021) 'Ecological status of surface waters in Europe'. Available at: https://www.eea.europa.eu/en/analysis/indicators (Accessed: 23 August 2024).

European Environment Agency (2023) 'Europe's Air Quality Status 2023'. Available at: https://www.eea.europa.eu/publications/europes-air-quality-status-2023 (Accessed: 5 August 2024).

European Environment Agency (2024) 'Chemicals in European surface water and groundwater'. Available at: https://www.eea.europa.eu/en/european-zero-pollution-dashboards (Accessed: 23 August 2024).

European Parliament (2021) 'Report on the implementation of the Ambient Air Quality Directives: Directive 2004/107/EC and Directive 2008/50/EC (A9–0037/2021)'. Available at: https://www.europarl.europa.eu/doceo/document/A-9-2021-0037_EN.html (Accessed: 26 June 2025).

European Union (2000) 'Directive 2000/60/CE of the European Parliament and of the Council of 23 October 2000 establishing a framework for Community action in the field of water policy', *Official*

Journal of the European Union L 327. Available at https://eur-lex.europa.eu/legal-content/EN/TXT/?uri=CELEX%3A32000L0060&qid=1731495956210 (Accessed: 13 November 2024).

European Union (2024) 'Directive 2024/2881 of the European Parliament and of the Council of 23 October 2024 on ambient air quality and cleaner air for Europe (recast)', *Official Journal of the European Union L* 2024/2881. Available at: https://eur-lex.europa.eu/eli/dir/2024/2881/oj (Accessed: 5 December 2024).

Fowler, D. et al. (2020) 'A chronology of global air quality', *Philosophical Transactions of the Royal Society A*, 378(2183), 20190314.

Fremantle, K., De Vito, L., Williams, B. and Longhurst, J. (2022) 'A framework for assessing the contribution of UK local authorities toward compliance with the EU ambient air quality directive', *Journal of Environmental Planning and Management*, 65(2), pp. 356–373.

Fuller, R. et al. (2022) 'Pollution and health: A progress update', *The Lancet Planetary Health*, 6(6), pp. e535–e547.

Hooghe, L. and Marks, G. (2001), *Multi-level governance and European integration.* Lanham: Rowman and Littlefield.

Jager, N.W. et al. (2016) 'Transforming European water governance? Participation and river basin management under the EU Water Framework Directive in 13 Member States', *Water*, 8(4), p. 156.

Jordan, A.J. and Lenschow, A. (eds.) (2008) *Innovation in environmental policy? Integrating the environment for sustainability.* Cheltenham: Edward Elgar.

Jordan, A.J. and Lenschow, A. (2010) 'Environmental policy integration: A state-of-the-art review', *Environmental Policy and Governance*, 20(3), pp. 147–158.

Knill, C., Steinbacher, C. and Steinebach, Y. (2020) 'Balancing trade-offs between policy responsiveness and effectiveness: The impact of vertical policy-process integration on policy accumulation', *Public Administration Review*, 81(1), pp. 157–160.

Kochskämper, E., Challies, E., Newig, J. and Jager, N.W. (2016) 'Participation for effective environmental governance? Evidence from Water Framework Directive implementation in Germany, Spain and the United Kingdom', *Journal of Environmental Management*, 181, pp. 737–748.

Lafferty, W. and E. Hovden (2003), 'Environmental policy integration: Towards an analytical framework', *Environmental Politics*, 12(3), pp. 1–22.

Lenschow, A. (ed.) (2002) *Environmental policy integration: Greening sectoral policies in Europe.* London: Earthscan.

Martínez-Fernández, J. et al. (2020) 'The role of the Water Framework Directive in the controversial transition of water policy paradigms in Spain and Portugal', *Water Alternatives*, 13(3), pp. 1–26.

Moss, T. (2004) 'The governance of land use in river basins: Prospects for overcoming problems of institutional interplay with the EU Water Framework Directive', *Land Use Policy*, 21(1), pp. 85–94.

Moss, T., Bouleau, G., Albiac Murillo, J. and Slavíkova, L. (2020) 'The EU water framework directive twenty years on: Introducing the special issue', *Water Alternatives*, 13(3), pp. 446–457.

Newig, J., Challies, E., Jager, N. and Kochskämper, E. (2014) 'What role for public participation in implementing the EU Floods Directive? A comparison with the Water Framework Directive, early evidence from Germany and a research agenda', *Environmental Policy and Governance*, 24(4), pp. 275–288.

Persson, Å. et al. (2018) 'Environmental policy integration: Taking stock of policy practice in different contexts', *Environmental Science and Policy*, 85, pp. 113–115.

Russel, D. (2016) 'Agriculture', in: Dunlop, C. and Radaelli, C. (eds.) *Handbook of regulatory impact assessment.* Cheltenham: Edward Elgar, pp. 228–239.

Russel, D., Den Uyl, R. and De Vito, L. (2018) 'Understanding policy integration in the EU: Insights from a multi-level lens on climate adaptation and the EU's coastal and marine policy', *Environmental Science and Policy, 82, pp. 44–51.*

Russel, D. et al. (2020) 'Policy coordination for national climate change adaptation in Europe: All process, but little power', *Sustainability*, 12(13), p. 5393.

Russel, D. and Jordan, A. (2009) 'Joining up or pulling apart? The use of appraisal to coordinate policy making for sustainable development', *Environment and Planning A*, *41*(5), pp. 1201–1216.
Steinbacher, C. (2023) 'Analytical perspectives on environmental policy integration', in: Jörgens, H., Knill, C. and Steinebach, Y. (eds.) *Routledge handbook of environmental policy*. Abingdon: Routledge, pp. 122–135.
Venghaus, S., Märker, C., Dieken, S. and Siekmann, F. (2019) 'Linking environmental policy integration and the water-energy-land-(food-) nexus: A review of the European Union's energy, water, and agricultural policies', *Energies*, 12(23), p. 4446.
Voulvoulis, N., Arpon, K.D. and Giakoumis, T. (2017) 'The EU Water Framework Directive: From great expectations to problems with implementation', *Science of the Total Environment*, 575, pp. 358–366.
Zingraff-Hamed, A., Serra-Llobet, A. and Kondolf, G.M. (2022) 'The social, economic, and ecological drivers of planning and management of urban river parks', *Frontiers in Sustainable Cities*, 4, 907044.

Anthony R. Zito and Benedetta Cotta

The challenges of implementing European Union environmental policy

Abstract: This chapter addresses the often overlooked but fundamentally vital aspect of European Union (EU) environmental policy, namely policy implementation. It takes the innovative approach of considering a range of barriers that the EU and the EU Member States, which are the chief arenas for responsibility of policy implementation, have faced over time. The chapter organizes the implementation history into (1) the period of EU environmental policy expansion and its implications for and considerations of implementation (1972–1995); (2) the period of the questioning about EU integration and the delivery of good policy (1995–2019) and (3) the contemporary period (2019 onwards). The chapter argues that the policy response and academic focus has over time focused more on the role of actors rather than the ongoing problems posed by policy problems and the chosen solutions. Relying on secondary and primary research, the chapter explores how various EU actors have sought to focus on the key implementation challenges and how they sought to overcome these barriers to policy delivery.

Keywords: Policy implementation; implementation barriers; policy actors; policy problems; problematic policy solutions

1 Introduction

One fundamental challenge to successful policy implementation, in the European Union (EU) and elsewhere, is that both policymakers and public policy scholars have tended to view implementation as a secondary consideration; implementation also raises politically uncomfortable questions about failure (Peters, 2021). Likewise, policy implementation, including evaluation (see Chapter 35), is in many dimensions challenging for developing both criteria and data to evaluate the policy outcomes over time (Crowley et al., 2021). Nevertheless, policy implementation is vital for realizing policy goals. Scholars differ in understanding the nature of implementation. One approach views the implementation effort as making laws apply in public and private spheres, with omissions and deviations reflecting implementation failure. An alternative emphasizes political dynamics: actors operate according to their own goals and interpretations of policy, making the identification of what constitutes failure problematic (Peters, 2024).

The EU environmental policy context relies on EU legislative outputs (regulations, directives and other instruments) being transposed and then implemented by Member State administrations (Zhelyazkova and Thomann, 2021). Member States have flexibility in selecting policy instruments to incorporate the obligations, rights and duties con-

https://doi.org/10.1515/9783111321523-039

tained in EU environmental legislation into national law. Similarly, national authorities responsible for implementing these measures have discretion in applying EU environmental legislation on the ground. The EU maintains a key role in this policy process by monitoring timely and correct implementation in the Member States as per the EU treaties, directly overseeing specific policy fields and providing the design and setting of policy objectives and instruments. Our encompassing view of policy implementation stresses the impact that a range of actors operating within the EU have on the process. This includes EU institutions that craft the policy output but also national and subnational administrations that implement the policy as well as firms and civil society that shape these policies. Depending on the policy instrument, for example, EU citizens can shape the implementation monitoring of EU regulatory policies or change behavior due to informational campaigns.

Considerable EU literature on this subject focuses on trends of implementation failure and efforts to rectify problems. This chapter innovates by presenting a comprehensive governance perspective on the factors that challenge implementation. Our analysis is over time because it is important to understand the changing nature of the implementation barriers, EU actors' efforts to circumvent these barriers and academic attempts to study them. We follow these trajectories chronologically. The chapter first focuses on the period of EU environmental policy creation and expansion (1972–1995), which reflects a limited policymaker and academic appreciation of implementation issues. Secondly, following Member States' pushback against EU policy expansion (e.g., the rise of the subsidiarity and competitiveness debates—see Chapters 1, 7 and 32) and certain political events, the EU witnessed a period of greater attention to implementation challenges (1995 to 2019). Finally, taking the von der Leyen Commission I as our starting point, we consider the contemporary and future trajectory (2019 onwards). The empirical evidence uses both secondary research and original elite interviews (listed in the Appendix under the designation political system and number).

Framework

One of the core academic debates concerning implementation is the question of 'top-down' approaches (i.e., focusing on legislatures and executive government providing direction that requires competent management; e.g., Pressman and Wildavsky, 1973; Mazmanian and Sabatier, 1983) and 'bottom-up' approaches (i.e., focusing on how actors in a given local context perceive their circumstances and act in a correspondingly varied manner; e.g., Lipsky, 1980). Both approaches share a pessimistic perspective on implementation and examine the causes of its failure. We conceptualize a set of barriers to EU environmental policy implementation reflecting both dynamics (see Table 1). This is an overview of potential implementation challenges that may or may not exist at a given time. Our perspective isolates which and when any of these considerations received EU environmental policymaker and academic focus. This is not an exhaustive list but one focusing on key implementation challenges. Equally, we have no prior expectation that any of these barriers will necessarily feature as an EU environmental policy priority. The academic literature has noted consistent patterns of Member State implementation divergence from EU legislative specifications. This chapter focuses on the varied circumstances that lead to these environmental implementation problems.

Our overview starts with barriers reflected in problem characteristics found with policy actors involved in implementation. The first two distinctions listed in Table 1 focus on the degree that the implementation actors (e. g., environmental ministries) hold sufficient resources (personnel hours, funding, appropriate equipment, knowledge etc.) and capacity to tackle specific policy projects and to monitor and enforce policies (Knill, Tosun and Heichel, 2008; Steinebach, 2022) versus wider questions of whether the actors and organizations involved have the skills, morale and material provisions to handle policy action more generally (Sabatier and Mazmanian, 1979; Peters, 2015). The next two characteristics center on coordination problems between the implementation actors. This may reflect differences in opinion and preferences (including abilities to veto policy change) between the responsible Member State and EU actors. Equally, there may be more basic challenges of having the actors and organizations communicating with each other due to environmental policies involving multiple actors, time constraints, other pressing demands etc. (Jordan and Schout, 2006). The fifth and sixth characteristics focus on actor behavior that limits policy implementation. Barriers can arise due to a lack of consensus-oriented decision-making; competition and confrontation may lead to disproportionate cost burdens, rather than cost-sharing (Jänicke, 1992; Börzel, 2002). Environmental norm entrepreneurs who persuade actors to redefine their interests and identities by providing scientific knowledge or by appealing to shared norms and identities may also be absent (Börzel, 2005). Finally, lawgivers must give some discretion to agents to administer the policy, creating potential degrees of policy drift from the legislative intent (McCubbins, Noll and Weingast, 1987; Peters, 2024).

The second category of challenges in Table 1 reflects the dynamics found in the environmental problems themselves. Environmental policy problems usually involve nested sets of issues and require large-scale, multi-actor responses to, for example, water pollution (May 2015). Equally there is the challenge of issues that involve nested, complex policy dynamics involving actors who are both causes of the problem as well as responsible for remedying it (e. g., makers of products and packaging) or when the understanding of the nature of the problem is incomplete and uncertain (Levin et al., 2012). A related but separate dimension is whether the implementation burdens involve costs spread over or concentrated on society members (e. g., climate policy emissions versus large combustion plant emissions; Ansell, Sørensen and Torfing, 2017). The final dynamic in this group concerns the timing and context of the policy intervention: policymakers, often motivated by short-term electoral needs, may opt for recognizable legislative outputs over harder-to-define implementation outcomes (Hudson, Hunter and Peckham, 2019).

The third category of barriers (see Table 1) isolates how policy solutions challenge implementation. Policymakers may establish policy objectives that do not appropriately reflect the actual policy context in which implementation occurs (Hudson, Hunter and Peckham, 2019; Sabatier and Mazmanian, 1979). A related dynamic involves the particular policy objective clashing and/or competing with other equally valued policy objectives. One of the bigger potential policy design omissions is an operationally clear definition of what constitutes policy success, as a benchmark for discerning what constitutes partial or complete failure (McConnell, 2010, 2015). Moving beyond the more macro-conceptualization of the policy and its objectives are more micro-questions. The policy design could involve elements that are problematic to implement, whether because the specific measures contain poorly specified solutions that are inappropriate to context or contain confusions reflecting messy compromises etc. (Howlett et al., 2015; Peters, 2021). Another dimension consists of the problems when policy measures translating European rules domestically interact with preexisting Member State legislation. When European rules conflict with existing domestic legislation, the resulting misfit creates high adaptational pressure from the EU. Greater misfit increases implementation challenges, leading to policy inertia (Pierson, 2000), retrenchment (Börzel, 2005) or layering (Daugbjerg and Swinbank, 2016). Table 1's last two elements highlight the nature of the process of implementing the policy solutions, particularly complex policy processes that have the scope for multiple-actor involvement and therefore a range of potentially conflicting interests and perceptions (McConnell, 2010). Equally, these processes may lack appropriate or useful mechanisms for transmitting feedback from policy problems and for adjusting (Ansell, Sørensen and Torfing, 2017; May, 2015).

Having presented a range of potential implementation barriers, we now examine how these barriers have manifested themselves in the eras we scrutinize and how EU actors have engaged with these challenges. Note that we fully expect that many implementation problems will reflect a combination of these barriers which often will interact, reinforce or contradict each other in a given policy implementation. Our focus is to see if there are key barriers or interactions of barriers at work and how the EU and Member States have responded. Although our analysis gives greater coverage to challenges that the EU has recognized and responded to, it is important to reflect on challenges that do not occur and the reasons and implications behind their absence.

2 1972–1995 environmental policy expansion era

In the 1970s, the European Economic Community's (EEC's) passed into law a range of ambitious environmental directives and regulations which necessarily brought policy implementation challenges to EU governance. Nevertheless, it was only in the mid-1980s that the problems of implementing this legislation started to feature in EU political discussions (Knill and Liefferink, 2007, pp. 150–151). As a new policy area, it

Table 1: List of potential environmental implementation barriers.

Problems of policy actors acting as barriers
Lack of resources for implementing actors
Lack of broader capacity by implementing actors and malfunctioning administrative routines
Lack of actor consensus and preference agreement about implementation
Lack of communication
Lack of cooperation and reciprocity between policymakers
Lack of norm entrepreneurs
Actor discretion problems and countervailing interests
Problems of policy problems acting as barriers
Size of the policy problem
Complexity of problem
Available knowledge about problem
Size of the group targeted to rectify problem
Issue attention to the problem
Problems of the policy solutions acting as barriers
Problematic objectives that do not reflect actual policy context
Specific objectives conflict with other objectives
No benchmark for what constitutes policy success
Poorly specified solutions
Incongruence with preexisting legislation
Policy implementation involves complex processes that contain opposition, disagreement
Implementation solutions lack adequate feedback and adjustment mechanisms

Source: Authors' own elaboration.

was difficult to understand the scope and impact of the environmental policy instruments, which also operated in a newer policy-making system. Accordingly, both the EU and the Member States focused their efforts on building a policy portfolio to respond to environmental problems. Simultaneously, the European Commission (EC) was striving to build a legal platform and justification for expanding this area of EU integration expansion, and various Member States were seeking to enhance their policy portfolios. Neither the EC nor the Member States had a strong incentive to highlight problems in the process (Jordan, 1999; Chapters 31 and 32). Nevertheless, the 1980s saw a change as environmental groups and the public developed higher EU policy expectations. Actors in the EC began to emphasize poor implementation and enforcement failures in the European integration process and in environmental policy itself (Jordan, 1999).

Problems of the policy actors as barriers

In the 1980s, countries like Denmark and Germany were environmental pioneers, influencing EU legislation by uploading their national policies (Börzel, 2002; Liefferink et al., 2009). A key challenge in implementing EU environmental policies is the varying degrees of preexisting national legislation, often requiring rule changes and actors' agreement. This barrier contains several dynamics: beyond the issue of EU legislation fitting with the Member State legislation (solution problem) are questions of views of the implementing Member State actors (lack of consensus in the implementation process) and the resistance of particular interest groups and political parties (countervailing interests).

For instance, Germany was among the first to introduce mandatory take-back, reuse and recycling regulations for packaging products; these shaped the 1994 European Packaging and Packaging Waste Directive ('Parliament and Council Directive 94/62/EC'; Newmayer, 2000). However, discrepancies between German and EU regulations, combined with efforts by Germany's Christian Democratic government to align national law with EU rules, met strong Bundesrat opposition (Haverland, 2000). The conflicting interests delayed the directive's domestic transposition, ultimately triggering an EU infringement procedure (Haverland, 2000). While stakeholders can delay EU environmental implementation, they can also act as norm entrepreneurs promoting compliance. For example, PRO Europe, the umbrella organization for national producer responsibility systems for recycling, reuse and recovery of certain products, led a five-year project organizing around fifty seminars and workshops in Central and Eastern European (CEE) countries. These events facilitated the implementation of the European Packaging Directive in these countries, highlighting local solutions (EU1).

Challenges to implementing EU environmental legislation are particularly evident in Member States with absent or limited preexisting environmental legislation such as Greece, Spain, Portugal, Italy and Ireland, often portrayed as environmental laggards (Börzel, 2002; Liefferink et al., 2009). These countries were characterized by low levels of socioeconomic development, inefficient administrations and insufficient technical expertise, personnel and infrastructure to implement the EU environmental legislation (Börzel, 2000). Greece, for example, has lacked personnel and expertise on environmental matters and cooperation between implementing bodies, hindering transposition of several European environmental directives (Pridham, 1996). Additionally, poor communication between the EU and national agencies, compounded by bureaucratic resistance, prevented diffusion of information on EU directive implementation in Greece (Pridham, 1996). The EC also identified differences in industrial structures and administrative capacity as barriers to implementing sector-specific environmental legislation in Member States (EU2; see also Chapter 14). Limited funding hindered implementation of the Drinking Water Directive ('Council Directive 98/83/EC') and Pollution Control programs in Italy (Dente and Lewanski, 1982; Pridham, 1996). Weak technical capacity can obscure implementation failures; Spain's 1980 implementation of the Drinking Water Directive appeared robust, though authorities lacked the means to detect violations of strict limits (Knill and Liefferink, 2007).

Problems of the policy problems as barriers

Given the growing importance the EU environmental agenda has accorded to policy problems, such as climate change, at a later chronological point in our survey it is tempting to de-emphasize the importance of these implementation barriers. Nevertheless, our verdict takes the challenges of the policy problem as an inherent policy reality, one obscured by the interaction of policy actors' solutions contributing to the barrier. Thus, the EC concentrated throughout this era more on cases where it could achieve success and where public attention and complaints gave impetus (Jordan, 1999). In this policy context, issues less prominent on the agenda or more difficult to tackle tended to receive less emphasis. Chemicals policy is a classic example that incorporates issue uncertainty and problem complexity (see Chapter 27). Despite being one of the EU's longest-standing set of environmental regulations (particularly 'Directive 67/548') and which witnessed the high-profile 1976 Seveso accident, the environmental implications of the increasingly vast array of chemicals were not understood in this period. Indeed, this policy uncertainty and complexity, despite the presence of a stronger EU regulatory regime, remain the case today as the number of chemicals being traded in the EU and the impact of exposure to the environment are still not understood. In emphasizing the scope of the policy problem, we also acknowledge the pressure of chemical industry and other interests to allow continued use of extant chemicals.

Even issues with high political visibility may have a substantial level of issue complexity and uncertainty that leads to suboptimal outcomes. A classic example is the German 'Forest dieback' which was a core environmental and political issue in the 1980s. Both German and eventually EU policy solutions focused on industrial emissions of sulphur dioxide and nitrogen oxides, pointing to relatively containable point sources (i. e., large power plants; Newig, 2007). While the regulation significantly reduced industrial pollution, the complexity of understanding forestry ecosystems suggests that other issues may still need targeting to protecting forests systemically.

Problems of the policy solutions as barriers

One of the inherent implementation challenges facing the EU is the prevailing use of the directive, which is obligatory in its objectives and goals but leaves leeway to the Member States in the choice of implementing instruments. This flexibility necessarily gives individual Member States scope to interpret the legislation, and divergence between implementation actors and the EU goals may emerge.

Equally, EU environmental legislation may be formulated in a way that makes implementation difficult. A classic example is the Drinking Water Directive. Researchers have found evidence that Member State representatives had not fully grasped the strict quality standards of the Commission proposals and their implications, resulting in a long implementation struggle (Golub, 1996; Knill and Liefferink, 2007). Member State administrations also took advantage of weaknesses in this legislation. The national administrations noted that the measurement procedures specified by the Directive were inadequate for establishing violations to these quality values (Knill and Lenschow, 2000).

3 1995–2019 environmental policy reflection

Since the mid-1990s, Member State reluctance to adopt the Fifth Environmental Action Program's ambitious goals, alongside economic challenges and difficulties in ratifying the Maastricht Treaty, has hindered EU environmental implementation (Hey, 2005). Qualitative research has highlighted an implementation deficit (Knill and Lenschow, 1998; Lampinen and Uusikylä, 1998), though longitudinal studies reveal a fluctuating trend in environmental infringements, declining in the late 1990s but peaking from the mid-2000s (Börzel and Buzogány, 2020). This variation partly reflects the Commission's shift toward more flexible, less harmonized legislation, granting Member States greater implementation autonomy (Knill and Liefferink, 2013). Additionally, Member States often 'domesticate' EU policies, adapting them to national contexts in ways that diverge from EU prescriptions (Bugdahn, 2005). Simultaneously, the EU explored other types of policy instruments to supplement or act as regulatory alternatives since 1989 (see Chapter 22). Although directives remain the dominant policy instrument, there have been some significant policy experiments such as the EU Emissions Trading Scheme (ETS; Wurzel, Zito and Jordan, 2013).

In the mid-2000s, transposition and implementation gaps resurged, coinciding with EU enlargement in 2004 and 2007 to ten CEE countries with weak environmental frameworks (VanDeveer and Carmin, 2012; Börzel and Buzogány, 2020). During the CEE countries' enlargement, actor-related dynamics associated with their distinct administrative and legal traditions, along with a lack of cooperation between EU and implementing actors, shaped how CEE countries implemented EU environmental legislation. In Poland, for instance, local environmental authorities were understaffed and lacked training. Recognizing these challenges, the EU provided technical assistance and personnel training at city, county and regional levels. These initiatives aimed to enhance EU environmental policy knowledge, particularly regarding secondary law and waste management planning. However, while well designed, these projects failed to achieve their objectives due to inadequate stakeholder cooperation, poor preparation of local beneficiaries and low-quality submitted documents (Cotta, 2018). Local authorities also lacked a sense of ownership over the EU-funded projects due to limited engagement in their management (Cotta, 2018). Additionally, inefficient communication between central, regional and local authorities and private waste management companies hindered implementation (EU6).

Along with capacity issues, the CEE candidate countries lacked financial resources to implement costly EU waste legislation and relied heavily on EU assistance. Hungary, for example, faced severe economic difficulties in the mid-1990s, prompting the Bokros Package (1995), which cut national funds and investments, making EU funding crucial for environmental infrastructure (HU1). During accession negotiations and after assuming membership, CEE countries received financial support from the EU for environmental capacity-building and infrastructure, including the construction of waste treatment facilities. However, limited planning capacity, expertise and bureaucratic complexity often led to lost EU funds and implementation gaps (HU1, HU2).

The 2008 global financial and economic crisis further exacerbated the situation in CEE and the other Member States, eroding national budgets for environmental policy implementation (Falkner, 2016; Burns, Eckersley and Tobin, 2020). Falkner (2016) found that the 2008–2015 Member State austerity measures led to public budget cuts, impacting EU climate and energy policies.

Problems of the policy problems as barriers

The wider context in this period was that the environmental policy sector's traditional focus on tackling problems from specific polluters of water, air, etc. in particular media contexts had to expand to confront the growing ecological problems of climate change, toxics and biodiversity, to take only three examples with their inherent levels of complexity and uncertainty. Moreover, many more societal elements (e. g., households) and interests contribute to these environmental issues (see Chapters 20, 23 and 27).

In the waste sector, for example, the policy problem's size and complexity have been major obstacles to Hungary and Poland's implementation of EU requirements. Both countries received EU funds to construct regional waste disposal sites, but problems and delays characterized their implementation. In Poland, errors contained at the submission stage of several EU-funded projects for municipal waste treatment demonstrated the complexity of understanding the problem. For instance, Cracow's project included outdated data, requiring revisions that postponed implementation until 2007 (EU7). Similarly, projects in the cities of Kalisz, Leszno and Toruń had procedural errors that needed correction (EU6). In Hungary, the concept of municipal waste management was misinterpreted as mere waste disposal into landfills, leading to EU-funded projects that did not include recovery and recycling options (HU3). Waste treatment facility ownership was also complex. Hungarian municipalities owned the facilities, but their lack of waste management expertise and the large number of stakeholders have often generated confusion and disputes over operational costs, ownership structure and profits (HU3).

Problems of the policy solutions as barriers

Our hypothesis, which requires research investigation beyond the scope of this chapter, is that the more flexible nature of the new policies was less likely to trigger explicitly defined implementation issues after 2008 compared to the already extant policies posing ongoing challenges, such as the Water Framework Directive. Nevertheless, clear evidence warns against taking this proposition too far. In what was admittedly viewed as a trial phase of the EU ETS, the Member State governments allocated significantly more trading allowances than the companies needed, and therefore the allowances' price became problematically low (see Chapter 20). Arguably this dynamic partly reflected an EU and Member State acceptance of the need to start generously, but there were also elements of learning the system and building necessary Member State implementation infrastructure (Wurzel, Zito and Jordan, 2013). The European Commission concluded that the 1999 voluntary agreement with the European automobile industry to reduce carbon dioxide was not delivering the anticipated regulations, leading it to switch to binding legislation that imposed more specific requirements on industry.

4 Policy evolution onwards from 2019

In December 2019, the Commission's European Green Deal Communication introduced a new ambitious European level environmental agenda (see Chapter 1 for details). A few months later, the Covid-19 pandemic hit. The EU responded in 2020 with a recovery package, Next Generation EU (NGEU), aimed at addressing the pandemic's consequences and fostering broader policy reforms in the Member States. NGEU and its financial instrument, the Recovery and Resilience Facility (RRF), also provided funding to environmental/climate policies (e.g., energy efficiency) in the Member States (Schramm and Terranova, 2024). However, not all Member States introduced ambitious environmental reforms, e.g., Italy (Cotta and Domorenok, 2022). Moreover, the Member State implementation remains problematic, as the Eighth Environment Action Program for the period 2022–2030 noted, stressing the need to improve EU environmental implementation, the quality of policy delivery and monitoring. Member States' implementation gaps were now further assessed by the EC's Environmental Implementation Review (EIR), in place since 2017.

Problems of the policy actors as barriers

The 2022 EIR notes several ongoing implementation issues. These include: a considerable Member States' environmental investment gap, and two-thirds of this gap relates to general pollution and protection of water bodies; insufficient transparency and public access to environmental information and lack of necessary infrastructure for appropriate landfill sites, with twelve Member States facing infringement proceedings; regional and local fragmentation of implementation with Hungary, Italy, Luxembourg and Spain highlighted (European Commission, 2022).

Financial constraints remain a significant barrier to implementing European energy policies (Hoicka et al., 2021; also see Chapter 26). Similarly, in the waste management sector, Poland's 2022 EIR highlighted challenges in closing noncompliant disposal facilities and ensuring proper aftercare. While Poland initially struggled with a lack of coordination between local authorities and private actors, stronger domestic regulations on municipal waste collection helped address these issues (PL1).

Broader political dynamics also shape environmental policy implementation. For example, growing research indicates that populist parties across Europe have increasingly challenged ambitious national and EU-level climate initiatives, complicating their execution (e.g., Lockwood, 2018; Forchtner, 2019; Forchtner, Kroneder and Wetzel, 2018; Huber et al., 2021). Yet, limited analysis exists of how populist governments and movements negatively affect environmental policy implementation. One study argues that right-wing populist parties can support environmental standards based on political strategy and electoral interests (Tosun and Debus, 2020). Evidence from Hungary shows a decline in the implementation of EU environmental policies, particularly in the water and waste sectors, following a re-nationalization of infrastructures, the weakening of market access for foreign stakeholders and reduced collaboration in environmental decision-making (Buzogány and Cotta, 2024).

Policy problems and policy solutions as barriers

Policy documents such as the EIR focus on getting political actors to manage challenges, emphasizing stronger environmental governance and better compliance in the Member States. The Commission's 2022 EIR also recommends Member State action to address policy problems related to the circular economy and waste management, marine ecosystem, industrial emissions and water quality management.

The complexity of many long-term environmental problems, reflecting both the range of actors involved—who often have separate interests and priorities than environmental ones—and the intricate ways these policy problems can interact and exacerbate each other, remains a significant policy reality in such prominent areas as climate change, biodiversity, toxics and waste policy. In the waste management sector, poor knowledge about the circular economy and insufficient coordination of policies for construction and demolition of waste management at the European level have caused uncertainties about the procedures to fulfil the 'end-of-waste' criteria in the Member States (Giorgi et al., 2022). Given the politically, as well as technically, difficult issues that involve addressing business practices, household consumption and agricultural production, we expect an ongoing mismatch of objectives, complex implementation processes that embed opposing interests and poorly specified solutions. This reflection on the mismatch of the policy problem and the policy solution currently gets less academic attention, and so the scope of the challenge is less defined.

5 Concluding reflections

Our review of the academic literature and the public discourse on EU environmental policy implementation suggests that both have focused on the problems created by the characteristics of the policy actors. Our analysis and primary evidence suggest that this indeed is of critical importance. Nonetheless, our analytical framework raises the question of whether there is sufficient policy and academic assessment of the ongoing implementation barriers created by difficult policy problems and flawed specification/design of policy solutions. Environmental studies of policy problems emphasize that the understanding of policy problems and the design and impact of policy solutions have changed over time, even in the relatively brief history of the environmental policy. For example, waste landfills have traditionally raised concerns about the potential leaching of various problematic substances into the soil due to improper disposal, but there has been a growing awareness of the potential climate emissions issues involved in such sites (e.g., Bognor et al., 2008). Given the evolution of knowledge about policy problems, how sure are we that the EU environmental policy responses have fully responded to the various dimensions of the environmental challenges, and particularly those involving nested problems? We need a large research effort to assess the changing understanding of the environmental policy problem and the ability of current EU tools to respond and adapt to changing circumstances. How well do EU environmental instruments learn and adjust to these new understandings?

Since the early 2000s the EU has shifted toward more flexible environmental instruments that address cost-effectiveness questions, such as broad framework laws that specify what the EU considers the most important environmental objectives. It would be worth further investigation as to how this has affected implementation. Such elements as formal transposition of EU measures may be less of an issue, but do the more contextualized Member State responses adequately deal with the environmental problem? Research needs to assess whether Member States have become more adept at implementation or more sophisticated at appearing to address issues and manipulate the process.

To illustrate some of the dynamics raised above, during the CEE accession process, interviewees noted the EC's flexible approach regarding the length of transitional periods (EU3 and EU4). Similarly, in infringement cases, the EC exercises flexibility in trusting Member States' data and collaborating with noncompliant states to avoid lengthy infringement procedures (EU3). This more flexible approach also led to the introduction of policy instruments with context-oriented adaptability in the Member States (Lenschow 2010). The EC improved the monitoring of environmental implementation through the development of the European Network for the Implementation and

Enforcement of Environmental Law (IMPEL) between Member States since 1992 and more recently candidate countries. Novel tools to monitor implementation (i. e., the EIR) and specific implementation task forces in the Directorate-General for Environment were also introduced (Lenschow, 2010). However, this improved flexibility also had negative implications. The monitoring tools were often established on a voluntary basis (e. g., IMPEL), and the Court of Justice of the EU long process of assessing infringements were not seen as deterrents for non-implementation. It created a double standard and a disparity between the strict Enlargement requirements for candidate countries and more lenient enforcement for Member States, exacerbating the EU's implementation deficit (EU3).

Another large research gap is the question of understanding how mixes of EU environmental and nonenvironmental instruments affect implementation. Since the late 1980s, increasing use of economic and informational instruments in environmental responses has occurred at a national and EU level. Likewise, the EU continues to prioritize other nonenvironmental objectives and instruments, such as supporting the agricultural sector. How do these mixes shape environmental policy implementation, intentionally and unintentionally?

The chapter also alerts us to another pending issue. As the EU currently discusses further enlargement in the Balkan region and in former Soviet countries such as Georgia, Moldavia and Ukraine, the Eastern enlargement teaches us that candidate countries need a clear vision of what they want to achieve with enlargement. This must be reflected in the capacity to develop strategic planning at national, local and regional levels. This is crucial in the environmental field where candidates need to develop a consensus and a stringent dialogue with civil society. Equally, in environmental sectors, such as waste, where private actors are key for implementing EU requirements, it is important that these stakeholders are involved in understanding the policy problems as well as cooperate in policymaking and implementation.

References

Ansell, C., Sørensen, E. and Torfing, J. (2017) 'Improving policy implementation through collaborative policymaking', *Policy & Politics*, 45(3), pp. 467–486.

Bogner, J., et al., (2008) 'Mitigation of global greenhouse gas emissions from waste: Conclusions and strategies from the Intergovernmental Panel on Climate Change (IPCC) Fourth Assessment Report. Working Group III (Mitigation)', *Waste Management & Research*, 26(1), pp.11–32.

Börzel, T.A. (2000) 'Why there is no "southern problem": On environmental leaders and laggards in the European Union', *Journal of European Public Policy*, 7(1), pp. 141–162.

Börzel, T.A. (2002) *States and regions in the European Union: Institutional adaptation in Germany and Spain.* Cambridge: Cambridge University Press.

Börzel, T.A. (2005) 'Europeanization: How the European Union interacts with its member states', in: Bulmer, S. and Lequesne, C. (eds.) *The member states and the European Union.* Oxford: Oxford University Press.

Börzel, T.A. and Buzogány, A. (2020) 'Compliance with EU environmental law: The iceberg is melting', in: Zito, A., Burns, C. and Lenschow, A. (eds.) *The future of European Union environmental politics and policy*. Routledge, pp. 129–155.

Burns, C., Eckersley, P. and Tobin, P. (2020) 'EU environmental policy in times of crisis', *Journal of European Public Policy*, 27(1), pp. 1–19.

Buzogány, A. and Cotta, B. (2024) 'Post-accession backsliding and European Union environmental policies', in: Obydenkova, A. (ed.) *Global environmental politics and international organizations*. Routledge, pp. 83–101.

Cotta, B. (2018). 'Wasted money, wasted time? The sustainability of EU assistance to Hungary and Poland's waste management sector', *Emecon: Employment and economy in Central and Eastern Europe*, 7(1), 1–18.

Cotta, B. and Domorenok, E. (2022) 'Catching up with the European Union's recovery and resilience agenda: Green transition reforms in the Italian National Recovery and Resilience Plan', *Contemporary Italian Politics*, 14(4), pp. 424–440.

Crowley, K., Stewart, J., Kay, A. and Head, B. (2021) *Reconsidering policy complexity, governance and the state*. Bristol: Policy Press.

Daugbjerg, C. and Swinbank, A. (2016) 'Three decades of policy Llyering and politically sustainable reform in the European Union's agricultural policy', *Governance*, 29(2), pp. 265–280.

Dente, B. and Lewanski, R. (1982) 'Administrative networks and implementation effectiveness: Industrial air pollution control policy in Italy', *Policy Studies Journal*, 11(1), pp. 116–129.

Falkner, G. (2016) 'The EU's problem-solving capacity and legitimacy in a crisis context: A virtuous or vicious circle?', *West European Politics*, 39(5), pp. 953–970.

Forchtner, B. (ed.) (2019) *Contemporary environmental communication by the far right in Europe*. London: Routledge.

Forchtner, B., Kroneder, A. and Wetzel, D. (2018) 'Being skeptical? Exploring far-right climate-change communication in Germany', *Environmental Communication*, 12(5), pp. 589–604.

Giorgi, S. et al. (2022) 'Drivers and barriers towards circular economy in the building sector: Stakeholder interviews and analysis of five European countries policies and practices', *Journal of Cleaner Production*, 336, 130395.

Golub, J. (1996) 'British sovereignty and the development of EC environmental policy', *Environmental Politics*, 5(4), pp. 700–728.

Haverland, M. (2000) 'National adaptation to European integration: The importance of institutional veto points', *Journal of Public Policy*, 20(1), pp. 83–103.

Hey, C. (2005) *EU environmental policies: A short history of the policy strategies'*, in: Scheuer S. (ed.) *EU Environmental Policy Handbook. A critical analysis of EU environmental Legislation—making it accessible to environmentalists and decision makers.* Brussels: European Environmental Bureau, pp. 17–30.

Hoicka, C.E. et al. (2021) 'Implementing a just renewable energy transition: Policy advice for transposing the new European rules for renewable energy communities', *Energy Policy*, 156, 112435.

Howlett, M., Mukherjee, I. and Woo, J. (2015) 'From tools to toolkits in policy design studies: The new design orientation towards policy formulation research', *Policy & Politics*, 43(2), 291-311.

Huber, R.A., Maltby, T., Szulecki, K. and Ćetkovic, S. (2021) 'Is populism a challenge to European energy and climate policy? Empirical evidence across varieties of populism', *Journal of European Public Policy*, 7, pp. 998–1017.

Hudson, B., Hunter, D. and Peckham, S. (2019) 'Policy failure and the policy-implementation gap: Can policy support programs help?', *Policy Design and Practice*, 2(1), pp. 1–14.

Jordan, A. (1999) 'The implementation of EU environmental policy: A policy problem without a political solution?', *Environment and Planning C: Government and Policy*, 17(1), pp.69–90.

Jordan, A. and Schout, A. (2006) *The coordination of the European Union: Exploring the capacities of networked governance*. Oxford: Oxford University Press.

Knill, C. and Lenschow, A. (1998) 'Coping with Europe: The impact of British and German administrations on the implementation of EU environmental policy', *Journal of European Public Policy*, 5(4), pp. 595 – 614.

Knill, C. and Lenschow, A. (2000) 'Do new brooms really sweep cleaner? Implementation of new instruments in EU environmental policy', in: Knill, C. and Lenschow, A. (eds.) *Implementing EU environmental policy: New directions and old problems.* Manchester: Manchester University, pp. 251 – 286.

Knill, C. and Liefferink, D. (2007) *Environmental politics in the European Union.* Manchester: Manchester University Press.

Knill, C., Tosun, J. and Heichel, S. (2008) 'Balancing competitiveness and conditionality: Environmental policy-making in low-regulating countries', *Journal of European Public Policy*, 15(7), pp. 1019 – 1040.

Lampinen R. and Uusikylä P. (1998) 'Implementation deficit—why Member States do not comply with EU directives?', *Scandinavian Political Studies*, 21(3), pp. 231 – 251.

Levin, K., Cashore, B., Bernstein, S. and Auld, G. (2012) 'Overcoming the tragedy of super wicked problems: Constraining our future selves to ameliorate global climate change', *Policy Sciences*, 45(2), pp. 123 – 152.

Liefferink, D., Arts, B., Kamstra, J. and Ooijevaar, J. (2009) 'Leaders and laggards in environmental policy: A quantitative analysis of domestic policy outputs', *Journal of European Public Policy*, 16(5), pp. 677 – 700.

Lipsky, M. (1980) *Street-level bureaucracy: Dilemmas of the individual in public services.* New York: Russell Sage Foundation.

Lockwood, M. (2018) 'Right-wing populism and the climate change agenda: Exploring the linkages', *Environmental Politics*, 27(4), pp. 712 – 732.

May, P. (2015) 'Implementation failures revisited: Policy regime perspectives', *Public Policy and Administration*, 30(3 – 4), pp. 277 – 299.

Mazmanian, D. and Sabatier, P. (1983) *Implementation and public policy.* Chicago: Scott Foresman.

McConnell, A. (2010) 'Policy success, policy failure and grey areas in-between', *Journal of Public Policy*, 30(3), pp. 345 – 362.

McConnell, A. (2015) 'What is policy failure? A primer to help navigate the maze', *Public Policy and Administration*, 30(3 – 4), pp. 221 – 242.

McCubbins, M., Noll, R. and Weingast, B. (1987) 'Administrative procedures as instruments of political control', *The Journal of Law, Economics, and Organization*, 3(2), pp. 243 – 277.

Newig, J. (2007) 'Symbolic environmental legislation and societal self-deception', *Environmental Politics*, 16(2), pp. 276 – 296

Peters, B.G. (2015) 'State failure, governance failure and policy failure: Exploring the linkages,' *Public Policy and Administration*, 30(3 – 4), pp. 261 – 276.

Peters, B.G. (2021) *Advanced introduction to public policy.* Cheltenham: Edward Elgar Publishing.

Peters, B.G. (2024) 'Institutionalism(s) and implementation: Sources of implementation failure'. In: Sager, F., Mavrot, C. and Keiser, L. (eds.) *Handbook of public policy implementation.* Cheltenham: Edward Elgar Publishing, pp. 157 – 169.

Pierson, P. (2000) 'Increasing returns, path dependence, and the study of politics', *American Political Science Review*, 94, pp. 251 – 267.

Pressman, J. and Wildavsky, A. (1973) *Implementation.* Berkeley: University of California Press.

Pridham, G. (1996) 'Environmental policies and problems of European legislation in Southern Europe', *South European Society & Politics*, 1(1), pp. 47 – 73.

Sabatier, P. and Mazmanian, D. (1979) 'The conditions of effective implementation: A guide to accomplishing policy objectives', *Policy Analysis*, 3(4), pp. 481 – 504.

Schramm, L. and Terranova, C. (2024)0' From NGEU to REPowerEU: Policy steering and budgetary innovation in the EU', *Journal of European Integration*, 46(6), pp. 943 – 961.

Steinebach, Y. (2022) 'Instrument choice, implementation structures, and the effectiveness of environmental policies: A cross-national analysis. *Regulation & Governance*, 16(1), pp. 225–242.

VanDeveer, S.D. and Carmin, J.A. (2012) 'EU environmental policy and the challenges of eastern enlargement', in: Jordan, A. and Adelle, C. (eds.) *Environmental policy in the EU.* London: Routledge, pp. 297–312.

Wurzel, R., Zito, A. and Jordan, A. (2013) *Environmental governance in Europe: A comparative analysis of the use of new environmental policy instruments.* Cheltenham: Edward Elgar Publishing.

Zhelyazkova, A. and Thomann, E. (2021) 'Policy implementation', in: Jordan, A. and Gravey, V. (eds.) *Environmental policy in the EU: Actors, institutions and processes.* Abingdon: Routledge, pp. 220–240.

Appendix: List of interviews

Reference No.	Affiliation	Place and date
EU1	PRO Europe	Brussels, 2013
EU2	European Commission, DG Environment	Brussels, 2011
EU3	European Commission, DG Environment, Strategic Planning and Programming Unit	Brussels, 2011
EU4	European Commission, DG Enterprise and Industry	Brussels, 2011
EU5	European Commission, DG Environment, Resource and Waste Management Unit	Brussels, 2013
EU6	European Commission, DG Regional and Urban Policy	Brussels, 2013
EU7	European Commission, DG Regional and Urban Policy	Brussels, 2013
HU1	Policy advisor for Hungary	Brussels, 2013
HU2	National Development Agency	Budapest, 2013
HU3	Ministry of Rural Development	Budapest, 2011
PL1	Polish waste management expert	Online, 2024

Jonas J. Schoenefeld

Environmental policy evaluation in the European Union: Actors, institutions and influence

Abstract: Policy evaluation, or the retrospective assessment of policies, has grown in importance in the European Union (EU) and its Member States. Starting from specific policy areas such as structural funding, evaluation now features in many environmental policy processes. EU initiatives such as those centered on better regulation, regulatory refits or evaluation clauses in legislation have institutionalized the practice over time. Today, numerous actors work with environmental policy evaluation, including the core EU institutions, courts and agencies. Nonstate actors have also discovered evaluation as a practice and a route to advance their interests, ranging from nongovernmental organizations to business associations to a cottage industry of evaluation institutes and public consultancies. This chapter takes stock of what we know about the actors and institutions involved in EU environmental policy evaluation and how they conduct and use evaluation. Doing so unpacks how insights on environmental policy evaluation practices, including the impact and politics of evaluations in the policy process, remain fairly scattered and fragmented in existing literatures. A governance perspective on evaluation appears particularly promising to address the gaps in our knowledge and understanding, moving beyond the limited interest of policy scientists and associated disciplines so far.

Keywords: Policy evaluation; policy monitoring; environmental policy; climate policy; European Union

1 Introduction

How do we know whether governmental efforts to protect the environment work and to what extent? While policy initiatives and their impacts are typically subject to considerable societal discourse in democracies, exposing and assessing the causal mechanisms through which public policies take effect remains a challenging task—especially concerning the environment, which sustains many policy and nonpolicy influences. As a response, practices of (environmental) policy evaluation have developed to meet this challenge over at least half a century around the globe. Policy evaluation comes in different varieties; one of the key distinguishing features is its temporal perspective. Ex post policy evaluation is conventionally understood as the "[c]areful retrospective assessment of the merit, worth and value of administration, output and outcome of government interventions, which is intended to play a role in future practical action situations" (Vedung, 1997, p. 3). This chapter focuses on such ex post evaluation, while excluding other forms of evaluation, notable ex ante evaluation or impact assessment,

https://doi.org/10.1515/9783111321523-040

(for more details on ex ante evaluation, see for example Dunlop and Radaelli, 2015; Turnpenny et al., 2009).

In 2016, the European Environment Agency (EEA) concluded that "[t]he evaluation of environment and climate policies is, today, a well-established discipline" (2016, p. 4). This assessment followed decades of development of the practice of policy evaluation in general and environmental policy evaluation in particular, both in the European Union (EU) institutions, but also in its Member States and, in some cases, other substate governance levels and actors (see also Feldman and Wilt, 1996). This chapter highlights and discusses key aspects of what we know about the 'discipline' (European Environment Agency, 2016) of environmental policy evaluation in the EU, how researchers have looked at it and in which directions it may evolve. Drawing on Hill and Varone (2017), the chapter focuses on the analysis *of* evaluation, rather than analysis *for* evaluation, which refers to the great range of methods and approaches that have been developed over time to conduct evaluation in different domains (e. g., Crabbe and Leroy, 2012; Knaap and Tschangho, 1998; Patton, 2008; Stockmann, 2022). Therefore, the point of departure is understanding evaluation as a phenomenon of governance: that is, a feature and practice of political institutions, public administration and other actors who ultimately seek to steer society's interaction with the environment in a sustainable direction.

From the beginning, policy evaluation came with a certain level of attractiveness for practitioners and also theorists, who saw it as a tool to rationalize policy-processes by being able to understand and focus on 'what works' (Sanderson, 2002). The dream has often been that of a rational, Weberian public administration that executes its tasks with precision and motivation—with policy evaluation as a tool within it that provides crucial knowledge to keep the machine running. This ideal of public administration and policy evaluation probably has never existed anywhere—just like idealized visions of firms in the private sector tend to only ever partially come true. Decades of scholarship have uncovered many additional public administration features, such as its own interests: for example, the aim to maximize budgets or staff to gain policymaking power and influence; the people within it, such as street-level bureaucrats like police officers or social workers who deliver services on behalf of the state and who may also pursue their own agendas (e. g., Lipsky, 1980) or their capacities to develop and execute innovative approaches (Mazzucato, 2018; Schoenefeld et al., 2024). From the environmental policy perspective, Max Weber's vision of a siloed public administration has proven increasingly problematic, given the many mounting and cross-sectoral challenges of climate change, biodiversity loss, or pollution, to name but a few. These issues do not fit into the typical silos of public administration and therefore require other—and often innovative—ways of working (e. g., Bickel et al., 2020).

The dream of a machine-like administration with the corresponding evaluation tools to rationalize administrative and political processes will probably persist as an idealist view, but we know today that it is not a realistic vision of what evaluation is or does. Rather, evaluation may be conceptualized as one (potentially important) input into policy processes, but only one alongside many other influences, such as interests, power and resources. Accordingly, Per Mickwitz (2021, p. 242) notes that "[e]nvironmental policy decision making is always political and involves many actors and many different interests, and a lot of other information than that provided by formal evaluations is used". One of the leading early evaluation scholars, Carol Weiss, explained early on: "The programs with which the evaluator deals are not neutral, antiseptic, laboratory-type entities. They emerged from the rough and tumble of political support, opposition, and bargaining" (Weiss, 1993, pp. 94–95). Such dynamics tend to persist during evaluation and when its practices and findings enter the policy process. Nevertheless, many important methodological and technical questions remain and have often been central to academic and practitioner debates on evaluation. It is mistaken to pigeonhole evaluation as a purely political or a purely technical endeavor. It contains elements of both, and one task of research is to unpack what their mix looks like in individual evaluations or entire evaluation systems.

The scholarly landscape on environmental policy evaluation in the EU therefore resembles a patchwork, with contributions appearing in different places and at different times. Meanwhile, practice has consolidated much more over time. To trace such developments and contribute to some defragmentation, this chapter proceeds as follows. Section 2 focuses on key moments in the historical emergence of environmental policy evaluation in the EU, and how these produced the current state of practice and corresponding scholarship. These include elements such as the better regulation drives of the European institutions, and the way in which policy evaluation has featured in different environmental action programs over time. Section 3 unpacks some of the key scholarly perspectives on environmental policy evaluation in the EU, including understanding evaluation patterns and actors, evaluation within the policy cycle, larger governance systems and political environments and, finally, the use of evaluation to understand what role evaluation may play in public policy processes. Section 4 concludes by looking ahead to what role evaluation may play in an age of environmental decline, driven by accelerating climate change and biodiversity loss and the efforts of human-based systems to implement responses to it. Doing so opens future research avenues but also insights for practitioners seeking to build, utilize and improve evaluation systems.

2 The emergence and state of environmental policy evaluation in the EU

Historically, the EU was not a policy evaluation leader, and nor did the domain of environmental policy evaluation lie within the EU. Evaluation as a public administration practice first emerged in the United States of America, where social science disciplines had developed rapidly in the post-war period. Simultaneously, there was also a significant expansion of the social state, with many different policies or 'programs' implemented to alleviate poverty, educate the population and keep it healthy. Such programs came with significant public expense, which eventually generated questions about the effects of such endeavors and therefore initiated evaluation as one way to generate corresponding knowledge (Knaap and Tschangho, 1998). Institutionally, the EU was an infant when evaluation began to grow on the other side of the Atlantic. Nevertheless, especially once a number of Southern European countries joined the EU in the 1980s and then Central and Eastern European countries followed in the 2000s, the corresponding spending on structural funding to support poorer members generated a demand for EU-level evaluation to assess the effectiveness of such funding (Batterbury, 2006; Summa and Toulemonde, 2002).

Meanwhile, the energy crises of the 1970s and a growing awareness of issues such as acid rain and climate change produced societal concern about the state of the environment and corresponding policymaking in the EU Member States. This dynamic also reached the European institutions, which presented a first Environmental Action Program in 1973 (Hoerber, 2012). Different types of assessments, starting from economic aspects, already featured in the first Environmental Action Program, but it took nearly a generation until evaluation appeared explicitly in the sixth program in 2002 (Schoenefeld and Jordan, 2019), and it has featured since (at the time of this writing, the eighth Environmental Action Program, running from 2022 until 2030, was in force). The EU had also been strengthening the role of evaluation in its institutions by introducing ideas and initiatives concerning 'smart regulation' and regulatory 'fitness checks' in the 2010s (Smismans, 2015), which linked with evaluative practices. Subsequently, the 'better regulation agenda' (Radaelli, 2018) served to further institutionalize evaluation in the European institutions. Pieces of environmental legislation, such as the Water Framework Directive, were among the first to be subjected to the new fitness checks (Valin and Huitema, 2024).

Scholars recognized early that evaluating EU policies tends to be challenging, because "EU policies and programs result from complex and long negotiation processes and are implemented through multiple chains of authorities linking the center to the ground. This makes the evaluability of European policies and programs generally poor" (Summa and Toulemonde, 2002, p. 423). Similar statements have been made about many environmental issues and policy areas whose 'wicked' properties (Rittel and Webber, 1973) challenge evaluators. Taken together, environmental policy evaluation in the EU faces this twofold complexity challenge.

3 Studying policy evaluation: Main research foci

The extant, fairly scattered scholarship on (environmental) policy evaluation in the EU may be grouped into aspects that relate to evaluation patterns and actors. A second group of perspectives on evaluation concerns policy process and politics, including ideas of evaluation in the policy cycle (and its discontents), evaluation use and the relationship between politics and evaluation. A third, newer and more holistic perspective aims to bring these perspectives together to understand the role of evaluation in broader governance systems. This section reviews the current state of knowledge and practice in turn.

Evaluation patterns and actors

The emergence of evaluation activities generated a demand for knowledge on the characteristics and patterns of such activities, often from a comparative perspective. However, unlike science with its curated research databases and libraries, no general and searchable repository exists for (environmental policy) evaluation documents in the EU. Consequently, researchers and practitioners interested in evaluation usually start by collecting evaluation documents, which has pragmatically been done for individual studies or in specific institutions. For example, Mastenbroek, van Voorst and Meuwese (2016) found 216 ex post legislative evaluations by the European Commission (EC) between 2000 and 2012 from different policy areas. Focusing on climate policy, Huitema et al. (2011) identified 259 evaluations of climate policies in Finland, Germany, Italy, Poland, Portugal and the United Kingdom (UK) between January 1998 and March 2007. They identified a clear growth in the number of evaluations over time but also differences in the numbers of evaluations per country and the types of actors that produced them. Fujiwara et al. (2019) found 236 evaluations of climate policies conducted by the EU and by Austria, the Czech Republic, France, Greece and the UK. They also identified growth over the years, with the EU as a particularly productive evaluator. Finally, Schoenefeld (2023) collected 618 climate policy evaluations between 1997 and 2014 at the EU-level, as well as in Germany and in the UK, once again demonstrating growth over time. These aforementioned authors analyzed the evaluations over various dimensions, including the actors involved (see below), evaluation methods and criteria, as well as public availability.

Meanwhile, practitioners also recognized the need to bring evaluative knowledge together. The EC provides its evaluations on its website, though not always in a structured way, given that no central repository exists (Mastenbroek, van Voorst and Meuwese, 2016). Many evaluations appear as EC Staff Working documents. Focusing on climate and environment policy, the EEA contracted a consultancy in 2018 to collect evaluations, which returned 495 evaluations that were then listed in a publicly available database (European Environment Agency, 2021). According to the website's technical information, the database was updated in 2020, adding 101 evaluations to the list, and a meta-analysis of the full database was published (Ramboll, 2020). The online database permits sorting and downloading the evaluation documents according to a range of different criteria. While there have been other attempts at creating such repositories, no institution has so far achieved a sustained collection of evaluations over time, meaning that current knowledge remains fragmented and most likely incomplete.

One particular focus in evaluation studies relates to evaluation actors or, in other words, asking who is involved in evaluation and how/why. One key actor and driver of evaluation in the EU has long been the EC as its main administrative body, which instituted a decentralized evaluation approach in the mid-1990s (Summa and Toulemonde, 2002). Over time, other institutions also became involved in evaluation, including notably the European Court of Auditors and the European Parliament (Fernandes, Eisele and Anglmayer, 2024; Stephenson and Schoenefeld, 2023). Then there are various research institutes, consultancies, universities and others which are typically involved as contractors to conduct evaluations (Huitema et al., 2011; Pleger and Sager, 2016). To understand the impetus for evaluation, Schoenefeld (2023) focused on evaluation funders, distinguishing between government-based and society-based funders in the area of climate policy evaluation. He found that government funders—notably the EU institutions and national ministries—accounted for the lion's share of evaluations. Societal funders also supported evaluations in relevant numbers, evaluations which turned out to be more critical of existing policy targets, highlighting their independence.

Evaluation in the policy process

For many, the classic way to conceptualize the role of evaluation in the policy process is the so-called policy cycle. The policy cycle is a heuristic of the policy process. It typically begins with agenda setting and then policy formulation, through to policy implementation, monitoring and, finally policy evaluation. In this idealized (but largely hypothetical) ideational world, evaluation draws on the past to provide input into new policy development as the cycle commences anew. Both scholars and practitioners have worked with this idea, for example by examining the extent to which ex post evaluation closes the regulatory policy cycle (Mastenbroek, van Voorst and Meuwese, 2016), by thinking about ways of linking ex ante and ex post evaluation (Smismans, 2015) or by instituting the 'evaluate first' principle in the Commission, which means that any new proposal requires an earlier ex post evaluation (Stephenson and Schoenefeld, 2023). While the policy cycle heuristic has stimulated useful work, most studies of practical policymaking have thoroughly debunked it. Other policy formulation and policymaking models, such as the advocacy coalition or multiple streams frameworks (see Weible, 2023 for an overview) demonstrate that policymaking typically does not proceed in a neat, stage-like fashion but is rather subject to other mechanisms and influences, such as the skilled work of policy entrepreneurs to advance their ideas by bringing together like-minded individuals, institutions and ideas. However, the work to conceptualize and study evaluation with a view to these different theories has only just begun.

Such efforts may benefit from another strand of work, which has focused on the concept of evaluation use, or the extent to which findings and insights from evaluations find their way into policy processes and how. With a view to justifying evaluation and its inevitable and non-negligible costs (Leeuw, 2010), evaluators proposed utilization-focused evaluation as one way to foreground use and therefore the utility of evaluation (Patton, 2008). Responding to such initiatives, a small number of researchers began to explore to what extent and how evaluation use materializes, focusing on different actors. Conceptually, Højlund (2014) explains that there are many different potential ways evaluation can be used, ranging from instrumental and conceptual to legitimizing, informational and strategic use. Empirically, Højlund (2015) finds that the EC used evaluation to learn internally, including in the environmental policy field. Zaki, Pattyn and Wayenberg (2024) present evidence that evaluation use varied over time, as a 'polycrisis' descended upon the EU. Faced with climate change, evidence was used to learn and craft the European Green Deal, the EU's major environmental policy package. However, as the Covid-19 pandemic hit and Russia invaded Ukraine in February 2022, provoking a Europe-wide energy crisis, EU actors mainly used evaluation-based evidence to justify existing institutional choices rather than to drive policy adjustment (Zaki, Pattyn and Wayenberg, 2024). Looking at the European Parliament, Zwaan, van Voorst and Mastenbroek (2016) question the idea of evaluation as a means to hold the EC to account: out of 220 evaluations they analyzed, only 16 percent appeared in Parliamentary questions, and even in these limited cases, the purpose was usually agenda-setting rather than to demand answers from the executive (Zwaan, Voorst and Mastenbroek, 2016).

Strategic elements of evaluation especially highlight its undeniably political features (Bovens, Hart and Kuipers, 2006). What may be considered political about evaluation depends on the underlying explicit or implicit definition of politics. First, following Lasswell (1965) in his classic formulation of politics as "who gets what, when and how", the role of evaluation links with interests and resource struggles. In such settings, the (dis)continuation or amendment of a policy as a function of an evaluation may impact the resources—monetary or otherwise—that certain actors get. Evaluation may thus impinge on these interests, and it may also be deployed strategically to one's interest-based advantage. Second, if politics is about what goes on in political institutions, such as parliaments or public administrations, one may study different uses there—whether for accountability, learning or strategy (Hoerner, 2019; van Voorst and Zwaan, 2019; Zwaan, Voorst and Mastenbroek, 2016). Third, if politics relates to that which is publicly discussed (see Mansbridge, 1999), then the extent to which evaluation supports deliberation, and especially public deliberation, becomes important (see Fischer, 2006). Several scholars, including those focusing on environmental issues, have pointed to variance in the extent to which evaluations are publicly available and/or used (Mastenbroek, van Voorst and Meuwese, 2016; Schoenefeld, 2023). Furthermore, de Francesco, Pattyn and Salamon (2024) demonstrate that monitoring and evaluation approaches focusing on the implementation of the Sustainable Development Goals in Belgium, the Netherlands and the UK came with significant political intentions to influence the international political discourse on the subject. However, domestic implementation appeared limited and fragmented, so much so that the quality of the monitoring and evaluation framework does not appear to affect general performance with a view to the targets (de Francesco, Pattyn and Salamon, 2024).

Looking across these different aspects, the work on evaluation's role in the policy process therefore remains incomplete and often the different scholarly strands of literature described above have coexisted with limited interaction. The conceptual advances that have been made—for example on the connection between evaluation use and politics to describe the political uses of evaluation (e.g., Schoenefeld and Jordan, 2019; Zwaan and Schoenefeld, 2024) demand more attention as a useful starting point to link and develop scattered literatures.

Evaluation in governance systems

Building on the above-mentioned insights, a few scholars have begun to think about policy evaluation's role in larger governance systems, some with a focus on environmental issues. This approach holds considerable promise to combine disconnected strands of debate and literature, both conceptually and with a view to empirical investigations. In one landmark study, Stame (2008) applied theories and thinking on federalism to investigate the role of evaluation in the EU. The goal was to understand how evaluation contributes to and potentially facilitates interactions between different levels. She demonstrates how the EU's institutional design has emerged from different influences, such as a perceived need for higher governance levels to control lower ones in the French public administration tradition or UK ideas on 'value for money'. She concludes that many evaluations in the EU remain (still) obligation-driven and recommends more theory-based evaluation—that is, evaluation that draws on theories of individual policies (Astbury, 2024)—as well as a stronger focus on context to realize the full potential of evaluation to make governance systems more effective (Stame, 2008).

Similarly, Schoenefeld (2023) used polycentric governance theory to explore the role of climate policy evaluation in the EU. The EU has been described as a relatively polycentric governance system, involving a range of different governance centers, which interact under a common set of overarching rules (Rayner and Jordan, 2013; van Zeben and Bobic, 2019). Using a large evaluations database (see above), Schoenefeld (2023) draws on polycentric governance theory to explore ideas of self-organization, context and interacting governance centers as key foundational ideas of polycentric governance with particular relevance for evaluation. He detects significant self-organization, and therefore pluralism, in climate policy evaluation in the EU, a medium level of attention to context and some indications that evaluation may facilitate interactions among different governance centers. Building on these insights, he offers a new definition of policy evaluation in polycentric governance systems:

> Policy evaluation in polycentric governance systems is a context-sensitive, systematic approach of assessing past policy impact, which uses the knowledge base from previous evaluations and may be conducted by state or societal actors to produce insights and recommendations for future policy development. (Schoenefeld, 2023, p. 201)

To what extent this normatively infused definition 'comes true' in other settings and policy fields is something for future researchers to explore. The governance view of evaluation helps illuminate different functions of evaluations in unison to unpack and understand their complementarities and synergies—but also potential antagonisms. Schoenefeld and Jordan (2019), for example, explored the connections among learning, accountability and political/strategic elements as functions of evaluation, concluding that a rationally optimal function of evaluation does not exist a priori, because precisely what function(s) evaluation fulfills is also, to a certain extent, subject to debate, interests and potentially the power play of the actors involved. Compared to more circumscribed policy process theories, the governance view offers a broader perspective on the role of evaluation by considering a potentially wider set of actors (including governmental and nongovernmental ones) and by focusing on elements such as interactions between governance centers and across different levels. This view is particularly well-suited to many environmental issues, which also tend to cross governance centers/levels and involve many actors.

4 Looking ahead

Our age of environmental decline involving such issues as climate change and the rapidly advancing, human-induced great extinction requires unprecedented levels of action and a true 'step change' in the way humans live (see Hartley and Torfing, 2016). Incrementalism will likely not lead to accomplishing the Sustainable Development Goals and venturing beyond them will be even more difficult. While policy scientists have long stressed that vast public policy changes tend to be unlikely in the absence of large-scale internal or external shocks, this chapter has highlighted the multiple possible roles for policy evaluation in delivering a sustainable future. Policy evaluation has been on the rise globally, with the EU as a particularly dynamic site of development.

For scholars, there is still great room for analyses *of* evaluation, that is, understanding the current evaluation landscape, its dynamic development and potential future directions. While much research, including in leading evaluation journals, focuses on methodological aspects of *how to conduct* evaluation as well as descriptive and analytical accounts of modern-day evaluation practices, outputs and effects still lag behind. Handbook resources, such as Varone, Jacob and Bundi (2023) or Newcomer and Mumford (2024), both building on earlier publications such as Furubo, Rist and Sandahl (2002) and Jacob, Speer and Furubo (2015), or a dedicated special issue on the politicization of evaluation in the EU (Stephenson, Schoenefeld and Leeuw, 2019) provide useful launchpads for future investigation. In doing so, scholars should apply the full thrust of theory and methods from political, governance and policy sciences (Ansell and Torfing, 2016; Levi-Faur, 2012; Weible, 2023) and adjacent disciplines, to develop a fuller, more in-depth understanding of evaluation across different substantial policy fields, in both environmental policy and beyond.

In so doing, important questions will arise. For example, with a view to collaborative governance (e. g., Emerson and Nabatchi, 2015) an empirical question is to what extent evaluations have become potential tools for collaboration and enabling discourse and exchange between different actors (see Fischer, 2006) while navigating other potential effects, such as a feeling of policing and control through evaluation, which could possibly stifle collaborative ambitions (see Schoenefeld and Jordan, 2019). Such investigations would also benefit from considering different governance levels. Extant literature and research often focus on the national level or international/regional institutions, such as the EU. However, evaluation also occurs at subnational levels, including federal states, counties and municipalities (e. g., Feldman and Wilt, 1996). Here, it is important to explore what forms evaluations take (given that resource levels may be lower in smaller-scale institutions), how evaluation contributes to governance processes and, harking back to Stame (2008), to what extent evaluation may strengthen the connection between different governance levels while also keeping in mind that accountability and control functions of evaluation may also be part of the game (Schoenefeld and Jordan, 2019). Precisely how to embed evaluation in larger governance systems thus remains a major future investigative area.

Policy accumulation is a newer phenomenon observed in the area of environmental policymaking and beyond (see Adam et al., 2019; Adam, Steinebach and Knill, 2018). In essence, policy accumulation means that the number of policies in many policy fields—including environmental policy—has been growing around the world. Cutting-edge research suggests that implementation capacities in public administration have not matched the growth of policies, potentially leading to 'bureaucratic overload' and then in some cases 'policy triage', where policymakers make hard choices about which policies to implement and which to postpone or neglect—including in the EU (Knill, Steinebach and Zink, 2024). In an age of tightening public budgets combined with multiple demands on public policymakers to implement cross-sectoral and wide-ranging policies and reach targets, it is becoming ever more difficult for public administrations to keep up.

Against this background, it would be useful to explore to what extent environmental policy evaluation is already helpful or could be helpful to assist difficult decisions in triage-type situations. So far, evaluators have rarely assessed multiple instruments and approaches simultaneously, drawing on previous evaluations and different data sources. A notable recent exception is Stechemesser et al. (2024), who conducted a global assessment of climate policy instruments and found that only a small number produced tangible effects. Such approaches are rare, and the extent to which policy evaluation informs, for example, the EEA's landmark and regular State of the Environment Report and the issues highlighted there (for the latest edition, see European Environment Agency, 2019) has not yet been assessed. In further exploring evaluation's role in such ways, it will also be important to explore to what extent evaluation itself may be subject to triage decisions, given that evaluation also tends to be a resource-intensive activity (Leeuw, 2010).

Environmental policy evaluation in the EU—and surely beyond—remains exciting and promising but still partially uncharted territory for political and policy science scholars and their colleagues in adjacent disciplines. Scholars should apply their full remit of tools and theories to explore policy evaluation with a view to actors, the policy process, governance-settings and more. Evaluation, as this chapter has attempted to demonstrate, has the potential to be much more than the last and often neglected stage of a stylized policy cycle.

References

Adam, C., Hurka, S., Knill, C. and Steinebach, Y. (2019) *Policy accumulation and the democratic responsiveness trap.* Cambridge: Cambridge University Press.

Adam, C., Steinebach, Y. and Knill, C. (2018) 'Neglected challenges to evidence-based policy-making: The problem of policy accumulation', *Policy Sciences*, 51(3), pp. 269 – 290.

Ansell, C. and Torfing, J. (eds.) (2016) *Handbook on theories of governance.* Cheltenham: Edward Elgar Publishing.

Astbury, B. (2024) 'Program theory', in: Newcomer, K.E. and Mumford, S.W. (eds.) *Research handbook on program evaluation.* Cheltenham: Edward Elgar, pp. 260 – 279

Batterbury, S.C.E. (2006) 'Principles and purposes of European Union cohesion policy evaluation', *Regional Studies*, 40(2), pp. 179 – 188.

Bickel, M.W. et al. (2020) 'Multilevel knowledge management for municipal climate action: Lessons from evaluating the operational situation of climate action managers in the German Federal State of Lower Saxony', *Journal of Cleaner Production*, 277, 123628.

Bovens, M., Hart, P. and Kuipers, S. (2006) 'The politics of policy evaluation', in: Moran, M., Rein, M. and Goodin, R.E. (eds.) *The Oxford handbook of public policy.* Oxford: Oxford University Press, pp. 319 – 335.

Crabbe, A. and Leroy, P. (2012) *The handbook of environmental policy evaluation.* London: Routledge.

de Francesco, F., Pattyn, V. and Salamon, H. (2024) 'The monitoring and evaluation challenges of the sustainable development goals: An assessment in three European countries', *Sustainable Development*, 32(3), pp. 1913 – 1924.

Dunlop, C.A. and Radaelli, C.M. (2015) 'Impact assessment in the European Union: Lessons from a research project', *European Journal of Risk Regulation*, 6(1), pp. 27 – 34.

Emerson, K. and Nabatchi, T. (2015) *Collaborative governance regimes.* Washington, DC: Georgetown University Press.

European Environment Agency (2016) *Environment and climate policy evaluation (18/2016).* European Union. Available at: https://www.eea.europa.eu/publications/environment-and-climate-policy-evaluation (Accessed: 7 January 2025).

European Environment Agency (2019) *The European environment: State and outlook 2020: Knowledge for transition to a sustainable Europe.* European Union. Available at: https://www.eea.europa.eu/soer/publications/soer-2020, https://doi.org/10.2800/96749 (Accessed: 7 January 2025).

European Environment Agency (2021) *EEA catalogue of European environment and climate policy evaluations.* European Union. Available at: https://poleval-catalogue.apps.eea.europa.eu (Accessed: 26 June 2025).

Feldman, D.L. and Wilt, C.A. (1996) 'Evaluating the implementation of state-level global climate change programs', *Journal of Environment and Development*, 5(1), pp. 46 – 72.

Fernandes, M., Eisele, K. and Anglmayer, I. (2024) 'How evaluation is understood and practised in the European Parliament', *Evaluation*, 30(2), pp. 253 – 268.

Fischer, F. (2006) *Evaluating public policy.* Mason: Cengage Learning.
Fujiwara, N. et al. (2019) 'The practice of climate change policy evaluations in the European Union and its member states: Results from a meta-analysis', *Sustainable Earth*, 2(1), pp. 1–16.
Furubo, J.-E., Rist, R.C. and Sandahl, R. (eds.) (2002) *International atlas of evaluation.* New Brunswick: Transaction Publishers.
Hartley, J. and Torfing, J. (2016) 'Innovation', in: Ansell, C. and Torfing, J. (eds.) *Handbook on theories of governance.* Cheltenham: Edward Elgar Publishing, pp. 236–244
Hill, M. and Varone, F (2017) *The public policy process.* Oxon: Routledge.
Hoerber, T. (2012) *The origins of energy and environmental policy in Europe: The beginnings of a European environmental conscience.* London: Routledge.
Hoerner, J. (2019) 'Adding fuel to the flames? Politicisation of EU policy evaluation in national parliaments', *Politische Vierteljahresschrift*, 60(4), pp. 805–821.
Højlund, S. (2014) 'Evaluation use in evaluation systems-the case of the European Commission', *Evaluation*, 20(4), pp. 428–446.
Højlund, S. (2015) 'Evaluation in the European Commission: For accountability or learning?', *European Journal of Risk Regulation*, 6(1), pp. 35–46.
Huitema, D. et al. (2011) 'The evaluation of climate policy: Theory and emerging practice in Europe', *Policy Sciences*, 44(2), pp. 179–198.
Jacob, S., Speer, S. and Furubo, J.-E. (2015) 'The institutionalization of evaluation matters: Updating the international atlas of evaluation 10 years later', *Evaluation*, 21(1), pp. 6–31.
Knaap, G. J. and Tschangho, J.K. (eds.) (1998) *Environmental program evaluation: A primer.* Urbana: University of Illinois Press.
Knill, C., Steinebach, Y. and Zink, D. (2024) 'How policy growth affects policy implementation: Bureaucratic overload and policy triage', *Journal of European Public Policy*, 31(2), pp. 324–351.
Lasswell, H.D. (1965) *World politics and personal insecurity.* New York City: The Free Press.
Leeuw, F. L. (2010) 'Benefits and costs of evaluation-an essay', *Zeitschrift für Evaluation*, 9(2), pp. 211–229.
Levi-Faur, D. (2012) *The Oxford handbook of governance.* Oxford: Oxford University Press.
Lipsky, M. (1980) *Street-level bureaucracy: The dilemmas of individuals in public service.* New York City: Russell Sage Foundation.
Mansbridge, J.J. (1999) 'Everyday talk in the deliberative system', in: Macedo, S. (ed.) *Deliberative politics: Essays on democracy and disagreement.* Oxford: Oxford University Press, pp. 211–239.
Mastenbroek, E., van Voorst, S. and Meuwese, A. (2016) 'Closing the regulatory cycle? A meta evaluation of ex-post legislative evaluations by the European Commission', *Journal of European Public Policy*, 23(9), pp. 1329–1348.
Mazzucato, M. (2018) *The entrepreneurial state: Debunking public vs private sector myths.* New York City: PublicAffairs.
Mickwitz, P. (2021) 'Policy evaluation', in: Jordan, A.J. and Gravey, V. (eds.) *Environmental policy in the EU: Actors, institutions and processes.* Fourth Edition. London: Routledge, pp. 241–258.
Newcomer, K.E. and Mumford, S.W. (eds.) (2024) *Research handbook on program evaluation.* Cheltenham: Edward Elgar.
Patton, M.Q. (2008) *Utilization-focused evaluation.* Thousand Oaks: Sage publications.
Pleger, L. and Sager, F. (2016) 'Betterment, undermining, support and distortion: A heuristic model for the analysis of pressure on evaluators', *Evaluation and Program Planning*, 69, pp. 166–172.
Radaelli, C. M. (2018) 'Halfway through the better regulation strategy of the Juncker Commission: What does the evidence say?', *Journal of Common Market Studies*, 56(S1), pp. 85–95.
Ramboll (2020) *Update of the European Environment Agency catalogue of available evaluations of European environment and climate policies.* Copenhagen: Ramboll.
Rayner, T. and Jordan, A.J. (2013) 'The European Union: The polycentric climate policy leader?', *Wiley Interdisciplinary Reviews: Climate Change*, 4(2), pp. 75–90.

Rittel, H.W.J. and Webber, M.M. (1973) 'Dilemmas in a general theory of planning', *Policy Sciences*, 4(2), pp. 155–169.

Sanderson, I. (2002) 'Making sense of "what works": Evidence based policy making as instrumental rationality?', *Public Policy and Administration*, 17(3), pp. 61–75.

Schoenefeld, J.J. (2023) *The evaluation of polycentric climate governance*. Cambridge: Cambridge University Press.

Schoenefeld, J.J. et al. (2024) 'Positive public administration for sustainable development: The crucial role of municipalities in driving success', in: Lucas, P., Nabachi, T., O'Flynn, J. and 't Hart, P. (eds.) *Pathways to positive public administration: An international perspective*. Cheltenham: Edward Elgar.

Schoenefeld, J.J. and Jordan, A.J. (2019) 'Environmental policy evaluation in the EU: Between learning, accountability, and political opportunities?', *Environmental Politics*, 28(2), pp. 365–384.

Smismans, S. (2015) 'Policy evaluation in the EU: The challenges of linking ex ante and ex post appraisal', *European Journal of Risk Regulation*, 6(1), pp. 6–26.

Stame, N. (2008) 'The European project, federalism and evaluation', *Evaluation*, 14(2), pp. 117–140.

Stechemesser, A. et al. (2024) 'Climate policies that achieved major emission reductions: Global evidence from two decades', *Science*, 385(6711), pp. 884–892.

Stephenson, P.J. and Schoenefeld, J.J. (2023) 'The role and functioning of evaluation in the European Union', in: Varone, F. Jacob, S. and Bundi, P. (eds.) *Handbook of public policy evaluation*. Cheltenham: Edward Elgar, pp. 266–284.

Stephenson, P.J., Schoenefeld, J.J. and Leeuw, F.L. (2019) 'The politicisation of evaluation: Constructing and contesting EU policy performance', *Politische Vierteljahresschrift*, 60(4), pp. 663–679.

Stockmann, R. (2022) *Handbuch zur Evaluation: Eine praktische Handlungsanleitung* (Vol. 16). Münster: Waxmann Verlag.

Summa, H. and Toulemonde, J. (2002) 'Evaluation in the European Union: Addressing complexity and ambiguity', in: Furubo, J.-E., Rist, R.C. and Sandahl, R. (eds.) *International atlas of evaluation*. New Brunswick: Transaction Publishers, pp. 407–425.

Turnpenny, J., Radaelli, C.M., Jordan, A.J. and Jacob, K. (2009) 'The policy and politics of policy appraisal: Emerging trends and new directions', *Journal of European Public Policy*, 16(4), pp. 640–653.

Valin, N. and Huitema, D. (2024) 'Lost in translation: Questioning the role of European evaluations in environmental policy change', *Journal of Environmental Planning and Management*. Advance online publication, 68(11), pp. 2545–2565.

van Voorst, S. and Zwaan, P. (2019) 'The (non-) use of ex post legislative evaluations by the European Commission', *Journal of European Public Policy*, 26(3), pp. 366–385.

van Zeben, J. and Bobic, A. (2019) *Polycentricity in the European Union*. Cambridge: Cambridge University Press.

Varone, F., Jacob, S. and Bundi, P. (eds.) (2023) *Handbook of public policy evaluation*. Cheltenham: Edward Elgar.

Vedung, E. (1997) *Public policy and program evaluation*. New Brunswick: Transaction Publishers.

Weible, C.M. (2023) *Theories of the policy process*. New York: Routledge.

Weiss, C.H. (1993) 'Where politics and evaluation research meet', *Evaluation Practice*, 14(1), pp. 93–106.

Zaki, B., Pattyn, V. and Wayenberg, E. (2024) 'Policy learning from evidence during polycrises: A case of EU environmental policy', *Policy Design and Practice*, 7(4), pp. 390–408.

Zwaan, P. and Schoenefeld, J.J. (2024) 'Explaining different usages of policy monitoring in the EU', *Journal of European Integration*, 46(8), pp. 1257–1273.

Zwaan, P., van Voorst, S. and Mastenbroek, E. (2016) 'Ex post legislative evaluation in the European Union: Questioning the usage of evaluations as instruments for accountability', *International Review of Administrative Sciences*, 82(4), pp. 674–693.

Susanna Vanhamäki

Implementing the concept of circular economy in European Union policy

Abstract: A proposed solution to the sustainability crisis involves embracing the concept of a circular economy, an economic system designed to regenerate resources by minimizing waste and maximizing the lifespan of products and materials. In our present economy, we extract materials, manufacture products and ultimately dispose of them as waste, following a linear process. Conversely, in a circular economy, products and materials are sustained within the system through processes such as maintenance, reuse, refurbishment, remanufacture and recycling. In a circular economy, the emphasis shifts to preventing waste generation.

This chapter dissects the circular economy concept, its origin and actual meaning. What is circularity compared to linearity? Why do we need to rethink the traditional processes? Furthermore, the emergence of the circular economy in the European Union policy context will be discussed. How have circular economy principles been integrated into European-level strategies and subsequently incorporated into national and regional policies? What are the policy implementation challenges? Can circular economy strategies foster societal transitions toward sustainability?

Keywords: Circular economy; circular economy policy; systemic change; holistic sustainability; resource efficiency

1 Circular economy emerging as a concept

The world is grappling with multiple crises, a trend likely to continue. Global challenges have arisen due to industrialization and urbanization. Human activities in the past century have led to climate change, biodiversity loss and energy and resource shortages. These issues prompt questions about the Earth's capacity and our role in maintaining harmony with nature. Referred to as the sustainability debate, this critical matter stems from technological advancements and economic growth (Du Pisani, 2006). There is widespread consensus on the necessity of transitioning to a more sustainable society, where a circular economy is proposed as one possible solution.

The background of the sustainability discussion justifies the importance of the development of a circular economy. The sustainability concept originates from concern about damage to the natural environment caused by the technological and economic development after the world wars (Du Pisani, 2006). In the 1960s and 1970s the world faced ecological disasters. The limitations of the Earth's carrying capacity were highlighted by the Club of Rome's 1972 report that focused on the exponential economic expansion and population growth (Meadows et al., 1972). This debate launched the discussion where the angle changed from general environmental concern to the increas-

https://doi.org/10.1515/9783111321523-041

ing search for solutions to bolster a different societal development that would be able to support economic development (Kenny, 1994; Du Pisani, 2006).

'Our Common Future', also known as the Brundtland Report, was published in 1987 by the United Nations and defined sustainable development as "development that meets the needs of the present without compromising the ability of future generations to meet their own needs" (World Commission on Environment and Development, 1987). The concept calls for environmental, social and economic sustainability to achieve sustainable development.

When applying sustainability principles to society and economy, challenges have occurred. Policymakers and academics combine environmental and sustainability discourses with industrial and economic policy to drive progress (Bina, 2013). However, the patterns of our conventional economy are not sufficient to deliver this. A general understanding among policymakers, academia and business has grown that the traditional way, the 'linear economy', of creating economic growth by extracting raw materials, manufacturing them to be used and finally throwing them away as waste—'take-make-dispose'—cannot lead to sustainable development (Millar, Mclaughlin and Börger, 2019; Neves and Marques, 2022). This widespread understanding, enhanced by academic research, led to the emergence of various sustainable economy concepts, for example, green economy, bioeconomy, (Loiseau et al., 2016; D'Amato et al., 2017; Billi, Mascareno and Edwards, 2021), industrial ecology (Geng and Doberstein, 2008; Blomsma and Brennan, 2017; D'Amato et al., 2017) and also cleaner production, which is seen as a predecessor of circular economy, especially at the company level (Su, Heshmati and Geng, 2013; Ghisellini, Cialani and Ulgiati, 2016).

In contrast to the linear economy, the circular economy proposes to design, make, use and reuse products and services to ensure they stay within the economy for as long as possible while minimizing environmental harm (Ellen MacArthur Foundation, 2012; Kirchherr, Reike and Hekkert, 2017). Both science and practice define circular economy to be an economic system that aims to close material loops, reduce the need for raw materials, reduce waste disposal and maintain the value of products and resources for as long as possible (Geng and Doberstein, 2008; Ellen MacArthur Foundation, 2012; Ghisellini, Cialani and Ulgiati, 2016; Kirchherr, Reike and Hekkert, 2017). 'R' frameworks have been used to describe the technical part of the circular economy, most often through the principles 'reduce, reuse and recycle' (Blomsma and Brennan, 2017; Ghisellini, Cialani and Ulgiati, 2016; Kirchherr, Reike and Hekkert, 2017). Moreover, Sardianou et al. (2023) point out that circular economy definitions are focused on waste management, resource scarcity and recycling. Despite the common association of the circular economy with recycling, recycling importantly does not rank among the foremost sustainable solutions. Instead, prioritization should be accorded to practices such as reuse, remanufacturing and refurbishment (Korhonen, Honkasalo and Seppälä, 2018).

The basic idea behind the circular economy dates back to the 19th century (Murray, Skene and Haynes, 2017). However, the origin of the circular economy concept is usually linked with Pearce and Turner (1990), who explained the operations of the environment as seen from an economics perspective (explained in, e.g., Su, Heshmati and Geng, 2013; Murray, Skene and Haynes, 2017; Ghisellini, Cialani and Ulgiati, 2016; Geissdoerfer et al., 2017; Merli, Preziosi and Acampora, 2018). The grounds behind the circular economy concept are effective use and recycling of resources (Merli, Preziosi and Acampora, 2018).

The circular economy concept has gained increased attention since its launch by the Ellen MacArthur Foundation in 2012. It was soon accepted as a possible solution to the environmental crises. Since 2015 the concept has been a central part of the European Union's (EU) environmental policy (Calisto Friant, Vermeulen and Salomone, 2021; Vanhamäki, 2021). Pursuing a circular economy can be seen as a means of achieving a more sustainable future.

The circular economy stands as a pivotal and frequently employed concept arising from the discourse surrounding sustainability. As it is an economic growth strategy focusing on the environment, the economic and environmental sustainability perspectives are embedded in the concept. Nevertheless, fostering the circular economy necessitates a comprehensive consideration of all perspectives of sustainability, including the social dimensions (Kirchherr, Reike and Hekkert, 2017). Yet, the social perspective is still weak despite the efforts of scientific research (Geissdoerfer et al., 2017; Merli, Preziosi and Acampora, 2018). The missing social sustainability perspective casts doubts upon the concept overall. Research has pointed out that the citizen perspective and changes in consumption need to be prioritized to enable a transformation toward a circular society (Kirchherr, Reike and Hekkert, 2017; Korhonen, Honkasalo and Seppälä, 2018; Schöggl, Stumpf and Baumgartner, 2020). The social dimension is needed to establish a holistically sustainable approach to circular economy (Blomsma and Brennan, 2017; Kirchherr, Reike and Hekkert, 2017; Merli, Preziosi and Acampora, 2018; Mies and Gold, 2021).

In addition to the holistic approach, the other essential perspective is to understand the circular economy as a systemic transition. The circular economy concept applies to three scale, or system, levels of implementation: micro-level, meso-level and macro-level (Geng and Doberstein, 2008; Su, Heshmati and Geng, 2013; Kirchherr, Reike and Hekkert, 2017). Micro-level actions comprise activities of a single actor; a company, product, or consumer while the meso-level includes actions implemented together with other actors, e.g., in industrial ecosystems such as industrial symbiosis where one company's waste is another's resource or where companies develop other kinds of symbiotic cooperation, for example, related to energy production and consumption (Geng and Doberstein, 2008; Su, Heshmati and Geng, 2013; Ghisellini, Cialani and Ulgiati, 2016; Kirchherr, Reike and Hekkert, 2017; Merli, Preziosi and Acampora, 2018; Hedlund et al., 2020). Furthermore, the macro-level actions include activities implemented in a larger context, on the local, regional or national level in networks or networks of ecosystems, referring to the structure of the entire economy (Su, Heshmati and Geng, 2013; Kirchherr, Reike and Hekkert, 2017; Merli, Preziosi and Acampora, 2018). Representing a systemic change to the circular economy concept, the systems perspective includes multilevel governance and supports interconnections between different level actors in society (Vanhamäki, 2021).

However, circular economy research is still relatively new. Significant contributions have primarily originated from governmental bodies and private enterprises (Korhonen et al., 2018; Calisto Friant, Vermeulen and Salomone, 2020). Within academic spheres, emphasis has predominantly centered on the practical instantiation of circular economy principles at the organizational and ecosystemic levels, alongside critical deliberations concerning the conceptual underpinnings of circularity (e. g., Ghisellini, Cialani and Ulgiati, 2016; Kirchherr, Reike and Hekkert, 2017; Korhonen, Honkasalo and Seppälä, 2018; Korhonen et al., 2018). Until recently, academia has not agreed on a single definition for what a circular economy means and includes (see e. g., Kirchherr, Reike and Hekkert, 2017; Korhonen, Honkasalo and Seppälä, 2018; Korhonen et al., 2018; Schroeder, Anggraeni and Weber, 2019). However, in 2021, Nobre and Tavares (2021) proposed a 'final' common sense definition based on the definitions of forty-four experts around the world. Still, Sardianou et al. (2023) continue to state that the concept does not have a generally accepted definition among scholars and practitioners. The challenge in defining the concept lies in the need to summarize all the essential aspects in a compact definition, the R framework and waste hierarchy, systemic and holistic perspectives.

The origin and setting of the circular economy concept requires understanding before moving on to the policy development and discussion. The contextual background of the strategy explains why it has become a core concept of EU environmental policy.

2 Circular economy in EU policy

On a global level, Germany was the first to include the idea of circularity in national laws in 1996 (Su, Heshmati and Geng, 2013). Following that China introduced circular economy principles in their law in 2009 (Su, Heshmati and Geng, 2013). Also, Chinese universities were leaders in academic publishing on circular economy between 2005 and 2013 (Merli, Preziosi and Acampora, 2018). China has implemented a top-down approach, whereas other countries have encouraged the development of the circular economy through bottom-up policies (Ghisellini, Cialani and Ulgiati, 2016).

Since 2008, the EU has taken the lead in its efforts to develop the circular economy, first under related concepts. The EU concept of the circular economy, along with its related policies, have been developed through the unique way the EU operates, which involves multiple institutions, like the European Commission (EC), European Parliament and the Member States.

In EU environmental legislation, several steps on the way toward circular economy policy were taken over the past decades before the actual concept was introduced. Directives addressing climate change (European Commission, 2008), prioritizing energy efficiency and the adoption of renewable energy sources (European Commission, 2011a; European Commission, 2008), and emphasizing waste management in accordance with the waste hierarchy (European Union, 2008) have set the path for cleaner production, resource efficiency and the advancement of the circular economy.

In 2011, the EC introduced a flagship initiative focusing on resource efficiency (European Commission, 2011b), signaling the official intention to establish a long-term framework for transitioning the EU toward a 'circular economy'. The initiative's aim was to develop Europe into a recycling society, with a primary objective of minimizing waste generation and harnessing waste as a valuable resource. The circular economy efforts were boosted by the think tank and global thought leader the Ellen MacArthur Foundation. Subsequently, the circular economy became integral to EU policies. Simultaneously, the launch of the European bioeconomy strategy (European Commission, 2012) influenced the policy discourse concerning biobased circularity, given the interconnectedness of both concepts within the broader sustainability discussion.

In 2014, the EC initiated a zero-waste program (European Commission, 2014), a comprehensive effort advocating for circular economy principles. The release of the first action plan followed in 2015 (European Commission, 2015). The action plan outlined a series of measures aimed at facilitating Europe's transition toward a circular economy. It delineated a concrete action program encompassing initiatives that targeted production, consumption, waste management, the secondary raw materials market and a revised legislative proposal on waste management (European Commission, 2015). Additionally, the annex to the action plan provided a timeline for the completion of these actions. By 2019, the fifty-four actions contained in the action plan had mostly been delivered (European Commission, 2019a; European Commission, 2020). These included, for example, a new waste framework including ambitious recycling rates, clarified legal status of recycled materials, strengthened waste prevention and waste management measures, as well as promoting the circular design of products, together with energy efficiency (European Commission, 2019a).

The EC adopted a new Circular Economy Action Plan in March 2020 (European Commission, 2020). It is one of the major parts of the European Green Deal, the EU's strategy to promote sustainable growth where overcoming climate change and environmental degradation are the drivers (see Chapter 20; European Commission, 2019b). The 2020 Action Plan was built on the actions implemented since 2015 and steered the focus more toward a sustainable circular economy, not only focusing on products but the entire product life cycle, while also emphasizing services. The plan focuses on sectors that use the most resources with high potential for circularity, such as electronics and Information and communications technology (ICT), batteries and vehicles, packaging, plastics, textiles, construction and buildings, food, water and nutrients. Furthermore, the 2020 plan aims to reduce total waste generation and halve the amount of residual (non-recycled) municipal waste by 2030. Consumers and public buyers are in focus, as the aim is to make circularity work in practice for citizens, regions and cities. The importance of systemic transition through stakeholder cooperation at EU, national, regional, local and international levels is emphasized. Furthermore, the plan highlights the EU aim to be the leader of global efforts on circular economy. The plan contains thirty-five actions, of which some have been adopted, some are proposed by the EC but not yet adopted and others are waiting for further processing (Watkins and Meysner, 2022). In May 2023, the EC published a revised circular economy monitoring framework to better track the transition progress (European Commission, 2023). The framework aims to monitor new indicators, such as material efficiency and waste prevention but also the contribution of a circular economy to sustainability, climate neutrality and resilience. Eurostat (2024) maintains updated data on the monitoring framework. Recent updates in EU circular economy policy are related to the Clean Industrial Deal aiming to support industries' renewal, reduce waste and extend the life of materials, an upcoming public procurement framework in 2026, emphasizing sustainability, resilience and European preference criteria, and adopting a circular economy act in 2026 to ensure that materials are used and reused efficiently and reduce our global dependencies (European Commission, 2025).

The EU circular economy approach has predominantly emphasized waste management (Marino and Pariso, 2020; Fitch-Roy, Benson and Monciardini, 2021; Sardianou et al., 2023). Following the 2020 action plan, the EU circular economy policy is now emphasizing incorporating a broader view on circular economy. However, considerable effort still remains to be made concerning waste management, as the implementation of the EC's waste and recycling initiatives has not been aligned in the Member States. There is an increasing need for clarity on how waste management and recycling initiatives relate to EU legislative actions, especially considering the sociopolitical and economic complexities involved (Sardianou et al. 2023).

The EU policies have also been criticized for a tendency to disproportionately prioritize technical and economic facets of circularity over social and cultural dimensions (see Chapter 5), such as citizen lifestyle transformations (Calisto Friant, Vermeulen and Salomone, 2021). Calisto Friant, Vermeulen and Salomone (2021) emphasize that while social and cultural challenges and inequalities are acknowledged within the policy framework, proposed solutions tend to pivot around prospective economic benefits rather than addressing wealth redistribution concerns. The social impacts and societal benefits of a circular economy have not yet been defined by researchers; thus, this poses a challenge to recognize and measure such benefits (Padilla-Rivera, Russo-Garrido and Merveille, 2020).

Leipold (2021) also highlights wider scholarly concern that the circular economy policy is unsuccessful in meeting environmental goals because it prioritizes economic goals through recycling targets but not environmental goals such as reduction. Criticism is directed toward EU circular economy policies for primarily updating directives and targets without embarking on transformative change endeavors beyond economic growth pursuits (Fitch-Roy, Benson and Monciardini, 2020; see Chapter 7). Despite the 2020 Circular Economy Action Plan emphasizing the significance of the recycling industry as a pivotal component, achieving a sustainable circular economy necessitates driving forward structural socioeconomic transformations.

3 From the EU level to national, regional and local circular economy strategies

To support sustainability and sustainable development in society, it is crucial to implement it into governance. In general, policymakers widely accept the circular economy concept and view it as a key concept in the aim for sustainability in society (Sauvé, Bernard and Sloan, 2016; Geissdoerfer et al., 2017; Korhonen, Honkasalo and Seppälä, 2018).

Some European nations were quick to implement specific circular economy policies. Denmark emerged as a pioneer by adopting a national-level circular economy strategy in 2013, followed by Finland and the Netherlands in 2016, and subsequently by Greece, France and Slovenia in 2018 (Fitch-Roy, Benson and Monciardini, 2021). In other countries, the focus has been on broader green and sustainable initiatives, also covering the circular economy. For instance, Portugal's Green Growth Commitment (Government of Portugal, 2015) emphasizes sustainable practices overall.

The EU and Member State-level policies have in turn inspired and pushed regional and local-level governance to form circular economy strategies. The first regional and local-level circular economy strategies or road maps were launched by big cities like Amsterdam and Paris and forerunner Finnish regions like Päijät-Häme and Southwest Finland (Amsterdam Circular, 2015; Mairie de Paris, 2017; Päijät-Häme Regional Council, 2021; Kiertotalouden Varsinais-Suomi, 2021).

Some European regions have also combined the implementation of the regional circular economy strategies with smart specialization (Vanhamäki, Rinkinen and Manskinen, 2021). The concept of Smart Specialization Strategies (S3) was introduced within the EU's Cohesion and Innovation policy framework. This initiative aims to ensure the strategic use of European Structural Funds and to direct investments in research and innovation toward fields that demonstrate the highest competitive advantage and future potential (Foray et al., 2012). If the circular economy is evident in the smart specialization strategy, regional research, development and innovation projects in the theme are naturally supported, as the regional policy sphere promotes circularity (Vanhamäki, Rinkinen and Manskinen, 2021). Furthermore, during the 2021–2027 programming period, smart specialization strategies continue to direct the allocation of structural funding toward specific themes and activities, with an enhanced emphasis on sustainability and green transition. Integrating the circular economy into the smart specialization strategy will undoubtedly facilitate and expand the availability of funding for regional implementation of circular economy-related projects.

Concretizing the regional strategy to circular economy actions requires roadmaps and action plans. Without the connection between strategy and action, the initiatives remain too abstract. Currently, most regions still struggle to build specific monitoring and evaluation measures and mechanisms for the circular economy (Vanhamäki, Rinkinen and Manskinen, 2021).

4 Challenges in implementing circular economy policies

Even if academics, practitioners and policymakers see the circular economy as a possible solution to develop sustainability, criticism toward the concept exists (see Chapter 5). The circular economy is often presented as a win-win policy where the environment and economy go hand in hand. However, circularity is not the only perspective, as it easily refers to recycling. The ideal of a circular economy fails if we continue, or increase, production and use of products as before (Zink and Geyer, 2017). A behavioral change is required to enable reduced environmental impact; producing and consuming less overall is vital. Moreover, Millar, Mclaughlin and Börger (2019) criticize the social perspectives. It is unclear if a circular economy is able to support social equity and welfare while promoting the economy and protecting the environment. Addressing this transformation and behavioral change is the hardest challenge for the concept. The transition to a circular economy requires a system-wide change—not only change at the individual level, but encouraging more circular behavior at an individual level can partly support a wider system transition (Wastling et al, 2018). In the wider system, transitional behavioral change is a critical element of the change.

The data presented in the EC revised monitoring framework for the circular economy reveal that, even if EU production has become more resource-efficient, materials consumption remains very high and requires reduction in the future (European Commission, 2023). Positive news is that the EU is managing waste more sustainably; however, differences between the Member States are significant (see Chapters 14, 25 and 34). Plastics are a waste stream that needs even more attention. Despite some advancements in circularity, the EU economy remains predominantly linear, with recycled materials constituting less than 12 percent of the total materials utilized. The trade of secondary raw materials is increasing, however slowly. Furthermore, the monitoring framework reveals that regarding investments, value added and jobs the circular economy sector has grown in recent years. For example, the circular economy sectors created around EUR 299 billion of added value in 2021, which means an increase of 27 percent compared with 2015 (European Commission, 2023).

The EU circular economy policy offers substantial benefits through its efforts to reduce waste, cut emissions, support circular business models and innovation, enhance awareness and implement a regulatory framework with targets. However, weaknesses in implementing the policy initiatives, especially regarding the national differences are evident. Commitment and greater harmonization of policies and regulations in Member States is crucial. Furthermore, the infrastructure, technological and economic possibilities for companies to evolve vary, as do the methods to increase awareness and education. Addressing these weaknesses is crucial for achieving the policy's long-term goals.

The understanding and implementation of the circular economy in policy and practice have evolved during the past decade toward a more a holistic perspective.

As the EU circular economy discussion was initially developing, several national and regional strategies were still focusing on waste management (Vanhamäki et al., 2019). Even if the circular economy concept was rapidly adopted, the full understanding of it is still developing. In the EU, the focus is no longer waste but increasingly addressing priorities higher up the waste hierarchy, such as reduce and reuse. However, so far, the circular economy does not adequately recognize the importance of absolute reduction of resource consumption to achieve a full circular economy transition.

Several initiatives, such as legislation, plans and other policies, that support or are related to the development of the circular economy were launched following the 2020 EU Action Plan. They address, for example, pollution, resource security, climate change and biodiversity loss. In particular, the linkage between biodiversity and the circular economy has gained attention lately (e. g., European Environment Agency, 2023). The circular economy is seen to be able to decrease the negative impacts of production and consumption on biodiversity loss. The Intergovernmental Science-Policy Platform on Biodiversity and Ecosystem Services argues that the biodiversity loss needs tackling through transformative economic, social, political and technological changes; relying on only conservation and restoration is insufficient to generate fundamental changes (Ellen MacArthur Foundation, 2021).

Biodiversity loss is an alarming global trend that needs to be taken seriously in all sectors (see Chapter 23). By reducing the need for resource extraction and decreasing waste, a circular economy supports the reduction of the current rate of biodiversity loss (European Environment Agency, 2023). Nature-positivity is a recent term which links the biodiversity perspectives with the circular economy (Ellen MacArthur Foundation, 2021). The root causes of biodiversity loss are tightly linked with the circular economy, eliminating waste, circulating products and materials and regenerating nature. However, the linkages have not yet been studied extensively and further research is needed (Ruokamo et al., 2023).

Finland offers an example of a national policy approach to promoting circular actions. The transition to a circular economy has been challenging to drive systematically as the diversity of contexts, directions and actions needed is vast. In Finland, the Ministry of the Environment and the Ministry of Economic Affairs and Employment has responded by involving stakeholders, policymakers and researchers in building consensus around the actions and networks. The Circular Economy Green Deal is a new national policy tool, a voluntary strategic commitment (Ministry of the Environment, 2024a). The approach is strongly science-based; research institutes have provided the knowledge on consumption of natural resources while also considering the economy's wellbeing and sustainability. The Circular Economy Green Deal aims to encourage public and private actor contributions to circular economy transition through promoting national level targets and setting organizational targets and indicators. Various organizations have participated in the process. These included most Finnish regions, major cities, key business and sectoral organizations, the largest forest sector companies and numerous operators in the construction sector. The first commitments were signed in September 2024 by, for example, companies in the fields of energy and plastic, and a medium-sized city (Ministry of the Environment, 2024b).

5 Conclusion

The circular economy needs to comprehend a systemic transition toward a more sustainable society. The EU was one of the global forerunners in implementing the circular economy into its policies. However, to achieve a holistic circular economy approach, all aspects affecting the economy need consideration, including consumers, materials, processes and strategy level (Schöggl, Stumpf and Baumgartner, 2020). Even if the EU circular economy policy is moving its focus toward reusing and reducing, there is still a long way to go to reduce resource consumption to achieve a full circular economy transition.

The analysis of the European circular economy policy landscape finds that the EC sees the need for more legally binding measures to support the transition to a circular economy (Watkins and Meysner, 2022). Even if the EU circular economy policy has been criticized for focusing on waste management, an increasing number of initiatives are focusing the attention higher up in the waste hierarchy, such as reducing and reusing. Still, the focus needs to move more toward the top of the hierarchy, that is, refusing and rethinking.

A current concern is how to support EU policy implementation. Several policies and regulations have been established, but they require proper implementation. It is time to move from vision to implementation. This concerns especially the local and regional levels where actual activities occur. However, since the 2020 Action Plan launch, the EU policy context, including circular economy implementation, has changed remarkably. First, the Covid-19 pandemic turned the focus to unpredicted risks and complicated supply chains. The war in Ukraine affected the market and prices of energy and food. The prolonged crises and constantly changing global landscape support the need for and importance of the circular economy transition from the perspective of safety and security of supply.

In practice, considerable effort is required to even take the first steps and organize effective waste management in the whole EU. However, if the policymakers in the somewhat lagging countries can grasp the big picture of the circular economy quicker than their colleagues, who have 'run the long way', these countries might be able to address higher parts of the waste hierarchy more effectively than their peers.

The circular economy is an economic growth strategy. It needs to work from the economic perspective; thus, the way society can steer economic profits to support holistic and systemic sustainability is key. Changing the consumer's mindset is a challenging and time-consuming process. Nevertheless, the circular economy should encourage companies to more sustainable solutions.

References

Amsterdam Circular (2015) *A vision and a roadmap for the city and region.* Available at: https://assets.website-files.com/5d26d80e8836af2d12ed1269/5ede5a03e4cd056426b86d8b_20152115%20-%20Amsterdam%20scan%20-%20report%20EN%20web%20single%20page%20-%20297x210mm.pdf (Accessed: 10 May 2024).

Billi, M., Mascareno, A. and Edwards, J. (2021) 'Governing sustainability or sustainable governance? Semantic constellations on the sustainability-governance intersection in academic literature', *Journal of Cleaner Production*, 279, 123523.

Bina, O. (2013) 'The green economy and sustainable development: An uneasy balance?', *Environment and Planning C: Politics and Space*, 31(6), pp. 1023 – 1047.

Blomsma, F. and Brennan, G. (2017) 'The emergence of circular economy: A new framing around prolonging resource productivity', *Journal of Industrial Ecology*, 21(3), pp. 603 – 614.

Calisto Friant, M., Vermeulen, W. J. and Salomone, R. (2020) 'A typology of circular economy discourses: Navigating the diverse visions of a contested paradigm', *Resources, Conservation and Recycling*, 161, 104917.

Calisto Friant, M., Vermeulen, W. J. and Salomone, R. (2021) 'Analysing European Union circular economy policies: Words versus actions', *Sustainable Production and Consumption*, 27, pp. 337 – 353.

D'Amato, D. et al. (2017) 'Green, circular, bio economy: A comparative analysis of sustainability avenues', *Journal of Cleaner Production*, 168, pp. 716 – 734.

Du Pisani, J.A. (2006) 'Sustainable development: Historical roots of the concept', *Environmental Sciences*, 3(2), pp. 83 – 96.

Ellen MacArthur Foundation (2012) *Towards the circular economy, Volume 1: An economic and business rationale for an accelerated transition.* Available at: https://www.ellenmacarthurfoundation.org/assets/downloads/publications/Ellen-MacArthur-Foundation-Towards-the-Circular-Economy-vol.1.pdf (Accessed: 18 April 2024).

Ellen MacArthur Foundation (2021) *The nature imperative: How the circular economy tackles biodiversity loss.* Available at: https://ellenmacarthurfoundation.org/biodiversity-report (Accessed: 10 May 2024).

European Commission (2008) '20 20 by 2020: Europe's climate change opportunity', *COM*(2008) 30 final. Available at: https://eur-lex.europa.eu/legal-content/EN/TXT/PDF/?uri=CELEX:52008DC0030 (Accessed: 12 June 2025).

European Commission (2011a) 'Renewable energy: Progressing towards the 2020 target', *COM*(2011) 31 final. Available at: https://eur-lex.europa.eu/LexUriServ/LexUriServ.do?uri=COM:2011:0031:FIN:EN:PDF (Accessed: 18 April 2024).

European Commission (2011b) 'A resource-efficient Europe—Flagship initiative under the Europe 2020 Strategy', *COM*(2011) 21 final. Available at: https://eur-lex.europa.eu/legal-content/EN/TXT/PDF/?uri=CELEX:52011DC0021&from=en (Accessed: 18 April 2024).

European Commission (2012) 'Innovating for sustainable growth: A bioeconomy for Europe', *COM*(2012) 60 final. Available at: https://ec.europa.eu/research/bioeconomy/pdf/official-strategy_en.pdf (Accessed: 18 April 2024).

European Commission (2014) 'Towards a circular economy: A zero waste programme for Europe', *COM*(2014) 398 final. Available at: https://eur-lex.europa.eu/resource.html?uri=cellar:50edd1fd-01ec-11e4-831f-01aa75ed71a1.0001.01/DOC_1&format=PDF (Accessed: 12 June 2025).

European Commission (2015) 'Closing the loop—An EU action plan for the circular economy', *COM*(2015) 614 final. Available at: http://eur-lex.europa.eu/legal-content/EN/TXT/?uri=CELEX%3A52015DC0614 (Accessed: 18 April 2024).

European Commission (2019a) 'Closing the loop: Commission delivers on Circular Economy Action Plan', Press release, 4 March 2019. Available at: https://ec.europa.eu/commission/presscorner/detail/en/IP_19_1480 (Accessed: 29 April 2024).

European Commission (2019b) 'The European Green Deal', *COM*(2019) 640 final. Available at: https://eur-lex.europa.eu/legal-content/EN/TXT/?uri=COM%3A2019%3A640%3AFIN (Accessed: 27 April 2024).

European Commission (2020) 'A new Circular Economy Action Plan: For a cleaner and more competitive Europe', *COM*(2020) 98 final. Available at: https://eur-lex.europa.eu/legal-content/EN/TXT/?qid=1583933814386&uri=COM:2020:98:FIN (Accessed: 27 April 2024).

European Commission (2023) 'A revised monitoring framework for the circular economy', *COM*(2023) 306 final. Available at: https://eur-lex.europa.eu/legal-content/EN/TXT/?uri=COM%3A2023%3A306%3AFIN&qid=1684143860344 (Accessed: 27 June 2024).

European Commission (2025) *Clean industrial deal.* Available at: https://commission.europa.eu/topics/eu-competitiveness/clean-industrial-deal_en (Accessed: 15 May 2025).

European Environment Agency (2023) *The benefits to biodiversity of a strong circular economy.* Available at: https://www.eea.europa.eu/publications/the-benefits-to-biodiversity (Accessed: 10 May 2024).

European Union (2008) 'Directive 2008/98/EC of the European Parliament and of the Council of 19 November 2008 on waste and repealing certain directives', *Official Journal of the European Union L* 312/3. Available at: https://eur-lex.europa.eu/legal-content/EN/TXT/?uri=celex%3A32008L0098 (Accessed: 27 April 2024).

Eurostat (2024) *Circular Economy Monitoring framework.* Available at: https://ec.europa.eu/eurostat/web/circular-economy/monitoring-framework (Accessed: 27 June 2024).

Fitch-Roy, O., Benson, D. and Monciardini, D. (2020) 'Going around in circles? Conceptual recycling, patching and policy layering in the EU circular economy package', *Environmental Politics*, 29(6), pp. 983–1003.

Fitch-Roy, O., Benson, D. and Monciardini, D. (2021) 'All around the world: Assessing optimality in comparative circular economy policy packages', *Journal of Cleaner Production*, 286, 125493.

Foray, D. et al. (2012) 'Guide to research and innovation strategies for smart specialisation (RIS3)', European Commission. Available at: https://s3platform.jrc.ec.europa.eu/en/w/guide-on-research-and-innovation-strategies-for-smart-specialisation-ris3-guide- (Accessed: 27 May 2024).

Geissdoerfer, M., Savaget, P., Bocken, N.M.P. and Hultink, E.J. (2017) 'The circular economy: A new sustainability paradigm?', *Journal of Cleaner Production*, 143(2), pp. 757–768.

Geng, Y. and Doberstein, B. (2008) 'Developing the circular economy in China: Challenges and opportunities for achieving "leapfrog development"', *International Journal of Sustainable Development & World Ecology*, 15(3), pp. 231–239.

Ghisellini, P., Cialani, C. and Ulgiati, S. (2016) 'A review on circular economy: The expected transition to a balanced interplay of environmental and economic systems', *Journal of Cleaner Production*, 114(2), pp. 11–32.

Government of Portugal (2015) 'Green growth commitment: executive summary'. Available at: https://www.greengrowthknowledge.org/sites/default/files/CrescimentoVerde_EN_Portugal.pdf (Accessed: 12 June 2025).

Hedlund, C., Stenmark, P., Noaksson, E. and Lilja, J. (2020) 'More value from fewer resources: how to expand value stream mapping with ideas from circular economy', *International Journal of Quality and Service Sciences*, 12(4), pp. 447–459.

Kenny, M. (1994) 'Ecologism', in: Eccleshall, R. (ed.) *Political ideologies: An introduction.* Second edition. London: Routledge, pp. 218–251.

Kiertotalouden Varsinais-Suomi (2021) *Circular economy in southwest Finland.* Available at: https://kiertotaloudenvarsinaissuomi.fi/in-english/ (Accessed: 10 May 2024).

Kirchherr, J, Reike, D. and Hekkert, M. (2017) 'Conceptualizing the circular economy: An analysis of 114 definitions', *Resources, Conservation and Recycling*, 127, pp. 221–232.

Korhonen, J., Honkasalo, A. and Seppälä, J. (2018) 'Circular economy: The concept and its limitations', *Ecological Economics*, 143, pp. 37–46.

Korhonen, J., Nuur, C., Feldmann, A. and Eshetu Birkie, S. (2018) 'Circular economy as an essentially contested concept', *Journal of Cleaner Production*, 175, pp. 544–552.

Leipold, S. (2021) 'Transforming ecological modernization "from within" or perpetuating it? The circular economy as EU environmental policy narrative', *Environmental Politics*, 30(6), pp. 1045 – 1067.

Loiseau, E., Saikku, L., Antikainen, R., Droste, N., Hansjürgens, B., Pitkänen, K., Leskinen, P., Kuikman, P. and Thomsen, M. (2016) 'Green economy and related concepts', *Journal of Cleaner Production*, 139, pp. 361 – 371.

Mairie de Paris (2017) *Paris circular economy plan.* Available at: https://cdn.paris.fr/paris/2019/07/24/38de2f4891329bbaf04585ced5fbdf0f.pdf (Accessed: 10 May 2024).

Marino, A. and Pariso, P. (2020) 'Comparing European countries' performances in the transition toward the circular economy', *The Science of the Total Environment*, 729, 138142.

Meadows, D.H., Meadows, D.L., Randers, J. and Behrens, W.W. (1972) *The limits to growth: A report for the club of Rome's project on the predicament of mankind.* New York, NY: Universe Books. Available at: http://www.donellameadows.org/wp-content/userfiles/Limits-to-Growth-digital-scan-version.pdf (Accessed: 17 April 2024).

Merli, R., Preziosi, M. and Acampora, A. (2018) 'How do scholars approach the circular economy? A systematic literature review', *Journal of Cleaner Production*, 178, pp. 703 – 722.

Mies, A. and Gold, S. (2021) 'Mapping the social dimension of the circular economy', *Journal of Cleaner Production*, 321, 128960.

Millar, N., Mclaughlin, E. and Börger, T. (2019) 'The circular economy: Swings and roundabouts?', *Ecological Economics*, 158, pp. 11 – 19.

Ministry of the Environment (2024a). *Circular economy green deal.* Available at: https://ym.fi/en/circular-economy-green-deal (Accessed: November 1, 2024)

Ministry of the Environment (2024b). 'The first pledgers of the circular economy green deal will reduce the use of natural resources and accelerate the transition to the circular economy'. In Finnish. Available at: https://ym.fi/-/kiertotalouden-green-dealin-ensimmaiset-sitoutujat-vahentavat-luonnonvarojen-kayttoa-ja-kiihdyttavat-kiertotalousmurrosta?languageId=fi_FI (Accessed: November 1, 2024)

Murray, A., Skene, K. and Haynes, K. (2017) 'The circular economy: An interdisciplinary exploration of the concept and application in a global context', *Journal of Business Ethics*, 140(3), pp. 369 – 380.

Neves, S.A. and Marques, A.C. (2022) 'Drivers and barriers in the transition from a linear economy to a circular economy', *Journal of Cleaner Production*, 341, 130865.

Nobre, G.C. and Tavares, E. (2021) 'The quest for a circular economy final definition: A scientific perspective', *Journal of Cleaner Production*, 314, 127973.

Padilla-Rivera, A., Russo-Garrido, S. and Merveille, N. (2020) 'Addressing the social aspects of a circular economy: A systematic literature review', *Sustainability*, 12(19), 7912.

Päijät-Häme Regional Council (2021) *Päijät-Häme Roadmap towards Circular Economy*. Available at: https://paijat-hame.fi/wp-content/uploads/2021/03/Roadmap_CE_eng.pdf (Accessed: 10 May 2024).

Pearce, D.W. and Turner, R.K. (1990) *Economics of natural resources and the environment.* Hemel Hempstead, Herts: Harvester Wheatsheaf.

Ruokamo, E. et al. (2023) 'Exploring the potential of circular economy to mitigate pressures on biodiversity', *Global Environmental Change*, 78, 102625.

Sardianou, E., Nikou, V., Evangelinos, K. and Nikolau, I. (2023) 'What are the key dimensions that CE emphasizes on? A systematic analysis of circular economy definitions', *Environment Systems and Decisions*. Available at: https://doi.org/10.1007/s10669-023-09956-5.

Sauvé, S., Bernard, S. and Sloan, P. (2016) 'Environmental sciences, sustainable development and circular economy: Alternative concepts for trans-disciplinary research', *Environmental Development*, 17, pp. 48 – 56.

Schroeder, P., Anggraeni, K. and Weber, U. (2019) 'The relevance of circular economy practices to the sustainable development goals', *Journal of Industrial Ecology*, 23(1), pp. 77 – 95.

Schöggl, J.P., Stumpf, L. and Baumgartner, R.J. (2020) 'The narrative of sustainability and circular economy: A longitudinal review of two decades of research', *Resources, Conservation and Recycling*, 163, 105073.

Su, B., Heshmati, A. and Geng, Y. (2013) 'A review of the circular economy in China: Moving from rhetoric to implementation', *Journal of Cleaner Production*, 42, pp. 215 – 227.

Vanhamäki, S. et al. (2019) 'Bio-based circular economy in European national and regional strategies', *International Journal of Sustainable Development and Planning*, 14(1), pp. 31 – 43.

Vanhamäki, S. (2021) *Implementation of circular economy in regional strategies*. PhD thesis. Lappeenranta-Lahti University of Technology LUT. Available at: https://urn.fi/URN:ISBN:978-952-335-771-6 (Accessed: 16 April 2024).

Vanhamäki, S., Rinkinen, S. and Manskinen, K. (2021) 'Adapting a circular economy in regional strategies of the European Union', *Sustainability*, 13(3), 1518.

Wastling, T., Charnley, F. and Moreno, M. (2018) 'Design for circular behaviour: Considering users in a circular economy', *Sustainability*, 10, 1743.

Watkins, E. and Meysner, A. (2022) 'European circular economy policy landscape overview', Institute for European Environmental Policy. Available at: https://ieep.eu/wp-content/uploads/2022/11/European-Circular-Economy-policy-landscape-overview.pdf (Accessed: 16 April 2024).

World Commission on Environment and Development (1987) 'Report of the World Commission on Environment and Development: Our common future', United Nations. Available at: https://sustainabledevelopment.un.org/content/documents/5987our-common-future.pdf (Accessed: 16 April 2024).

Zink, T. and Geyer, R. (2017) 'Circular economy rebound', *Journal of Industrial Ecology*, 21(3), pp. 593 – 602.

Paul Tobin and Ebba Minas

No longer an ever-increasing *acquis?* The expansion, dismantling, termination and stasis of European environmental policies

Abstract: We explain·the development and nuances of each direction of policy change, namely expansion, dismantling, termination and stasis, and we map these directions against the European Union's (EU) environmental policy trajectories since 1992. In particular, we analyze policy dismantling, which has been a focal area of EU environmental politics research since the early 2010s. We examine the dominant conceptualization of policy dismantling, which emphasizes the 'visibility' and 'deliberateness' of dismantling, and we reflect upon the challenges faced by scholars in researching such characteristics empirically. Turning to future research, we discuss the growing possibilities of large-N policy analysis via advanced computational methods, which can identify previously hidden patterns of policy change within the vast body of EU legislation. This chapter holds important implications for scholars and practitioners of EU environmental policy change who wish to understand the creation—and removal—of environmental policies.

Keywords: Dismantling; European Union environmental policy; expansion; policy change; regulations

1 Introduction

Since the 1957 *Treaty Establishing the European Community* that created the European Union's (EU) forerunner, the EU has been committed to "ever-closer union amongst the peoples of Europe'. The European project's primary tool for achieving this goal is the creation of new policies that build connections and 'spillover' into new policy areas (see Scholten and Scholten, 2017). Hence, if the EU has subsequently become a global environmental superpower (Zito, 2013), then *policies* are the source of its strength. Indeed, the EU has been labeled a 'regulatory state' because of the importance of regulation and policy to securing its goals (McGowan and Wallace, 1996; Majone, 2002). In short, to achieve 'ever closer union', the EU has become an 'ever increasing union' in terms of its *acquis* (body, or collection) of policies. Yet, because of this breadth of policy competencies, characterizing the nature of environmental change at the European level is fraught with difficulty. As Yves Steinebach and Christoph Knill (2017, p. 434) caution, "The biased assessment of change either towards [environmental policy] expansion or dismantling has to be avoided by considering the developments in both directions". This chapter seeks to support scholars wishing to undertake analyses of EU environmental policy change, in whichever 'direction' those changes may take place.

https://doi.org/10.1515/9783111321523-042

During the 1990s, there was a widespread expectation that the body of EU environmental legislation—the *acquis*—would continue to steadily expand over time to match growing European competencies and environmental challenges (Weale, 1999). However, the 2008/09 global financial crisis (GFC) saw a shift in narratives around environmental protection, and scholarship began to explore additional directions of *policy change* beyond expansion (see also Chapter 4). In a foundational volume, Michael Bauer et al. (2012) conceptualized *policy dismantling*, which they divided into four ideal types according to the deliberateness and visibility of any policy dismantling, a conceptualization that has subsequently become widely used to analyze environmental protection (see Burns, Tobin and Sewerin, 2019a, Burns, Eckersley and Tobin, 2020; Burns and Tobin, 2020; Gravey and Jordan, 2016; Pollex and Lenschow, 2020; Schaub, Tosun and Jordan, 2024). This research has in turn spurred a whole new research agenda on how to make policies 'durable' prior to any future dismantling (Jordan and Moore, 2020). Environmental policy was at the heart of the research on policy dismantling, as it had been the target of much rhetorical discussion at the EU level during the 2010s. Around the time of the United Kingdom's (UK) Brexit referendum, policymakers were keen to 'cut the green tape' to reduce regulatory 'burden' and reassure European publics that were being bombarded with anti-EU discourses (Maccaferri, 2019).

Related to, but distinct from the concept of policy dismantling is another conceptualization that enables examination of policy cessation. With the development of large-N datasets of EU policies, and the computing power to analyze them, scholars returned to an older, less conceptually nuanced but still usefully descriptive phenomenon: *policy termination* (Bardach, 1976; Brandsma, Pollex and Tobin, 2023). Despite possessing less refinement regarding the motivations for the cessation of a policy than in the case of *dismantling*, policy termination nevertheless provides a useful means of examining the final stages of a policy's life, perhaps once its goals have been achieved or, alternatively, because it is achieving its goals too well. Finally, although instances of policy dismantling were identified at both EU and national levels (Burns, Tobin and Sewerin, 2019b), scholars have found instances of *stasis* in certain contexts (Gravey and Jordan, 2016). This absence of policy change is just as integral to understanding the direction of policymaking as expansion, dismantling and termination.

This chapter contains four parts. We begin by examining the EU's environmental policy change trajectories since 1992 (the year of the EU's foundation via the Maastricht Treaty). This part is divided into three sections and explores policy expansion, then dismantling and the related—but distinct—phenomenon of policy termination, before focusing on the EU's experience of the dynamic nature of policy stasis. Second, we critically examine the form of policy change that has received the most scholarly attention since the 2008/2009 GFC, namely policy dismantling. Third, we offer reflections on potential future research on policy change, particularly considering the recent developments that have been made in large-N computing power. Finally, we conclude by discussing the developments that occurred during the 2024 European Parliamentary elections and selection of the commission president and what these developments may augur for future EU environmental policy change.

2 The EU's environmental policy change trajectories since 1992

Greater research precision regarding policy change was made possible with the distinction made by Knill, Tosun and Bauer (2009) between *policy density* (the number of pieces of legislation proposed or passed) and the *policy intensity* of specific measures (the level of their ambition). In so doing, scholars conducting comparative policy analysis—be it between actors, between levels of governance, or between points in time—could more systematically track policy change. For example, consider which would have the more beneficial environmental impact: a policymaker creating more policies than another, but which lack ambition, or a policymaker making fewer policies, but which are extremely ambitious? There is no correct answer per se, but the distinction between policy density and policy intensity at least affords scholars an opportunity to attempt a response. Yet, before attempting to determine the direction of EU environmental policy changes, a scholar must first decide what is meant by *environmental policy.*

Operationalizing environmental policy can be a challenging topic. For instance, a hydroelectric dam may reduce greenhouse gas emissions in the electricity supply, thus making it an effective climate policy, but in doing so, may destroy various habitats, damaging biodiversity. Are policies about hydroelectric power environmental policies? Relatedly, the environment has been increasingly *integrated* into other policy areas to avoid 'siloing' and hopefully improve environmental effectiveness (Dupont and Jordan, 2021; Rietig, 2019). However, this means that environmental activities are often included within the budgets of 'non-environmental' departments and ministries; locating these instances and separating them out can be extremely challenging for researchers. For example, the main aim of industrial policies is economic growth and increased competitiveness, which can be achieved through such measures as new technologies and greater energy efficiency. Despite not being classified as environmental policies, they can reduce greenhouse gas emissions and thereby interest scholars studying environmental policies (Meckling, 2021).

Because of this difficulty in demarcating environmental policy, one approach often taken is to follow the EU's own understanding of environmental policies. For example, Charlotte Burns and Paul Tobin (2020, p. 7) analyze a list of climate policies identified by the European Commission but also note that the list is not exhaustive. Another approach is to derive data from the EUR-Lex (n.d.) website and search for certain keywords pertaining to the environment or to search for policies linked to particularly environmental committees or Directorates-General or labeled as being within the EU's "Environment, consumers and health protection" policy area. However, the former approach runs the risk of overlooking environmental policies that have been integrated into other areas, while the latter approach would include health policies, which may not be how the scholar envisions 'environmental policy'. Whichever path is taken, transparency and replicability are watchwords for a researcher to prioritize when identifying and describing their process for demarcating what counts as 'environmental policies'.

We now explore policy expansion, dismantling and termination and stasis/status quo in turn. For each, we provide exemplar policy developments that reflect the relevant instance of policy change, across a range of environmental policy issues, including climate change, biodiversity protection and air and water quality. As we are charting multiple environmental policy areas, it is impossible to state an overall trajectory since 1992 that is applicable to all policy areas. However, broadly speaking, the pattern we see is one of a steadily expanding (greater 'density') environmental *acquis* and one in which, for the most patterns, policies have become more ambitious (greater 'intensity'). As Lenschow, Burns and Zito (2020) note, dismantling is challenging at the EU level, for both institutional and ideational reasons. Yet, patterns of stasis and instances of dismantling have been found, which are contrary to the transformational environmental protection that is needed for the EU to achieve its long-term goals.

Policy expansion

Research on European environmental policy expansion has built on, and worked in tandem with, research on the expansion of European welfare policy (Jensen et al., 2014). Following Weale's (1999) exploration of the expansion of EU environmental policy, there had been a broad assumption that the EU's environmental *acquis* would steadily expand. This assumption derived from expectations of increasing 'spillover' of competencies up to the European level, growing scientific understanding about environmental problems and the rising material living standards of citizens leading to more 'post-material' values (Inglehart, 1981; for critique, see Kidd and Lee, 1997). This expectation was broadly supported throughout the 2000s, and, despite research on other directions of policy change since the early 2010s, studies have continued to find overall patterns of EU environmental policy expansion. Expansion is understood as increases to the number of policies (density) and also ambitiousness (intensity). As we explore now, empirical studies have found many nuances for characterizing and explaining the nature of policy expansion beyond simple increases in the number of policies.

Patterns of policy expansion have been found across a variety of environmental policy fields. Burns, Eckersley and Tobin (2020) found a "significant drop in the density of EU environmental policy proposals" following the GFC. They found that new policies were still being proposed, just at a rate that was fluctuating; hence, the *acquis* continued to expand. Of these policy proposals between 2004 and 2014, they found that 'chemicals' regulation was the largest area of expansion in the 2004–2009 Parliamentary session, while 'climate' jumped to being the area of most proposed policy in 2009–2014. Indeed, regarding climate change and energy policy, Peter Slominski (2018) found the EU policy trajectory to be broadly unchanged despite the aftermath of the GFC; the main impact had been on discourses around policy, not changes to the policy documents.

Steinebach and Knill (2017) conducted a thorough investigation of environmental policy expansion (and dismantling) for each year between 1980 and 2014. They found the "most significant punctuation in policy expansion can be observed in 1996"; they propose that this peak was due to the adoption of Council Directive 96/61/EC that required the application of the most effective and advanced technology to be used when issuing permits for industrial installations. Also assessing EU environment-industry policy, Viviane Gravey and Brendan Moore (2019) find the field to have expanded between 1995 and 2016, albeit with a shift toward a greater proportion of policies being non-legislative rather than legislative in origins. Over the same period, they also found an expansion of EU air quality policies but with a continuing dominance of legislative policies in this area. These analyses collectively highlight the utility of examining not just the *direction* of EU environmental policy change but also the policy area, Parliamentary session, policy discourses, landmark events and legislative or non-legislative origins of any policies that are created. There is more to understanding policy expansion than simply the growth in number of policies.

Policy dismantling and termination

Following the conceptualization put forward by Knill, Tosun and Bauer (2009) that distinguished between policy density and intensity, the 2010s saw a rapid growth of 'policy dismantling' studies to capture policy change that went backwards as well as forwards. This topic was especially timely; following the GFC, EU policymakers talked of cutting the 'burden' of environmental regulations (Burns and Tobin, 2016), while David Cameron, Prime Minister of the UK (then a EU Member State), spoke in 2013 of needing to 'cut the green crap' under the aegis of his austerity agenda. Accordingly, scholars were keen to assess the extent to which any such dismantling was *actually* occurring or whether these stances were instead rhetorical.

Policy dismantling has gone on to become understood as entailing a 'reduction' or 'diminution' of policies that leaves some vestige of the policy behind (Jordan, Bauer and Green-Pedersen, 2013, p. 795). To add greater analytical insights to this process, Bauer and Knill (2012) proffered a '2 x 2' typology (see Table 1) of policy dismantling. Dismantling may result from an explicit decision by policymakers to pursue that end, or not, and the dismantling may be high, or low, visibility. This framework enables scholars to characterize the nature of any dismantling in such a manner that aids comparison across types of actors, policy areas and time. For example, Burns, Eckersley and Tobin (2020) found little evidence for *active dismantling* (i. e., deliberate and highly visible), but did find that the average intensity (ambitiousness) score of EU environmental policies fell from 3.00 (out of 5) during 2004 and 2009, to 2.34 during 2009 and 2014. They describe this as being a form of *dismantling by default*; policymakers had not decided to remove existing policy in a deliberate manner, and the overall trajectory would necessarily be 'low visibility', yet ambitions did wane.

Table 1: The four types of policy dismantling developed by Bauer and Knill (2012).

	High visibility	Low visibility
Dismantling decision	Active dismantling	Dismantling by arena shifting
No dismantling decision	Dismantling by symbolic action	Dismantling by default

Studies employing the Bauer and Knill (2012) policy dismantling typology are commonly small-to-medium-N in nature, due to the need to assess the characteristics of each policy being dismantled. For example, Gravey and Moore (2019, p. 28) found limited instances of EU environmental policy dismantling, but the few cases found appeared to be dismantling by default, "such as the EU failing to keep up with reinforced WHO standards for ambient air". While the instances of EU environmental policy dismantling are sparse in number to date, the Bauer and Knill (2019) typology enables a more fine-grained understanding to be obtained regarding the nature of any instances that are found. Jan Pollex and Andrea Lenschow (2020) analyze *ecodesign* policies aimed at producers and *ecolabel* legislation targeted toward consumers. In doing so, they differentiate between the legislative development of policies, where they find no dismantling and the *implementation* of these extant policies, suggesting that instrument setting may be an aspect in which dismantling is occurring. As such, they propose that "dismantling research benefits from in-depth policy research [...] [to] uncover dismantling strategies that easily remain hidden from political attention" (Pollex and Lenschow, 2020, p. 20) Hence, research on policy dismantling is necessarily suited to small-to-medium-N studies of policies, such that these characteristics can be explored in detail.

While the above explorations of policy dismantling were being undertaken during the 2010s, scholars did not analyze 'policy termination' of EU environmental policy. Indeed, Andrew Jordan, Bauer and Green-Pedersen (2013, p. 797) suggested that "the whole approach [of policy termination] has largely run out of steam". This accurate reflection derived from the reality that termination is a simple binary assessment of whether a policy has been completely removed, or not (Bardach, 1976). Consequently, termination lacks the rich description enabled by the 2 x 2 policy dismantling typology and was resultantly replaced by the newer approach. However, the subsequent development of web scraping methods and large-N computational power has enabled the simple binary assessment of termination to be applied to the large dataset that is the EU *acquis*. While research in this area is still nascent, Brandsma, Pollex and Tobin

(2023) investigated the extent of policy termination across more than 120,000 EU policies between 1971 and 2021. They found policy termination to be a limited reality for EU environmental policy; just 13/3,657 (0.35 percent) of policies in the "environment, consumers and health protection" policy area were terminated during the period. While analyses of policy dismantling find informative instances of dismantling and can characterize the deliberateness and visibility of this process, the early work on policy termination suggests that EU environmental policy is remarkably resilient, at least against being repealed entirely.

Policy stasis

Policy areas other than environmental protection offer insights for understanding 'policy stasis'. Regarding social policy, Carsten Jensen et al. (2014, p. 528) propose the existence of 'expansionary dismantling', "where new policies and instruments are used to compensate reform losers and to obfuscate cutbacks". Indeed, this understanding builds on Giuliano Bonoli's (2001, p. 240) argument that policy change can be a mix of expansion, stasis and dismantling, where focusing down to the instrument level shows that even in the same policy field, policy may be expanding and dismantling at the same time. The study of EU Ecodesign policy by Pollex (2022) epitomizes this scenario, whereby voluntary measures expanded but entailed lenient standards, thus enabling 'shallow dismantling' via policy expansion. Hence, although the *interrelating dynamics* between such directions can be explored in still greater detail regarding environmental policy, several studies have found overall patterns of stasis.

Referring to *status quo* rather than the word 'stasis', the study by Gravey and Jordan (2016) has become a landmark piece on policy stasis in EU environmental policy, due to its empirical comprehensiveness and critical conceptual insights into the nature of policy change. Gravey and Jordan (2016) examine dismantling (accorded a score of -1), status quo (0) and expansion (1) across three dimensions—density, scope and settings—and two levels—legislation as a whole and constitutive instruments—finding widespread but limited dismantling that in many policy areas could be characterized as being stasis overall. Burns, Eckersley and Tobin (2020) and Burns and Tobin (2020) similarly use a numbering system in their coding of policy intensity, using 1 for dismantling, 2 for stasis and then 3, 4 and 5 for increasing degrees of policy intensity. Burns, Eckersley and Tobin (2020) found an increase over time in the percentage of environmental policies that were coded 2 (meaning stasis), from 19.4 percent of policy proposals in 2004–2009, to 40.6 percent in 2009–2014. Burns and Tobin (2020) found the same pattern regarding EU climate policy when comparing the period 1998–2009 with 2009–2015.

The meaning behind any periods of EU environmental policy stasis is open to interpretation. Burns, Tobin and Sewerin (2019a, pp. 6–7) suggest that "[c]ontinuation of the status quo [...] may be considered as ambitious: there may be no need to create new legislation, if existing policies are already working effectively". Burns, Eckersley and Tobin (2020) found this narrative to be prevalent amongst EU policymakers, whereby the establishment of a 'mature' body of EU legislation meant there was a shift in emphasis from the mid-2010s onwards, away from favoring the creation of new policies and toward *implementing* the policies that had already been created. However, stasis may be interpreted as a loss of ambition or capacity to act on climate change (see Burns, Tobin and Sewerin, 2019a; Burns, Eckersley and Tobin, 2020). Regarding climate change, for example, much of the early emissions reductions achieved before 2020 could be considered 'low hanging fruit', necessitating a ratcheting up of ambition over time. If the EU does not keep pace with the required upwards trajectory of increasing climate ambition, then stasis may quickly become inadequate in the face of potentially catastrophic environmental problems.

3 Reflections on 'policy dismantling'

As discussed above, Bauer and Knill (2012) typologized policy dismantling according to whether it follows a dismantling *decision* and whether it is *visible* to the public. This distinction enables the politics behind policy dismantling to be analyzed, which is especially important in a context of policy backlashes, which have been particularly prevalent against climate policies since the start of the 2020s (Patterson, 2022). Nevertheless, the typology is necessarily and deliberately a *descriptive* approach, from which explanations may then be developed after establishing the change that has occurred. In this section, we reflect upon three dimensions that scholars wishing to employ a policy dismantling approach need to consider if using the typology. These considerations are: the challenges faced by scholars in operationalizing types of dismantling, the difficulties of accessing data, and the benefits of engaging with additional descriptions of dismantling processes, in addition to deliberateness and visibility.

Having already noted the challenges of operationalizing 'environmental policy', let us turn to operationalizing the dividing features of policy dismantling. First, what counts as 'visible' dismantling? While Bauer and Knill (2012) emphasize the importance of visibility and refer to the amount of 'political attention' received, deciding as a scholar whether dismantling is visible can be easier said than done. To whom does the dismantling need to be visible? Political scientists may perceive dismantling to be visible, considering their detailed tracing of policymaking events, but a European citizen may disagree. Gravey and Jordan (2020) offer welcome measures for addressing this quandary by bringing reframing and venue-shopping into their study of policy dismantling. Nevertheless, considering the integration of environmental issues into other policy areas (Dupont and Jordan, 2021), does environmental policy dismantling need to affect just environmental policies, or can it occur when other policies are being dismantled? If the latter is the case, then could we also question how 'deliberate' the dismantling is? For example, environmental policies may be dismantled as part of a broader streamlining agenda. Continuing this vein, what counts as 'deliberate'? For scholars, affixing deliberateness to an action is fraught with difficulty. For example, environmental policy dismantling during the 2010s in the EU, Germany, Denmark and France was deemed to be 'dismantling by default', where "policymakers were distracted from maintaining previously high standards, rather than actively seeking to diminish existing levels of ambition" (Burns, Tobin and Sewerin, 2019b, p. 201). Hence, in practice, 'deliberate' is commonly understood to be the dismantling of policies that coincides with a narrative favoring this activity. Having scholarly certitude over which labels to allocate is difficult. We encourage researchers to reflect openly about the decision-making process they employed when allocating one of the four ideal-typical forms of dismantling to a specific case.

Second, building from the data-access issues that hinder determination of the 'deliberateness' of policy dismantling, there are practical data access issues to be considered regarding 'visibility', too. In their study of environmental policy dismantling, Peter Eckersley and Tobin (2019, p. 458) note that "[w]e may lack empirical evidence of dismantling by arena shifting because—by definition—it requires scholars to look beyond high-level policies or items of legislation agreed by elite actors and instead examine how decisions are interpreted, implemented and enforced 'on the ground'". Although this reflection regards national-level policymaking and dismantling being 'shifted' to the local government arena, the principle also applies to EU-level policymaking when dismantling is shifted to the national-level arena. Indeed, from the mid-2010s onwards, there has been a marked emphasis on policy implementation as a priority for the European Commission, which is implicitly and sometimes explicitly used to mean national-level policymaking, as it is the Member States that must enact new EU policies (Newig and Koontz, 2014; Zhelyazkova and Thomann, 2021).

Finally, there is a lack of conceptualization of the politics behind dismantling, and the qualitative ways in which dismantling can vary, depending on whether the policy at hand is being changed via a legislative or non-legislative process. For example, rather than—or even, in addition to—deliberateness and visibility, one may wish to consider whether a policy has been *depoliticized* by policymakers and whether dismantling is more likely via a political arena in which voters can shape outcomes, or not. For example, we may wish to consider whether dismantling is occurring in a forum that is directly accessible to elected representatives and/or the public, or if it is administered by technocrats, such as 'comitology committees' (see Burns and Tobin, 2020). The usage of unelected, technical forums for dismantling policy represents a potentially insidious means of evading democratic oversight, if it is occurring deliberately (see Burns and Tobin, 2020; Pollex and Lenschow, 2020). Meanwhile, as noted earlier, Gravey and Moore (2019) differentiated between types of policy expansion according to whether proposals were via legislative or non-legislative means. And 'devolving' power to local levels may grant greater regional agency, but if those arenas do not have the capacity or resources to enact these new powers, we may consider the policy to be essentially dismantled (Eckersley and Tobin, 2019). Consequently, further research into the nature of the arena responsible for policy change is important but under-researched.

4 Future research on EU environmental policy change

Further research on the nature of EU environmental policy change is especially welcome across policymakers, fields of environmental policy and the nature of the interactions between policy change 'directions'. Indeed, as discussed in the section above on policy termination, the possibility of accessing and analyzing the entire *acquis* of European environmental policy affords huge new possibilities to researchers. We discuss the growing possibilities of large-N policy analysis via advanced computational methods, which can identify previously hidden patterns of policy change within the vast body of EU legislation (see Brandsma, Pollex and Tobin, 2023). In their analysis of 120,000 EU policies since 1971 captured from the EUR-Lex (n.d.) website, Brandsma, Pollex and Tobin (2023) identify 3,657 policies within the "environment, consumers, and health protection" policy area. Other states, such as Australia, the UK and the United States, likewise have created online repositories of legislation and policy data. Using web scraping skills obtained via computer programming languages (see Brooker, 2020 for guidance) or simply 'exporting' data as this function becomes more widespread, new large-N analyses can be conducted that identify previously hidden patterns within environmental policymaking (Tobin et al., 2024). These studies can engage to a greater degree with questions around temporality, due to the long-term nature of the data as well as the roles of institutions, different European Parliamentary party groupings and specific environmental issue areas. Indeed, the scale of the EU's legislative *acquis* has become so large that advanced computational methods not only hold promise but will be increasingly necessary for conducting environmental policy analyses.

A second area deserving of greater future inquiry is the nature of the EU's environmental policy change in the context of, and/or shaped by, external relations (see Chapter 29). Often, the literature on the EU as an environmental actor examines the Union's activities as somewhat of a monolithic entity, commonly with regards to climate change rather than other environmental policy areas and frequently around a framing of being a leader, pioneer, follower or even a leader-mediator 'leadiator' (Bäckstrand and Elgström, 2013). Yet, a nuanced exploration of the relationship between policy change within the EU and the resultant changes in the stances of the EU in conducting external action would be most welcome. Moreover, the nature of this relationship can be reversed to explore how external conferences and negotiations affect policy change within the EU's borders. If the EU continues to improve its environmental performance, particularly regarding climate change, it is foreseeable that, as a bloc, it will be increasingly less perceived as a crucial actor in the international arena, for example, because of its diminishing status as a direct source of greenhouse gas emissions. Accordingly, the relationship between policy change and external dimensions will be especially noteworthy.

5 Conclusion

Following the 2024 EU election, the new EU Parliament composition and the reelection of Ursula von der Leyen as Commission President suggest that a new policy agenda is coming. While climate change and the environment remain high on the political agenda, the rise of nationalist, euroskeptic, populist and radical right-wing parties could complicate future implementation of ambitious environmental policies. How this altered political landscape will impact the environmental policy trajectory of the EU remains to be seen.

This chapter highlights the need for a nuanced analysis of policy change, differentiating between policy expansion, dismantling, termination and stasis, with a particular focus on policy dismantling. Since 1992, the EU has generally experienced an increase in environmental policy density and intensity, despite fluctuations. Studies on policy dismantling in the 2010s highlighted the nuanced nature of policy change, revealing that dismantling often occurs subtly. While complete policy termination is rare, these subtle reductions in policy ambition suggest a more complex reality than mere expansion. Additionally, the analysis of policy stasis indicates periods of minimal change, either reflecting effective existing policies or a lack of political will. Overall, the EU's environmental policy trajectory highlights the importance of considering the interplay of various policy changes and the methodological challenges in capturing these dynamics.

The nature of EU environmental policy change presents many opportunities for further research, particularly through advanced computational methods for large-N policy analysis. These methods enable researchers to uncover hidden patterns within the large body of EU legislation, providing insights into the temporality of policy changes, institutional roles and specific environmental issues. Another area for future inquiry is the relationship between the EU's internal policy changes and its external relations. Examining how the EU's evolving environmental policies influence its global stance, and vice versa, will provide a more comprehensive understanding of the EU as an environmental actor.

References

Bardach, E. (1976) 'Policy termination as a political process', *Policy Sciences*, 7(2), pp. 123–131.

Bäckstrand, K. and Elgström, O. (2013) 'The EU's role in climate change negotiations: From leader to "leadiator"', *Journal of European Public Policy*, 20(10), pp. 1369–1386.

Bauer, M.W., Jordan, A., Green-Pedersen, C. and Héritier, A. (eds.) (2012) *Dismantling public policy: Preferences, strategies, and effects*. Oxford: Oxford University Press.

Bauer, M.W. and Knill, C. (2012) 'Understanding policy dismantling: An analytical framework', in: Bauer, M.W., Jordan, A., Green-Pedersen, C. and Héritier, A. (eds.) *Dismantling public policy: Preferences, strategies, and effects*. Oxford: Oxford University Press, pp. 30–56.

Bonoli, G. (2001) 'Political institutions, veto points and the process of welfare state adaptation', in: Pierson, P. (ed.) *The new politics of the welfare state*. Oxford: Oxford University Press, pp. 238–264.

Brandsma, G.J., Pollex, J. and Tobin, P. (2023) 'Overlooked yet ongoing: Policy termination in the European Union', *Journal of Common Market Studies*, 61(5), pp. 1360 – 1376.
Brooker, P.D. (2020) *Programming with Python for social scientists.* London: SAGE.
Burns, C., Eckersley, P. and Tobin, P. (2020) 'EU environmental policy in times of crisis', *Journal of European Public Policy*, 27(1), pp. 1 – 19.
Burns, C. and Tobin, P. (2016) 'The impact of the economic crisis on European Union environmental policy', *Journal of Common Market Studies*, 54(6), pp. 1485 – 1494.
Burns, C. and Tobin, P. (2020) 'Crisis, climate change and comitology: Policy dismantling via the backdoor?', *Journal of Common Market Studies*, 58(3), pp. 527 – 544.
Burns, C., Tobin, P. and Sewerin, S. (eds.) (2019a) 'Measuring the impact of the crisis on European environmental policy', in: Burns, C., Tobin, P. and Sewerin, S. (eds.) *The impact of the economic crisis on European environmental policy.* Oxford: Oxford University Press, pp. 1 – 18.
Burns, C., Tobin, P. and Sewerin, S. (2019b) 'European environmental policy at a rime of crisis: Benign neglect, or a leader losing pace?', in: Burns, C., Tobin, P. and Sewerin, S. (eds.) *The impact of the economic crisis on European environmental policy.* Oxford: Oxford University Press, pp.198 – 216.
Dupont, C. and Jordan, A., (2021) 'Policy integration', in: Jordan, A. and Gravey, V. (eds.) *Environmental policy in the EU: Actors, institutions and processes.* Abingdon: Routledge, pp. 203 – 219.
Eckersley, P. and Tobin, P. (2019) 'The impact of austerity on policy capacity in local government', *Policy & Politics*, 47(3), pp. 455 – 472.
EUR-Lex (n.d.) *EUR-Lex: Access to European Union law.* Available at: https://eur-lex.europa.eu/homepage.html (Accessed: 05 September 2024).
Gravey, V. and Jordan, A.J. (2016) 'Does the European Union have a reverse gear? Policy dismantling in a hyperconsensual polity', *Journal of European Public Policy*, 23(8), pp. 1180 – 1198.
Gravey, V. and Jordan, A.J. (2020) 'Policy dismantling at EU level: Reaching the limits of "an ever-closer ecological union"?', *Public Administration*, 98(2), pp. 349 – 362.
Gravey, V. and Moore, B. (2019) 'Full steam ahead or dead in the water? European Union environmental policy after the economic crisis', in: Burns, C., Tobin, P. and Sewerin, S. (eds.) *The impact of the economic crisis on European environmental policy.* Oxford: Oxford University Press, pp. 19 – 41.
Inglehart, R. (1981) 'Post-materialism in an environment of insecurity', *American Political Science Review*, 75(4), pp. 880 – 900.
Jensen, C., Knill, C., Schulze, K. and Tosun, J. (2014) 'Giving less by doing more? Dynamics of social policy expansion and dismantling in 18 OECD countries', *Journal of European Public Policy*, 21(4), pp. 528 – 548.
Jordan, A., Bauer, M.W. and Green-Pedersen, C. (2013) 'Policy Dismantling', *Journal of European Public Policy*, 20(5), pp. 795 – 805.
Jordan, A.J. and Moore, B., 2020. *Durable by design?: Policy feedback in a changing climate.* Cambridge: Cambridge University Press.
Kidd, Q. and Lee, A.R. (1997) 'Postmaterialist values and the environment: A critique and reappraisal', *Social Science Quarterly*, pp. 1 – 15.
Knill, C., Tosun, J. and Bauer, M.W. (2009) 'Neglected faces of Europeanization: The differential impact of the EU on the dismantling and expansion of domestic policies', *Public Administration*, 87(3), pp. 519 – 37.
Lenschow, A., Burns, C. and Zito, A. (2020) 'Dismantling, disintegration or continuing stealthy integration in European Union environmental policy?', *Public Administration*, 98(2), pp. 340 – 348.
Maccaferri, M. (2019) 'Splendid isolation again? Brexit and the role of the press and online media in re-narrating the European discourse', *Critical Discourse Studies*, 16(4), pp. 389 – 402.
Majone, G. (2002) 'A European regulatory state?', in: Richardson, J. (ed.) *European Union: power and policymaking.* Abingdon: Routledge, pp. 263 – 277.
McGowan, F. and Wallace, H. (1996) 'Towards a European regulatory state', *Journal of European Public Policy*, 3(4), pp. 560 – 576.

Meckling, J. (2021) 'Making industrial policy work for decarbonization', *Global Environmental Politics*, 21(4), pp. 134–147.

Newig, J. and Koontz, T.M. (2014) 'Multi-level governance, policy implementation and participation: The EU's mandated participatory planning approach to implementing environmental policy', *Journal of European Public Policy*, 21(2), pp. 248–267.

Patterson, J.J. (2022) 'Backlash to climate policy', *Global Environmental Politics*, 23(1), pp. 68–90.

Pollex, J. (2022) 'Simultaneous policy expansion and reduction? Tracing dismantling in the context of experimentalist governance in European Union environmental policy', *Journal of Common Market Studies*, 60(3), pp. 604–633.

Pollex, J. and Lenschow, A. (2020) 'Many faces of dismantling: Hiding policy change in non-legislative acts in EU environmental policy', *Journal of European Public Policy*, 27(1), pp. 20–40.

Rietig, K. (2019) 'The importance of compatible beliefs for effective climate policy integration', *Environmental Politics*, 28(2), pp. 228–247.

Schaub, S., Tosun, J. and Jordan, A. (2024) 'Climate action through policy expansion and/or dismantling: Country-comparative insights: An introduction to the special issue', *Journal of Comparative Policy Analysis: Research and Practice*, 26(3–4), pp. 215–232.

Scholten, M. and Scholten, D. (2017) 'From regulation to enforcement in the EU policy cycle: a new type of functional spillover?', *Journal of Common Market Studies*, 55(4), pp. 925–942.

Slominski, P. (2018) 'Energy and climate policy: Does the competitiveness narrative prevail in times of crisis?', in: Falkner, G. (ed.) *EU policies in times of crisis.* Abingdon: Routledge, pp. 125–140.

Steinebach, Y. and Knill, C. (2017) 'Still an entrepreneur? The changing role of the European Commission in EU environmental policy-making', *Journal of European Public Policy*, 24(3), pp. 429–446.

Tobin, P., Duit, A., Kelly, N. and Kelly, C. (2024) 'Exploring the role of businesses in polycentric climate governance with large-*N* data sets', *Global Environmental Politics*, 24(3), pp. 168–190.

Weale, A. (1999) 'European environmental policy by stealth: The dysfunctionality of functionalism?', *Environment and Planning C: Government and Policy*, 17(1), pp. 37–51.

Zhelyazkova, A. and Thomann, E. (2021) 'Policy implementation', in: Jordan, A. and Gravey, V. (eds.) *Environmental policy in the EU.* Abingdon: Routledge, pp. 220–240.

Zito, A.R. (2013) 'The European Union as an environmental leader in a global environment', in: Oosthoek, J. and Gills, B.K. (eds.) *The globalization of environmental crisis.* Abingdon: Routledge, pp. 81–94.

Ekaterina Domorenok and Anthony R. Zito

Conclusions: European Union environmental policy research and policy agenda

Abstract: This concluding chapter reflects on some of the underlying patterns discernible in the varied chapters of this European Union (EU) environmental policy *Handbook*. The *Handbook* chapters stress that EU environmental policy persists in the effort to protect the environment, integrate policies and innovate in the face of tensions reflecting diverging interests and anthropocentric perspectives. The policy and broader political approaches suggest the importance of geopolitical dynamics, greater integration of values and temporal analysis. The policy observations stress the importance of the international arena, new challenges and policy packages and mixes in shaping the future trajectory of EU environmental policy.

Keywords: Public policy theory; geopolitical dynamics; policy mixes and packages; moral values and policymaking; practical policy observations

1 Introduction

The core objective of this *Handbook* has been to look back at the policy and scholarly developments of European Union (EU) environmental policy and reflect on what this can tell us about the current and future trajectories of this policy area. The reality of EU environmental policy is that it is a mosaic of different institutions, ideas, perspectives, interests, policies and tools; the academic study of this policy sector is equally varied and evolving. This conclusion points to some of the broader patterns that can be discerned in the chapters. Firstly, section two isolates some important trends that merit further scientific investigation and political debate in the years to come. We then examine the theoretical implications and possibilities for academic research in section three. Finally, section four offers observations about critical policy developments for practitioners and other readers to focus on.

2 Vital trends in EU environmental policymaking

The first strong message from the *Handbook* chapters is that the ongoing and increasing complexity of both global and local environmental policy challenges has necessitated a greater range of intricate policy designs and an increase in the mixes of policies and policy tools (see the various chapters on specific policy problems in Section C). Furthermore, as the chapters in Section B illustrate, the governance of EU environmental policy has evolved in-step with these and other policy transformations. The interplay between institutional and noninstitutional actors has become increasingly

https://doi.org/10.1515/9783111321523-043

complex throughout the different policy phases, as environmental issues have progressively intertwined with other policy sectors following the shift from the environmental to the sustainability agenda. In response to these challenges, as several contributions to the *Handbook* show, this process has culminated with the adoption of the European Green Deal (EGD), prompting a wide scholarly and policy debate on the ambition, coherence and consistency of the EU's environmental commitment in a long-term perspective.

Although the overall EU policy intent has been focused on the overarching goals of environmental protection and climate mitigation and adaptation, the related policy measures involved tensions. Multiple trade-offs relate to the linkage and balance between environmental risks, social costs and economic concerns. Additionally, there are specific sectoral concerns (which focus on water, agriculture etc.) and broader EU strategic rationales, which include questions of strategic geopolitical survival against the perceived security threats of Russian and China. A number of policy observations flow from these overall trends.

The persistence yet restriction of the EU environmental policy agenda

The chapters, particularly those by Gravey (Chapter 4) and by Tobin and Minas (Chapter 37), investigating EU environmental policy during recent decades of political and economic turbulence and recent political and economic challenges detect only a marginal occurrence of policy termination (i. e., the cessation of actual policy measures) and active policy dismantling (a reduction or diminution of policy measures). Protection of the environment continues to be a high priority for a substantial portion of the EU populace and many interest groups. Whatever its ultimate trajectory and achievements, the EGD represents a major policy step to boost climate and environmental governance. Nevertheless, the chapters point us to the fact that in many environmental problems the governance ambition has diminished. The chapter by Pollex and Lenschow (Chapter 32) stresses that a more subtle dynamic can exist at the EU level. A *de facto* dismantling occurs when the European Commission chooses not to adjust environmental protection and technological standards in line with new understandings and developments or when EU policymakers choose not to develop and agree on follow-on measures that were articulated in the original intent of specific environmental legislation.

Although the EGD has signaled a renewed ambition to push forward on both climate and environmental policy measures, there is a broader governance and political significance to it. Several *Handbook* contributions point out that the EGD and the instruments the EU has launched (in response to the Covid-19 pandemic and, more recently, the war between Russia and Ukraine) have marked a new phase in the evolution of environmental policies. This phase has been characterized by increased political tensions around a trilemma composed of environmental protection, economic growth and social costs and risks of decarbonization. After announcing an ambitious environmental legislative agenda at the beginning of its first mandate, the Commission led by Ursula von der Leyen significantly downplayed environmental priorities at the end of its first term as a consequence of growing conflicts and tensions in the European Parliament (EP) and the Council of the European Union, as well as the increased political and societal contestation across the Member States.

The struggle for policy integration

Despite challenges, the EU policymaking process has pushed to integrate policy efforts and priorities that the accumulation of EU environmental and climate legislation achieved. Various chapters in the volume illustrate that, after decades of incorporating environmental issues into individual sectors, the EU has progressively adopted a broader integrated approach, acknowledging the complexity of the sources of environmental pollution, harm and risks, along with the associated need for cross-sectoral and multilevel policies to address the climate crisis. More specifically, as chapters in Section C and de Vito and Russel (Chapter 33) demonstrate, the EU has adopted a more nuanced approach to environmental policy integration in several relevant subfields, including, air, water and biodiversity protection. The EU has increasingly engaged with health, transport, territorial planning and development policies, paving the way for new policy standards in food, waste and chemicals policies. Nevertheless, this effort at greater integration of sectoral approaches and priorities faces an ongoing challenge of differing values and interests.

Fundamental strategic tensions: ideas

Taking the value and ideational dimension first, the nature of these struggles (see Section A chapters, especially those by Jörgens and Rocha Trindade, Gravey, and Bailey) highlights profound normative tensions between ecological and economic values underlying the debate on how economic growth can be decoupled from environmental degradation while at the same time ensuring social justice. Jörgens and Rocha Trindade discuss how the required transformations call into question the established policy paradigms and principles, demanding a move from the dominant anthropocentric "worldview" to a more ecocentric approach.

Additional normative, conceptual and practical challenges arise from the need to address urgent but still insufficiently explored issues. These include the criteria for the ethical management of human–nonhuman animal conflicts, sound policies and principles for nonhuman nature or a conceptual framework to integrate environmental protection and specific concerns related to more vulnerable societal groups, including women (Kronsell and Gunnhildur Magnusdottir) or migrants (Blocher, Andreolla Serraglio and Beckmann).

Overall, many of the *Handbook* chapters conclude that the EU's policymaking remains trapped in its path-dependent trajectory (Zito, Chapter 2), struggling to overcome the consolidated ecological modernization imperatives, and showing limited or even decreasing environmental ambition. Due to institutional evolution of the EU environmental policy sector prior to the Single European Act, EU environmental policy has had a long history of being linked and therefore subordinate to the EU's market dynamics. In the recent Commission (i.e., the Barroso, Juncker and von der Leyen Commissions), there have been moves to highlight a better regulation agenda that seeks to protect the economic competitiveness of EU producers (chapters by Bailey, Bürgin and Pollex and Lenschow). There are several important but implicit narratives at work in such policy agendas. Some focus on viewing environmental protection as a burden on the economy; others perceive economic growth and competitiveness as prerequisites for environmental governance. The concept of the circular economy, while promising various environmental benefits, nevertheless adheres to these narratives (Vanhamäki, Chapter 36). The EU continues to focus on specific, nonradical problem-solving with an emphasis on securing economic growth and environmental protection.

Paradigmatic alternatives do exist, but Section A chapters stress how anthropocentric approaches have dominated EU environmental policy so far. Policies informed by more of an ecocentric worldview remain largely marginal and underdeveloped. The thrust of these chapters suggests that actors seeking to change this EU environmental policy status quo need to take a pluralist and strategic approach, but equally one that is not simply evolutionary and incremental in nature.

Inherent strategic tensions: interests and power

The *Handbook* chapters in Sections B and D underline the importance and power of particular economic and political interests found in both the EU environmental and other policy sectors. Kovacic (Chapter 5) stresses how such considerations are embedded fundamentally in the EU handling of science and knowledge that underpin policymaking. Joltreau and Smith (Chapter 16) underline the prominence of business actors in shaping regulatory knowledge about the EU economic production processes as well as the domestic context. Beunen and Bazzan (Chapters 23, 28) highlight the continued power of interest groups and stakeholders such as farmers, foresters and hunters, which then are translated into national interests and EU-level positions. Carter and Farstad (Chapter 11) stress the recently increased scope and power of right-wing parties.

An important message shared in several *Handbook* chapters is to abandon the assumption that the efforts to protect national interests in both the decision-making and actual governance are centered in the Southern or Eastern Member States. Börzel and Hofmann (Chapter 14) note how northern states, such as Sweden with its long association with pioneering green policy choices, are operating legal end-runs to protect certain industries. National interests are an integral reason for the failure to address wider international challenges that are discussed below, such as climate change migration and population displacement.

Scope for environmental actors and entrepreneurship

Although the *Handbook* emphasizes the reality of ongoing constraints on EU environmental change, chapters continue to find evidence of the drive toward a more advanced environmental governance by a range of actors in the EU. Despite the critical issues outlined above, we see the gradual empowerment of the European Commission in the environment and climate fields (Bürgin), along with the EP's increased environmental ambition over time. Although the EP's credentials as an "environmental champion" have been recently challenged by the fragility of the pro-environmental coalition and remain to be tested against the new political equilibrium after the 2024 election (Carter and Farstad), the EP has played a crucial role in shaping the content of central EGD dossiers, including the Fit for 55 package, for which it sought more ambitious targets and a broader scope, aiming to secure early and continuous progress. Wurzel, Liefferink and di Lullo (Chapter 12) stress that entrepreneurship and pioneering behavior by individual Member States and coalitions have featured strongly in the trajectory of EU environmental policymaking, although this effort may vary in its degree and intensity while facing opposition from other Member States. One of the important messages of the chapters on the Member States is that environmental policy promotion and implementation occur across all the Member States, and even the smaller Member States can have a significant (disproportionate to their size) entrepreneurial environmental impact in the EU institutional context.

Equally important, as the complexity of EU environmental policy governance has significantly increased, it has led to a more intricate and varied set of policy actions involving experts (Kovacic, Chapter 5), non-governmental organizations (NGOs) (Berny, Chapter 17), business (Joltreau and Smith, Chapter 16), local governments (van der Heijden, Chapter 15) and communities (Blocher, Andreolla Serraglio and Beckmann, Chapter 22). In acknowledging the resistance from interest groups, *Handbook* chapters find that other actors are coming to the fore and are likely to do so in the future. There are businesses that are likely to set the circular economy agenda and to encourage more ambitious environmental targets. Prontera and Domorenok (Chapter 26) note the move toward network building and public-private cooperation that involves creating multi-stakeholder platforms, public-private partnerships and pan-European industry alliances. Cities have the scope to become climate leaders in experimentation with respect to environmental governance. Environmental NGOs have played a role in building EGD proposals on previous EU initiatives and evaluating EU policy progress.

This has brought to the forefront fundamental questions about the democratic quality and accountability of environmental policymaking in the EU across different territorial levels. Although the number and scope of deliberative channels and arenas for this wide range of actors to be involved in environmental decision-making processes have progressively increased, the extent to which this has enhanced the awareness, ownership and power of these actors remains to be understood (see Torney, Buzogány and Parks, Chapter 9, and Machin, Chapter 18).

This democratic challenge also points to the fundamental source of likely governance change for the EU environmental climate and environment sectors. Torney, Buzogány and Parks and Machin suggest several pathways for EU citizens to involve themselves more fully in the policy direction of the EU. These authors and Almiron and Paez (Chapter 19) suggest that a more critical, reflective and engaged public has the potential to bring power and hope to progress environmental protection and a more ecocentric governance focus. Indeed, it is such citizen engagement that provided much of the political impetus in 2019 for the EGD program.

Climate policy agenda prioritization

Handbook findings (see in particular Chapters 20 by Wettestad and Gulbrandsen and 30 by Tosun) emphasize how the EU climate agenda has emerged and consolidated over the last two decades, progressively expanding from mitigation objectives and targets, including the establishment of the European Emissions Trading System to a broader decarbonization policy mix, involving in particular the energy, transport, building, agriculture and aviation sectors. However, as Wettestad and Gulbrandsen emphasize, the sheer number of and the overlaps between old and new climate mitigation instruments, especially because of the recent legislative agenda stemming from the EGD, pose the problems of coverage, ambitiousness and coherence of the EU environment and climate agendas. The more recent, equally complex and often controversial climate adaptation measures have been led by the ambition of delivering a "transformative" change, to match, as Rayner and Groen (Chapter 21) argue, the gravity and breadth of the climate crisis. This ambition necessarily involves engaging with an even broader range of policies, including spatial planning, climate emergencies, resources management and socioeconomic systems. These developments have pushed the EU beyond the logic of compliance, which was the typical though not always effective policy approach, in the first three decades of EU environmental regulation (see Börzel and Hofmann, Chapter 14). They have moved the EU toward alternative market-oriented and voluntary policy instruments targeting cities (van der Heijden, Chapter 15), subnational authorities (Eckersley, Chapter 13) and business (Joltreau and Smith, Chapter 16). This change has been particularly relevant for the progressively strengthened connection between the single market regulations and dynamics, on the one hand, and the green transition, on the other, with increasing tensions between the competitiveness and sustainability rationales in the content of EU economic policies and governance (see Deters and Heidebrecht, Chapter 31). In fact, a range of problems and trade-offs related to the greening of EU industrial policies have emerged with the framework of the circular economy package, indicating the need to change the established models of production and consumption (Vanhamäki, Chapter 36). The external dimension of EU environmental policy, analyzed by Delreux in Chapter 29, aligns with these trends, illustrating how EU standards intentionally and unintentionally have spread beyond EU borders through multiple instruments, though the coherence and consistency of the latter has been widely criticized and questioned.

In noting these overarching trends, a core pattern identified in the *Handbook* is that climate change governance has tended to take a greater portion of the EU's policy formulation and negotiation agenda compared to the traditional policy problems labeled environmental policy. Overall, as the analysis presented by the chapters by Bürgin, Carter and Farstad and Tosun illustrates (Chapter 10, 11 and 30), the environmental drive of the EU's institutions has significantly shrunk over the last decade, giving way to a growing focus on and commitment to climate issues, which entails the increasing prioritization of social and economic measures aimed at offsetting decarbonization costs. Demirbilek, Benson and Fritsch (Chapter 24) stress the comparative lack of policy innovation to tackle water policy compared to the climate crisis. This prioritization has negative consequences for efforts to enhance environmental protection in other policy problems such as waste and biodiversity (see Chapter 25 by Broka and Chapter 23 by Beunen), a reality that is even more significant when we acknowledge that such policy problems shape and contribute to climate change and are shaped by the climate crisis.

3 Theoretical implications and possibilities

To capture the multifaceted dimensions of environmental policy and its evolution since its inception in the 1970s, the chapters in this *Handbook* employ a variety of theoretical and analytical angles, contributing to a broader reflection on the nature of political and policy change in the EU. These include, but are not limited to, a range of public policy approaches. Certain chapters focused on outcomes and current situational challenges through the lenses of policy turbulence and policy termination, dismantling and expansion (see especially Tobin and Minas, Chapter 37). Other policy approaches involved looking at policy processes such as policy evaluation and the policy and political dynamics that shape them. Zito and Cotta (Chapter 34) typologize a range of implementation barriers that policymakers must overcome while de Vito and Russel (Chapter 33) stress the importance of differentiating horizontal, vertical and mixed integration of EU policy mechanisms and processes. Several chapters sought to operationalize the EU's current and future policy trajectory through approaches that assess EU policy change processes (e.g., Chapter 4 by Gravey and Chapter 6 by Rietig). Policy change and success have proved to be determined not only by political factors and the logic of compliance, but also by knowledge, resources and capacities of public administrations and other noninstitutional actors involved in policy processes across different territorial levels. Over the last two decades, policy diffusion, learning and networking have been among the main engines of environmental policy change as indicated in the learning, climate adaptation and energy chapters. The EU is experimenting with demonstration projects in the areas of urban governance and the creation of EU Missions for the promotion of healthy soil that all seek to trigger a range of far-reaching diffusion and learning effects. Such policy entrepreneurship, as discussed in Chapter 21 by Rayner and Groen, Chapter 9 by Torney, Buzogány and Parks and 32 by Pollex and Lenschow, suggests the need for a more systematic examination of the role more experimental governance plays in current EU policymaking.

At the same time, many *Handbook* chapters went beyond policy analysis to embrace a range of broader political dimensions. Eckersley, van der Heijden and Wurzel, Liefferink and di Lullo (Chapters 13, 15 and 12) stress both the interdependence of the various policy levels operating in the EU but also the power relations that operate to create constraints and opportunities. The chapters by Berny and by Deters and Heidebrecht (Chapters 17 and 31), to highlight only two, emphasize the importance of a clear path-dependent trend shaped by the EU institutional process, marked by occasional disruptions and numerous barriers to setting and achieving more ambitious environmental goals. More recently, the growing turbulence and polycrisis of the post-Paris Agreement period, combined with rising geopolitical and geoeconomic tensions and social and economic concerns over the costs of decarbonization and green transitions, have decisively sidelined ecological priorities. This has led some *Handbook* authors (e.g., Jörgens and Rocha Trindade, Bailey in Chapters 3 and 7) to focus on changes of ideas and paradigms that inform the overarching EU policy values and choices. Similarly, the micro-policy level, which encompasses individual perceptions, commitment and ownership of specific values, along with political and ideological orientation, have proved to be fundamental for understanding environmental policies and governance. The *Handbook*'s analyses of the nature of citizenship (Machin, Chapter 18) and democratic governance (Torney, Buzogány and Parks, Chapter 9) speak directly to this question.

At least three dimensions stand out in the *Handbook* chapters as being both important theoretical pathways as well as involving current *lacunae* in the field: the importance of geopolitical dynamics, values and time. The stories of the evolution of EU environmental policy and climate change are fully embedded in the geopolitical changes and international pressures that shape EU integration and policy. Climate and other forms of global migration are only one development that will have an impact on the EU population's environmental, social and political welfare. However, much more attention needs to be paid to the implications of the EU's environmental international presence. Delreux (Chapter 29) emphasized the multivenue strategy that the EU has operated, noting that many of its successful unilateral actions are facing increasing resistance and hostility from both third party (i.e., non-EU) state and non-state actors. The chapters by Blocher, Andreolla Serraglio and Beckmann (Chapter 22) and by Demirbilek, Benson and Fritsch (Chapter 24) note the colonial and neocolonial implications of EU strategies and engagement with the rest of the world, particularly the Global South. A greater social and political economy study of the impact of EU measures is called for.

This discussion of the international implications of EU policy choices brings us directly into the question of having more explicit and critical analyses of the values underpinning EU environmental policy. The chapters looking at paradigms (Chapter 3), ideational challenges (Chapter 7) and citizenship (Chapter 18) all call for critical reflections on the underpinning values and perspectives informing EU environmental policy. They stress that the traditional anthropocentric approach has tended to highlight established interests and power. Part of this discussion must be an extension of rights and voice to those elements of human society as well as the biosphere that have been marginalized by EU policies. Kronsell and Magnusdottir (Chapter 8) and Paez and Almiron (Chapter 19) highlight the marginalization of critical elements of both human society and the ecosphere inherent in the dominant EU environmental policy approach. A wider, more inclusive notion of justice for all elements of human society but also for all species must face the intergenerational consequences of current and future policy action. A much stronger addition of both ecocentric and intersectional approaches would start challenging traditional thinking. The *Handbook* chapters accept that this is not going to involve an instant revolution but rather a strategic placement of new understandings and values in the decision-making process and in some of the most vital policy areas, such as biodiversity.

Finally, theoretical approaches that embrace and use the temporal dimension to understand how EU environmental policy has evolved over time are crucial. Berny, Joltreau and Smith (Chapter 17 and 16) stress the need to look over the longer term at how the interactions between interests and EU policymakers lead to a reproduction or change in the EU environmental institutions. The chapters by Deters and Heidebrecht and by Pollex and Lenschow (Chapters 31 and 32) suggest not only that there is a path-dependent dynamic that shapes current EU environmental outputs, but that there are significant changes that are easily overlooked when one only takes broad snapshots. Rietig in Chapter 6 warns of the dangers of trying to judge the impact of learning in too short a timescale. The deeper levels of policy learning, which might involve a shift in world view and environmental philosophy, may take some time to manifest themselves in policy actions. All of the aspects mentioned above represent some of the major gaps in our knowledge of EU environmental policies, and they would all benefit from systematic qualitative and quantitative study.

4 Practical policy observations

This *Handbook* has sought to review the policy developments and academic analysis of specific dimensions of EU environmental policy. In making these assessments of policy dimensions over time, several broad policy observations surface.

Multidimensional environmental policy in an international global arena

Our chapters on climate change, most especially on international migration, but also chapters on water, energy and other policy sectors demonstrate that international actions and strategies are an essential part of EU policymaking going forward. There are several implications to this reality that need unpacking. First is the need to integrate geopolitical analysis and strategies into environmental policy and vice versa. Many of the important technological advances that are planned for boosting renewable energy, smart systems and data management (enhanced potentially by machine learning) will involve rare earth minerals. The reality that planetary sources are substantially located in other parts of the world, including China and Africa, or involve deep-sea mining in the oceans and near-space mining, raises the fundamental question of the EU's continued, peaceful access to such supplies. The EU, as demonstrated in its framework regulation on critical earth mineral supplies (see European Union, 2024) recognizes this necessity with respect to a green transition, but there is a wider set of implications of geopolitical cooperation and competition that are often kept apart from environmental policymaking. The necessity of more integrated strategic thinking will only become more apparent over time.

A second important strand is the acknowledgement, articulated by Delreux in Chapter 29, that the EU is moving toward a greater use of unilateral venues and measures which have extraterritorial effects on third countries. Thus, we see the creation of the Carbon Border Adjustment Mechanism as well as the creation of the Regulation on Deforestation Free Products that impose costs of adjustment on third party actors. This again will place a greater burden on EU diplomatic and negotiating efforts as other international actors seek opportunities and venues to contest these measures. Part of the turbulence that the EU will face is the rise of international leadership that has clear and opposing strategic objectives. Gravey suggests some important strategic steps, emphasizing the need to define the most vital priorities that need to be pursued across all EU international policy activity.

A third dimension that must be kept in mind for the future is the role of the EU enlargement dynamic. *Handbook* chapters such as the one by Wurzel, Liefferink and di Lullo (Chapter 12), have spoken about the enlargement political dynamics and how they have shaped EU decision-making. The chapters by Börzel and Hofmann and by Zito and Cotta (Chapter 14 and 34) have stressed the effort on both the part of new Member States and the EU to ensure a convergence around the EU environmental *acquis*. As Delreux stresses, much of the significant international impact the EU has had has been through the enlargement mechanism. Whatever the geopolitical likelihood of Ukraine, Moldova, Georgia and the remaining third-country Balkan states joining the EU in the long term, history tells us that this is a fundamental opportunity to promote environmental protection, but that it takes substantial political and policy resources and planning. Nevertheless, environmental policy has proven itself to be one of the positive and popular EU integration measures, despite substantial political and interest group resistance. Can the EU better prepare for such an effort, and does the EU have the capacity?

Mixes and packages require evaluation knowledge and coordination

One of the policy patterns woven through the *Handbook* chapters is the importance of policy packaging and policy mixes. The EGD is the most ideal-typical and current example of policy packaging, with its combination of revised and new climate measures such as the Carbon Border Adjustment Mechanism and the Social Climate Fund (see Wettestad and Gulbrandsen, Chapter 20). A different kind of EU policy grouping strategy (see Rayner and Groen, Chapter 21) is the EU Mission Framework where the EU has harnessed Horizon Research Innovation money to give diverse EU actors opportunities to experiment with their visions for innovating in the areas of climate change, the oceans and waters, climate change adaptation and climate neutral, smart cities (European Commission, 2025).

However, such efforts speak to a larger policy challenge that the EU faces. Too little is understood about the intended and unintended consequences of having multiple polices at work, 'policy mixes', at the same time and within and across the environmental and other EU policy sectors (Flanagan, Uyarra and Laranja, 2011). Such measures can reinforce other measures operating to deal with the same or different policy problems and priority that the EU faces, but equally they can undermine such efforts (Zito and Eckersley, 2025). Elements of the EGD have mobilized farmers and foresters to push their Member State and EP representatives to curtail the EU environmental ambition. *Handbook* chapters such as the one by van der Heijden (Chapter 15) highlight the problem of having a wide range of climate policies now operating at the local level. Nevertheless, there is a crucial lack of clarity about the role and relevance of these measures and how the interaction and competition between them works. Schoenefeld (Chapter 35) stresses the lack of evaluation that exists about having multiple policy instruments and approaches in simultaneous operation and the question of whether the accumulation of policy measures across the various EU priorities is overstretching the implementation capacity of those responsible for delivering policy benefits. Academic research on how policies interact does exist (note especially Schmidt and Sewerin, 2019), but a more concerted, cross-sectoral effort that focuses on unintended consequences is needed.

There is a danger in simply viewing this policy observation as a micro-level administrative challenge, although such knowledge-building and evaluation is vital. The *Handbook* chapters on climate change note the fundamental lack of information exchange and coordination between the efforts to protect the environment and what are considered more traditional security concerns in the face of the Russian security threat and increasing population migration. The *Handbook* findings stress that the consequences of environmental disasters, political insecurity and other global phenomena will at various points overcome the efforts to keep these policy areas separate and compartmentalized. The *Handbook* has stressed the importance of the EGD project in not only addressing climate targets but also bringing wider environmental goals and policies into this mix. There is an EU tendency, certainly by some policy actors, to see the environment and climate as distinctive policy fields. There is a continued urgent need to see the interdependent dynamics caused by these policy problems and the benefit of policy coordination.

Coda: The necessity for hope and persistence

The *Handbook* chapters make clear the persisting gaps between the necessary EU environmental targets on so many indicators (climate emissions, chemical regulation, waste production and biodiversity to name only a few) and the current EU policy achievement. As educators, as well as being students of EU environmental policy, the editors and authors in this *Handbook* are all too aware of the danger that underlining these ongoing realities and challenges may create despondency in our students and readers, especially those in younger generations, about the future. The *Handbook* does make clear the need for fundamental adjustments to the production and consumption of the riches of the Earth, as well as the persuasive engagement with institutional, ideational and interest group resistance to such revolutionary, ecocentric thinking.

Nonetheless, the *Handbook* policy sector chapters note the considerable improvement in policy processes, standards and outcomes in areas such as chemicals and water since the environment became a European Community environmental priority in 1972. Furthermore, this web of institutions and regulations are needed to achieve future environmental gains. As Biermann (2021) and others argue with respect to the wider global governance and public policy system, it is counterproductive to simply dispense with current EU environmental institutions and policies. Environmental problems do require both the proactive and remedial administration of chemical regulation etc. that currently operate, however limited their current focus.

Perhaps even more importantly, the EU peoples as individual and groups have the power to make a substantial difference, and not simply by voting in national parliaments and the European Parliament. In terms of innovation in the approach toward more ecocentric policies and a reshaping of societal environmental impact, the *Handbook* chapters suggest the substantial impact that both small and partial steps can have in moving forward. The chapters stress the importance of continuing to maintain and improve upon climate and environmental measures in particular areas where the new linkages can gain greater purchase. This progression must involve local and individual efforts as well as international, multilateral strategies. Such a move requires the identification of neglected areas and beings—having for example a more explicit policy approach to female-dominated, often low-carbon areas of the economy where women may predominate. This in turn creates both performative and learning dynamics that are important for the EU moving forward. An actively engaged citizenry and policymaking elite can learn by doing: realizing the potential that they have unleashed by such measures can strengthen a movement toward both an elite and mass understanding of the EU's role in protecting the environment and lead to increased EU policy ambition and accomplishment.

References

Biermann, F. (2021) 'The future of "environmental" policy in the Anthropocene: Time for a paradigm shift', *Environmental Politics*, 30(1), pp. 58 – 77.

European Commission (2025) 'EU Missions in Horizon Europe', Brussels: European Commission. Available at: https://research-and-innovation.ec.europa.eu/funding/funding-opportunities/funding-programmes-and-open-calls/horizon-europe/eu-missions-horizon-europe_en (Accessed: 25 July 2025).

European Union (2024) 'Regulation (EU) 2024/1252 of the European Parliament and of the Council of 11 April 2024 establishing a framework for ensuring a secure and sustainable supply of critical raw materials and amending Regulations (EU) No 168/2013, (EU) 2018/858, (EU) 2018/1724 and (EU) 2019/1020. L 2024/1252', *Official Journal of the European Union.* Available at: https://eur-lex.europa.eu/legal-content/EN/TXT/?uri=CELEX%3A32024R1252&qid=1720020986785 (Accessed: 25 July 2025).

Flanagan, K., Uyarra, E. and Laranja, M. (2011) 'Reconceptualising the "policy mix" for innovation', *Research Policy*, 40 (5), pp. 702 – 713.

Schmidt, T.S., and Sewerin, S. (2019) 'Measuring the temporal dynamics of policy mixes: an empirical analysis of renewable energy policy mixes' balance and design features in nine countries', *Research Policy*, 48(10), 103557.

Zito, A. and Eckersley, S. (2025) 'Framing European Heritage and identity: Cultural policy instruments of the European Union', *Journal of Common Market Studies.* Available at: https://doi.org/10.1111/jcms.13767.

List of Contributors

Núria Almiron is Professor of Ethics and Political Economy of Communication in the Department of Communication at Pompeu Fabra University (Spain) and co-director of the UPF-Centre for Animal Ethics. Her research focuses on persuasive communication, interest groups and public affairs, approached from a critical animal studies perspective.

Diogo Andreolla Serraglio is a Research Analyst at the Potsdam Institute for Climate Impact Research (PIK) in Germany. His work focuses on advancing the understanding of human mobility in the context of disasters, climate change and environmental degradation and contributes to global policy and practice in this field.

Ian Bailey is Professor of Environmental Politics at the School of Geography, Earth and Environmental Sciences, University of Plymouth (United Kingdom). His main areas of research include national climate and energy politics, carbon markets, environmental policy implementation and social engagement with energy transitions.

Giulia Bazzan is Assistant Professor of Public Governance at Tilburg University (Netherlands), where she coordinates the MSc in Public Governance and conducts research on institutional design, policy effectiveness and sustainability transitions. Her work combines comparative public policy and configurational methods to explore how governance arrangements shape outcomes in complex, multi-level systems.

Annabel Beckmann is a social worker with an M.A. in Social Work, Social Policy and Management. Her research interests focus on human rights, migrant rights and global and European migration politics, with particular emphasis on human mobility in the context of climate change and intersectional approaches to antidiscrimination and feminist practice.

David Benson is Associate Professor at the University of Exeter in Penryn, Cornwall (United Kingdom). His interdisciplinary research focuses on environmental politics, policy and governance.

Nathalie Berny is Professor of Sociology at Sciences Po Rennes (France) and member of the National Centre for Scientific Research (CNRS) at Arènes. She is associate member of Maison Française d'Oxford (United Kingdom). Her research interests revolve around interest group politics, social movement theory, environmental policies and organization studies.

Raoul Beunen is Professor of Environmental Governance at the Open Universiteit Nederland. His research explores the potentials and limitations of environmental policy and planning in the perspective of adaptive governance and sustainability.

Julia M. Blocher is a Scientist at the Potsdam Institute for Climate Impact Research (PIK) in Germany, where she leads interdisciplinary research on climate-related migration, displacement and planned relocations. Her research emphasizes the socially differentiated impacts of climate change, focusing on social strata, gender and social equity, cultural factors and Indigeneity.

Tanja Börzel is Professor of Political Science at the Otto Suhr Institute for Political Science, Freie Universität Berlin (Germany). Her research focus lies in the fields of European integration, governance, compliance and diffusion. She is also director of the Cluster of Excellence "Contestations of the Liberal Script" (SCRIPTS) that examines the nature, causes and potential consequences of deepening contestations of liberal orders at the domestic and international level in a global, comparative and historical perspective.

Emanuela Bozzini is Associate Professor at the University of Trento (Italy) where she teaches environmental sustainability and public policy analysis. She has previously been a research assistant at the University of Essex (United Kingdom), a Fulbright-Schuman fellow at the University of Maryland (USA) and a research fellow at the University of Cardiff (United Kingdom). Her research interests focus on EU environmental policy, risk regulation and the use of scientific evidence in policymaking, with a specific attention to chemicals and agro-food issues.

Anna Broka is a researcher at Vidzeme University of Applied Sciences in Latvia, based in the Institute of Social, Economic and Humanities Research (ViA HESPI). Her research explores how ecosystems and multidimensional environmental factors, including climate change, influence the welfare and well-being of marginalised groups, with a focus on policy analysis, youth transitions and social equity.

Alexander Bürgin is Associate Professor at Zeppelin University, Friedrichshafen (Germany). His main research areas include the social legitimacy of EU governance, the EU political system, EU environmental and energy policies, the EU's external influence and EU–Turkey relations.

Aron Buzogány is Assistant Professor for Political Science at BOKU University Vienna (Austria), where he leads the European Environmental Policy Group. His research is on EU-level decision-making, national implementation and external impact of EU environmental, energy and climate policies.

Neil Carter is Professor of Politics at the Department of Politics and International Relations, University of York (United Kingdom). His research focuses on green parties, environmental politics and policy in the UK and European Union and the party politics of climate change.

Benedetta Cotta is Assistant Professor in Political Science in the Department of Political Science, Law and International Studies at the University of Padova (Italy). Her research primarily focuses on the implementation of European environmental policies in the Member States from Central and Eastern Europe and the emergence of eco-social policies in the European Union.

Tom Delreux is Professor of Political Science and EU politics at the University of Louvain (Belgium). His research interests include the EU's external relations, EU environmental policy, EU institutions and international environmental politics.

Burçin Demirbilek is Associate Professor in the Department of Political Science and Public Administration, Çankırı Karatekin Üniversitesi (Türkiye). Her research focusses on environmental policy, EU-Turkey relations, water management and water policy.

Henning Deters is a political scientist at the University of Vienna (Austria), Centre for European Integration Research (EIF). He studies environmental politics, judicial politics, multilevel governance and European integration.

Laura De Vito is Senior Research Fellow at the University of the West of England, Bristol (United Kingdom). Her research focuses on issues of environmental policy and governance and decision-making for sustainable futures.

Maurizio di Lullo is a lawyer and linguist by training. He has worked at the General Secretariat of the Council of the EU since 1999. For fifteen years he participated in UN climate conferences and negotiations of EU climate legislation. Since 2020, he has followed Home Affairs issues (borders/ Schengen/Covid-19) with, inter alia, work on the EU Digital Covid Certificate.

Ekaterina Domorenok is Associate Professor of Political Science in the Department of Political Science, Law and International Studies at the University of Padova (Italy). She co-directs the Observatory on Sustainability, Equality and Social Justice (OSES). Her research primarily focuses on public policy, with a particular attention to sustainability, climate change and eco-social transitions.

Peter Eckersley is Associate Professor of Public Policy and Management at Nottingham Business School, Nottingham Trent University (United Kingdom). His research focuses on central-local government relations, climate policy, local governance, policymaking and public accountability.

Fay Farstad is Associate Professor in the Department of Comparative Politics at the University of Bergen (Norway). Her research focuses on comparative environmental and climate change policy and politics, also at the EU level, with a particular focus on the role played by political parties.

Oliver Fritsch is a Senior Lecturer in Environmental Policy, Law and Impact Assessment at Murdoch University, Australia. He specializes in environmental policy and planning, with a particular focus on water resources, biodiversity, local and regional transport and energy.

Viviane Gravey is a Senior Lecturer in the Department of Politics and International Studies at Queen's University Belfast (United Kingdom). Her research focuses on the relationship between policy change and shocks to policymaking systems.

Lisanne Groen is Assistant Professor of International Environmental Governance at the Department of Environmental Sciences at the Open Universiteit Nederland. Her research centers around issues of global, EU and national climate change mitigation and adaptation, biodiversity and plastic pollution policy and governance, including international negotiations.

Lars H. Gulbrandsen is Research Professor and Research Director at the Fridtjof Nansen Institute (Norway). His research interests are within the fields of environmental politics, forest politics and policy, nonstate certification schemes and climate and energy politics.

Sebastian Heidebrecht is Assistant Professor at the University of Vienna (Austria), Centre for European Integration Research (EIF). He works on EU politics and governance, with a focus on the EU's evolving digital policy approach.

Andreas Hofmann is Assistant Professor in European Union Studies at Leiden University (the Netherlands). His primary research interest is the role of courts in political processes and judicial procedures as a mode of solving political conflicts.

Thibaut Joltreau is Assistant Professor of Geopolitics and International Business at EDHEC Business School in Lille, France. His research explores the interrelations between industrial policy, business models and the evolving geography of production.

Helge Jörgens is Associate Professor at the Department of Political Science and Public Policy of Iscte—University Institute of Lisbon and an integrated researcher at the Centre for Research and Studies in Sociology (CIES-Iscte) (Portugal). His research interests include comparative and international environmental and climate policies, the role and influence of international public administrations and the diffusion and transfer of public policies.

Zora Kovacic is Ramón y Cajal Research Fellow of the Urban Transformation and Global Change (TURBA) lab of the Economics and Business Faculty at the Universitat Oberta de Catalunya (Spain). Her research centers on the science-policy interface, environmental governance, post-normal science and governance in complexity.

Annica Kronsell, Professor of Political Science and of Environmental Social Science at the School of Global Studies, University of Gothenburg (Sweden), is interested in how public institutions can govern climate and sustainability issues, applying ecological feminist and critical theories mostly in a Nordic and European context.

Andrea Lenschow is Professor of European Politics and Integration and currently Vice President for International Affairs, Diversity and Academic Staff Development at Osnabrück University (Germany). Her research interests focus on European Union integration and governance, environmental politics and policy, global sustainability and supply chain governance.

Duncan Liefferink is Associate Professor in the Environmental Governance and Politics group at the Institute for Management Research, Radboud University Nijmegen, the Netherlands. His main research focuses on European and comparative environmental politics.

Amanda Machin is Professor of Political Sociology at the Department of Sociology and Social Work, University of Agder in Norway. She is interested in the dynamics, theories, discourses, imaginaries, protests, identifications, performances and bodies of ecological and radical democratic transformation.

Gunnhildur Lily Magnusdottir is Associate Professor in Political Science at the Department of Global Political Studies at Malmö University (Sweden). Her research centers around European climate policymaking and in particular climate institutions and how they understand and work with the social dimensions of climate change.

Ebba Minas is a PhD student in the Department of Political Science at Stockholm University (Sweden). Her research focuses on comparative climate politics and political economy, with a particular emphasis on industrial decarbonization.

Eze Paez is Ramón y Cajal Fellow at the Law & Philosophy Group of Pompeu Fabra University and board member of the UPF-Centre for Animal Ethics (Spain). His work explores the political status of nonhuman animals from a republican perspective, as well as our duty to mitigate naturogenic wild animal suffering.

Louisa Parks is Professor in Political Sociology at the School of International Studies and the Department of Sociology and Social Research at the University of Trento (Italy). Her research interests center around citizen activism and its links to global environmental governance, and she has published books and articles on these themes. Her current projects include work on activism and representation in the Convention on Biological Diversity and the impacts of the European Green Deal.

Jan Pollex is an interim professor of European Politics and Integration at Osnabrück University (Germany). His research interests focus on European politics, environmental and climate policy and environmental movements and political parties.

Andrea Prontera is Associate Professor of Political Science in the Department of Political Science, Communication and International Relations of the University of Macerata (Italy). His main research interests lie in the areas of international political economy, EU public policy and energy policy. His latest book is *Green Superpowers: China, the European Union, and the United States in the Global Energy Transition* (Oxford University Press, 2024).

Tim Rayner is a Research Fellow at the Tyndall Centre for Climate Change Research and School of Environmental Sciences, University of East Anglia (United Kingdom). His research interests encompass both mitigation and adaptation dimensions of national and European Union climate policy and politics.

Katharine Rietig is Professor of Sustainability and International Politics at Newcastle University (United Kingdom). Her research sits at the intersection of international relations, global governance and European public policy.

Inês Rocha Trindade is a Research Assistant at the Centre for Research and Studies in Sociology at Iscte—University Institute of Lisbon (CIES-Iscte) (Portugal). Her research focuses on environmental and climate policy, with an emphasis on eco-sufficiency, policy paradigms and policy change.

Duncan Russel is Professor of Environmental Policy at the University of Exeter (United Kingdom). His research focuses on environmental policy and governance in European contexts.

Jonas J. Schoenefeld, PhD, is Project Leader and Scientist at the Institute for Housing and Environment (IWU) in Darmstadt (Germany) and a Visiting Researcher at the Tyndall Centre for Climate Change Research, School of Environmental Sciences, University of East Anglia (United Kingdom). His research interests focus on various aspects of environmental governance from the EU to the municipal level, with a particular focus on policy implementation, monitoring and evaluation.

Andy Smith is Research Professor in Political Science at the Centre Émile Durkheim in Sciences Po Bordeaux (France). His research is centered upon local climate policymaking and on ecological transitioning within specific industries such as agro-food and construction.

Paul Tobin is Senior Lecturer in Politics at the University of Manchester (United Kingdom). He specializes in the comparative politics of environmental policy, especially regarding climate change leadership and also, in contrast, the dismantling and obstruction of climate action.

Diarmuid Torney is Associate Professor in the School of Law and Government at Dublin City University (Ireland) and Director of the DCU Institute for Climate and Society. His research focuses on climate change and environmental politics, policy and governance, including the intersection of climate change and democratic governance, democratic innovations and deliberative democracy.

Jale Tosun is Professor of Political Science at Heidelberg University (Germany) and Adjunct Professor at the University of Oslo (Norway). Her research agenda comprises comparative public policy, public administration, comparative political economy, governance and European Union integration.

Jeroen van der Heijden is Honorary Professor of Public Governance at the School of Regulation and Global Governance (also known as RegNet) at the Australian National University. His research explores the interplay between urban, climate and regulatory governance, with particular emphasis on their interrelations and implications for public policy and practice.

Susanna Vanhamäki is Principal Lecturer in Circular Economy at LAB University of Applied Sciences, Lahti (Finland). Her research focuses on systemic change toward sustainability and circularity, emphasizing strategic stakeholder collaboration.

Jørgen Wettestad is Research Professor at the Fridtjof Nansen Institute (Norway). He has published widely on international, EU and national environmental, climate and energy policy.

Rüdiger Wurzel is Professor of Comparative European Politics and Jean Monnet Chair in European Union Studies in the School of Politics and International Studies at the University of Hull (United Kingdom). He has published widely on environmental issues, the EU and German politics.

Anthony R. Zito is Professor of European Public Policy at the School of Geography, Politics and Sociology at Newcastle University (United Kingdom). His research centers around issues of public policy, European Union integration, environmental politics and policy, global governance and expert networks.

Index

Note: Page numbers in *italics* indicate figures, **bold** indicate tables in the text, and references following "n" refer to the notes.

https://doi.org/10.1515/9783111321523-044